ETHNICITY, LAW AND HUMAN RIGHTS

ETHNICITY, LAW AND HUMAN RIGHTS

The English Experience

SEBASTIAN POULTER
Reader in Law
University of Southampton

CLARENDON PRESS · OXFORD
1998

Oxford University Press, Great Clarendon Street, Oxford OX2 6DP

Oxford New York
Athens Auckland Bangkok Bogota Bombay Buenos Aires
Calcutta Cape Town Dar es Salaam Delhi Florence Hong Kong
Istanbul Karachi Kuala Lumpur Madras Madrid Melbourne
Mexico City Nairobi Paris Singapore Taipei Tokyo Toronto Warsaw
and associated companies in
Berlin Ibadan

Oxford is a trade mark of Oxford University Press

Published in the United States by
Oxford University Press Inc., New York

A catalogue record for this book is available from the British Library

Library of Congress Cataloging in Publication Data
Poulter, Sebastian M.
Ethnicity, law, and human rights : the English experience /
Sebastian Poulter.
p.   cm.
Includes bibliographical references.
ISBN 0–19–825773–2
1. Minorities—Legal status, laws, etc.—Great Britain.
2. Muslims—Legal status, laws, etc.—Great Britain.   3. Hindus—
Legal status, laws, etc.—Great Britain.   4. Sikhs—Legal status,
laws, etc.—Great Britain.   5. Rastafari movement—Great Britain.
6. Human rights—Great Britain.   I. Title.
KD4095.P68   1998
342. 41 ' 087–dc21   97-38242
ISBN 0–19–825773–2

Typeset by J&L Composition Ltd, Filey, North Yorkshire

Printed in Great Britain
on acid-free paper by
Bookcraft Ltd, Midsomer Norton, Bath

Preface

Recent years have witnessed an increased tendency on the part of many peoples and individuals to identify with their particular ethnic groups or communities. An appreciation of their cultural heritage, a concern for the preservation of their distinctive customs and traditions, and a commitment to maintain their deeply-held values and beliefs has led them to stake out claims upon the wider polity for greater recognition of their ethnicity. Indeed, there is now widespread public awareness that a majority of modern states do not reflect single nations, but are ethnically heterogeneous in character and possess profound religious, linguistic, and cultural divisions.

In England, during the past thirty years, there has been a growing interest in how such relatively recently formed ethnic communities as the Muslims, Hindus, Sikhs, and Rastafarians are faring in a comparatively novel and strange environment, and what response there has been on the part of the majority community. My own investigations have been particularly directed at examining the reaction of the English legal system to the presence of these four groups here. Of course, two other ethnic communities, the Jews and the gypsies, have been established in this country for a much longer period. In this book, a central cultural concern of some members of each of these six minority ethnic communities is placed under the spotlight and examined in the context of the relevant provisions of English law. While much has been written over the past quarter of a century or so on the subject of ethnic relations in Britain by political scientists, sociologists, anthropologists, and educationalists, there has been relatively little analysis of the subject by lawyers, whose principal interests in ethnic minorities have lain in the related but distinct areas of immigration and anti-discrimination law. Furthermore, what has so far been written from a legal standpoint appears to have had only limited impact upon research within these other disciplines. This is surprising, bearing in mind both the significance of the legal dimension in framing and implementing policies in the field of ethnic relations and the important symbolic role of English law as the embodiment of certain standards and values for which Britain claims worldwide renown. Legal analysis can also provide a degree of clarity and precision of exposition in a subject often bedevilled by obfuscating sociological jargon, impenetrable to all save specialists in the subject. In addition, the discipline of law can usually offer a sharper focus not only because of its coercive and binding nature, but also because it tends to operate most directly when clashes between cultures are particularly acute.

English law embodies values, principles, and rules which have been developed and refined over a considerable period of time through democratic political debate and detailed interpretation by analytical judicial minds, in order to deal with disputes and problems in a specifically English context. Yet how is it to cope with newcomers from other countries and civilizations, who may have very different conceptions, values, perspectives, traditions, and beliefs? The old adage 'When in Rome, do as the Romans do' cannot be pressed too far in the modern world, when what is at stake is religious freedom or cultural identity, and English law is likely, if it is not sufficiently sensitive and adaptable, to find itself on a collision course with people of deep convictions, who feel that their cultural values and practices cannot simply be jettisoned once they have begun a new life on foreign soil.

This book attempts to illuminate the conflicts which are liable to arise in such circumstances through the medium of two particular techniques. Part I analyses the policies, principles, and legal rules which have been developed to handle the ethnic diversity which characterizes England today, and it places them in the wider context of the protection afforded to ethnic minorities by international human rights law, as it has evolved during the course of the twentieth century. This affords the reader an opportunity of appreciating both what legally ought to be done and what may properly be accomplished in terms of international standards and norms, as well as what is actually happening under current English law in relation to ethnic differences.

Part II is devoted to six detailed 'case studies', in which specific matters of major cultural significance to Jews, gypsies, Muslims, Hindus, Sikhs, and Rastafarians respectively, are addressed primarily in terms of their potential to generate a conflict with English legal provisions. Each of these studies follows a similar pattern, in which the historical background to the particular community's presence in England is explored, the attitudes of the majority community are examined, and the specific issue generating the potential conflict is described, before the impact of English law on the question is analysed. Since legal rules and principles evolve in a particular social and political context, a deeper appreciation of their significance can be achieved if the social background of the community concerned is understood and if there is a detailed survey of the political dimension of the enactment of English legislation in terms of public discussion, parliamentary debates, and the activities of pressure groups and influential individuals. Insofar as English law has adapted to the cultural needs of the ethnic communities this study reveals how and why this has come about. Where English law has proved less flexible, an attempt is made to discover why such a rigid stance has been adopted. It is vital to appreciate the interplay of various forces in these equations, as well as the connections which exist between modern legal developments and arguments, on the one hand, and historical events and perceptions, on the other. This rounded approach should afford the possibility of a fresh perspective from which to view the broad field of ethnic relations in England today.

In assessing whether the current provisions of English law deal adequately with each of the six contentious situations analysed in Part II, some comparisons are drawn with the legal position in other countries, as well as with the standards set by international human rights law. In the final chapter, in Part III, an attempt is made to chart the way ahead. The dangers of failing to find satisfactory solutions to each of the issues addressed by the case studies are the alienation of certain sections of the population, the risk in some instances of creating separate ghettoes in English towns and cities, and friction in foreign relations with other states, as well as possible outbreaks of civil strife, each of which could have very harmful effects upon the social fabric and economic wellbeing of the country at large.

It is important to indicate at the outset that this book is concerned with ethnic differences relating to matters of culture (in a broad sense), rather than with 'racial' differences related to skin 'colour'. The chapters in Part II cover topics such as family organization, religious worship, diet, dress, personal appearance, and general lifestyle, which typically form the basis of an ethnic group's claim to the possession of distinctive cultural traditions. 'Ethnicity' and 'race' are thus perceived to be very different concepts, albeit with a certain degree of overlap. This work is not, therefore, an analysis of legal measures designed to reduce racial discrimination (although some reference is made to this subject), nor does it examine questions of colour prejudice in Britain.

I should like to express my thanks to Yvonne Baatz, Catherine Barnard, Ralph Beddard, Penny Green, Andrew Halpin, Urfan Khaliq, and Jonathan Montgomery for their kindness in commenting on drafts of individual chapters. I also owe an immense debt of gratitude to Marion Dalton and Margaret Newton for their patient and painstaking transformation of an untidy manuscript into a presentable form for publication. Completion of the book would not have been possible but for the support and encouragement of my wife, Jane, who has helped in so many ways.

Part of Chapter 3 first appeared in volumes XXV-XXVII (1990–1992) of

The Irish Jurist (N.S.) (Round Hall Press, Dublin, 1994) and part of Chapter 6 was previously published as a contribution to *Islamic Family Law,* edited by Chibli Mallat and Jane Connors (Graham & Trotman, London, 1990).

S.P.

Contents

PART III: THE WAY AHEAD

Table of Cases

Table of Statutes

UK Statutes

OTHER NATIONAL STATUTES

AUSTRALIA

CANADA

Table of International Instruments

PART I
General Survey

PART I
Country Studies

1

Introduction

People have been coming to settle in Britain for centuries. They have come from near and far, individually and in groups, fleeing from political or religious persecution and in search of economic advancement.[1] Among the many groups of immigrants who entered this country between 1400 and 1900 mention may be made of the arrival of wandering bands of gypsies during the fifteenth century,[2] the importation of African slaves and servants from the sixteenth century onwards,[3] the influx of Huguenot refugees from France during the sixteenth and seventeenth centuries,[4] and the re-admission of Jews in the middle of the seventeenth century for the first time since the banishment imposed upon them by Edward I in 1290.[5]

Around the turn of the twentieth century many Jews fled to Britain from pogroms in Eastern Europe[6] and others followed later, their numbers being swelled during the 1930s by those who escaped from Nazi persecution in Germany. Immediately after the 1939–45 War a large number of political refugees and exiles from Eastern Europe settled here. They were followed from 1948 onwards by economic migrants from the colonies and the New Commonwealth.[7] To begin with they came principally from Jamaica and other islands in the Caribbean, but there were also smaller contingents from the Indian subcontinent, Cyprus, Malta, and Hong Kong (amongst others). Just

---

[1] For excellent synopses, see Kiernan, V., 'Britons Old and New' in Holmes, C. (ed.), *Immigrants and Minorities in British Society* (London, 1978), ch 2; Patterson, S., 'Immigrants and Minority Groups in British Society' in Abbott, S. (ed.), *The Prevention of Racial Discrimination in Britain* (London, 1971), 41–53.

[2] See Okely, J., *The Traveller-Gypsies* (Cambridge, 1983), 3.

[3] See generally, Walvin, J., *Black and White: The Negro and English Society 1555–1945* (London, 1973); Shyllon, F., *Black People in Britain 1555–1833* (London, 1977). Much earlier, Africans had served as soldiers during the Roman occupation of Britain, notably in one of the legions that was stationed at Hadrian's Wall; see Fryer, P., *Staying Power: The History of Black People in Britain* (London, 1984), 1–2.

[4] See Gwynn, R., *Huguenot Heritage* (London, 1985).

[5] See e.g. Hyamson, A., *A History of the Jews in England* (London, 1908); Roth, C., *A History of the Jews in England* (Oxford, 1941).

[6] For immigration in the more modern period, see generally, Holmes, C., *John Bull's Island: Immigration and British Society, 1871–1971* (Basingstoke, 1988).

[7] See generally, Rose, E., *Colour and Citizenship* (London, 1969), Part II.

before immigration controls were introduced by the Commonwealth Immigrants Act 1962 the pace of immigration from India and Pakistan began to quicken appreciably and it continued to be very substantial even after this enactment, principally through vouchers and the admission of wives and children and other dependent relatives. The late 1960s and early 1970s saw the arrival of many East African Asians, who had either found themselves squeezed out of their jobs through the process of 'Africanization' in Kenya and Tanzania or else had been forcibly expelled from Uganda by Idi Amin. More recently, sizeable numbers of refugees have fled here from Vietnam, Iran, Sri Lanka, Somalia, and the former Yugoslavia.

THE NATURE OF ETHNICITY

The precise nature of ethnicity is intensely problematic. That the concept defies simple definition and explanation is apparent from the diverse approaches to the subject taken by writers over the past thirty years or so.[8] However, for present purposes it is sufficient to explore briefly some of its legal, dictionary, and census meanings simply with a view to clarifying the scope of the analysis which forms the focus of this work.

The only context in which the meaning of ethnicity has had to be judicially determined in England, as part of the process of statutory interpretation, has been in the field of race relations legislation. In an attempt to provide a satisfactory, all-embracing definition of the complex concept of racial discrimination, Parliament has resorted to a wide-ranging formula, which seeks to outlaw discrimination which is related to a person's 'colour, race, nationality or ethnic or national origins'.[9] Such language has been described as 'rubbery and elusive'[10] and in the leading case of *Mandla v Dowell Lee*[11] in 1983 the House of Lords was called upon to decide exactly what is meant by 'ethnic' origins in the Race Relations Act 1976. Lord Fraser's opinion in that case was strongly influenced by the conclusions reached four years earlier by the New

---

[8] See e.g. Shibutani, T. and Kwan, K., *Ethnic Stratification: A Comparative Approach* (New York, 1965); Barth, F. (ed.), *Ethnic Groups and Boundaries* (London, 1969); Glazer, N. and Moynihan, D. (eds), *Ethnicity: Theory and Experience* (Massachusetts, 1975); Van den Bergh, P., *The Ethnic Phenomenon* (New York, 1981); Banton, M., *Racial and Ethnic Competition* (Cambridge, 1983); Rex, J., *Race and Ethnicity* (Milton Keynes, 1986); Rex, J. and Mason, D. (eds), *Theories of Race and Ethnic Relations* (Cambridge, 1986); Smith, A., *The Ethnic Origin of Nations* (Oxford, 1986); Hutnik, N., *Ethnic Minority Identity: A Social Psychological Perspective* (Oxford, 1991); Eriksen, T., *Ethnicity and Nationalism* (London, 1993); Hutchinson, J. and Smith A. (eds), *Ethnicity* (Oxford, 1996).   [9] Race Relations Act 1976, s 3(1).
[10] See *Ealing London Borough v Race Relations Board* [1972] AC 342 at 362 per Lord Simon, who was commenting on similar wording in Race Relations Act 1968, s 1(1).
[11] [1983] 2 AC 548.

Zealand Court of Appeal in *King-Ansell v Police*.[12] In interpreting similar language in a New Zealand statute, the Court there had recourse to dictionary definitions of 'ethnic' and the same approach was followed in *Mandla v Dowell Lee*. Perusal of the first edition of the *Oxford English Dictionary* by the judges in both cases revealed three phases in the evolution of the word. The earliest meaning, dating from 1470 (if not before) is given as 'pertaining to nations not Christian or Jewish; Gentile, heathen, pagan'. Since this definition is no longer in current, popular usage and its adoption would lead to the bizarre result that Jews would clearly not be protected by the race relations legislation, it was rejected by both courts as totally inappropriate.[13] A second definition, dating back to the middle of the nineteenth century, is 'pertaining to race; peculiar to a race or nation; ethnological'. This definition is unhelpful for two reasons. First, it adds nothing to the other words already in the statutory formula, namely 'colour, race, nationality or . . . national origins' and is thus superfluous in the context of race relations legislation. Secondly, it would tend to confine cases of racial discrimination to situations where there is scientific proof of possession by a community of distinctive genetic and biological characteristics, when there are very few, if any, distinctions which are scientifically recognized as racial. Both courts concluded, therefore, that 'ethnic' should be interpreted in a much broader and more 'popular' sense.[14]

The third definition, only given in the 1972 *Supplement* to the first edition of the *OED* (not the original *Dictionary* itself[15]) and whose earliest usage was apparently in 1935, is 'pertaining to or having common racial, cultural, religious or linguistic characteristics, [especially] designating a racial or other group within a larger system'. While this modern definition held far greater appeal for both courts in its recognition of broadly 'cultural' as well as 'racial' factors,[16] it was capable, upon a literal interpretation, of affording 'ethnic' rather too wide a meaning, since a group defined solely by reference to religious characteristics would qualify for protection, whereas all the judges knew very well that the legislation in question was not designed to outlaw purely religious discrimination.[17]

The application of the Race Relations Act 1976 to specific instances of discrimination on the basis of 'ethnic origins' and the precise interpretations

[12] [1979] 2 NZLR 531.
[13] *King-Ansell v Police* at 533, 537–8, 541; *Mandla v Dowell Lee* at 561.
[14] *King-Ansell v Police* at 533; *Mandla v Dowell Lee* at 561.
[15] The original *OED* was published under the title *A New English Dictionary on Historical Principles* between 1888 and 1928.
[16] *King-Ansell v Police* at 535, 536, 538, 543; *Mandla v Dowell Lee* at 562.
[17] *King-Ansell v Police* at 533, 541; *Mandla v Dowell Lee* at 562, 568.

placed upon this phrase are considered at various places later in this work,[18] but the important point to make at this stage is that the concept of ethnicity used in the book's title is derived from the broad, modern, more culturally-orientated one designated in the third definition given in the 1972 *Supplement* to the first edition of the *OED* and repeated in the second edition of the *Dictionary* published in 1989. Appropriately, the second edition also defines 'ethnic minority (group)' as 'a group of people differentiated from the rest of the community by racial origins *or cultural background*' (emphasis added). So far, English courts and tribunals have only given rulings that Sikhs[19], Jews[20], and gypsies[21] constitute 'ethnic' groups and are thus entitled on this ground alone to the protection of the Race Relations Act. On the other hand, tribunal and court decisions indicate that Muslims[22] and Rastafarians[23] are not included, essentially because they are perceived as purely religious groups. The position of Hindus has not yet been considered in any proceedings under the Act. Nevertheless, all these groups or communities come within the broad compass of ethnicity adopted in this book and are allocated separate chapters in the case studies in Part II. This is because the focus of the work is upon those cultural traditions, values, and religious beliefs of the minority communities which distinguish them from the majority community, as opposed to differences based upon 'race', colour, or nationality, and regardless of whether discrimination against a particular minority is classified as 'racial' discrimination in the eyes of English law.

It needs to be acknowledged that in an essay published in 1969, which has had a profound impact upon the modern anthropological approach to ethnicity, Fredrik Barth sought to move the emphasis away from the cultural content of ethnicity towards trying to find explanations for the maintenance of social boundaries between different groups.[24] A major plank in his argument was that members of an ethnic group could, through contact with other groups, cease to exhibit their separate cultural traits and yet still perceive themselves as distinctive and different from their neighbours. Moreover, members of an ethnic group could disperse into very different ecological environments and significantly alter their cultural behaviour in consequence, but nevertheless maintain

---

[18] See below, pp 303–7, 351–4   [19] *Mandla v Dowell Lee* (above).
[20] *Seide v Gillette Industries Ltd* [1980] IRLR 427; *Mandla v Dowell Lee* [1982] 3 All ER 1108 at 1113 (CA); [1983] 2 AC 548 at 561 (HL); *Simon v Brimham Associates* [1987] IRLR 307.
[21] *Commission for Racial Equality v Dutton* [1989] 1 All ER 306.
[22] *Nyazi v Rymans Ltd* (EAT, 10 May 1988, unreported); *Tariq v Young* (Birmingham Industrial Tribunal, 19 Apr 1989, unreported); *Commission for Racial Equality v Precision Manufacturing Services* (Sheffield Industrial Tribunal, 26 July 1991, unreported); *J H Walker Ltd v Hussain* [1996] IRLR 11.
[23] *Dawkins v Department of the Environment* [1993] IRLR 284.
[24] *Ethnic Groups and Boundaries*, 9–38.

a common allegiance to their original ethnic group. It is probable, there-fore, that the self-ascription of difference and the maintenance of social boundaries constitute key ingredients of ethnicity. Even so, reference to a past, real or imagined, in which a community functioned on the basis of distinctive cultural traditions would seem to be equally essential to the recognition of these boundaries. Moreover, in the context of the present work the particular cultural practices examined in Part II remain central to the ethnic identities of very many members of the groups concerned. They continue to differentiate themselves, and indeed are distinguished by outsiders, on the basis of their adherence to cultural norms such as those discussed in Chapters 4 to 9.

It is also worth stressing at this stage the situational and instrumental characteristics commonly attributed to the concept of ethnicity by anthropologists.[25] The particular features of a group's culture, which are identified as significant by members and outsiders, and precisely where the boundary is drawn with other groups, especially the majority community, often depend upon the context or situation in which an issue arises. Furthermore, a group may choose to emphasize, adapt or even distort or invent[26] specific cultural traits, in order to achieve certain goals or objectives in its dealings with the wider society and state institutions. Ethnic identity is a malleable phenomenon and cultures can obviously be employed, mobilized, manipulated, or modified to suit strategic purposes, as the studies in Part II demonstrate.

A graphic illustration of several of these definitional difficulties is furnished by the 'ethnic question' used in the 1991 national census. Respondents were asked, for the first time in such a census in Britain, to identify their 'ethnic group' by reference to a list of nine possible categories. Such a procedure inevitably imposes an absolute, rather than situational, character upon ethnicity, as one leading analyst has pointed out—

One may be Welsh in England, British in Germany, European in Thailand, White in Africa. A person may be Afro-Caribbean by descent but British by upbringing . . . . Similarly, a person may be an East African Asian, an Indian, a Sikh or a Ramgarhia.[27]

Of the nine categories employed in the census, one was simply 'White', with no scope for internal differentiations within, for example, the various European or North American identities. Since there was no separate

<hr>

[25] See generally, Banks, M., *Ethnicity: Anthropological Constructions* (London, 1996).
[26] See e.g. Sollors, W. (ed.), *The Invention of Ethnicity* (New York, 1989); Alexander, C., *The Art of Being Black: The Creation of Black British Youth Identities* (Oxford, 1996).
[27] Peach, C., 'Introduction' in Peach, C. (ed.), *Ethnicity in the 1991 Census* (London, 1996), vol 2, 1 at 5.

category of 'Arab', many respondents from the Middle East classified themselves as 'White', while others appreciated that this answer would not correspond with the intentions of the framers of the census question and therefore designated themselves instead as members of a residual category of 'Others'.[28] The category of 'Indian' clearly could not encompass crucial differences in religion, language, or place of origin, nor could the category 'Black-African' reflect the profound cultural distinctions which exist between the many peoples from that continent. Indeed, not one of the groups represented in the case studies in Part II of this work was identified as a separate ethnic category in the census. In reality, the pragmatic focus of the census question was upon colour, race, and national origins rather than upon culture, tradition, or religious affiliation. Despite their very limited value for present purposes, the census figures for England and Wales are given below so that readers are at least aware of the broad statistical information uncovered by the inclusion of a purportedly 'ethnic' question.[29]

Ethnic Group	Numbers
White	46,875,667
Indian	830,205
Pakistani	455,363
Bangladeshi	161,701
Black African	205,447
Black Caribbean	492,471
Black (other)[30]	215,191
Chinese	146,462
Other ethnic groups	507,770

A 'religious' question was not included in the 1991 census, nor are any official government statistics kept concerning religious affiliation in this country,[31] no doubt partly because such figures would need to be viewed with great caution.[32] They can specify how many people claim

---

[28] Al-Rasheed, M., 'The Other-Others: hidden Arabs?' in *Ethnicity in the 1991 Census*, vol 2, ch 9.

[29] Office of Population, Censuses and Surveys, *1991 Census: Ethnic Group and Country of Birth, Great Britain* (London, 1993), 830–1, 858–9; for further details, see generally the four volumes on *Ethnicity in the 1991 Census* (London, 1996).

[30] At least a quarter (and perhaps a much higher proportion) of those in this category are young people of Afro-Caribbean descent who were born in Britain; see Ballard, R. and Kalra, V., *The Ethnic Dimensions of the 1991 Census: A Preliminary Report* (Manchester, 1994), 7–8; Peach, C. 'Black-Caribbeans: class, gender and geography' in *Ethnicity in the 1991 Census*, vol 2, 25 at 26–7.

[31] The estimates regularly published in *Social Trends* are based upon figures supplied by the various religious faiths and denominations themselves.

[32] A question about religious affiliation may, however, be included in the 2001 census.

to belong to a particular faith, but they cannot indicate the strength of a person's inner commitment nor the extent to which individuals comply with the 'normal' observances of that faith.[33] The 1991 census figures are thus not of much direct relevance for present purposes, in view of the fact that five of the six groups considered in Part II are held together to a large degree by religious ties and the sixth group, gypsies, had no means of separately identifying themselves on the census form. Estimates of the membership of the various ethnic groups examined in Part II are given in their respective chapters, but in the main they are unofficial[34] and too much reliance should not be placed upon them.

It has become commonplace in England today to refer to both the 'non-White' groups identified in the 1991 census and those examined in Part II of this book as 'ethnic minority communities' or 'minority ethnic communities' and this convention is followed here because the terminology is so widely used and understood. However, to refer to these groups as 'communities' may tend to disguise important divisions within some of these minorities,[35] such as those based on national origins, sect, clan, caste, gender,[36] and age.[37] Even the common bonds of Hinduism, Sikhism, and Islam may often be less important in the everyday lives of Asian settlers here than the much narrower loyalties of caste, sect, and descent-group.[38] There are obvious dangers in readily assuming that the only identity possessed by any individual person is membership of a particular ethnic community, defined by reference to its adherence to a specific 'culture'.[39] As will be seen, this is an important consideration when the issue of 'group rights' is addressed in subsequent chapters.[40] Even so, it is thought that the ethnic groups considered in Part II possess a sufficient degree of distinctiveness to justify the appellation of 'communities', at least in a loose sense, so long as their internal heterogeneity is borne in mind.

[33] See e.g. Sillitoe, A., *Britain in Figures* (Harmondsworth, 1973), 13.

[34] The figures for gypsies are provided by the Department of the Environment; see below, ch 5.

[35] See e.g. Rex and Mason, 30; Ignatieff, M., 'Why "community" is a dishonest word', *Observer*, 3 May 1992.

[36] See e.g. Saghal, G. and Yuval-Davis, N., *Refusing Holy Orders: Women and Fundamentalism in Britain* (London, 1992).

[37] See e.g. Knott, K. and Khokher, S., 'Religion and ethnic identity among young Muslim women in Bradford' (1993) *New Community* 593.

[38] See Ballard, R. (ed.), *Desh Pardesh: The South Asian Presence in Britain* (London, 1994), 4, 29; see also Lewis, P., *Islamic Britain: Religion, Politics and Identity among British Muslims* (London, 1994), *passim*.

[39] See generally, Hutnik, N., *Ethnic Minority Identity: A Social Psychological Perspective* (Oxford, 1991); Baumann, G., *Contesting Culture: Discourses of Identity in Multi-ethnic London* (Cambridge, 1996); Appiah, K., 'Identity, Authenticity, Survival' in Guttman, A. (ed.), *Multiculturalism*, 2nd ed. (Princeton, 1994), 149–63.

[40] See below, especially, chs 3 and 6.

Ethnicity, Law and Human Rights

From a legal perspective, as we shall see, in several respects the most important characteristics of the ethnic minority communities today are not so much the (predominantly) brown or black skins of their members but the adherence by many of them to certain customs, traditions, religious beliefs, and value systems which are greatly at variance from those of the majority community.[41] As Sir Thomas Bingham (now Lord Bingham CJ) commented in 1993—

. . . it is probably true that post-war immigration, particularly from the Indian sub-continent and the West Indies, has made us a more heterogeneous people than we have ever been. And it is surely true that some of these more recent citizens have shown less willingness to be submerged in the prevailing British way of life, and more desire to preserve their own traditions of language, custom and religion, than most of their predecessors have been inclined to do.[42]

It seems increasingly clear that, faced with continued prejudice,[43] discrimination,[44] and even violent attacks[45] from sections of the majority community, many members of the ethnic minority communities are responding by emphasizing their distinctive religious and cultural identities[46], sometimes even by means of deliberate separation from the mainstream of British life. They are harnessing their cultural resources to devise collective strategies of active resistance to racial hostility, discrimination, and disadvantage in order to enable them to circumvent patterns of oppression and exclusion. They are finding that 'membership of an ethnic network is a valuable asset in the maintenance of a positive sense of personal identity and self-worth, especially in the face of systematic denigration'.[47] Furthermore, the first signs are appearing of the

[41] For a valuable empirical study of the attitudes of two generations of 'British Asians' towards the maintenance of their cultural identities and the retention of religious and social traditions, see Stopes-Roe, M. and Cochrane, R., *Citizens of This Country: The Asian-British* (Clevedon, 1990).

[42] 'The European Convention on Human Rights: Time to Incorporate' (1993) 109 *LQR* 390 at 391–2.

[43] See e.g. Jowell, R. *et al* (eds), *British Social Attitudes: The 9th Report* (Aldershot, 1992), 181–93; Institute for Public Policy Research, *Survey on Prejudice* (London, 1997).

[44] See e.g. Brown, C., *Black and White Britain* (London, 1984); Brown, C. and Gay, P., *Racial Discrimination: 17 Years After the Act* (London, 1985); Modood, T., Berthoud, R., *et al, Ethnic Minorities in Britain: Diversity and Disadvantage* (London, 1997), ch 4.

[45] See e.g. 'Racial Attacks and Harassment', Third Report of the House of Commons Home Affairs Committee, HC 71 of 1994; Modood, Berthoud, *et al*, ch 8.

[46] See Modood, T., Beishon, S. and Virdee, S., *Changing Ethnic Identities* (London, 1994), ch 6.

[47] Ballard, R., 'New Clothes for the Emperor?: The conceptual nakedness of the race relations industry in Britain' (1992) *New Community* 481 at 487; see also Modood, T., *Racial Equality: Colour, Culture and Justice* (London, 1994), 12–13.

rewards of such strategies in terms of economic success for some of the newer minority communities.[48] The ill-treatment of minorities here does not, of course, provide even a major part of the explanation for this phenomenon of cultural retention. For most Asians of the older genera-tions in Britain their countries of origin provide strong moral reference points in terms of furnishing potent influences upon their behaviour here.[49] The vitality of their links with kinsfolk and villagers in the Indian subcontinent ensures that they maintain high standards of conduct so that the honour of their families is preserved intact. Compliance with traditional norms of behaviour is important if they are not to suffer a loss of standing and prestige among members of their own communities, both here and overseas.

However, there is a much more positive side to the preservation of ethnic minority cultures and values than the two 'defensive' mechanisms just mentioned. Many members of these communities see themselves as proud inheritors of major ancient civilizations. They naturally dislike being portrayed in the British media merely as victims of racism or else as posing a threat to the majority community. One consequence of this is that many Asians have come to resent being designated simply as 'black', a blanket term hitherto widely used (notably by the political Left) to refer to those from the Indian subcontinent, as well as Africans and Afro-Caribbeans. The idea that they should be included within a group defined by reference to, arguably, its most negative characteristics (victim or threat) rather than by stressing its most positive characteristics (cultural or religious identity) is now anathema to many.[50] On the other hand, one group whose members are particularly proud to call them-selves 'black', the Rastafarians, seek to emphasize certain distinctive cultural traits, both as a means of distancing themselves from some of the values of mainstream society and as a mechanism for the re-discovery of their African roots.

Over the next few years ethnic identity and cultural diversity can therefore be expected to set the political agenda in relation to the min-ority communities just as forcefully as discrimination on the basis of colour or 'race'. As Modood has pertinently put it, 'the road to social integration and race equality politics has to go through ethnicity, not

[48] See Modood, T., 'The Indian Economic Success: a challenge to some race relations assumptions' (1991) 19 *Policy and Politics* 177.

[49] See e.g. Jeffery, P., *Migrants and Refugees: Muslim and Christian Families in Bristol* (Cambridge, 1976); Anwar, M., *The Myth of Return: Pakistanis in Britain* (London, 1979); Bhachu, P., *Twice Migrants: East African Sikh Settlers in Britain* (London, 1985); Robinson, V., *Transients, Settlers and Refugees: Asians in Britain* (Cambridge, 1986); Shaw, A., *A Pakistani Community in Britain* (Oxford, 1988).

[50] See e.g. Modood, T., 'Alabama Britain', *Guardian*, 22 May 1989; Modood, Berthoud, *et al*, 294–7.

against it'.[51] In similar vein, Gilroy has pointed out that 'racial subordination is not the sole factor shaping the choices and actions of Britain's black settlers and their British-born children. . . . Black expressive cultures affirm while they protest'.[52]

POLICY OPTIONS

Many different expressions have been coined over recent decades in an attempt to describe the variety of policy options available to the British state and its institutions in dealing with the implications of an ethnically diverse population. Absorption, acculturation, adaptation, assimilation, integration, multiculturalism, and pluralism are among the most widely used terms. However, no consensus exists as to the exact meanings to be attributed to several of these words, leading to a growing sense of bewilderment among writers and their readers as well as commentators and their audiences. In the present work the inventory of these concepts will be scaled down to the two which seem to have the greatest potential for illuminating the subject, but the justification for this pruning should not be interpreted as merely a search for simplification. While the overall objective is certainly one of clarification, it will be argued that this can only be achieved by recognizing the diversity of implications inherent in each of the two broad approaches selected. It is precisely because the implications of common terms have not usually been spelt out in a coherent fashion that so much confusion currently reigns. Since so many of the most important repercussions of these alternative approaches lie in the field of law, it is hoped that a careful legal analysis may offer a particularly valuable insight into the practical significance of the two different policy options discussed.[53]

(a) Assimilation

A policy of assimilation is generally understood as entailing the 'absorption' of the minorities into the mainstream culture of the majority community. Minority groups are required to surrender the distinctive

---

[51] Modood, note 50 above. See also Modood, T., ' "Black", racial equality and Asian identity' (1988) *New Community* 397 and 'Catching up with Jesse Jackson: being oppressed and being somebody' (1990) *New Community* 85.

[52] *There Ain't No Black in the Union Jack: the cultural politics of race and nation* (London, 1987), 153, 155.

[53] For illuminating analyses of the options, see Parekh, B., *Colour, Class and Consciousness* (London, 1984), ch 15; Parekh, B., 'Britain and the Social Logic of Pluralism' in *Britain: A Plural Society* (London, 1990), 58–76. See also Honeyford, R., *Integration or Disintegration* (London, 1988), ch 2.

characteristics of their separate identities and blend into the wider society. It is taken for granted that the dominant culture of the majority is superior to that of the minorities and that it is desirable to ensure an homogeneous society through 'acculturation' on the part of the minorities. The acceptance of the minorities by the majority and by the state as full members of the broader society is made conditional upon the abandonment of their cultural differences. Separate group identities are to be obliterated. Alien customs and traditions are viewed rather like jokers in a pack of cards, needing to be discarded for proper participation in the game of social and political life. That many white people in Britain still consider assimilation through 'adaptation' to be a moral obligation on the part of migrants and their descendants today is apparent from the frequently heard utterance of the old adage—'When in Rome, do as the Romans do'.

A variety of ulterior motives may obviously be ascribed to some assimilationists, including feelings of prejudice and xenophobia. In this regard it is worth noting that, according to a survey report compiled during 1991, more than 90 per cent of respondents perceived British society as racially prejudiced and almost a third classified themselves as racially prejudiced.[54] In a further survey conducted in 1991 Britain was perceived as a racist society by 56 per cent of Asians, 67 per cent of whites and 79 per cent of Afro-Caribbeans.[55] However, there are at least four rational arguments in favour of varying degrees of assimilation which merit serious consideration. First, there may be genuine concern that failure by members of some minorities to assimilate with respect to certain important English values may involve a departure from minimum standards of acceptable behaviour.[56] Secondly, it may be argued that the vital principle of 'equality before the law' will be jeopardized if minorities are accorded special exemptions and privileges by the English legal system, on the basis of their adherence to traditional practices or religious rituals. Such equality has long been regarded as a cardinal virtue of the English legal system and more than a century ago Dicey made particular reference to it as part of the fundamental concept of the

[54] See Jowell, 181–3.
[55] See Amin, K. and Richardson, R., *Politics for All: Equality, Culture and the General Election 1992* (London, 1992), 22, 44.
[56] In *The Morality of Freedom* (Oxford, 1986) Raz argues that assimilation may be justified where the culture of a minority community imposes undue restrictions upon the personal liberty of its members (at 423–4). Note also the comment by Conor Cruise O'Brien—'When we are told to respect the cultures of groups we are being told to respect things which may include, for example, the Hindu caste system, the treatment of women in Islam and a number of other cultures, female circumcision in certain cultures, ostracism of twins . . . and so on', 'What Rights should Minorities Have?' in Ashworth, G. (ed.), *World Minorities* (Sunbury, 1977), 1, xvii.

'rule of law'.[57] Thirdly, anxiety may be expressed about the degree to which some members of minority groups can attain economic advancement and prosperity and break free from a cycle of disadvantage and discrimination if they insist upon retaining their separate customs and identities. The suggestion here is that white employers, for example, may be less willing to recruit minority workers whom they fear may make cultural or religious demands upon them or may not 'fit in' and work well with other employees.[58] Fourthly, there may be a feeling that the active promotion of separate ethnic identities may foster divisiveness and be incompatible with the degree of general social cohesion required for the maintenance of a sense of national unity.[59]

During the early years of post-1945 immigration it was widely assumed in official circles that assimilation would be the appropriate policy for Britain to adopt.[60] Most of those who came to settle here during the 1950s and early 1960s originated from the Caribbean. A history of slavery and three centuries of British colonial rule had already deprived Afro-Caribbeans of many of their original cultural traditions and led to their substantial Anglicization.[61] They thought of themselves primarily as British, they spoke the English language as their mother-tongue (albeit in a special dialect or *patois*), and in Christianity they felt that they shared a common religious faith with white Britons. There appeared to be no profound cultural differences and it seemed that assimilation would quickly remove most minor differences, without

---

[57] See Dicey, A., *An Introduction to the Study of the Law of the Constitution*, 10th ed. (London, 1959), ch IV.

[58] For examples of discrimination of this type, see Commission for Racial Equality, *Chartered Accountancy Contracts* (London, 1987), 18–20; Commission for Racial Equality, *Second Review of the Race Relations Act 1976* (London, 1991), 13–14.

[59] This may perhaps be regarded as a rather Machiavellian argument since he advised his prince to eliminate cultural differences in the population and submerge cultural groups into an homogeneous polity on the grounds that national unity was crucial in defence of the republic in a predatory international environment—see Machiavelli, N., *The Prince and the Discourses* (Lerner, M., ed.; New York, 1940), xxxiv. For some on the right-wing of modern British politics the very concept of 'nationhood' excludes those who are culturally different from the majority community even if they possess British nationality; see generally, Gordon, P., *White Law: Racism in the Police, Courts and Prisons* (London, 1983), 143–7; Gilroy, P., *op cit*.

[60] See e.g. Patterson, S., *Immigration and Race Relations in Britain 1960–1967* (London, 1969), 108–15. It is worth noting that in 1949 a Royal Commission, set up to consider what measures might be introduced to influence future population trends, stressed the importance of ensuring that immigrants were 'of good human stock and were not prevented by their religion or race from intermarrying with the host population and becoming merged in it'; *Report of Royal Commission on Population*, Cmnd 7695 of 1949, 124.

[61] See e.g. Pryce, K., *Endless Pressure: A Study of West Indian Life-styles in Bristol* (Harmondsworth, 1979), 2–5; Hiro, D., *Black British, White British* (London, 1991), ch 2.

undue difficulty.[62] Hence, in 1964 the Commonwealth Immigrants Advisory Council, for example, referred in one of its reports to its basic assumption that—

. . . a national system of education must aim at producing citizens who can take their place in society properly equipped to exercise rights and perform duties which are the same as those of other citizens. If their parents were brought up in another culture or another tradition, children should be encouraged to respect it, but a national system cannot be expected to perpetuate the different values of immigrant groups.[63]

However, by the mid-1960s a policy of assimilation was becoming much harder to sustain in the light of the arrival of large numbers of Muslims, Hindus, and Sikhs from the Indian subcontinent. Their distinctive religious beliefs, disparate cultural traditions, and diverse languages set them much further apart from the white population and these factors prompted a reassessment of what a realistic policy should endeavour to achieve. It would be much more difficult to promote assimilation against the wishes of sizeable ethnic and religious groups from South Asia than to apply it to migrants from the Caribbean, whose main difference from the majority community lay merely in the colour of their skin. Moreover, historical evidence suggested that assimilation could often prove counter-productive, with minorities tending to become far more determined to hold fast to their ethnic identities than if no official efforts had been made to cut them adrift from their cultural heritage.[64]

(b) Cultural pluralism

From the mid-1960s onwards policy-makers have increasingly tended to distance themselves from an assimilationist approach in their public pronouncements and have moved steadily towards a broad philosophy of cultural pluralism (initially described as 'integration'). Those who subscribe to this approach emphasize the importance of according proper respect to the distinctive cultures and identities of members of the ethnic communities. They regard this as the appropriate response to

[62] The following comment made in the House of Commons in 1965 by Sir John Vaughan-Morgan seems typical—'West Indians . . . may be at the opposite end to us in the racial spectrum, but . . . without exception they are the most assimilable of all immigrants'; HC Debs, 709, col 361. In her study of early West Indian migrants Patterson did, however, draw attention to several distinctive cultural traits, e.g. in relation to family structure, sex relations, and religious affiliation and practice—see *Dark Strangers* (London, 1963).
[63] *Commonwealth Immigrants Advisory Council Second Report*, Cmnd 2266 of 1964, para 10.
[64] A well-known example was the unsuccessful attempt to stamp out the foreign cultures of immigrants to America during the period 1910–20; see Hartmann, E., *The Movement to Americanize the Immigrant* (New York, 1967).

diversity in a liberal democracy in which individual choice, freedom of expression, concern for human dignity, justice, and religious toleration are cherished as important values. While they are naturally concerned to uphold the principle of equality before the law in a formal (Diceyan) sense, they also seek genuine equality for minorities in terms of social justice. Often this may require the law to afford minority cultures, traditions, and values equal respect and recognition with those of the majority, if justice is to be done in individual cases. Identical treatment, irrespective of cultural or religious differences, may commonly represent an inappropriate legal response.[65] Advocates of cultural pluralism not only seek to affirm the value of greater diversity in enriching national life, they also reject the notion that minorities should be encouraged to surrender or disguise their identities in order to gain economic advancement. It would, in their view, be unwise to assume that prejudice and discrimination on the part of white employers are caused principally by cultural differences rather than skin colour. Such differences may well be put forward merely as a smokescreen to mask blatant racist attitudes. However, even where cultural factors do influence recruitment decisions (for instance, at the interview stage), pluralists would unhesitatingly reject the widely prevalent attitude of managers towards ethnic minority job-applicants encapsulated in the following statement—

I don't care whether they are yellow, green, purple or what have you, as long as they can do the job and are willing to muck in like everyone else, and not harp on about their differences, or make special pleading or demand privileges but try to become just like the rest of us.[66]

Finally, pluralists believe that a spirit of national unity, cohesion, and solidarity can be generated by the promotion of a common culture of respect for and tolerance of diversity. This can be cultivated through a common educational system, exposure to the mass media, involvement and interaction in the same economic environment, and participation in the same broad political society.[67] Even so, while 'unity through diversity' rather than a pattern of uniformity is the objective sought by pluralists, they do acknowledge that there may be a few occasions when the maintenance of minimum standards of behaviour may require some particularly abhorrent or obnoxious cultural traditions to be abandoned by those who have come to live in this country.

---

[65] See e.g. Van Dyke, V., *Human Rights, Ethnicity and Discrimination* (London, 1985), 20–1.
[66] See Modood, T., 'Cultural Diversity and Racial Discrimination in Employment Selection' in Hepple, B. and Szyszczak, E. (eds) *Discrimination: The Limits of Law* (London, 1992), 237.   [67] See Raz, J., *Ethics in the Public Domain* (Oxford, 1994), 172–3.

THE MODERN APPROACH

The shift from assimilation to cultural pluralism was heralded in official circles in a notable speech in 1966 by the Labour Home Secretary, Roy (now Lord) Jenkins, in which he described the latter concept in terms of 'integration'. He commented—

Integration is perhaps a rather loose word. I do not regard it as meaning the loss, by immigrants, of their own national characteristics and culture. I do not think we need in this country a melting pot,[68] which will turn everybody out in a common mould, as one of a series of carbon copies of someone's misplaced vision of the stereotyped Englishman . . . . I define integration, therefore, not as a flattening process of assimilation but as equal opportunity, coupled with cultural diversity, in an atmosphere of mutual tolerance.[69]

First signs of a change of approach, away from assimilation and towards pluralism, were apparent among MPs a year earlier during the course of a debate in the House of Commons on the subject of immigration control. While Roy Hattersley still spoke of assimilation being the objective,[70] his Labour colleague Dr M S Miller indicated that integration should not involve loss of separate cultural identities.[71] On the Conservative side, whereas Peter Thorneycroft (later Lord Thorneycroft) referred to 'the problem of absorbing these new cultures within our existing community . . ., within the fabric of the civilization of which we . . . are so proud',[72] Norman St John Stevas (now Lord St John of Fawley) emphasized the potential enrichment of British society which the preservation of ethnic minority cultures would bring.[73]

Express public support for a policy of cultural pluralism has since been proffered by four Conservative Ministers at the Home Office, Timothy Raison[74] in 1980, Douglas Hurd[75] and John

[68] This is, of course, a reference to the assimilationist policies adopted in the United States during the early years of this century and exemplified by Israel Zangwill's play *The Melting Pot*, first performed in New York in 1908. The idea of a melting pot or crucible, in which a new American would be moulded out of a fusion of people from many different ethnic groups, appears to be as old as the Republic itself, but the task has never been successfully achieved. While some distinctive cultural traits have been abandoned and the strength of some national and linguistic identities has declined, America remains a country where ethnic divisions are of considerable importance. In the words of Glazer, N. and Moynihan, P., *Beyond the Melting Pot* (Massachusetts, 1963), 290—'The point about the melting pot is that it did not happen'.

[69] See Jenkins, R., *Essays and Speeches* (London, 1967), 267.

[70] HC Debs, 709, cols 378–9, 381, 384.   [71] Ibid, cols 404, 408.

[72] Ibid, col 336.   [73] Ibid, cols 416–8.

[74] 'Cultural diversity, adaptation and participation' (1980) *New Community* 96 ('settling in Britain, taking UK citizenship and generally being British, does not mean that people are expected to abandon deeply held religious and cultural traditions. We expect people to want to cherish the cultural and religious beliefs of their forefathers. This is a right which we hold very dear in Britain; and a right for which our ancestors fought very hard').

[75] Speech given at Birmingham Central Mosque on 24 Feb 1989, reprinted in *New Life*,

Patten[76] in 1989, and Michael Howard in 1994.[77] Moreover, a Home Office policy document in 1990 declared—

The Government's fundamental objective is that Britain should be a fair and just society where everyone, irrespective of ethnic origin, is able to participate freely and fully in the economic, social and public life of the nation while having the freedom to maintain their own religious and cultural identity. Members of ethnic minorities, a growing proportion of whom were born in the United Kingdom, are an integral part of British society.[78]

The policy was also endorsed by John Major as Prime Minister when he commented in 1991—

We have to consider what integration means. It does not mean everyone being like everyone else. Uniformity is not integration . . . it is like a successful team, all the different players have recognised roles to play, they have contributions to make and they are accepted by each other as equal parts of the whole.[79]

In 1995 an official government report to an important international body stated unequivocally—

It is a fundamental objective of the UK Government to enable members of ethnic minorities to participate freely and fully in the economic, social and public life of the nation, with all the benefits and responsibilities which that entails, while still being able to maintain their own culture, traditions, language and values.[80]

In the light of these public pronouncements, it seems very likely that cultural pluralism will represent official government policy in this field for the foreseeable future. Naturally, however, differences of emphasis can be expected between the political parties, as well as varying forms of commitment to the detailed implementation of such a policy since, as we

3 Mar 1989 ('No-one is asking for you to abandon either your faith or your traditions. Britain has a long tradition of receiving immigrants . . . . In no case has the majority living here sought to eradicate minority customs or beliefs').

[76] Letter to leading British Muslims, reprinted in *The Times*, 5 July 1989 ('Modern Britain has plenty of room for diversity and variety . . . . No-one would expect or want British Muslims, or any other group, to lay aside their faith, traditions or heritage . . . . I would emphasise that greater integration in the sense of a fuller participation in British life does not mean forfeiting your faith or forgetting your roots. Muslims cannot and should not be expected to do this, nor Hindus or Sikhs, Catholics or Jews'). Similar sentiments are expressed in 'Aspects of Islam in Britain', Foreign and Commonwealth Office Booklet No. 72/90 (London, 1990), 1.

[77] Speech at conference organized by the Runnymede Trust on 23 Sept 1994, reprinted in (1994) 279 *Runnymede Bulletin* 8–9 ('Our aim, both as individuals and as a society, must be to ensure that the values of the different cultures which make up the UK are protected and respected').

[78] Home Office, 'Policy Criteria for the Administration of Section 11 Grant', 2.

[79] Speech on 25 Sept 1991, reported in (1991) 250 *Race and Immigration* 4–5.

[80] Home Office, *13th UK Periodic Report to the UN Committee on the Elimination of All Forms of Racial Discrimination Relating to the Period up to 31 July 1994* (London, 1995), 1.

shall see, the precise implications of the policy leave considerable scope for disagreement about which particular legal measures are appropriate.[81] It is certainly arguable that recent years have witnessed some diminution of practical support for pluralism on the part of Conservative administrations.[82]

One of the best expressions of the pluralist approach is to be found in *Education for All*, the authoritative and influential Report of the Committee of Inquiry into the Education of Children from Ethnic Minority Groups[83] (the 'Swann Report') in 1985. After emphasizing that the Committee had found the sense of ethnic identity among many members of the ethnic minority groups to be 'very strong'[84] and unlikely to dissolve in the face of influences emanating from the majority community, the Report commented—

We would . . . regard a democratic pluralist society as seeking to achieve a balance between, on the one hand, the maintenance and active support of the essential elements of the cultures and lifestyles of all the ethnic groups within it, and, on the other, the acceptance by all groups of a set of shared values distinctive of the society as a whole. This then is our view of a genuinely pluralist society, as both socially cohesive and culturally diverse.[85]

A clear implication of this vision, as the Swann Committee acknowledged, is that the ethnic minority communities cannot expect to preserve unchanged all the elements of their cultural traditions since this would, in some instances, prevent them from taking on the shared values of the wider society.[86] There are, therefore, limits to the acceptance of cultural diversity which may need to be imposed in support of the overriding public interest in promoting social cohesion. The Report decisively rejected a deliberate policy of assimilation on the ground that it would amount to 'a denial of the fundamental freedom of all individuals to differ on aspects of their lives where no single way can justifiably be presented as universally appropriate'.[87] Even so, it recognized that there were many in the majority community who still favoured the assimilationist approach[88] and during recent years there have been

---

[81] See below, ch 2.

[82] See e.g. the repeal of the statutory duty placed upon local authorities to provide camp sites for gypsies, discussed in ch 5, and the reduction of funding allocated under s 11 of the Local Government Act 1966, discussed in ch 2.

[83] Cmnd 9453 of 1985.   [84] At 4.   [85] At 6.

[86] At 5.   [87] At 4.

[88] At 6. There have been very few public attitude surveys on this question, but one such report indicated that 40 per cent of white respondents disagreed with the idea that 'people of Asian and West Indian origin should preserve as much of their own culture as possible'—see Brown, C., *Black and White Britain: The Third PSI Survey* (London, 1984), 273, 289. For higher percentages in a more recent survey, see Jowell, R. *et al* (eds), *British Social Attitudes: The 13th Report* (Aldershot, 1996), 108.

several utterances by Conservative politicians (some of them quite senior) along these lines.[89] They do not, however, represent official Conservative Party policy and some idea of how far Conservative thinking has developed is apparent from the following declaration made by a commentator who is generally regarded as one of the representatives of the 'New Right'—

Assimilation can be ruled out since it implies a compulsion that can only obtain in closed, totalitarian states. In open and free societies, committed to freedom and dignity of the individual, assimilation is not possible—both ethical and pragmatic considerations forbid it. Moreover, since it suppresses contrasting world views, customs and cultural forms, the success of assimilation can deprive the dominant society of a means of enriching itself. It does not, then, even make sense.[90]

PLURALISM WITHIN LIMITS

Having established a clear distinction between the broad concepts of assimilation and cultural pluralism, it is important next to stress the extent of their convergence. Very few, if any, pluralists currently subscribe to an interpretation of the theory of 'cultural relativism',[91] in terms of which all cultural traditions and practices are accorded equal weight and value on the grounds that no cross-cultural judgements can be independent, impartial, and objective.[92] Rather, as the Swann Report indicated,[93] there is agreement that there are limits to a policy of pluralism and these arise out of the need to maintain a cohesive society founded on shared fundamental values.[94] Where society imposes these

[89] See e.g. John Biffen, *Independent*, 5 Oct 1987 (minorities should accept 'the social and cultural standards' of the 'host country'); Sir John Stokes, *Independent*, 30 May 1989 ('those who settle here must obey our laws and customs'); John Townend, HC Debs, 159, col 1105, 8 Nov 1989 ('it behoves the newcomers to become English . . . . They should accept our laws, our history, our traditions and our tolerance'); Norman Tebbit, *The Field*, May 1990 ('in recent years our sense of insularity and nationality has been bruised by large waves of immigrants resistant to absorption, some defiantly claiming a right to superimpose their culture, even their law, upon the host community').   [90] Honeyford (1988), 40.
[91] Cultural relativism is discussed further below, pp 107–19.
[92] A position not far removed from cultural relativism was espoused by Lustgarten, L., 'Liberty in a Culturally Plural Society' in Griffith, P. (ed.), *Of Liberty* (Cambridge, 1983), 91, 101, where he argued that the only exceptions to a policy of cultural pluralism should be practices which result in 'severe physical abuse or worse' (e.g. suttee and female circumcision) or where institutional accommodation of cultural diversity would be 'wholly impracticable'. However, he subsequently modified this stance to allow a wider range of exceptions, in line with the broad thrust of the arguments set out below—see his chapter, 'Racial Inequality, Public Policy and the Law: Where Are We Going?' in Hepple and Szyszczak, *Discrimination*, 457.   [93] At 6.
[94] See e.g. Parekh (1984), 228–31 and (1990), 71; Gross, F., *Ideologies, Goals and Values* (Westport, 1985), ch 17.

values its stance will, of course, be an assimilationist one, refusing to countenance particular instances of diversity and insisting upon a pattern of uniformity.

Assimilation, too, has its limits as a general policy option. Few assimilationists would press their philosophy into the deepest and most personal aspects of the lives of members of minority communities. They would not seek, for instance, to alter people's religious convictions[95] through state programmes designed to convert Jews, Muslims, Hindus, Sikhs, and Rastafarians to Christianity or to restrict their right to worship. Nor would they generally aim to alter the manner in which members of minorities organize their daily lives within the family circle, in terms of social relations between family members and the upbringing of children. A distinction is normally made between the private sphere and the public domain, on the basis of which conformity to majority values and norms is required in the case of activities within the latter but not those within the former.[96] Inevitably, of course, there can be considerable difficulty in deciding whether a particular activity falls within one sphere or the other,[97] many matters relating to the treatment of wives and the upbringing of children falling unequivocally somewhere between the two.[98]

One consequence of the existence of this limited zone of convergence, this area of common ground between most assimilationists and pluralists, is that current British policy is perhaps best described as being one of cultural pluralism with assimilationist exceptions designed to uphold minimum standards and sustain national coherence. Expressed rather more succinctly, it represents 'cultural pluralism within limits'. However, this pithy description of the broad tenor of present British policy in this field leaves a large number of more penetrating questions unanswered. On precisely what basis are exceptions to the pluralist philosophy to be admitted in practice? How can it adequately be determined whether minimum national standards are breached by a particular traditional practice, which therefore needs to be suppressed? Another way of posing the dilemma is to ask exactly where the limits of tolerance lie. Even if

---

[95] See e.g. Parekh (1990), 63.

[96] See e.g. Honeyford (1988), 37, 45–6. For discussion of the usefulness of the distinction, see further below, pp 26–9.

[97] See generally, Benn, S. and Gaus, G. (eds), *Public and Private in Social Life* (London, 1983); Cochran, C., *Religion in Public and Private Life* (New York, 1990).

[98] Feminists (and others) have recently expressed considerable disquiet at the manner in which English law is prone to marginalize women's concerns by confining them to a private or domestic sphere—see e.g. O'Donovan, K., *Sexual Divisions in Law* (London, 1985). For a liberal justification of legal intervention in the private sphere, see Gardner, J., 'Private Activities and Personal Autonomy: At the Margins of Anti-Discrimination Law' in Hepple and Szyszczak, *Discrimination*, ch 9.

state interference with minority cultures can sometimes be justified, is there an important division between the private sphere and the public domain, in terms of which the law may only regulate the latter and must eschew intervention in the former because it is confined to purely personal matters? Another problem concerns the notion of equality. If equality is an important justification for a policy of pluralism, how can that be reconciled with the view that assimilation appears to offer the most direct route to legal equality by treating everyone in an identical manner? How does the concept of 'legal neutrality' fit into the equation? If it possesses any relevance, should it be an active neutrality or a passive one? Since the law pays such great attention to the notion of 'rights', it also needs to be established whether these are the rights of individuals or of groups. If both individual and collective rights exist side by side, is there inevitably a tension between them and how can this be resolved? Is there a distinction between a right and a privilege?

Three of these broad issues are addressed in the remainder of this chapter, namely the search for minimum standards, the attempt to draw a distinction between public and private domains, and the implications of tolerance (including the question of neutrality). Legal interpretations of rights, equality, and minimum standards are explored in Chapters 2 and 3.

THE SEARCH FOR MINIMUM STANDARDS AND SHARED VALUES

As we have seen, the pluralist standpoint generally accepts the need for some limits to be set to cultural diversity and the Swann Committee referred to the shared values, which are a distinctive feature of our society as a whole and which must be accepted by all in the interests of national cohesion. Another way of expressing this idea is to insist that cultural tolerance cannot become a 'cloak for oppression and injustice'[99] within the minority communities themselves, nor must it endanger the integrity of the 'social and cultural core'[100] of English values. Where are these shared values and minimum standards to be located? The following interpretation of the concept of 'modified pluralism' has been proffered by Parekh, a member of the Swann Committee—

British society, like any other society, has a certain definite conception of the good life to which its members subscribe and which influences the way they live. Although its members hold and endeavour to live up to different personal ideals,

[99] Lester, A. and Bindman, G., *Race and Law* (Harmondsworth, 1972), 18.
[100] Patterson, S., 'Immigrants and minority groups in British society' in Abbott, S. (ed.), *The Prevention of Racial Discrimination in Great Britain* (London, 1971), 30.

there are certain basic values to which they all adhere, and which form the basis of their decisions concerning what personal ideals they can legitimately hold . . . . British society is therefore entitled to insist that every one of its members, immigrant as well as native, must conform to what it regards as its basic, minimal values. What these values are and how they can be elicited are difficult philosophical questions . . ., but we will all agree that monogamy, legal and moral equality of all men, equality of sexes, and basic civil liberties are some of them. It has taken Britain centuries of struggle to secure these values a firm institutional basis, and she is morally entitled to insist that nothing should be done to weaken her adherence to them.[101]

Parekh's list of British values is a good starting point because of the very broad reach of his reference to 'basic civil liberties'. By clear implication this would cover such fundamental values as democracy, the rule of law, natural justice, freedom of expression, and religious toleration. These may be regarded as forming the bedrock of British values, at least as expressed in public institutional form and reflected in legal principles. The recognition of English as the national language should also be included in this category. It is important, however, to acknowledge that individual members of the general public may well not appreciate the implications of such values when the principles to be derived from them have to be applied in concrete cases, or else they may profoundly disagree with one another as to what the implications should be. A study in the United States in 1960, for example, found that while Americans were agreed upon the value of democracy, they displayed an alarming lack of consensus about its implications.[102] They virtually all agreed that public officials should be chosen by means of majority vote, but around half of respondents also stated that only people who were well informed should be allowed to vote, and as many as 80 per cent declared that a duly elected black person should not be allowed to take office.[103] Similarly, although almost all respondents agreed with the abstract democratic principles of free speech, including the right of minorities to criticize the majority, more than a third felt that people should not be allowed to make speeches against religion and over half wanted to ban the advocacy of communism.[104] Hence the general endorsement of the principle of democracy seems to have been no more than a token declaration, so vague as to be worthless in arguing that any real consensus exists among the population as a whole about the practical content of 'shared values'. It is important, therefore, to appreciate that the process of attributing 'shared values' to the community at large is a

---

[101] *Colour, Culture and Consciousness*, 229–30.
[102] Prothro, J. and Grigg, C., 'Fundamental principles of democracy: bases of agreement and disagreement' (1960) 11 *Journal of Politics* 276.
[103] Ibid at 282–5. [104] Id.

somewhat artificial one and that these values are best seen simply as a reflection of the formal institutional expression of such philosophical ideas, rather than what individual members of society actually believe.[105] The difficulty of extrapolating any clear principles from widespread social acceptance in this country has also been adverted to by Galligan—

The divisions within British society over such matters as the legal enforcement of morality, the rights and wrongs of abortion, surrogate motherhood, and any number of other matters, are deep and unbridgeable. The same divisions apply to questions about civil liberties. But if there is little by way of agreed principles for balancing competing values, how is it to be done? One approach would be to look beyond the diversity of views popularly held and try to reconstruct from the basic institutions, practices and beliefs of the society a set of deep political principles. Some guidance might be derived in this way, but it is bound to be limited since, even at this critical level, it is not clear that society is based on any set of coherent and consistent principles sufficiently clear and specific to assist in practical decisions.[106]

Galligan's principal concern lay with the wide discretion conferred upon public officials in the field of public protest, marches, and demonstrations and his preferred solution was to place reliance, in the balancing of competing values, on the process of decision-making through democratic principles of accountability.[107] While this is clearly important in practical terms, especially in that field, the focus of the present study is rather different. The concern is with the broad sweep of policies and principles to be adopted by Parliament and the courts in framing and developing a structure which can direct an institutional response to the legal issues presented by a multicultural society. Here the limited guidance that can be afforded by 'deep political principles', as expressed in concepts such as the rule of law, natural justice, non-discrimination, sexual equality, freedom of expression, and religious tolerance, can be useful. How far greater specificity can be achieved to deal with concrete problems is addressed in Chapter 2.

The relationship between 'shared values', understood in an institutional sense, on the one hand, and minority cultures, on the other, should be seen as a reciprocal one. Shared values of the type described will

---

[105] This was perhaps insufficiently appreciated by Parekh when he subsequently argued (1990, 75) that accepting Parliamentary democracy was not part of British identity, on the grounds that 'many a Briton prefers a more participatory and less centralised form of government'. The shared values need to be viewed as they are expressed in institutional form at any given time, rather than as individuals might wish to see them altered or reformed in the future.

[106] 'Preserving public protest: the legal approach' in Gostin, L. (ed.), *Civil Liberties in Conflict* (London, 1988), 47.

[107] Id; for a similar emphasis upon following proper procedural rules, see Gross, 311–13.

obviously influence the manner in which the practice of minority traditions evolves here. Sometimes the impact will be direct, as where English
law prevents or inhibits such behaviour, while at other times the forces
of public opinion, state education, and discussions within individual
families will lead to modifications and adaptations. Parekh has graphically described the extent to which this latter process is already well
advanced—

Contrary to popular impression, great changes are afoot within ethnic communities, and every family has become a terrain of subdued or explosive struggles.
In any family, husband and wife, parents and children, brothers and sisters are
having to renegotiate and redefine their patterns of relationship in a manner that
takes account both of their traditional values and those characteristic of their
adopted country. Different families reach their own inherently tentative conclusions, exchange ideas and experiences, learn from each other's failures and
successes, and grow at their own pace.[108]

On the other hand, ethnic traditions, beliefs, and values must not be
denied the opportunity of influencing the future content of the shared
institutional values of the country as a whole.[109] These values are not
immutable and just as women's perspectives have profoundly affected
their development during the course of the twentieth century, so the
viewpoint of the ethnic minority communities can be expected to achieve
similar results during the course of the next century.

In his Reith Lectures on 'The Persistence of Faith' in 1990, the then
Chief Rabbi elect, Jonathan Sacks, drew attention to the conflicts inherent in a pluralist approach and suggested a way out of the deadlock
which is liable to arise when the interests of individuals and groups
collide. The solution he advocated was—

. . . to think of a plural society not as one in which there is a Babel of conflicting
languages, but rather as one in which we each have to be bilingual. There is a
first and public language of citizenship which we have to learn if we are to live
together. And there is a variety of second languages which connect us to our
local framework of relationships: to family and group and the traditions that
underlie them. If we are to achieve integration without assimilation, it is important to give each of these languages its due . . . . Keeping this first language alive
means significant restraints on all sides. For Christians, it involves allowing other
voices to share in the conversation. For people of other faiths it means coming to
terms with a national culture. For secularists, it means acknowledging the force
of commitments that must, to them, seem irrational. For everyone, it means
settling for less than we would seek if everyone were like us, and searching
for more than our merely sectional interests: in short, for the common good.[110]

---

[108] (1990), 71.   [109] Ibid, 74.
[110] *The Persistence of Faith* (London, 1991), 66, 68.

There are clear dangers to the social cohesion of the country as a whole if too great a stress is placed on ethnic differences and if individuals from the various ethnic groups identify themselves so strongly with their own distinctive communities (and are so identified by others) that there is little appreciation of the role they can and should be playing in forging and reinforcing a new sense of national identity.[111] Pluralism should not be interpreted as emphasizing separate identities to such an extent that it dilutes the commitment of all to tackling issues of national concern and to widespread patterns of mutual interdependence and co-operation, nor should it restrict those who wish to become assimilated within the mainstream culture from freely pursuing this course of action.[112] However, the demands of most members of minority groups for greater recognition of their cultural values and traditions spring from a desire for greater integration within the wider society, rather than separation from it.[113] They usually seek relatively minor adjustments in majority practices in order to meet their needs and have no wish to reject or destabilize English society as a whole.

PUBLIC AND PRIVATE DOMAINS

We have already seen that even assimilationists recognize the need for minority groups to be able to pursue certain 'private' activities free from any pressure to conform with majority values. Freedom of religious belief, the right to worship in accordance with the tenets of a non-Christian faith, and the liberty to use languages other than English in private communications are obvious examples of spheres where it is felt that state interference would be unjustified. Indeed, it seems clear that one of the cardinal features of the modern liberal democratic state, whose development began in the seventeenth century and was furthered by the rationality of the Enlightenment, is the pronounced separation between the public and private spheres of life.[114] The democratic revolutions of the eighteenth century enshrined the distinction between the public and the private in the life of modern Western nations and this led in turn to the often rigid separation of church and state. Hence Article 10 of the French Declaration of the Rights of Man and the Citizen proclaimed in 1789—

---

[111] See generally, Goulbourne, H., *Ethnicity and Nationalism in Post-Imperial Britain* (Cambridge, 1992).   [112] See Rex, J., *Race and Ethnicity* (Milton Keynes, 1989), 134.
[113] See Kymlicka, W., *Multicultural Citizenship* (Oxford, 1995), 67, 95–8, 176–9.
[114] See generally, Morris, P., 'Judaism and pluralism' in Hamnett, I. (ed.), *Religious Pluralism and Unbelief* (London, 1990), 179–201.

No person shall be molested for his opinions, even such as are religious, provided that the manifestation of these opinions does not disturb the public order established by law.

However, the importance of the proviso in this article is clear. There are obvious difficulties in consistently sustaining an approach that the state should not intervene in matters pertaining to religion, simply because these are inherently private and thus sacrosanct. The state may feel entitled to argue that certain practices which are justified in the name of religion fall below minimum standards and do so much damage that they need to be outlawed. More vulnerable members of the community, such as women and children, may require the protection of the law to prevent harm being done to them. Sometimes this harm may occur in the context of the regulation of interspousal relations[115] or the treatment or upbringing of children[116] and hence within a sphere which would *prima facie* constitute part of the 'private' domain of people's lives. Despite this, intrusions into the personal lives of members of minorities may sometimes be as necessary as in the case of members of the majority community. If the adage 'an Englishman's home is his castle' no longer reflects the legal position for the majority, neither can it govern domestic relations within ethnic communities.[117]

Just as some assimilationists have wrongly assumed that matters apparently within a 'private' domain should be left totally free from state pressure to conform with majority values, so some pluralists have erroneously argued that the law has no place in upholding cultural diversity in the 'public' domain. One pluralist has argued, for example, that any suggestion that 'individuals or groups should receive differential treatment in the public domain is a move away from the multicultural ideal towards the plural society of colonialism'.[118] As we shall see, this is to confuse the legal recognition of cultural diversity with the doctrine of *apartheid*.[119] The policy of cultural pluralism can only be made to work successfully in some public spheres, including certain economic arrangements, through differential treatment on the part of English law. In the field of employment, for example, if the law were to treat everyone in an identical manner, regardless of cultural and religious differences (for example, in relation to dress or uniform), genuine

---

[115] e.g. through polygamy, forced marriages, or extrajudicial divorce—see further below, ch 6.

[116] e.g. through female circumcision, child-marriage, or withdrawal from school.

[117] For an illustration of the intervention of the English courts against the wishes of the ultra-orthodox community of Hasidic Jews in Stamford Hill in North London, in a case involving child sexual abuse, see Boggan, S., 'A Law unto Themselves', *Independent on Sunday*, 11 Aug 1991.

[118] Rex, J., 'The concept of a multi-cultural society' (1987) *New Community* 218 at 222.

[119] See below, ch 3.

equality of opportunity could not be achieved.[120] Yet we have seen that the pluralist ideal set out by Roy Jenkins in 1966 emphasized both equal opportunity and cultural diversity as twin pillars of a policy of integration. While principles of race equality may well require that the law almost invariably be 'colour-blind', the imperatives of ethnic pluralism dictate that it cannot ignore important cultural differences if justice is to be attained. The precise distinction between differential treatment designed to secure the protection of ethnic identities and cultures, on the one hand, and identical treatment designed to combat unwarranted discrimination, is explored further in Chapter 3.

There are two further reasons why the attempt to draw a sharp distinction between public and private domains is doomed to failure and should therefore be abandoned in the analysis of policies for an integrated multicultural society. First, as we have seen already, there is no satisfactory way of classifying activities as belonging within one zone or the other. Family matters and religious practices and observances cannot be viewed as private matters, of no concern to the legal system or public institutions, when they relate to, for example, the treatment of women and children, the education of pupils at school, absences from work for purposes of worship, reactions to blasphemy, or the disposal of dead bodies. Equally, when members of ethnic communities enter into the public domain to pursue civic, economic, and legal roles, they do not automatically shed their identities in terms of religion, culture, language, and dress codes and these factors may all need to be taken into account by public authorities, civil institutions, employers, and the court system.

Secondly, a rigid separation of public and private domains denies the perspectives of the minority communities themselves. For them, it is vital that their cultural identities be publicly and openly recognized by the wider society in a positive fashion, if they are to flourish in this country and play a constructive role in the life of the nation. To confine their cultures to the margins of society, largely screened from public view, is not only to belittle them in a patronizing fashion but also to deny the possibility of mainstream British culture being enriched through contact with minority cultural traditions.[121] Furthermore, several minority faiths draw no distinction between religious and secular activities, viewing their religions as a way of life and certainly not merely as a private matter. The strengths and virtues of many members of these communities which are so visible in the public sphere in terms of, for example, hard work, enterprise, self-help, economic advancement, the value attached to education, the acquisition of academic and professional qualifications, discipline, and respect for the law, can only be

---

[120] See below, ch 2.   [121] See Parekh (1990), 67–8, 70–1.

sustained by the cultural resources, family networks, social cohesion, and community spirit derived from the private domain.[122] Hence, while it may be possible for sociologists to construct models of separate public and private domains, the division is not a useful one in terms of framing realistic policies for a multicultural society.[123]

THE IMPLICATIONS OF TOLERANCE

It will be recalled that one ingredient of the definition of integration given by Roy Jenkins in 1966 was 'an atmosphere of mutual tolerance'. In this section the concept of tolerance is outlined, together with the standard justifications usually accorded to it, before its implications for the pursuit of a general policy of cultural pluralism are explored.

The question of tolerance only arises in circumstances of diversity and it broadly involves taking an indulgent attitude of 'live and let live' towards the behaviour of others, despite the fact that their actions excite feelings of disapproval, dislike, or disgust.[124] The tolerator has the power to interfere with, influence, or control the offending practice, but elects to refrain from exercising that power. In a liberal democracy such abstention is regarded as a virtue as well as the proper stance to be adopted, both on the part of individuals and on the part of state authorities, subject to limits laid down by law. In historical terms, liberalism has always been closely identified with the values of individual liberty and toleration, and these concepts are particularly associated with the political philosophies of John Locke and John Stuart Mill.

Locke's *Letter on Toleration*, written in 1685, was composed during a period of great religious antagonism both in Britain and in other parts of Europe, following the revocation in the same year of the Edict of Nantes (1598), which marked the ending of a period of toleration towards Protestant dissenters and sparked off the persecution of Huguenots in Catholic France.[125] Locke was vigorously opposed to such religious intolerance, on the ground that coercion could only bring about insincere protestations of faith rather than a true conversion. Outward observances were merely hypocritical and would not save souls or bring about salvation. Mere professions of belief under threat of persecution

---

[122] Ibid, 65–6.

[123] It is significant that Rex, for long a protagonist of the two domains thesis, eventually accepted that it was 'too naive and simplistic'—see Rex, J., 'The Political Sociology of a Multi-Cultural Society' (1991) 2 *European Journal of Intercultural Studies* 7. For an example of his earlier stance see note 118 above.

[124] See Mendus, S., *Toleration and the Limits of Liberalism* (Basingstoke, 1989), 8–9.

[125] See generally, Cranston, M., 'John Locke and the Case for Toleration' in Mendus, S. and Edwards, D. (eds), *On Toleration* (Oxford, 1987), ch 6.

or suppression were valueless in this regard. Locke's criticism of religious intolerance was thus based on the sheer irrationality of the process.

The notion that religious intolerance may well be irrational is often connected with the view that rational discussion and argument will help in the search for truth. Tolerance of a variety of viewpoints, perspectives, and lifestyles opens up new options and helps individuals to appreciate the fallibility of previous ideas and choices. Intolerance can thus be seen as intellectual arrogance, a blindness to the possibility of error. In this sense tolerance is allied to scepticism about whether any group has a monopoly of truth or of the ideal pattern of living.[126]

Most of the other common justifications of toleration in a liberal society are strongly linked with Mill's essay *On Liberty* (1859). His approach was greatly influenced by what he felt was a growing pattern of dull uniformity prevailing in Victorian England, in which there was a tendency for people to impose their opinions and inclinations upon others. He inveighed against the despotism of custom and public opinion and advocated in their place individuality, diversity, and eccentricity.[127] This led him to consider the acceptable limits of societal interference with individual liberty and hence to formulate his famous 'harm principle'. He wrote—

The object of this essay is to assert one very simple principle, as entitled to govern absolutely the dealings of society with the individual in the way of compulsion and control, whether the means used be physical force in the form of legal penalties or the moral coercion of public opinion. That principle is that the sole end for which mankind are warranted, individually or collectively, in interfering with the liberty of action of any of their number is self-protection. That the only purpose for which power can be rightfully exercised over any member of a civilised community, against his will, is to prevent harm to others. His own good, either physical or moral, is not a sufficient warrant . . . . The only part of the conduct of anyone for which he is amenable to society is that which concerns others. In the part which merely concerns himself, his independence is, of right, absolute. Over himself, over his own mind and body, the individual is sovereign.[128]

Mill's interpretation of tolerance is thus that it will promote greater individuality and diversity and free people from the tyranny of popular opinion and custom, as well as of state intervention, to the general benefit of society at large.

Although he did not himself use the phrase, Mill set great store by the

---

[126] See e.g. King, P., *Toleration* (London, 1976), 114, 120, 126; Mendus and Edwards, 5–6.
[127] See *On Liberty*, Himmelfarb, G. (ed.) (Harmondsworth, 1985), especially 63–4, 120–2, 136–40.   [128] At 68–9.

notion of 'personal autonomy', arguing that the only lifestyle worth following is one freely chosen. As he put it, a person's 'own mode of laying out his existence is best, not because it is the best in itself, but because it is his own mode'.[129] This choice can, of course, only be made if a policy of toleration has enabled a wide selection of alternative lifestyles to flourish and hence be available for making a selection. Only in such a manner can human nature expand and realize its fullest potential.[130] For Mill intolerance is immoral, but this formed only part of his wider vision of liberty which extends well beyond requiring people to endure behaviour on the part of others which they find distasteful or misguided. Mill's argument on the basis of autonomy is 'sometimes thought to be the specifically liberal argument for pluralism: the one argument which is not shared by non-liberals, and which displays the spirit of the liberal approach to politics'.[131]

Moreover, it is Mill's conception of liberty which has substantially contributed to the definition of a liberal state as one which is open, diverse, plural, and equally hospitable to all the beliefs and activities which its members espouse.[132] A central perception within the liberal tradition is thus that in such a state the government should not normally favour one life-style above another. People should be permitted to lead their own lives in their own ways, so long as they do not harm others. The state should maintain a position of 'neutrality' and not discriminate in favour of one set of religious or moral preferences and against another. It should be neutral *vis-à-vis* competing conceptions of what is entailed by the 'good life'. 'Neutrality' is, however, a notoriously vague and ambiguous concept.[133] For Locke and Mill it meant that the state should be neutral in motivation,[134] whereas a modern liberal theorist such as Dworkin would favour seeking a more neutral outcome.[135] For him neutrality may require active intervention to equalize opportunities for everyone to realize their own version of the good life. His requirement of neutrality springs from his belief that liberalism is founded on a view of persons as entitled to equal concern and respect.[136] This does not mean that neutrality invariably connotes equal (i.e. identical) treatment.[137] Rather, what is needed to achieve genuine neutrality is treatment as an

---

[129] Ibid, 133.   [130] Ibid, 122.

[131] See Raz, J., 'Autonomy, Toleration and the Harm Principle' in Mendus, S. (ed.), *Justifying Toleration: Conceptual and Historical Perspectives* (Cambridge, 1988), 155. For further development of the argument that personal autonomy provides the best foundation for the doctrine of liberty, see Raz, J., *The Morality of Freedom* (Oxford, 1986).

[132] See Mendus (1989), 69.   [133] Ibid, chs 4 and 5.   [134] Ibid, 113–14.

[135] See Dworkin, R., *Taking Rights Seriously* (London, 1977), ch 7.

[136] Ibid, 198–9, 227, 272–3.

[137] To employ a medical analogy, a doctor who gave all patients identical treatment would hardly be according them equal concern.

equal. Precisely how this is to be achieved in practical terms is contro-versial,[138] but it at least alerts us to the range of possible implications inherent in a modern liberal view of toleration. In this regard, it is necessary to outline the limits of toleration.

At one end of the spectrum lie those instances where toleration is not required at all. We have already seen that there are bound to be some forms of behaviour which are regarded as 'beyond the pale'. Mill's contribution to the debate about the proper limits of tolerance lies in the application of the harm principle, indicating that interference can only be considered justifiable if there is harm to others. Exactly what constitutes harm for this purpose is bound to be open to many different interpretations and there has been much controversy as to whether only physical harm is meant to be encompassed or whether moral harms can be included, such as the causing of offence, disgust, or disapproval.[139] Is there any value-free account of what amounts to harm? While there may be no easy answer here to such a theoretical question, serious attempts to solve this problem have been made through the laws and constitutions of liberal democracies, as well as in international human rights law, and the insights afforded by these provisions are considered further in Chapters 2 and 3. One situation in which it is generally accepted that tolerance may be inappropriate is where those to whom it might be extended would themselves deny it to others. To afford tolerance in such circum-stances would be a self-defeating exercise, if it put at risk the continued existence of a liberal society.[140] It seems clear that Locke subscribed to this view and indeed envisaged an even wider role for the law in curbing religious practices. While denying the right of the state to force a person to renounce religious opinions, he thought that the law might properly prohibit the publication of such opinions if this was necessary for the peace, safety, and security of the people, as well as penalize actions that were injurious to the public good.[141]

Recently, Kymlicka has argued cogently that liberal principles cannot justify the imposition of 'internal' restrictions by minority groups upon the basic civil rights of their own members, for this would be to deny individuals the personal autonomy to which liberalism is broadly com-mitted.[142] To restrict religious freedom or to deny education to girls, for example, would violate a key reason why liberals wish to protect cul-tural membership, namely to afford individuals an informed choice as to

[138] See further below, ch 3.
[139] See e.g. Horton, J. and Mendus, S. (eds), *Aspects of Toleration* (London, 1985), ch 6; Mendus (1989), 121–4.   [140] See Mendus and Edwards, (1987), 7, 11–12.
[141] Cranston, (1987), 104, 109.
[142] *Multicultural Citizenship* (Oxford, 1995), chs 3, 8.

how to lead their lives. As he has explained, tolerance would be inappropriate in this context, since—

Liberalism is committed to (perhaps even defined by) the view that individuals should have the freedom and capacity to question and possibly revise the traditional practices of their community, should they come to see them as no longer worthy of their allegiance.[143]

On the other hand, there may equally be difficulties at the other end of the spectrum in determining the limits of toleration in a positive rather than a negative sense. Once it is clear that toleration is appropriate, how extensive and fulsome should this tolerance be in practice? Conventionally, toleration in a legal sense has merely involved the duty to refrain from harming others, aptly summarised in the Latin maxim *sic utere non nocere alium* ('so use your own that you do not harm another'). However, Lord Scarman has argued powerfully that the concept needs to be expanded—

The problem . . . is that the sort of toleration that I have been describing, essentially negative in character, is no longer enough for civilised man. Man today requires more of the law than that he be left alone to pursue his way of life as he sees fit. Today he asks of the law positive rights enforceable against the state, against his employer, and indeed on occasions against the rest of us.[144]

Lord Scarman's thesis is that the legal concept of toleration should evolve from merely playing a permissive role to a more active endorsement of diversity, so that minorities can survive with their distinct identities intact and their members can flourish in a climate of equal opportunities.[145] The idea that toleration is not inherently a passive stance is epitomized by Voltaire's famous statement 'I disapprove of what you say, but I will defend to the death your right to say it'.

One of the most trenchant modern criticisms of Mill's standpoint on liberty argues that he greatly exaggerated the place of personal autonomy in the lives of ordinary people.[146] In practice, they are not free to choose their own lifestyles as easily as he suggested. As individuals, they form part of groups or communities in society that are held together by very strong bonds, from which they cut themselves adrift at their peril. Most people cannot simply cast off the deeply held moral and religious beliefs and traditional customs which have held their communities together for generations. Nor should they be encouraged to do so, if this would leave them without any feeling of worth or identity in an environment which may not be fully responsive to their needs. People are interdependent and need a sense of belonging, a consciousness of

---

[143] Ibid, 152. [144] 'Toleration and the Law' in Mendus and Edwards (1987), 54.
[145] Ibid, 57. [146] See Mendus (1989), chs 4 and 6.

identity and solidarity, which extends beyond their mere individuality. As we have seen, the task of the modern multicultural state is to achieve the correct balance between the loyalties of a common appreciation of citizenship based around a set of shared core values, on the one hand, and the claims derived from the separate cultural identities of ethnic minorities, on the other.[147] The important point to make here is that toleration in a modern sense may require more than passive neutrality on the part of the law, in the face of existing provisions and realities which prevent minorities from achieving their potential and making a full contribution to the wider society. Tolerance must reach out far enough to prevent minorities experiencing alienation and give them a feeling of being welcomed, respected, and valued for their own distinctive characteristics and contributions to diversity.[148]

A simple illustration of the inadequacy of passive neutrality relates to the basic organization of the working week with its Christian definition of Sunday as the principal day of rest. This has important implications for Jews (and other Sabbatarians) for whom Saturday represents the Sabbath, as well as for Muslims whose main time for congregational prayers at the mosque is around midday on Fridays. Unless the law is responsive to the needs of traders[149] and employees[150] from these minority faiths, in enabling them to organize their work in accordance with their religious tenets, Jews and Muslims will be more likely to feel alienated from mainstream society than integrated within it.

While Mill's powerful defence of liberty and enthusiastic endorsement of the value of diversity in society would appear to support a policy of cultural pluralism along the lines outlined earlier, especially in the light of his recognition of the importance of individuals being free to act in combination with one another in pursuit of their distinctive lifestyles,[151] this would in fact represent something of a distortion of his views. He championed the cause of individuality, especially where individuals were acting in opposition to custom or counter to popular opinion. He regarded the despotism of custom as hindering the development and progress of individuals and their prospects of attaining happiness and hence as operating to the detriment of society at large,[152] arguing that—

---

[147] See also Miller, D., 'Socialism and toleration' in Mendus (1988), ch 11.
[148] See Mendus (1989), 159–60.
[149] For the exemption for Jews from the Sunday trading laws, see Sunday Trading Act 1994, sched 1, para 2(2)(b); sched 2, Part II, replacing Shops Act 1952, s 53.
[150] For an example of an unsuccessful claim by a Muslim employee to have the right to take time off work for Friday prayers, see below, ch 3.
[151] At 142.   [152] See at 64, 120, 122, 125, 136.

The human faculties of perception, judgement, discriminative feeling, mental activity, and even moral preference are exercised only in making a choice. He who does anything because it is the custom makes no choice.[153]

His most striking illustration of the bane of custom was the Chinese practice of binding the feet of women, stunting their natural growth, both physical and mental.[154] The Chinese ideal of making all people alike was anathema to him.[155] However, while Mill's hostility to mindless adherence to custom clearly needs to be borne in mind when considering the rights of individuals who find themselves in conflict with the traditions of their ethnic group,[156] his strictures should be seen in the context of his broad toleration of religious diversity. Hence, while he obviously admired eccentricity and innovation above conformity, there is no reason to believe that he despised those who had freely chosen a particular lifestyle, involving certain religious practices and traditions, after due consideration. He certainly gave specific endorsement to the notion of religious education and to the instruction of pupils in the faith of their parents.[157]

More recently, Kymlicka has sought to demonstrate that modern liberalism is perfectly capable of recognizing the fundamental significance of cultural membership and of justifying legal measures designed to protect minority cultures.[158] He argues cogently that it is only through having a rich and secure cultural structure that people can become fully aware of the choices available to them and can intelligently examine their value,[159] commenting—

The notion of respect for persons *qua* members of cultures, based upon the recognition of the importance of the primary good of cultural membership, is not . . . an illiberal one. It doesn't say that the community is more important than the individuals who compose it . . . . The argument simply says that cultural membership is important in pursuing our essential interest in leading a good life, and so consideration of that membership is an important part of having equal consideration for the interests of each member of the community.[160]

According to Raz, cultures are entitled to liberalism's respect because of the vital role they play in shaping the content of individual freedom.[161] Indeed Mill himself emphasized the importance of a common cultural membership based on collective feelings of nationality derived from historical experiences and recollections, both pleasant and painful.[162]

---

[153] At 122.   [154] At 135.   [155] See at 137–8.
[156] See further below, ch 3.   [157] See at 178.
[158] *Liberalism, Community and Culture* (Oxford, 1991); *Multicultural Citizenship* (Oxford, 1995).   [159] (1991) at 165.
[160] Ibid, 167–8.   [161] See *Ethics in the Public Domain*, 163.
[162] See *Utilitarianism, On Liberty, Considerations on Representative Government*, Williams G. (ed.) (London, 1993), 391.

CONCLUSIONS

Many members of Britain's ethnic minority communities seem certain to wish to retain several aspects of their distinctive cultural identities and religious traditions for the foreseeable future. Official policy has shifted away from encouraging the assimilation of such minorities towards a pluralist approach, in which the goal of integration is represented by the promotion of equal opportunity coupled with cultural diversity in an atmosphere of mutual tolerance between the majority and the minorities. However, a culturally diverse population also requires strong elements of social cohesion around a set of shared core values, which impose certain uniform standards in the wider public interest. There are limits beyond which a tolerant attitude is inappropriate. Although such limits are hard to define with precision, they are best seen as arising from the formal, institutional values reflected in the key political and legal concepts employed in a modern liberal democracy, such as free and regular elections to government, the rule of law, natural justice, non-discrimination, freedom of expression, and religious toleration. Since ethnic, cultural, and religious pluralism finds its strongest justification in broadly liberal sentiments it must itself be bounded by notions of basic civil liberties. A successful policy of pluralism needs to acknowledge openly the potential conflicts which may arise and try to settle them amicably. It also needs to stress the commitment of all to the solution of national concerns and the importance of developing widespread patterns of co-operation and interaction among the various communities.

Pluralism may sometimes justify differential treatment between communities in order to create genuine equality of opportunity and sustain religious freedom, and this may require the establishment of special legal rights. On the other hand, legal intervention may also be needed to impose certain minimum standards of formally equal protection in the personal and family affairs of members of minority communities. The traditional separation of activities into public and private domains thus possesses little value in determining the proper response of the state to cultural diversity. The same is broadly true in respect of the traditional stance of neutrality expected of a liberal state, in terms of which governments should not favour one set of religious preferences over another. Difficulties arise in determining what type of legal provisions would amount to such 'favouritism', since if neutrality is perceived as precluding intervention to secure genuine equality for members of minority faiths a policy of pluralism may be seriously jeopardized.

Mill's definition of a liberal state as one that is open, diverse, plural, and equally hospitable to a wide variety of beliefs and practices can be seen as an endorsement of a policy of cultural diversity and his 'harm principle' provides a useful starting point from which to assess the legal limits to tolerance. Although Mill deprecated blind adherence to custom, both he and modern liberal theorists accept the importance of cultural identity for individuals in pursuing their own goals. Obviously the rights of individuals and groups can conflict with one another and this issue is addressed in Chapter 3. Before proceeding to that aspect, attention needs next to be turned to charting the developments which have occurred within English law in the treatment of cultural diversity.

2

Developments in English Law

The aims of this chapter are to chronicle the principal developments which have occurred within English law in its handling of ethnic or cultural differences and to identify the various legal techniques which are available to give effect to the two broad policy options outlined in the previous chapter. While the modern approach endorses cultural pluralism there are, as we have seen, limits to this process and assimilationist measures may sometimes be needed to uphold minimum standards, as part of the wider public interest, in the light of shared institutional values.

The first section explores the evolution of English legal attitudes towards cultural diversity by concentrating upon the role of the courts in three particular areas. In each of them the judges have been called upon to determine whether or not to recognize and uphold a diversity of customs, usages, and traditions. The second section focuses on the work of Parliament and illustrates how the legislature has, in recent decades, passed enactments reflecting both pluralist and assimilationist philosophies. The third section seeks to demonstrate the variety of techniques which are available to implement each of these approaches and thus draws attention to the ambiguity inherent in the use of blanket terminology to describe policies whose legal implications can be far more complex than they appear at first sight.

JUDICIAL STANCES IN RELATION TO CULTURAL DIVERSITY

(a) Local English customs[1]

Despite the mass of legislation enacted in modern times, the bedrock of the English legal system remains the common law developed over many centuries through the decisions given by the English judiciary in individual cases. The roots of the common law system lie in local customs, derived from a variety of sources, which were in operation prior to the advent of William the Conqueror in 1066. However, the Norman Conquest had a dramatic impact upon the development of the common law

---

[1] See generally, Allen, C., *Law in the Making*, 7th ed. (Oxford, 1964), ch II.

because thereafter the King was able, by building upon existing rudimentary Anglo-Saxon institutions, to lay the foundations of a strong central government and administration. The resulting centralization of judicial power and authority eventually led to the growth of legal rules which were applicable throughout the country and were thus 'common' to all its inhabitants. At the time, this process of unification distinguished England sharply from continental Europe where each particular area continued to be regulated by its own distinctive customs. By the middle of the twelfth century a book entitled *De Legibus et Consuetudinibus Angliae*, compiled by several authors but generally attributed to Glanvill, referred to the fixed customs of the King's Court as constituting *'jus et consuetuedo regni'* and these gradually replaced the great mass of local customs. However, in the main, neither the local customs themselves nor the local courts which administered them were formally abolished; rather the jurisdiction of the royal courts simply grew and superseded them, so that over a period of three centuries they had almost totally disappeared.

Today local customs are only upheld and enforced on isolated occasions and they thus constitute only a very minor, subsidiary source of modern law. Nevertheless, the manner in which they are regulated sheds valuable light upon the approach adopted by the English judges towards the practices followed by local communities, who naturally represent only small minorities within the population as a whole. Local customs, if they are to be recognized by the courts, must today satisfy the standard tests of immemorial antiquity, uninterrupted continuance, certainty, and reasonableness.[2] It is through the last of these four requirements that the courts are able to exercise a constant supervision and control over local variations from the general law of the land and prevent the application of customs which 'offend justice and common sense'.[3] It is clear that judicial insistence that local customs should not be unreasonable springs from a notion that the wider public interest may sometimes demand that minority practices, however long established, should give way in the face of overriding considerations relating to the dictates of fairness and reason and the welfare of all. Application of the doctrine of 'public policy' is the real ground upon which a proven local custom may properly be denied legal recognition by the courts.[4]

---

[2] See *Halsbury's Laws of England* (4th ed.), 12, paras 406–44.
[3] See *Produce Brokers Co v Olympia Oil and Coke Co* [1916] 2 KB 296 at 301.
[4] Allen, 155–6.

(b) Indigenous customs during the period of colonialism and empire[5]

During the colonial era, while it was the normal practice of the British Crown to introduce English law into its overseas possessions as 'the law of general application', the indigenous inhabitants were usually permitted to retain their personal and customary laws, save in certain extreme cases. Exceptions were made in respect of customs and practices which were felt to be particularly objectionable and these were usually banned by specific legislation. In this way the burning of widows ('*sati*'), punishment by mutilation, and religious blackmail were prohibited in India,[6] slavery and trial by ordeal were outlawed in West Africa,[7] and witchcraft and voodoo ('*obeah*') were criminalized in Africa and the West Indies respectively.[8] Customs authorizing forced marriages[9] or preventing certain categories of 'social outcasts' from intermarrying within the wider community[10] were similarly outlawed by statute in various parts of Africa.[11] Aside, however, from such attempts to legislate the demise of a few 'barbarous' customs, the imperial and colonial courts were commonly empowered by statute to exercise a continuing control over the enforcement of customary law in their respective territories. The mechanism for this supervisory function was the so-called 'repugnancy clause'. This usually provided that the indigenous or customary law of the inhabitants was only to be applied in the future insofar as it was not 'repugnant to justice, equity and good conscience'.[12] Sometimes the clause was phrased in a slightly different way, though the consequences seem to have been much the same. Three examples of repugnancy clauses may be given by way of illustration.

The Indian Punjab Laws Act 1872 provided in section 5—

In questions regarding succession, special property of females, betrothal, marriage, divorce, dower, adoption, guardianship, minority, bastards, family

---

[5] See generally Allott, A., *New Essays in African Law* (London, 1970), ch 5; see also Elias, T., *British Colonial Law* (London, 1962), ch 6; Daniels, W., *The Common Law in West Africa* (London, 1964), ch 10; Roberts-Wray, K., *Commonwealth and Colonial Law* (London, 1966), 575–9.

[6] See Rankin, G., *Background to Indian Law* (Cambridge, 1946), chs X-XII. Although '*sati*' (or '*suttee*') was outlawed in British India in 1829, at least forty instances of it have occurred since Independence. In 1987 the Indian Government hurried to reinforce the ban by enacting the Commission of Sati (Prevention) Act following the much-publicised *sati* of Roop Kanwar in Rajasthan on 4 Sept 1987.   [7] See Daniels, 290–1.

[8] See e.g. Elias, 106–8 and the Jamaican '*Obeah*' Law of 1898 (Cap 266).

[9] See Phillips, A. and Morris, H., *Marriage Laws in Africa* (London, 1971), 99–100.

[10] See Daniels, 273.

[11] For details of other practices banned in Africa, see Gann, L. and Duignan, P., *The Rulers of British Africa 1870–1914* (London, 1978), 353–4.

[12] For the origins of this expression and its application in British India, see Derrett, D., 'Justice, Equity and Good Conscience' in Anderson, N. (ed.), *Changing Law in Developing Countries* (London, 1963), ch 7; Rankin, 16.

relations, wills, legacies, gifts, partition, or any religious usage or institution, the rule of decision shall be—

(a) Any custom applicable to the parties concerned, which is not contrary to justice, equity or good conscience, and has not been declared to be void by any competent authority;
(b) the Muhammadan law . . . and the Hindu law . . . .[13]

The Gold Coast Supreme Court Ordinance 1876 stated in article 19—

Nothing in this Ordinance shall deprive the Supreme Court of the right to observe and enforce the observance, or shall deprive any person of the benefit, of any law or custom existing in the Colony, such law or custom not being repugnant to natural justice, equity and good conscience . . . .

The Tanganyika Order in Council 1920 provided in article 24—

In all cases, civil and criminal, to which natives are parties every Court shall . . . be guided by native law so far as it is applicable and is not repugnant to justice and morality or inconsistent with any Order in Council or Ordinance . . . .

By way of further variation, Maori customs in New Zealand and aboriginal customs in New Guinea were only allowed continued application by the colonial authorities to the extent that they were not repugnant to 'general principles of humanity'.[14]

Colonial judges were, of course, faced at the outset with the question whether the relevant repugnancy clause demanded the application of English or local standards of 'justice, equity and good conscience' or 'justice or morality'. One of the best known judicial pronouncements on the subject was made by Wilson J in the Tanganyikan case of *Gwao bin Kilimo v Kisunda bin Ifuti*[15] in 1938. He stated—

Morality and justice are abstract conceptions and every community probably has an absolute standard of its own by which to decide what is justice and what is morality. But unfortunately, the standards of different communities are by no means the same. To what standard, then, does the Order in Council refer—the African standard of justice and morality or the British standard? I have no doubt whatever that the only standard of justice and morality which a British court in Africa can apply is its own British standard. Otherwise we should find ourselves in certain circumstances having to condone such things, for example, as the institution of slavery . . . .[16]

---

[13] It is worthy of note that the laws specified in para (b) were not subjected to the 'justice, equity and good conscience' test laid down in para (a).
[14] See New Zealand Government Act 1846, s 10; New Guinea Native Administration Regulations 1924, reg 57(2).   [15] [1938] 1 TLR (R) 403.
[16] See also Allott, A., 'What is to be done with African customary law?' [1984] *JAL* 56 at 59, where the additional point is made that the powers entrusted to the courts by the various repugnancy clauses were in practice only exercised to a very limited degree in Africa.

However, by 1962 the Judicial Committee of the Privy Council had warned in an appeal from Nigeria that—

. . . the principles of natural justice, equity and good conscience applicable in a country where polygamy is generally accepted should not . . . be readily equated with those applicable to a community governed by the rule of monogamy.[17]

In the same year Elias (who was later to be elected as the President of the International Court of Justice) felt able to write[18]—

It may be said that, generally, British colonial policy . . . has not been to judge the validity of local law and customs by the standards of Western thought or Christian ethics, but by the canons of decency and humanity considered appropriate to the situation in hand . . . . It is not often easy to decide what ought to be the true morality in a particular colony's conditions. A constant judicial dilemma is to strike a nice balance between what is reasonably tolerable and what is essentially below the minimum standard of civilised values in the contemporary world.

It is clear that the same concerns for reasonableness and justice which apply to the regulation of local English customs were employed by the colonial courts to ensure that indigenous customs were not unreasonable, repugnant, or immoral. Broad public policy considerations guided the decisions of the courts in both instances.

(c) Conflict of laws principles

English courts apply conflict of laws principles to determine the outcome of cases with a foreign element. In some instances this may mean that they decide the issues on the basis of the rules of another legal system, if that system is selected as the appropriate legal regime to govern the particular case. In a number of such cases decided since 1945 English judges have been faced with the question whether or not to apply foreign laws and customs, which were *prima facie* the correct ones to select under established conflict of laws principles, yet which caused them some qualms because they were so different from English law. In each of the following six examples it is possible to discern a clear pattern in the reasoning of the judges involved.

In *Baindail v Baindail*[19] a Hindu man who had entered into a potentially polygamous marriage in India came to England and married a second 'wife' here. The second marriage could only be declared a nullity under English law at the instance of the second 'wife' if the first marriage was regarded as valid by the English courts. Lord Greene MR indicated

---

[17] *Dawodu v Danmole* [1962] 1 WLR 1053 at 1060.
[18] *British Colonial Law*, 104.   [19] [1946] P 122.

that the question whether or not to recognize the Hindu marriage, despite its polygamous nature, had to be decided 'with due regard to common sense and some attention to reasonable policy'.[20] The marriage was recognized.

In *Cheni v Cheni*[21] a marriage had occurred in Egypt between an uncle and his niece who were Sephardic Jews. The couple had later come to live in Britain. Although such a marriage falls within the prohibited degrees of consanguinity in domestic English law, it was perfectly valid in terms of Egyptian law because of its acceptability under Jewish law. Sir Jocelyn Simon P upheld the validity of the marriage in the eyes of English law through the application of conflict of laws principles and indicated that the test to be applied in such cases was whether the outcome was unconscionable in terms of English public policy. The true test, he declared was—

whether the marriage is so offensive to the conscience of the English court that it should refuse to recognise and give effect to the proper foreign law. In deciding that question the court will seek to exercise common sense, good manners and a reasonable tolerance. In my view it would be altogether too queasy a judicial conscience which would recoil from a marriage acceptable to many peoples of deep religious convictions, lofty ethical standards and high civilisation.[22]

In *Varanand v Varanand*[23] a couple were divorced in London, quite informally and without going through the normal court procedure, by means of a process of mutual consent according to the customary law of Thailand, the country of their domicile. Scarman J upheld the validity of the divorce at English common law, pointing out that the judicial discretion to refuse recognition to a foreign status was one to be most sparingly exercised and confined to cases involving an infringement of public policy or natural justice.[24]

A few years later, in *In the Estate of Fuld (deceased) (No. 3)*, the same judge remarked—

It is not, however, to be thought that blind adherence to foreign law can ever be required of an English court. Whether the point be described in the language of public policy, 'discretion' or 'the conscience of the court', an English court will refuse to apply a law which outrages its sense of justice or decency.[25]

---

[20] At 129; see also *In re Langley's Settlement Trusts* [1962] Ch 541 at 554, 558.
[21] [1965] P 85.　　　[22] At 99.　　　[23] (1964) 108 *SJ* 693.
[24] Subsequently, Parliament took a less tolerant stance towards such divorces. A ban on the recognition of extrajudicial divorces occurring within the British Isles was imposed by statute in 1973 and is now to be found in section 44(1) of the Family Law Act 1986; see further below, ch 6.　　　[25] [1968] P 675 at 698.

In *Alhaji Mohamed v Knott*[26] a Muslim marriage had been contracted in Nigeria between two Nigerian domiciliaries at a time when the bride was only just thirteen. Three months later the couple arrived in England so that the husband could pursue a course of study. A juvenile court ordered that the wife be placed in the care of a local authority following the discovery that her husband had taken her to a doctor to be fitted with a contraceptive device. The ground relied upon by the Court was that the girl was 'in moral danger'. The decision was reversed on appeal by the Divisional Court. Lord Parker C J stressed the necessity of viewing the marriage through the perspective of Nigerian Muslims and rejected the notion that such marriages were 'repugnant' or 'abhorrent'.[27] He held that the marriage was entitled to the fullest recognition by the English courts, as indeed were the sexual relations which were a natural corollary. The girl could hardly be said to be in moral danger merely because she carried out her wifely duties.[28]

In *Bumper Development Corp Ltd v Commissioner of Police of the Metropolis*[29] an important twelfth century bronze idol had been wrongfully removed from the precinct of a ruined Hindu temple in India and brought to London, where it was purchased in good faith by the plaintiffs. While the idol was in the possession of the British Museum for purposes of appraisal and conservation, it was seized by the Metropolitan Police as part of a policy of returning stolen religious artefacts to their lawful owners in India. When the plaintiffs sought the return of the idol, a claim of superior title was made by the ruined temple where it had been discovered. The preliminary question for the English court was whether, in the words of Purchas LJ, 'something which on one view is little more than a pile of stones'[30] had the legal capacity to sue in this country. Whereas under Indian law a Hindu temple is recognized as a juristic entity and is capable of suing through an officer properly appointed under that law, in English municipal law legal personality is restricted to individuals or institutionalized groups of individuals formed into corporate bodies; hence purely inanimate objects do not qualify. The Court of Appeal held that this presented no barrier to a suit brought by the temple here because there was no 'offence to English public policy in allowing a Hindu religious institution to sue in our courts for the recovery of property which it is entitled to recover by the law of its own country. Indeed we think that public policy would be

---

[26] [1969] 1 QB 1.   [27] At 15–16.

[28] Subsequently, the British Government adopted a less indulgent approach towards such a relationship. In 1986 the possibility of such a person under the age of sixteen being admitted to the UK as a spouse was removed by a change in the Immigration Rules—see HC 306 of 1986–6, discussed below.

[29] [1991] 4 All ER 638.   [30] At 647.

advantaged'.[31] In support of this approach Purchas LJ cited a statement made by Cardozo J in an American case as follows[32]—

The courts are not free to refuse to enforce a foreign right at the pleasure of the judges, to suit the individual notion of expediency or fairness. They do not close their doors unless help would violate some fundamental principle of justice, some prevalent conception of good morals, some deep-rooted tradition of the common weal.[33]

The upshot of the case was that the temple's claim to have a title to the idol superior to that of the plaintiff corporation was upheld by the Court of Appeal.

It is well established in the field of conflict of laws that the English courts possess a reserve or 'disabling' power, in terms of which they can decline to uphold or enforce an otherwise applicable rule of foreign law.[34] What the six cases cited above tend to indicate is not only a broadly tolerant attitude towards the recognition of foreign laws and customs on the part of English judges over recent decades but also the limits to that tolerance. Basically, the same criteria have been adopted in this sphere as with local customs in England and indigenous customs in the British empire and colonies. Tolerance is bounded by notions of reasonableness, common sense, and justice. The line is to be drawn at what is repugnant, abhorrent, or offensive to the conscience of the court. Ultimately the question is one of 'public policy', of the need to safeguard the public interest. Moreover, this approach has recently been expressly reflected in several statutory provisions. For instance, the Family Law Act 1986 provides that even where a foreign divorce, annulment, or separation satisfies the basic (and sometimes quite stringent) requirements for recognition, the English courts retain a discretion to refuse recognition where it would be 'manifestly contrary to public policy' to do otherwise.[35]

(d) Public policy and human rights

Public policy is an elusive and wide-ranging concept which confers a great deal of discretion upon the judiciary[36] and the very lack of precision

---

[31] At 648. [32] Ibid.

[33] *Loucks v Standard Oil Co of New York* (1918) 224 NY 99 at 111.

[34] See *Dicey and Morris on The Conflict of Laws*, 12th ed. (London, 1993), 88–96; *Cheshire and North's Private International Law*, 12th ed. (London, 1992), 128–37.

[35] Section 51(3)(c); for other examples, see Adoption Act 1976, s 53(2)(a); Private International Law (Miscellaneous Provisions) Act 1995, s 14(3)(a)(i).

[36] See e.g. *Sharif v Sharif* (1980) 10 *Fam Law* 216; *R v Registrar General, ex parte Smith* [1990] 2 All ER 170.

in the doctrine has predictably given rise to much criticism and concern.[37] Early in the nineteenth century, Burrough J commented that public policy was 'a very unruly horse, and when once you get astride it you never know where it will carry you'.[38] To this remark Lord Denning, more recently, offered a characteristic riposte—'With a good man in the saddle, the unruly horse can be kept in control. It can jump over obstacles . . . and come down on the side of justice'.[39] This metaphorical exchange naturally prompts the question whether, in the cases which will inevitably arise in future years involving judicial recognition of ethnic minority cultural traditions in England, any greater specificity can be given to the doctrine so that justice is indeed accomplished. Are there any cardinal values in English public policy which can be identified with more particularity than the general attributes of order, justice, and personal freedom which form an integral part of a liberal democracy?[40] What exactly are the limits to legal acceptance of cultural diversity in a tolerant society? The answers which would be given in other Western democracies to such profound questions would usually entail reference to a written constitution. It is there that the judges would expect to be able to locate the higher values of the nation, against which might be tested the ordinary laws of the land and the practices of public authorities. In particular, such constitutions would contain a 'bill of rights', a list of the fundamental human rights and freedoms which the state undertakes to guarantee to all those within its jurisdiction.

In the absence of such a constitution in this country, it is not perhaps surprising that on several occasions during the past twenty-five years eminent English judges should have explicitly drawn a connection between the dictates of English public policy and the provisions of those international human rights treaties to which the United Kingdom is a contracting party. For example, in *Blathwayt v Lord Crawley* Lord Wilberforce referred to the guarantee of freedom of religion in the European Convention on Human Rights and stated—

. . . I do not doubt that conceptions of public policy should move with the times

---

[37] See generally, Knight, W., 'Public Policy in English Law' (1922) 38 *LQR* 207; Winfield, P., 'Public policy in the English common law' (1928–9) 42 *Harvard LR* 76; Lloyd, D., *Public Policy* (London, 1953); Kahn-Freund, O., 'Reflections on Public Policy in the English Conflicts of Laws' (1953) 39 *Transact Grotius Society* 39; (1974) III *Hague Recueil des Cours* 426–31; Nygh, P., 'Foreign Status, Public Policy and Discretion' (1964) 13 *ICLQ* 39; Holder, W., 'Public Policy and National Preferences: The Exclusion of Foreign Law in English Private International Law' (1968) 17 *ICLQ* 926; Carter, P., 'The Role of Public Policy in English Private International Law' (1993) 42 *ICLQ* 1.

[38] See *Richardson v Mellish* (1824) 2 Bing 229 at 252.

[39] *Enderby Town Football Club Ltd v Football Association* [1971] Ch 591 at 606–7.

[40] See e.g. Stein, P. and Shand, J., *Legal Values in Western Society* (Edinburgh, 1974), 1.

and that widely accepted treaties . . . may point the direction in which such conceptions, as applied by the courts, ought to move.[41]

In *Oppenheimer v Cattermole* Lord Salmon expressly held that on grounds of public policy no recognition should be afforded by English law to a Nazi decree depriving Jews of German nationality because it amounted to 'so great an offence against human rights.'[42] In *Attorney General v BBC* Lord Scarman stated—

If the issue should ultimately be, as I think in this case it is, a question of legal policy, we must have regard to the country's international obligation to observe the European Convention as interpreted by the European Court of Human Rights.[43]

In *Schering Chemicals v Falkman Ltd* Lord Denning MR made the same point when he said—

We are here concerned with a question of policy . . . On such a question, I take it that our law should conform as far as possible with the provisions of the European Convention on Human Rights.[44]

In the light of these statements, it is possible to argue that collectively those human rights and freedoms which the United Kingdom has undertaken to respect, by adherence to international treaties and conventions, constitute a significant portion of the hard core of English public policy, in contrast to those aspects of economic doctrine and political ideology which tend to fluctuate from one administration to another. The imminent incorporation of the European Convention on Human Rights into English law can only serve to reinforce this position.[45]

Bearing in mind that the number of major international human rights conventions is quite small, and that for a British Government to repudiate such a convention would be both unthinkable and unprecedented, the general impact of habitually having regard to them in cases involving public policy issues seems likely to generate some consistency and predictability in an area where the greatest danger would appear to be uncontrolled judicial discretion. Whether this approach will commend itself to the courts in the field of ethnic minority cultures is not yet clear, but the first sign of such a development was faintly visible in 1991 in *R v Chief Metropolitan Stipendiary Magistrate, ex parte Choudhury.*[46] The Chief Metropolitan Stipendiary Magistrate had refused to issue a summons for the private prosecution of Salman Rushdie and his publishers for

---

[41] [1976] AC 397 at 426. [42] [1976] AC 249 at 282–3.
[43] [1981] AC 303 at 354. [44] [1981] 2 All ER 321 at 331.
[45] Legislation is expected in 1998. For detailed examination of use of the Convention by the English courts prior to incorporation, see Hunt, M., *Using Human Rights Law in English Courts* (Oxford, 1997). [46] [1991] 1 QB 429.

blasphemy for allegedly vilifying the Muslim faith and the Prophet Muhammad in his novel *The Satanic Verses*. The Divisional Court upheld the Magistrate's action on the basis that the common law offence of blasphemy is clearly confined to the protection of the Christian religion[47] and it ruled as a matter of law that the crime could not be extended judicially to other faiths. The Court did, however, appear to acknowledge *en passant* that the case might be regarded as raising an issue of public policy and that it was therefore necessary to consider the implications of the provisions of the European Convention.[48] The Court was specifically referred to Article 9 of the Convention on freedom of religion and Article 14 on freedom from discrimination, but it finally concluded that the Convention did not require signatories to create an offence of blasphemy against Islam.[49]

MODERN LEGISLATION REFLECTING PLURALIST AND
ASSIMILATIONIST APPROACHES

The legislative changes which have been introduced during the past thirty years or so to deal with ethnic minority cultural traditions can be seen as reflecting both philosophies. On the one hand, there are several instances where Parliament has enacted provisions designed to recognize and support cultural diversity. On the other hand, there are a number of examples of assimilationist provisions aimed at outlawing or denying legal significance to ethnic and religious traditions. Sometimes both tendencies are apparent in the same Act and, notably in the case of the Local Government Act 1966 and the Education Reform Act 1988, attempts have been made to achieve a balance between them and, particularly in relation to the latter, a somewhat uneasy compromise obtains. The pattern of these developments is set out below.

(a) Enactments endorsing cultural pluralism

In 1968 Parliament acknowledged for the first time the desire of many gypsies to maintain their nomadic lifestyle by imposing upon all local authorities a duty, under the Caravan Sites Act of that year, to provide adequate sites for gypsies residing in or resorting to their areas.[50] Hitherto the official assumption had been that gypsies would, over time, settle down as members of the house-dwelling community and

---

[47] See e.g. *R v Gathercole* (1838) 1 Lew CC 237.   [48] At 318, 320–2.
[49] The 'Rushdie Affair' is discussed further below, ch 3.
[50] See Part II of the Act, especially s 6(1), as amended by Local Government Act 1972, sched 30.

that they should be encouraged to do so. However, in 1994 a sharp reversal of policy led to local authorities being relieved of further duties in the provision of gypsy sites[51] and the adoption of a much more assimilationist stance.[52]

In 1972 the ancient and notoriously unjust rule in *Hyde v Hyde*[53] was abolished by the Matrimonial Proceedings (Polygamous Marriages) Act, which allowed the courts to grant matrimonial relief to parties to actual or potentially polygamous marriages contracted abroad.[54] Since polygamy had long been perceived by the judiciary as such an odious, alien custom that parties could not even be granted maintenance or divorce by the English Courts in respect of potentially polygamous but actually monogamous marriages, this was a major advance.[55]

Four years later Parliament enacted two further Acts with profound significance, one in a practical sense and the other symbolically. The first of these, the Race Relations Act 1976, incorporated into English law the novel concept of 'indirect discrimination'.[56] This renders unlawful certain apparently neutral acts done by employers and others, which are not designed to discriminate against ethnic minorities but which nevertheless have a disproportionately adverse impact upon them because of their cultural and religious backgrounds. In particular, the Act's provisions have the effect of making it unlawful for employers and educational establishments to impose standardized rules about uniforms, dress, and appearance with which members of minority groups cannot conscientiously comply, unless such rules can be demonstrated to be 'justifiable'.[57]

The other piece of legislation in 1976, the Motor-Cycle Crash Helmets (Religious Exemption) Act, was passed in order to relieve turbaned Sikhs from the duty being imposed on all motor cyclists to wear helmets complying with high safety standards.[58] Parliament took the view that the health and safety considerations underlying the obligation to wear a helmet were outweighed by the religious concern felt by many orthodox Sikhs about having to discard their turbans.[59]

More recently, the Sikh community has built upon the precedents

---

[51] Criminal Justice and Public Order Act 1994, s 80(1).

[52] For detailed analysis of the law relating to gypsy encampments, see below, ch 5.

[53] (1866) L R 1 P & D 139.

[54] S 1, now embodied in Matrimonial Causes Act 1973, s 47.

[55] See Poulter, S., '*Hyde v Hyde*: A reappraisal' (1976) 25 *ICLQ* 475.

[56] See s 1(1)(*b*). For detailed analysis of the concept, see below, ch 8.

[57] See further below, ch 8.

[58] See now Motor Cycles (Protective Helmets) Regulations 1980, enacted pursuant to Road Traffic Act 1972, s 32.

[59] The exemption is now contained in Road Traffic Act 1988, s 16(2) and is discussed further below, ch 8.

established by the 1976 Acts and persuaded Parliament to pay further attention to its needs. One of the five distinctive symbols of Sikhism ('the five Ks') is the *kirpan* (a small sword or dagger), which should be carried as a matter of religious obligation by all orthodox Sikhs. The Criminal Justice Act 1988, which contains provisions designed to penalize those who carry knives and other sharply-pointed instruments in public places, deals with the *kirpan* by means of a specific exemption for those carrying sharply-pointed articles for 'religious reasons'.[60] Similarly, section 11 of the Employment Act 1989 contains an exemption for turbaned Sikhs from the duty recently imposed upon all those working on construction sites to wear safety helmets.[61] Furthermore, any employer who refuses to employ a Sikh on a construction site simply because he is unwilling to wear a safety helmet in place of his turban will be barred from even being able to argue that such a policy is 'justifiable' on grounds of safety under the indirect discrimination provisions of the Race Relations Act.[62]

In 1989 the Children Act imposed a new obligation upon all local authorities to give due consideration to the religious persuasion, racial origin, and cultural and linguistic background of any child whom they were looking after, or preparing to look after, in making any decision about that child's future.[63] This direction supplemented earlier statutory provisions barring local authorities from causing children in their care to be brought up in any religious creed other than that in which they would have been brought up, had they not been in public care.[64] The Children Act 1989 also required voluntary organizations to give due consideration to the religious persuasion, racial origin, and cultural and linguistic background of any child being accommodated by them, in reaching any decisions about the child.[65]

The Broadcasting Act 1990 required the Independent Television Commission to do everything possible to ensure that every licensed TV service exercises due responsibility with respect to the content of any religious programmes and, in particular, that these do not involve any abusive treatment of the religious views and beliefs of those belonging to a particular religion or religious denomination.[66]

The Private International Law (Miscellaneous Provisions) Act 1995

---

[60] Section 139(5)(b).
[61] Construction (Head Protection) Regulations 1989, discussed further below, ch 8.
[62] Employment Act 1989, s 12.
[63] S 22(5)(c). Local authorities must also bear in mind these same factors when satisfying themselves whether the needs of privately fostered children are being met—see Children (Private Arrangements for Fostering) Regulations, S 1 2050 of 1991, reg 2(2)(c).
[64] Children Act 1948, s 3(7); Children and Young Persons Act 1969, s 24(3); see now Children Act 1989, s 33(b)(a).
[65] S 61(3)(c).   [66] S 6(1)(d).

gave wider recognition to Muslim and other potentially polygamous marriages contracted abroad. This involved substantial amendment of an assimilationist provision which had been introduced by the Matrimonial Proceedings (Polygamous Marriages) Act 1972. While, as we have seen, the main aim of that Act was to allow the courts to afford matrimonial relief to parties to polygamous marriages, section 4 of the Act had struck a sharp blow against cultural pluralism. It had incorporated a new situation into the statutory list of grounds upon which a marriage is void, namely where either party to an actual or potentially polygamous marriage contracted abroad was at the time of the marriage domiciled in England and Wales.[67] Although section 4 purported to be merely a re-statement of the pre-existing common law position, its enactment seemed to have occurred without sufficient regard to the extent of its application. The provision was framed so widely that it was liable to bar, for example, Muslims from the Indian subcontinent who had acquired a domicile of choice here, from returning to their countries of origin to enter into a first marriage through an Islamic wedding. This restricted them in their choice of ceremony since an Islamic form of marriage cannot validly be contracted in England.[68] Fortunately, in *Hussain v Hussain*[69] the Court of Appeal had managed, through ingenious if dubious reasoning, to restrict the ambit of the bar to potentially polygamous marriages abroad contracted by women domiciled in England, not men placed in similar circumstances. However, the outcome was highly anomalous and the Law Commission proposed further reform,[70] which was eventually effected by the 1995 Act. In section 5, it now provides that a marriage entered into abroad between parties, neither of whom is already married, is not void here merely on the grounds that it has been entered into under a law that permits polygamy and that one or both of the parties are domiciled in England and Wales. First marriages in polygamous form contracted in such circumstances will, therefore, now be recognized as valid in English law.

(b) Enactments promoting assimilation

In 1973 section 16 of the Domicile and Matrimonial Proceedings Act introduced a rule into English family law which removed the rights of Muslims and other minorities to follow exclusively their own norms and procedures in relation to divorce. This provision reversed the previous common law rule that English law would generally recognize the validity

---

[67] See now Matrimonial Causes Act 1973, s 11(d).
[68] *R v Bham* [1966] 1 QB 159.   [69] [1983] Fam 26.
[70] See Poulter, S., 'Polygamy—New Law Commission Proposals' (1983) 13 Fam Law 72.

of extrajudicial divorces obtained here, provided they were acceptable to the law of the couple's domicile.[71] Henceforth, no proceeding in the British Isles would be regarded as validly dissolving a marriage unless it was instituted in a court of law. This meant a ban both on the Muslim *talaq*[72] and on consensual forms of divorce used by many societies in different parts of the world.[73] During the course of the Parliamentary debates on this provision the promoter of the measure justified the ban on the basis of the need to ensure 'that the proceedings themselves satisfy our normal requirements of justice' and indicated that one of the reasons for finding extrajudicial divorces objectionable was that they 'can enable a wife to be discarded by the unilateral action of her husband'.[74]

Twelve years later the Prohibition of Female Circumcision Act 1985 was enacted in the wake of reports that a small number of such operations had been occurring within this country. Prior to 1985 female circumcision was probably a common law crime or an offence under the Offences Against the Person Act 1861, but many felt it was desirable, in the absence of any judicial precedent, to put the matter beyond doubt by means of a well-publicized and unequivocal enactment. During the course of the Parliamentary debates on the subject a Government spokesman described female circumcision as 'not compatible with the culture of this country' and 'thoroughly repugnant to our way of life',[75] and the promoter of the legislation justified the ban on the ground that female circumcision amounted to 'cruel, inhuman or degrading treatment', contrary to Article 5 of the Universal Declaration of Human Rights.[76] Although the Act creates special exemptions for operations needed for a person's physical or mental health, no account is to be taken in assessing mental health of anyone's belief that the operation is required 'as a matter of custom or ritual'.[77]

From a practical point of view by far the most significant assimilationist tendencies have come in the field of immigration law.[78] The Immigration Act 1971 empowers the Secretary of State to make rules[79] and since 1971 a variety of changes to the Immigration Rules have restricted entry to the United Kingdom in such a way as to strike at the family customs and traditions of several of the minority communities, with the result that the unity of many families has been destroyed.

[71] See e.g. *Varanand v Varanand* (1964) 108 SJ 693; *Qureshi v Qureshi* [1972] Fam 173.
[72] See further below, ch 6.
[73] The ban is now contained in Family Law Act 1986, s 44(1).
[74] See HC Debs, 850, col 1630; 860, col 1086.
[75] HL Debs, 447, col 86 (Lord Glenarthur).
[76] HL Debs, 441, col 674 (Lord Kennet).   [77] S 2(2).
[78] See generally, Jackson, D., *Immigration Law and Practice* (London, 1996).
[79] S 3(2).

The most notorious of these provisions has been the 'primary purpose' rule, in terms of which spouses were refused entry clearance certificates to join partners in this country unless the entry clearance officer was satisfied that 'the marriage was not entered into primarily to obtain admission to the United Kingdom'.[80] A similar rule applied to the entry of fiancés and fiancées who sought to come to this country to marry and reside with a partner here.[81] These rules clearly had an adverse impact upon the traditional pattern of arranged marriages favoured by several ethnic minority communities. In 1993 an authoritative report published by JUSTICE castigated the rules as 'grossly unfair and unnecessary' and called for their abolition because 'they lead to a quantity of human misery that more than outweighs any mischief which they prevent'.[82] They were finally abrogated in 1997.[83] Another example of the assimilationist tendency is found in the manner in which the traditional pattern of Asian extended families has come under pressure from rules which specify that the accommodation which immigrants come to in the United Kingdom must, in many instances, be owned or occupied 'exclusively', rather than jointly.[84]

Two further changes in immigration law are worthy of note because they demonstrate the determination of the authorities to exclude from entry parties to certain unacceptable types of marriage. From 1986 persons under the age of sixteen have been barred from entering the United Kingdom in reliance upon their status as a spouse of someone living here.[85] This followed the discovery early in that year of a twelve-year-old Iranian bride and a thirteen-year-old Omani bride, each living in England with her student husband.[86] Sixteen is the 'age of consent' for lawful sexual intercourse[87] and the minimum age for marriage in England,[88] and it was felt to be intolerable to have these child brides performing their wifely duties here.[89] Further, in 1988 steps were taken to prevent second and subsequent wives of polygamous men from joining their husbands here for settlement purposes.[90] The policy underlying

---

[80] See 'Statement of Changes in Immigration Rules', HC 395 of 1994, para 281.

[81] Ibid, para 290.

[82] Young JUSTICE, *The primary purpose rule: a rule with no purpose* (London, 1993), 18. For a powerful critique of the rule, see generally Sachdeva, S., *The Primary Purpose Rule in British Immigration Law* (Stoke-on-Trent, 1993). The application and interpretation of the rule was modified in 1992; see HC Debs 210, cols 523–4 (written answers).

[83] 'Statement of Changes in Immigration Rules', HC 26 of 1997, paras 1, 3.

[84] See e.g. HC 395 of 1994, paras 281(v), 290(vi), 297(iv), 317(iv).

[85] HC 306 of 1985–6; see now HC 395 of 1994, para 277.

[86] See e.g. *The Times*, 6 and 20 March 1986.   [87] Sexual Offences Act 1956, s 6(1).

[88] Matrimonial Causes Act 1973, s 11(a)(ii).

[89] Cf *Alhaji Mohamed v Knott* [1969] 1 QB 1 discussed above.

[90] Immigration Act 1988, together with amendments to Immigration Rules, HC 555 of 1988; see now HC 395 of 1994, paras 278–80.

this change was to prevent a husband simultaneously having two or more wives living with him in the United Kingdom on the grounds that actual polygamy is not 'an acceptable social custom in this country'.[91]

While several of the 'assimilationist' provisions outlined above are clearly motivated by a desire to maintain minimum standards of behaviour, others are not. The 'primary purpose' rule in immigration law was originally prompted by the desire to restrict male immigration and section 4 of the Matrimonial Proceedings (Polygamous Marriages) Act 1972, in its attempt to invalidate marriages which would merely have been potentially rather than actually polygamous, seems to have been a thoughtless mistake which has, fortunately, been rectified by the Private International Law (Miscellaneous Provisions) Act 1995.[92]

(c) Attempts to strike a balance

(i) Section 11 of the Local Government Act 1966

Section 11 of the Local Government Act 1966 (as amended[93]) provides that the Secretary of State may pay grants towards expenditure on additional staff to those local authorities which, in his opinion, are 'required to make special provision in the exercise of any of their functions in consequence of the presence within their areas of persons belonging to ethnic minorities whose language or customs differ from those of the rest of the community'.[94] The grants are generally paid on approved posts at the rate of 50 per cent (previously 75 per cent) of salary costs[95] and the total expenditure on the part of central and local government is currently well in excess of £100 million per annum, despite recent cuts.[96] Around 80 per cent of this is devoted to improving the English language competence of children from non-English speaking backgrounds.[97] This is very much in line with the Government's revised objective under section 11, following a policy review in 1990, which is to assist members of ethnic minority communities to enter fully into and benefit from the mainstream of national life by increasing their opportunities for educational, economic, and social development.[98]

A concentration of funding upon programmes designed to improve people's command of the English language strongly suggests an assim-

---

[91] See HC Debs, 122, col 785 (Douglas Hurd MP).   [92] S 5.

[93] By Local Government (Amendment) Act 1993, s 1.

[94] For a review of the development of section 11 funding, see Bagley, C., *Back to the Future: Section 11 of the Local Government Act 1966: Local Authorities and Multicultural/Antiracist Education* (Slough, 1992).   [95] Home Office Circular No. 78/1990, para 21.

[96] 'Guide to Section 11 Funding: The 1992/93 Section 11 Allocation', Local Authorities Race Relations Information Exchange Research Report No. 3 (1992), 2.   [97] Ibid, 3.

[98] Home Office, 'Policy Criteria for the Administration of Section 11 Grant' (1990), 3.

ilationist perspective. Indeed in 1990 the Government openly acknowledged that section 11 funding was not intended to be used, as it had previously been, for the active promotion of cultural pluralism—

The Government fully recognises the benefits that derive from the maintenance of religious, artistic, cultural and linguistic traditions among ethnic minority communities. It does not, however, consider Section 11 grant to be an appropriate use for initiatives aimed at such purposes.[99]

On the other hand, such grants are still being made available for various limited purposes which demonstrate Government acceptance of the fact that some members of the ethnic minority communities will continue to have cultural needs which are different from those of the majority community. Applications may be made, for instance, in respect of projects which strengthen ties between schools and parents whose lack of English or cultural differences make such links hard to establish, or which provide interpreting or translation services, or which promote the delivery of personal social services (for example for children and the elderly), which are appropriate for people from a variety of cultural backgrounds.[100] Hence, the way in which the criteria for grants are applied reflects, to some degree, a pluralist approach, even if the bulk of the funding is devoted to the promotion of the use of the English language as a key mechanism for achieving equality of opportunity.[101]

(ii) The religious education provisions of the Education Reform Act 1988[102] (now incorporated in the Education Act 1996)

Collective worship

The 1988 Act retained the requirement laid down in the Education Act 1944 that all pupils at state schools must take part in an act of collective worship on each school day, subject to a right of parental withdrawal.[103] As before, in LEA schools the act of worship must not be distinctive of any particular denomination, but under current law it is required to be 'wholly or mainly of a broadly Christian character'.[104] This does not mean, however, that every single day's worship has to be Christian in character. It is sufficient if, 'taking any school term as a whole', most acts

---

[99] Ibid.   [100] Ibid, 5, 9, 13–16, 35.

[101] Since 1994 a proportion of s 11 funding has formed part of the 'Single Regeneration Budget'.

[102] For a detailed examination and critique, see generally, Hamilton, C., *Family, Law and Religion* (London, 1995), ch 7; Poulter, S., 'The religious education provisions of the Education Reform Act 1988' (1990) 2 *Education and the Law* 1; Harte, J., 'Worship and Religious Education under the Education Reform Act 1988—a Lawyer's View' (1991) 13 *British Journal of Religious Education* 152.

[103] Education Act 1996, ss 385(1), 389(1).   [104] Ibid, s 386(2).

of worship are wholly or mainly of a broadly Christian character.[105] 'Broadly Christian' worship is meant to be of such a nature that pupils from non-Christian backgrounds can participate and it can thus contain some non-Christian elements.[106] Furthermore, despite the express reference to Christianity (of which there was no explicit mention in the 1944 Act), there are two other provisions specifically designed to take account of the diversity of faiths represented in the pupils of many schools. First, in working out the precise forms of collective worship to be adopted, individual LEA schools may themselves decide what is appropriate and in the process have due regard to the family background of their pupils.[107] Secondly, an LEA school may be exempted from the 'broadly Christian' requirement if the LEA's Standing Advisory Council on Religious Education (SACRE) decides this would be appropriate.[108] Then the worship can either be distinctive of a non-Christian religion or else give no particular emphasis to any one faith. Moreover, the exemption may either relate to the school as a whole or to 'any class or description of pupils' there.[109]

Religious education classes

The 1988 Act retained compulsory religious education classes, which now form part of the 'basic curriculum', albeit subject to the right of parental withdrawal.[110] In LEA schools the classes must, as before, follow an 'agreed syllabus' formulated by a locally convened conference of four committees.[111] These committees are now appointed to represent the LEA, the teachers' associations, the Church of England, and such other Christian denominations and other religions and denominations of such religions as appropriately reflect the principal religious traditions of the area.[112] The greatest change made by the 1988 Act was that any new agreed syllabus produced after 29 September 1988 must 'reflect the fact that the religious traditions in Great Britain are in the main Christian, whilst taking account of the teaching and practices of the other principal religions represented in Great Britain'.[113]

This opaque phrasing has naturally provoked controversy as to its

---

[105] Education Act 1996, s 386(4).

[106] See DFE Circular 1/94, 'Religious Education and Collective Worship', paras 54, 62, 63 and 65; *R v Secretary of State for Education, ex parte R and D* [1994] ELR 495.

[107] Education Act 1996, s 386(5), (6).

[108] Ibid, s 387. S 390(1) places a legal duty upon every LEA to constitute a SACRE and in terms of s 390(4)(a) each SACRE must include a group representing such Christian denominations and other religions and denominations of such religions as, in the opinion of the LEA, will appropriately reflect the principal religious traditions in the area.

[109] Education Act 1996, s 387(1)(a).

[110] See now Education Act 1996, ss 352, 376–81, 389(1).

[111] Ibid, ss 375, 376.   [112] Ibid, sched 31, para 4.   [113] Ibid, s 375(3).

precise meaning, but it seems to have been deliberately designed not only to reflect the centrality of the Christian tradition in this country but also to achieve a measure of flexibility to suit the needs of different local communities.[114] Although Christianity is referred to explicitly and is thus afforded greater prominence, the legality of an agreed syllabus does not fall to be tested by asking whether it is 'mainly Christian' but rather whether 'a reasonable amount of attention' is devoted to teaching based on Christian traditions.[115] The appropriate balance between Christianity and the other principal religions is to be determined at the local level, but clearly none of the religions can be totally excluded from the syllabus. While in most instances it will be proper to devote most attention to Christianity, this will not be appropriate in all cases.[116]

(iii) The national curriculum provisions of the Education Reform Act 1988 (now incorporated in the Education Act 1996)

The law requires all maintained schools to teach pupils the secular 'core' and other 'foundation' subjects which comprise the 'national curriculum' established by statute.[117] English is naturally designated as a core subject,[118] but this is balanced by the requirement that all pupils between the ages of eleven and sixteen must study an approved modern foreign language as one of their other foundation subjects.[119] Several non-European languages have already been approved by delegated legislation, including Arabic, Bengali, Chinese, Gujerati, Hindi, Japanese, Punjabi, Turkish, and Urdu.[120] These may be offered by schools provided they also offer one of the official languages of the European Community.[121]

The content of the core and other foundation subjects, such as history and geography, is determined by orders made by the Secretary of State for Education and Employment after receiving advice from the Qualifications and Curriculum Authority.[122] There has been considerable concern on

---

[114] See the statement in the House of Lords by the promoter of the provision, the Bishop of London, HL Debs, 498, col 639; Hull, J., 'The Religious Education Clauses of the 1993 Education Bill' (1993) 15 *British Journal of Religious Education* 1.

[115] See Hull, J., 'Should Agreed Syllabuses be Mainly Christian?' (1991) 14 *British Journal of Religious Education* 1.

[116] See HC debs, 221, cols 1255–6 (written answers). DFE Circular 1/94 is misleading in stating (para 35) that—'As a whole and at each key stage, the relative content devoted to Christianity in the syllabus should predominate'.

[117] See Education Act 1996, ss 353, 354.   [118] Ibid, s 354(1)(*a*).

[119] Ibid, ss 354(2)(*c*), 355(1)(*c*), (*d*).

[120] Education (National Curriculum) (Modern Foreign Languages) Order, SI 2567 of 1991, Sched.   [121] Ibid, para 2(2), (3).

[122] Education Act 1996, ss 356; Education Act 1997, ss 21–3. QCA replaced the School Curriculum and Assessment Authority in this role in 1997.

the part of many educationalists and members of the ethnic minority communities that these subjects should possess an appropriate multicultural dimension and much debate as to how far this has been achieved.[123] One leading expert commented in 1993 that the curriculum had 'failed to take full account of the plurality of cultures which exist in this country', being 'narrow and biased in favour of the white, middle-class population'.[124] In particular, non-British and non-European topics tended to be confined to optional courses, which were often not selected by schools. On the other hand, at the same time some educationalists indicated that they could clearly see the prospect of incorporating multicultural perspectives into virtually all aspects of the curriculum.[125] Following the implementation of the Dearing Report[126] (which recommended that the national curriculum be reduced by around one-third), teachers should have greater opportunities for the inclusion of multicultural material in a wide range of subjects, but whether or not they will seize the opportunity remains to be seen. The legislation itself requires that ministers, local education authorities, governing bodies, and headteachers, in exercising their functions with regard to the curriculum generally, should ensure that every school possesses a 'balanced and broadly based' curriculum which promotes the spiritual, moral, and 'cultural' development of pupils and of society, and prepares pupils for the experiences of adult life.[127] Moreover, the notion that a multicultural dimension should permeate the whole curriculum was encouraged by guidance issued by the National Curriculum Council in 1990 which stated—

. . . in order to make access to the whole curriculum a reality for all pupils, schools need to foster a climate in which equality of opportunity is supported by a policy to which the whole school subscribes and in which positive attitudes to gender equality, cultural diversity and special needs of all kinds are actively promoted. For example, introducing multicultural perspectives into the curriculum is a way of enriching the education of all pupils. . . . Teachers have a major role to play in preparing young people for adult life; this means life in a multi-

---

[123] In 1988 the Secretary of State for Education instructed the National Curriculum Council to take account, in its advice to him, of 'the ethnic and cultural diversity of British society and of the importance of the curriculum in promoting equal opportunities for all, regardless of ethnic origin or gender'; however, as a result of right-wing opposition to multicultural education, the report of a group appointed to draw up guidelines for schools on the subject was never published—see Tomlinson, S., 'The Multicultural Task Group: The Group That Never Was' in King, A. and Reiss, M. (eds), *The Multicultural Dimension of the National Curriculum* (London, 1993), ch 2.

[124] See Pumfrey, P. and Verma, G. (eds), *Cultural Diversity and the Curriculum: The Foundation Subjects and Religious Education in Secondary Schools* (London, 1993), 25.

[125] See generally, King and Reiss (above).

[126] Dearing, R., *The National Curriculum and its Assessment: Final Report* (London, 1994).

[127] Education Act 1996, s 351.

cultural, multilingual Europe, which in its turn is interdependent with the rest of the world.[128]

The preceding two sections have demonstrated that both Parliament and the courts have played their part in the development of legal principles and rules which sometimes endorse cultural pluralism and at other times promote assimilation. In the previous chapter assimilationist tendencies were primarily justified by reference to a need for a cohesive and unified society to maintain minimum values and standards and we have seen how the courts (and to some limited extent the legislature) have made an attempt at least to outline what these norms entail.[129] This process is of great practical significance, for it determines the limits of the principal and guiding policy of cultural pluralism. Cultural pluralism itself was justified in Chapter 1 by reference to the importance attached in a liberal democracy to the ideals of individual choice, freedom of expression, and religious toleration.

Assimilationists and pluralists may often disagree about the meaning of equal treatment of minorities, the former demanding that everyone be treated uniformly so as to foster a pervasive sense of nationhood, and the latter insisting on genuine equality, sometimes in the form of specific differential treatment, in the belief that unity through diversity is more likely to achieve social justice and harmony. This section explores the variety of methods available for the implementation of assimilationist and pluralist policies in the hope of illuminating the range of implications each policy may have.

(a) Suppression

Where a minority practice is regarded as 'beyond the pale', as falling so far outside the minimum standards of acceptable behaviour that it must be suppressed, a policy of assimilation may simply take the form of treating the conduct in question as a criminal offence. In most instances no alteration of English law will be required, for the minimum acceptable

---

[128] National Curriculum Council, Guidance Document No. 3: 'The Whole Curriculum' (London, 1990).

[129] In the legislative examples given above, only the briefest reference has been made to the factors which may have motivated Parliament to enact the specific provisions mentioned. More detailed exploration of the wide range of considerations influencing the law-making process is to be found in several of the 'case studies' in Part II.

standards will already be embodied in its criminal provisions.[130] In criminal proceedings it has long been the general approach of the courts to apply a uniform and consistent standard in determining guilt or innocence, regardless of the ethnic origins of the accused or whether the conduct in question might be justifiable in terms of the values, religious beliefs or cultural traditions of the accused.[131] Occasionally, a special statutory measure may need to be enacted in order to place beyond doubt the ban on a particular minority practice, a notable recent example being the Prohibition of Female Circumcision Act 1985.

(b) Invalidity

Where a minority practice is regarded as unacceptable but does not necessarily warrant the imposition of criminal sanctions, a common technique is to deny legal validity to the conduct in question so that the person performing the act is deprived of the legal recognition sought. The best examples of this technique can be found in family law where, for example, validity can be denied to a marriage or a divorce which, for one reason or another, fails to comply with minimum standards. Child marriages,[132] polygamy,[133] and extrajudicial divorces[134] occurring in England are all dealt with in this manner.

(c) Exclusion

Another expedient method of preventing unacceptable practices occurring within this country is simply to exclude the persons liable to indulge in them from entering the United Kingdom. As we have seen, the immigration rules now bar the entry of spouses under the age of sixteen, as well as the second or subsequent wives of polygamists. It is also possible to ban the import of certain toxic substances, such as traditional medicines or cosmetics containing dangerous levels of lead, mercury or arsenic.[135] Some Asian products have already been dealt with in this manner.[136]

---

[130] See, for example, s 57 of the Offences Against the Person Act 1861, designed to maintain the long-standing ban on polygamy, derived from canon law, by making bigamy a criminal offence.

[131] See *R v Esop* (1836) 7 C & P 456; *R v Barronet and Allain* (1852) Dears CC 51; *R v Senior* [1899] 1 QB 283. For modern illustrations, see *R v Dad and Shafi* [1968] Crim LR 46 and *R v Moied* (1986) 8 Crim AR (S) 44 (kidnapping) and *Bradford Corporation v Patel* (1974, unreported but noted in *TES*, 11 Jan 1974), in which a Muslim father was convicted of an offence under the Education Act 1944 for failing to ensure the attendance of his fifteen year old daughter at a co-educational school to which she had been allocated by the LEA, despite his religious objections to such schools.　　　[132] Matrimonial Causes Act 1973, s 11(a)(ii).

[133] Ibid, s 11(b).　　　[134] Family Law Act 1986, s 44(1).

[135] See e.g. Medicines Act 1968, ss 62 and 129.

[136] See e.g. Medicines (Bal Jivan Chamcho Prohibition) (No 2) Order 1977.

(d) Laissez-faire

Where there is no good reason to take objection to a minority cultural practice, both assimilationists and pluralists may readily take the view that, if the particular practice is permissible within the current law, nothing needs to be done. English law is a flexible and liberal system and no further accommodation or adaptation may be needed on either side for a satisfactory *modus operandi* to be achieved. As Sir Robert Megarry VC pointed out in *Malone v Metropolitan Police Commissioner*—

England . . . is not a country where everything is forbidden except what is expressly permitted; it is a country where everything is permitted except where it is expressly forbidden.[137]

Sir John Donaldson MR struck the same note in *A-G v Guardian Newspapers Ltd (No. 2)* when he stated—

The starting point of our domestic law is that every citizen has a right to do what he likes, unless restrained by the common law . . . or by statute.[138]

He later referred to 'this universal basic freedom of action'.[139]

Under existing legal provisions, which are expressed in general terms applicable to all, religious minorities are entitled to freedom of worship; to construct, own, and manage religious buildings;[140] to register such buildings[141] and claim exemption from liability for the payment of local rates;[142] to celebrate religious festivals;[143] and to swear their own distinctive oaths in judicial proceedings (whether as plaintiff or defendant, witness or juror).[144] No special provision is needed here for minorities to enjoy equal rights with the majority community. The same approach of equal treatment is adopted towards the validity of arranged marriages,[145] the legality of male circumcision, the entitlement of parents to withdraw children from religious education at state schools,[146] the right to establish independent schools,[147] and the lawfulness of cremation.[148] A policy of non-intervention suffices.

---

[137] [1979] Ch 344 at 357.   [138] [1990] 1 AC 109 at 178.   [139] Ibid.

[140] Subject, of course, to the planning laws; see further, ch 7.

[141] Places of Worship Registration Act 1855.

[142] Local Government Finance Act 1988, s 51 and sched 5, para 11. The premises must be places of 'public' worship—see *Church of Jesus Christ of Latter-Day Saints v Henning* [1964] AC 420; *Broxtowe BC v Birch* [1983] 1 All ER 641.

[143] See e.g. Education Act 1996, s 444(3)(c) entitling pupils to be absent from school on any day set apart for religious observance by the religious body to which the parents belong.   [144] Oaths Act 1978, s 1.

[145] *Singh v Singh* [1971] P 226. 'Forced marriages' are, however, voidable under Matrimonial Causes Act 1973, s 12(c)—see *Hirani v Hirani* (1983) 4 FLR 121, discussed further below, ch 6.   [146] Education Act 1996, s 389(1).

[147] Education Act 1996, s 466 imposes an obligation to register the school with the Department for Education and Employment.   [148] Cremation Acts 1902 and 1952.

(e) Non-discrimination

While most areas of English law are even-handed in their provision for minorities and majority alike, there may be a few spheres in which the law has not been updated to take account of the growth of the newer minority communities in recent decades. It may thus be in need of reform to eliminate discriminatory rules and to provide for formal equality. Perhaps the most striking example of religious discrimination lies in the law of blasphemy which, as we have seen, only protects Christianity (and Anglican doctrine in particular) from vilification. Similarly, the Church of England is placed in a specially privileged position in the appointment of ministers as prison chaplains[149] and in determining the content of religious education in state schools.[150] There are also special rules governing marriage formalities which favour Jews and Quakers[151] (as well as Anglicans).[152] In all these instances the current state of English law can only be explained by reference to historical circumstances and the 'Establishment' of the Church of England and many people today regard these privileges as anomalous, discriminatory, and unwarrantable[153] in a society which has become both multicultural and predominantly secular.[154]

(f) Specific differential treatment

It is perhaps only at this point in the range of legal techniques available that the pluralist clearly parts company from the assimilationist. The pluralist may argue that in certain limited circumstances the law should make specific provision for members of ethnic groups, with a view to affording them genuine as opposed to merely formal equality. Such differential treatment is felt to be justifiable on rational grounds, either as a means of supporting the maintenance and preservation of valuable parts of minority cultures or as a method of ensuring fairness and justice, and it is this which distinguishes the present category from the elimination of the discriminatory provisions criticized in the previous category.

---

[149] Prison Act 1952, ss 7, 10.   [150] Education Act 1996, sched 31, para 4(2)(*b*).
[151] Marriage Act 1949, ss 26(1), 35(4), 43(3), 75(1)(*a*).   [152] Ibid, Part II.
[153] The current discriminatory state of the blasphemy law was criticized both by Lord Scarman in *Whitehouse v Lemon* [1979] AC 617 at 658 and by the Law Commission in Report No. 145 'Offences against Religion and Public Worship' (1985), para 2.3. A bill designed to abolish the office of prison chaplain and to promote religious equality in prisons was promoted by Lord Avebury in 1991, but without success—see Prisons (Freedom of Religion) Bill, HL Bill 6 of 1991.
[154] The following comment was made by Purchas LJ in *Bumper Development Corp Ltd v Commissioner of Police of the Metropolis* [1991] 4 All ER 638, discussed above, '. . . no distinction between institutions of the Christian church and those of other major religions would now be generally acceptable' (at 648).

Since such differential provision may last indefinitely, it should be distinguished sharply from the notion of special temporary measures designed to make up for past discrimination through various programmes of 'reverse' or 'positive' discrimination or 'affirmative action'.[155] The latter forms of compensatory justice, intended to assist historically disadvantaged groups, are only meant to last until the objective of securing equal treatment in a formal sense has been accomplished.[156] By contrast, specific differential treatment can be permanent.

Several examples can be given of this type of adaptation of English law in response to the concerns of members of minority communities. As we have seen, Parliament has created specific exemptions for turbaned Sikhs who ride on motor cycles and who work on building sites.[157] The indirect discrimination provisions of the Race Relations Act 1976 similarly give members of some ethnic minority groups specific rights not to be discriminated against on the basis of dress or appearance, unless the discrimination can be shown to be justifiable.[158] There are specific statutory exemptions for Jews and Muslims from the requirement to stun animals and poultry prior to slaughter[159] and Jews are permitted to open large shops on Sundays without being in breach of the Sunday trading laws, provided they close on Saturdays.[160] There are also specific references to minority faiths in the religious education provisions of the Education Act 1996.[161]

Differential treatment is also a feature of the courts' sentencing process in criminal cases. When considering the appropriate sentence to impose upon a convicted person, the judges are prepared to take into account a variety of specific considerations of a cultural nature, which may result in mitigation of the punishment meted out. The defendant's foreign origin, adherence to ethnic or religious customs or traditional values, and ignorance of English law are all matters which the court may properly bear in mind.[162] On this basis, in *R v Adesanya*[163] a Nigerian mother was given an absolute discharge following her conviction of the offence of assault for scarifying the faces of her two young sons pursuant to Yoruba tribal custom. Similarly, in *R v Bibi*[164] a Muslim widow had

[155] See generally, Greenawalt, K., *Discrimination and Reverse Discrimination* (New York, 1983); Edwards, J., *Positive Discrimination, Social Justice, and Social Policy* (London, 1987).
[156] See e.g. Race Relations Act 1976, ss 37, 38; Convention on the Elimination of All Forms of Racial Discrimination, Art 1(4); Thornberry, P., *International Law and the Rights of Minorities* (Oxford, 1991), ch 29.   [157] See further below, ch 8.
[158] See further below, ch 8.
[159] See Slaughter of Poultry Act 1967, s 1 and Slaughterhouses Act 1974, s 36, discussed further below, ch 5.
[160] Sunday Trading Act 1994, sched 1, para 2(2)(b); sched 2, Part II, replacing Shops Act 1950, s 53.   [161] See e.g. ss 375(3), 390(4)(a).
[162] See e.g. *R v Bailey* [1964] Crim LR 671; *R v Derriviere* (1969) 53 Crim AR 637.
[163] (1974, unreported but noted in (1975) 24 *ICLQ* 136).   [164] [1980] 1 WLR 1193.

the prison sentence imposed on her by the Crown Court for involvement in the import of illicit drugs substantially reduced by the Court of Appeal, once it became clear that she had been so completely socially isolated through the doctrine of *purdah* and so dependant upon her brother-in-law, who had organized the import of the drugs, that she bore little moral responsibility for the offence.

Recognition of specific cultural factors is also afforded by the courts in assessing the level of damages to be awarded to plaintiffs in tort cases. In *Bakhitiari v The Zoological Society of London*[165] a young Iranian girl had lost three fingers as a result of being bitten by a chimpanzee while on a visit to the zoo. Although plastic surgery had covered the affected area, she was left with an unsightly stump. The Court awarded her a larger sum than would have been awarded to a white girl, in view of the apparent revulsion felt in Iranian society towards any physical blemish in women and the effect of that revulsion upon her prospects of marriage.[166] In *Seemi v Seemi*[167] a Muslim woman was awarded £20,000 in an action for slander brought against her former husband, who had falsely accused her of not being a virgin on her wedding night. The Court bore in mind the impact which a slur of this sort would have on a Muslim wife and her family, recognizing that it would be regarded by her community as a very grave insult in a way which would not be true of most accusations of this nature made in England. A final illustration of the recognition of cultural diversity is afforded by the decision of the Criminal Injuries Compensation Board in *Thompson*[168] to award a Rastafarian victim of assault general damages of £1,500 to reflect the depression and humiliation he had suffered when his dreadlocks were cut off in a knife attack upon him.

(g) State-funded differential treatment

It will be recalled that the Swann Committee's vision of a pluralist society encompassed the maintenance and active support of minority cultures.[169] This may often entail public funding to be effective and a number of examples are available of situations in which financial support from the state is either required or authorized by existing law. Central government funds are made available to pay for the costs of

---

[165] (1991) 141 *NLJ* 55.

[166] No doubt, the decision can be criticized for its national and sexual stereotyping. For a less contentious case, compare the award of an extra £5,000 by way of general damages to the African plaintiff in *Opoku v Diecasting Tool and Engineering Co (Southgate) Ltd* (unreported but noted in *Guardian*, 4 Dec 1980), because the loss of three of his fingers in an industrial accident would preclude him from being installed as an Ashanti chief in Ghana.

[167] (1990) 140 *NLJ* 747.   [168] [1989] *CLY* 1207.   [169] See above, ch 1.

an interpreter in criminal proceedings where the accused does not understand the English language.[170] Courts are expected to purchase copies of the Qur'an and other holy books so that non-Christian witnesses can swear religious oaths. Until 1994 local authorities were obliged by statute to provide adequate sites for gypsy encampments[171] and between 1978 and 1993 the Exchequer had contributed £78 million towards the capital costs of establishing such sites.[172] Considerable public funding is channelled into the support of voluntary aided schools run by Jewish organizations, as well as those owned by Anglican and Roman Catholic foundations.[173] Moreover, many teachers of religious education in state schools are paid to give information to all their pupils about non-Christian faiths as part of the religious education syllabus.[174] Public funding is also provided for translations to be made of the annual reports of school governors, where the LEA directs that such translations should be produced for the benefit of parents who are not fluent in English.[175] Parents of registered pupils are entitled to copies of such reports free of charge.[176] As we have seen, central government grants are available under section 11 of the Local Government Act 1966 to enable local authorities to make specific provision for the needs of their ethnic minority communities.

While most (if not all) of the instances of differential treatment outlined in categories (f) and (g) above would receive warm endorsement from the majority of pluralists, they would be repudiated by many assimilationists. Moreover, those who subscribe to the view that it is appropriate to maintain a clear division between the public and private domains may well reject notions of differential treatment, on the ground that it represents unjustified state involvement in matters which ought to be left to the private sphere.[177] On this basis, for example, Sikhs would possess no legal rights to wear turbans at work, at school, or on motor cycles, only being entitled to do so in relation to purely 'private' activities. The immense difficulties involved in sustaining and justifying such an approach have been outlined in the previous chapter.

---

[170] Prosecution of Offences Act 1985, s 19(3)(*b*). For the vital importance of finding an interpreter who speaks and understands the same dialect as well as the same language as the accused, see *R v Begum (Iqbal)* (1991) 93 Cr App R 96. In that case the lack of such competence on the part of the interpreter led to the defendant's trial for murder being declared a nullity and her conviction being quashed. For the right of persons detained by the police not to be interviewed without an interpreter, provided at public expense, where they have difficulty in understanding English, see para 13 of Code C made pursuant to the Police and Criminal Evidence Act 1984.

[171] Caravan Sites Act 1968, Part II, discussed further below, ch 5.

[172] HC Debs, Standing Committee 'B', 11 Feb 1994, col 692.

[173] See Education Act 1996, s 65.   [174] Ibid, s 375(3).

[175] Ibid, s 161(3)(*b*).   [176] Ibid, s 161(4)(*a*).

[177] See e.g. Honeyford, R., *Integration or Disintegration* (London, 1988), ch 2.

CONCLUSIONS

In determining whether to give effect to local English customs as a minor source of law, to uphold indigenous traditions overseas during the period of colonialism and empire, or to recognize foreign laws and customs today under conflict of laws principles, the English judges have adopted a broadly tolerant approach, but they have drawn the line at what has been felt to be unreasonable, repugnant, abhorrent, or unconscionable. The critical test has ultimately been whether the custom in question offended against the general public interest. The courts have naturally declined to endorse practices which, in their view, were manifestly contrary to public policy. The imprecision of the public policy doctrine has naturally led to criticism and some limited clarification has recently been furnished by various pronouncements in the House of Lords and the Court of Appeal, in which a link has been made between modern conceptions of public policy and internationally recognized human rights treaties to which the United Kingdom is a contracting party. This trend is welcome and may prove helpful in the future judicial handling of ethnic diversity.

In the legislative field, both pluralist and assimilationist tendencies have been apparent over the past thirty years or so. The assimilationist measures can, at least partly, be justified within the conception of pluralism outlined in the previous chapter, namely 'pluralism within limits', as well as being consistent with the judicial approach of refusing to countenance cultural practices which offend against public policy because they are unconscionable or violate human rights standards.

The law possesses a wide spectrum of techniques which can be employed to handle diverse ethnic and cultural practices, ranging from their suppression through the application of criminal penalties, at one extreme, to their promotion through the allocation of state funding, at the other. Examples have been given of how English law has responded to ethnic diversity through the use of seven different techniques displaying varying degrees of goodwill, tolerance, and antipathy towards particular customs and traditions. Particular prominence has been accorded to the concept of 'differential treatment' as a means of moulding English law to meet the specific cultural needs of minority groups.

A framework has now been established, in terms of which it is possible to undertake the detailed analysis of particular controversies which form Part II of this book. The implications of the basic guiding policy of modified pluralism have been explored and the relevant developments and techniques of English law have been explained. However, before incorporating the six case studies within this framework, it is desirable to pursue in greater detail several of the issues already mentioned insofar as they pertain to human rights and group rights. These aspects are addressed from the broad perspective of international law in the following chapter.

3
Human Rights and Minority Rights

In each of the 'case studies' presented in the chapters which comprise Part II of this work, consideration is given to the human rights dimension of the particular issue being addressed. In this way it is hoped that the analysis can be afforded greater depth through a comparison of English legal provisions with principles operating in international human rights law.

The present chapter begins with a justification of the choice of international human rights law as constituting the major comparative frame of reference, supplementing those comparisons which are drawn in Part II with the domestic laws of selected individual countries. Next there is an analysis of the system of minority protection operated by the League of Nations from 1919 to 1939, a scheme which may be regarded as embodying the first modern regime on the subject. This is followed by an examination of the shift away from explicit concern for minorities towards greater concentration upon the notion of human rights for all under the United Nations system. Despite this change of focus, the International Covenant on Civil and Political Rights, which is sponsored by the United Nations, does possess an article on minority rights, and this is subjected to detailed analysis, together with subsequent UN declarations. Developments within the Council of Europe are then explored, including the omission of any specific minority rights article from the European Convention on Human Rights and recent attempts to make good this deficiency through the Framework Convention for the Protection of National Minorities in 1995 and the drafting of a new Protocol to the European Convention itself.

Subsequently, an attempt is made to grapple with some of the major philosophical problems posed by any legal recognition of special rights for minority communities and their members. How can any differential treatment for minorities be reconciled with the principles of equality and non-discrimination? Does such treatment involve according privileges to minorities and how does it differ from the doctrine of *apartheid*? Can cultural pluralism and equality of opportunity be promoted simultaneously, as Roy Jenkins proposed in his definition of 'integration'?[1] International human rights law should be able to offer some answers

[1] See above, ch 1.

to these questions, as well as to the thorny problem of 'group rights'. Do such collective rights co-exist alongside the rights of individuals? If the rights of individuals clash with the claims of groups how are such conflicts to be resolved?

The chapter concludes with an assessment of whether human rights standards can make a valuable contribution to debates about ethnocentricity and cultural relativism. Can reference to such standards offer an escape from the criticism that, whenever English law refuses to countenance a minority tradition or ethnic practice, this amounts to a form of unjustified cultural imperialism? Are there some principles which are of universal application or is the very notion of human rights an exclusively Western one?

JUSTIFICATIONS FOR A HUMAN RIGHTS DIMENSION

The incorporation of a human rights dimension can be justified on a number of different, though related, grounds. First, since the subject-matter of this book falls squarely within the broad field of civil liberties, international human rights law is a natural and logical choice for comparison in view of its close substantive connection with the various topics under discussion.[2]

Secondly, recent years have witnessed an increasing tendency on the part of English courts to make reference in their judgments both to the European Convention on Human Rights itself and to decisions made under it by the European Commission and the European Court of Human Rights.[3] The United Kingdom ratified the Convention in 1953[4] and its incorporation by statute into municipal law is imminent.[5]

Thirdly, the provisions of the Convention carry considerable moral weight because they have been subscribed to by some forty countries in Europe and thus represent a minimum standard of rights and freedoms accepted across a large number of liberal democracies. The moral weight of this regional standard is transformed into a universal or near-universal standard when the spotlight is turned away from the European Convention and focused instead upon truly international treaties, ratified by large numbers of nations from many different parts of the world[6], such as the International Covenant on Civil and Political

---

[2] For examples of the adoption of this approach, see Feldman, D., *Civil Liberties and Human Rights in England and Wales* (Oxford, 1993); Chambers, G. and McCrudden, C. (eds), *Individual Rights and the Law in Britain* (Oxford, 1994).   [3] See above, ch 2.
[4] Cmnd 8969 of 1953.   [5] Legalisation is expected in 1998.
[6] The ratification figures below relate to the position on 1 Jan 1996: see Marie, J-B., 'International Instruments Relating to Human Rights: Classification and Status of Ratifications as of 1 January 1996' (1996) 17 *Human Rights LJ* 61.

Rights[7], the International Covenant on Economic, Social and Cultural Rights,[8] the International Convention on the Elimination of All Forms of Racial Discrimination,[9] the Convention against Discrimination in Education,[10] the Convention on the Elimination of All Forms of Discrimination against Women,[11] and the Convention on the Rights of the Child.[12] In Palley's words—

> The international community has created a *universal* international *legal ethic* on human rights standards and is well on the way to creating international human legal rights . . . . To sum up, there are moral rights or human rights, which we invoke in order to evaluate or to argue for change; there are legal rights, accorded by the positive law of states . . . ; there are international human rights standards set out in formal international declarations or treaties which, because as yet they only bind some states, are still not universal in their operation; and there are international human rights which have arisen out of international customary law and treaties binding all states.[13]

A fourth reason for introducing a human rights dimension relates to the lack of a written constitution containing a bill of rights in England. Hence, prior to the incorporation of the European Convention, there has been no written guarantee of religious freedom in English law, nor any general provision expressly prohibiting discrimination on grounds of religion. English law has largely developed its principles during a period when there were relatively few adherents to non-Christian faiths resident in this country. Its provisions may, therefore, as we have seen, sometimes have fallen short of according equal treatment to members of non-Christian minority communities.[14] In these circumstances members of minority faiths had no option but to have recourse to the European Commission of Human Rights in Strasbourg if, perhaps having unsuccessfully relied upon the Convention before the English courts, they wished to press further a claim based on principles of religious freedom. To date, ten such applications have been submitted to the Commission by members of the minorities discussed in Part II of this book. Muslims have complained about insufficient facilities for prayers in prison,[15] of not being allowed time off work to visit a mosque for Friday prayers,[16] of not being permitted to marry at the age of fourteen,[17] and of not being

---

[7] Cmnd 3220 of 1967; ratified by 132 states.
[8] Cmnd 3220 of 1967; ratified by 134 states.
[9] Cmnd 4108 of 1969; ratified by 146 states.
[10] Cmnd 1760 of 1962; ratified by 85 states.
[11] Cmnd 8440 of 1982; ratified by 151 states.
[12] Cm 1976 of 1992; ratified by 185 states.
[13] Palley, C., *The United Kingdom and Human Rights* (London, 1991), 37, 55.
[14] See above, ch 2.   [15] *Ali v UK*, application 5112/71.
[16] *Ahmad v ILEA* [1978] QB 36; *Ahmad v UK* (1981) 4 EHRR 126, discussed below, pp 104–6.
[17] *Khan v UK* (1986) 48 Dec & Rep 253.

protected by the blasphemy laws.[18] Jews have twice alleged failure on the part of the prison authorities to respect their dietary rules.[19] Hindus have claimed that unnecessary restrictions were being placed on their freedom to worship at a particular temple,[20] and that an employee was forced to join a trade union contrary to his religious beliefs.[21] A turbaned Sikh contested the legal obligation which used to be imposed upon all motor cyclists to wear a safety helmet[22] and another Sikh raised religious objections to wearing prison clothing and having to clean his cell.[23] In the event, none of these applications was upheld by the Commission, but at least the applicants had the opportunity of grounding their arguments upon the existence of a legal right to religious freedom and in one case a friendly settlement was reached involving the payment of substantial compensation by the British Government.[24]

A fifth justification lies in the familiar claim that 'all human rights exist for the protection of minorities'.[25] In a democracy it is arguable that the majority can, to a large extent, be left to look after itself through the ballot box. Of course, the term 'minorities' in the sense referred to here is a label which covers not only ethnic groups but also those who differ from or disagree with the majority on a wide range of matters and hence perceive themselves to be in a vulnerable position. In arguing the case for 'taking rights seriously', Dworkin contends that the institution of rights is crucial 'because it represents the majority's promise to the minorities that their dignity and equality will be represented. When the divisions among the groups are most violent, then this gesture, if law is to work, must be most sincere'.[26]

MINORITY PROTECTION UNDER THE LEAGUE OF NATIONS

Although a tradition of protecting the rights of minorities by means of treaty was reasonably well established in international law by the turn of the twentieth century,[27] the period immediately after the First World War witnessed considerable development and improvement.[28] Indeed it may

---

[18] *R v Chief Metropolitan Stipendiary Magistrate, ex parte Choudhury* [1991] 1 All ER 306; *Choudhury v UK* (1991) 12 *Human Rights LJ* 172; see further below, pp 101–4.

[19] *X v UK* (1976) 5 Dec & Rep 8; *DS and ES v UK* (1990) 65 Dec & Rep 245.

[20] *ISKCON v UK* (1994) 76–A Dec & Rep 90, discussed below, ch 7.

[21] *Chauhan v UK* (1990) 65 Dec & Rep 41.

[22] *X v UK* (1978) 14 Dec & Rep 234, discussed below, ch 8.

[23] *X v UK* (1982) 28 Dec & Rep 5.   [24] *Chauhan v UK* at 45.

[25] Sieghart, P., *The Lawful Rights of Mankind* (Oxford, 1985), 168.

[26] Dworkin, R., *Taking Rights Seriously* (London, 1977), 205.

[27] See generally, Capotorti, F., *Study on the Rights of Persons belonging to Ethnic, Religious and Linguistic Minorities* (New York, 1991), 1–4; Thornberry, P., *International Law and the Rights of Minorities* (Oxford, 1991), ch 2.   [28] Thornberry, ch 3.

be said that it reached its zenith at this time. The League of Nations system included treaties for the protection of minorities living within several states in Central and Eastern Europe including Austria, Bulgaria, Czechoslovakia, Greece, Hungary, Poland, and Romania. It also encompassed 'declarations' with a similar effect in respect of Albania, Estonia, Latvia, and Lithuania which were extracted from these states by the Allied Powers as a condition of their admission to the League of Nations.

These treaties and declarations contained several standard articles.[29] One of these obliged the states in question to grant all inhabitants 'free exercise, whether public or private, of any creed, religion or belief', whose practices were not 'inconsistent with public order or morals'.[30] Another article provided that all nationals were to be equal before the law and were to enjoy the same civil and political rights without distinction as to race, language, or religion.[31] Adequate facilities were to be given to those whose mother tongue was not the official language for the use of their own language, either orally or in writing, before the courts. A further article declared that nationals who belonged to racial, religious, or linguistic minorities were to enjoy 'the same treatment and security in law and in fact as other nationals'.[32] In particular, the same article stated, they were to have 'an equal right to establish, manage and control at their own expense charitable, religious and social institutions, schools and other educational establishments with the right to use their own language and to exercise their religion freely therein'. In towns and districts with a considerable proportion of nationals whose mother tongue was not the official language, adequate facilities were to be provided by the state, as part of the public education system, to ensure that instruction was given to the children of those nationals in primary schools through the medium of their own language.[33] This was not, however, to prevent the state from making the teaching of the official language compulsory in those schools. In those parts of the country where there was a considerable proportion of nationals belonging to racial, religious, or linguistic minorities, these minorities were to be assured of an equitable share in the enjoyment and application of the sums which might be provided out of public funds for educational, religious, and charitable purposes. In those states with significant Jewish minorities there was a further article which provided that Jews should not be compelled to perform any act which constituted a violation of their Sabbath, nor placed under any disability by reason of their refusal

---

[29] See Thornberry, 399–403 where the Polish Minorities Treaty 1919 is set out in appendix 1.

[30] See e.g. Polish Minorities Treaty, Art 2.   [31] Ibid, Art 7.

[32] Ibid, Art 8.   [33] Ibid, Art 9.

to attend courts of law or perform any legal business on their Sabbath.[34] Where there was a significant Muslim population, suitable provision was to be made for regulating their family law and questions of personal status in accordance with Muslim usage.[35]

What is so striking about these provisions to a modern eye is how extensive they were. Equality before the law for all and non-discrimination were firmly guaranteed, but this was only half the picture. The other half was represented by specific rights to protect the cultural traditions of the minorities, including the use of their languages in court, respect for the Jewish Sabbath and for Muslim personal laws, the provision of mother tongue teaching for primary school children, separate schools, and even a direct share of public funds for the minorities' own educational, religious, and charitable purposes. In terms of the assimilation-pluralism spectrum of 'legal techniques' set out in the previous chapter, the League treaties and declarations operated to the very limits of the pluralist model.[36]

The League of Nations was responsible for enforcing the guarantees in the treaties and declarations, and disputes arising out of them could be referred by the Council of the League to the Permanent Court of International Justice for an advisory opinion. The Court's opinion in the *Minority Schools in Albania*[37] case in 1935 represents the *locus classicus* in judicial analysis of the concept of equal treatment for minorities under the League system and therefore warrants careful examination. Having subscribed to the standard form articles outlined above, Albania had amended its constitution in 1933 and provided for the abolition of all private schools in the country, including those run by the Greek minority. When challenged with a violation of its declaration, the Albanian Government sought to justify its constitutional amendments by arguing that since all private schools run by the majority community were being abolished, as well as those managed by the Greek and other minorities, no possible breach of the declaration could arise. No discrimination would be involved because all private schools were being accorded equal treatment.

This line of argument commended itself to the British judge on the Permanent Court, Sir Cecil Hurst, who took the view that the whole purpose behind the Albanian declaration was to prevent discrimination against the Greek and other minorities. In granting the minorities 'an equal right' to manage their own schools, the declaration could not have

---

[34] Ibid, Art 10. For the important influence of Jews in the creation of the League system of minority protection, see Baron, S., *Ethnic Minority Rights* (Oxford, 1985), 14–18.

[35] See e.g. Minorities in Albania Declaration 1921, Art 2.

[36] They thus comfortably spanned techniques (d) to (g) set out at pp 59–65 above.

[37] (1935) PCIJ, Ser A/B, No. 64.

been intended to mean that the minorities were guaranteed continuity in the exercise of this right once the majority community had been completely deprived of it. As Sir Cecil explained—

The word 'equal' implies that the right so enjoyed must be equal in measure to the right to be enjoyed by somebody else. *'They shall have an equal right'* means that the right to be enjoyed by the people in question is to be equal in measure to that enjoyed by some other group. A right which is unconditional and independent of that enjoyed by other people cannot with accuracy be described as an 'equal right'. 'Equality' necessarily implies the existence of some extraneous criterion by reference to which the content is to be determined.[38]

This was a perfectly logical conclusion to reach upon a literal interpretation of the phrase 'equal right'. However, Sir Cecil found himself in a minority of three judges who dissented from the opinion of the Court expressed by the eight judges in the majority. The Court looked to the wider spirit, both of the declaration as a whole and of the League's overall system for protecting minorities, and reached precisely the opposite conclusion. In its view the right of the minority to manage its own schools was an unconditional right, which could not be taken away simply to achieve an identical result for all private schools. As the Court explained—

The idea underlying the treaties for the protection of minorities is to secure for certain elements incorporated in a State, the population of which differs from them in race, language or religion, the possibility of living peaceably alongside that population and co-operating amicably with it, while at the same time preserving the characteristics which distinguish them from the majority, and satisfying the ensuing special needs. In order to attain this object, two things were regarded as particularly necessary, and have formed the subject of provisions in these treaties. The first is to ensure that nationals belonging to racial, religious or linguistic minorities shall be placed in every respect on a footing of perfect equality with the other nationals of the State. The second is to ensure for the minority elements suitable means for the preservation of their racial peculiarities, their traditions and their national characteristics. These two requirements are indeed closely interlocked, for there would be no true equality between a majority and a minority if the latter were deprived of its own institutions, and were consequently compelled to renounce that which constitutes the very essence of its being as a minority.[39]

The Court then turned its attention to the way in which 'true equality' was to be achieved for minorities under the standard articles in the League treaties and declarations. As we have seen, one of these articles provided for 'the same treatment and security in law and in fact'. The Court declared—

---

[38] At 25.   [39] At 17.

Equality in law precludes discrimination of any kind; whereas equality in fact may involve the necessity of different treatment in order to attain a result which establishes an equilibrium between different situations. It is easy to imagine cases in which equality of treatment of the majority and of the minority, whose situation and requirements are different, would result in inequality in fact . . . . The equality between members of the majority and of the minority must be an effective, genuine equality . . . ; that is the meaning of this provision.[40]

The particular right to maintain and manage separate schools was an important illustration of the application of the principle of equal treatment 'in law and in fact' because such schools were indispensable to the Greek community. The abolition of these institutions and their replacement by government schools would deprive the minority of the institutions appropriate to its needs, whereas the majority would continue to have its own needs supplied by the institutions created by the state. In the Court's words—

Far from creating a privilege in favour of the minority, as the Albanian Government avers, this stipulation ensures that the majority shall not be given a privileged situation as compared with the minority.[41]

The Court therefore rejected the Albanian Government's defence to the charge that the abolition of private schooling was lawful under its Declaration.

While the League system of minority protection perhaps worked tolerably well for a time, at least in coping with everyday frictions, it had virtually ceased to function by the outbreak of the Second World War.[42] Indeed, in the view of most expert commentators and the public at large the system was a failure in practical terms, in the sense that it neither secured the enforcement of the minority rights which had been guaranteed, nor managed to reduce international tensions and keep the peace.[43] In large part this was probably due to the fact that the system had been imposed by the victorious Allied Powers upon only a few states in the wake of the outcome of the 1914–18 war and this bred considerable resentment. These states felt that their sovereignty was being unduly restricted in a rather humiliating manner and that their efforts to achieve national unity were being undermined. Many members of the majority populations tended to see the minorities as dependent upon external pressures and hence potentially disloyal, as well as being bent on exploiting and abusing their 'privileges'. Indeed, the Nazis encouraged the German-speaking minorities in Czechoslovakia and

[40] At 19.   [41] At 20.   [42] Thornberry, 46.
[43] See e.g. Claude, I., *National Minorities: An International Problem* (Massachusetts, 1955), ch 3; Baron, 17–22; Bilder, R., 'Can Minorities Treaties Work?' in Dinstein, Y. and Tabory, M. (eds), *The Protection of Minorities and Human Rights* (Dordrecht, 1992), 65–7.

Poland to make excessive demands upon their governments and then used failure to meet these demands as a pretext for aggression against these states. Ultimately, however, it was the lack of a general political will to make the League system effective which resulted in its collapse, as Bagley has explained—

> It is unjust to view the failure of the minority system of the League . . . independently of the general international conditions of its time. The minorities protection system was but a part of the world structure established at Paris. Inevitably [it] depended on the general state of international order and relations, and inevitably when that order disintegrated the system collapsed with it, like one floor of a toppling building. The between-war world was witness to an appalling phenomenon of retrogression, a backsliding of morals and politics. Dictatorships replaced democracies, hate and intolerance flourished, power over-rode reason, and passionate nationalism crushed the growing bloom of international co-operation. That minorities should suffer in such a climate was inevitable.[44]

For present purposes, however, the appropriate conclusions to draw from this early exercise in minority protection are both encouraging and instructive. First, international law had, even by this period, grappled with the conceptual difficulty of distinguishing between formal equality and genuine equality for minorities and had elected to spell out a wide range of standard provisions designed to afford minorities equality 'in fact' in a very positive manner, as well as to ban discrimination against them. Secondly, the lesson which would be learnt from the ultimate failure of the system would not be to abandon minority protection altogether but rather to broaden the scope of protection afforded, so as to benefit everyone through the universal promotion of human rights, while still seeking to ensure that minorities were properly safeguarded. Thirdly, it is clear that the political climate must be conducive towards the attainment of such objectives if they are to be implemented successfully.

In a liberal democracy such as that which prevails in modern Britain there is no good reason for believing that the state is not fully capable of sustaining a commitment towards upholding both human rights and minority rights. As we have seen, the general stance of government policy is favourable to the development of cultural pluralism, and English law has already demonstrated its capacity to deliver legal provisions designed to guarantee minorities equality 'in fact' through specific differential treatment, as well as formal equality through principles of non-discrimination.[45]

---

[44] Bagley, I., *General Principles and Problems in the Protection of Minorities* (Geneva, 1950), 126. [45] See above, ch 2.

The fact that English law currently fails to accord minorities several of the specific rights contained in the standard articles of the League system should not necessarily be a cause for surprise or alarm. As indicated earlier, the League system marks the high-water mark of positive provisions for minority protection and, as we shall see, these provisions do not all form part of modern international human rights law. It should be borne in mind that the minority populations protected by the League had generally been established and settled in the countries concerned for a very considerable period of time and were recognized as distinctive communities. Many of the ethnic minority communities in Britain, on the other hand, are the product of migration since 1945. In the case of the oldest minority, the Jews, their Sabbath is in large part respected through English legal provisions.[46] Moreover, separate schools for minorities can be established in the independent sector and there are several Jewish voluntary aided schools within the state sector.[47] Language rights, in terms of the use of mother tongue in schools and in court proceedings, are accorded to the Welsh in Wales.[48] For other linguistic minorities, while there is no legal right to mother tongue teaching at primary school level, an interpreter can be demanded for an accused in a criminal case who does not understand the English language.[49]

HUMAN RIGHTS UNDER THE UNITED NATIONS CHARTER

As indicated earlier, the movement after the Second World War was firmly away from the limited task of seeking to protect minorities in a small number of European countries towards the far grander concept of the universal protection of human rights everywhere. As the United States' representative, Mrs Eleanor Roosevelt, emphasized in 1947 during a discussion by the UN General Assembly of a draft article on minorities, which had been submitted for inclusion in the Universal Declaration of Human Rights, the best solution to the problem of minorities was 'to encourage respect for human rights'.[50] After considerable division of opinion on the question had been expressed during these debates, the Universal Declaration ultimately contained no specific article on minorities. As Thornberry has explained—

---

[46] See e.g. Sunday Trading Act 1994, sched 1, para 2(2)(*b*); sched 2, Part II; *Barker v Warren* (1677) 2 Mod Rep 271 (adjournment of court to avoid sitting on Saturday); cf *Ostreicher v Secretary of State for the Environment* [1978] 1 All ER 591.

[47] See above, ch 2.

[48] See Education Act 1996, s 354(1)(*b*), (2)(*d*); Welsh Language Act 1993, s 22.

[49] Prosecution of Offences Act 1985, s 19(3)(*b*).   [50] UN Doc A/C 3/SR 161, 726.

The minority right to an identity was omitted from the Declaration because of the negative repercussions of the League regime, cold war politics, and a rather euphoric belief that the ascription of rights to individuals *qua* individuals, without setting them in their full cultural or religious group contexts, was necessary and sufficient to meet post-war conditions.[51]

Instead, the issue of minority protection was referred for further study to the UN Sub-Commission on the Prevention of Discrimination and the Protection of Minorities, a subordinate body of the UN Commission on Human Rights,[52] which had itself strongly favoured the inclusion of such an article in the Universal Declaration.[53] Nevertheless, the Declaration did, of course, contain a number of articles particularly pertinent to minority protection, albeit expressed in universal terms. These included non-discrimination provisions[54] and guarantees of freedom of religion,[55] expression,[56] and association,[57] as well as of the rights of all freely to participate in the cultural life of their country.[58]

Soon after its creation in 1947 the Sub-Commission drew a clear distinction between its twin roles.[59] On the one hand, prevention of discrimination required steps to be taken to suppress or eliminate any conduct which denied or restricted a person's right to equality simply because of his or her membership of a particular group. On the other hand, the protection of minorities demanded that members of non-dominant groups who sought differential treatment so that their traditional characteristics of race, nationality, religion, and language were preserved should be suitably accommodated. However, two limitations upon the grant of such protection were clearly recognized. First, differential treatment could only be granted if it would not prejudice the welfare of the community as a whole. Secondly, those members of minorities who wished, of their own volition, to become assimilated within the majority community should not be prevented from doing so, for this in turn would amount to discrimination.

Following the proclamation of the Universal Declaration in 1948, work began on transforming the rights outlined within it into more detailed binding treaty obligations through the mechanism of the two International Covenants, one on Civil and Political Rights and the other on Economic, Social, and Cultural Rights. This task was finally accomplished in 1966 and both Covenants entered into force ten years later. At the instigation of the UN Commission on Human Rights and the Sub-Commission on the Prevention of Discrimination and the Protection of

---

[51] At 242.   [52] Ibid, 137.   [53] Ibid, ch 12.
[54] Arts 2 and 7.   [55] Art 18.   [56] Art 19.
[57] Art 20.   [58] Art 27.
[59] See Alston, P. (ed), *The United Nations and Human Rights: A Critical Appraisal* (Oxford, 1992), 213–14.

Minorities, a specific provision on minorities was duly incorporated into the International Covenant on Civil and Political Rights. Article 27 of the Covenant runs as follows—

In those States in which ethnic, religious or linguistic minorities exist, persons belonging to such minorities shall not be denied the right, in community with the other members of their group, to enjoy their own culture, to profess and practise their own religion, or to use their own language.

For the first time, therefore, a provision seeking to guarantee the protection of minorities and their separate identity was contained in a treaty intended to be of universal application. Several difficult questions are, however, raised by the phrasing of Article 27.

First, while the Article is clearly intended to recognize the claims of groups or communities within a state, the right is not spelt out, in terms, as a collective right. The right is expressed as adhering instead to individuals who belong to minority groups and is thus of the same nature as the other rights guaranteed in the Covenant, which are accorded to individuals rather than to other entities. In the light of this individualistic approach, the minority itself cannot be said to possess a right of its own to the preservation of its separate identity. There are sound political reasons for this, as Capotorti has explained—

The fact of granting rights to minorities and thus endowing them with legal status might increase the danger of friction between them and the state, in so far as the minority group, as an entity, would seem to be invested with authority to represent the interests of a particular community *vis-à-vis* the state representing the interests of the entire population. Moreover, the freedom of each individual member of a minority to choose between voluntary assimilation with the majority and the preservation of his own distinctive characteristics might be disregarded by the organs of the entity formed by the minority group, in its concern to preserve the unity and strength of the group.[60]

Even so, the community preservation aspect lies at the core of Article 27. In its authoritative 'General Comment' on Article 27, adopted in 1994,[61] the Human Rights Committee indicated that while the rights were conferred upon individuals 'as such', the protection of these rights was directed to 'ensure the survival and continued development of the cultural, religious and social identity of the minorities concerned, thus enriching the fabric of society as a whole'.[62]

Thornberry has described the rights in Article 27 as—

---

[60] Capotorti (1991), 35.
[61] General Comment No. 23 (50); UN Doc CCPR/C/21/Rev 1/Add 5, reprinted in (1994) 15 *Human Rights LJ* 234.　　　　　　　　　　　　　　[62] Ibid, paras 1, 3 and 9.

. . . a hybrid between individual and collective rights because of the 'community' requirement: the right of a member of a minority is not exercised alone; enjoyment of culture, practice of religion, and use of language presupposes a community of individuals endowed with similar rights. The rights may, therefore, be described as benefiting individuals but requiring collective exercise.[63]

Several other rights guaranteed by the Covenant may be said to be of the same hybrid nature, while not being specifically linked to minority group protection. For example, freedom of assembly[64] and association[65] can hardly be exercised other than collectively, although these are rights granted to individuals. Similarly, the right to manifest one's freedom of religion in public 'in community with others'[66] can only be regarded as a collective right despite its allocation to individuals.

Secondly, the opening words of Article 27 display a hesitancy, almost a trepidation, about mentioning the possible presence of minority communities within a state. An earlier draft began in much more robust fashion with the phrase 'Persons belonging to ethnic, religious or linguistic minorities shall . . . .'[67] The reason for the change of phrasing is not hard to fathom. Several states, notably those in Latin America, were unwilling even to recognize the existence of minorities within their borders, describing themselves simply as 'countries of immigration'.[68] Australia and France took a similar view. Indeed France went so far as to attach a reservation to its ratification of the International Covenant in order to declare that Article 27 was 'not applicable so far as the Republic is concerned'.[69] In a subsequent report to the UN Human Rights Committee, France elaborated its position by explaining that, under the terms of its constitution, the Republic—

was indivisible, secular, democratic and social. It shall ensure the equality of all citizens before the law, without distinction . . . of origin, race or religion. It shall respect all beliefs. Since the basic principles of public law prohibit distinction between citizens on grounds of origin, race or religion, France is a country in which there are no minorities . . . .[70]

However, in its 'General Comment', the Human Rights Committee declared this contention to be erroneous, pointing out that the existence of a minority within a state depends upon the establishment of objective

---

[63] At 173.   [64] Art 21.   [65] Art 22.   [66] Art 18(1).
[67] See Thornberry, 149–50.   [68] Ibid, 154–6.   [69] Ibid, 245.
[70] Id. While the historiography of France has traditionally emphasized the homogeneity of the nation, this has tended to mask religious, ethnic, and regional differences. The Catholic Church is accorded a special status under French law (e.g. in the fields of education and taxation), nationals whose origins lie in north Africa are often treated as foreigners in French political and social discourse, and Bretons have long cherished their separate language and culture; see generally, Silverman, M., *Deconstructing the Nation: Immigration, Racism and Citizenship in Modern France* (London, 1992).

criteria rather than upon a decision of the state itself.[71] The Committee also made it clear that in order to qualify for protection under Article 27 individuals need not be citizens or even permanent residents of the state in which they are members of a minority.[72] The artificiality of distinguishing for this purpose between, for example, those members of the Asian communities in the United Kingdom who possess British nationality and those who do not is plain.

The fact that, unlike France, the United Kingdom clearly recognizes the existence of ethnic, religious, and linguistic minorities within its jurisdiction is apparent from its periodic reports to the UN Human Rights Committee under Article 40 of the International Covenant. In its first report in 1977, for instance, its statement strongly echoed the speech made by Roy Jenkins about 'integration' in 1966 in declaring—

Although it is hoped that minority groups will ultimately be fully integrated into British society, integration is seen not as a flattening process of assimilation, but as equality of opportunity accompanied by cultural diversity in an atmosphere of mutual tolerance.[73]

Thirdly, the guarantee in Article 27 is expressed in rather negative terms, in the sense that members of minorities are not to be 'denied' the specific rights allotted to them. These 'cultural' rights are not spelt out in the same assertive vein as are, for example, the rights to life and liberty or to freedom of assembly and association. However, if Article 27 is to be accorded any significance beyond the mere repetition of freedoms guaranteed by other articles, such as freedom of religion,[74] freedom of expression,[75] and freedom from discrimination,[76] it must be given some 'positive' content.[77] The objective behind the Article is the achievement of a real rather than a fictitious equality for members of minorities, so that they do not have to surrender their distinctive identities. In this sense it is, at least to some extent, the UN equivalent and direct descendant of the guarantees contained in the League treaties and declarations. In its 'General Comment' the Human Rights Committee indicated that positive measures may be necessary to protect a minority's identity and way of life, together with the maintenance and development of its culture.[78] Even so, Article 27 is expressed in very vague and general terms and no consensus has yet developed among states as to its detailed content.[79] Uniformity of treatment cannot therefore be expected on the part of states, nor is it required. Thornberry has aptly summarized

---

[71] Paras 4.1 and 5.2; see also McGoldrick, D., *The Human Rights Committee* (Oxford, 1991), 138–9.   [72] Paras 5.1–5.2.
[73] See *Yearbook of the Human Rights Committee 1977–8* (New York, 1986), II, 111.
[74] Art 18.   [75] Art 19.   [76] Art 26.
[77] See Thornberry, 180–3.   [78] Paras 6.1, 6.2, 7.   [79] Thornberry, 184–6.

the position by categorizing Article 27 as 'weak' and its lack of specificity as leaving 'a wide discretion to states as to the modalities of its application.'[80]

Fourthly, Article 27 is remarkable in not being expressly encumbered by the usual list of permissible restrictions and limitations, which afford the state a range of justifications for interfering with most human rights. However, it seems clear that such restrictions have to be implied and this is borne out by the *travaux préparatoires*. Several states indicated in General Assembly debates at the United Nations that the same limitations applied as under Articles 18 and 19 on freedom of religion and freedom of expression respectively. These restrictions applied naturally to majorities and minorities alike.[81] Hence a state could legitimately curtail the rights of minorities by laws designed to protect public order, safety, health, or morals, or the fundamental freedoms of others.[82] Nor can minority communities utilize their rights under Article 27 to engage in activities aimed at the destruction of the rights and freedoms of others, a matter regulated as follows by Article 5(1)—

Nothing in the present Covenant may be interpreted as implying for any State, group or person the right to engage in any activity or perform any act aimed at the destruction of any of the rights and freedoms recognised herein or at their limitation to a greater extent than is provided for in the present Covenant.

However, it seems clear that there are no precise guidelines in the Covenant which clarify the balance to be struck between the interests of minorities in cultural preservation, on the one hand, and those of the state and majorities in maintaining social cohesion, minimum standards, and national unity, on the other.[83]

In spite of all the deficiencies in Article 27 mentioned above, it clearly binds the United Kingdom and the 130 or so other states which have ratified the Covenant. Although some writers have suggested that Article 27 represents general international customary law and thus binds states not parties to the Covenant,[84] this claim seems rather doubtful.[85] Rather, Article 27 should be seen as part of a gradual process of evolution towards a universal norm, a process which builds from an accumulation of widely ratified treaties, UN declarations, and extensive state practice. As part of this process reference may usefully be made to two UN declarations in particular, the first being the Declaration on Race and Racial Prejudice adopted by the UNESCO General Conference in 1978. The Declaration proclaims boldly in Article 1(2) that—'All individuals and groups have the right to be different, to consider themselves as

---

[80] Thornberry, 387.   [81] Ibid, 151.   [82] Ibid, 202.
[83] Ibid, 195–6.   [84] Ibid, 219–21.   [85] Ibid, 246.

different and to be regarded as such'. Article 1(3) elaborates upon this right by declaring—

Identity of origin in no way affects the fact that human beings can and may live differently, nor does it preclude the existence of differences based on cultural, environmental, and historical diversity nor the right to maintain cultural identity.

However, diversity of lifestyles and the right to be different should not, the Declaration states, serve as a pretext for racial prejudice and cannot justify any discriminatory practice either in law or in fact.[86] The practice of forced assimilation is condemned in the preamble to the Declaration, while the right to maintain cultural identity is spelt out more clearly in Article 5(1). This emphasizes the need for everyone to respect—

the right of all groups to their own cultural identity and the development of that distinctive cultural life within the national and international context, it being understood that it rests with each group to decide in complete freedom on the maintenance and, if appropriate, the adaptation or enrichment of the values which it regards as essential to its identity.

The stress upon the 'complete freedom' of 'groups' to determine their own cultural identity presents some difficult problems in its potential to create a clash with both individual rights and those of the state, an issue which is discussed further below,[87] but it should be noted that the Declaration is not intended to be a legally binding document. The accompanying Resolution for Implementation of the Declaration merely urges states to ratify the relevant anti-discrimination instruments and the taking of measures in the municipal systems of member states.[88]

The second UN declaration of note is the General Assembly's Declaration on the Rights of Persons Belonging to National or Ethnic, Religious and Linguistic Minorities, adopted in 1992.[89] This is designed to elaborate in greater detail the obligations of states under Article 27 and stresses the duty of states to take appropriate legislative and other measures to protect both the existence and the identity of minorities.[90] Persons belonging to minorities must have the right to establish and maintain their own associations as well as free and peaceful contacts with other members of their group at home and abroad.[91] States must take measures to create favourable conditions to enable members of minority groups to express their characteristics and to develop their culture, language, religion, traditions, and customs, save where specific practices are in violation of national law and are contrary to

---

[86] Art 1(2).   [87] See below, pp 92–8.   [88] Thornberry, 298.
[89] GA Resolution 47/135 (18 Dec 1992), reprinted in (1993) 14 *Human Rights LJ* 54–6.
[90] Ibid, Art 1.   [91] Art 2(4), (5).

international standards.[92] Adequate opportunities must be afforded for mother-tongue learning and teaching and, where appropriate, states should take measures in the field of education to encourage knowledge of the history, traditions, language, and culture of their minorities.[93] There should be no discrimination against members of minorities in the exercise of their cultural rights.[94]

Apart from the International Covenant on Civil and Political Rights and these two UN Declarations, there are several other treaties and declarations which form part of the UN system for the protection of minorities. They fall into two separate categories. First, there are provisions designed to promote cultural diversity and the 'right to be different'. For example, under Article 13(1) of the International Covenant on Economic, Social and Cultural Rights state parties recognize the right of everyone to education and agree that education should enable all persons to participate effectively in a free society and should 'promote understanding, tolerance and friendship among all nations and all racial, ethnic or religious groups'. Under the Covenant state parties also agree to respect the liberty of parents 'to ensure the religious and moral education of their children in conformity with their own convictions'.[95] The UN Declaration on the Elimination of Intolerance and Discrimination Based on Religion or Belief[96] also elaborates in far greater detail the freedom of religion accorded in Article 18 of the Covenant on Civil and Political Rights.

The second group of provisions is designed to outlaw discrimination on the basis of religious beliefs or ethnic origin, as well as on the basis of race, thus promoting formal equality for minorities. Such provisions are to be found in the Covenant on Economic, Social and Cultural Rights,[97] the Declaration on the Elimination of Intolerance and Discrimination Based on Religion,[98] the International Convention on the Elimination of All Forms of Racial Discrimination,[99] and the Convention against Discrimination in Education.[100]

HUMAN RIGHTS UNDER THE EUROPEAN CONVENTION AND THE COUNCIL OF EUROPE

Bearing in mind the political climate which surrounded the drafting of the European Convention immediately after the 1939–45 war, it is not

---

[92] Art 4(2).   [93] Art 4(3), (4).   [94] Art 2(1).   [95] Art 13(3).
[96] UN Doc A/36/51 (1981); see generally, Dickson, B., 'The United Nations and Freedom of Religion' (1995) 44 *ICLQ* 327.   [97] Art 2(2).
[98] Art 4(1).   [99] Art 2.
[100] Art 3. It is noteworthy that, while segregation of children at school by race is prohibited by the Convention (Art 1(1)(c)), separate but equal schooling of children on the basis of language, religion, or sex is permissible (Art 2(a), (b)).

surprising that a specific minorities' protection Article was not included. In this regard the Convention, which was opened for signature by member states of the Council of Europe in 1950, closely followed the policy adopted two years earlier in framing the Universal Declaration of concentrating upon human rights for all rather than minority rights for a few. Of course, many of the human rights guaranteed in the Convention directly assist minorities in asserting and maintaining their separate identities, such as the rights to freedom of religion[101] and expression,[102] the rights to freedom of association and assembly,[103] the right to respect for private and family life,[104] and the right to the free assistance of an interpreter where an accused cannot understand or speak the language used in criminal proceedings.[105] All these rights are expressed in virtually the same terms as they are in the International Covenant on Civil and Political Rights. Similarly, the obligation of state parties under the First Protocol to the Convention to respect the right of parents to ensure education of their children in conformity with their own religious and philosophical convictions[106] mirrors that expressed in the International Covenant on Economic, Social and Cultural Rights.[107] Moreover, as is the case under the Covenants, the European Convention contains a basic non-discrimination clause. Article 14 provides—

The enjoyment of the rights and freedoms set forth in this Convention shall be secured without discrimination on any ground such as sex, race, colour, language, religion, political or other opinion, national or social origin, association with a national minority, property, birth or other status.

While it is plain from the face of this Article that the principle of non-discrimination is guaranteed only *vis-à-vis* the rights and freedoms covered by the Convention, there is no need for a violation of another article of the Convention to be established before Article 14 can become operative. The Commission and the Court of Human Rights have each indicated in separate findings, for instance, that Article 14 can be violated if a restriction which is permissible under another article is imposed in a discriminatory fashion.[108]

In the *Belgian Linguistic Case (No 2)*[109] the Court explained that, despite the very broad wording of Article 14, the Convention does not forbid every difference in treatment on each of the grounds specified there because this would obviously lead to absurd results. National authorities

---

[101] Art 9.   [102] Art 10.   [103] Art 11.   [104] Art 8.
[105] Art 6(3)(*e*). See also Art 5(2) which affords everyone who is arrested the right to be informed promptly of the reasons for his arrest and of any charges against him 'in a language which he understands'; this right is reinforced by Art 6(3)(*a*).
[106] Art 2.   [107] Art 13(3).
[108] *Grandrath v Federal Republic of Germany* (1967) 10 YBECHR 626 at 678; *Belgian Linguistic Case (No 2)* (1968) 1 EHRR 252.   [109] See previous note.

often need to differentiate between people in different situations and thus the important question relates to defining the precise circumstances when this is permissible under Article 14. The Court ruled that 'the principle of equality of treatment is violated if the distinction has no objective and reasonable justification'.[110] Not only must the difference in treatment pursue a legitimate aim, there must also be a 'reasonable relationship of proportionality between the means employed and the aims sought to be realised'.[111] These principles have been reiterated on a number of occasions in subsequent cases.[112] Hence the Convention does not stand in the way of national laws differentiating between ethnic and religious groups with a view to protecting minorities, provided these principles are properly observed. On the other hand, state parties are not obliged by the Convention to take positive steps of this nature, as they clearly were under the standard articles of the League of Nations treaties and declarations and as they appear to be under Article 27 of the International Covenant. In the *Belgian Linguistic Case* itself, while the Court found that Belgium had unlawfully discriminated against some French-speaking children in the provision of schooling contrary to Article 14, the Court held that the combined effect of Article 14 and the First Protocol did not produce a guarantee for parents that their children could be educated by the state in the language of their choice.[113] Other decisions make it equally clear that there is no general right for those whose mother tongue is not the official language of the state to use their own language in dealings with public authorities[114] and national courts.[115] This marks a sharp contrast with the position under the League of Nations system, where the protection afforded to linguistic minorities was far greater. On the other hand, the following general statement by the Court in the case of *Young, James and Webster v UK* shows that it is fully aware of the needs of members of minority groups—

Although individual interests must on occasion be subordinated to those of a group, democracy does not simply mean that the views of a majority must always prevail: a balance must be achieved which ensures the fair and proper treatment of minorities and avoids any abuse of a dominant position.[116]

Furthermore, in *G and E v Norway* the Commission indicated that under Article 8 'a minority group is, in principle, entitled to claim the right to respect for the particular life style it may lead as being "private life",

---

[110] At 284.   [111] Id.

[112] See e.g. *Marckx v Belgium* (1980) 2 EHRR 330 at 343; *Abdulaziz, Cabales and Balkandali v UK* (1985) 7 EHRR 471 at 499.   [113] At 282.

[114] *Inhabitants of Leeuw-St Pierre v Belgium* (1965) 8 YBECHR 338.

[115] *Isop v Austria* (1962) 5 YBECHR 108; *K v France* (1984) Dec & Rep 203; *Bideault v France* (1986) 48 Dec & Rep 232.   [116] (1981) 4 EHRR 38 at 57.

"family life" or "home".[117] However, a widespread feeling that the rights of minorities were being afforded insufficient protection by the Convention, coupled with a concern about the general resurgence of racism, xenophobia, and anti-semitism across the continent and in particular at the occurrence of 'ethnic cleansing' in the former Yugoslavia, have recently led to a number of initiatives on the part of the Council of Europe.[118]

In 1990 the Parliamentary Assembly recommended member states to take all necessary legislative, administrative, judicial, and other measures to create favourable conditions to enable minorities to express their identity and to develop their education, culture, language, traditions, and customs.[119] States should abstain from pursuing policies of forced assimilation; rather they should fully implement the provisions of Article 27 of the International Covenant.[120] By 1992 the Parliamentary Assembly had moved forward to the development of a two-pronged approach. First, it recommended that an additional protocol be appended to the European Convention, specifically framed for the protection of minorities.[121] Secondly, it proposed that the Committee of Ministers should draft and rapidly adopt a declaration setting out the basic principles relating to the rights of minorities to which member states adhered and which should serve as a yardstick against which future applications for membership of the Council of Europe could be judged.[122]

In relation to the latter project, the first summit meeting of Heads of State and Government of the member states of the Council of Europe, held in Vienna in 1993, instructed the Committee of Ministers to proceed beyond a mere declaration of principles to the drafting of a 'Framework Convention', which would be open for signature by non-member states, notably those in Eastern Europe, as well as member states.[123] In 1995 the Committee of Ministers approved a draft prepared by an ad hoc committee of experts, which was then opened for signature.[124] The Convention, which came into force during 1997, constitutes the first legally binding multilateral instrument devoted to the protection of national

---

[117] (1984) 35 Dec & Rep 30 at 35.

[118] See generally, Gomien, D., 'The Rights of Minorities under the European Convention on Human Rights and the European Charter on Regional and Minority Languages' in Cator, J. and Niessen, J. (eds), *The Use of International Conventions to Protect the Rights of Migrants and Ethnic Minorities* (Strasbourg, 1994), ch VI.

[119] Recommendation 1134 (1990), Art 13(ii).   [120] Art 13(iv), (v).

[121] Recommendation 1177 (1992), Art 12.   [122] Arts 13, 14.

[123] Vienna Declaration, 9 Oct 1993, appendix II, reprinted in Council of Europe, 'Information Sheet No. 33' (1993), 153 at 156–7.

[124] Framework Convention for the Protection of National Minorities, European Treaty Series 157 (1995); see generally, Gilbert, G., 'The Council of Europe and Minority Rights' (1996) 18 *Human Rights Quarterly* 160.

minorities in general and it contains a detailed statement of legal principles, which contracting states commit themselves to implement through national legislation and government policies. Unfortunately, no definition of a 'national minority' is provided in the Convention because of the impossibility of finding a form of words acceptable to all the member states of the Council of Europe. However, while this is clearly a major defect, the Convention's provisions furnish important evidence of the continuing development of international law principles governing the treatment of minorities. Stress is placed upon the protection of minorities through safeguarding not the rights of the group as such but the rights of the members of minority groups, which may be exercised either individually or in community with others.[125] Article 4 contains strong echoes from the opinion given by the Permanent Court in the *Minority Schools in Albania* case.[126] Equality before the law, equal protection of the law, and non-discrimination are guaranteed first. The principle of non-discrimination is not tied to other rights and is thus more extensive than the protection afforded by Article 14 of the European Convention. Article 4(2) then provides—

The Parties undertake to adopt, where necessary, adequate measures in order to promote, in all areas of economic, social, political and cultural life, full and effective equality between persons belonging to a national minority and those belonging to the majority. In this respect, they shall take due account of the specific conditions of the persons belonging to national minorities.

Such special measures as are required to give members of minorities full and effective equality are not to be considered as themselves constituting acts of discrimination.[127]

Under Article 5 state parties undertake to promote the conditions necessary for persons belonging to national minorities to maintain and develop their culture and preserve the essential elements of their identity, namely their religion, language, traditions, and cultural heritage. Parties should refrain from policies or practices of forced assimilation. Voluntary assimilation is, of course, permissible and every person belonging to a national minority has the right to choose whether or not to be treated as such.[128] Article 6(2) requires states to take appropriate measures to protect persons who may be subject to threats or acts of discrimination, hostility, or violence as a result of their ethnic, cultural, linguistic, or religious identity. Other articles cover such matters as freedom of religion and of expression, access to the media, the use of minority languages, multicultural education, and the establishment of

---

[125] Arts 1, 3(2).   [126] (1935) PCIJ, Ser A/B, No. 64, discussed above.
[127] Art 4(3).   [128] Art 3(1).

separate schools.[129] The only limitations, restrictions, and derogations which states are allowed to make to the rights and freedoms set out in the Convention are those permitted by international law, in particular the European Convention, on public policy grounds.[130] Members of minorities are, of course, under a duty to respect national legislation and the rights of others.[131] Periodic monitoring of compliance with the Framework Convention is entrusted to the Committee of Ministers, to whom state parties must submit regular reports on steps taken to implement its provisions.[132] There is, however, no provision for rights of individual petition nor for decisions by a judicial tribunal, as under the European Convention, and this is clearly a substantial weakness.[133]

A large part of the inspiration behind the Framework Convention lay in a desire, reflected at the Vienna summit meeting, to convert into legal principles certain political commitments concerning minorities which had been adopted by the Conference on Security and Co-operation in Europe (CSCE). At a meeting in Copenhagen in 1990 the CSCE had affirmed that—

. . . respect for the rights of persons belonging to national minorities as part of universally recognized human rights is an essential factor for peace, justice, stability and democracy . . . . The participating States will adopt, where necessary, special measures for the purpose of ensuring to persons belonging to national minorities full equality with the other citizens in the exercise and enjoyment of human rights and fundamental freedoms.[134]

Many of the detailed principles incorporated in the Framework Convention had earlier been set down in the Copenhagen Document. Hence, a consensus-building process which had begun life during the early 1970s as a broad East-West inter-governmental dialogue on military security and human rights had developed after the end of the Cold War into a mechanism for dealing with the phenomenon of minority claims, which threatened both the maintenance of security and proper adherence to human rights norms.

One likely limitation on the effectiveness of the Framework Convention, as we have seen, is that it does not create personal rights for individuals, enforceable through judicial machinery. Implementation of its provisions is left to states, which thus retain a measure of discretion, subject to a reporting and monitoring system whose efficacy has yet to

---

[129] Arts 7–14.   [130] Art 19.   [131] Art 20.   [132] Arts 24–26.
[133] The Convention was criticized on this score by the Parliamentary Assembly in Recommendation 1255 (1995), Art 7.   [134] See (1990) 29 *ILM* 1305 at 1318.

be tested.[135] It is this aspect which has given greater salience to the second of the 1992 Parliamentary Assembly's projects, namely the drafting of an additional protocol to the European Convention itself, which would automatically be buttressed by the Convention's own enforcement mechanisms of rights of individual petition coupled with binding Court decisions and remedies. By 1993 the Assembly had prepared a draft of the new protocol, the key provision of which declared—

Every person belonging to a national minority shall have the right to express, preserve and develop in complete freedom his/her religious, ethnic, linguistic and/or cultural identity, without being subjected to any attempt at assimilation against his/her will.[136]

The draft protocol was presented to the summit meeting held in Vienna in 1993. However, rather than adopting the Assembly's draft, the meeting merely decided to instruct the Committee of Ministers 'to begin work on drafting a protocol complementing the . . . Convention . . . in the cultural field by provisions guaranteeing individual rights, in particular for persons belonging to national minorities'.[137] This represented a marked shift of emphasis towards a universalist rather than a particularist approach to the issue, stressing the need to recognize the cultural rights of all rather than exclusively those of minorities.[138]

The Committee of Ministers, in its turn, delegated the task of drafting to the same ad hoc committee of experts (CAHMIN) which had drafted the Framework Convention, but without the same success. Work on the project was officially suspended in 1996 because it did not seem possible to add substantially to the protection already afforded by the Convention.[139] The ad hoc committee had managed to draft new articles on such minor and uncontroversial matters as the right to a name, freedom to learn a language of one's choice and to use it (other than in dealings with public authorities), and the right to establish cultural institutions. However, no consensus could be reached on the central issue of the inclusion of an article guaranteeing respect for a person's cultural identity and the right to express it through a cultural activity.[140] The principal problems related to doubts as to whether such a provision could be made suffi-

---

[135] Art 26 provides for the Committee of Ministers to be assisted by an expert advisory committee, but the precise powers of this committee, its degree of independence, and the influence it is likely to wield are unclear.

[136] Recommendation 1201 (1993), Art 3(1); under Art 14 restrictions could, however, be imposed on the usual public policy grounds—see further below.

[137] Vienna Declaration, op cit, 157.

[138] See Marquand, D., 'Human rights protection and minorities' [1994] PL 359.

[139] Council of Europe, 'Human Rights Information Sheet No. 38' (1996), 135.

[140] For details of the discussions, see Ad Hoc Committee for the Protection of National Minorities (CAHMIN), meeting reports, (94) 35; (95) 9, 16, 21, 22.

ciently precise to be justiciable and whether it added anything of substance to the existing guarantees covering family life, religion, expression, assembly, and association. For some members, a right to cultural identity would possess an important symbolic and political value, while others were concerned at the prospect of encouraging division and secessionist tendencies or about the budgetary implications of any possible positive obligations states might incur. In any event, the Parliamentary Assembly subsequently indicated its dismay at this impasse and expressed the strong hope that work would soon recommence on the project.[141]

THE BOGEY OF *APARTHEID*

Through its ratification of the European Convention and the Framework Convention, the United Kingdom has bound itself not to discriminate between individuals contrary to Articles 14 and 4 respectively, but this does not bar it from taking a variety of measures to protect the cultural identities of minority groups, provided the conditions laid down in the *Belgian Linguistic Case* are satisfied. Furthermore, on the basis of Article 5 of the Framework Convention and Article 27 of the International Covenant it appears bound to take such measures, albeit that under these provisions it is left to each state's discretion to decide precisely what measures to take. A wide range of such measures already taken by Parliament and the English courts was outlined in the previous chapter. However, those who oppose such differential treatment commonly allege that it amounts to a form of *apartheid* and is thus impermissible. It is important, therefore, to clarify the distinction between the two concepts and nail this canard. As we have seen, the European Court in the *Belgian Linguistics Case* insisted that differential treatment must possess 'an objective and reasonable justification' and the doctrine of *apartheid* clearly failed this test. The distinctions made by *apartheid* were based purely on a system of racial classification related essentially to the colour of a person's skin and his or her supposed biological 'race'.[142] The division of South Africans by law into whites, coloureds, Asians, and blacks and their enforced segregation for the purposes, *inter alia*, of voting, residence, employment, marriage, sexual relationships, and the use of public facilities was arbitrary and irrational. It was for this reason that it was almost universally condemned as discriminatory

---

[141] Recommendation 1300 (1996), Art 4.

[142] See South Africa's Population Registration Act 1950 and generally, Dugard, J., *Human Rights and the South African Legal Order* (Princeton, 1978), ch 4.

and unlawful.[143] It was a coercive system imposed by a white government upon non-white racial groups against their wishes, whereas specific measures of minority protection are made available for members of ethnic communities for them to use if they so wish.[144] The crucial difference between *apartheid* and minority protection measures was perhaps best summarized by Judge Tanaka in his judgment in 1966 in the *South West Africa Cases (Second Phase)*.[145] In defending its application of *apartheid* in South West Africa before the International Court of Justice, the South African Government had argued that the doctrine did not violate international norms on equality. In the course of his opinion Judge Tanaka commented—

The principle of equality does not mean absolute equality, but recognises relative equality, namely different treatment proportionate to concrete individual circumstances. Different treatment must not be given arbitrarily; it requires reasonableness, or must be in conformity with justice, as in the treatment of minorities . . . In these cases, the differentiation is aimed at the protection of those concerned, and it is not detrimental and therefore not against their will. Discrimination according to the criterion of 'race, colour, national or tribal origin' in establishing the rights and duties of the inhabitants of [South West Africa] is not considered reasonable and just. Race, colour etc. do not constitute in themselves factors which can influence the rights and duties of the inhabitants as in the case of sex, age, language, religion, etc. If differentiation be required, it would be derived from the difference of language, religion, custom, etc., not from the racial difference itself. In the policy of *apartheid* the necessary logical and material link between difference itself and different treatment which can justify such treatment in the case of sex, minorities, etc., does not exist.[146]

Apartheid was unwanted, unreasonable, arbitrary, and invidious, whereas specific differential treatment designed to preserve ethnic and cultural identities and traditions is wanted, reasonable, rational, and just. Whereas the former doctrine created unwarranted privileges for a minority at the expense of the majority community, the latter accords minorities genuine equality with the majority community.

THE SPECTRE OF 'GROUP RIGHTS'

If the bogey of *apartheid* easily dissolves in the light of clear analysis, the spectre of 'group rights' is perhaps rather more difficult to banish from

---

[143] See e.g. International Convention on the Elimination of All Forms of Racial Discrimination, Art 3; see also International Convention on the Suppression and Punishment of the Crime of *Apartheid* (1973), ratified by 99 states.

[144] See e.g. Framework Convention, Art 3(1).   [145] (1966) ICJ Reports 4.

[146] At 311–2.

the scene. We have already seen that several human rights guaranteed to individuals can only be exercised effectively on a collective basis. However, the notion of collective or group rights has tended, in the liberal tradition, to be viewed with a considerable degree of suspicion and hostility.[147] As we have seen, liberalism is characterized by a profound attachment to individualism, to the belief that individual persons are the ultimate units of moral worth.[148] As Kymlicka has explained[149]—

There seems to be no room within the moral ontology of liberalism for the idea of collective rights. The community, unlike the individual, is not a 'self-originating source of valid claims'.[150] Once individuals have been treated as equals, with the respect and concern owed them as moral beings, there is no further obligation to treat the communities to which they belong as equals. The community has no moral existence or claims of its own. It is not that the community is unimportant to the liberal, but simply that it is important for what it contributes to the lives of individuals, and so cannot ultimately conflict with the claims of individuals. Individual and collective rights cannot compete for the same moral space, in liberal theory, since the value of the collective derives from its contribution to the value of individual lives.

One obvious reason for rejecting the concept of group rights is their close association with *apartheid*. Under the South African Group Areas Act 1950 and related legislation, for example, different racial groups were physically segregated in terms of their access to housing, social amenities, and recreational facilities.[151] The provision of 'separate but equal' schooling for black people in the American South was similarly viewed by liberals as morally repugnant and was declared unconstitutional by the US Supreme Court in *Brown v Board of Education*[152] in 1954. However, we have already seen that there is a clear distinction to be drawn between such arbitrary and coercive doctrines based on race and colour, on the one hand, and rational and positive policies designed to safeguard the cultures of minority communities at their own request, on the other. While the former policy confers a 'badge of inferiority'[153] upon the community in question, the latter approach affords it genuine equality. Even so, the main thrust of the argument against group rights in terms of their potential conflict with individual rights still stands. Liberals fear that, if collective rights are recognized, individuals may find that their

---

[147] For discussion of the variety of meanings attributable to group rights as well as some of the dangers inherent in according recognition to such rights, see Montgomery, J., 'Legislating for a Multi-faith Society: Some Problems of Special Treatment' in Hepple and Szyszczak, *Discrimination*, ch 11; Kymlicka (1995), chs 2 and 3.

[148] See above, ch 1.   [149] Kymlicka (1991), 140.

[150] Rawls, J., 'Kantian Constructivism in Moral Theory' (1980) 77 *Journal of Philosophy* 543.

[151] See e.g. Horrell, M., *Laws Affecting Race Relations in South Africa* (Johannesburg, 1978), chs XI and XIV.

[152] (1954) 347 US 483.   [153] See Kymlicka (1991), 145; Kymlicka (1995), 59–60.

own personal interests and identities have become submerged within those of the group.[154] An individual's culture and ethnicity are, after all, only one portion of that person's own distinctive identity and there are dangers in allowing the group to dictate what cultural rights an individual should be free to exercise.[155]

An illustration of this dilemma is afforded by the examination in Chapter 6 of the claim by some Muslim organizations that all British Muslims should automatically have their family affairs regulated by a separate system of Islamic personal law. Such a scheme might well be viewed as repressive rather than liberating, particularly by some Muslim women, who might feel that their interests were likely to be better served by the general provisions of English family law. Any situation in which exclusive jurisdiction over the lives of individuals is handed over to the leaders of a group, who then have the power to determine whether or not a person should be deemed to be a member of that group, is potentially dangerous. The right to dissent, to be a 'minority within a minority' must therefore be preserved, not stifled, and everyone must be afforded equal access to the general law of the land. The clear consent of the individual to be governed by the dictates of the group is a vital ingredient if any form of group rights is to be acknowledged. Group determinism cannot be permitted to prevail over individual choice and personal autonomy.[156] Hence, while it is appropriate that the concept of group rights should facilitate the voluntary, collective enjoyment by members of a group of their individual rights, it is not the function of international human rights law to protect a group from internal strife by enforcing discipline upon its members through coercion.

Individual liberty must, moreover, mean more than merely possessing the right to sever all connections with an ethnic community and disavow all its beliefs, values, doctrines, and traditions. Certainly an individual should be free to become fully assimilated within the wider society, but such an extreme course of action is unlikely to appeal to most people with ethnic minority origins. Many such individuals will wish to remain full members of their own ethnic communities, while commonly seeking to modify and adapt traditional norms and value systems to meet the changing social environment in which they find themselves in a liberal democracy such as modern Britain.

In a valuable study of ethnic identity Hutnik has suggested a model of four possible cultural adaptation styles which might be adopted by

---

[154] See Goulbourne, H., 'Varieties of pluralism: the notion of a pluralist, post-Imperial Britain' (1991) *New Community* 211 at 224–5.
[155] See Berting, J. (ed), *Human Rights in a Pluralist World: Individuals and Collectivities* (London, 1990), 251–8.   [156] See Capotorti (1991), 42–3.

individual members of ethnic minorities.[157] The 'assimilationist' style is followed by those who adapt themselves completely to the majority group. The 'dissociative' style is the one adopted by those who keep exclusively to the culture of their own minority group. The 'acculturative' style is followed by those who identify with the cultures of both the majority and the minority, while the 'marginal' style is adopted by those who identify with the culture of neither group. Hutnik argues convincingly that ethnic minority self-categorization can persist long after cultural adaptation has occurred through acculturation and even possibly after assimilation. Retention of a sense of ethnic identity can occur independently of the dissociative style, so that, for example, 'the ethnic minority individual may feel strongly Indian (say) but be very British in his/her behaviour and other attitudes'.[158]

Community solidarity based on the notion of group rights should not, therefore, curtail the individual's freedom of expression, the right to marry outside one's community or faith, and the liberty to change or abandon one's religion. There must be room for recognizing the ethnic identities of Jews who are not *kosher*[159], Muslims who consume alcohol, Sikhs who are cleanshaven and bareheaded, Hindus who marry outside their caste, gypsies who are housedwellers, and Rastafarians who do not wear dreadlocks. Above all, individuals should not be precluded from making positive contributions to the evolution of their own ethnic cultures simply because they are tied to a doctrine of rigid and restrictive collective rights.

The need to appreciate the malleable nature of culture is of vital importance. Cultures are not static, they are constantly preserving themselves from becoming ossified through the injection of new variations, interpretations, and pragmatic adjustments to their surroundings. This phenomenon of 'cultural transformation' applies to religious beliefs and practices, to the use of language, and to social customs and traditions, as well as to the creative arts. As Kallen has explained—

A living culture is a changing culture; and it is a changing culture . . . because of the transactions wherewith living, altering individuals transform old thoughts and things while labouring to preserve them and to produce new. Cultures live

---

[157] Hutnik, N., *Ethnic Minority Identity: A Social Psychological Perspective* (Oxford, 1991), 124.

[158] Ibid, 159; see also Modood, T., Berthoud, R., *et al*, *Ethnic Minorities in Britain: Diversity and Disadvantage* (London, 1997), 328–38.

[159] For evidence of a strong sense of ethnic identity among Jewish women in England, regardless of whether they believe in the basic principles of the Jewish faith or observe traditional rituals, see Schmool, M. and Miller, S., *Women in the Jewish Community: Survey Report* (London, 1994), 15–26.

and grow in and through the individual, and their vitality is a function of individual diversities of interests and associations.[160]

Culture should not be reified, since it represents a continuous process whereby individuals reinterpret their traditions, values, and beliefs in the light of their social environment and personal histories.

The solution to this problem must lie in balancing the claims of groups against those of individuals, acknowledging that both have an important role to play in the pursuit of human happiness and fulfilment. Kymlicka has explained how a liberal society needs to recognize the inevitable element of genuine conflict involved, rather than shy away from any acceptance of collective rights—

People are owed respect as citizens and as members of cultural communities. In many situations, the two are perfectly compatible, and in fact may coincide. But in culturally plural societies, differential citizenship rights may be needed to protect a cultural community from unwanted disintegration. If so, then the demands of citizenship and cultural membership pull in different directions. Both matter and neither seems reducible to the other . . . . Such conflicts are, in fact endemic to the day-to-day politics of culturally plural societies, and various schemes of minority rights can be understood and evaluated in this light.[161]

In his view what is required is a flexible response on the part of the law, which will uphold the legitimate claims of cultural membership through recognition of certain group rights, while avoiding systems of racial discrimination (such as *apartheid* or segregation) or of cultural oppression.[162]

It is precisely this flexible, integrated approach which international human rights law endeavours to provide. As Thornberry has pointed out—

. . . minority rights need to be brought into balance with human rights or, more correctly, to be seen as part of human rights. Whatever respect must be paid to the rights of groups, the stance of modern international law is clear in according primacy to individual choice: respect for group rights does not justify 'group determinism', the overriding of individual choice by claims of the group.[163]

In this light it is worth attempting to clarify exactly what degree of recognition has been accorded to group rights, as such, in international law.[164] Most fundamentally, the right of national, ethnic, racial, and religious groups to their very existence is specifically recognized in the

[160] Kallen, H., *Cultural Pluralism and the American Idea* (Philadelphia, 1956), 55.
[161] At 151–2.
[162] Ibid, 255; see also his *Multicultural Citizenship*, chs 3 and 4.
[163] At 394; see also Steiner, H., 'Ideals and Counter-Ideals in the Struggle Over Autonomy Regimes for Minorities' (1991) 66 *Notre Dame LR* 1539.
[164] No account is given here of the rights of 'peoples' to 'self-determination', since such groups fall outside the compass of this work.

Convention on the Prevention and Punishment of the Crime of Genocide 1948.[165] The Convention has been ratified by 120 states and there is no doubt that the prohibition of genocide is of universal application.[166] Secondly, the right to cultural identity, most clearly expressed in Article 27 of the International Covenant on Civil and Political Rights and in the Framework Convention, is an attempt to achieve a reconciliation between group rights and individual rights.[167] In Thornberry's words—

The right to identity conceals the collective right behind the rights of individuals. The group is the 'unacknowledged presence' behind the individual rights. Collective rights are a substantive, if not a 'formal' aspect of the legal reality. The greater part of this reality is given over to individual rights. 'Minority rights' are substantive and indirect, not formal and direct.[168]

Minorities were not accorded the status of 'subjects' of international law even under the League of Nations regime for minority protection[169] and such groups are not accorded international personality under modern law by Article 27.[170] On the other hand, it has been pointed out that when states comment on Article 27 in periodic reports submitted to the Human Rights Committee under Article 40 of the Covenant, they do in fact provide information about the situation of minority groups rather than particular individuals and this supports the notion that the practice of states 'before international bodies shows that Article 27 is understood as a group protection provision'.[171] Moreover, Article 1 of the 1992 UN Declaration on the Rights of Persons Belonging to National or Ethnic, Religious and Linguistic Minorities obliges state parties to protect the identity of such minorities within their respective territories and to encourage conditions for the promotion of that identity. Thirdly, the right not to be discriminated against on the grounds of race, colour, religion, or language is also expressed as the right of individuals in the International Covenants[172] and the International Convention on the Elimination of All Forms of Racial Discrimination.[173] However, in practice individuals are normally subjected to such forms of discrimination because of their

---

[165] Cmnd 4421 of 1970.

[166] Thornberry, ch 7; Lerner, N., *Group Rights and Discrimination in International Law* (Dordrecht, 1991), ch 9.   [167] Thornberry, 394; Lerner, 15.

[168] At 396.   [169] Id.

[170] Sohn, L., 'The Rights of Minorities' in Henkin, L. (ed), *The International Bill of Rights* (New York, 1981), 274. The clearest enunciation of a group's independent right to cultural identity is to be found in the UNESCO Declaration on Race and Racial Prejudice, Art 5(1) discussed above, pp 82–4, where the point was made that the Declaration was not intended to be binding. It is drafted in highly ambiguous language—see Thornberry, ch 33.

[171] Ermacora, F., 'The Protection of Minorities before the United Nations' (1983) IV *Receuil des Cours* 247 at 323.   [172] ICCPR, Arts 2(1), 26; ICESCR, Art 2(2).

[173] Art 1(1). The Convention does, however, specifically refer to 'racial groups' in Arts 1(4) and 2(2) dealing with measures of 'affirmative' action; see generally, Lerner, ch 13.

group membership rather than their personal attributes and thus the group interest lies behind the formal protection afforded to individuals.[174] Furthermore, Article 20(2) of the International Covenant on Civil and Political Rights might be viewed as designed to afford protection to groups when it provides—

Any advocacy of national, racial or religious hatred that constitutes incitement to discrimination, hostility or violence shall be prohibited by law.

CONFLICTING RIGHTS AND CLAIMS

We have seen that international law has long recognized the claims made by ethnic groups to retain their own separate identities and that it tends today to give effect to such aspirations by conferring rights upon the individual members of such groups. Not infrequently, however, such rights and claims are liable to clash with the interests of individuals within other groups, particularly those of the majority community and hence perhaps also with the general welfare of the society as a whole. In conflictual situations such as these the law is called upon to determine the boundaries of particular rights, claims, and interests. While the definition of the limits of rights is a routine function of any legal system,[175] the task is often an extremely onerous one in this field and difficult decisions have to be made, with profound implications for members of minority and majority communities alike. Dworkin has prudently cautioned that the institution of rights 'requires an act of faith on the part of the minorities, because the scope of their rights will be controversial whenever they are important . . . .'[176]

It is clear that no international consensus has yet developed on ranking the different human rights into some sort of hierarchial structure, in such a way as to enable easy resolution of any conflicts between them.[177] Superficially, it might be attractive at least to accord precedence to those rights which are nonderogable in the sense that they cannot be suspended in times of emergency.[178] However, Meron has explained that even this approach is flawed—

The international community as a whole has neither established a uniform list of nonderogable rights[179] nor ranked nonderogable rights ahead of derogable

---

[174] Lerner, 27.

[175] See generally, Gostin, L. (ed), *Civil Liberties in Conflict* (London, 1988).

[176] *Taking Rights Seriously*, 205.

[177] See Meron, T., 'On a hierarchy of international human rights' (1986) 80 *AJIL* 1.

[178] See ICCPR, Art 4; ECHR, Art 15.

[179] Freedom of religion, for example, is a derogable right under ECHR, Art 15(1), but is nonderogable under ICCPR, Art 4(2).

rights. If a derogable right conflicts with a nonderogable right, the latter will not necessarily prevail . . . .[180]

Even so, international law is not totally bereft of techniques for resolving the conflicts which may arise and it tackles the problem in a number of different ways. At the most fundamental level the law will not tolerate attempts to undermine the essential framework of human rights itself. The 'culture of freedom' represented by liberal conceptions of human rights cannot be neutral in the face of efforts to subvert its very foundations. Article 5(1) of the International Covenant on Civil and Political Rights therefore declares—

Nothing in the present Covenant may be interpreted as implying for any State, group or person any right to engage in any activity or perform any act aimed at the destruction of any of the rights and freedoms recognised herein or at their limitation to a greater extent than is provided for in the present Covenant.[181]

Hence any ethnic group whose philosophy involved, for example, complete denial of elementary democratic freedoms, such as free elections and freedom of expression, would not be able to rely upon any of the rights contained in the Covenant with a view to achieving such objectives.[182]

Secondly, whereas some of the rights guaranteed in the international treaties are expressed in unqualified or virtually unqualified terms, others are restricted by limitation or 'saving' clauses, which allow states to curtail their exercise in certain prescribed sets of circumstances. In particular, four freedoms of great significance for ethnic minority communities, namely those of expression, religion, association, and assembly, may be restricted by law, so far as is necessary in a democratic society, in the interests of such considerations as public safety, the prevention of disorder or crime, the protection of health or morals, or for the protection of the rights and freedoms of others.[183] Where an absolute or unqualified right (or one with minimal qualifications) conflicts with one of these four, it seems fairly clear that the former should prevail, since the latter is expressly capable of being limited in order to protect the

---

[180] At 16.

[181] Art 5(1) of the International Covenant on Economic, Social and Cultural Rights is in identical terms, as is Art 17 of the European Convention on Human Rights.

[182] In *Kuhnen v Federal Republic of Germany* (1988) 56 Dec & Rep 205, an application based on the European Convention, the European Commission ruled that a journalist, who had been convicted of a criminal offence for publishing pamphlets advocating the reintroduction of national socialism and racial discrimination, could not succeed in his claim that his freedom of expression had been violated; the German authorities were held to have been entitled to restrict his freedom *inter alia* because his activities were aimed at the general destruction of the rights and freedoms set forth in the Convention.

[183] See e.g. ECHR, Arts 9(2), 10(2) and 11(2). The wording of each is slightly different.

rights of others.[184] Hence if members of an ethnic group were to claim that as part of their cultural expression or religious tradition they were entitled to indulge in human sacrifice, the destruction of twins, female infanticide, the summary execution of apostates,[185] the automatic suicide of widows, the severing of limbs as a punishment, the genital mutilation of girls, or servitude, they would find such claims were 'trumped' by unconditionally (or virtually unconditionally) guaranteed rights held by their victims to life, to freedom from torture or inhuman or degrading treatment or punishment, or to freedom from slavery.[186] In relation to genital mutilation, it is notable that precisely this method of curtailing a broad right to cultural identity by means of other protective articles is employed in the Convention on the Rights of the Child. Article 30, entitled 'Minority Rights', declares in very general terms—

In those States in which ethnic, religious or linguistic minorities . . . exist, a child belonging to such a minority . . . shall not be denied the right, in community with other members of his or her group, to enjoy his or her own culture, to profess and practise his or her own religion, or to use his or her own language.

Prima facie, this Article might justify the circumcision of a young girl if that custom was followed by her ethnic or religious group, but Article 24 entitled 'Health', after guaranteeing a child's right to the enjoyment of 'the highest attainable standard of health',[187] provides—

States Parties shall take all effective and appropriate measures with a view to abolishing traditional practices prejudicial to the health of children.[188]

This coded reference to the obligation to prohibit genital mutilation is further supplemented by Article 19, which commits state parties to taking appropriate measures to protect children from all forms of physical or mental violence, injury, or abuse.

Two further illustrations may be given of situations in which claims made on behalf of an ethnic group, based on the generalized right to cultural identity under Article 27 of the International Covenant on Civil and Political Rights, would have to give way to more specific rights. A claim to be entitled to force a girl to marry under customary or religious norms[189] would be 'trumped' by the many specific provisions in human

---

[184] See e.g. Harris, D., O'Boyle, M., and Warbrick, C., *Law of the European Convention on Human Rights* (London, 1995), 296–7. Since advocacy of racial or religious hatred is unconditionally banned by ICCPR, Art 20(2), such speech cannot be defended as part of freedom of expression under Art 19, since the latter can be limited in order to respect the rights of others, as well as to protect public order.

[185] The right to change one's religion is expressly guaranteed by ICCPR, Art 19(2) and ECHR, Art 9(1).   [186] See ECHR, Arts 2, 3 and 4; ICCPR, Arts 6, 7 and 8.

[187] Art 24(1), (2). See also ICESCR, Art 12.   [188] Art 24(3).

[189] See further below, ch 6.

rights treaties which insist that all marriages require the free and full consent of the intended spouses.[190] Secondly, the traditional practice of gypsies not to educate their children[191] would have to give way to the unequivocally expressed right of all children to education.[192] It is argued in Chapter 6 below that this approach of according priority to unqualified specific rights over qualified general rights is appropriate to resolve the clash between the guarantee of sexual equality in marriage and family relations, on the one hand, and freedom of religion, on the other, which arises when Muslim organizations demand a separate and independent system of personal law for British Muslims.[193]

Much more difficult to resolve are clashes between rights of roughly the same order of importance. A recent instance of this is the conflict between freedom of religion and freedom from religious discrimination, on the one hand, and freedom of expression, on the other, so graphically exemplified by the 'Rushdie Affair'.[194] In such situations detailed investigation is required to establish precisely how the conflict of rights is to be resolved in particular circumstances. The relevant legal provisions need to be interpreted, often in the light of decided cases, and there may naturally be scope for considerable disagreement about what the correct outcome should be. The task for lawyers is no different here from that exercised in interpreting the provisions of a municipal legal system in a civil liberties case, as the following analysis of blasphemy law and, in particular, the litigation arising out of the 'Rushdie Affair' should demonstrate.

The publication of Salman Rushdie's novel, *The Satanic Verses*, in 1988 caused grave offence to many Muslims across the world through what they felt was a highly abusive and disrespectful portrayal of Islam and

---

[190] ICCPR, Art 23(3); ICESCR, Art 10(1); Convention on Consent to Marriage 1970, Art 1(1); International Convention on the Elimination of All Forms of Discrimination against Women, Art 16(1)(*b*).   [191] See below, ch 5.

[192] ICESCR, Art 13; ECHR, Art 2 of First Protocol; Convention on the Rights of the Child, Art 28.

[193] On the challenge posed to Islamic doctrines by claims to sexual equality, see generally, Esposito, J., *Women in Muslim Family Law* (Syracuse, 1982); Mernissi, F., *Women and Islam: An Historical and Theological Enquiry* (Oxford, 1991); Mayer, A., *Islam and Human Rights* (London, 1991), chs 5, 6; Ahmed, L., *Women and Gender in Islam* (New Haven, 1992).

[194] For a variety of illuminating perspectives on the affair, see the reports of three seminars organized by the Commission for Racial Equality, *Law, Blasphemy and the Multi-Faith Society* (London, 1990), *Free Speech* (London, 1990) and *Britain: A Plural Society* (London, 1990). See also Akhtar, S., *Be Careful with Muhammad* (London, 1989); Appignanesi, L. and Maitland, S., *The Rushdie File* (London, 1989); Lee, S., *The Cost of Free Speech* (London, 1990); Ruthven, M., *A Satanic Affair* (London, 1990); Webster, R., *A Brief History of Blasphemy* (Southwold, 1990); Bowen, D. (ed), *The Satanic Verses: Bradford Responds* (Bradford, 1992); Horton, J. (ed), *Liberalism, Multiculturalism and Toleration* (Basingstoke, 1993), chs 7–12; Modood, T., 'British Asian Muslims and the Rushdie Affair' (1990) 61 *Political Quarterly* 143.

the Prophet Muhammad. It led, *inter alia*, to violent protest demonstrations, to the public burning of copies of the book in Bolton and Bradford, and in February 1989 to the pronouncement of death sentences upon the author and his publishers in the form of a *fatwa* issued by the spiritual leader of Iran, Ayatollah Khomeini. In England, after unsuccessful attempts to have the book withdrawn or banned, an aggrieved Muslim, Abdul Choudhury, instituted proceedings by way of judicial review to try to force the authorities to prosecute Rushdie and his publishers for the offence of blasphemy. The courts ruled, however, that the offence only protected Christianity, not Islam, and that the magistrate who had refused to issues summonses for this reason had acted properly.[195] Choudhury thereupon made a complaint to the European Commission of Human Rights, alleging that the United Kingdom was in breach of Articles 9 and 14 of the Convention through a failure to uphold the freedom of religion of Muslims as a result of its discriminatory blasphemy law. The Commission's task, therefore, was to resolve the apparent conflict between these articles and Article 10, which makes it clear that authors are entitled to impart their ideas without interference on the basis of their right to freedom of expression.

The exercise of freedom of expression, however, carries duties and responsibilities and the state is therefore entitled to curtail it in order to safeguard, *inter alia*, the rights of others.[196] Hence when, in an earlier case, the publisher and editor of *Gay News* had complained about the denial of their right to freedom of expression under the European Convention, following their conviction of blasphemous libel in the English courts in *Whitehouse v Lemon*,[197] their application to the European Commission was flatly rejected as being manifestly ill-founded.[198] However, this ruling merely established the state's right to restrict freedom of expression by means of a law making blasphemy an offence.[199] It did not indicate whether or not a state was bound to do so pursuant to its obligation to guarantee freedom of religion.[200] This question was only addressed when the Commission was subsequently confronted in

---

[195] *R v Chief Metropolitan Stipendiary Magistrate, ex parte Choudhury* [1991] 1 QB 429.

[196] ECHR, Art 10(2); for decisions of the European Court of Human Rights stressing the vital importance of freedom of expression, while upholding the validity of state restrictions in the particular circumstances of each case, see *Handyside v UK* (1976) 1 EHRR 737; *Muller v Switzerland* (1991) 13 EHRR 212.   [197] [1979] AC 617.

[198] (1982) 5 EHRR 123.

[199] For subsequent decisions of the European Court to the same effect, see *Otto-Preminger Institut v Austria* (1995) 19 EHRR 34 and *Wingrove v UK* (1997) 24 EHRR 1.

[200] In *Whitehouse v Lemon* Lord Scarman had earlier indicated his view (at 665) that the right to freedom of religion, by necessary implication, imposed a duty upon all to refrain from insulting or outraging the religious feelings of others, but this had been doubted by the Law Commission: see Working Paper No. 79 'Offences against Religion and Public Worship', para 6.6.

Choudhury v UK[201] with an application alleging that the failure of English law to prohibit blasphemy against Islam violated principles of religious freedom.

The Commission held that the right to freedom of religion under Article 9 of the Convention did not extend to guaranteeing a right to bring any specific form of proceedings (such as a prosecution for blasphemy) against those who, by authorship or publication, offended the sensitivities of an individual or a group of individuals. The obligation of a state not to interfere with freedom of religion (save on certain prescribed grounds) thus did not entail a duty to make blasphemy a criminal offence. Hence, the manner in which an apparent conflict between two basic freedoms of broadly the same order of importance was resolved in this case was by defining the precise ambit of the particular rights. In a legal sense there simply was no clash at all, since freedom of religion under the Convention did not encompass the right to prohibit others from scurrilous vilification of a religious faith by rendering such conduct a criminal offence. The application failed because it was 'incompatible *ratione materiae*'[202] with the terms of the Convention. However, in the subsequent case of *Otto-Preminger-Institut v Austria*,[203] in which the issues related to a blasphemous film which grossly disparaged God, Christ, the Virgin Mary, and the Eucharist, the European Court appeared to take a rather different view of the relationship between Articles 9 and 10. In rejecting the applicant's claim that seizure of the film by the Austrian authorities amounted to a breach of Article 10, the Court declared—

The respect for the religious feelings of believers *as guaranteed in Article 9* can legitimately be thought to have been violated by provocative portrayals of objects of religious veneration; and such portrayals can be regarded as malicious violation of the spirit of tolerance, which must also be a feature of democratic society[204] (emphasis added).

The Court indicated that among the duties and responsibilities imposed upon the exercise of freedom of expression by Article 10(2) was the obligation to 'avoid as far as possible expressions that are gratuitously offensive to others and thus an infringement of their rights, and which therefore do not contribute to any form of public debate capable of furthering progress in human affairs'.[205] This meant that in certain democratic societies it might be considered necessary to prevent improper attacks on objects of religious veneration. Ultimately, the Court simply had to weigh up the conflicting interests of Articles 9 and 10,

---

[201] (1991) 12 *Human Rights LJ* 172.   [202] At 173.   [203] (1995) 19 EHRR 34.
[204] At 56.   [205] At 57.

while allowing the state a margin of appreciation in striking the appropriate balance.[206]

In *Choudhury v UK* the applicant had also alleged a violation of Article 14 of the Convention, guaranteeing non-discrimination, on the ground that English blasphemy law protected Christianity alone and thus discriminated against other faiths. However, the Commission ruled that this complaint was inadmissible for the same reason, namely that it fell outside the provisions of the Convention. Article 14 of the Convention, as we have seen, is not an independent, free-standing guarantee of non-discrimination. It only bars discrimination in relation to other rights contained within the Convention. Hence, since the right to prosecute for blasphemy was not guaranteed by Article 9 of the Convention as part of freedom of religion, the discriminatory nature of the English offence did not engage any responsibilities under Article 14. While this latter part of the Commission's decision is not easy to reconcile with previous rulings that Article 14 can be violated if a restriction permissible under another Article is imposed in a discriminatory manner[207] and may thus be highly debatable,[208] the point being made here is that controversies arising from the clash of different human rights are capable of resolution through a process of judicial interpretation and are not therefore in any real sense irreconcilable.[209] Disputes can be brought to European and other human rights institutions which can make a legal ruling on the issues.

The same principles and procedures of institutional interpretation apply to the equally difficult task of determining whether or not a particular freedom has been lawfully restricted upon one or more of the broad public interest grounds identified in the saving clauses which are appended to many of the rights and freedoms guaranteed. Defensive arguments will inevitably be made by states to the effect that they are justified in limiting the exercise of several rights on grounds such as public health, safety, order, or morals or else on the basis that they are protecting the general public interest or the specific rights of others. Several situations of this nature are discussed in Part II of this book and only one illustration is therefore given here to demonstrate how controversial such determinations are liable to be.

In *Ahmad v ILEA*[210] the applicant, a devout Muslim who had been employed by ILEA as a full-time teacher at several of its primary schools, complained of unfair dismissal following his resignation (under

---

[206] At 57–8.   [207] See above, p 85.

[208] For criticism, see Poulter, S., 'Towards Legislative Reform of the Blasphemy and Racial Hatred Laws' [1991] *PL* 371 at 374–5; Harris, Boyle, and Warbrick, 360; cf Feldman, D., *Civil Liberties and Human Rights in England and Wales* (Oxford, 1993), 696–7.

[209] Feldman, 40.   [210] [1978] QB 36.

protest) after ILEA sought to make him change his status to that of a part-time teacher, working only four and a half days a week instead of five. The reason why ILEA had pressed this alteration on him, with a resulting reduction in salary, was that he was regularly absenting himself from his school classes early on Friday afternoons in order to visit a nearby mosque for Friday prayers. Section 30 of the Education Act 1944 (re-enacted as section 146 of the Education Act 1996) seeks to guarantee that a teacher in the state system will not 'receive any less emolument' by reason only of his 'attending . . . religious worship' and this provision is automatically incorporated in the contracts of all such teachers. However, the majority of the Court of Appeal felt unable to apply section 30 at its face value in affording protection to the applicant and the Court ruled that his dismissal had not been unfair. In a vigorous dissenting judgment, Scarman LJ (as he then was) expressed alarm that the result of the case would render it impossible for devout Muslims to become or remain full-time teachers. He argued that education authorities should make suitable administrative arrangements to ensure that Muslims could attend Friday prayers, that pupils would be taught, and that other staff were not unduly burdened, even if this involved extra public expenditure in employing a few more teachers.

A central issue in this case for all the judges was the impact of Article 9 of the European Convention guaranteeing freedom of religion. Scarman LJ took the view that the majority decision would be 'almost certainly a breach of our international obligations'.[211] As to the relevance of the European Convention in English law he declared—

. . . it is no longer possible to assume that because the international treaty obligations of the United Kingdom do not become law unless enacted by Parliament our courts pay no regard to our international obligations. They pay very serious regard to them; in particular, they will interpret statutory language and apply common law principles, wherever possible, so as to reach a conclusion consistent with our international obligations . . . .[212]

While Scarman LJ emphasized the importance of the guarantee of freedom of worship in Article 9(1), Lord Denning MR and Orr LJ stressed the significance of the restrictions authorized by Article 9(2), which states—

Freedom to manifest one's religion or beliefs shall be subject only to such limitations as are prescribed by law and are necessary in a democratic society in the interests of public safety, for the protection of public order, health or morals, or for the protection of the rights and freedoms of others.

---

[211] At 50.   [212] At 48.

In their view the rights of ILEA under the contract and the rights of the pupils to be taught prevailed over Ahmad's freedom of religion.

When Ahmad ultimately took his complaint to the European Commission, alleging a violation of Article 9(1), it was the stance taken by the majority of the Court of Appeal, not Scarman LJ, which was finally vindicated.[213] Ahmad's application was dismissed as manifestly ill-founded on the basis that ILEA was entitled to rely on its contract being fulfilled and had given due consideration to Ahmad's religious freedom by offering him a part-time post. The upshot seemed to be that Ahmad's exercise of his freedom of worship had to be subordinated to the contractual rights of the authority, which were entitled to protection under the provisions of Article 9(2).

The scale of the difficulties presented by saving clauses is perhaps best summed up by Palley—

Despite international consensus on the specified criteria for restrictions, any evaluation of the relationship between rights and restrictions will always be controversial: criteria or rules have to be selected as relevant; those criteria have to be interpreted and choice made between conflicting interpretations; the facts and circumstances have to be discovered . . .; then there has to be an evaluation of the criteria in relation to the circumstances; account has . . . to be taken of the consequences . . . . Decision-making is not easy and one should not too lightly assume that decision-makers are either wicked or weak.[214]

At a more general level, Finnis has proffered the following suggestion about how best to approach the inevitable conflicts which exist in any appraisal of human rights—

There is . . . no alternative but to hold in one's mind's eye some pattern, or range of patterns, of human character, conduct, and interaction in community, and then to choose such specification of rights as tends to favour that pattern, or range of patterns. In other words, one needs some conception of human good, of individual flourishing in a form (or range of forms) of communal life that fosters rather than hinders such flourishing. One attends not merely to character types desirable in the abstract or in isolation, but also to the quality of interaction among persons; and one should not seek to realize some patterned 'end-state' imagined in abstraction from the processes of individual initiative and interaction, processes which are integral to human good and which make the future, let alone its evaluation, incalculable.[215]

---

[213] *Ahmad v UK* (1981) 4 EHRR 126.

[214] Palley, C., *The United Kingdom and Human Rights* (London, 1991), 161–2; for greater scepticism about the process, see Murphy, T., 'Toleration and the Law' in Horton, J. and Crabtree, H. (eds), *Toleration and Integrity in a Multi-Faith Society* (York, 1992), ch 9, esp at 56–9.   [215] Finnis, J., *Natural Law and Natural Rights* (Oxford, 1986), 219–20.

QUESTIONS OF ETHNOCENTRICITY AND RELATIVISM

It has been argued in the previous two chapters that the guiding policy of cultural pluralism has limits and that there are some situations in which English law should not countenance certain 'foreign' customs and practices because they fall below the minimum standards which can be derived from the set of institutionalized core values deemed to be shared by all those living in Britain. Of course, one of the inherent dangers in assessing and evaluating the laws, traditions, and cultures of other peoples lies in the adoption of an ethnocentric approach, in terms of which automatic and thoughtless assumptions are made about the superiority of the appraiser's own community's patterns of behaviour, values, and beliefs. For example, in the Tanganyikan case of *Gwao bin Kilimo v Kisunda bin Ifuti*,[216] mentioned in the previous chapter, Wilson J (a British colonial judge) held it to be repugnant to English conceptions of justice that a particular African tribal custom provided for a father's property to be attached in execution of a judgment debt of his son, remarking—

Is it just according to our ideas to take away a man's property in order to compensate a party who has suffered injury at the hands of the man's son, the son being of full age and fully responsible in law for his own actions? I hold most strongly the opinion that it is not just.

This judicial application of the colonial 'repugnancy clause' has been subjected to some well-founded criticism on the basis that the judge failed to consider the customary rule in its proper social, economic, and legal context. As one commentator has pointed out—

If it could be shown, for instance, that the herd allegedly owned by the father . . . was family property in the sense that it was built up by contributions of the father's family past and present, would a rule that cattle from it could be used in meeting the obligations of other members of the family be unjust or repugnant to morality? . . . the true significance of [the judge's] statement [was] the unwillingness of the court to accept the notion inherent in the asserted custom that a person's property is not his 'private property' to the extent that it may be used to meet a range of obligations wider than those which English law would consider strictly his. The judge's action must, then, be seen as a judicial attempt to impose notions of private property on a society still communally-oriented.[217]

The decisions of the English courts in cases concerning local customs are similarly prone to be tainted by the mark of ethnocentricity. In the

---

[216] [1938] 1 TLR (R) 403.
[217] Sawyer, A., 'Judicial Manipulation of Customary Family Law in Tanzania' in Roberts, S. (ed.), *Law and the Family in Africa* (The Hague, 1977), 121–2.

famous *Tanistry case*[218] in the seventeenth century an English court ruled that the Irish custom of tanistry, which involved succession by the 'eldest and worthiest' male (*senior et dignissimus*) who was of the same name as the deceased, was unreasonable and hence inapplicable.[219] The English judges were accustomed to the principle of primogeniture and, as Allen has remarked—

... no modern reader can fail to detect in the case a deep-seated prejudice against a custom which outraged feudal law by admitting a gap in the seisin, and by excluding daughters from the inheritance on the failure of heirs male; indeed as Maine observes, 'the judges thoroughly knew that they were making a revolution, and they probably thought that they were substituting a civilised institution for a set of mischievous usages proper only for barbarians.'[220]

It has been contended by some theorists that when a person from one cultural background criticizes an aspect of another culture, such condemnation must inevitably be ethnocentric and in reality constitutes a form of 'cultural imperialism'.[221] This is the position taken by 'cultural relativists', who argue that most evaluations are relative to the cultural background out of which they arise[222] and that because of the great variety of cultural values there can be no moral absolutes; hence it is important to recognize that the object of criticism may well be considered perfectly moral in terms of its own system. The only means of escape from ethnocentricity, the argument continues, lies in the discovery of universally shared standards.[223]

This naturally raises the question whether the introduction of a human rights perspective, as a standard of comparison to be set alongside English law, can help to solve the problem of ethnocentricity. Can a convincing argument be made that the human rights dimension introduces an objective international standard against which other cultures may be validly tested? It will be recalled that the distinguished Nigerian jurist Elias commented in relation to the colonial 'repugnancy clause' that the dilemma for the courts was to 'strike a nice balance between what is reasonably tolerable and what is essentially below the minimum

[218] *Le Case de Tanistry* (1608) Davis 28.
[219] For clarification of what transpired in the case, see Newark, F., 'The Case of Tanistry' (1952) 9 *NILQ* 215. English law had, at least notionally, been brought to Ireland in 1171 by Henry II and in 1541 Henry VIII had taken the title 'King of Ireland'.
[220] *Law in the Making*, 7th ed. (Oxford, 1964), 144–5.
[221] See e.g. Renteln, A., 'Relativism and the Search for Human Rights' (1988) 90 *American Anthropologist* 56 at 63–4.
[222] See Herskovits, M., *Cultural Relativism: Perspectives in Cultural Pluralism* (New York, 1972), 14.
[223] See generally, Renteln, A., *International Human Rights: Universalism versus Relativism* (London, 1990); see also Milne, A., *Human Rights and Human Diversity* (Basingstoke, 1986).

standard of civilised values in the contemporary world'.[224] Can international human rights treaties be regarded as setting this 'minimum standard of civilised values'?

There is widespread acceptance of the view that the modern notion of human rights is at least derived from Western concepts and values. Pollis and Schwab robustly assert that human rights—

. . . as a twentieth-century concept and as embedded in the United Nations can be traced to the particular experiences of England, France and the United States . . . . Thus to argue that human rights has a standing which is universal in character is to contradict historical reality. What ought to be admitted by those who argue universality is that human rights as a Western concept based on natural right *should* become the standard upon which all nations ought to agree, recognising, however, that this is only our particular value system.[225]

The first formal modern document on the subject, the Universal Declaration of Human Rights 1948, was drawn up at a time when most developing countries were still colonial territories and thus not represented at the United Nations. Only forty-eight states voted in favour of the Declaration, out of the fifty-six states which were members of the organization at that time.[226] Western nations, especially the United States, were very much to the fore in the drafting process[227] and the Declaration can thus be portrayed, at least in its inception, as embodying essentially Western values.

Certainly, the European Convention, which was drawn up soon afterwards and was modelled on the Universal Declaration, operates exclusively within the confines of the member states of the Council of Europe and may therefore accurately be depicted as representing those Western values which form the basis of European liberal democracies. However, most of the rights and freedoms contained in both the Universal Declaration and in the European Convention are now mirrored in the International Covenant on Civil and Political Rights, a treaty whose terms were hammered out in the United Nations between 1948 and 1966 at a period when Western states were in the process of becoming merely a small minority. The Covenant has since been ratified by over 130 states, at least fifty of which can be described as developing countries. Furthermore, many of these fundamental human rights are also contained in the

---

[224] *British Colonial Law*, 104, quoted above, ch 2.

[225] Pollis, A. and Schwab, P. (eds), *Human Rights: Cultural and Ideological Perspectives* (New York, 1980), 4.

[226] No state voted against, but eight states abstained—Saudi Arabia, South Africa, and six Eastern European states.

[227] See Humphrey, J., 'The Universal Declaration of Human Rights: Its History, Impact and Juridical Character' in Ramcharan, B. (ed), *Human Rights: Thirty Years after the Universal Declaration* (The Hague, 1979), 23–4.

African Charter on Human and Peoples' Rights, which has been ratified by almost all African countries. As we have seen, several of the other international conventions have been ratified by a wide range of countries from different parts of the world.[228]

In the light of this, it might be argued with some conviction that international human rights norms should be accepted as establishing external standards which, if not necessarily universal,[229] are at least shared by a large number of peoples of different cultural backgrounds. However, some cultural relativists are wary of even using the widespread ratification of human rights treaties as a method of validating a set of shared standards. As Renteln has put it—

Even the claim that because political elites have ratified human rights documents human rights are therefore universal is suspect. There is no guarantee that the elites ratify for reasons other than political expediency. Moreover, it is far from clear that the values of elites correspond to the traditional value systems in the countries they represent.[230]

There would appear to be a number of objections to this analysis. First, while political 'expediency' may occasionally lead to the ratification of a human rights treaty, it is far more likely that most ratifications spring from political awareness and sensitivity. Governments are concerned to demonstrate, both to their own citizens and to the outside world, that they are conscious of the fundamental values which their own people share with the rest of mankind, or at least with those in the same geographical region. Renteln's reference to 'expediency' suggests that there is something to be gained politically from ratification, but it is hard to see what benefit a government can expect other than the respect of the public, at home and abroad. Almost certainly ratification will lead to a mass of practical problems in the future, as treaty obligations are breached by the state and news of violations leaks out. The state is then faced not only with adverse comment and charges of hypocrisy in the media but also with legal complaints which may well need to be addressed in an international forum. As Henkin has argued—

Acceptance, even hypocritical acceptance, is a commitment in principle to which one can be held accountable. Hypocrisy requires concealment that can be uncovered.[231]

---

[228] See above, pp 69–70.

[229] For denials of such universality, see generally Pollis and Schwab, ch 1; Renteln (1990), ch 2.

[230] Renteln, A., 'A Cross-Cultural Approach to Validating International Human Rights: The Case of Retribution Tied to Proportionality' in Cingranelli, D. (ed), *Human Rights: Theory and Measurement* (Basingstoke, 1988), 10.

[231] Henkin, L., 'The Universality of the Concept of Human Rights' (1989) 506 *Annals of the American Academy of Political and Social Sciences* 10 at 13.

Secondly, it is important to appreciate that human rights treaties represent formal, binding legal obligations, to which each state party has agreed to adhere in its treatment of those subject to its jurisdiction. In this sense it is obvious that the commitment must be made by the elite, in the form of the government, since this is the only way in which the state's international responsibility can be engaged. Other states are entitled to rely upon official declarations of such standards and can hardly be expected to go behind them in search of popular, non-elitist values as a reflection of that society's moral beliefs.

Thirdly, it is quite erroneous to focus upon 'traditional' value systems in the search for universal human rights. Profound changes have occurred in the attitudes and moral sentiments of people from all parts of the world during the course of the twentieth century and in particular since 1945. Western notions of individual freedom and worth have spread to other continents, as part of the general process of cultural globalization, and have received endorsement through the widespread ratification of human rights instruments, as well as through the practice of states in the form of constitution-making and the enactment of legislation. Indeed, it is arguable that the human rights enumerated in the Universal Declaration in 1948 now form part of customary international law as a result of the practice of states, especially in their participation in international organizations.[232] Banton has rightly emphasized that the spread of human rights ideals is now a vital factor in the equation, an aspect which Renteln tends to overlook—

It no longer makes sense to conceive of a world comprised of discrete societies. Almost all ethnic groups are now caught up in the desire to be modern and to enjoy a high standard of living. Elites play a crucial part in realising the unity of mankind. I doubt whether it is profitable to search for abstract principles when technological change is creating so many new moral problems and so many of them derive from conflicts of rights. Further progress in human rights depends not upon what has hitherto been accepted, but upon the skill and altruism of elites in seizing opportunities to persuade others that in given circumstances general rights must take precedence over particular rights.[233]

Howard has also argued cogently that human rights are a modern concept, universally applicable in principle, which has arisen as a result of the social evolution of the entire world towards state societies—

To seek an anthropologically based consensus on rights by surveying all known human cultures . . . is to confuse the concepts of rights, dignity, and justice. One can find affinities, analogues, and precedents for the actual content of

---

[232] See e.g. Humphrey in Ramcharan (1979), ch 1; Renteln (1990), 29; cf Cassese, A. *International Law in a Divided World* (Oxford, 1986), 299.
[233] See (1991) *New Community* 177.

internationally accepted human rights in many religious and cultural (geo-graphic and national) traditions; but the actual content of *human* rights . . . is particular and modern, and represents a radical rupture from the many status-based, non-egalitarian, and hierarchical societies of the past and present.[234]

Vincent too has expressed concern about whether it any longer makes sense to identify a distinct cultural context and background within which a people's moral values find their authentic definition—

The doctrine of cultural relativism asserts . . . that rules about morality vary from place to place. This seems an uncontroversial assertion. But if the general moral prescription drawn from it is that we should adopt in each place the rules of that place, this is clear and helpful only if the boundaries between one place and another are clear. When, as in the contemporary world, the downward seepage of a global cosmopolitan civilization has obscured even further cultural bound-aries that were previously hardly clear, this aspect of the doctrine of cultural relativism is misleading if not always chaotic.[235]

There is widespread support for the view that one of the main effects of the standards adopted in the United Nations has been to underline the universal validity of human rights.[236] The idea that people in the West should refrain from criticizing developing countries for violations of human rights, on the basis that their subjects do not qualify for protec-tion because of the traditional values of the society in question, betrays considerable arrogance. As Hatch has bluntly put it—'Although we may do harm by expressing judgments across cultural boundaries, we may do as much or more harm by failing to do so'.[237] Relativism may too easily contain a bias in favour of supporting the status quo, when there is no evidence that customary practices are viewed favourably within a particular society and when there may be a popular clamour for change.[238]

Donnelly has pointed out that arguments based on cultural relativism are far too often made by cynical political leaders, who have long abandoned their own traditional cultures and who employ the concept merely as a device to mask self-interest and arbitrary rule—

We must not be misled by complaints of the inappropriateness of 'western' human rights made by repressive regimes whose practices have at best only

---

[234] 'Dignity, Community and Human Rights' in An-Na'im, A. (ed), *Human Rights in Cross-Cultural Perspectives* (Philadelphia, 1992) 81.

[235] Vincent, R., *Human Rights and International Relations* (Cambridge, 1986), 54.

[236] See Ramcharan, (1979), 11, 213; Meron, T., *Human Rights and Humanitarian Norms as Customary Law* (Oxford, 1989), ch II. The same point emerges clearly in the 'Bangalore Principles', the product of a high level Commonwealth judicial colloquium: see Common-wealth Secretariat, *Developing Human Rights Jurisprudence* (London, 1988), ix-x.

[237] *Culture and Morality: The Relativity of Values in Anthropology* (New York, 1983), 136.

[238] Ibid, 116–7, 134.

the most tenuous connection to the indigenous culture; communitarian rhetoric too often cloaks the depredations of corrupt and often westernized or deracinated elites.[239]

Vincent argues that tolerance derived from cultural relativism can be interpreted as 'the cowardice of moral abstention'[240] and, as another commentator has aptly put it, sceptical relativism can only lead to 'sub-standards for sub-humans'.[241] Arguments based on cultural preservation are surely no more acceptable today than those used in the past (and now discredited), which relied upon national sovereignty as a defence to human rights violations. Even so, it is important ultimately to recognize that several of the principles which are found in widely ratified human rights treaties may well not reflect universal values. For example, millions of children in a large number of countries are currently subjected to genital mutilation[242] and to exploitative and unhealthy labour, in the belief that these practices are either perfectly harmless or else positively beneficial for the upbringing of the children themselves.[243] Similarly, Islam apparently precludes the possibility of Muslims changing their faith and undergoing religious conversion, upon pain of possible punishment by death for apostasy.[244] Examples such as these should certainly make one pause for thought before asserting too categorically that there are universal sentiments about the contents of fundamental human rights. A variety of different conclusions can nevertheless be drawn from recognizing such examples of diversity in moral values and cultural standards.

[239] 'Cultural Relativism and Universal Human Rights' (1984) 6 *Human Rights Quarterly* 400 at 411.   [240] At 55.
[241] Ramcharan, 213. For powerful critiques of relativism, see Teson, F., 'International Human Rights and Cultural Relativism' (1985) 25 *Virginia Journal of International Law* 869; Mayer, A., *Islam and Human Rights: Tradition and Politics* (London, 1991), ch 1; Howard, R., 'Cultural Absolutism and the Nostalgia for Community' (1993) 15 *Human Rights Quarterly* 315.
[242] See e.g. Dorkenoo, E. and Elworthy, S., *Female Genital Mutilation: Proposals for Change* (London, 1992); Brennan, K., 'The Influence of Cultural Relativism on International Human Rights Law: Female Circumcision as a Case Study' (1989) 7 *Law and Inequality* 367.
[243] See Renteln (1990), 56–60.
[244] According to sound Islamic tradition (*sunna*) the Prophet Muhammad said—'kill the person who changes his religion'; see Al-Bukhari, *Sahih* (Beirut, nd), Part 9, 19. The Qur'an itself is far from consistent on the subject—compare *Surah* II: 256 'Let there be no compulsion in religion' with *Surahs* II: 6–7; III: 177 and IX: 74, which refer to 'grievous punishment' for apostasy. See also Mayer (1991), ch 8; Khadduri, M., *War and Peace in the Law of Islam* (Baltimore, 1955), 149–52; An-Na'im, A., 'The Islamic Law of Apostacy and its Modern Applicability: A case from the Sudan' (1986) 16 *Religion* 197; An-Na'im, A., 'Religious Minorities under Islamic Law and the Limits of Cultural Relativism,' (1987) 9 *Human Rights Quarterly* 1 at 8; Akhtar, S., *Be Careful with Muhammad* (London, 1989), ch 4, especially at 71–2, where it is argued that apostasy is only punishable by death if it is 'aggravated' by treachery or by ideological enmity to Muslims or the Islamic state or by any attempt to bring Islam into serious disrepute etc.

First, by no means all versions of cultural relativism preclude criticism of the practices and beliefs of other communities. Renteln has argued, for instance, that relativism does not necessarily force its adherents to foreswear moral criticism, nor does it automatically prescribe a policy of toleration, as is commonly supposed.[245] What it does require is merely an open appreciation that any criticism is being offered from the moral perspective of the critic's own cultural values, or at least from values external to the society whose norms are being criticized. In this sense such criticism may be said to be subjective and ethnocentric rather than objective and universal. Renteln argues that acknowledging the ethnocentricity of criticism does not necessarily render it impotent, adding— 'It is better to be honest about the local source of the criticism than to pretend it is universal'.[246] Hence, the first conclusion to extract from the relativist approach may simply be that critics of other cultures should not be too frightened by accusations of ethnocentricity, especially if the standards being employed as the basis of criticism are not merely those of the critic's own society but are shared by many other countries and peoples and are formally declared in widely ratified international conventions. Relativism can thus be seen as descriptive rather than prescriptive, emphasizing the extent to which people unconsciously adopt the standards of their own culture rather than dictating a tolerant response simply because cultural standards differ.[247] It is not a case of *'tout comprendre, c'est tout pardonner'*. Otherwise *apartheid* should have been condoned on the basis that it had become an integral part of the culture of white society in South Africa. The issue of tolerance is a quite separate question and is a matter of policy, the limits of which have already been discussed in Chapter 1. Misconceptions about the precise connection between relativism and tolerance have arisen simply because the theory of relativism can sometimes usefully be employed as a vehicle for the encouragement of a broadly respectful and tolerant approach, but this is certainly not a necessary consequence.[248]

A second possible conclusion to draw from the relativist approach is that any attempted identification of the moral values of different societies may be a somewhat artificial process. In Chapter 1 the question of societal values was addressed in the context of a search for shared minimum standards in Britain. It emerged that it was difficult if not impossible to draw any conclusions about the existence of a popular consensus about underlying moral and political principles, even in a democracy. It was therefore safer to envisage the existence of a formal acceptance of such values on the basis of institutional structures, rather

[245] (1990), ch 3.   [246] (1990), at 77.   [247] Ibid, 73–5.
[248] See generally, Hatch, chs 4, 5.

than strive to locate a genuine consensus on the basis of public opinion polls and social surveys.

A third approach to relativism is to attempt to work out a balance between the desire to accord a wide range of human rights the status of universal norms on the basis of formal declarations and international treaties, on the one hand, and the need to recognize at least some variations on the grounds of cultural differences, on the other. Donnelly, for example, has suggested that one might start with a presumption of universality, yet be prepared to countenance limited deviations, for instance through a process of interpretation and the creation of a small number of exceptions of a minor nature.[249] He argues that the Universal Declaration represents 'a minimal response to the convergence of basic crosscultural human values'[250] and hence that the rights outlined there should be presumed to apply universally. It is far from easy, however, to identify precise areas in which deviations and exceptions should be countenanced.

Such an approach would have important practical implications for the implementation of the provisions of international agreements. As a party to the major human rights treaties, the United Kingdom is bound to comply with their terms and could not plead as a defence to an alleged breach that it was seeking to give effect to a minority cultural practice in order to avoid a charge of ethnocentricity. However, it might well be possible to argue that minority cultural values are relevant in interpreting precisely what content should be given to the particular rights guaranteed. In several of its decisions, the European Court of Human Rights has indicated that local community attitudes and beliefs concerning, for example, corporal punishment and homosexuality, are relevant in the application of the European Convention.[251] Even so, fairly rigorous 'European' standards have been upheld in the light of practices adopted in the majority of state parties.[252]

Greater flexibility can probably be expected in interpreting the International Covenant on Civil and Political Rights, both on the basis of the inclusion of Article 27 and on the ground that this treaty was intended to apply in a wide range of economic, social, and cultural environments.[253] However, a clear indication that such arguments cannot be pressed too far is provided by the observations of the United Nations Human Rights

---

[249] (1984) 6 *Human Rights Quarterly* 400.   [250] At 416–7.

[251] See e.g. *Tyrer v UK* (1978) 2 EHRR 1; *Dudgeon v UK* (1981) 4 EHRR 149; *Campbell and Cosans v UK* (1982) 4 EHRR 293.

[252] Ibid; see also *Inze v Austria* (1987) Ser A 126, where the Court held that the traditional moral attitudes and convictions of the rural population of Carinthia could not justify discrimination against illegitimate children in the inheritance of farms.

[253] See generally, Australian Law Reform Commission, *Report No. 31: The Recognition of Aboriginal Customary Laws* (Canberra, 1986), 1, 126–41.

Committee in its consideration in 1991 of the first periodic report submitted by the Sudan, pursuant to its obligations as a party to the International Covenant on Civil and Political Rights.[254] Two of the questions raised by the Committee were whether the Sudanese Penal Code, which is now based on Muslim *shari'ah* law, was not discriminatory in certain respects and whether it applied equally to members of the non-Muslim population. Other questions addressed the permissibility under the Penal Code of public flogging, crucifixion, and amputations and whether the crime of apostasy by a Muslim was compatible with the right to freedom of religion. In responding to the Committee, the Sudanese representative argued that human rights 'was a field in which there was a risk of partiality or double standards, particularly with regard to the treatment of a number of Third World countries'.[255] He claimed that countries should be freely permitted to choose their own legal systems based on their convictions, traditions, and customs and he contended that, in the light of the increased emphasis being accorded to the *shari'ah* in Islamic countries, there should be a review of the rights contained in international human rights instruments because these had been adopted prior to this development.[256] Many of the punishments prescribed by Islamic law could not be considered cruel or degrading because they had been imposed by God. Apostasy was punishable by death because it was equivalent to treason in endangering the fabric of Muslim society.

This line of argument provoked a sharp retort from the Committee.[257] The Committee insisted that it viewed Islam as a progressive religion, which did not pose an obstacle to the implementation of the Covenant in Islamic countries. Many states in the Islamic world had participated in the drafting of the Covenant and, if certain of its provisions had been deemed irreconcilable with Islamic law, states parties could have entered reservations. Furthermore, the Committee declared—

. . . although a State might defend its culture and national religion, in doing so, it could not deviate from the fundamental common values in the Covenant, which were applicable to the entire international community. Such values should, moreover, be reflected in domestic legislation.[258]

The Committee felt, however, that it ought to be possible for the Sudanese authorities and the Committee jointly to find a way of reconciling the Sudan's freedom to live within a social system of its own choice with the Committee's obligation to ensure respect for human rights. On the other hand, certain punishments under the Sudanese Penal Code did constitute 'cruel or degrading treatment' contrary to the Covenant, and

---

[254] *Report of the Human Rights Committee*, GA Off Rec, 46th session, Supplement No. 40 (New York, 1991) 124–8.   [255] At 126.
[256] Ibid.   [257] At 127–8.   [258] At 127.

the provisions on apostasy also violated the Covenant's guarantee of freedom of religion. While the Committee could seek to take into account various cultural factors in its interpretation of the provisions of the Covenant, it was 'obliged to apply the principles of the Covenant without any distinctions among State parties.'[259]

A similar approach is to be found in the following statement in the Vienna Declaration and Programme of Action,[260] adopted by consensus at the World Conference on Human Rights held in 1993—

All human rights are universal, indivisible and inter-dependent and inter-related. The international community must treat human rights globally in a fair and equal manner on the same footing, and with the same emphasis. While the significance of national and regional particularities and various historical, cultural and religious backgrounds must be borne in mind, it is the duty of States, regardless of their political, economic and cultural systems, to promote and protect all human rights and fundamental freedoms.[261]

CONCLUSIONS

Extensive provision for the protection of minorities was established under the League of Nations between 1919 and 1939. A legal regime of cultural and religious pluralism was created, with minority groups being accorded specific rights, which allowed them to preserve their separate identities through recognition of the importance of their languages, faiths, schools, holy days, and even personal laws. These specific rights were not regarded as affording privileges to minority groups, but rather as guaranteeing them genuine equality or 'equality in fact', in addition to the assurance of non-discrimination in a formal sense. The ultimate political failure of the League of Nations system inevitably brought the minorities' protection regime to an end, but the consequence of this was not the abandonment of the notion of protecting minorities, but rather the extension of legal guarantees for all through the universal promotion of human rights. The Universal Declaration of Human Rights was proclaimed by the United Nations in 1948 and the rights outlined there were transformed into binding treaty provisions in the two International Covenants, which were opened for signature in 1966 and came into force ten years later. Article 27 of the International Covenant on Civil and Political Rights provided the first explicit guarantee of the rights of members of ethnic, religious, and linguistic minorities to the

---

[259] At 128.   [260] Reprinted in (1993) 14 *Human Rights LJ* 352.
[261] Para 5; for further discussion, see Beetham, D. (ed.), *Politics and Human Rights* (Oxford, 1995), 86–8, 204–18.

preservation of their separate cultural identities in a treaty intended to be of universal application. It is, however, a rather weak article. Its vague and negative phrasing leaves the extent of its application largely to the discretion of states. While it probably does not yet represent customary international law and therefore only binds states that have ratified the Covenant, Article 27 can be seen as part of the general movement in international law towards a universal norm of ensuring legal respect for cultural differences through international guarantees of the 'right to be different'.

The European Convention, drafted in the immediate aftermath of the 1939–45 war, followed the pattern of the Universal Declaration and did not contain a specific article on the protection of minorities. However, many of its provisions indirectly safeguard the rights of members of minority groups. Moreover, the article on non-discrimination does not preclude state parties from differentiating between ethnic and religious groups with a view to protecting minorities, provided the distinction has an objective and reasonable justification and is not imposed in an arbitrary fashion. Recently, the Council of Europe has taken steps to try to strengthen legal safeguards for national minorities through the preparation of a possible new protocol to the European Convention and the completion of the Framework Convention for the Protection of National Minorities, the latter being open to ratification by non-members of the Council as well as members. Even so, in the liberal tradition the notion of group rights has tended to be viewed with suspicion, partly in the light of its association with arbitrary distinctions based on racial classifications (as in the case of *apartheid*) but also through anxiety about the possible conflicts between such group rights and the human rights of individuals and how these might be resolved. International human rights law has endeavoured to tackle this potentiality for conflict by means of a balanced and flexible response, which accords primacy to the choice of individuals while recognizing the reality of the collective interest which lies behind the formal rights guaranteed to individuals.

Rights often appear to conflict with one another and one person's claim to freedom of expression, for example, may clash with the assertion by others that their religious freedom has been violated, as happened in the 'Rushdie Affair'. International human rights law has developed techniques of interpretation designed to resolve such conflicts and ultimately bodies such as the European Commission and Court of Human Rights can give definitive rulings on controversial issues.

There may be significant advantages to be gained from employing human rights standards embodied in widely ratified international conventions to deflect charges of ethnocentricity, when English law takes exception to cultural practices and refuses to countenance them on the grounds that they are unconscionable or contrary to public policy. While the doctrines of cultural relativism are useful in alerting critics of other cultures to the need to be aware of the limits of their own perspectives, the human rights dimension certainly widens these perspectives. In any event, cultural relativism does not invariably demand the approval or toleration of alien traditions. Broadly speaking, the habit of bearing in mind international human rights provisions is likely to be beneficial to minority communities since the treaties and conventions in question accord several rights of major importance for the continued flourishing of ethnic groups.

PART II

Case Studies in Relation to Particular Groups

4

Jews: The Controversy Over Religious Methods of Slaughter

It seems probable that there were a few Jews in Britain in Roman times,[1] but the earliest establishment of Jewish communities here occurred in the wake of the Norman Conquest.[2] French Jews crossed the Channel to operate as financiers and moneylenders in England and they played an important role not only as bankers to the Crown but also in expanding and developing an unsophisticated economy.[3] As usurers, they attracted considerable popular hostility and regularly needed royal protection. On the other hand, a succession of Angevin kings gravely exploited them until the time eventually arrived when they were no longer of much economic value to the Crown,[4] whereupon they were banished from the realm by a decree from Edward I in 1290, an act which amounted to a clear abuse of the royal prerogative.[5] During this medieval period of settlement the Jews had been granted a large measure of autonomy in the legal regulation of their internal affairs, being entitled to rely upon the application of Talmudic law in their own courts in matters such as marriage, succession, and contracts.[6] However, their total numbers were small, never exceeding 5,000.[7]

The middle of the seventeenth century witnessed the re-settlement of Jews in England, following representations to Oliver Cromwell seeking their re-admission. Although Cromwell gave no formal permission for them to re-enter the country, in the light of formidable English opposition, he personally favoured their return (for both political and economic reasons) and he intimated informally that if they behaved inconspicuously no official action would be taken against them.[8] No fundamental

---

[1] See Applebaum, S., 'Were there Jews in Roman Britain?' (1951–2) XVII *Transactions of the Jewish Historical Society of England* 189.

[2] See generally, Roth, C., *A History of the Jews in England* (Oxford, 1941), 1–131.

[3] See Freedman, M. (ed.), *A Minority in Britain* (London, 1955), 7–8.

[4] In 1275 the statute *de Iudaismo* had imposed a ban on usury by Jews, which greatly reduced their resources.

[5] See Dummett, A. and Nicol, A., *Subjects, Citizens, Aliens and Others* (London, 1990), 31–2.

[6] Roth, 10, 116–7.

[7] Brook, S., *The Club: The Jews of Modern Britain* (London, 1989), 15.

[8] Roth, 154–66; Freedman, 10–11.

change in this tacit arrangement occurred upon the Restoration of the Monarchy in 1660. However, since Charles II was of a tolerant disposition in religious matters this emboldened the Jewish community to function more openly.[9] They soon leased from Christian owners both a house for use as a synagogue and a field to serve as a burial ground. Samuel Pepys was able to gain admittance to the synagogue and he observed worship there, without any difficulty, in 1663.[10] When, during the following year, the heads of the congregation were molested at their worship and threatened with prosecution under the laws against religious non-conformity, the wardens of the synagogue successfully petitioned the Crown for protection. The King declared that he had given no orders for their molestation and announced that they could expect the same favour as they had formerly enjoyed, so long as they conducted themselves 'peaceably and quietly with due obedience to His Majesty's Laws and without scandal to his government'.[11] This royal dispensation afforded the Jews valuable security, but it needed to be reinforced in 1673 when leaders of the Jewish community in London were indicted on a charge of riot for simply joining together in an act of public worship.[12] A true bill of indictment was found against them by a grand jury and this prompted a further petition to the Crown on their part. This time the King in Council responded with an order that the Attorney General should stop all proceedings against them by entering a *nolle prosequi*. This was duly done and their freedom to worship was thus upheld.

A few years earlier Jewish witnesses in proceedings before the Court of King's Bench had been permitted by the Chief Justice to take an oath on the Old Testament[13] (as in medieval times[14]) and in a subsequent case the venue of the proceedings was altered from London to Middlesex because all the sittings in London were on Saturdays and one of the witnesses was unwilling to testify on the Jewish sabbath.[15] While a new era of religious toleration was ushered in with the Glorious Revolution of 1688, the provisions of the Toleration Act of that year did not extend to Jews and they had to wait until 1846 for formal legislative confirmation of the *de facto* freedom of worship allowed them by the Stuart kings almost two centuries earlier.[16]

---

[9] See generally, Henriques, H., *The Jews and the English Law* (Oxford, 1908), 125–52.

[10] *The Diary of Samuel Pepys*, R. Latham and W. Matthews eds, (London, 1971), IV, 335.

[11] Henriques, 147–8.

[12] Henriques 2, 149–50. A similar order was issued by James II in 1685 when an attempt was made to prosecute members of a Jewish congregation under the non-conformity laws—see Henriques, 3, 153–4.   [13] *Robeley v Langston* (1668) 2 Keb 314.

[14] See *Omychund v Barker* (1744) Willes 538 at 543.

[15] *Barker v Warren* (1677) 2 Mod Rep 271.

[16] Religious Disabilities Act 1846; see generally, Henriques, 158–76.

Until the middle of the nineteenth century, at least in theory, many forms of employment were closed to observant Jews because the holders of a great variety of offices were required, by law, to subscribe to Christian oaths before taking up their posts.[17] This applied to all Crown appointments and most professions, as well as to the retail trade in the City of London. Ultimately these religious obstacles, many of which could in practice be circumvented with little difficulty from 1728 onwards, were abolished by statutes such as the Jewish Disabilities Removal Act 1845 and the Jewish Relief Act 1858. The traditional requirement that Members of Parliament should subscribe to a Christian oath of allegiance before being allowed to take their seats led to a lengthy struggle before the first Jewish MP, Baron Lionel de Rothschild, eventually took his seat in 1858, some eleven years after he had been duly elected.[18] It was not, therefore, until the mid-nineteenth century that Jewish 'emancipation' was finally achieved.

Between 1881 and 1905 around 100,000 Jews fled to this country from pogroms and political and economic restrictions in Russia and other parts of Eastern Europe, adding very substantially to the existing Jewish community of about 60,000.[19] The large numbers involved alarmed the existing settled community, whose members had successfully integrated into mainstream English society and who were fearful of the impact of such a dramatic influx of impoverished, Yiddish-speaking refugees.[20] Indeed the Anglo-Jewish 'establishment' took active steps to try to dissuade too many refugees from settling permanently here, encouraging them either to travel on to the United States or else to return to Eastern Europe. The British government was also concerned at the situation and eventually the Aliens Act 1905 was enacted, giving immigration officers power to refuse entry to 'undesirable' immigrants.[21] However, its provisions had been considerably softened during its passage through Parliament[22] and the only aliens defined as 'undesirable' were those who had arrived as passengers on 'immigrant ships'[23] and were unable to support themselves and their dependants, or were mentally ill or were likely to become a charge on the rates or a danger to the public on account of their ill health, or had previously been expelled from Britain following the commission of a criminal offence.[24] Moreover, lack of means or likelihood

---

[17] Henriques, 198–208.   [18] See Henriques, 265–305.

[19] See generally, Gartner, L., *The Jewish Immigrant in England 1870–1914*, 2nd ed. (London, 1976); Lipman, V., *A History of the Jews in Britain since 1858* (Leicester, 1990), ch 3. Many Russians blamed the Jews for the assassination of Tsar Alexander II in 1881, although only one of the five conspirators was Jewish.   [20] Brook, 22–3.

[21] S 1(1).   [22] See Dummett and Nicol, 103–4.

[23] For reasons of administrative convenience, 'immigrant ships' were defined as those carrying more than twenty alien steerage passengers, see s 8(2).   [24] S 1(3).

of being a charge on the rates were excluded as grounds for refusing entry to political or religious refugees.[25]

By the outbreak of war in 1939 over 50,000 Jews from Germany, Austria, and Czechoslovakia had also sought refuge here from Hitler's anti-semitism and Nazi expansionism.[26] This brought the total Jewish population in this country up to around 400,000, but since the early 1950s the size of the Jewish community has declined by around a quarter to an estimated 300,000 today.[27]

THE ATTITUDES OF THE MAJORITY COMMUNITY

At the end of the twelfth century Jewish residents were far from popular with their Christian neighbours and in several instances massacres and other forms of persecution took place. Partly this can be attributed to jealousy at the comparative prosperity of many Jews, often at the apparent expense of those who needed to borrow from them and had to pay a high rate of interest. Passions were especially inflamed at the time of the Crusades, with many Christians feeling that it was wrong for 'Jews to enjoy their ill-gotten riches undisturbed at home, while the soldiers of the Cross were facing untold dangers to combat Moslem infidels overseas'.[28] In 1190 outbreaks of violence against Jews occurred in several towns and cities, with the worst excesses being perpetrated at York where all the Jewish inhabitants died and their attackers then proceeded to the Cathedral to make a bonfire of the bonds of indebtedness which the Jews had deposited with the sacristan.[29]

The medieval period also witnessed a number of occasions on which Jews were accused, without the slightest justification, of the ritual murder of Christian children.[30] Vengeance was then wrought upon the innocent suspects. Following a decision of the Lateran Council of 1215, Jews were forced to wear a 'badge' to distinguish them from the rest of the population. Initially this had to take the form of a piece of white cloth or parchment worn on the outer garment, but in 1275 Edward I's statute *de Iudaismo* stipulated that the 'badge of shame' should be of yellow taffeta, six fingers long and three inches broad, and should be worn over the heart by all Jews over the age of seven.[31]

Turning to the period after the Resettlement, it seems to have been the general view of commentators that, in contrast with many other coun-

---

[25] S 1(3).   [26] Brook, 31–2.
[27] See Waterman, S. and Kosmin, B., *British Jewry in the Eighties* (London, 1986), 6–7; Massil, S. (ed), *The Jewish Year Book 1996* (London, 1996), 183.   [28] Roth, 20.
[29] Ibid, 20–4.   [30] Ibid, 9, 13, 55–6, 78, 90.   [31] Ibid, 95–6.

tries, anti-semitism has been of only minimal significance in Britain.[32] Leading historians have been at pains to stress the tolerance of the majority community and the satisfactory way in which Jews have generally come to be accepted as full members of society.[33] Much emphasis was laid upon the valuable contributions made by Jews to their adopted country and hence the degree to which they had earned the right to emancipation and civil equality. Insofar as obstacles had been placed in their path, these could not be attributed to any widespread hostility on the part of either the government or the public at large. Writing about the first half of the eighteenth century, for example, Roth felt able to claim—

. . . from the moment of the Resettlement there was probably no country in Europe in which the Jews received better treatment than England. Even in Holland they were excluded from certain towns and provinces, and in Turkey they received only the restricted rights of unbelievers. In Germany and Italy the Ghetto system still prevailed; from Spain, Portugal, and much of France, there was complete and even barbarous exclusion; Polish Jewry was terrorized and almost rightless; Danish Jewry was insignificant. In England, on the other hand, the Jews were under the protection of the law, could settle anywhere they pleased, and enjoyed virtual social equality. Not infrequently, indeed, some zealot published a conversionist pamphlet in which their beliefs were reviled, or a fanatical antiquarian advocated the enforcement of the restrictive legislation which existed on the statute-book. But that was all. Only on one or two isolated occasions was there any mob violence—never, however, receiving governmental sanction or connivance, or resulting in loss of life.[34]

However, another leading scholar of Anglo-Jewry, James Parkes, has drawn attention to the underlying feelings of the majority community—

On the whole it must be said that the Jewish community was accepted because such acceptance was in accord with the English spirit of liberty, and not because there was any general affection for Jews as such. On the whole they were regarded with contempt, and the more ostentatious religions continued to regard them with hostility as the enemies of the Christian faith well into the nineteenth century.[35]

Turning to more modern times, popular anti-semitic sentiment was aroused both during the period of immigration from Russia at the turn of the twentieth century (culminating in the restrictions imposed in the Aliens Act 1905) and in the depression of the 1930s when Mosley and his British Union of Fascists were able to whip up hostility towards the Jews, especially in the East End of London. Concern was expressed at

---

[32] See e.g. Brook, ch 28. Cf Kushner, T., 'The impact of British anti-semitism 1918–1945' in Cesarani, D. (ed), *The Making of Modern Anglo-Jewry* (Oxford, 1990), 191.
[33] See e.g. Roth, 267.   [34] Ibid, 202–3.   [35] In Freedman (ed), 49.

the intrusion of an alien culture, as well as at the economic competitive-
ness of people who relied on self-help, hard work, self-denial, and
deferred gratification.[36] In both instances, however, no major cata-
strophe occurred and the crisis passed off reasonably quickly. Parkes
thus felt able to conclude in quite sanguine terms—

... there are shadows on the picture. But they are not enough to reverse the
general verdict that the Jew in England has found more kindness than hostility,
more understanding than contempt, more opportunities than restriction.[37]

Two contemporary historians take a rather different view. Holmes has
concluded from a study principally relating to the sphere of public
affairs and organized politics from 1876 to 1939 that there was a clear
tradition of anti-semitism in British society during this period[38] and
Kushner's researches suggest that this tradition persisted throughout
the Second World War.[39]

So far as the situation today is concerned, there would appear to be a
number of different strands in any continuing hostility on the part of
members of the majority community. First, there still seems to be a
feeling among some people (probably confined mainly to the older
generation) that despite the length of their presence in this country the
Jews are essentially a separate nation of foreigners and can never be
truly British.[40] This anachronistic attitude may have been somewhat
reinforced by the creation of the State of Israel and by the impression
that since most British Jews strongly support Israel they may have
somewhat divided loyalties. Secondly, a quite legitimate revulsion at
some of Israel's recent actions, such as its invasion of Lebanon in 1982
and its oppressive conduct in the former 'occupied territories' of West
Bank and Gaza, may extend in the general direction of Anglo-Jewry
simply because the leaders of the Jewish community in Britain usually
seem prepared to defend Israeli policies at all costs.[41] In dealings with its
neighbours and with the Palestinians, Israel has often displayed a
'macho arrogance' (to use the words of Sir Evelyn de Rothschild[42])
and the excesses of Zionism are distasteful to many in modern Britain.
The full dimensions and implications of the Holocaust remain largely
unacknowledged in the mainstream of British thought[43] and although
there is widespread support for the State of Israel, public opinion here is
greatly exercised about the plight of the Palestinians in their search for a

---

[36] See Holmes, C., *John Bull's Island: Immigration and British Society 1871–1971*
(Basingstoke, 1988), 65–73, 296–7.   [37] In Freedman (ed), 51.
[38] *Anti-Semitism in British Society, 1876–1939* (London, 1979).
[39] *The Persistence of Prejudice: Antisemitism in British Society During the Second World War*
(Manchester, 1989).   [40] See e.g. Brook, chs 27–30.
[41] Brook, chs 26 and 27.   [42] Quoted in Brook, 377.   [43] Brook, 421.

genuinely independent homeland. There is a widespread impression that Israeli intransigence continues to confound their aspirations. Thirdly, among a very small section of the majority community here a rabid antisemitism persists and appears to be rising, as the following report reveals—

... between 1984 and 1992 there was an 85% increase in the reporting of antisemitic incidents—incidents such as physical attacks on Jewish individuals, desecration of Jewish cemeteries, arson attacks on Jewish property, and daubing of graffiti on Jewish buildings. In the same period there was an increase in the dissemination of virulent antisemitic literature sent through the post to Jewish individuals and organisations.[44]

On the other hand, another recent report, based on interviews with a representative sample of the British population, concluded that feelings about Jews were 'markedly positive and compare very favourably with views in other countries', adding that 'a large plurality of Britons see anti-Semitism as a negligible factor in British society today,' albeit that it was thought to be more likely to increase rather than decease over the next few years.[45] Only 8 per cent of those interviewed considered that Jews behaved in a manner which provoked hostility in this country, though 12 per cent would prefer not to have Jews as neighbours.[46] As we shall see, these figures are far lower than those for some of the other minorities discussed in this book.

While a few in Britain may still regard Jews as foreigners, the general attitude appears to be that the members of Anglo-Jewry have, over the centuries, integrated particularly well into British society so that today they appear almost indistinguishable from other citizens. Many of them have chosen to assimilate of their own accord, by becoming less observant of their religion and its traditions, by letting their synagogue membership and attendance lapse, and by marrying outside the community.[47] Indeed the number of those in Britain who acknowledge themselves to be Jews is in overall decline.[48] Within the Jewish community itself there are, of course, a variety of degrees of orthodoxy.[49] At one end of the spectrum stand the small ultra-orthodox communities such as the Chasidim, who maintain the same lifestyle as their forbears did two centuries ago in Poland. At the other end are found those who are

---

[44] Runnymede Commission on Antisemitism, *A Very Light Sleeper: The persistence and dangers of antisemitism* (London, 1994), 11.
[45] Golub, J., *British Attitudes toward Jews and other Minorities* (New York, 1993), 5.
[46] Ibid, 3, 10, 18.
[47] Brook, *passim*, especially ch 30; around one-third of Jews are not affiliated to any synagogue or major Jewish organization (at 428).
[48] Brook, 430; Waterman and Kosmin, 6–7.
[49] See Brook, chs 4–11; Lipman, 240–1.

members of Reform or Liberal synagogues, the progressive wing of Anglo-Jewry, accounting for nearly a quarter of all Jews in Britain. In the centre lies by far the largest group under the banner of the United Synagogue, a federation of orthodox Ashkenazi synagogues representing those Jews with their origins in northern Europe. The Sephardi communities, derived from southern Europe, North Africa, and the Middle East, maintain their own separate institutions.

The fact that the more orthodox and observant Jews respect their own sabbath,[50] worship in their own synagogues, swear oaths in court on the Old Testament, run their own schools, and celebrate their marriages in accordance with Jewish law[51] does not appear to cause any resentment on the part of the majority community. However, one particular area of Jewish religious practice, the slaughter of animals for food by the method known as *shechita*, has stirred up considerable controversy over the years and continues to attract public criticism. As will be seen, the complaints voiced by animal welfare campaigners have in the past sometimes been contaminated by anti-semitic sentiments,[52] and this aspect needs to be borne in mind as part of any appraisal of the current legal position.

THE PRACTICE OF *SHECHITA*

For observant Jews, at least among the more orthodox members of the community,[53] meat is only regarded as fit for consumption (*kosher*) if the animal has been slaughtered in a particular manner.[54] This involves cutting its throat with an exceptionally sharp knife, in rapid uninterrupted movements which sever its windpipe and gullet, as well as its carotid arteries and jugular veins, the main blood vessels supplying and draining its head and brain. The speed of the incision produces a very sudden and substantial fall in blood pressure which quickly results in a loss of consciousness. Death then soon intervenes.

---

[50] In *Tower Hamlets Council v Rabin* (1989) ICR 693 at 695 Wood J commented that 'some 17% of Jews are orthodox and sabbath observing'.

[51] On Jewish marriages, see ch 6 below.

[52] See Kushner, T., 'Stunning Intolerance: a century of opposition to religious slaughter' (1989) 133 *Jewish Quarterly* 16.

[53] Most members of the Reform and Liberal synagogues do not keep strictly to the dietary laws (*kashrut*). A recent survey of the practices of 1,350 Jewish women in England from a variety of backgrounds found that 43 per cent purchased all their meat from *kosher* butchers, but there appears to be a greater willingness to eat non-*kosher* food outside the home—see Schmool, M. and Miller, S., *Women in the Jewish Community: Survey Report* (London, 1994), 100–5.

[54] See generally, Horowitz, G., *The Spirit of Jewish Law* (New York, 1953), 115–7; Homa, B., *Shechita* (London, 1967); Lawrence, J., *Some Aspects of Shechita* (London, 1971).

An essential characteristic of *shechita* is that the animal's blood begins to drain away prior to its unconsciousness. In the Book of Genesis it is written—'But flesh with the life thereof, which is the blood thereof shall ye not eat'[55] and Leviticus contains a similar injunction against the consumption of blood.[56] Although there is no Biblical description of *shechita*, there is a reference to it in Deuteronomy in the following verse—

If the place which the Lord thy God hath chosen to put his name there be too far from thee, then thou shalt kill of thy herd and of thy flock, which the Lord hath given thee, as I have commanded thee, and thou shalt eat in thy gates whatsoever thy soul lusteth after.[57]

The words 'as I have commanded thee' imply the existence of a divinely ordained method and orthodox Jews have, since time immemorial, regarded *shechita* as a matter of legal obligation.

The person entrusted with the task of *shechita*, known as a *shochet*, is as much a religious functionary as a slaughterman. He must be someone of high moral character and with consistent religious practice and observance. He is trained for the office, he has to qualify by means of an examination, and he has to be certified and appointed by the appropriate religious authorities.[58] As an observant Jew he would, of course, be very well aware of the numerous scriptural provisions enjoining kindness to animals.[59]

THE LEGAL EXEMPTION AND ITS ORIGINS

The Slaughterhouses Act 1974 lays down that as a standard practice no animal in a slaughterhouse or knacker's yard shall be slaughtered otherwise than instantaneously by means of a mechanically operated instrument in proper repair, unless it has first been instantaneously rendered insensible to pain until death supervenes, by a process of stunning or such other means as are prescribed by regulations made under the terms of the Act.[60] In practical terms, this means that animals being slaughtered for meat must be made unconscious before they are bled. This is achieved either by mechanical means in the form of a captive-bolt pistol or through electric shock treatment. This statutory provision applies to cattle, sheep, goats, swine, and horses. A similar provision in the Slaughter of Poultry

---

[55] Ch 9, v 4.   [56] Ch 7, v 26.   [57] Ch 12, v 21.

[58] For an account of the historical development of the supervision of *shechita* in England, see Hyamson, A., *The London Board for Shechita 1804–1954* (London, 1954).

[59] See e.g. Exodus, ch 23, v 12; Deuteronomy, ch 22, v 4, 10 and ch 25, v 4; Proverbs, ch 12, v 10.   [60] S 36(1).

Act 1967 applies to the slaughter, for purposes of preparation for sale for human consumption, of domestic fowl and turkeys kept in captivity.[61] The objective is, of course, in both instances to try to ensure a humane method of slaughter and any person who slaughters an animal or bird in contravention of these provisions commits a criminal offence.[62]

The statutory system of 'pre-stunning' is unacceptable to Jews because of the religious requirement that the animal or bird must be completely sound and healthy and must not have suffered any injury before slaughter, if it is to be regarded as capable of producing meat which is *kosher*. In order to accommodate *shechita* and obviate any need for pre-stunning both Acts furnish specific exemptions for the slaughter, without the infliction of unnecessary suffering, of a bird or an animal 'by the Jewish method for the food of Jews and by a Jew duly licensed for the purpose' by a special Rabbinical Commission.[63] Similar exemptions are given to Muslims so that they can maintain their religious tradition of *dhabh* and produce *halal* meat.[64]

The statutory origins of the exemptions for both Jews and Muslims lie in the earliest piece of English primary legislation on the humane slaughter of animals for the meat-trade, namely the Slaughter of Animals Act 1933. This in turn was modelled on prior Scottish legislation in the form of the Slaughter of Animals (Scotland) Act 1928. Before 1933 the welfare of animals in English slaughterhouses was governed by local byelaws made pursuant to the Public Health Act 1875.[65] These byelaws provided for animals to be 'effectually stunned' prior to slaughter, but granted an exemption from this requirement for *shechita*. This exemption can thus be seen as an early example of the phenomenon of specific differential treatment described in Chapter 2.

---

[61] S 1(1).   [62] Slaughter of Poultry Act, s 1(3); Slaughterhouses Act, s 36(4).

[63] The Commission's membership is designed to make it representative of both the Ashkenazi and Sephardi communities and of the ultra-orthodox as well as the ortho-dox—see 1974 Act, sched 1 and sched 3, para 4. Decisions of the Commission about whom to licence and what conditions to impose will generally be unchallengeable in the courts so long as the Commission exercises its discretion reasonably in the interests of meeting the requirements of the Jewish community—see *R v Rabbinical Commission for the Licensing of Shochetim, ex parte Cohen, The Times*, 22 Dec 1987.

[64] The wording of the Muslim provision is rather old-fashioned in referring to 'Moham-medans'. In *Malins v Cole and Attard* (1986) CLY 94 a Muslim slaughterman was convicted of an offence under the Slaughter of Poultry Act because the chicken he was caught selling had not been slaughtered 'for the food of' Muslims, as required by the Act. It had been bought by and slaughtered for a man wearing a crucifix (who later turned out to be an RSPCA inspector), without any check having been made by the slaughterman that it would in fact be used for the food of Muslims. It is well known that some Hindus and Sikhs buy *halal* meat from Muslim butchers, but no offence appears to be committed if at the time of slaughter the slaughterman intends the meat to be for Muslims. Similarly, much *kosher* meat is sold on the general market—see below.

[65] See s 169, incorporating s 128 of the Towns Improvement Clauses Act 1847.

In 1904 an official committee was established by the Admiralty to assess the adequacy of the nation's meat supply in the event of war. Part of its brief was to 'ascertain the most humane and practicable method of slaughtering animals for human food and to investigate and report upon the existing slaughterhouse system'.[66] In their report the Committee's members declared that they were

. . . aware that in dealing with [*shechita*] they cannot help trenching upon very delicate ground, but it has been their earnest desire to avoid, as far as possible, giving any offence to Jewish susceptibilities. They feel, however, that considerations of humanity must be regarded as paramount, and that no unnecessary suffering could be condoned on the ground that it was incidental to the observance of any religious custom.[67]

Although the Committee recommended that stunning should be required in all cases,[68] opposition from the Board of Deputies of British Jews was successful in blocking this proposal.[69] Instead, a circular was issued in 1908 to all local councils by the Local Government Board indicating that, if they chose to introduce byelaws governing slaughterhouses, stunning should not be made obligatory where slaughter was carried out by a Jew, duly licensed by the Chief Rabbi, 'when engaged in the slaughtering of cattle intended for the food of Jews according to the Jewish method of slaughtering, if no unnecessary suffering is inflicted'.[70] In 1922 in the case of *Dodd v Venner*[71] the legality of making a distinction between Jews and others in this regard was upheld by the Divisional Court and the position remained one of regulation by local public health byelaws until the passing of the 1933 Act. That enactment was a private members' measure introduced by Lieutenant-Colonel Moore and the following comment made by him in moving the second reading of the bill was virtually the only reference to *shechita*—

Clause 6 has created some alarm. In this Clause we exempt Jews and Mohammedans. It is not wise at the present time to interfere with the fundamental religious beliefs of any race, and the question of killing is a ritual of the Jewish and Mohammedan community which is fundamental to their religion.[72]

---

[66] *Report of the Admiralty Committee on the Humane Slaughtering of Animals*, Cd 2150 of 1904, 3.   [67] Ibid, 10.

[68] Ibid, 11.

[69] See Board of Deputies, *Report on the Jewish Method of Killing Animals* (London, 1905); for discussion of the composition and operation of the Board today, see Brook, ch 16, who describes it as constituting 'the lay leadership of Anglo-Jewry' (at 211).

[70] See model byelaw 9B, discussed by Alderman, G., 'Power, Authority and Status in British Jewry: The Chief Rabbinate and Shechita' in Alderman, G. and Holmes, C. (eds), *Outsiders and Outcasts* (London, 1993), 12 at 20–1.   [71] (1922) 127 LT 746.

[72] HC Debs, 246, col 715.

OPPOSITION TO *SHECHITA*

There has been intermittent public opposition to *shechita* in England for well over a hundred years, but the degree of this antagonism has waxed and waned considerably at different periods.[73] The RSPCA, which was founded[74] in 1824, has mounted a series of campaigns against *shechita*[75] and has been joined by other animal welfare organizations, such as the Humane Slaughter Association[76] and Compassion in World Farming. Private members' bills to remove or limit the statutory exemption for *shechita* have been introduced in Parliament on no fewer than six occasions since 1955.[77] The responsibility for defending *shechita* has principally rested upon the shoulders of the *shechita* committee of the Board of Deputies, which has successfully co-ordinated the discreet lobbying of MPs.[78] In this they have been helped both by the Council of Christians and Jews and by the fact that in recent years the Jewish community has been well represented in the House of Commons.[79] It is doubtful, however, whether Parliament would have been willing to contemplate such an interference with religious freedom through what would have been widely perceived as a direct attack upon Judaism.[80]

The campaign against all forms of religious slaughter intensified in the 1970s with the discovery by animal welfare groups that Muslim entrepreneurs had developed a very substantial export market for *halal* meat with countries in the Middle East and North Africa. Indeed by 1983 a National Opinion Poll revealed that 77 per cent of respondents were altogether opposed to religious slaughter.[81] Although no British government has yet shown itself to be leaning in favour of repealing the statutory exemption, a decision was taken in 1979 to establish a government-sponsored 'quango' in the form of the Farm Animal Welfare Council, as a direct response to pressure from animal welfare groups. Its report is discussed below.

What part, if any, has anti-semitism played in the opposition to *shechita*? It has often been pointed out that the RSPCA ceased campaigning

[73] Kushner, T., 'Stunning Intolerance' (1989) 133 *Jewish Quarterly* 16.

[74] It is surely significant (and somewhat ironic) that one of its founders was a Jew, Lewis Gompertz.

[75] See e.g. *Legalised Cruelty* (London, 1948); *Humane Slaughter* (Horsham, 1981); *Ritual Slaughter* (Horsham, 1984); *Farm Animals: Religious Slaughter* (Horsham, 1995).

[76] See *Slaughter By Religious Methods* (South Mimms, 1995).

[77] See Charlton, R. and Kaye, R., 'The politics of religious slaughter: an ethno-religious case study' (1985–86) *New Community* 490.   [78] Ibid.

[79] See Alderman, G., *The Jewish Community in British Politics* (Oxford, 1983), 174–5. Since 1930 there have never been fewer than sixteen Jewish MPs; in 1974 there were forty-six.

[80] Alderman, G., 'The defence of *shechita*: Anglo Jewry and the "humane conditions" regulations' (1995) *New Community* 79 at 82.

[81] See Duffy, M., *Men and Beasts: An Animal Rights Handbook* (London, 1984), 28, 41.

against *shechita* during the 1930s so as to disassociate the organization sharply from Nazi persecution.[82] Only pro-Nazi British groups used the issue directly to attack the Jewish community here. Even so, Kushner has shown how, despite a voluntary restraint on political campaigning, the RSPCA was not above making some use of the anti-semitism which was present in the country at large to put further pressure on the Jewish community.[83] In correspondence between the RSPCA and the Board of Deputies during 1938–39 it was suggested by the chairman of the RSPCA that, if the Jews would only agree to give up the practice of *shechita*, they would be able to improve their relations with the wider society. The implicit corollary of their failure to do so was that they would then fully deserve the hostility being expressed towards them by those who were avowedly anti-semitic. Around this time there was certainly a cross-fertilization of ideas between anti-semitic political organizations and animal welfare groups and similar arguments were employed in their respective publications.[84] Almost certainly the same difficulty of attempting to separate the various strands of opposition to *shechita* remains today and it has been further compounded by the racist overtones evident in campaigns against the Muslim method of slaughter.[85]

Undoubtedly the most important attack upon *shechita* in recent years has come from the Farm Animal Welfare Council's *Report on the Welfare of Livestock When Slaughtered by Religious Methods*, published in 1985.[86] Dr Sidney Torrance, a former chairman of the Board of Deputies' *shechita* committee, immediately branded the Council's recommendations as 'probably the most serious threat which observant Jews in Britain have had to face'.[87] The Report's principal conclusion was that, although there was a dearth of scientific evidence to indicate at precisely what stage in the process of losing consciousness animals cease to feel pain, loss of consciousness following severance of the major blood vessels in the neck is not immediate and animals may experience pain for as long as ten to eleven seconds (in the case of cattle), fourteen seconds (in the case of sheep) and seventeen seconds (in the case of calves) after their throats have been cut, even in the best conditions.[88] The Council's ultimate assessment was that these periods were 'unacceptably long' and that humane slaughter could best be achieved by effective stunning in all cases.[89] It therefore recommended that the Government should require

---

[82] See e.g. Charlton and Kaye at 491; Kushner at 17.   [83] Kushner, ibid.
[84] See e.g. Ward, M., *Jewish Kosher—should it be permitted to survive in a new Britain?* (Ilfracombe, 1945); Kushner, ibid.
[85] See e.g. Klug, B., 'Overkill—the polemic against ritual slaughter' (1989) 134 *Jewish Quarterly* 38.   [86] (London, 1985).
[87] *Jewish Chronicle*, 12 July 1985.   [88] *Report*, 19–20.   [89] Ibid, 20.

the Jewish and Muslim communities to review their methods of slaughter so as to develop alternatives which would permit effective stunning. The findings of these communities should then be presented to Ministers so that the current legislative exemptions could be repealed within a period of three years.[90] The Council justified its stance in the following terms—

> The up-to-date scientific evidence available and our own observations leave no doubt in our minds that religious methods of slaughter, even when carried out under ideal conditions, must result in a degree of pain, suffering and distress which does not occur in the properly stunned animal. We accept that the religious requirements and intentions of both the Muslim and Jewish communities are such as to cause as little pain and suffering as possible to the animals being slaughtered. In our discussions, some members told us that if they could be convinced that their methods of slaughter caused unnecessary suffering they would respond to the demand for change. We believe our findings show conclusively that change is needed. However, we have to acknowledge that over the centuries the acts associated with religious slaughter have assumed a cultural significance in their own right and have become symbols that are important in the traditions of those who adhere to those religions. We have to recognise that in these circumstances the change we would like to see cannot be achieved overnight. We see no reason however, given goodwill, why such change could not be achieved and become legally enforceable within a period of three years.[91]

The Farm Animal Welfare Council also expressed concern in their Report over a number of subsidiary issues. Three of these are worthy of mention here. The first related to the type of pen in which cattle are placed prior to slaughter. Certain designated rotary pens, which had originally been introduced in the interests of humane slaughter,[92] were found to be unsatisfactory on welfare grounds because they involve the unnatural inversion of the animals so that they are lying on their backs with their necks extended, a position likely to cause them both terror and discomfort.[93] The Council recommended that the use of rotary pens be discontinued and that they should be replaced by pens which restrained animals in a standing position.[94] Secondly, the Council found that animals were sometimes shackled and hoisted onto the bleeding rail before they had fully lost consciousness.[95] It recommended that an interval of at least twenty seconds (in the case of sheep and goats) and thirty seconds (in the case of calves and adult bovines) should elapse for this purpose.[96] Thirdly, the Council pointed out that a substantial proportion of meat produced by means of religious slaughter is marketed to the general

---

[90] *Report*, 25.   [91] Ibid, 25.
[92] Under the Slaughter of Animals (Prevention of Cruelty) Regulations 1958.
[93] *Report*, 15–16.   [94] Ibid, 25.   [95] Ibid, 19.   [96] Ibid, 26.

public without any indication of its origins. Apparently the proportion of *kosher* meat which is made available on the general market may be as high as two-thirds.[97] The hindquarters are invariably treated as non-*kosher* and a quantity of rump steak is thus released to the general public, who are ignorant of its provenance. The Council felt that consumers were entitled to be aware of the method of slaughter employed and recommended that all meat offered for sale from carcasses slaughtered by religious methods should be clearly labelled accordingly.[98]

The Government's response to the Council's Report was given in a Parliamentary answer by Mr John MacGregor, the Minister of Agriculture, Fisheries and Food, in 1987.[99] By that time the Government had received many representations on the subject and had an opportunity to consult Jewish and Muslim leaders in great detail on the question. However, on this occasion the traditional approach of quiet diplomacy and negotiation employed by the Board of Deputies and the Chief Rabbi attracted considerable criticism from several quarters of Anglo-Jewry, in which it was felt that a more belligerent defence of all aspects of *shechita* was required.[100] Members of certain dissident pressure groups decided to deal directly with the Ministry and they ultimately secured some significant concessions in relation to the subsidiary issues.[101] In any event, at this stage, while the Minister broadly committed the Government to the implementation of the Council's recommendations relating to the subsidiary issues (with the exception of the labelling proposal which was ruled out as impracticable), he declined to impose a requirement of stunning upon the Jewish and Muslim communities. He commented—

The religious communities have made clear that elements of their slaughter requirements are fundamental obligations, forming part of their religious law which it is not open to them to alter. They have also rejected the Council's assessment of the welfare implications of religious slaughter . . . . [T]he Government has to recognise the serious implications for the religious communities if they were no longer allowed to prepare meat as their faiths require. We do not believe that we would be justified in imposing such a burden on these

---

[97] Ibid, 8–9.   [98] Ibid, 27.
[99] HC Debs, 121, cols 405–7 (written answer, 29 Oct 1987).
[100] See generally, Alderman (1994) at 83–9.
[101] This was subsequently accomplished by the Slaughter of Animals (Humane Conditions) Regulations, SI 1242 of 1990, Part IV. For Parliamentary discussion of the regulations, see HL Debs, 521, cols 610–21 (13 July 1990). For discussion of the agreement reached earlier between the Government and the Chief Rabbi on these subsidiary issues, see Kaye, R., 'The politics of religious slaughter of animals' (1993) *New Community* 235 at 236–7; Alderman (1994) at 83–5. The 1990 regulations have been replaced by the Welfare of Animals (Slaughter or Killing) Regulations, SI 731 of 1995, sched 12.

communities. We do not therefore propose to ask Parliament to reverse the attitude which it has taken to this issue in the past.[102]

The Farm Animal Welfare Council's proposal that *shechita* be deprived of its current legislative exemption rested essentially upon the argument that humane slaughter can best be achieved by effective stunning. However, as the response submitted by the Chief Rabbi, purportedly on behalf of the entire Jewish community,[103] was quick to point out, the Council's scientific case was deeply flawed, being selective, partial, and inconclusive. Its working party did not contain any of the leading scientific experts in the field, it relied upon only three sets of experiments (the significance of whose results was highly controversial), and it acknowledged openly that there was 'a lack of scientific evidence to indicate at what stage in the process of losing consciousness the ability to feel pain ceases'.[104] Yet, without any citation of experiments which had reached very different conclusions from those relied upon by the Council, it felt able to make such a sweeping recommendation as mandatory stunning in all cases.

The Council placed considerable reliance upon experiments conducted with the electro-encephalograph (EEG) and the electro-corticogram (ECoG), instruments which record electrical activity in the brain. However, there is widespread agreement amongst neurologists that one cannot equate EEG or ECoG readings with loss of consciousness.[105] Electrical activity can be detected even when the animal has been properly anaesthetised. Moreover, even using the EEG as a method for trying to evaluate pain, a German researcher, Professor W. Schulze (whose work was commissioned by the West German Government but was not mentioned in the Council's Report) had concluded in 1985—'. . . *shechita* is painless according to EEG recordings and the absence of any defensive movements in sheep and calves, and constitutes a suitable method of slaughter'.[106] It is certainly arguable that blood pressure is a more reliable indicator than the EEG or ECoG in determining the onset of unconsciousness and in *shechita* the severance of the blood vessels in the neck causes an immediate and complete cessation of blood flow to the brain.[107]

Research since 1985 appears to have established a clear difference in

[102] HC Debs, 121, col 406.
[103] *Comments by the Jewish Community on the FAWC Report* (1985), 3, 10–13.
[104] At 20.   [105] See *Comments by the Jewish Community*, 10 and appendix E.
[106] Ibid, 11–12 and appendix F.   [107] Ibid, 13.

the responses evoked in brain activity between adult cattle depending on whether or not they had been stunned. Investigations have revealed that some cattle slaughtered by means of *shechita* took over two minutes to lose evoked responses in the brain, whereas in those which had been stunned the loss of evoked activity was virtually instantaneous.[108] However, while it is known that electrical responses are evoked in the higher centres of the brain when an animal feels pain and that the total absence of such responses is an unequivocal indicator of insensibility, it is not proven that the mere presence of recorded responses reveals conscious perception of pain because, for example, they can be demonstrated to occur in anaesthetised animals. Even so, relying upon this research, the Commission of the European Communities Scientific Veterinary Committee recommended to the European Parliament in 1990 that the legal exemptions from stunning should be abolished in all the Community's member states.[109] This seemed somewhat surprising in view of the Committee's acknowledgement of the fact that, while evoked responses are the most appropriate measure of brain function in this context, their presence merely demonstrates the 'possibility' that an animal can feel pain. The recommendation was rejected.[110]

   The other important element in the scientific equation is the efficacy of the normal stunning method. The Farm Animal Welfare Council had itself, in an earlier report, been highly critical of the practical application of the stunning technique.[111] There is considerable evidence to suggest that on a day-to-day basis stunning very often does not function humanely. Mistakes are by no means uncommon, such as failures through 'missed shots' (with the captive bolt pistol) or 'missed shock' (in the case of electrical stunning). Both types of failure cause undoubted pain to the animal and a further attempt has then to be made to stun it properly.[112] The stunning procedure is not as precise a technique as *shechita* and those involved in performing it are almost certainly less strongly imbued with a sense of responsibility for the welfare of animals than the *shochetim*.[113] As previously noted, the latter are rigorously trained, have to be of high moral character and integrity and are subject to a system of supervision and licensing by a Rabbinical Commission. Their licences can be revoked if any irregularity or dereliction of duty is uncovered. By contrast, secular slaughtermen seem liable to rush the

---

[108] Daly, C., Kallweit, E., and Ellendorf, F., 'Cortical function in cattle during slaughter; conventional captive bolt stunning followed by exsanguination compared with shechita slaughter' (1988) 122 *Veterinary Record* 325.

[109] Personal communication to the author from the Chairman of the Committee, 21 Jan 1991.   [110] See further below.

[111] *Report on the Welfare of Livestock (Red Meat Animals) at the Time of Slaughter* (London, 1984).   [112] At 31–8.

[113] See Dresner, S. and Siegel, S., *The Jewish Dietary Laws* (New York, 1966), 27–8.

process (because they are paid according to piece-rates) and tend to display little concern for the welfare of the animals consigned to them.[114] They often fail to keep the stunning tongs on the animal for a long enough period to achieve loss of consciousness through electrocution. There are reports of conscious animals falling off the bleeding rail or drowning in the scalding tank, to the general unconcern of the stunners. The only event which slows down their frenetic, de-humanizing routine comes in the form of a six-monthly welfare and hygiene check by inspectors from the Ministry of Agriculture. As one commentator has aptly put it— 'Slaughterhouses are not temples of technological excellence and the niceties of stunning are often skimped'.[115] The argument that scientific research has shown *shechita* to be less humane than stunning is, clearly, not proven. Indeed precisely the opposite claim could just as plausibly be made on the basis of current knowledge.

Turning to the religious argument, the Farm Animal Welfare Council took the view that the Jewish rules prohibiting stunning could simply be adapted to suit modern circumstances if the scientific evidence (as they believed) proved that *shechita* involved cruelty to animals.[116] The Council's argument was essentially that ancient Jewish principles about the need for kindness to animals needed to be updated in the way they were implemented today, if they were to meet current standards. This presupposes that the Jewish rules on the subject are capable of being modified to suit different times and circumstances. The Council saw these rules as being largely dependent upon Rabbinical oral tradition and seems to have imagined that a decision to amend them could thus be taken by a committee of British rabbis acting on behalf of Anglo-Jewry as a whole. It suggested that the Jewish rules were of greater symbolic and cultural significance than of real practical importance in the contemporary world.

The response of the Jewish community was that the Council's approach to this aspect of the question was based on a fundamental misconception of the status of *shechita* in Jewish law, partly explained perhaps by the absence of any Jewish representation on the Council's working party. In the words of the response—

We take exception to the wrongful relegation of the laws of *shechita* to the realm of symbol and culture, which is unacceptable to us in the context of Jewish life and thought. The proper preparation of meat, and the associated restrictions imposed on us by Jewish law, are far more than symbolic or cultural in nature. Their true rationale, as expressed in the Bible . . . is to ennoble and invest with

[114] See Tyler, A., 'Slaughterhouse tales', *Independent*, 13 Mar 1989.
[115] Long, A., 'Taking the horror out of the ritual slaughter of animals', *Independent*, 28 Aug 1987.   [116] See *Report*, 21, 25.

spiritual meaning all aspects of life, by the transformation of the physical act of eating into an expression of Divine service. . . . The Jewish dietary laws are designed to generate an overall raising of moral behaviour and integrity, and with a better understanding of their significance they would not have been dismissed as a mere historical symbol of purely cultural value.[117]

Addressing the legal status of the dietary prescriptions, the response proceeded—

In this connection, it should also be stressed that the detailed rules relating to the method of *shechita* form a basic and integral part of the corpus of Jewish *law*. The rules are not merely general 'traits', 'principles' or 'religious categories' (as wrongly described in . . . the Report), but constitute binding legal prescriptions. . . . The 'Oral Law' explaining and interpreting the Biblical references is, in the framework of Jewish jurisprudence, as binding in practice, and as Divine in authority and origin, as the Written Law . . . the so-called 'Oral' law was committed to writing and carefully codified both in general principle and in detail almost two thousand years ago, and it is in every respect an exact and precise legal system. . . . It has been accepted since time immemorial that the laws of *shechita*—whatever their textual sources or origin—are a fundamental part of Jewish law and practice which cannot be done away with without violating the entire structure of Jewish law. . . . Any adjustment of Jewish law must be effected within the framework and rules of the system. The role of the Rabbis is to administer the law and not to make or unmake it. It must be borne in mind that we are dealing with rules which are spelled out in precise and explicit detail, and which constitute, in the Jewish view, a part of eternal and unalterable Divine law incumbent on all Jews. No agency in the world can alter imperatives laid down as binding in the codes of Jewish law.[118]

SOME FOREIGN COMPARISONS

In the light of the complex issues involved in deciding whether or not to make a special exception for religious methods of slaughter, it seems worthwhile making brief reference to the laws of some other states and the European Union before examining the human rights dimension of the problem.

It is clear that in the vast majority of western countries religious exemptions from the requirement of stunning are embodied in the law.[119] This applies to the domestic legislation of all the members of the European Union (except Sweden), and the EC Directive on the protection of animals at the time of slaughter contains a specific provision declaring that the general requirement of stunning or instantaneous

[117] *Comments by the Jewish Community*, 4.   [118] Ibid, 4–5.
[119] See *FAWC Report*, 38–40.

killing does not apply in the case of animals subject to particular methods of slaughter which are required by certain religious rites'.[120] A similar exemption is contained in the European Convention for the Protection of Animals for Slaughter.[121] *Shechita* is exempted in Australia and New Zealand and it is expressly recognized as humane in a very positive fashion in both Canada[122] and the United States.[123] In Norway, by contrast, there is no provision for religious slaughter, but the legislation banning *shechita* there was introduced in 1930 at the instigation of a politician, Quisling, who was a Nazi sympathizer.[124]

THE HUMAN RIGHTS DIMENSION

Article 9(1) of the European Convention on Human Rights provides that everyone has a right to freedom of religion, including the right to manifest this religion in practice and observance. Article 9(2) restricts this right by declaring—

Freedom to manifest one's religion or beliefs shall be subject only to such limitations as are prescribed by law and are necessary in a democratic society in the interests of public safety, for the protection of public order, health or morals, or for the protection of the rights and freedoms of others.

Article 18 of the International Covenant on Civil and Political Rights is in similar vein, but its limitation clause refers to the 'fundamental' rights and freedoms of others as the basis for protective legislation rather than merely rights and freedoms in general. Article 27 of the same Covenant further buttresses religious freedom by providing—

In those States in which ethnic, religious or linguistic minorities exist, persons belonging to such minorities shall not be denied the right, in community with the other members of their group, to enjoy their own culture, to profess and practise their own religion, or to use their own language.

There can be no doubt that for observant Jews *shechita* is a significant aspect of their practice of religion, involving not only deep beliefs about man's relationship with God, as well as with other animals, but also the organization of social and family life. Moreover, the strength of the principles governing *shechita* is reinforced by their incorporation as part of Jewish law as well as reflecting an aspect of immemorial tradi-

---

[120] 93/119/EC (1993), Art 5(1), (2).   [121] (1979), Art 17.
[122] Humane Slaughter Regulations 1959.
[123] Federal Humane Slaughter Act 1958; *Jones v Butz* 374 F Supp 1284 (1976).
[124] See *Comments by the Jewish Community*, 19. Legislation banning *shechita* in Nazi Germany in 1933 was reversed in the Federal Republic in 1960.

tion. Any limitations placed on *shechita* by English law would have to be shown to be 'necessary in a democratic society' in order to satisfy the stringent terms of the European Convention. The concept of necessity entails both a pressing social need and a degree of proportionality between the aim being pursued by the state and the legal interference with the right in question.[125] The hallmarks of a democratic society, according to the jurisprudence of the European Court of Human Rights, are pluralism, the tolerance of different outlooks and philosophies, and broadmindedness.[126] Tolerance requires considerable forbearance in the face of practices which offend the sensibilities of many members of the public. A justification of the type set down in Article 9(2) would first have to be put forward to establish a 'legitimate aim'. Here there are two possibilities, namely 'public morality' and 'the rights of others'. The latter justification in this context might possibly refer to three different concepts. First, it might mean the rights of Gentiles not to have their moral scruples about cruelty to animals offended by practices which they felt to be inhumane. If so, it adds nothing to the right to have restrictions imposed in defence of public morality. Secondly, the rights of Gentiles might perhaps extend to not being at risk of eating *kosher* meat unknowingly through the absence of any system of labelling. Here there is certainly a basis for arguing that consumers should have adequate information so that they can make a choice as to whether or not they wish to eat *kosher* meat, as the Farm Animal Welfare Council specifically recommended. Thirdly, the rights of others might just conceivably be stretched to encompass the rights of animals as well as human beings. This would raise the wider issue as to whether animals do indeed possess legal rights, or, if the wording of the International Covenant is followed, 'fundamental' rights.

If such 'animal rights' were indeed recognized, logic would surely dictate that it should be illegal for human beings to kill any animals for food, for the right to life is usually regarded as the most precious right of all. Yet this is nowhere the law and never has been. Animals cannot easily be regarded as legal 'subjects', for they lack the capacity to litigate to enforce legal rights or to give instructions in this regard.[127] Instead they are usually viewed as the 'objects' or beneficiaries of legal rules, in the sense that the law can impose duties upon human beings in such a

[125] See *Sunday Times v UK* (1979) 2 EHRR 245 at 275, 277–8.
[126] See e.g. *Handyside v UK* (1976) 1 EHRR 737 at 754; *Young, James and Webster v UK* (1981) 4 EHRR 38 at 57.
[127] This argument cannot, of course, be regarded as conclusive since the same incapacity often affects young children, the mentally-ill, and the senile. In *The Case for Animal Rights* (London, 1983) Regan argues that animals (like incapacitated human beings) have a moral right to respectful treatment, having the status of 'moral patients' rather than 'moral agents'.

way that the welfare of animals is protected.[128] Certainly, there is no evidence to suggest that the 'rights of others' in the European Convention was intended to cover animals.

However, even if the ascription to animals of legal rights is difficult to sustain, there is clear authority for the proposition that 'public morality' is promoted and enhanced by the humane treatment of animals.[129] In *Re Wedgewood*[130] a bequest in a will for the 'protection and benefit of animals' was upheld as creating a valid charitable trust on the broad basis that it created for a general public purpose beneficial to the community. The testatrix had wanted to support the movement for humane slaughter and her right to do so in this manner was endorsed by the Court of Appeal. Lord Cozens-Hardy MR declared that—

... apart from authorities which are binding upon us, I should be prepared to support the trust on the ground that it tends to promote public morality by checking the innate tendency to cruelty.[131]

Swinfen Eady LJ added—

A gift for the benefit and protection of animals tends to promote and encourage kindness towards them, to discourage cruelty, and to ameliorate the condition of the brute creation, and thus to stimulate humane and generous sentiments in man towards the lower animals, and by these means promote feelings of humanity and morality generally, repress brutality, and thus elevate the human race.[132]

If, therefore, public morality were to be the essential ground of a 'legitimate aim' for restricting shechita, it would need to be demonstrated both that the Jewish method was definitely less humane than the process of stunning and that the general public's ethical standards regarding the treatment of animals had attained a degree of coherence from which it was clear that *shechita* was a mere historical anomaly. Otherwise, the banning of *shechita* would surely represent a disproportionate response to the aim being pursued. At present neither of these points can be established. The scientific evidence, as we have already seen, is wholly inconclusive on the first issue. As to the second, public opinion is far from united on the appropriate minimum standards for the treatment of animals. Animal welfare organizations are still having to campaign vigorously against 'factory farming' (and other forms of intensive rear-

---

[128] See Rollin, B., *Animal Rights and Human Morality* (New York, 1981), 76–81; Goodkin, S., 'The evolution of animal rights' (1987) 18 *Columbia Human Rights Law Review* 259 at 267; Brown, L., *Cruelty to Animals* (Basingstoke, 1988), 48–50.

[129] For a survey of the political and moral dimensions of the debate about 'animal rights', see Clarke, P. and Linzey, A. (eds), *Political Theory and Animal Rights* (London, 1990).

[130] [1915] 1 Ch 113.   [131] At 117.

[132] At 122. For US cases deciding that public policy there is similarly opposed to cruelty to animals, see *Humane Society of Rochester v Lyng* 633 F Supp 480 (1986).

ing) and against the close confinement of animals during their transportation to slaughter, as well as against 'field sports' (such as fox-hunting), and experimentation on animals for the purpose of testing new cosmetics.[133] So long as such activities remain lawful, it would be extremely hard to argue that 'public morality' necessitated a ban on *shechita*. Even savagely beating a hedgehog, a harmless creature held high in the affections of the general public, was only made an offence as recently as 1996.[134]

Furthermore, although the European Court of Human Rights has pointed out that it is not possible to identify a 'uniform European conception of morals',[135] in the present instance, as we have seen, there is a broad consensus in Western European countries that *shechita* should be allowed.

CONCLUSIONS

Through its dietary laws (*kashrut*), Judaism attempts to attach religious importance to the act of eating by teaching Jews reverence for all living creatures. As Dresner and Siegel have explained—

[Judaism] says we have the power to hallow the act of eating, that we can find a way of ennobling and raising this prosaic act which will lend it meaning and significance, an aspect of holiness, that we may even succeed in transforming it into a means of serving God. For man is not merely an animal, even a *rational* animal . . . ; he is better defined as a *religious* animal—an animal, yes, with all the functions and frailties of animals, but a 'religious' animal, one which has the wonderful power to take his animal functions and turn them into something holy. The glory of man is his power to hallow. We do not live to eat; we eat to live. Even the act of eating can be sanctified; even the act of eating can become a means of achieving holiness. . . . The laws of *kashrut*—which forbid the eating of blood, limit the number of animals which may be eaten and provide for a humane method of slaughter and a specially trained slaughterer—have helped to attain Judaism's goal of hallowing the act of eating by reminding the Jew that the life of the animal is sacred and may be taken to provide him with food only under these fixed conditions. From this he learns reverence for life, both animal and human.[136]

For English law to remove the existing statutory exemption granted to *shechita*, in the face of its deep religious significance for many Jews,

---

[133] For discussion of the current state of English law on these issues, see Blackman, D., Humphreys, P., and Todd, P. (eds), *Animal Welfare and the Law* (Cambridge, 1989).
[134] Wild Mammals (Protection) Act 1996, abrogating *Hudnott v Campbell*, *The Times*, 27 June 1986.   [135] *Muller v Switzerland* (1991) 13 EHRR 212 at 228.
[136] *The Jewish Dietary Laws* (New York, 1966), 21, 38–9.

would be to assert a degree of moral superiority which cannot be justified at the present time. In the future it is, of course, possible that scientific developments in the measurement of animal pain may establish a clear and indisputable disparity between *shechita* and stunning to the detriment of the former, in which case the question would need to be reconsidered. Furthermore, legal rights may eventually come to be attributed to animals in much the same way that the law has had to evolve to recognize the rights of both those people who were formerly enslaved and those whose lives were severely circumscribed on the basis that they constituted the weaker sex. After the legal repudiation of racism and sexism, the law may ultimately move on to outlaw 'speciesism'.[137] The upshot of such reforms might be that, while killing animals painlessly for food would still be permitted, the infliction of any pain and suffering as part of this process would be regarded as legally wrong, even in circumstances where it is currently justified as 'necessary' for the wellbeing of human society.[138] At present, however, the case for removing the legal exemption accorded to *shechita* has not been sufficiently made out.[139] The justification for specific differential treatment to be accorded to this important aspect of religious practice rests on secure enough foundations for the provisions of the Slaughter of Poultry Act 1967 and the Slaughterhouses Act 1974 to be maintained intact for the time being.[140] Suppression of such a vital part of Jewish religious observance through the criminalization of *shechita* would not be justifiable.[141]

---

[137] See e.g. Singer in Clarke and Linzey, 162–3.

[138] See generally, Pedley, D., 'Animal rights: some are more equal than others' (1990) 140 *NLJ* 1415. The current exceptions only allow *shechita* provided no 'unnecessary suffering' is involved.

[139] See also Zellick, G., *The Law, Religion and the Jewish Community* (London, 1987), 11.

[140] Sufficient justification exists, by analogy, for preserving the exemption accorded to Muslims, although some concern has been expressed over the lack of training, expertise, and supervision of some Muslim slaughtermen—see *Farm Animal Welfare Council Report* (1985), 21.

[141] Greater threats to the future supply of *kosher* meat may come indirectly from increased costs. This has already occurred as a result of the need for the installation of upright pens and might be accentuated by the introduction of labelling in relation to meat sold on the general market—see Alderman (1994) at 82, 89; Rocker, S., 'Shechita defence lobby moves up a gear', *Jewish Chronicle*, 19 Aug 1994, 15.

5

Gypsies: The Pursuit of a Nomadic Lifestyle

Records of the presence of gypsies in England date back to at least the beginning of the sixteenth century.[1] Their ancestors had left northern India around five hundred years earlier and had spread out across Europe. The first arrivals here claimed to be Christian pilgrims from Egypt, but had in reality left the Balkans in the wake of Turkish occupation.[2] Initially, perhaps, the prospect of helping indigent Christian pilgrims who were begging for alms may have evoked a sympathetic response from those here who believed their story and were familiar with the idealization of poverty promoted three centuries earlier by Saint Francis of Assisi.[3] However, by the middle of the sixteenth century the status of pilgrims was in steep decline and begging was increasingly frowned upon. Severe sanctions were being imposed upon gypsies by authorities throughout Europe,[4] and England was to prove no exception.

Hence, within a very short time of the gypsies' advent to this country they were faced with a steady stream of repressive legislation directed at outlawing altogether both them and their way of life. An Act passed in 1530 during the reign of Henry VIII decreed that 'outlandish people calling themselves Egyptians' should quit the realm within sixteen days of the Act's proclamation, upon pain of imprisonment and forfeiture of all their goods and chattels.[5] Similarly, any gypsies entering the country after the Act's promulgation were to suffer the same penalties if they remained for longer than fifteen days after being ordered out. In 1554 a further Act was felt to be necessary, since gypsies were again entering the country 'using their old-accustomed devilish and naughty practices and devices, with such abominable living as is not in any Christian Realm to be permitted, named or known . . . .'[6] This time the punishment was for any gypsy to be automatically deemed and judged a felon and to suffer pain of death and loss of lands and goods, without benefit and privilege of sanctuary or clergy. An exception was

---

[1] See Okely, J., *The Traveller-Gypsies* (Cambridge, 1983), 3; Fraser, A., *The Gypsies,* 2nd ed. (Oxford, 1995), 112–13.
[2] See Holmes, C., *John Bull's Island: Immigration and British Society 1871–1971* (Basingstoke, 1988), 24.   [3] Fraser, 127.
[4] Fraser, chs 5, 6.   [5] 22 Hen 8 c 10.   [6] 1 & 2 Ph & M c 4.

made for those gypsies who, within twenty days of the Act's proclamation, left their 'naughty, idle and ungodly life and company' and who were placed in the service of some honest and lawful occupation. In 1562 it was considered necessary to pass further legislation to cover those who were 'counterfeiting, transforming or disguising themselves by their apparel, speech or behaviour' so as to convey the impression that they were 'vagabonds, commonly called or calling themselves Egyptians'.[7] This suggests that the term 'Egyptian' had already been expanded in normal parlance to encompass those who were following a gypsy lifestyle in this country but were not in fact of foreign origin.[8] In 1596 at York Quarter Sessions no fewer than 106 gypsies were condemned to death at a single sitting, though most were later reprieved for the sake of their children.[9] Only the nine who were of foreign origin were actually executed.[10] The Acts of 1530 and 1554 remained on the statute-book for over three hundred years until they were repealed as obsolete in 1856.[11]

Although there are no official figures for the numbers of gypsies resident in England today, an authoritative study prepared for the European Commission in 1995 concluded that there were 33,000 gypsies living in caravans and a further 30,000 living in houses,[12] while a research report for the Department of the Environment in 1991 had put the number of caravan-dwellers at 'perhaps 40,000 individuals at most'.[13] Regular bi-annual counts of the numbers of gypsy caravans are made by the Department (based on figures supplied by local authorities) and in recent years these have consistently shown totals of around 12,000–13,000 such vehicles.[14]

More than twenty years ago, a major study by Adams and others concluded that the gypsies

. . . are not simply a social group but a cohesive ethnic group with membership based primarily on descent . . . They have a distinct cultural identity and maintain by intent their separation from the majority society. Their value system is in many ways different from that of the majority society and their purposes and goals are centred in their own society. Travelling remains the ideal and most

[7] See 5 Eliz c 20, s 3.

[8] See Okely, 3–4; Mayall, D., 'The making of British gypsy identities c 1500–1800' (1992) 11 *Immigrants and Minorities* 21 at 25–6.

[9] Ministry of Housing and Local Government, *Gypsies and Other Travellers* (London, 1967), 3.   [10] See Fraser, 133.

[11] 19 & 20 Vict c 64. The 1562 Act was repealed in 1783 by 23 Geo 3 c 51.

[12] See Kenrick, D. and Bakewell, S., *On The Verge: The Gypsies of England*, 2nd ed. (Hatfield, 1990) 10. In 1994 a Government minister stated in Parliament that 50–60 per cent of gypsies lived in houses—see HC Debs, 248, col 373.

[13] Todd, D. and Clark, G., *Gypsy Site Provision and Policy* (London, 1991), 12.

[14] See Hawes, D. and Perez, B., *The Gypsy and the State* (Bristol, 1995), 40.

caravan-dwelling gypsies travel for at least part of the year. They are adaptive people and have a viable family-based economy which in many cases requires geographical mobility. The travelling way of life and the gypsies' distinct identity seem likely to have more persistence than has hitherto been realized. The majority of caravan-dwelling gypsies demonstrate little or no desire for assimilation.[15]

Although the number of gypsies who have settled down permanently, either in houses or in caravans, has increased sharply in recent years, as a result of restrictions on camp sites, many gypsies still maintain a pattern of itinerancy, at least for some weeks each year. Among their traditional occupations are scrap-metal breaking and dealing, clearance of other discarded goods and waste, external building and gardening (such as laying of tarmac drives, gravelling, tree-pruning, and roofing), seasonal agricultural work (including fruit picking), hawking of goods, and fortune-telling.[16] Until recently they have been particularly well placed to undertake many of these activities because they are able to exploit both their mobility and their minimal overhead expenses and cater for gaps in supply and demand in spheres where any permanent large-scale business would be uneconomic or insecure.[17] However, there is evidence that during the past few years their seasonal agricultural activities have been hit by increased mechanization, scrap-metal breaking has been restricted in certain locations by environmental controls, and in the urban areas unemployment among house-dwellers has made casual work harder to find.[18]

Most gypsies have replaced the wagons and horses of former days with motorized caravans or trailers, which are both comfortable and well equipped.[19] In terms of their customary 'ideology of travelling'[20] they regard themselves as free to roam to and fro from one part of the country to another, camping *en route* wherever they please. Traditionally, they have camped by the roadside, on grassy verges, on commons and farms, on derelict land, and in urban clearance areas, as well as on private land they had bought themselves.[21] As will be seen, their rights to continue these customary practices have been severely curtailed by legislation and a substantial (if still insufficient) number of alternative sites have recently been established by various local authorities.

---

[15] *Gypsies and Government Policy in England* (London, 1975), 267.
[16] *Gypsies and Other Travellers*, ch 5; Adams, ch 5; DoE Circular 1/94, para 6.
[17] Adams, 114.
[18] See Viney, T. and Dermody, G., 'Beyond the Pale' (1986–87) 65 *Poverty* 9.
[19] *Gypsies and Other Travellers*, 11–12, 19–20. [20] Ibid, 1–2. [21] Ibid.

THE ATTITUDES OF THE MAJORITY COMMUNITY

Long-standing hostility towards gypsies on the part of officialdom is manifest from the repressive sixteenth century legislation already mentioned. Further evidence, of more recent times, is furnished by the official reaction to the arrival of a small band of a few hundred German gypsies of Macedonian origin who came here between 1904 and 1906, following their expulsion from Holland.[22] Soon after landing they were driven across county boundaries by police forces acting on behalf of their local authorities. Subsequently, the Chief Constable of Northampton was to write to the Home Office, in relation to a later group, that they were 'a most objectionable band to have roaming around the country . . . they live by masterful begging and thieving . . . [and represent] a standing menace to law and order'.[23]

How far such hostile views were an accurate reflection of the attitudes of the public at large is far from clear, in view of a statement made by the honorary secretary of the Gypsy Lore Society in 1907—

Public opinion has changed, and the Romani wanderers are now regarded with indulgent toleration; the barriers of prejudice that existed on both sides are being broken down . . . .[24]

The majority community has probably held ambivalent attitudes towards gypsies for centuries, with fluctuations occurring more strongly one way or the other in the light of the circumstances of time and place. In the words of a recent editorial—

Gypsies arouse strong feelings. For some people they are romantic vagabonds, descendants of the magicians and suave charmers of the ancient East who retain contact with nature and access to mysteries that the rest of us have lost. Others fear them as outsiders with an alien language and impenetrable customs who pose an ill-defined threat to our ordered society.[25]

While no serious objection can be levelled at the freedom of movement enjoyed by gypsies while they are actually on the road, the question as to where they should be allowed to stop and establish their camps is one of acute controversy. Many members of the house-dwelling community, even if they are broadly sympathetic to the plight and aspirations of the gypsies in general terms, vehemently oppose the idea of having a gypsy encampment sited in the immediate vicinity of their own homes. They would not, however, usually express the same opposition to the camping and caravanning activities of holidaymakers. Indeed the ethos

---

[22] See Holmes, C., 'The German Gypsy Question in Britain 1904–06' (1978) *Journal of the Gypsy Lore Society* 248.   [23] See ibid at 258.
[24] See Adams, 8.   [25] *Independent*, 24 Aug 1992.

of 'getting closer to nature', the feeling of physical well-being derived from the open-air life, as well as the simple pleasure of 'going as one pleases' while on holiday, pervade the sentiments of the house-dwelling society to a marked degree.[26] It is, therefore, pertinent to ask why those who pursue these romantic ideals as a general lifestyle should generate greater criticism and resentment on the part of others than those who are only able to follow this pattern of living for a few weeks each year. Why is the presence of gypsies often regarded as so unwelcome?

The standard allegations made against gypsies are typically of three kinds.[27] The first is that they have a tendency to frighten house-dwellers. Gypsies often have a rather strange appearance and perhaps rough ways of talking and behaving and some may adopt bullying and threatening tactics in dealing with house-dwellers, leading to apprehension of possible assault. If they travel in large groups this pattern of behaviour may spread particular alarm. Secondly, they may constitute a nuisance and perhaps even a health hazard in the neighbourhood. Sometimes they may need to pester residents for water and they may indulge in insanitary or offensive personal habits such as urinating and defecating in the open. Occasionally where they possess horses they may allow these to roam freely through the streets, break through fences, and graze in farmers' fields without obtaining prior permission. Their dogs may also run around without any supervision and cause fear and annoyance to members of the general public. In some instances gypsies may indulge in petty pilfering and theft, though they tend to be blamed for such offences even when there is no real evidence that they are responsible, and there is no reason to suppose that their crime rate is any higher than that of the rest of the community. The third objection may perhaps be categorized as 'environmental' or 'aesthetic'. It is that gypsies despoil the amenities of an area by littering it with old car bodies and other items of scrap and that these constitute an eyesore, both while the gypsies are on the site and when they leave their rubbish behind. The whole place is strewn with messy debris and its contents amount to a form of environmental pollution. Fires are often lit to burn the upholstery and tyres of cars that are being scrapped and this creates an unpleasant stench over a wide area. On the other hand, it would appear that the gypsies make a contribution to the economy of the country through their work on scrap-metal, and the collection of waste material for recycling is widely

---

[26] Sandford, J., *Gypsies* (London, 1973), 5, 184.

[27] See generally *Gypsies and Other Travellers*, 1–2, 43–45; HC Debs, 759, cols 1919–2004; 176, cols 227–61; Cripps, J., *Accommodation for Gypsies: A Report on the Working of the Caravan Sites Act 1968* (London, 1977), hereafter 'Cripps Report', 12; *Page Motors Ltd v Epsom and Ewell Borough Council* (1982) 80 LGR 337; DoE, *The Accommodation Needs of Long-Distance and Regional Travellers* (London, 1982).

accepted as a necessary part of our modern industrial society.[28] It is clearly in the public interest that one of the mainstays of the gypsy economy is retained and encouraged rather than that the bulk of them are left to rely on social security.

Conflict between gypsies and the settled population appeared to grow during the 1980s and early 1990s, perhaps accentuated by the adverse publicity attracted by the antics of 'New Age Travellers', who were often mistakenly linked in the public mind with ethnic gypsies. However, there were also a variety of demographic, economic, and social factors at work, which contributed to the greater visibility of gypsy encampments, including the spread of commuter housing into rural areas, the reduction in woodlands, the loss of traditional gypsy sites to new housing, the general tightening of planning controls for gypsy sites, and the consequent movement of gypsies onto highway verges where they could easily be seen from passing cars. To add to all these considerations, a further salient factor has been suggested—

More housing owner-occupation and long-distance commuting has probably increased residents' sensitivity to the protection of their amenities, and contributed to a growing attitude that caravans are an 'alien feature' in the countryside.[29]

In any event a recent report, based on interviews with a representative sample of the general population, found a greater level of intolerance towards gypsies than any other minority group.[30] Of those interviewed 65 per cent indicated that they would prefer not to have gypsies as neighbours and 57 per cent maintained that gypsies behave in a manner which provokes hostility towards them.[31]

THE DEVELOPMENT OF MODERN POLICY AND LEGISLATION ON ENCAMPMENTS

During the nineteenth century government policy was indisputably assimilationist[32] and considerable use was made of section 4 of the Vagrancy Act 1824.[33] In terms of this section (which is still in force) every person 'pretending or professing to tell fortunes, or using any subtle craft, means or device, by palmistry or otherwise, to deceive

---

[28] *Gypsies and Other Travellers*, 38; *Cripps Report*, 6.
[29] Home, R., 'Planning Aspects of the Government Consultation Paper on Gypsies' [1993] *JPL* 13 at 14.
[30] See Golub, J., *British Attitudes toward Jews and other Minorities* (New York, 1993).
[31] Ibid, 6–7, 14–15.
[32] See Mayall, D., *Gypsy-Travellers in Nineteenth Century Society* (Cambridge, 1988).
[33] For the severity of its operation, see Mayall, 147, 152; gypsies had, of course, been subject to statutes on vagrancy and vagabondage since their arrival here—see Fraser, 134–6.

and impose on any of Her Majesty's subjects' as well as every person 'wandering abroad and lodging . . . in the open air, or under a tent, or in any cart or waggon and not giving a good account of himself or herself' is to be deemed to be a rogue and a vagabond and hence liable to criminal penalties. Today those in the first category are liable upon summary conviction to be imprisoned for a maximum term of three months, while those in the second category are liable to fines.[34]

During the 1960s central government policy was ambivalent, sometimes acknowledging that gypsies had the right to follow their traditional way of life, while at other points encouraging a settled pattern of existence.[35] Public attitudes, however, were hardening, as Adams has explained—

. . . increasing distaste for the activities and way of life of Travellers was evident in the many Parliamentary Questions in the House [of Commons] asking for additional powers to control their unauthorized encampments. Local authorities were coming under increasing pressure from housedwellers to move Travellers out of the locality; it may be that the increasing number of owner occupiers were particularly concerned at the damage to local amenities. Lined up in these ranks were many local authorities, several police forces, the National Farmers Union, the Rural District Councils Association, and most of the press. . . . It seems that during the 1960s intolerance of the Gypsy way of life and harassment of those on the roads were increasing.[36]

On the other hand, ranged against these forces were Kent County Council, the Gypsy Council, and the National Council for Civil Liberties (NCCL).[37] Kent had a relatively large gypsy population and by providing some official sites had attracted an extra influx of gypsies, who had been evicted from adjacent areas. The County Council was busy rallying local MPs to press the Government for action to compel other counties to share the burden of providing sites. The Gypsy Council was organizing resistance to evictions and gained considerable publicity in the process. It was also putting pressure on the Government for the speedy creation of a network of 200 temporary sites spread throughout the country. The Gypsy Council had also become affiliated to the NCCL and had briefed the NCCL to act on its behalf in legal and Parliamentary affairs. In 1967, within a year of the landmark speech by the then Home Secretary, Roy Jenkins, rejecting a policy of assimilation of minorities and promoting cultural diversity,[38] the NCCL passed a resolution at its annual general meeting calling for recognition of—

. . . the rights of gypsies and other travellers to participate in our multiracial society as a minority group with a distinctive culture and style of living, including

---

[34] Criminal Justice Act 1982, s 70.   [35] Adams, 10–13.   [36] Ibid, 10.
[37] Ibid, 13–14.   [38] See above, ch 1.

those families that choose to travel, take up seasonal and casual work and maintain their traditions of self-employment and full mobility.[39]

Later that year the Ministry of Housing and Local Government published a report[40] which was to mark the beginning of a decisive shift in policy. It incorporated the findings of a recent census which had revealed a population of around 15,000 (although undercounting was clearly acknowledged[41]) and concluded—

The prime need is for camp sites to enable the travellers to avoid the use of unlawful sites. . . . Until a wide network of special sites is provided, there should be an end to the present system of perpetually moving the travellers from one unlawful stopping place to the next. . . . A variety of provisions is probably the best answer: housing for those who wish to be housed; permanent pitches for those waiting to be housed or who prefer site life and do little or no travelling; and short stay pitches for those who travel continually from place to place and have no wish to settle . . . .[42]

This Report led more or less directly to the enactment of Part II of the Caravan Sites Act 1968, until recently the cornerstone of modern legislation on gypsy encampments. Although this was a private member's bill, the Government provided assistance in drafting and piloting the measure through Parliament. The promoter of the bill was Eric Lubbock, later to become Lord Avebury but then Liberal MP for Orpington, who was not only particularly familiar with the position of gypsies through having a constituency in Kent but was also the Chairman of NCCL's Parliamentary Civil Liberties Group. He was already planning to introduce a private member's bill on security of tenure for other caravan-dwellers and was persuaded by the Government to extend his measure to gypsies in the absence of sufficient Parliamentary time for a Government bill on the subject.[43] The measure had all-party support and its third reading in both Houses was unopposed.[44]

In a striking application of the concept of state-funded differential treatment, described in Chapter 2, the key section of the Act imposed a duty on local authorities to provide adequate accommodation in the form of caravan sites for gypsies 'residing in or resorting to their area'.[45] In introducing the bill, Eric Lubbock explained that it would 'give relief to quiet neighbourhoods and beautiful countryside which have suffered from invasions of the travelling people, while at the same time it will

---

[39] See Adams, 14.   [40] *Gypsies and Other Travellers* (London, 1967).
[41] Ibid, 4–5, 7.   [42] Ibid, 55, 66.   [43] See Adams, 15–16.
[44] See HL Debs, 293, col 1020; 295, col 640.
[45] Section 6(1). Initially the duty was imposed upon county councils and London boroughs, but was later extended by Local Government Act 1972, sched 30 to metropolitan boroughs.

give those travelling people a recognized place in the community'.[46] Although no time limit for the provision of sites was specified in the Act, both a 'carrot' and a 'stick' were made available.[47] The carrot took the form of enhanced powers for local authorities to remove gypsies and their caravans from unauthorized encampments once they had been afforded sufficient authorized sites.[48] The stick was represented by the Minister's power to direct dilatory authorities to make adequate provision.[49] Eric Lubbock expressed confidence that the Minister's power would only need to be used 'as a last resort. Once the duty is laid on local authorities I think they will get on and do the job'.[50] However, as we shall see, this confidence turned out to be wildly misplaced, even though there was a delay of more than a year before the Act finally came into operation on 1 April 1970, designed to give enough time for proper funding arrangements to be made to enable councils to embark on the programme of providing sites.

Before considering the details of the 1968 Act[51], it is important to draw attention to the provisions of various other pieces of legislation regulating gypsy encampments set up elsewhere than on local authority land. Only then will it become clear just how significant the 1968 provisions regarding these sites were prior to their repeal in 1994 and the extent to which the gypsies' traditional pattern of itinerancy had been restricted and curtailed by other statutes. As will be shown, the following appraisal is a very fair one—

The position of gypsies with regard to the law of encampment is . . . distinctive. Their travelling existence makes it difficult if not impossible to conform, because these laws strike at the very root of their nomadic way of life. While the law no longer outlaws the gypsies as persons, it has progressively reduced the opportunity to occupy land legally, and the offences which can be committed through unauthorized camping have greatly increased.[52]

(a) Camps on privately-owned land

Before the Second World War some gypsies had acquired their own plots of land and installed their caravans there without undue hindrance. Others found a private owner who was willing to allow them to pitch camp on his land.[53] Since 1945, however, the proliferation of planning controls has meant that sweeping powers to regulate the use of land have been vested in local authorities, and gypsies who wish to camp on

[46] HC Debs, 759, cols 1930–1. [47] Ibid. [48] S 10 of the Act.
[49] Ibid, s 9(2). [50] HC Debs, 759, col 1929.
[51] See generally Forrester, B., *The Travellers' Handbook* (London, 1985); Brand, C., *Mobile Homes and the Law* (London, 1986). [52] Adams, 157.
[53] Ibid, 268.

privately-owned land are very often frustrated by the planning laws. The Caravan Sites and Control of Development Act 1960 makes it an offence for any occupier of land to cause or permit any part of the land to be used as a caravan site unless he has first obtained a 'site licence'.[54] The local authority may not, however, issue such a licence unless the occupier is already entitled to the benefit of planning permission for the use of the land as a caravan site under the town and country planning legislation.[55] While the authority must generally issue a site licence within two months of an application being made, provided such planning permission is in force,[56] such permission may well not be at all easy to obtain. To take but one minor example of the many restrictions on such use which exist, a long-standing model byelaw, adopted until recently by several county and borough councils, provided as follows—

No gypsy or squatter or other such person dwelling in a tent . . . or in a van, caravan or similar vehicle, shall occupy any land within 300 yards of any dwelling house so as to cause injury, disturbance or annoyance to the inmates of such house after being requested to depart by any inmate of the house or by his servant or by any constable on his behalf.[57]

It was not until 1993 that this byelaw was finally held by the High Court to be *ultra vires* and hence void because it was partial and discriminatory,[58] but the ordinary planning controls usually represent a very substantial impediment to gypsy encampments on private land and the vast majority of their planning applications are rejected.[59] The sanctions for breach of these controls include fines and eviction, and in *Runnymede Borough Council v Ball*[60] the Court of Appeal held that a local authority could obtain an injunction to evict gypsies from their own land, where they were clearly intending to use it in breach of planning controls, without the necessity of first prosecuting them under the town and country planning legislation. The Planning and Compensation Act 1991 has further strengthened planning enforcement powers to remedy breaches of planning controls, in particular by enabling planning authorities to prohibit the use of land as a residential caravan site, if necessary immediately, through the issue of a 'stop notice'.[61]

Although the 1960 Act was not specifically aimed at gypsies but rather

---

[54] S 1(1), (2). For interpretation of these provisions in cases where gypsies were trespassing upon the occupier's land, see *Test Valley Investments Ltd v Tanner* [1964] Crim LR 62 and *Bromsgrove District Council v Carthy* [1975] 30 P & CR 34. Certain exemptions are listed in the first schedule to the Act, one of which covers caravans parked on land occupied by someone for whom the caravanner is doing seasonal agricultural work.

[55] S 1(3) of the 1960 Act.   [56] S 3(4).   [57] See *Cripps Report*, 5.

[58] *R v Bristol City Council, ex parte McDonough* [1993] CLY 3891.

[59] See Todd and Clark, 12–13.

[60] [1986] 1 All ER 629; see also *Waverley B C v Hilden* [1988] 1 All ER 807.   [61] S 9.

at the problem of house-dwellers resorting increasingly to caravans during a housing shortage, its provisions had a marked adverse impact on gypsies. Those who had for years frequented or lived on sites which they either owned or rented suddenly found themselves on the wrong side of the law and liable to new penalties.[62] Their camps were closed and they were forced to move elsewhere. Apart from private land, the most natural places for gypsies to stop were on common land and on roadside verges, to which attention will next be turned.

(b) Camps on commons

As a result of the nineteenth century enclosure movement vast areas of the country ceased to be common land at all. Moreover, various enactments dating back to the Commons Acts of 1826 and 1899 empowered local authorities to make byelaws in relation to commons within their areas. These byelaws often restricted the rights of gypsies and others to camp there. More recently, section 23 of the Caravan Sites and Control of Development Act 1960 has authorized rural district councils to make orders prohibiting the stationing of caravans on certain commons within their areas for the purposes of human habitation. Contravention of such an order amounts to an offence and any person found guilty is liable upon summary conviction to a fine.[63] In *Guildford Borough Council v Valler*[64] Sedley J commented that—

... it is a matter of history that local authorities made energetic use of the s 23 power, ditching and fencing commons and thereby depriving the gypsy population of the majority of the stopping places which had been available to them for centuries and had made their peripatetic life possible . . . .

So far as urban commons are concerned, section 193(4) of the Law of Property Act 1925 makes it an offence, without lawful authority, to drive any caravan or other vehicle upon such land or to camp or light a fire there.

(c) Camps by the roadside

In terms of section 72 of the Highway Act 1835[65] an offence was committed—

... if any hawker, higgler, gypsy, or other person travelling shall pitch any tent, booth, stall or stand, or encamp upon any part of the highway . . .

[62] See Okely, 106–7.   [63] S 23(3).   [64] *The Times*, 18 May 1993.
[65] 5 & 6 Will 4 c 50.

The wording of this provision was amended slightly in the largely consolidating Highways Act 1959, so that section 127 of the latter Act provided as follows—

If, without lawful authority or excuse . . . a hawker or other itinerant trader or a gypsy pitches a booth, stall or stand, or encamps, on a highway he shall be guilty of an offence and shall be liable in respect thereof to a fine . . . .

A highway means any road, path or track over which all members of the public have the right to pass and repass without seeking permission[66] and would include, for example, a lay-by.

During the late 1960s a controversy developed over the meaning to be attributed to the term 'gypsy' in section 127. In the case of *Mills v Cooper*[67] a magistrates' court had dismissed a charge laid against the defendant under the section, on the basis that in a previous hearing under the same section the prosecution had failed to establish that the defendant was in fact a gypsy. The justices felt that to pursue the case again at the second hearing, albeit that it related to a different period of time, would be oppressive and an abuse of the process of the court. They clearly took the view that if it could not be established that the defendant was a gypsy in December 1965 the same result would inevitably be reached *vis-à-vis* his status in March 1966. On appeal, however, the Divisional Court took a different view, holding that the word 'gypsy' in the context of section 127 did not mean a member of the Romany race but rather a person leading a nomadic life without a fixed abode. Accordingly, being a gypsy was not an unalterable status and the fact that the defendant could not be proved to have been a gypsy in December 1965 did not mean that he was not a gypsy three months later. Lord Parker CJ considered that it would be impossible to establish satisfactorily whether a person was really of the Romany race. He added, possibly rather naively, that it was 'difficult to think that Parliament intended to subject a man to a penalty in the context of causing litter and obstruction on the highway merely by reason of his race.'[68] Diplock LJ similarly denied that the word 'gypsy' could bear its ordinary dictionary meaning of a member of the Romany race because this would mean that in 1959 Parliament would have amended the wording of the 1835 Act (which referred to 'gypsy or other person') so as to discriminate against persons by reason of their racial origin alone. He also raised the practical problem of how pure-blooded a Romany would have to be to fall within the definition.

This ruling in 1967 clearly worried both the Race Relations Board and

---

[66] See e.g. *Ex parte Lewis* [1888] 21 QBD 191.   [67] [1967] 2 All ER 100.
[68] At 103.

some commentators, in seemingly denying gypsies the right to recognition as an ethnic group.[69] Obviously not all persons leading a nomadic life without any fixed abode are gypsies and thus the Divisional Court's definition seemed as flawed as that of the magistrates. In the context of section 127 it would appear that two elements were intended to be required, both membership of a distinct ethnic group and itinerancy (since many gypsies do settle in houses, as we have seen). The explanation given by Diplock LJ for the removal of the words 'other person' from the 1959 Act is neither accurate nor convincing. The words omitted were in fact 'or other person travelling', that is other itinerants. The probable explanation for their omission was that the words were redundant.[70] All those itinerants whom Parliament wished to include were already specified with sufficient particularity.

In any event, the wording of the section was clearly felt by gypsies and their supporters, as well as civil liberties' organizations, to be offensive and discriminatory and following a recommendation in a government report in 1977 that the word 'gypsy' be removed,[71] this reform was accomplished when the provision was re-enacted as section 148 of the Highways Act 1980. However, gypsies may still, in appropriate cases, fall into the remaining categories of 'hawker or other itinerant trader'. Furthermore, it needs to be remembered that wilful obstruction of a highway and the depositing there of rubbish (or of anything else) to the interruption of users are also offences under the Highways Act 1980.[72] Additionally, camping on roadside verges and central reservations between dual carriageways in urban areas was made an offence by the Road Traffic Act 1974,[73] thus removing what might otherwise have been fresh opportunities for gypsy camps to be established following road improvement schemes.

(d) Camps on local authority sites[74]

Until 1994 the powers and duties of local authorities with respect to the establishment of caravan sites in their areas were derived from two Acts of Parliament. The first, the Caravan Sites and Control of Development Act 1960, was designed with holidaymakers rather than gypsies in mind and merely empowered local authorities to provide sites for caravans.[75] The principal object of the Act was in fact to introduce more stringent controls over caravanning generally and to

[69] See Edmonds, R., 'Gypsies and the Law' (1968) 31 *MLR* 567; Adams, 272–3.
[70] Edmonds at 570.   [71] *Cripps Report*, 28.   [72] Ss 137, 148.
[73] S 7, amending the Road Traffic Act 1972; see now Road Traffic Act 1988, ss 19, 20.
[74] For discussion of the realities of the situation in five London boroughs, see generally Hyman, M., *Sites for Travellers* (London, 1989).   [75] S 24.

ensure that sites were positioned in suitable locations and that they possessed adequate facilities. To this end, as we have seen, the Act in effect made it compulsory for both planning permission and a site licence to be obtained for all existing and future sites.[76] The second and far more important piece of legislation, Part II of the Caravan Sites Act 1968, imposed upon every council of a county, Metropolitan district and London borough a duty to exercise its powers under the 1960 Act so far as might be necessary in order to provide 'adequate accommodation' for gypsies 'residing in or resorting to' its area.[77] Mindful of the decision in *Mills v Cooper*, gypsies were broadly defined in section 16 of the Act as persons of a 'nomadic habit of life, whatever their race or origin', excluding members of an organized group of travelling showmen or persons engaged in travelling circuses travelling together as such. Whether a person followed a nomadic lifestyle was a matter of fact and degree and the courts ruled that those gypsies who had lost this habit through permanent settlement were excluded.[78] On the other hand, those who were seasonally nomadic[79] or who would be travelling but for special circumstances, such as the old age or infirmity of a family member,[80] were held to be included within the statutory definition.[81] Metropolitan districts and London boroughs were only required to provide accommodation for a maximum of fifteen caravans each at any one time.[82] While the 1968 Act extended the powers of local authorities by enabling them to provide working space and facilities for the operation of normal gypsy activities,[83] no duty was imposed with respect to such provision.

Although Part II of the 1968 Act did not contain any time-limit within which local councils were required to provide the necessary sites (despite the well-known reluctance of many authorities), an incentive for them to comply reasonably promptly was offered in the form of the prospect of obtaining a 'designation order'. Such an order could be made by the Minister in relation to certain specified areas, whenever it

[76] Ss 1(1) and 3(3).

[77] S 6(1), as amended by the Local Government Act 1972, sched 30.

[78] See *Cuss v Secretary of State for the Environment and Wychavon District Council* [1991] *JPL* 1033; *Horsham District Council v Secretary of State for the Environment, Independent,* 31 Oct 1989.   [79] See *Greenwich London Borough v Powell* [1989] AC 995 at 1010–11.

[80] See *R v Shropshire County Council, ex parte Bungay* (1991) 23 HLR 195.

[81] Travelling showmen apparently did not come within the definition even when they were not travelling 'as such' but as itinerant gypsies—see *Hammond v Secretary of State for the Environment* [1989] *JPL* 519. 'New Age Travellers' and 'hippies' could, however, sometimes come within the terms of the statutory definition—see *North Yorkshire County Council v Capstick* (1986, unreported); *R v Gloucester County Council, ex parte Dutton* (1992) 24 HLR 246, but only if they travelled in cohesive groups and there was some connection between their wandering and the means by which they made or sought their livelihood—*R v South Hams District Council, ex parte Gibb* [1994] 4 All ER 1012.

[82] S 6(2). The Minister was empowered to give exemptions from even this limited duty, but no such exceptions were ever granted.   [83] S 6(4).

appeared to him either that adequate provision of accommodation had already been made or that in all the circumstances it was not necessary or expedient to make any such provision.[84] The effect of an order was to make it an offence for any person 'being a gypsy' to station a caravan within the designated area for the purpose of residing for any period (a) on any land situated within the boundaries of a highway; or (b) on any other unoccupied land; or (c) on any occupied land without the consent of the occupier.[85]

The only defence specifically mentioned in the Act was where the caravan was stationed on the land in consequence of illness, mechanical breakdown or other immediate emergency and the accused removed it or intended to do so as soon as reasonably practicable.[86] A person found guilty of an offence was liable on summary conviction to a substantial fine and, if the offence was continued after the conviction, this amounted to a further offence.[87] As an additional sanction a magistrates' court order might authorize the local authority to take such steps as were reasonably necessary to remove any caravan stationed in contravention of the above provisions.[88] Anyone who intentionally obstructed a person acting in the exercise of any power conferred by such an order was liable to a substantial fine and a constable could arrest without a warrant anyone whom he reasonably suspected to be guilty of committing such an obstruction.[89] These provisions were undoubtedly perceived by local authorities as a much more effective way of removing gypsies from unauthorized encampments than by taking action under the Highways Act,[90] the Road Traffic Act, local byelaws, or public health[91] or litter legislation.[92] Designation was therefore well worth striving for.

[84] S 12. For an illustration of the designation of a London borough on the basis that it was not necessary or expedient to make any provision having regard to the small and recent gypsy population of the borough, see *R v London Borough of Camden, ex parte Maughan* (1991) 23 HLR 95.
[85] S 10(1). For an interpretation of the meaning of 'unoccupied' land, see *R v Beaconsfield Justices, ex parte Stubbings* (1987) 85 *LGR* 821.   [86] S 10(2).
[87] S 10(3). The maximum fine was originally £50, but by 1991 it had been increased to £1000; Criminal Justice Act 1991, s 17.
[88] S 11(1). In *R v Highbury Corner Magistrates, ex parte Ward* (1984, unreported) Mann J held that a magistrates' court had no discretion to refuse to make such an order under s 11 if a breach of s 10 had been established.
[89] S 11(4), (5), as substituted by s 174 of the Local Government, Planning and Land Act 1980.
[90] Aside from the question of prosecuting for offences under ss 137 and 148, the local authority has power under s 143 to require the removal of any unauthorized structure from a highway and gypsy caravans have been held to fall within this section—see *R v Welwyn Hatfield District Council, ex parte Brinkly* [1983] *JPL* 378.
[91] In terms of s 268 of the Public Health Act 1936 the local authority can issue an abatement notice in respect of a statutory nuisance created by the overcrowding of a van or tent or where it has become prejudicial to the health of its inmates or where there is an absence of proper sanitary accommodation.
[92] See Environmental Protection Act 1990, Part IV. Greater powers are, however,

During the Parliamentary debates preceding the Act it was argued that it was unjust to impose criminal liability in respect of these provisions upon gypsies as a class of persons, when holidaymakers who camped without authorization within a designated area would not be guilty of an offence.[93] However, such a double standard was justified by Lord Kennet, Parliamentary Secretary at the Ministry of Housing and Local Government, on the basis of the positive discrimination in favour of gypsies in the rest of the Act.[94] Local authorities needed to be given these increased powers over unauthorized encampments as a *quid pro quo* if they were to be compelled to undertake the burdensome and expensive duties that were being thrust upon them.

It will be recalled that as well as being offered the 'carrot' of designation, local authorities were also liable to be threatened with the 'stick' of a directive from the Minister, ordering them to provide sites. Such a directive was enforceable through mandamus.[95] Although the general assumption in 1968 seems to have been that once the Act came into force site provision would proceed fairly rapidly,[96] this did not turn out to be the case. In 1977 the Cripps Report commented on the parlous position which had then been reached—

Six-and-a-half years after the coming into operation of Part II of the 1968 Act, provision exists for only one-quarter of the estimated total number of gypsy families with no sites of their own. Three-quarters of them are still without the possibility of finding a legal abode, unless on the relatively few sites provided by other gypsies, on the dwindling number of farm sites, or on sites provided for non-gypsy caravans where they are rarely welcome. Only when they are travelling on the road can they remain within the law; when they stop for the night they have no alternative but to break the law . . . . Whatever the difficulties, the figures demonstrate a failure, and a growing failure to perform a statutory duty. They also give some measure of the task ahead: the provision of upwards of 300 permanent gypsy sites, with transit sites and stopping places in addition.[97]

The Report attributed much of the blame for the poor performances of local authorities to the pressures of public opinion. Large numbers of suggested sites were being eliminated from further consideration by the force and determination of opposition from local residents. Even those which were finally selected were often thoroughly unsuitable, being situated excessively close to sewage plants, refuse destructors, motorways, main road intersections, and major railway tracks.[98]

available under s 2 of the Refuse Disposal (Amenity) Act 1978 (offence of unauthorized dumping of part or whole of abandoned motor vehicle) and s 3 of the Control of Pollution Act 1974 (offence of unlicensed deposit of controlled waste).   [93] See Adams, 19.

[94] HL Debs, 293, col 1051; 294, col 1273.   [95] S 9(2).   [96] Adams, 21.
[97] At 9, 11.   [98] Ibid, 11.

The Cripps Report was at pains to point out that government policy was now to 'accept the gypsy's right to a nomadic existence for as long as he wishes to continue it. There is no intention to put pressure on him to settle or assimilate unless or until he wishes to do so . . . .'[99] However, Okely has suggested that such a pluralist philosophy had barely begun to be digested by many of those entrusted with the implementation of the Act—

Up to the mid 1970s at least, while no clear policy was acknowledged, the underlying assumption among influential officials in central and local government was that gypsies would eventually be assimilated into the dominant sedentary society. Site provision was equated with settlement, and in turn equated with assimilation.[100]

At all events, no directive had yet been issued to any local authority by the Minister using his powers under section 9(2) of the Act. The Cripps Report was in no doubt that the reluctance of Ministers to give a lead and use their 'reserve power' was an important contributory factor in the paucity of sites, noting that 'they have been too tolerant towards local authorities who have consistently ignored or evaded duties laid upon them by the Act.'[101]

In order to speed up the provision of sites, the Cripps Report recommended that quotas be allocated to each county by the Secretary of State after discussions with local authorities.[102] This proposal was accepted by the Government[103] and discussions with local authorities took place in 1979. The Government also accepted a recommendation that it should renew attempts to persuade local authorities to desist, so far as possible, from enforced movement or harassment of gypsies during the period taken to establish the quotas and set up the agreed number of sites.[104] As a result, several authorities operated 'non-harassment' policies in terms of which they did not take action unless the unauthorized encampment was creating a hazard to road safety or public health, or constituted an intolerable public nuisance by virtue of its size, location, nature, or persistence, or would be damaging to the public interest if allowed to remain for an extended period, or would damage the authority's property or prejudice its use and enjoyment by legitimate tenants or occupiers.[105]

The most controversial question, however, concerned the issue of 'designation'. The Report recommended that the powers of the Secretary of State in this regard be restricted by the imposition of further

[99] At 1, 7.   [100] At 113.   [101] At 15.   [102] Ibid, 23.
[103] See DoE Circular 57/78.   [104] *Cripps Report*, 24; DoE Circular 57/78.
[105] See e.g. the policy of Gloucester County Council described in *R v Gloucester County Council, ex parte Dutton* (1992) 24 HLR 246.

preconditions before such an order could be made.[106] However, many local authorities regarded the designation powers as potentially their most effective weapon in evicting gypsies from unauthorized encampments and did not wish to see them diluted in any way. They also pressed for designation to be more flexibly available on a district or part-county basis, rather than limited to the county-wide basis laid down in the 1968 Act. One reason for this was that many district councils had been unwilling to co-operate fully with their county councils without this bait as an incentive. The Government eventually bowed to their demands and designation on a district basis was introduced by section 175 of the Local Government, Planning and Land Act 1980, provided a joint application was made by the county and district together.[107] However, it remained the position that the Minister had first to be satisfied that there was 'adequate' accommodation in the area for gypsies. The concept of adequate accommodation was elaborated in a Departmental Circular in 1978 as follows[108]—

The powers that flow from designation are severely discriminatory against one group of people, and their use is justifiable only on the basis that the duty of the responsible local authority with regard to that group has been fully implemented . . . . 'Adequate' provision should have the effect that no gypsy residing in or resorting to the area is without a suitable place to go. For this purpose it is first necessary to establish the extent of the need for accommodation and to distinguish between local gypsies with long standing connections with the area and those visiting it, whether for a lengthy period or a few days . . . . Sites of high quality intended for permanent occupation may be inappropriate for the needs of gypsies in transit or of those unable to accommodate satisfactorily to the stricter regime necessarily prevailing on a well-organised site . . . .

In a subsequent Departmental Circular in 1981 it was pointed out that three different types of site were likely to be needed—residential (long-stay with full facilities), transit (short-stay with minimum facilities),[109] and emergency stopping places (with few or no facilities). Both circulars also stressed, rather disingenuously, the value of gypsies owning and running their own private sites wherever feasible and drew attention to this method of relieving the pressure on local authorities for suitable provision.[110]

By the beginning of 1986, although the position had improved con-

---

[106] At 26–7; see also the criticisms of designation in Adams, 275–6.

[107] By the same section the Minister's power to issue directions was extended even to designated areas.   [108] DoE Circular 57/78.

[109] DoE Circular 8/81; see also DoE, *The Accommodation Needs of Long-Distance and Regional Travellers* (London, 1982).

[110] For a review of the difficulties with regard to establishing private sites, see Home, R., 'Planning Problems of Self-Help Gypsy Sites' [1982] *JPL* 217.

siderably over the previous decade, there were still around 3,000 families in need of accommodation who were having to camp on unauthorized sites.[111] Moreover, only a small percentage of the sites provided were of the temporary or transit type, despite the fact that these are preferred by most gypsies and cost far less than the permanent sites.[112] The explanation for this lay in the fact that the highest priority for obtaining a full refund of the capital costs of creating a site, through an Exchequer grant, was given to the 'residential' sites, while such grant would only be paid for temporary or transit sites if a recognized and specific need had been identified.[113] Designations were not being reviewed or withdrawn, even when they no longer reflected the situation which prevailed when they were granted and there was no longer adequate accommodation in the area concerned.

By around this time the House of Commons Select Committee on the Environment was sufficiently disturbed at the continued shortfall of accommodation to request a 'modest review' of the effectiveness of Government policy towards the provision of sites.[114] Professor Wibberley was asked by the Department to submit a report analysing the responses to consultation on the subject.[115] In his report he was particularly concerned to emphasize the need for designation to operate fairly and efficiently if it was to continue to be an acceptable mechanism. Comments in some of the responses which were received suggested that some district councils might be deliberately under-counting the number of gypsies resorting to their areas in order to gain designation more easily. He proposed that better and more frequent counts of gypsy families be made, that there should be periodic reviews of designated districts, and that designation should be withdrawn from those authorities which were no longer complying with the target figures for their areas.[116] The Government's initial response was, however, predictably bland and non-committal,[117] although the Secretary of State did acknowledge that the most important contribution that could be made to resolving difficulties between gypsies and the settled community remained 'the provision of properly serviced sites as quickly as possible'.[118]

It is against this background that attention needs to be turned to consider both how local authorities were using the law to remove gypsies from unauthorized encampments and how the gypsies themselves

---

[111] See DoE, *Count of Gypsy Caravans in England* (Jan 1986).   [112] See Okely, 113–7.
[113] DoE Circular 8/81, para 19.
[114] *Third Report of the House of Commons Environment Committee on the DoE's Main Estimates, 1985–86*, HC 414 of 1984–85, para 18.
[115] *A Report on the Analysis of Responses to Consultation on the Operation of the Caravan Sites Act 1968* (London, 1986).   [116] Ibid, paras 3.8–3.11.
[117] DoE News Release 65, 6 Feb 1987.
[118] HC Debs, 109, col 858 (written answers).

were using the courts to try to resist eviction and speed up the provision of authorized sites.

(e) The general law of trespass

Whenever gypsies camp, without permission, on land which is not their own, they are, of course, trespassers and can be evicted through proceedings brought under the civil law. Indeed it is proceedings of this nature which have traditionally been most commonly employed by local authorities to move gypsies on, rather than those available under the criminal law. In 1970 both the Rules of the Supreme Court (RSC) and the County Court Rules (CCR) were supplemented by a new rule, which provided a more expeditious procedure than had formerly been available for the recovery of land from squatters and other trespassers.[119] In terms of RSC Order 113 and CCR Order 24, possession may be obtained through either the High Court or a county court with great speed and guaranteed predictability. Prosecutions under the criminal law are invariably much slower in coming to court and may occasionally fail on a technical point of law. Under Orders 113 and 24 (as amended) proceedings can be brought against defendants without even specifically naming them, with the summons merely being sealed in a transparent envelope affixed to a stake in the ground, a considerable advantage with a fluctuating group of people such as gypsies.[120] Furthermore, such proceedings may be expected to attract less publicity than the pressing of criminal charges and this the local authority may well prefer.

Nevertheless, in 1986 the law of trespass was strengthened, following the antics of a convoy of 'hippies' who were attempting to make a pilgrimage to Stonehenge,[121] so that trespassers could be more easily prosecuted than hitherto. Section 39 of the Public Order Act 1986 provided that trespassers would be guilty of a criminal offence, rendering them liable to up to three months' imprisonment, if they failed to leave, as soon as reasonably practicable, land they had entered upon illegally, after a direction to do so had been given by the senior police officer present at the scene. Such a police direction could be given only if the senior officer reasonably believed that two or more persons had entered land as trespassers and were present there with the common purpose of residing there for any period, that reasonable steps had been taken by or on behalf of the occupier to ask them to leave and—

---

[119] See generally, Pritchard, A., *Squatting* (London, 1981), 22–42.

[120] See SI 2289 of 1986.

[121] See generally, NCCL, *Stonehenge: a report into the civil liberties implications of the events relating to the convoys of summer 1985 and 1986* (London, 1986).

(a) that any of those persons had caused damage to property on the land or used threatening, abusive, or insulting words or behaviour towards the occupier, a member of his family, or an employee or agent of his, or

(b) that those persons had between them brought twelve or more vehicles on to the land.

The word 'vehicle' was defined to include a caravan[122] and although this new statutory offence was aimed directly at bands of 'hippies' rather than at gypsies, it was clearly liable to be used against the latter in suitable circumstances,[123] even though guidelines issued by the Association of Chief Police Officers indicated otherwise.[124] It did not, however, extend to trespass on land forming part of a highway.[125] The principal advantage of the creation of the new offence from the point of view of individual farmers and other landowners (including local authorities) lay in a saving of the legal costs which would be incurred in bringing civil proceedings. On the other hand, the police were called upon to make difficult judgments as to whether a trespass had occurred under the civil law and considerable resentment and misunderstanding could result from confrontations with both 'hippies' and gypsies.[126]

(f) Litigation in the courts

Only very slowly did the courts begin to respond sympathetically to gypsy arguments designed to demonstrate that intervention was required both by judges and by the Minister, if local authorities were to be pressed to comply with their statutory duty to provide enough sites. Early on, the very existence (albeit unused) of the Minister's 'reserve power' under section 6 of the 1968 Act, to give directions to local authorities enforceable by mandamus, was held to restrict other remedies, such as a private right of action, being employed in an attempt to force the hand of local authorities. In *Kensington and Chelsea London Borough Council v Wells*[127] the Court of Appeal ruled that the duty imposed upon local authorities was not susceptible of enforcement at the instance of individual gypsies because it was clear that the statute had provided the Minister with the sole remedy. Indeed, in the view of Roskill LJ, a local authority could not even be said to be in breach of its duty until the Minister had invoked his reserve power, at any rate in the

---

[122] S 39(5).

[123] For an illustration of its use against gypsies, see Daly, M., *Anywhere But Here: Travellers in Camden* (London, 1990), 9–10.

[124] See Sandland, R., 'Travelling: back to the future' (1994) 144 *NLJ* 750.

[125] S 39(5)(b).

[126] Section 39 was repealed and replaced by an even more stringent provision in the Criminal Justice and Public Order Act 1994—see below. [127] (1974) 72 *LGR* 289.

absence of 'quite inordinate delay'.[128] While subsequently the avenue of judicial review of the exercise of administrative powers by local authorities was strongly upheld by Woolf J in *R v Secretary of State for the Environment, ex parte Ward*[129] and by Mann J in *R v Secretary of State for the Environment, ex parte Lee*,[130] so as at least to ensure that they reached their decisions in a proper manner,[131] this mechanism was only available in exceptional circumstances and the remedies, being discretionary, were likely in practice to be too restricted to speed up the provision of sites to any significant extent. However, in *Lee's* case Mann J at least ruled that, in order to assess whether a council was in breach of its duty under the 1968 Act, the correct approach was to ask directly whether there was adequate accommodation for gypsies residing in or resorting to the relevant area, adding—

So simple an approach seems to me appropriate, having regard to the language of the statute and to the consideration that the court is not dealing with a mere technicality but with the ability of people to have secure accommodation for their homes (as presumably Parliament intended) and with the removal of the often grossly injurious environmental impact upon the public and local residents of unauthorized gypsy encampments.[132]

The judge took the view that the duty of a council was not an inchoate one, dependent upon a direction from the Secretary of State (as Roskill LJ had previously suggested in *Wells*), nor was it implicitly qualified so that it only required the council to do what was reasonably practicable, as McCullough J had indicated in the earlier case of *R v Secretary of State for Wales, ex parte Price*.[133] However, while Mann J boldly quashed the decision of the Secretary of State not to issue a direction under section 9 (because the decision had been based on the mistaken assumption that the council was not in breach of its duty), he declined to grant an order of mandamus compelling the Secretary of State to issue a direction. Only the Secretary of State could decide whether this was necessary in all the circumstances.

Subsequently, in *R v Hereford, Worcester and Surrey County Councils, ex parte Smith and Hilden*[134] Henry J expressed strong criticism of the long delay in the provision of sites—

The social damage caused by there not being sufficient sites to accommodate the nation's gypsies goes beyond the obvious effect of homelessness on the families concerned and on the conscience of the community . . . . If moved on, they and their children will suffer from society's failure to provide for them, and the effect of forced departures on education and employment opportunities will not only

---

[128] At 289–90.   [129] [1984] 2 All ER 556.   [130] (1987) 54 P & CR 311.
[131] See also *R v London Borough of Brent ex parte McDonagh* (1989) 21 HLR 494.
[132] At 324.   [133] [1984] JPL 87.   [134] (1988) COD 3.

perpetuate the cycle of deprivation, but is likely in itself to foster unlawful and anti-social behaviour in them. Their plight will or should be an affront to the national conscience. On the other hand, if allowed to remain as trespassers, not only are the tolerated sites likely to be in the wrong place . . . and therefore both objectionable and conspicuous, but the community will be indignant to witness necessary laws not being enforced . . . . I do not believe that Parliament could have envisaged that making adequate provision for gypsies should take this long, and surely the time must have now come when the Department will be intensifying its pressure on the counties nation-wide to demonstrate that this relatively small but serious problem must be solved, and its solution must be given priority.

Perhaps the most constructive ruling in favour of gypsies occurred in 1987 in *West Glamorgan County Council v Rafferty*.[135] In that case the Council had sought to evict gypsies who were trespassing on land earmarked for redevelopment, following the dismantling of a steel works. They were alleged to have caused nuisance and damage to neighbouring occupiers and to be making it difficult for the Welsh Development Agency to persuade firms to acquire premises in the area. In assessing whether the Council's decision to bring proceedings for possession should be quashed for 'unreasonableness', the Court of Appeal weighed up the factors in favour of eviction against those which ran counter to eviction and indicated that the only reasonable conclusion would be against eviction, if this were to be carried out with no provision for alternative accommodation. Amongst the factors militating against eviction were that over a period of fifteen years the Council had failed to carry out its duty under section 6 of the 1968 Act, so that if evicted there was no site within the Council's own boundaries to which the gypsies could lawfully go; it was probable that it was this failure which had led to the trespass in the present case; and eviction would cause substantial hardship to a substantial number of families involving both the trespassers themselves and those who would have to receive them elsewhere in the county. The evidence indicated that it was practicable to contain the caravans in question within a selected part of the area and quite unnecessary to evict all the families from the entire area at the same time.

Although the Court of Appeal concluded that the decision of the Council to take proceedings to evict the gypsies should be quashed for unreasonableness, the case certainly did not establish that councils would be barred in future from evicting gypsies unless and until they had complied with their obligations under the 1968 Act.[136] Each set of proceedings for eviction would have to be judged on its own merits at

---

[135] [1987] 1 All ER 1005.
[136] Ibid, at 1023; see also Brand, C., 'How are gypsies faring now?' (1986) 136 *NLJ* 995 and 997.

the time when it was brought. Hence, in *Mole Valley District Council v Smith*[137] the Court of Appeal upheld an injunction granted to a district council to evict gypsies who were camping on their own land in the Green Belt in contravention of the planning laws, even though the council in question was in clear breach of its duties under the Act. Similarly, in *R v Essex County Council, ex parte Curtis*[138] the Council's decision to evict gypsies from a lay-by under the Highways Act 1980 was upheld as reasonable by the Court despite the Council's admitted long-standing breach of its duties under the 1968 Act. Where gypsies had no right to occupy land and were clearly trespassing, their only recourse if they wished to resist an order for repossession of the land by its owner was to bring proceedings by way of judicial review,[139] but this remedy was only sparingly exercised in view of the availability of the right to make representations to the Secretary of State.[140]

Ultimately, in the late 1980s the pressure generated by the cases of *Lee* and *Rafferty* did lead Ministers to start issuing directions under section 9(2) of the Act, first to West Glamorgan and then to Hertfordshire.[141] Some seventeen years after the Act came into force litigation was at last persuading the Government to take some firm action against dilatory local authorities. However, none of the Ministerial directions contained specific time limits for implementation, nor did the Government ever apply to the courts for orders of mandamus to enforce provision of sites. Enforcement of the statutory duty had certainly proved elusive, while at the same time the use of the designation powers to prosecute gypsies had risen from a mere four charges in 1980 to an average of 200 a year during 1986 to 1991.[142]

(g) Recommendations for improving local authority provision

In 1989 research was commissioned by the Department of the Environment to address two fundamental questions. First, what were the main hindrances to site provision? Secondly, how could local authorities be assisted and encouraged to meet their statutory obligations in this regard? The resulting Report, published in 1991, identified a number of key issues.[143] Many district councils, rather than having to face any organized mass opposition to gypsies in their areas appeared merely to

---

[137] (1992) 24 HLR 442.   [138] (1992) 24 HLR 90.

[139] *Avon County Council v Buscott* [1988] QB 656.

[140] See *R v Horsham District Council, ex parte Wenman* (1992) 24 HLR 669.

[141] Subsequently, directions were issued to a few other counties, notably Surrey and Avon; see HL Debs 558, cols 478–9 (Lord Avebury).

[142] See Beale, A. and Geary, R., 'Abolition of an Unenforced Duty' (1995) 145 *NLJ* 47.

[143] Todd, D. and Clark, G., *Gypsy Site Provision and Policy: Research Report* (London, 1991), ch 3.

be under strong pressure from one or two forceful local residents, who fought tenaciously against site provision. Even so, there was little evidence of councils adopting a positive policy of educating residents about the statutory duties placed upon local authorities and promoting the benefits of site provision over unauthorized camping. Much more could have been done in terms of adopting pro-active strategies to lead and manage public opinion on the issue. The hostility shown to gypsies by several London boroughs and the inadequate level of provision made for them there meant that many resided in adjacent counties, thus accentuating the burdens placed upon them and causing considerable resentment there.

A critical factor in the success or failure of a gypsy sites policy was the amount of political will mobilized in its support and for many years inactive authorities had been able to rely on the apparent reluctance of the Department of the Environment to use its reserve powers to bring recalcitrant councils into line. Indeed some councils had objected to the lack of robust action by the Department partly on the grounds that their own efforts were made to seem less praiseworthy or necessary and partly because the whole legislative framework risked being weakened by the lax supervision afforded by the Department. However, the climate was changing as increasing activity in the courts had led to a tougher stance on the part of the Minister in issuing directions.[144] Ministerial directions were reported to have 'concentrated minds wonderfully'[145] and they had galvanized other authorities, as well as the ones directed, into taking action.

Some authorities were concerned at the slow pace of eviction procedures under both the civil law and the designation procedures and some limited use had therefore been made of section 39 of the Public Order Act, notably by one London borough. The provision of transit sites appeared to have been accorded a very low priority within councils compared to residential sites, with much opposition to them being expressed at district and parish level because of local perceptions of crime, nuisance, damage, and dirt. While few people in local government appeared happy to accept the responsibility for making an unpopular decision concerning the establishment of a transit site, the consequences of this lack of commitment to their creation 'for a population defined as nomadic' were regarded as 'extremely serious' by the authors of the Report.[146]

The Report recommended that various steps should be taken to

---

[144] The *Third Report from the House of Commons Environment Committee in the DoE's Main Estimates, 1990–91* had also recommended much more vigorous use of the Minister's power; see HC Debs, 176, col 228.   [145] Todd and Clark, 51.
[146] Ibid, 54.

ameliorate the situation.[147] Among the most important were the following. National performance standards should be developed by the Department of the Environment to be used as a baseline for comparing levels of achievement and for identifying those authorities which were proceeding unusually slowly. This would be preferable to the existing practice of the Department simply reacting to pressure from the courts in particular cases. Secondly, in view of the difficult situation prevailing in London, with totally different policies and political philosophies prevailing in adjacent boroughs, the Department should try to reach an overall agreement with all the London boroughs on a total target for the capital, with an appropriate distribution within the individual boroughs based on the latest gypsy count figures. Thirdly, since so many councils appeared confused about the designation process, the Department should prepare a comprehensive guide to the subject describing clearly both the application procedure and the terms upon which designation was granted or withheld, as well as the place of designation in the overall pattern of a statutory duty to make adequate provision for gypsies.

The main thrust of the Report was that progress would only be made if a firm lead was given to authorities by the Department and if councils were afforded a much clearer idea of the precise and compelling nature of their statutory responsibilities. The authors of the Report also prepared simultaneously some guidelines for good practice by local authorities.[148] These included the compilation by each council of a policy document, which would state a target date by which it would have fulfilled its statutory duty. Each council would have to obtain from the Department a clear indication of what information was needed to determine whether its own provision was adequate. Stress was also laid upon proper consultation with the gypsies themselves, upon establishing sound site selection procedures, and upon the adoption of a positive strategy towards creating favourable local public opinion towards the provision of sites.[149]

Meanwhile, the House of Commons Environment Committee had published another very critical report in the middle of 1990, in which it commented—

Progress towards adequate provision is still painfully slow. Our own calculations led us to the conclusion that at the present rate of new provision it would take

[147] Todd and Clark, ch 4.

[148] Todd, D. and Clark, G., *Good Practice Guidelines for Gypsy Site Provision by Local Authorities* (London, 1991).

[149] For a description of the positive approach adopted by West Sussex which led to its early designation, see Godfrey, J., 'Flourishing sites help gypsies settle', *Local Government Chronicle*, 30 Sept 1988, 14.

about twenty-five years to solve the problem; the Department did not demur from our estimate.[150]

The Committee was heartened to see the Department taking a more robust line with defaulting local authorities, but it felt that the time had come 'to set a realistic timetable for site provision, with the threats of much more vigorous use of the Secretary of State's powers of direction against laggard authorities'.[151]

(h) A radical reversal of policy

In 1992 the Department of the Environment issued a consultation paper[152] containing proposals which were depicted as representing 'a significant shift in policy'.[153] In reality, however, they amounted to a total *volte-face*, since they advocated the repeal of the whole of Part II of the 1968 Act.[154] They also came as a complete surprise.[155] Although the Conservative Party manifesto at the 1992 general election had included an undertaking to review the Act 'with the aim of reducing the nuisance of illegal encampments',[156] such a radical reversal of previous policy had not seemed a likely outcome in view of the conclusions reached in the Research Report commissioned by the Department of the Environment and published only the previous year.

The consultation paper highlighted three considerations which had prompted a desire to seek a fundamental change in the law. First, the failure of local authorities to implement their statutory obligations was conveniently glossed over through use of the bald statement that site provision was simply 'not keeping pace with the growth in the number of caravans'.[157] The Government acknowledged that, in January 1992, of the estimated 13,500 gypsy caravans in England and Wales (housing around 9,900 families), 4,500 of these caravans were still having to be parked on unauthorized sites.[158] Only 38 per cent of local authorities had achieved designation, tending to suggest that almost all the remaining 62 per cent had failed to fulfil their statutory duties, although this was not expressly admitted. The second strand apparent in Government thinking was that the advent of significant numbers of 'New Age Travellers' had complicated the problem since, although the 1968 Act was not designed with them in mind,[159] they might sometimes be entitled to

---

[150] *Third Report of the House of Commons Environment Committee on the DoE's Main Estimates, 1990–91*, HC 373 of 1989–90, para 52.   [151] Ibid, para 56.
[152] 'Gypsy Sites Policy and Illegal Camping: Reform of the Caravan Sites Act 1968' (London, 1992).   [153] Para 30.
[154] Para 24.   [155] See e.g. HL Debs, 554, col 469 (Lord Avebury).
[156] *The Best Future for Britain* (London, 1992), 23.   [157] Para 9.
[158] Para 8.   [159] Para 12.

its benefits.[160] The tendency of members of the majority community to conflate the two groups and to attribute the behaviour of one group to the other seems to be widespread. Certainly, 'New Age Travellers' have a very tarnished image among Conservative voters in rural areas and their antics must have contributed to pressure on the Government for decisive action to be taken to curb unlawful encampments.[161] Thirdly, and perhaps most importantly, the consultation paper raised the fundamental question whether, as a matter of political principle, site provision should be public rather than private, especially since 'many gypsies have settled on permanent sites'.[162] There was, the paper argued, no good reason why they should be able to remain there indefinitely. This theme was developed in the following proposition—

People who adopt a nomadic existence should be free to do so, provided they live within the law in the same way as their fellow-citizens. The choice should not, however, entail a privileged position under the law or an entitlement to a greater degree of support from the taxpayer than is made available to those who choose a more settled existence. Travellers, like other citizens, should seek to provide their own accommodation, seeking planning permission where necessary like anyone else.[163]

This line of reasoning is, however, far from straightforward. The paper proposed not only to remove the statutory duty of councils to provide sites for gypsies, but also to tighten up controls upon unauthorized camping by the imposition of some draconian sanctions. Seizure of caravans was contemplated in view of the difficulty of enforcing fines against a moving population.[164] The likely outcome, far from removing a privilege from gypsies, would instead be to confer a privilege upon the housedwelling population. The latter would continue to be able to maintain their lifestyle intact, taking vacations in their caravans without let or hindrance in a large variety of well-serviced and scenically located camp sites specifically catering for the needs of holidaymakers. Gypsies, by contrast, would have their nomadic lifestyle undermined through constant police harassment, prosecution, and conviction, leading to the possible impounding of their caravans and homelessness, if not imprisonment. As we have seen, equality before the law does not require identical treatment of everyone regardless of their different ethnic and cultural characteristics.[165] Recognition of such differences is essential if the state's general policy of pluralistic integration is to be adopted and implemented. Here the consultation paper seemed to be somewhat

---

[160] See e.g. *R v Gloucester County Council, ex parte Dutton* (1992) 24 HLR 246.
[161] See Thomas, P., 'Housing Gypsies' (1992) 142 *NLJ* 1714; Thomas, P. and Campbell, S., *Housing Gypsies* (Cardiff, 1992), 4–6.   [162] Para 9.
[163] Para 23.   [164] Para 21.   [165] See above, ch 1.

anachronistic in its notion that gypsies should be encouraged 'to settle and, in time, to transfer into traditional housing . . . so that they became integrated into the community'.[166] Integration does not entail assimilation and uniformity of behaviour, as John Major, as Prime Minister, had himself made clear only a few months before the consultation paper was published.[167] As Thomas has pointed out—

The tolerance of housedwellers towards gypsies is limited, as is our willingness to recognise and acknowledge that gypsies are different. . . . Willingness to accept difference as a component part of a well rounded society competes with our anxiety to make others more like us. The resistance of gypsies to conform to alien norms is consistent and frustrating. . . . There is an inherent danger in encouraging gypsies to be more like housedwellers by becoming housedwellers. Such a programme will not work and is rejected by gypsy people.[168]

As for the question of taxpayers' support in the form of publicly-funded sites, far less expenditure had been made per capita for gypsies in this regard than for members of the housedwelling community through council housing, mortgage interest relief for owner-occupiers, and subsidies to housing associations. Even so, there are obvious advantages in making more private sites available for those gypsies who can afford to pay for them and who wish to settle, as many now do, in one place for at least a substantial part of the year. Indeed, the National Gypsy Council has strongly advocated the merits of small private sites on the grounds that there would be better conditions there than on most public sites.[169] Generally, gypsies are not keen to live on public sites, 'claiming that they are often dirty, over-crowded and in environmentally poor locations'.[170] The reason so many have to reside there lies in the lack of any alternative venues where they can camp lawfully. However, the consultation paper was disingenuous in its suggestion that gypsies should seek planning permission for private sites 'like everyone else'. The practical problems entailed in obtaining such permission, despite the long-standing endorsement of the concept of private sites by the Department of the Environment are enormous.[171] The opposition encountered from local residents when coupled with environmental and traffic safety factors is usually sufficient to prevent the necessary permission being granted. As if that

[166] Para 27.
[167] See his speech reported in (1991) 250 *Race and Immigration* 4–5 and quoted in ch 1 above.   [168] *Op cit* at 1715.
[169] See Todd and Clark, *Research Report* 18.
[170] Home, R., 'Planning Aspects of the Government Consultation Paper on Gypsies' [1993] *JPL* 13 at 15.
[171] See Home, 16; Todd and Clark, 12–13, where it is estimated that permission is refused in around 90 per cent of applications, albeit with somewhat better prospects on appeal.

were not reason enough for concern at the viability of this option, the paper even proposed to remove the one very small feature of the planning system which operated in favour of gypsies, namely the possibility of occasionally countenancing sites in rural areas, such as Green Belts, where normally the most protective and restrictive regime applies.[172]

Despite widespread and vigorous opposition to all these proposals,[173] the Government determined to press ahead with its radical changes.[174] The planning guidance rules were amended as from January 1994 and Part II of the Caravan Sites Act 1968 was repealed by the Criminal Justice and Public Order Act 1994, which also removed the power of the Secretary of State to pay grants to local authorities for the provision of sites and tightened the sanctions upon unauthorized camping. Attention will next be turned to charting each of these developments in greater detail.[175]

(i) Planning guidance

At the beginning of 1994 a circular from the Department of the Environment[176] issued fresh planning guidance, designed to apply equally to local authority sites and private sites. Local planning authorities were advised to expect an increase in applications for private sites following the repeal of Part II of the 1968 Act and were notified of the importance of making adequate provision for gypsies in their development plans, both through the formulation of broad strategic policies and in more detailed elaboration.[177] Ideally, local plans should identify suitable locations, but where this was not possible, realistic criteria should at least be established for selecting such locations. Vacant land or surplus local council land might be appropriate. Account should be taken of the numbers of gypsy caravans in each area, as recorded in the regular six-monthly counts undertaken by local authorities, as well as of any

---

[172] Para 29.

[173] See HC Debs, 229, cols 969–70. There were negative responses from 93 per cent of county councils, 92 per cent of local authorities in London, and 71 per cent of district councils, as well as from police and childcare organizations and many others. For published criticisms, see e.g. Thomas, *op cit*; JUSTICE, 'Response to Consultation Paper on the Reform of the Caravan Sites Act 1968' (1992); Poulter, S., 'Gypsy Sites: An Unacceptable Volte-Face' (1992) 260 *Runnymede Bulletin* 10; Liberty, 'Rights and Freedoms of Gypsies and Travellers' (1993); Holgate, G., 'The Government's Consultation Paper "Reform of the Caravan Sites Act 1968"—A Solution to Gypsy Site Provision?' [1993] *Conv* 39, 111; Home, 17–18.

[174] For preliminary discussion of the changes in a debate upon a Private Member's bill, see HC Debs 218, cols 587–651.

[175] For a general critique of these developments, see Hawes, D. and Perez, B., *The Gypsy and the State* (Bristol, 1995).   [176] DoE Circular 1/94.

[177] Paras 4, 9–10.

tradition of sites occupied by gypsies.[178] In a departure from previous guidance, however, the circular specifically stated—

As a rule it will not be appropriate to make provision for gypsy sites in areas of open land where development is severely restricted . . . . Gypsy sites are not regarded as being among those uses of land which are normally appropriate in Green Belts. Green Belt land should therefore not be allocated for gypsy sites in development plans.[179]

Previously, it had been acknowledged that gypsy sites might be appropriate, and indeed necessary, in rural and Green Belt locations, albeit not as a matter of right. In a circular in 1977 the following guidance had been given by the Department of the Environment—

In certain counties there are areas of open land (including Green Belts, Areas of Outstanding Natural Beauty, etc.) where the land use policies which apply are severely restrictive to development. It may be necessary, however, to accept the establishment of gypsy sites in such areas, particularly where they come close to urban fringes. Otherwise, because of the pressure for sites around built-areas, it may be difficult to prevent unauthorized camping in far less suitable locations. On the other hand, there will clearly be a special obligation to ensure that the arguments in favour of a departure from the development plan are convincing.[180]

A similar stance was taken in a further circular the following year, in response to the Cripps Report, in which the Department declared—

. . . sites suitable in other respects may conflict with Green Belt or other planning policies. But the special need to accommodate gypsies—and the consequences of not accommodating them—should be taken into account as a material consideration in reaching planning decisions.[181]

Although the 1992 consultation paper referred to this approach as affording gypsies a 'privileged position',[182] its precise legal status was far from clear. In *Varey v Secretary of State for the Environment*[183] it was held not even to amount to a 'concession', let alone a special entitlement, and merely required sympathetic consideration to be given to applications from gypsies in such circumstances.[184] In practice, gypsies were far more likely to be the object of unfavourable than favourable treatment at the hands of the planning authorities.[185] In any event, the relevant parts

---

[178] Paras 11–12.   [179] Para 13.   [180] Circular 28/77, appendix, para 32.
[181] Circular 57/78, response to recommendation 4.13(d).
[182] At para 29.   [183] [1990] *JPL* 119.
[184] For an instance where the court upheld the grant of permission within the Green Belt and overruled the Secretary of State, see *Beech v Secretary of State for the Environment* [1993] EGCS 214.
[185] See Barnett, H., 'A Privileged Position? Gypsies, Land and Planning Law' [1994] *Conv* 454.

of both circulars were withdrawn by the 1994 circular, in which sites on the outskirts of built-up areas are mentioned as being more appropriate, with the clear proviso that 'care is taken to avoid encroachment on the open countryside'.[186] Regard should be had to access and highway considerations, the potential for noise and other disturbance from vehicles, and on-site business activities such as scrap-metal dealing.[187] The circular reiterated, albeit in slightly different terminology, the threefold classification of suitable types of sites which had previously been identified in a circular in 1981,[188] namely sites for settled occupation, temporary stopping places, and transit sites.[189] Authorities should not refuse private applications on the grounds that they considered public provision in the area to be adequate or because alternative accommodation was available elsewhere on the authorities' own sites.[190] However, proposals for gypsy sites should continue to be determined solely in relation to land-use factors and, while such sites might be acceptable in some rural locations, the granting of permission must be consistent with agricultural, archaeological, countryside, environmental, and Green Belt policies and the aim should always be 'to secure provision appropriate to gypsies' accommodation needs while protecting amenity'.[191]

In view of this, considerable doubts have been expressed, in Parliament and elsewhere, as to whether these new guidelines will make any real impact upon the needs of gypsies.[192] As Home has explained—

Subsuming gypsy accommodation within policies for caravan sites in general will not help gypsies provide for themselves, because of the likely pressure of demand from other mobile home and holiday caravan occupiers . . . . Policy should, therefore, recognise that gypsies are an identifiable social group with particular land use planning requirements, and that treating them the same as anyone else in relation to the planning system will in practice put them at a disadvantage, not least because development land for caravan sites will never have the same value as for conventional housing.[193]

Some imaginative thought clearly needs to be given to the location of some new sites in open countryside. Suggestions might include redundant army land, disused airfields, derelict industrial sites in the Green Belt, and agricultural land set aside pursuant to the Common Agricultural Policy of the European Union.[194]

---

[186] Para 14.   [187] Paras 6, 15–16.   [188] DoE Circular 8/81.
[189] Paras 17–18.   [190] Para 21.   [191] Para 22.
[192] See e.g. HL Debs, 555, cols 1529–63.   [193] At 16–17; see also Barnett at 455, 464.
[194] See e.g. HL Debs, 556, col 1196 (Lord Hylton).

(ii) Repeal of Part II of the 1968 Act

Widespread concern as to the viability of leaving future provision of further sites entirely to the private sector led to concerted opposition from many quarters to the repeal of Part II of the 1968 Act. This resistance culminated in an initial defeat for the Government in the House of Lords at the report stage of the Criminal Justice Bill, when an amendment proposed by Lord Stanley of Alderley, with cross-party support, to delay the repeal for five years was passed by 133 votes to 104.[195] The broad aim of the amendment was to give enough time for an objective assessment to be made as to whether local authorities were adjusting their development plans and granting planning permissions in a higher proportion of individual cases to enable a sufficient number of private sites to be established to meet national needs. However, the House of Commons refused to accept the amendment[196] and the House of Lords eventually gave way and voted not to re-insert it.[197]

As a result, section 80(1) of the Criminal Justice and Public Order Act 1994 has repealed Part II of the 1968 Act, notably the statutory duty placed upon local authorities to provide sites, as well as the ministerial power to give directions to councils in this regard. The provisions relating to designation have similarly been abrogated. This leaves local authorities in the position in which they were formerly, namely in possession of a discretionary power under the Caravan Sites and Control of Development Act 1960, which they rarely used prior to 1968. It seems very unlikely that such a power will now be extensively utilized and, if private site provision remains roughly at current levels or sees only a modest increase, there is every reason to expect the same types of problem as prompted the enactment of Part II of the 1968 Act in the first place.

There will probably be an increase in open conflicts between local housedwellers and gypsies, with caravans being hounded by police forces from one area to another.[198] Indeed, during the course of the Parliamentary debates on the bill, the Minister baldly asserted that one of the purposes of the legislation was to give the police power to 'move people on', rather than haul them before the courts.[199] In any event, the financial costs to local authorities in bringing court proceedings[200] and through police involvement are likely to be very considerable.[201] No doubt, few councils will actually close existing public sites, since they

---

[195] HL Debs, 555, cols 1259–64.   [196] HC Debs, 248, cols 355–79.
[197] HL Debs, 558, cols 477–92.
[198] See JUSTICE, 4–6; Holgate, 115; Home, 16–17; HC Debs, 241, cols 315–9.
[199] HC Debs, Standing Committee 'B', 11 Feb 1994, col 706.
[200] These are detailed below.   [201] HL Debs, 555, col 1517.

would then have to repay the Exchequer grant allocated for their establishment, make arrangements to accommodate those made homeless, and fulfil their statutory duties towards any children involved, but the message conveyed to the general public by the repeal of the statutory duty is that recalcitrant authorities have managed to evade their obligations to an unpopular minority group with impunity. This may breed considerable resentment on the part of those adjacent councils which have made strenuous efforts to fulfil their duties and find that their reward comes in the form of increasing numbers of gypsies being pushed in their direction.[202]

(iii) Termination of Exchequer grant

In his interim report in 1976, Sir John Cripps had expressed grave concern that the slow rate of public site provision was aggravating tensions between housedwellers and gypsies and therefore recommended that drastic financial measures should be introduced to speed up the process.[203] Since the movement of gypsies around the country meant that their accommodation needs represented a national rather than a local problem and since expediency dictated an initiative on the part of central government to help overcome popular opposition at the local level, a case could be made for the capital costs of site provision being met by the Exchequer. This led him to report as follows—

There is an urgent need to remedy a rapidly deteriorating situation, fraught with possibilities of violence; and there is every indication that no remedy will be found in time within existing arrangements. This suggests the need for a high rate of grant but limited in time as an added inducement to the more rapid provision of sites. In view of the current financial constraints on local authorities, I have concluded that nothing less than a grant of 100 per cent for five years towards the capital costs of sites is likely to achieve the required targets. The rate of grant (if any) for subsequent years could be reviewed towards the end of the period.[204]

This recommendation was accepted by the Department of the Environment and an Exchequer grant at the rate of 100 per cent to cover capital costs was introduced in 1978. The grant was described as 'a very exceptional rate and . . . in earnest of the Government's determination to secure quick and effective remedies'.[205] However, the projected five-

---

[202] This outcome was described as 'obnoxious' by Lord Congleton—see HL Debs, 555, col 1558.   [203] *Cripps Report*, 40.

[204] Ibid, 43.

[205] DoE Circular 57/78, para 4. Initially the grant was made under annual Appropriation Acts, but from 1980 onwards the power to pay grant was contained in Local Government, Planning and Land Act 1980, s 70.

year time span proved far too optimistic and, as we have seen, the annual growth in the number of sites remained small. The scheme was therefore extended indefinitely. One reason why it proved a less success-ful incentive than anticipated was that, under the system of block grants, gypsy sites were included as part of an authority's capital expenditure and therefore had to compete with other capital projects in terms of priorities.[206] Moreover, the Department of the Environment insisted on keeping costs down to a bare minimum, which could mean greater maintenance expenditure for local councils in the longer term.[207] How-ever, by the end of 1993 the total amount of grant paid to local autho-rities had reached £78 million[208] and the Government decided to bring the scheme to an end. Although this may seem a substantial sum of money, it is very small in comparison with the total expenditure during the same period on council housing (or indeed with the revenue fore-gone through mortgage interest relief), and the public provision of a pitch on an authorized site was obviously far cheaper than the construc-tion of a council house. In any event, not only the right of local autho-rities to claim the Exchequer grant but even the power of central government to pay it on a discretionary basis were removed by section 80(5) of the Criminal Justice and Public Order Act, after the Minister had unwarrantably castigated the scheme as an 'open-ended commitment unparalleled elsewhere in the public sector'.[209]

(iv) Extension of criminal sanctions for unauthorized encampments

The Government's manifest concern to reduce the nuisance caused by unlawful encampments led it inexorably to seek to strengthen the crim-inal law in this field. The repeal of Part II of the 1968 Act spelt the demise of the designation provisions and obviously some alternative criminal sanctions were needed to replace them. In the Government's view the clearest deficiency of the designation provisions lay in the fact that so few local authorities (under 40 per cent) had earned the right to employ them by carrying out to the full their duties under the 1968 Act. Tough sanctions were needed by all authorities if the campaign to be waged against unlawful caravanners was to be successful. Perhaps just as important a limitation upon the utility of the designation weapons, however, arose from their range of application. They could only be employed against persons of a 'nomadic habit of life' and it was far from clear from the limited case law prior to 1994 whether, for example,

---

[206] See Forrester, 44–5.   [207] See Hyman, 80–2.
[208] HC Debs, Standing Committee 'B', 11 Feb 1994, col 692.   [209] Ibid, col 713.

'hippies' and 'New Age Travellers', as well as ethnic gypsies, came within their ambit.[210]

To overcome these restrictions in the 1968 Act, the Criminal Justice and Public Order Act confers broadly similar powers regarding the removal of caravans as operated under the designation provisions, but it extends them to all local authorities and makes them applicable not merely to gypsies but to any persons 'for the time being residing in a vehicle or vehicles', if they are on land forming part of a highway, or any other unoccupied land, or on any occupied land without the consent of the occupier.[211] As a result, any local authority is empowered to give a direction for such persons to leave the land and remove their vehicles (and any other property they have with them), by serving a notice upon them.[212] A person who knows that such a direction has been given which applies to him and who then fails, as soon as practicable, to leave the land or remove the vehicles or other property (or after removal re-enters the land with a vehicle within three months of the direction) is thereby guilty of an offence and liable to a maximum fine of £1,000.[213] As under the 1968 Act, it is a defence for an accused to show that failure to leave or remove a vehicle or other property was due to illness, mechanical breakdown, or other immediate emergency.[214] Magistrates' courts are empowered to make orders for the removal of vehicles and those residing in them, upon a complaint by a local authority, if they are satisfied that a direction given by an authority is being contravened.[215] The court may then issue an order authorizing the local authority to take such steps as are reasonably necessary to ensure the removal order is complied with.[216] Wilful obstruction of anyone exercising powers pursuant to such an order also constitutes an offence and consequent liability, upon conviction, to a maximum fine of £1,000.[217]

In its consultation paper the Department of the Environment had envisaged even more stringent sanctions for non-compliance with these directions and orders—

... fine enforcement action by the courts against a moving population is very difficult and the last resort for fine default—imprisonment—may be reached in a high proportion of cases. An alternative penalty would be to seize the caravan; such action would also prevent the offence being repeated .... The seized caravans would be returned when the offender(s) satisfied the court that he (they) either had a legal place to camp or alternative accommodation.[218]

---

[210] See e.g. *R v Gloucester County Council, ex parte Dutton* (1992) 24 HLR 246; *R v South Hams District Council, ex parte Gibb* [1994] 4 All ER 1012.   [211] S 77(1).
[212] S 77(2).   [213] S 77(3).   [214] S 77(5).   [215] S 78(1).
[216] S 78(2).   [217] S 78(4).   [218] Para 21.

This suggestion was vigorously condemned by many critics as likely to lead to increased homelessness and the possibility of children having to be taken into care.[219] The decision not to proceed with such draconian measures was one of the very few concessions made by the Government as a result of the 'consultation exercise'.[220]

There is one technical difference between the 1994 Act's provisions and the former designation process. Whereas unauthorized camping was automatically an offence if an area had been designated, under the 1994 Act a trigger mechanism has been inserted and no offence is committed unless and until a local authority issues a direction for a person to leave through the service of a notice. This gives the local authority a discretion whether or not to take enforcement action. Of course, under the 1968 Act local authorities possessed a similar discretion in deciding whether or not to prosecute offenders and in many instances did not do so. Indeed, during the course of the debates on the bill in the House of Lords, a Government spokesman acknowledged that 10 per cent of all gypsy caravans were stationed on 'tolerated sites'[221] and he insisted that this policy of toleration would continue, adding—

The Department of the Environment intends to issue advice to local authorities repeating the existing advice that they should use the new powers to evict gypsies with great care, particularly where they are encamped unobtrusively on council land, and that they should continue to look for ways to minimise nuisance, by providing, for instance, temporary emergency stopping places where gypsies stay for short periods.[222]

A new circular was duly issued, which reminds local authorities that they should use their powers in a humane and compassionate fashion, primarily to reduce nuisance and to afford greater protection to private landowners.[223] While they would usually be justified in evicting from unauthorized sites gypsies who refused to move onto an authorized site in their area, councils should not evict gypsies needlessly and should remember that they could well have educational, housing, and social service responsibilities to individual gypsy families.[224] Where gypsies are camping unlawfully on council land and are not causing an uncontrollable nuisance, this could be tolerated for short periods in preference to forcing them to move to another area where they might

---

[219] See e.g. JUSTICE, 8–9.
[220] HC Debs, Standing Committee 'B', 11 Feb 1994, col 702.
[221] HL Debs, 555, cols 1546, 1559 (Earl Ferrers).   [222] Ibid, col 1526.
[223] DoE Circular 18/94, para 9.
[224] Ibid, paras 6, 8, 10–13. Failure to take account of such responsibilities at the time when a direction to leave is issued is likely to lead to it being quashed by the courts—see *R v Lincolnshire CC and Wealden DC, ex parte Atkinson, Wales and Stratford* [1997] JPL 65.

cause greater nuisance.[225] On such tolerated sites councils should consider providing basic services.[226]

Even if these concessions are borne in mind, the criminal law cannot provide an acceptable solution to the underlying problem of a shortage of sites.[227] Moreover, as if these new extended powers were not enough, the 1994 Act has further strengthened the criminal law of collective trespass by replacing section 39 of the Public Order Act 1986 with an even more stringent provision applicable to those who have, between them, six or more vehicles on land on which they are trespassing, rather than the twelve vehicles specified in the previous Act.[228] Apart from being subjected to criminal penalties for failing to comply with a police officer's direction to leave the land,[229] trespassers are liable to have their vehicles seized by the police.[230] Since gypsies often travel in groups, these provisions are liable to have a direct impact upon them.

(v) Towards assimilation through a move into housing

It is not difficult to construct an argument that the changes introduced in 1994 were designed not only to discontinue the pluralist, publicly-funded, specific differential treatment which the 1968 Act had accorded to gypsies (henceforth equating them with 'hippies', 'New Age Travellers', and indeed any other campers or caravanners), but also to push them towards greater assimilation with the majority community[231] by using the criminal law to suppress their nomadic tradition.[232] It will be recalled that, according to one leading commentator, officials in local and central government, even as recently as the 1970s, tended to equate site provision with settlement and eventual assimilation.[233] In its 1992 consultation paper, the Department of the Environment commented that—

The 1968 Act was intended to provide a network of sites to enable gypsies to move around or settle but in practice many gypsies have settled on permanent sites and 90 per cent of local authority pitches in England are used for residential as opposed to transit purposes.[234]

This is clearly meant to convey the impression that over the previous thirty years or so most gypsies had settled down permanently as a matter of choice. However, the fact is that the Exchequer grant was almost exclusively devoted to the establishment of permanent sites[235]

---

[225] DoE Circular 18/94, para 6.   [226] Id.   [227] See JUSTICE, 7.
[228] S 61(1)(b).   [229] S 61(4).   [230] S 62.
[231] For a denial that this was the Government's aim, see HL Debs, 555, col 542 (Earl Ferrers).
[232] In terms of the spectrum of legal techniques outlined at pp 59–66 above, moving from (f) and (g) to (a).   [233] Okely, 113, quoted earlier.
[234] Para 9.   [235] See Holgate, 111.

and the free movement of gypsies was severely curtailed by the lack of transit sites and the enforcement action taken by the police and local authorities, either under the civil law or pursuant to the designation provisions. Building upon this insecure foundation of apparently voluntary settlement, the consultation paper drew attention to the possibility that settled gypsies might be encouraged to move into houses, especially in view of the difficulty of obtaining permission for private sites due to local opposition.[236] The paper acknowledged that transferring into traditional housing 'may not be easy for people who are accustomed to a nomadic life-style'[237] and therefore declared that it might be necessary for the Government to provide advice on education, health, and housing which encouraged gypsies and other travellers 'to settle and, in time, to transfer into traditional housing'.[238] Indeed, the paper then proceeded to consider the feasibility of introducing a limited form of financial assistance towards the purchase of permanent housing for gypsies on similar lines to the scheme for council tenants,[239] though this idea was later abandoned.[240] Pressures to move into housing seem certain to be resisted by the vast majority of gypsies currently living in caravans, but even if significant numbers succumbed in desperation, such a shift would surely prove extremely difficult to implement in practice, in view of the current general shortage of rentable housing stock.[241] Nor would the gardens of most houses be suitable for gypsies to carry on their traditional economic activities, such as scrap-metal work.

(vi) Critical response

As we have seen, there was considerable opposition to the Government's change of policy. In particular, the relevant clauses of the Criminal Justice and Public Order Bill were subjected to a barrage of criticism in the House of Lords during the committee and report stages, with hardly a word being uttered in their defence by anyone other than the Government spokesman.[242] Attention was drawn to the irony of the Government's insistence that gypsies live 'within the law' at the very moment when those local authorities which had failed to fulfil their legal duties over a period of twenty-five years were being rewarded by an alteration of the law in their favour.[243] Lord Avebury, the promoter of the 1968 Act, described the 1994 changes as 'mean and despicable provisions which have no place on the statute book of a nation which prides itself on its

---

[236] Para 27.   [237] Id.   [238] Id.   [239] Para 28.
[240] See HC Debs, Standing Committee 'B', 10 Feb 1994, col 702.
[241] See Thomas, 1714–15; Thomas and Campbell, 6–12, 14–15; Home 16.
[242] See HL Debs, 555, cols 1111–50, 1168–1200, 1516–63.
[243] HL Debs, 555, cols 1112, 1133 (Lord Irvine).

treatment of minorities'.[244] The Bishop of Liverpool remarked that a 'civilised country is properly measured by how it treats its minorities, especially minorities who, for various reasons have attracted unpopularity'[245] and he clearly felt that the new policy failed this test. Earlier, Lord Irvine had commented that 'at one stroke the provisions destroy the tradition that non-conforming minorities are not to be persecuted'.[246]

THE HUMAN RIGHTS DIMENSION

During the past decade several applications have been made by gypsies to the European Commission of Human Rights, alleging violations of the Convention on the part of the United Kingdom. Reliance has principally been placed on Articles 8 and 14. Article 8(1) provides that everyone has the right to respect for his private and family life and 'his home'. Article 8(2) authorizes the imposition of a limited range of restrictions upon this right as follows—

There shall be no interference by a public authority with the exercise of this right except such as is in accordance with the law and is necessary in a democratic society in the interests of national security, public safety or the economic well-being of the country, for the prevention of disorder or crime, for the protection of health or morals, or for the protection of the rights and freedoms of others.

Article 14 provides that, in the enjoyment of the rights listed in the Convention, there must be no discrimination on any ground such as, *inter alia*, race, national or social origin, association with a national minority, or other status. Discrimination against gypsies undoubtedly falls within one of these categories, fitting perhaps most comfortably within the extended meaning of 'racial' discrimination adopted in the International Convention on the Elimination of All Forms of Racial Discrimination, which includes distinctions made on the basis of 'ethnic origin'.[247] As we have seen,[248] the European Court of Human Rights has ruled that distinctions between different groups are only permissible if a legitimate aim is being pursued, if the distinction possesses an objective and reasonable justification, and if there is a reasonable degree of proportionality between the means employed and the aim sought to be realized.[249]

---

[244] HL Debs, 555, col 1118.   [245] Ibid, col 1119.   [246] HL Debs, 554, col 503.
[247] Art 1(1). For confirmation that gypsies constitute an ethnic group under the Race Relations Act 1976, see *Commission for Racial Equality v Dutton* [1989] 1 All ER 306.
[248] See above, ch 3.
[249] See e.g. *Belgian Linguistic Case (No 2)* (1968) 1 EHRR 252 at 284; *Marckx v Belgium* (1980) 2 EHRR 330 at 343; *Abdulaziz, Cabales and Balkandali v UK* (1985) 7 EHRR 471 at 499.

Although there is no specific article in the European Convention designed to protect minority rights along the lines of Article 27 of the International Covenant on Civil and Political Rights, the Commission expressed the view in *G and E v Norway*[250] that under Article 8 'a minority group is, in principle, entitled to claim the right to respect for the particular life style it may lead as being "private life", "family life" or "home"'.[251]

Against this background how have English gypsies fared in their applications under the Convention? In *P v UK*[252] the applicants had been settled on a local authority site in Greenwich for over fifteen years when they were suddenly evicted by the council without any reason being given. They were seasonal workers who travelled in one of their two caravans for up to five months a year in search of employment. The other caravan was left on the council site. The essence of their complaint was that the security of tenure of gypsies on public sites provided under the Caravan Sites Act 1968 was very limited in comparison with that enjoyed by occupiers of other sites covered by the Mobile Homes Act 1983. Whereas those in the latter category could only be evicted for breach of their tenancy agreement and could transmit their security of tenure by means of sale or gift of their caravan, those in the former category could be evicted through a court order upon four weeks' notice, without the need for any reason being given. The applicants complained that their 'arbitrary' eviction constituted an interference with their right to respect for their home contrary to Article 8(1), as well as being discriminatory contrary to Article 14, in that non-gypsy caravanners were more securely protected by the Mobile Homes Act.

The Commission rejected the application as manifestly ill-founded for the following reasons. Interference with a person's private life and home could be justified under Article 8(2) if it was necessary to protect the rights of others. Here the council's right under the tenancy agreement to evict occupiers upon four weeks' notice was indeed necessary, in view of its duties under the 1968 Act to provide adequate sites for all gypsies residing in or resorting to their area. It was for this reason that the site was run on the basis that tenants could only leave the site for more than twenty weeks each year with the express written consent of the council. Earlier, in ruling against the applicants' contention that they were entitled to the protection of the Mobile Homes Act, the House of Lords had borne in mind the fact that local authorities would find it very difficult to discharge their duties under the 1968 Act if many of their residents had acquired a degree of permanency in their occupation (despite prolonged absence), thus precluding others from being catered

---

[250] (1984) 35 Dec & Rep 30.   [251] At 35.   [252] (1991) 67 Dec & Rep 264.

for adequately.[253] So far as the allegation of discrimination was concerned, the European Commission pointed out that the difference in security of tenure related not to a particular tenant's 'status' but to the classification of the site. Gypsies who resided on caravan sites other than those provided by local authorities pursuant to the Caravan Sites Act would enjoy the same security of tenure there as non-gypsies. Hence no violation of Article 14 had occurred.

In *Smith v UK*[254] the applicant had been threatened with eviction from a local authority site in Bedfordshire, part of which was being closed down. She alleged a violation of Article 8 on the basis that there were no other suitable public sites in the surrounding area and since Bedfordshire had been designated under the 1968 Act she would be committing an offence if she were to camp on an unauthorized site anywhere in that county.[255] In effect, her nomadic way of life was being criminalized in such circumstances and she was being denied the right to reside in a caravan in the part of the country where she had been brought up and where other members of her family lived. Moreover, she argued, the designation provisions were discriminatory in being targeted solely at gypsies. However, her application was rejected on the ground that she herself had not been a victim of any violation of the Convention, since the local authority had allowed her to remain on its site following judicial review proceedings and she had not indicated a desire to move elsewhere.

In *Buckley v UK*[256] the applicant had moved in 1988, together with her three children, to live in her caravans on land in South Cambridgeshire which was owned and occupied by her sister's family, who already had the necessary planning permission to station their own caravans there. The applicant had then acquired part of this land and stationed her three caravans on it. However, her subsequent application for planning permission to do so was refused by the district council in 1990 and its decision was upheld on appeal by the Secretary for State. The principal reasons justifying the refusal related to questions of amenity (detraction from the rural and open quality of the landscape) and highway safety (access to the site being too narrow for two vehicles to pass one another). The Secretary of State also found that the concentration of gypsy sites in the area had reached the desirable maximum and therefore ruled that the

---

[253] See *Greenwich London Borough Council v Powell* [1989] AC 995 at 1012.
[254] Application No. 18401/91.
[255] An earlier complaint by the same applicant that, even in undesignated areas, the lack of sites and constant forced removal of gypsies from unauthorized encampments constituted violations of the Convention had been rejected as inadmissible—see *Smith v UK*, Application No. 14455/88.   [256] (1997) 23 EHRR 101.

need for additional sites for gypsies should not outweigh these planning and highway objections.

The applicant was fined for failure to comply with a planning enforcement notice in 1992 and the following year the area of South Cambridgeshire was designated under the 1968 Act. Her application to the European Commission alleged a violation of Article 8, in that she was neither allowed to live in a caravan on her own land nor permitted to do so elsewhere in South Cambridgeshire because all the council sites were either full or dangerous, and unauthorized camping was a criminal offence as a result of designation. In its defence, the Government contended that members of minority groups could not claim immunity from general planning controls and that the refusal of planning permission and issue of enforcement notices were justified by the interests of public safety on the road, the economic wellbeing of the country, and the protection of the environment. As for the framework of regulation, including the system of designation orders, this represented a proportionate response to the need to protect public safety on the roads as well as the rights of others.

By the narrow margin of seven votes to five, the Commission concluded that a violation of Article 8 had occurred. It accepted that living in a caravan was an integral and deeply-held part of the applicant's gypsy life-style and that the traditional life-style of a minority could attract the guarantees concerning private life, home, and family life contained in Article 8. Although the issue of enforcement notices against her had pursued a legitimate governmental aim, this interference was excessive and disproportionate and therefore not necessary in a democratic society, even allowing the state the normal margin of appreciation. A fair balance had to be struck between the demands of the general interest of the community and the requirements of the protection of the individual's fundamental rights. In assessing whether an excessive burden was being placed upon the applicant, the Commission had to consider whether there was any practical alternative open to the applicant, bearing in mind that her options were restricted by her traditional gypsy life-style. Designation had been granted in South Cambridgeshire not upon the grounds that adequate provision had been made for gypsy accommodation in the district, but on the basis that it was not 'expedient' under section 12 of the 1968 Act for the district to make any such provision. In reality, insufficient accommodation was available to meet the needs of all gypsies residing in or resorting to the district. Despite this, it would be a criminal offence for the applicant to move onto waste land or the side of a road anywhere in the vicinity. Moreover, it would have been unreasonable to expect the applicant to apply for one of the few vacant places, as they became available, on one of the official sites nearby, bearing in mind that she was a single mother with three children, in view of the recent levels of disorder, crime, and violence in that neighbourhood. That site offered her distinct disadvantages compared to her current location on her own land close to other members of her family. Against this background, the Commission considered that the factors weighing in favour of the public interest in planning controls were of a slight and general nature. The highway safety aspect appeared weak and the strength of the general amenity argument was greatly reduced by the fact that this was not an area of untouched countryside or of particular scenic beauty in view of other authorized gypsy sites in the vicinity. The Commission expressly indicated that 'special considerations arise in the planning sphere regarding the needs of gypsies',[257] as the Government's own policies had themselves acknowledged.

The Commission's decision was reversed on referral to the Court. By six votes to three, the Court decided that no violation had occurred. In its view, the procedural safeguards provided for in the regulatory framework of English planning legislation had afforded Buckley due respect for her interests under Article 8. The special needs of gypsies had been sufficiently considered, but Buckley's own needs had to be balanced against the general interest in conforming with planning policies. Article 8 did not necessarily go so far as to permit individuals' preferences as to their place of residence to override the general interest. The means employed by the planning authorities to achieve their legitimate aims were not disproportionate and the margin of appreciation accorded to the state had not been exceeded.

However, the Court did at least accept that a gypsy's caravan, albeit stationed illegally on an unauthorised site, constituted a 'home' which was entitled to respect under Article 8(1). Thus, any interference with it under planning laws did need to be justified under Article 8(2). Hence, although the Court (unlike the Commission) did not allude expressly to the Commission's earlier statement in *G and E v Norway* (quoted above) concerning a minority group's life-style being entitled to protection under Article 8, much the same principle is established for gypsies if their caravans are recognized as their homes for purposes of the Article, even if unlawfully parked.

It will be recalled that in a circular issued in 1978 the Department of the Environment had itself accepted that the powers flowing from designation were 'severely discriminatory against one group of people' and therefore their use could only be justified if the duty of a local authority towards that group had been 'fully implemented'.[258] A key part of the applicant's argument in *Buckley v UK* was that, despite designation,

---

[257] At 120.   [258] DoE Circular 57/78.

there was an admitted shortfall of sites for gypsies in South Cambridge-shire. Hence, while designation might have a legitimate aim in regulating unauthorized camping, its discrimination against gypsies could be shown to be a disproportionate response to the problem if designation operated unfairly in practice by penalizing those gypsies who resided in the area and yet could not find a safe site in which to live and bring up their families. On this point, however, both the Commission and the Court ruled that since the applicant had not herself been prosecuted or subjected to any order for removal under the designation provisions, they would not review the propriety of these provisions *in abstracto*.

In any event, by repealing the designation provisions in 1994 the Government was able to claim publicly that it had eliminated formal discrimination against gypsies and substituted criminal sanctions for unauthorized camping which were of universal application covering 'hippies', 'New Age Travellers', and holidaymakers, as well as gypsies. However, as we have seen,[259] identical treatment with others may not always meet the legitimate needs of minorities and may in certain circumstances violate their human rights. Whether the nomadic life-style of gypsies is viewed as a particular form of private or family life, which is entitled to special protection under Article 8(1), on the basis of the Commission's statements in *G and E v Norway*[260] and *Buckley v UK*, or simply that gypsy caravans are 'home', as the Court ruled in *Buckley's* case, it will be for the state to demonstrate that any interference, albeit expressed in neutral terms, is 'necessary in a democratic society' pursuant to Article 8(2). If the impact of the 1994 Act is to destroy or gravely imperil the nomadic lifestyle of gypsies by making it virtually impossible for many of them to camp anywhere without being liable to prosecution, violations of Article 8 may be found to have occurred in individual cases. In 1993 the Council of Europe drew attention to—

. . . the special place among . . . minorities . . . reserved for Gypsies. Living scattered all over Europe, not having a country to call their own, they are a true European minority but one that does not fit in the definitions of national or linguistic minorities.[261]

Looking at the whole question from a wider international perspective, it needs to be borne in mind that there are two salient articles in the International Covenant on Civil and Political Rights. Article 12(1) provides—

---

[259] See generally chs 1–3 above.   [260] (1984) 35 Dec & Rep 30 at 35.
[261] See para 2 of Recommendation 1203 (1993), adopted by the Parliamentary Assembly, 2 Feb 1993; for further statements by the Council of Europe, see Thornberry, P. and Estebanez, M., *The Council of Europe and Minorities* (Strasbourg, 1994), ch 8.

Everyone lawfully within the territory of a state shall, within that territory, have the right to liberty of movement and freedom to choose his residence.[262]

In terms of Article 12(3) this right must not be subject to any restrictions except those which are provided by law, are necessary to protect national security, public order, public health or morals, or the rights and freedoms of others, and are consistent with the other rights in the Covenant. One of those 'other rights' is contained in Article 27 which declares—

In those states in which ethnic, religious or linguistic minorities exist, persons belonging to such minorities shall not be denied the right in community with the other members of their group, to enjoy their own culture, to profess and practise their own religion, or to use their own language.

While, as we have seen,[263] the ambit of this provision is far from clear, it reflects a growing international trend towards recognizing a pattern of cultural diversity within the confines of modern nation states. The objective behind the Article is the achievement of a real rather than a merely formal equality for members of such minority groups so that they do not have to surrender their distinctive identities. It encourages respect for the 'right to be different'. In its General Comment on Article 27, the Human Rights Committee stated in 1994 that 'culture' could manifest itself in many forms, including 'a particular way of life associated with the use of land resources' and that such cultural rights might require 'positive legal measures of protection'.[264] While 'New Age Travellers' and 'hippies' also seek to follow a different pattern of life from that of the bulk of the majority population, they do not constitute an ethnic, religious, or linguistic minority group. Hence, while their preference for a nomadic existence is certainly entitled to respect in a democratic society, specific differential treatment in law to preserve a distinctive cultural tradition is not required in their case, as it is for gypsies.[265]

Moreover, in 1990 the particular problems of gypsies were singled out for special mention in the document produced at the Copenhagen Meeting of the Conference on Security and Cooperation in Europe (CSCE).[266] This document committed participating states of the CSCE (now OSCE) to the protection of the rights of persons belonging to national minorities, including the right to preserve their ethnic and cultural identity 'free from any attempts at assimilation against their will'.[267]

---

[262] A similar provision exists in Art 2 to the Fourth Protocol of the European Convention, but the UK has not ratified this Protocol because of difficulties in implementing Art 3(2) in relation to the right of nationals to enter their country of nationality.
[263] See above, ch 3.   [264] Para 7.
[265] See e.g. HL Debs, 555, col 1553 (Lord Avebury).   [266] See (1990) 29 *ILM* 1305.
[267] At 1320.

CONCLUSIONS

The pursuit of a nomadic lifestyle for at least part of the year by no more than a few thousand caravan-dwelling gypsies should not pose an insuperable problem for a democratic country with a total population of some fifty million people. In view of the widespread prejudice to be found on the part of many members of the majority community, substantial efforts are required to influence public opinion locally towards the acceptance of gypsy sites as preferable to the constant hassle of expecting police forces and the courts to evict gypsies from unauthorized encampments. Elementary considerations of humanity demand that gypsy families be accorded a greater degree of security for their encampments and their itinerancy than currently exists.

A far greater level of tolerance towards gypsies is needed. Indeed, a policy of 'live and let live' must be actively cultivated and fostered if Britain is to be entitled to claim that it is a civilized country. In this regard, the gypsies constitute an important test case. The provision of public sites, acquired with taxpayers' money, side by side with private sites, far from 'undermining gypsies' responsibility to provide for themselves' (as alleged by the Government[268]), can be justified as a practical measure in view of the immense difficulties gypsies face in obtaining the necessary planning permission for private sites. Since many gypsies wish to settle on a permanent basis at least for a substantial part of the year, most public sites should be of a long-stay nature, but a nationwide network of short-stay and transit sites with reasonable services is also required to meet the needs of those who are travelling.[269]

At present, public sites are generally full and vacancies only rarely arise.[270] Provision needs to be made quickly for the 4,000 families who are currently camping illegally. This can only be achieved if firm pressure is placed upon local councils by central government, through legal mechanisms or otherwise.[271] Many sites will have to be located in open countryside.[272]

Gypsies have faced persecution and forced assimilation in most countries in Europe and in many places their treatment has been far worse than in Britain.[273] 'Encouraging' gypsies to become assimilated to the housedwelling population by punitive legislation directed against their traditional nomadic life-style is unacceptable. Human rights provisions indicate that, in addition to the universal rights to respect for private and family life, and to freedom of movement, which must be granted without

---

[268] 'Reform of the Caravan Sites Act', para 30.   [269] See Todd and Clark, 17–18.
[270] Home, 14.   [271] Ibid, 16–17.   [272] Ibid, 18.
[273] For a recent account, see Fonseca, I., *Bury Me Standing: The Gypsies and Their Journey* (London, 1995).

discrimination, gypsies should be guaranteed the right to maintain their identity as a distinctive ethnic minority and to enjoy their own culture. Their nomadic lifestyle and their camps should not be hindered or suppressed through the criminal law, save where this is justified on the basis of a pressing social need. In 1975 the hope was expressed that, with the removal of all remaining discriminatory legislation against gypsies, Britain might 'perhaps become the first country to permit the Gypsies their own separate way of life, travelling or settled by choice, together with full civil rights and opportunities'.[274] Sadly, almost a quarter of a century later, that goal appears far away.

[274] Adams, 291.

6

Muslims: The Claim to a Separate System of Personal Law

Although it is not entirely clear how far back the Muslim presence in Britain extends, there were certainly some Indian Muslims living in England during the eighteenth century.[1] Most of them were servants and *ayahs* (maids), brought to this country by army officers and nabobs who had made their fortunes as mercantile agents and clerks in the service of the East India Company.[2] A few others may have worked as entertainers performing at pageants and shows. *The Servants' Pocket Book* of 1761 specifically refers to various London taverns at which music and dancing took place, as the 'wonted haunts of Moormen [Muslims] and Gentoos [Hindus]'.[3] There were also a number of East Indian seamen, known as Lascars, many of whom were Muslims, who were among London's poor in the 1780s.[4] These sailors had been recruited by the East India Company and been laid off and left to fend for themselves while their ships were docked in English ports.[5] Some remained here permanently. They were ill-treated and despised by the majority community, although eventually a Parliamentary Committee was established to investigate their plight and to recommend improvements in their position.[6]

In 1764 a case arose at the Old Bailey in which the key issue was whether or not a Muslim could lawfully undertake to tell the truth in court by swearing an oath on the Qur'an rather than the Bible.[7] A man named Ryan and his wife were on a charge of theft and since this was then a capital offence the two judges trying the case referred the issue about the form of the oath to a bench made up of the twelve most important judges in the land, namely those of the Courts of King's

---

[1] See Fryer, P., *Staying Power: The History of Black People in Britain* (London, 1984), 27, 31, 69, 77–9.

[2] See Visram, R., *Ayahs, Lascars and Princes: Indians in Britain 1700–1947* (London, 1986), ch 2.

[3] Quoted by Hecht, J., *Continental and Colonial Servants in Eighteenth Century England* (Massachusetts, 1954), 54.   [4] See Visram, ch 3.

[5] See Nielsen, J., *Muslims in Western Europe* (Edinburgh, 1992), 4.

[6] *Report from the Committee on Lascars*, 1814–15 (No. 471).

[7] *R v Morgan* (1764) 1 Leach 54.

Bench, Common Pleas, and Exchequer. The 'Twelve Judges' unanimously decided that a Muslim could indeed be lawfully sworn on the Qur'an. The Muslim involved in the case was in fact the owner of the property alleged to have been stolen and he was bringing a private prosecution, which eventually resulted in the conviction of the accused couple. Somewhat surprisingly his name was John Morgan and part of the property stolen consisted of a quantity of Bengal coins. Perhaps the tentative conclusion can be drawn that he was a Welsh convert to Islam, who had acquired the coins while living in India. At all events the case appears to be the first of which there is a recognized law report involving a Muslim resident in England.[8]

During the second half of the nineteenth century Queen Victoria had a number of Indian servants and attendants who were Muslims.[9] She seems to have depended upon them considerably, both for her knowledge of Indian affairs and for gaining advice upon matters of policy. The most prominent among them was Abdul Karim, who was appointed to the post of Her Majesty's Indian Secretary (or 'Munshi') in 1888. He rapidly gained the Queen's confidence and favour and gave her lessons in Hindustani (Urdu). She used to visit him at his home and she commissioned a portrait of him in oils. She even used to study and discuss confidential state papers with him, until her ministers put pressure on her to stop what they regarded as a most reprehensible practice. Clearly, however, he exercised some influence over the Monarch right up to the time of her death.

During the latter part of the nineteenth century the number of Muslim seamen living here increased substantially following the opening of the Suez Canal in 1869. Yemeni Arabs and Somalis were recruited by British shipping companies through Aden and small settled communities began to be formed, notably in Cardiff and South Shields.[10] A similar pattern developed with the settlement in Liverpool of West African Muslims. The first English mosques were established in Woking in 1889 and in Liverpool a few years later. The Shahjehan mosque in Woking was built by Dr Leitner, a Hungarian Orientalist scholar with funds provided by the ruler of Bhopal, while the Liverpool mosque was constructed by a British convert, Shaykh Abdullah (Henry William) Quilliam, who had

---

[8] Although the 'Twelve Judges' did not expressly refer to it, there had in fact been an earlier reported English decision in which a Muslim had been allowed to swear an oath on the Qur'an: *Fachina v Sabine* (1738) 2 Strange 1104. However, in that case the Muslim in question had been living in Gibraltar at the time.

[9] See Vadgama, K., *India in Britain* (London, 1984), 20, 25–7, 30–1; Visram, 30–3.

[10] See Nielsen, 4; Halliday, F., *Arabs in Exiles: Yemeni Migrants in Urban Britain* (London, 1992), ch 2.

been appointed Shaykh to the United Kingdom by the Sultan of the Ottoman Empire, as well as Persian Consul in Liverpool by the Shah.[11]

The large-scale migration to Britain of Muslims from the Indian sub-continent began during the early 1960s. The sons of poor hill-farmers from Pakistan left their villages in the hill districts of Mirpur and Campbellpur in the West and of Sylhet in the East (which became part of the independent state of Bangladesh in 1971).[12] Around 130,000 Pakistanis had arrived by 1967, many just before controls were introduced by the Commonwealth Immigrants Act 1962. Other sizeable groups of Muslims arrived around this time or subsequently from the Indian states of Gujarat and Punjab, as well as from East Africa, Cyprus, Malaysia, several Arab countries, Iran, and Nigeria.[13]

The best estimate of the total size of the Muslim population of Great Britain, based on the 1991 census figures relating to ethnic origin and country of birth, is between one and 1.5 million, of whom nearly one-third have their origins in Pakistan.[14]

THE ATTITUDES OF THE MAJORITY COMMUNITY

In his celebrated study, *Orientalism*,[15] Edward Said has amply demon-strated how, from the Middle Ages to modern times, Western writers, administrators, and politicians have systematically defined the East (and especially the Arab peoples of the Middle East) as embodying quintes-sentially 'alien' values, beliefs, customs, and modes of thought. As a branch of academic scholarship 'Orientalism' has, for more than a cen-tury, presented Westerners with a stereotyped image of 'the East' which is distinctly unflattering. Naturally such a negative portrait helped to justify the colonial domination which characterized much of the region for long periods of its more recent history. Lord Cromer, for example, who was Governor of Egypt from 1882 to 1907, felt able to write at the end of his term of office—

Sir Alfred Lyall once said to me: Accuracy is abhorrent to the Oriental mind. Every Anglo-Indian official should always remember that maxim. Want of accu-racy, which easily degenerates into untruthfulness, is, in fact, the main charac-teristic of the Oriental mind. The European is a close reasoner; his statements of fact are devoid of ambiguity; he is a natural logician, albeit he may not have studied logic; he loves symmetry in all things; he is by nature sceptical and

---

[11] Nielsen, 4–5.   [12] See Rose, B., *Colour and Citizenship* (London, 1969), 58–60.
[13] Nielsen, 40–1.

[14] See Anwar, M., 'Muslims in Britain: 1991 Census and other statistical sources', CSIC Paper No. 9 (1993), 3–7; Peach, C. and Glebe, G., 'Muslim Minorities in Western Europe' (1995) 18 *Ethnic and Racial Studies* 26 at 28, 32, 34–5.   [15] (Harmondsworth, 1985).

requires proof before he can accept the truth of any proposition; his trained intelligence works like a piece of mechanism. The mind of the Oriental, on the other hand, like his picturesque streets, is eminently wanting in symmetry. His reasoning is of the most slipshod description. Although the ancient Arabs acquired in a somewhat high degree the science of dialectics, their descendants are singularly deficient in the logical faculty. They are often incapable of drawing the most obvious conclusions from any simple premises of which they may admit the truth. Endeavour to elicit a plain statement of facts from an ordinary Egyptian. His explanation will generally be lengthy, and wanting in lucidity. He will probably contradict himself half-a-dozen times before he has finished his story. He will often break down under the mildest process of cross-examination. The Egyptian is also eminently unsceptical. He readily becomes the dupe of the magician and the astrologer. Even highly educated Egyptians are prone to refer the common occurrences of life to the intervention of some supernatural agency. In political matters, as well as in the affairs of everyday life, the Egyptian will, without inquiry, accept as true the most absurd rumours. He will, indeed, do more than this. He will often accept or reject such rumours in the inverse ratio of their probability, for, true to his natural inconsistency and want of rational discrimination, he will occasionally develop a flash of hardy scepticism when he is asked to believe the truth.[16]

Lord Cromer sustained his hyperbole with yet more unfavourable comparisons between East and West—

Contrast again the talkative European, bursting with superfluous energy, active in mind, inquisitive about everything he sees and hears, chafing under delay, and impatient of suffering, with the grave and silent Eastern, devoid of energy and initiative, stagnant in mind, wanting in curiosity about matters which are new to him, careless of waste of time and patient under suffering. Or, again, look at the fulsome flattery, which the Oriental will offer to his superior and expect to receive from his inferior, and compare the general approval of such practices with the European frame of mind, which spurns both the flatterer and the person who invites flattery. This contemptible flattery, 'the nurse of crime', as it was called by the poet Gay, is, indeed, a thorn in the side of the Englishman in Egypt, for it prevents Khedives and Pashas from hearing the truth from their own countrymen.[17]

Muslims were, for many centuries, principally identified in the West as the monstrous Saracen enemy against whom a heroic struggle had been waged during the Crusades.[18] Islam was perceived as a wholly misguided version of Christianity and came to symbolize in Western minds 'terror, devastation, the demonic, hordes of hated barbarians'.[19] The Prophet Muhammad was consistently viewed as no more than a shame-

---

[16] Baring, E., *Modern Egypt* (London, 1908), 146–7.   [17] Ibid, 148.
[18] For an analysis of the distortion of such Western perceptions and their continuing relevance today, see Armstrong, K., *Holy War: The Crusades and their Impact on Today's World* (London, 1988).   [19] Said, 60.

ful imposter, the disseminator of a false revelation, and a cunning apostate.[20]

Indeed Norman Daniel has demonstrated in great detail how, during the twelfth and thirteenth centuries, medieval Christian historians distorted what was known about Islamic doctrine and the life of the Prophet so as to create a thoroughly disreputable image.[21] They adopted a polemical style to castigate Muslim history and beliefs. As Daniel has explained, for example,—

The life of Muhammad was seen as an essential disproof of the Islamic claim to Revelation. It was often treated as the most important disproof of all. To this end writers believed and wished to show that Muhammad was a low-born and pagan upstart, who schemed himself into power, who maintained it by pretended revelations, and who spread it both by violence and by permitting to others the same lascivious practices as he indulged in himself.[22]

In an extension of this thesis, Rana Kabbani has examined the myths perpetrated about the Islamic East in more recent times by Western travellers, poets and painters, who wanted their works to be popular with audiences in their home countries.[23] In stressing the differences between the two worlds, Western observers particularly emphasized the lascivious sensuality and inherent violence of the East. These were useful images to employ in the promotion of imperialism in the nineteenth century, for if 'it could be suggested that Eastern peoples were slothful, preoccupied with sex, violent and incapable of self-government, then the imperialist would feel himself justified in stepping in and ruling.'[24] A portrait of the East as both exotic and erotic is plain for all to see in works such as those of Sir Richard Burton,[25] but equally striking is the following damning comment made by David Roberts, the renowned Victorian painter of classical ruins and Eastern landscapes—

Splendid cities, once teeming with a busy population and embellished with temples and edifices, the wonder of the world, now deserted and lonely, or reduced by mismanagement and the barbarism of the Muslim creed to a state as savage as the wild animals by which they are surrounded. Often I have gazed at these till my heart actually sickened within me.[26]

It is against this background of deep hostility towards Islam and antagonistic perceptions of the Arab world, with which Western culture has

---

[20] Ibid, 59–73; Ruthven, M., *A Satanic Affair* (London, 1990), 35.
[21] *Islam and the West: The Making of an Image* (Edinburgh, 1960). [22] At 79.
[23] *Europe's Myths of Orient* (London, 1986). [24] Ibid, 6.
[25] See e.g. *A Plain and Literal Translation of the Arabian Nights' Entertainments* (London, 1884–6). Burton did, however, expressly reject the notion that Islam was a religion of pure sensuality—see *The Jew, The Gypsy and El Islam* (W.H. Wilkins, ed, London, 1898), 326–8.
[26] As quoted in Ballantine, J., *The Life of David Roberts, RA* (Edinburgh, 1886), 104–5.

been imbued over many centuries, that modern British attitudes need to be examined. Despite the existence of a strong pro-Arab tendency at the British Foreign Office stretching back to the time of T. E. Lawrence and beyond, popular English sentiment against Muslims would appear to have increased rather than decreased in recent years. A survey in 1993, based on interviews with a representative sample of the general population, found that around 30 per cent would prefer not to have Arabs or Pakistanis as neighbours.[27] Moreover, 28 per cent of those interviewed held the view that Pakistanis behave in a manner which provokes hostility towards them, while 21 per cent thought this was true in the case of Arabs.[28] Another recent report identified a widespread rise in 'islamophobia', namely a dread or hatred of Islam and Muslims.[29] This was found to be particularly evident in the media, but was also prevalent throughout all sections of society.[30] Islam tended to be portrayed as a static, monolithic, and intolerant faith, which was implacably hostile to the West and willing to exploit religion for strategic, political, and military advantage.[31] By ignoring the diversity of views, values, and practices among Muslims themselves, criticisms of events within countries such as Algeria, Iran, Iraq, Libya, Saudi Arabia, and Sudan can all too easily be interpreted as coded attacks on Muslims living in Britain, without the slightest justification.[32]

Riffat Hassan has graphically summarized the position in the following terms—

Given the reservoir of negative images associated with Islam and Muslims in 'the Collective Unconscious' of the West, it is hardly surprising that, since the demise of the Soviet Empire, 'the World of Islam' is being seen as the new 'Enemy' which is perhaps even more incomprehensible and intractable than the last one. The routine portrayal of Islam as a religion spread by the sword and characterized by 'Holy War', and of Muslims as barbarous and backward, frenzied and fanatic, volatile and violent, has led, in recent times, to an alarming increase in 'Muslim-bashing'—verbal, physical, and psychological—in a number of Western countries.[33]

[27] See Golub, J., *British Attitudes towards Jews and other Minorities* (New York, 1993), 8, 13.

[28] Ibid, 16, 21. For a rare sample survey of British attitudes towards Islam and Muslims, see Iqra Trust, 'Research on Public Attitudes to Islam' (London, 1991). When asked what image of Islam came spontaneously to their minds, while 19 per cent of respondents mentioned religious devotion and dedication, 14 per cent referred to fanaticism and extremism and 13 per cent to the inflexibility and restrictiveness of Islamic doctrine.

[29] Runnymede Commission on British Muslims and Islamophobia, *Islamophobia: its features and dangers* (London, 1997). [30] At 7.

[31] Ibid, 8–12.   [32] Ibid, 9.

[33] 'Rights of Women Within Islamic Communities' in Witte, J. and van der Vyver, J. (eds), *Religious Human Rights in Global Perspective: Religious Perspectives* (The Hague, 1996), 361 at 368.

On the other hand, it needs to be acknowledged that, in many instances, criticisms of Islamic regimes for human rights violations are entirely justified; in particular, certain unacceptable forms of punishment and ill-treatment of minorities tend to be defended by specific reference to religious norms.[34]

So far as Muslims living in England today are concerned, three matters in particular are prone to be the subject of adverse comment by members of the majority community. The first is the hostile response accorded by some British Muslims to Salman Rushdie following the publication of his book *The Satanic Verses*. Their support for the *fatwa* issued by Ayatollah Khomeini and what is perceived as their intolerance in repudiating Rushdie's right to free speech have attracted considerable criticism. Several strands in that controversy have already been addressed in Chapter 3 of this book. The second criticism relates to the alleged cruelty to animals which is felt to be involved in the Muslim method of slaughter. The broad issue of religious slaughter has been examined in Chapter 4, with particular reference to Jewish practice, and need not therefore be explored further here. The third relates to apprehension that certain of the precepts associated with the doctrine of *purdah* and some of the rules of Islamic law itself may place Muslim women in an unacceptably inferior position to their menfolk.[35] Vague notions about harems, the seraglio, and 'Oriental despotism' still colour the attitudes of many members of the majority community because they have passed into the collective store of knowledge of the West through centuries of repetition in a variety of cultural forms. Whether or not such fears about the welfare of Muslim women are indeed justified lies, of course, at the very heart of the examination in this chapter of the merits of a claim for the introduction of a separate Islamic system of personal law for Muslims living in England. At this juncture, it is merely important to note that public opinion in the majority community has been formed by negative images of Islamic beliefs and practices stretching back for many centuries. Whether such adverse views can be justified objectively today clearly requires the most careful and rigorous examination.

THE CLAIM TO A SEPARATE ISLAMIC SYSTEM OF PERSONAL LAW

During the 1970s the Union of Muslim Organisations of UK and Eire (UMO) held a number of meetings which culminated in a formal

---

[34] See e.g. ch 3 above; Qur'an, *Surahs* IV: 15, XXIV: 2 (adultery); V: 41 (severing of limbs for theft).

[35] For modern accounts of Islam's alleged 'tradition of misogyny' by Muslim feminists, see Mernissi, F., *Women and Islam: An Historical and Theological Enquiry* (Oxford, 1991); Ahmed, L., *Women and Gender in Islam* (New Haven, 1992).

resolution to seek official recognition of a separate system of Islamic family law, which would automatically be applicable to all British Muslims.[36] A proposal along these lines was subsequently submitted to various British Government ministers, with a view to having it placed before Parliament for approval and enactment. The demand was repeated in a meeting with Home Office ministers in 1989[37] and reiterated publicly in 1996.[38] The remainder of this chapter begins with an analysis of some of the considerations underlying UMO's demand, including an assessment of the adequacy of existing legal provision for Muslims in England. It then explores the possible reasons why UMO's claim has been unsuccessful, analyses their cogency, and makes special reference to the human rights dimension of the issue and, for comparative purposes, to the current debate about the future of Islamic personal law in India.

The claim to a separate Islamic system of personal law may be seen as arising from a variety of different causes.[39] First, in many non-Western societies and communities those traditional customs, religious beliefs, moral values, and legal principles which specifically pertain to the family and matters of personal status are held in very high esteem. They are often regarded as embodying the quintessential culture of a distinctive group of people, something not to be surrendered lightly or discarded, even when members of the group are living outside their country of origin. This is perhaps especially likely to be the case when religious belief, legal principle, and family relations are closely intertwined, as they are in Islamic doctrine.

Secondly, it may be argued that as other aspects of Islamic law, notably in the commercial and criminal spheres, have generally given way to Western-style codes in many countries with Muslim majorities in modern times,[40] so the particular area of Muslim family law has come to seem even more precious and worthy of preservation worldwide.

Thirdly, many Muslims living in England today are familiar with legal regimes in Asia and Africa which are of a pluralistic nature and which permit family relations within different religious and ethnic communities to be regulated by a variety of distinctive systems of personal law.[41] In India, to take perhaps the most obvious example, the present

---

[36] See UMO, *Why Muslim Family Law for British Muslims* (London, 1983). UMO was founded in 1970 and now represents over 200 different Muslim organizations.

[37] See Hiro, D., *Black British, White British* (London, 1991), 192.

[38] See *British Muslims Monthly Survey* (Dec 1996), 15–16.

[39] See generally, Lewis, B., 'Legal and Historical Reflections on the Position of Muslim Populations under Non-Muslim Rule' in Lewis, B. and Schnapper, D. (eds), *Muslims in Europe* (London, 1994), ch 1.

[40] See e.g. Esposito, J., *Women in Muslim Family Law* (Syracuse, 1982), 49, 75–6.

[41] See e.g. Hooker, M., *Legal Pluralism* (Oxford, 1976), chs II and III.

pattern of legal pluralism in family matters was given statutory force by the British Parliament during the days of Empire.[42] If this system was perfectly acceptable to the British authorities during the period of the Raj, Muslims see no reason why it should not prove workable in the United Kingdom itself now that the number of people belonging to religious minorities here has become really substantial.

Fourthly, many Muslims view the issue principally in terms of religious freedom and claim a proud record of religious toleration towards members of other monotheistic faiths, dating back over many centuries.[43] They therefore expect Islam's past respect for Jewish and Christian minorities in Muslim lands to be reciprocated today in the West.[44]

Finally, there are powerful practical reasons involving a rejection of the perceived alternatives. Muslims in England are currently presented with images (some of which are admittedly greatly exaggerated by the media) of a majority community whose scale of values in family and personal matters appears to be poles apart from their own. Sex education at school, widespread availability of contraceptives, teenage love affairs, prostitution, pornography, child abuse, easy abortion, marital breakdown, extra-marital cohabitation, children born out of wedlock, and neglect of the elderly all receive such prominent publicity that minorities might easily gain the impression that these are characteristic features of life in the community at large which are deliberately fostered as an integral part of legal policy. Finding themselves apparently surrounded by such 'evils', many Muslims believe that a sensible method of avoiding contamination would be to operate within a system of Islamic law, which they feel lays down a higher scale of values than those prevailing in the majority community, for whom the principles of English law were obviously primarily designed.[45]

In this regard, many devout Muslims sincerely believe that the best way of preserving their own families and communities from the corrupting forces at work in the wider society is to protect their women by regulating their lives rather narrowly and strictly.[46] Family honour is of

---

[42] See e.g. 21 Geo III c 70, s 17; Muslim Personal Law (Shariah) Application Act 1937.

[43] See e.g. Faruqi, I., 'The rights of non-Muslims under Islam' in *Muslim Communities in Non-Muslim States* (London, 1980), 43–66; Weeramantry, C., *Islamic Jurisprudence: An International Perspective* (Basingstoke, 1988), 85–91.

[44] It is important, however, not to exaggerate Islam's tolerance in this regard, since even Christians and Jews had to pay a poll-tax as a form of tribute and submission to Muslim rule and unbelievers had minimal rights or protection; see e.g. Khadduri, M., *War and Peace in the Law of Islam* (Baltimore, 1955), chs XIV–XV; Hourani, A., *A History of the Arab Peoples* (Massachusetts, 1991), 47, 117–19; An-Na'im, A., 'Religious Minorities under Islamic Law and the Limits of Cultural Relativism' (1987) 9 *Human Rights Quarterly* 1 at 11–13.

[45] A survey in 1989 indicated that in a case of conflict between Islamic law and English law, 66 per cent of Muslims would follow the former—see Hiro, 192.

[46] See e.g. Shaw, A., *A Pakistani Community in Britain* (Oxford, 1988), 140–1, 172.

the greatest importance and women are the repositories of that honour.[47] Men are the guardians. The structure of Muslim families has, therefore, long been based on ideas and practices which are strongly patriarchal and give men dominance over women. However, it is important to appreciate the historical context of progressive social reform in which this rigid 'sexual divide' came about, a matter succinctly explained by Esposito—

Qur'anic reforms corrected many injustices in pre-Islamic society by granting women rights to which they were entitled—the right to contract their marriage, receive dower, retain possession and control of wealth, and receive maintenance and shares in inheritance. At the same time, however, family laws were formulated to meet a woman's needs in a society where her largely domestic, child-bearing roles rendered her sheltered and dependent upon her father, her husband, and her close male relations. Thus family law reflected women's dependent position. . . . Since men had more independence, wider social contacts, and higher status in the world, their social position was translated into greater legal responsibilities . . . as well as more extensive legal privileges proportionate to those responsibilities. . . . In its attempts to meet the needs of a particular social milieu, Muslim family law reflected the social mores of the time—the traditional roles of men and women and the function of the extended family in a patriarchal society.[48]

The allocation of separate duties and responsibilities to men and women in classical Islamic law remained virtually unchallenged until the twentieth century (as indeed it did for many centuries in English law), because they closely parallelled the accepted roles of the sexes and the functions of the family in a basically unchanging society. However, profound alterations in the status and role of women in recent times have undermined these long established notions and it is the degree to which Muslim law and English law have responded to these developments which informs much of the discussion which follows.

THE ADEQUACY OF CURRENT ENGLISH LEGAL PROVISION
FOR MUSLIMS AND THEIR FAMILIES

The aim of this section is to describe some of the main principles and rules of English family law, with a view to contrasting them with the position under Islamic or Muslim law (*shari'ah*) and hence drawing attention to the degree to which they appear to be adequate or inadequate to meet the needs of Muslims living in England. The analysis will

[47] See e.g. Hourani, 105; Saghal, G. and Yuval-Davis, N. (eds), *Refusing Holy Orders: women and fundamentalism in Britain* (London, 1992), 133, 187–8.   [48] At 48.

focus on 'domestic' English law rather than the 'conflict of laws' and thus only consider, for example, marriages and divorces occurring in England rather than those which take place overseas.[49]

(a) Marriage

(i) Formalities

The basic law governing the solemnization of marriages in England is set out in the Marriage Acts 1949–96. These Acts stipulate detailed rules concerning where a marriage may take place, who should conduct the ceremony, at what time of day it may occur, and the nature of the celebration. Essentially, most weddings, other than those conducted in an Anglican church or chapel, must be performed in a register office or a place of public worship duly registered for the solemnization of marriages,[50] and must be solemnized between 8 am and 6 pm in the presence of either a registrar or an 'authorized person' (usually a minister of religion), with the couple exchanging vows according to a standard form of words prescribed by statute. However, two religious denominations are exempt from all these regulations, namely Quakers and 'persons professing the Jewish religion'.[51] Their special privileges go back at least as far as Lord Hardwicke's Marriage Act 1753. As a result their ceremonies may occur at any hour of the day or night; they need not take place in any particular building; they do not require the presence of any official appointed by or notified to the state authorities; and the form of the wedding merely has to follow the usages of the Society of Friends or the usages of the Jews, as the case may be.[52]

Whereas in the eighteenth century the privileges accorded to Jews and Quakers reflected religious toleration, in the twentieth century they symbolize religious discrimination. There can surely be no justification for the preservation today of what has now become a rather embarrassing historical anomaly. There is no good reason why some religious minorities should be exempt from the normal legal requirements, but not others. Since in Islamic law a marriage can be contracted merely in the presence of witnesses and requires no other formalities,[53] Muslims

---

[49] For marriages contracted overseas, see Poulter, S., *English Law and Ethnic Minority Customs* (London, 1986), chs 2, 3; for divorces obtained overseas, see Family Law Act 1986, Part II, discussed by Poulter, S., 'Recognition of Foreign Divorces: The New Law' (1987) 84 *Law Soc Gaz* 253.

[50] In 1992 (the latest year for which official figures are available), 82 mosques were registered for this purpose out of a total of 460 certified as places of public worship under the Places of Worship Registration Act 1855.

[51] Marriage Act 1949, s 26(1)(c), (d).   [52] Ibid, ss 26(1), 35(4), 43(3), 75(1)(a).

[53] Pearl, D., *A Textbook on Muslim Personal Law*, 2nd ed. (London, 1987), 41.

would no doubt appreciate being accorded the same privileges in this regard as Jews and Quakers. A far greater degree of uniformity should therefore be introduced into this aspect of English law. One problem which does arise, however, is that Muslim marriages may occur without either the bride or the groom being present at the ceremony. The wedding (*nikah*) can take place simply through an exchange of declarations between representatives acting on behalf of the couple.[54] Proxy marriages are not at present recognized by English law and it seems unlikely that abolition of this rule would be contemplated, unless adequate safeguards could be introduced to ensure that both parties had freely consented to the marriage.

(ii) Capacity to marry

English law makes no concessions to other laws or traditions in relation to capacity to marry in England. A marriage in which either party is under the age of sixteen or is within the prohibited degrees of relationship as defined in the Marriage Acts 1949–86, or is already married to someone else, will automatically be null and void.[55] Furthermore, it seems clear that English law will completely disregard the Islamic prohibition on marriages between Muslim women and non-Muslim men and thus any such marriage entered into in England is fully valid here. Of course, in Islamic law parties may marry under the age of sixteen and a husband may take up to four wives simultaneously.[56] The difficulties involved in accommodating these possibilities in England are examined further below.

(iii) Arranged marriages and forced marriages

Arranged marriages are treated as perfectly valid in themselves. However, if an arranged marriage taking place in England is pushed to the point of compulsion, so that the marriage is being forced upon one of the parties against his or her wishes, the marriage is voidable, with the result that the unwilling party is entitled to obtain a decree of annulment if proceedings are instituted within three years of the marriage.[57] The ground for annulment is that the party concerned did not validly consent to the marriage in consequence of 'duress'. After being restrictively

---

[54] Pearl, D., *A Textbook on Muslim Personal Law*, 41.

[55] Matrimonial Causes Act 1973, s 11. Concern about foreign marriages where the bride is under sixteen or where the marriage is actually polygamous has also led to changes in the immigration rules designed to prevent such couples settling in the UK—see HC 395 of 1994, paras 277–80, discussed above, ch 2.   [56] Pearl, 42–3, 77.

[57] Matrimonial Causes Act 1973, ss 12, 13.

interpreted by the judges for many years,[58] the concept of duress was given a far more liberal construction by the Court of Appeal in the case of *Hirani v Hirani*[59] in 1983. A Hindu woman of nineteen, who had been having an affair with a Muslim man, was threatened by her parents with eviction from the family home if she did not marry the Hindu husband whom they had chosen for her. The Court, in granting her an annulment after she had gone through the ceremony of marriage, indicated that the crucial question in cases of alleged duress was whether the threats or pressures which had been made or applied were so great as to destroy the reality of consent to marriage by overbearing the will of the individual concerned.[60] In this case they had clearly done so.

Broadly speaking, the consent of both spouses is an essential element in a Muslim marriage. However, there are instances where a minor child may be validly married simply on the basis of his or her guardian's consent, without the minor having any voice in the matter.[61] Where such a marriage does occur Muslim law grants the child the 'option of puberty', which means that upon subsequently attaining puberty[62] the minor may elect to have the marriage set aside, provided the marriage has not yet been affirmed by voluntary consummation. However, under the Hanafi school of Islamic jurisprudence, as applied in the Indian subcontinent, this option is only available to a child who has been married off by a guardian other than the father or grandfather.[63] Hence these two male relations do have the power to impose upon their issue, without the latter's consent, a fully valid and binding marriage from which there is no escape save through a divorce. This offends against English notions of freedom of choice in marriage and, as we shall see, is unlikely to prove acceptable for marriages entered into in England.

(b) Divorce

Whereas under Muslim law a divorce can be obtained in a number of different ways, notably extrajudicially through *talaq* (unilateral repudiation by the husband), *khul'* (divorce at the instance of the wife with the husband's agreement and on the basis that she will forego her right to dower), and *mubar'at* (divorce by mutual consent),[64] there is only one way of obtaining a divorce in England. This is through a decree or order

[58] See e.g. *Singh v Singh* [1971] P 226; *Singh v Kaur* (1981) 11 *Fam Law* 152.
[59] (1983) 4 FLR 232.
[60] This approach subsequently found favour with the Scottish Court of Session in *Shahid Mahmud v Rahat Bano Mahmud* [1994] SLT 599.
[61] Nasir, J., *The Islamic Law of Personal Status* (London, 1986), 46.
[62] Puberty is set at the age of twelve for boys and nine for girls—see Esposito, 16.
[63] Pearl, 44.   [64] See Pearl, ch 7; Nasir, ch 6.

granted by a court of civil jurisdiction on the ground that the marriage has irretrievably broken down.[65] Mutual agreement may provide the foundation of a divorce, but the parties are not free to remarry until the order has been made by the court. Some form of judicial process is considered essential, partly as a brake upon precipitate action by the spouses (or oppression by one of them in seeking consent to divorce) and partly as a mechanism for ensuring that the welfare of children is adequately safeguarded[66] and that the material outcome is reasonably fair.[67]

(c) Children

In disputes about responsibility for children, for example where the mother and father separate or divorce, the English courts determine the children's future home and upbringing on the basis that the welfare of the individual child is the paramount consideration.[68] A wide variety of factors are incorporated by the courts into the notion of a child's 'welfare', including its 'background',[69] and there have been decisions which clearly indicate that the judges feel it is desirable for children whose parents come from different religious backgrounds to maintain links with both cultural heritages, for instance through orders which recognize joint responsibility and the need for contact to continue with both parents.[70] In no reported case has a Muslim parent yet argued that upon divorce or separation the English courts should give special weight to those provisions of Muslim law which tend to allocate younger children automatically to the mother and older children automatically to the father, with the exact age of transfer between parents being dependent upon the particular school of Islamic jurisprudence applicable to the community to which the family belongs.[71] It is very doubtful if such rules would carry much weight with an English judge. Over recent decades the statute laws of several Arab and Islamic countries have modified classical Muslim law by raising the age at which children go to the father rather than the mother.[72]

---

[65] Family Law Act 1986, s 44(1); Matrimonial Causes Act 1973, s 1 (to be replaced in 1999 by Family Law Act 1996, s 3).
[66] Matrimonial Causes Act 1973, s 41 (as amended), to be replaced in 1999 by Family Law Act 1996, s 11.   [67] Matrimonial Causes Act 1973, Part II.
[68] Children Act 1989, s 1.   [69] Ibid, s 1(3)(d).
[70] See e.g. *Jussa v Jussa* [1972] 2 All ER 600; *H v H* (1975) 5 *Fam Law* 185.
[71] See Pearl, 96–7; Nasir, 167–9.
[72] See Anderson, J., *Law Reform in the Muslim World* (London, 1976), 141–3.

(d) Financial provision on divorce and separation

The English courts possess a wide discretion, within certain guidelines laid down by Parliament,[73] to decide whether to make orders for financial provision upon separation and divorce and, if so, how large an amount should be specified. So far as a period of separation during marriage is concerned, both English law and Islamic law oblige a husband to support his wife in appropriate circumstances. Under English law a young wife without children might well be expected to go out to work to reduce her husband's liability and would have her notional earning capacity taken into account by the court if she refused to do so, but a Muslim wife might be able to satisfy an English court that she should not have to do this, in the light of the values and practices of wives in her own family and community.[74] It is quite commonly accepted in many Muslim communities that wives should not go out to work to earn a living and that the husband should be solely responsible for the family's income.

After a divorce Muslim law only obliges a husband to support his wife during the three month period of *'iddat* during which she is precluded from remarriage.[75] However, he does have to pay her any deferred dower (*mahr*) due to her in consequence of the marriage contract.[76] English courts have been prepared to order the payment of such dower[77] and would undoubtedly take account of such lump sum payments in their overall assessment of what would be an appropriate division of the couple's capital and income resources and in deciding what financial and property orders should be made. Although the trend in English law is towards encouraging divorced wives to become self-sufficient and financially independent of their former husbands and thus financial orders for only a limited period are becoming increasingly common, the courts have to consider whether such orders would be appropriate in all the circumstances and what hardship might be caused to the wife by stopping all maintenance.[78] It therefore seems unlikely that they would pay specific regard to the very limited nature of the duty to maintain divorced wives under Muslim law, save where a very substantial payment of deferred dower had already been made.

---

[73] Matrimonial Causes Act 1973, Part II, as amended by Matrimonial and Family Proceedings Act 1984; Domestic Proceedings and Magistrates' Courts Act 1978.
[74] cf *Khan v Khan* [1980] 1 All ER 497 where the court refused to take 'judicial notice' of such a Muslim custom. The decision might have gone the other way if appropriate evidence had been presented.   [75] Nasir, 137–8.
[76] Ibid, ch 4.
[77] See *Shahnaz v Rizwan* [1965] 1 QB 390; *Qureshi v Qureshi* [1972] Fam 173.
[78] Matrimonial Causes Act 1973, as amended, ss 25, 25A.

(e) Inheritance

English rules govern the inheritance both of 'immovable property' (such as land and houses) situated here and of movable property (wherever situated), if at the time of death the deceased was domiciled here. Hence the estates of many Muslims resident in Britain may fall to be administered under the provisions of English law. Islamic law, which basically operates a very elaborate system of allocating mathematical shares to a variety of relatives,[79] can only apply directly in respect of immovable property situated overseas or, in the case of movables, where the deceased died domiciled in a country where the Muslim law of succession is administered.

While English rules for the distribution of an estate on intestacy are far removed in many respects from the Muslim law of intestate succession, there is nothing in English law to prevent a Muslim from making a valid will bequeathing his or her property in accordance with the Islamic pattern of inheritance. The terms of such a will would, however, be open to challenge by means of a claim for 'family provision' made by relatives or dependants who were able to prove that the will did not make reasonable financial provision for them.[80] Under Muslim law the share of a widow as an heir is comparatively small and only amounts to one-eighth of the net estate (increased to one-quarter if there are no children or agnatic grandchildren).[81] Hence a Muslim widow living in England might in appropriate circumstances be able to bring a successful application for family provision if she felt financially insecure.[82] Muslim law itself allows a person to make a will, but the bequests must not exceed one-third of the value of the net estate.[83] However, to a limited extent this may enable a testator to make greater provision for a surviving spouse than is available under the intestacy system.[84]

POSSIBLE REASONS FOR THE REJECTION OF UMO'S DEMAND

During the 1970s the response by British Government ministers to the proposal submitted by UMO for the introduction by Parliament of a system of Islamic family law applicable to all British Muslims was

---

[79] See Pearl, ch 8.

[80] See Inheritance (Provision for Family and Dependants) Act 1975, s 1.

[81] See Pearl, 150. Had her husband's marriage been polygamous this share would be divided with the other widows.

[82] Under Muslim law children have a duty to support needy parents (see Nasir, 179–80), but they might fail to do so in practice.   [83] Pearl, 143.

[84] In classical Sunni law no bequest could be made to heirs, but this rule has been abolished in several Muslim countries; no such rule ever operated in Shi'i law.

extremely negative,[85] as it appears to have been when the issue was raised again in 1989. The proposal appears to have been rejected out of hand on the ground that the suggested legislation would not be 'appropriate'. What justifications can be offered for such resistance and how convincing are they?

First, it seems to have been argued that the proposal ran counter to the English tradition of a unified system in family matters in terms of which a uniform set of rules is applied to all, regardless of their origins, race, or creed.[86] This would not seem to be an adequate reason in itself, especially since (as we have seen in relation to the rules governing the solemnization of marriages by Jews and Quakers), it is not wholly accurate. However, this argument is perhaps rather more convincing if it asserts that a basically uniform system has helped in the past to create a more cohesive society and that it is still needed today, more especially as part of the process of nation-building required to integrate the newer minorities into the general framework of English life and some of its most important values. Family law relates to one of the essential organizational structures of social and legal administration and to allow one religious denomination to separate itself off completely in this manner might be felt to be unacceptably divisive. As Hiro has commented 'were the government to permit different family laws it would be laying the foundation of social segregation'.[87]

A second problem with the proposal for the introduction of Islamic family law in England is the practical difficulty of working out which system of Muslim family law would be applicable. Apart from the fundamental division between Sunnis and Shi'is, there are a number of different 'schools' of Islamic law. For example, the majority of British Sunnis originate from the Indian subcontinent and the Middle East and are likely to follow the Hanafi school, while those Sunnis from African countries will tend to adhere to the Maliki school, with those from the Far East being subject to the Shafi'i school. Furthermore, many countries where Muslim law is applied have, during the course of the twentieth century, modernized and reformed it by means of local statutes or ordinances.[88] Which of these many different versions would be administered in England? Would the choice of law in each case depend upon the nationalities, domiciles, or countries of origin of the parties and, if so,

---

[85] See *Why Muslim Family Law for British Muslims* (London, 1983).
[86] Ibid, 4.   [87] *Black British, White British*, 312.
[88] See generally Nasir (1986). In some countries such reforms have, however, been abrogated by moves towards greater Islamization; in relation to Pakistan, for example, see Pearl, D, 'Three Decades of Executive, Legislative and Judicial Amendments to Islamic Family law in Pakistan' in Connors, J. and Mallat, C. (eds), *Islamic Family Law* (London, 1990), ch 15.

what would happen to all those Muslims who were born here or who now possess a British passport and an English domicile? There would clearly be a grave risk of introducing both immense complexity and much artificiality into the selection of the correct system for the resolution of individual disputes. The dangers of imposing an alien system upon individual British Muslims should not be underestimated.[89]

Thirdly, would cases be decided by the existing civil courts or by a specially established religious court staffed exclusively by Muslims? If the former, one can easily envisage the controversy that might surround their interpretations of the finer points of Muslim law and the resulting accusations that they were not fit to judge such cases. However, the latter solution might be just as likely to result in recrimination because the various Muslim communities in England possess different ethnic and cultural backgrounds and might well disagree with one another about whether the legal rules were being correctly interpreted and applied, even by people who were meant to be their own judicial representatives. Some idea of the divisions within the British Muslim 'community' can be gleaned from the following passage in a newsletter issued by the Islamic Cultural Centre attached to the London Central Mosque—

The administrators, the *'ulama,*[90] the imams and numberless committees of our mosques and organisations have failed the community dismally. Instead of creating a unified infrastructure for the benefit of the community and all its needs, they have fostered discord, diversity, distrust and dishonesty, which cannot be described as other than disgraceful.[91]

In the light of such practical problems, it is possible that many Muslims might prefer to have their disputes ultimately resolved by English judges applying English law. However, this suggestion should not be taken to imply that the initial approach to many family disputes should not be through the particular Muslim community concerned and its various welfare organizations and agencies. In many instances these should be able to offer counselling, mediation, and arbitration resulting in a satisfactory settlement of the problem.[92]

---

[89] Cf Nielsen, 106.   [90] Muslim scholars.

[91] Newsletter No. 39 (April 1988). On the fragmentation of the Muslim communities in Britain, see also Darsh, S., *Muslims in Europe* (London, 1980), 78–82; Nielsen, 44–8 and generally, Lewis, P., *Islamic Britain* (London, 1994); Geaves, R., *Sectarian Influences within Islam in Britain* (Leeds, 1996). The position of the substantial Ahmadi community would be particularly fraught, since their status as Muslims is officially denied in some Muslim countries.   [92] See further below, pp 234–5.

THE HUMAN RIGHTS DIMENSION

A fourth difficulty with the proposal for the introduction of Islamic family law into Britain is perhaps the most insuperable of all and relates to its content. Muslim family law appears to contain a number of substantive principles and rules which violate some of the fundamental human rights and freedoms set out in international treaties to which the United Kingdom is a contracting party, such as the International Covenant on Civil and Political Rights, the Convention on the Elimination of All Forms of Discrimination Against Women, and the European Convention on Human Rights. This is especially so in relation to those Muslim provisions which seem to discriminate against women, for the achievement of sexual equality is a matter of deep concern in modern Britain. Examples of rules that are unlikely to find favour here for this reason are those permitting polygamy, forced marriages (as opposed to arranged marriages), marriages of girls before puberty, and divorce through unilateral repudiation by the husband (*talaq*), as well as the ban on Muslim women marrying non-Muslim husbands. In response Muslims are likely to present two lines of defence.

First, they may adopt the broad position that Islam itself, correctly understood, does not discriminate against women and that any appearances to the contrary represent distortions of the faith. However, this line of argument presents acute difficulties in seeking to identify the appropriate canons of interpretation, for so much depends upon which Islamic sources are regarded as authoritative. As Mayer has explained—

Increasingly, feminists and modernists seem to believe that the Qur'an and the example of the Prophet provide material favourable for feminist and modernist positions, whereas the juristic tradition and the associated cultural norms, which developed in the context of traditional societies in the Muslim world, provide material for the opponents of feminism and modernism. The Qur'an, as divine Revelation, is obviously a central source of guidance. It is also a source that devotes considerable attention to the status of women, and it is noteworthy that the Qur'anic changes in women's status are in the direction of enhancing their rights and elevating their status and dignity. In an environment where women were so devalued that female infanticide was a common and tolerated practice, the Qur'an introduced reforms that prohibited female infanticide, permitted women for the first time to inherit, restricted the practice of polygamy, curbed abuses of divorce by husbands, and gave women the ownership of the dower, which had previously been paid to the bride's father.[93]

[93] Mayer, A., *Islam and Human Rights: Tradition and Politics* (London, 1991), 110. The Qur'an is not, however, free from verses endorsing male dominance such as *Surah* II: 228 which states that ' . . . men have a degree of advantage over women' and *Surah* IV: 34 which declares—'Men are the protectors and maintainers of women because God has given

A leading Muslim feminist, Leila Ahmed, has argued convincingly that there is a fundamental tension in Islam between its ethical or spiritual vision of sexual equality, on the one hand, and the unequal hierarchical structure of the family laws which were instituted in early Islamic society, on the other.[94] She has demonstrated how, throughout history, those who have held power in Muslim societies have ignored the former dimension and maintained intact the latter. This latter 'establishment Islam', which is 'authoritarian, implacably androcentric and hostile to women'[95] needs to be subverted by the ethical vision, if Islam is in practice to be rendered compatible with modern notions of human rights for both men and women.[96]

However, while it is natural for feminists (and others) to blame the subsequent juristic tradition for distorting the original, authentic values of the Qur'an and the Prophet, it is these very traditions which are often drawn upon by conservatives. Moreover, recent trends towards greater Islamization of national legal and political systems have tended to put into reverse the secular moves towards a pattern of greater sexual equality witnessed in many Muslim countries since the end of the nineteenth century.[97] Hence Muslims who advocate sexual equality are increasingly coming under attack as being—

servile imitators of the West who lack loyalty to and pride in the Islamic tradition. Feminists are condemned as agents of Western cultural imperialism, who aim to destroy sound customs and *shari'a* principles in the name of promoting enlightened interpretations of Islamic requirements.[98]

A second line of defence which can be deployed by Muslims is to draw attention to those human rights provisions which tend to support their cause. It will be recalled that one of the standard articles in the system of League of Nations treaties and declarations for the protection of minorities related to Muslim personal law.[99] It stated that, where there was a significant Muslim population, suitable provision was to be made for regulating their family law and questions of personal status in accordance with Muslim usage.[100] This was an important early expression of the notion of affording religious minorities equality 'in fact', but the League scheme collapsed more than half a century ago and a more complex system now operates. Under both the International Covenant

---

the one more strength than the other . . . therefore the righteous women are devoutly obedient. . . . As to those women on whose part ye fear disloyalty and ill-conduct, admonish them first . . . and last beat them. . . .' On the subordination of Muslim wives, see generally, Mir-Hosseini, Z., *Marriage on Trial: A Study of Islamic Family Law* (London, 1993).

[94] *Women and Gender in Islam* (New Haven, 1992), 62–3, 66–7, 88, 225, 238–9.
[95] Ibid, 225.   [96] Ibid, 238–41.
[97] Mayer, 112–13, and see further below, pp 229–33.   [98] Mayer, 113.
[99] See above, ch 3.   [100] See e.g. Minorities in Albania Declaration 1921, Art 2.

on Civil and Political Rights and the European Convention, freedom of religion is guaranteed[101] and in the case of the Covenant this is buttressed by the additional protection afforded to minorities by Article 27. This authorizes differential treatment for minorities so as to afford them genuine equality and such treatment may also be accorded to minorities under the Convention, provided any legal distinction avoids the taint of discrimination by possessing an objective and reasonable justification.[102]

However, as we have seen, while modern human rights law does acknowledge the existence of certain group rights, it generally accords primacy to the rights of individuals and views a person's religious affiliation and ethnic background as merely part of that individual's distinctive identity.[103] To insist that all British Muslims should automatically be subject to a separate Islamic system of personal law, regardless of the wishes of individual Muslims, would seem to go beyond what is currently permissible, since it would run counter to the guarantee of equal access to the law, regardless of religious affiliation, which is afforded by Article 26 of the International Covenant on Civil and Political Rights. The only option open to a Muslim who wished to be governed by English family law rather than Muslim personal law in a particular case would be to abjure the faith, which would surely be far too much to ask of anyone. As Lord Mackay LC has explained—

. . . there may be good reason why groups are treated differently, for instance, out of respect for religious convictions. But the process, in terms of access to the machinery of justice, ought to be the same for everyone.[104]

A further problem with placing particular reliance on the principle of freedom of religion[105] lies in the conflict which arises in this context with another important principle, that of sexual equality. The treaty provisions giving individuals the freedom to practise their religion contain substantial limitation clauses which permit legal restrictions to be imposed if they are necessary to safeguard, *inter alia*, public morals and the fundamental rights and freedoms of others.[106] Religious freedom is thus a very general and necessarily qualified right, whereas the right to sexual equality in relation to marriage and family life is very specific and unqualified.[107] The state is thus entitled to insist that no one

---

[101] ICCPR, Art 18; ECHR, Art 9.   [102] See above, ch 3.

[103] See above, ch 3.

[104] 'The Role of the Profession in Securing Access to Justice' in *Conference Papers of the Ninth Commonwealth Law Conference* (Auckland, 1990), 59.

[105] See e.g. *Why Muslim Family Law for British Muslims*, 4.

[106] European Convention, Art 9(2); International Covenant, Art 18(3).

[107] See e.g. European Convention, Arts 12, 14; International Covenant, Art 23(4); International Convention on the Elimination of All Forms of Discrimination against Women, Art 16.

should automatically be subjected to sexually discriminatory laws simply on the basis of religious affiliation. The International Covenant on Civil and Political Rights itself provides that state parties must take appropriate steps to ensure equality of rights and responsibilities of spouses as to marriage, during marriage, and at its dissolution.[108] A similar provision on the duty to eliminate discrimination against women in all matters relating to marriage and family relations is to be found in the International Convention on the Elimination of All Forms of Discrimination against Women.[109] The central question thus resolves itself into whether the Muslim rules mentioned above do or do not involve such discrimination. Of course, not all distinctions based on sex are unlawful. As we have seen, differentiation between the sexes has been held to be permissible provided a legitimate aim is being pursued, the distinction possesses an objective and reasonable justification, and there is a reasonable degree of proportionality between the means employed and the aim sought to be realized.[110]

The prohibition on Muslim women marrying non-Muslim husbands (unless they convert to Islam), while Muslim men may marry non-Muslim wives, provided they are Christians or Jews,[111] appears transparently discriminatory. Its underlying justification in religious terms is that Islam takes it for granted that children will assume the religious faith of their father. Hence the only way of ensuring that a Muslim woman's children will remain within the faith is for her to marry another Muslim. Can this rationale for the rule justify the distinction in terms of human rights law? While it would seem legitimate for members of any religious denomination to aim to keep their children loyal to their faith, the methods by which Muslims try to achieve this objective seem both unreasonable and disproportionate. The rule restricting intermarriage wrongly assumes that all who marry will invariably have children and the rule itself is premised on the assumption that the parent with the

---

[108] Art 23(4). Guarantees of sexual equality are also afforded by Arts 2, 3, and 26. Significantly, reference to all these articles was made by the Supreme Court of Mauritius in *Bhewa and Alladeen v Government of Mauritius* [1991] *Commonwealth Law Bulletin* 43 in rejecting a claim that failure to introduce a system of Islamic personal law for Mauritian Muslims amounted to a violation of the guarantee of religious freedom contained in the Constitution of Mauritius.   [109] Art 16(1), set out in full below.

[110] See above, ch 3; see also *Marckx v Belgium* (1980) 2 EHRR 330 at 343; *Abdulaziz, Cabales and Balkandali v UK* (1985) 7 EHRR 471 at 499. In the latter case the Court declared (at 501) that 'the advancement of the equality of the sexes is today a major goal in the member states of the Council of Europe. This means that very weighty reasons would have to be advanced before a difference of treatment on the ground of sex could be regarded as compatible with the Convention'.

[111] Technically, Muslim men may only marry '*kitabiyya*' (women of 'the Book'), an expression which some interpret as also including Zoroastrians—see *Surah* IV: 5 of the Qur'an; Nasir, 63–4.

power to determine a child's religion should automatically be the father. Yet a Muslim woman marrying an agnostic husband might well be able to reach an agreement with him that any children should be brought up as Muslims. Equally, there is no good reason why a Christian woman who marries a Muslim husband should automatically agree to her children being brought up as Muslims.

Secondly, the acceptance by Islam of polygamy, however limited the husband's entitlement may be under Muslim law[112] and however uncommon it may be in actual practice, is discriminatory, for it allows one of the spouses to take further partners with full legal recognition and thus fundamentally change the nature of the couple's family life together, while denying such a right to the other spouse. None of the usual justifications put forward by Muslims in favour of polygamy carry conviction. In modern Britain there is no surplus population of women resulting from loss of men in battle, which calls for spinsters to be saved from promiscuity by attachment to already married men. There is no greater reason why a husband whose wife is barren should be entitled to take a second wife than there is for a wife whose husband is impotent or sterile to take a second husband. Nor can one sensibly take it for granted that men have more voracious sexual appetites than women, which can only be gratified by maintaining relationships with several partners concurrently. Furthermore, it hardly seems a sufficient response for Muslims to draw an analogy between polygamy and the existence of mistresses in Western societies.[113] This is to confuse the law with what goes on in practice—and the Western practice is non-discriminatory in this regard, for wives take lovers on the side too. Polygamy in England today does not possess any objective or reasonable justification.[114]

Thirdly, the form of divorce known as *talaq*, under which a husband may unilaterally repudiate his wife without showing cause, without the need to have recourse to any court or extraneous authority, and without any requirement of notification to his wife, is clearly discriminatory since it is not available to a wife. It is a weak defence to this charge for Muslims to argue either that wives can divorce their husbands in a

---

[112] A maximum of four wives is laid down in *Surah* IV: 3 of the Qur'an. In some Muslim countries modern statutes have decreed that the permission of a court must be sought before a man takes a second or subsequent wife—see Anderson, 111–14.

[113] See *Why Muslim Family Law for British Muslims*, 28, 42.

[114] See generally, Parekh, B., 'Equality, Fairness and the Limits of Diversity' (1994) 7 *Innovation* 289 at 298–306. In *Rabia Bibi v UK*, Application No. 19628/92, the European Commission of Human Rights upheld the ban on the formation of polygamous households in England imposed by Immigration Act 1988 (see p 53 above) No violation of the right to respect for family life had occurred through the refusal of admission to the UK of a second wife of the applicant, a Bangladeshi Muslim. The ban was justified on the basis that it was necessary for the protection of public morals in preserving the monogamous culture of the UK.

similar manner, provided they stipulate for such a right in their marriage contracts, or that to pronounce a *talaq* may be costly for a husband in terms of his resultant liability to pay deferred dower.[115] Again this confuses law with practice and the practical realities are that few Muslim wives have sufficient bargaining power to enable them to insert such clauses in their marriage contracts and often the amount of dower is too small to provide a major disincentive to divorce. The notion, sometimes put forward, that to pay it would commonly bankrupt the husband seems extremely far-fetched.[116]

Fourthly, Muslim principles whereby minors may be married while still under the age of puberty and without their consent, although broadly applicable to children of both sexes, operate in practice mainly in respect of girls. In this sense they may be regarded as oppressive of women. Forced marriages are, in any event, prohibited by several human rights treaties including the International Covenant on Civil and Political Rights[117] and the Convention on Consent to Marriage, Minimum Age for Marriage and Registration of Marriages.[118] Moreover, the European Commission of Human Rights has ruled that Muslims cannot claim that their religious freedom has been violated under the Convention simply because English law prevents marriages of girls under the age of sixteen. In *Khan v UK*[119] an application from a Muslim man who had been denied the right to marry a girl aged fourteen, as authorized under Islamic law, was rejected as manifestly ill-founded on the ground that marriage could not be considered merely as a form of religious practice.[120] The right to marry is regulated by a separate article of the Convention,[121] which leaves the requirements for the validity of marriages to be determined by national laws.

The wide gulf which exists between Muslim and Western approaches to these matters can be graphically illustrated by reference to developments with regard to the ratification by states of the Convention on the Elimination of All Forms of Discrimination Against Women. The Convention, which came into force in 1981, has so far been ratified by over 150 nations including around twenty 'Muslim' states.[122] So far as these Muslim countries are concerned, their practice has generally been to

---

[115] *Why Muslim Family Law for British Muslims*, 27.

[116] Research by the Human Rights Commission of Pakistan suggests that in 92 per cent of marriages there the amount of dower is set at around £1, i.e. it is merely a token sum; see *The Times*, 11 Oct 1989. However, the dower agreed by some British Muslims may amount to several thousand pounds.   [117] Art 23(3).

[118] Art 1(1).   [119] (1986) 48 Dec & Rep 253.

[120] 'Practice' does not cover every action 'which is motivated or influenced by a religion or belief'—see *Arrowsmith v UK* (1978) 19 Dec & Rep 5 at 19.   [121] Art 12.

[122] See Marie, J-B., 'International Instruments Relating to Human Rights: Classification and Status of Ratifications as of 1 January 1996' (1996) 17 *Human Rights LJ* 61.

attach a reservation to the whole or part of Article 16 of the Convention, a key provision which not only imposes a general duty on states to take appropriate measures to eliminate discrimination against women in all matters relating to marriage and family relations, but also lists particular instances in relation to which this should be done. Article 16 provides as follows—

1 States Parties shall take all appropriate measures to eliminate discrimination against women in all matters relating to marriage and family relations and in particular shall ensure, on a basis of equality of men and women:

(a) The same right to enter into marriage;
(b) The same right freely to choose a spouse and to enter into marriage only with their free and full consent;
(c) The same rights and responsibilities during marriage and at its dissolution;
(d) The same rights and responsibilities as parents, irrespective of their marital status, in matters relating to their children; in all cases the interests of the children shall be paramount;
(e) The same rights to decide freely and responsibly on the number and spacing of their children and to have access to the information, education and means to enable them to exercise these rights;
(f) The same rights and responsibilities with regard to guardianship, wardship, trusteeship and adoption of children, or similar institutions where these concepts exist in national legislation; in all cases the interests of the children shall be paramount;
(g) The same personal rights as husband and wife, including the right to choose a family name, profession and an occupation;
(h) The same rights for both spouses in respect of the ownership, acquisition, management, administration, enjoyment and disposition of property, whether free of charge or for a valuable consideration.

2 The betrothal and the marriage of a child shall have no legal effect, and all necessary action, including legislation, shall be taken to specify a minimum age for marriage and to make the registration of marriages in an official registry compulsory.

The fullest explanation of the reasoning which underlies Muslim anxieties about the content of Article 16 can be found in the reservation attached by Egypt.[123] The reservation draws attention to the provisions of the *shari'ah* (or code of Islamic law), in terms of which women are accorded rights 'equivalent to' those of their spouses so as to ensure 'a just balance' between them. The reservation goes on to declare—

[123] See 'Declarations, reservations, objections and notifications of withdrawal of reservations relating to the Convention on the Elimination of All Forms of Discrimination against Women', CEDAW/SP/1996/2, 16–17.

This is out of respect for the sacrosanct nature of the firm religious beliefs which govern marital relations in Egypt and which may not be called in question and in view of the fact that one of the most important bases of these relations is an equivalency of rights and duties so as to ensure complementarity which guarantees true equality between the spouses. . . .

The reservation then turns to the specific questions of maintenance, dower, and divorce, commenting—

The provisions of the *shari'ah* lay down that the husband shall pay bridal money to the wife and maintain her fully and shall also make a payment to her upon divorce, whereas the wife retains full rights over her property and is not obliged to spend anything on her keep. The *shari'ah* therefore restricts a wife's right to divorce by making it contingent on a judge's ruling, whereas no such restriction is laid down in the case of the husband.

Similar reservations to Article 16 have been made by several other Muslim countries. Bangladesh has indicated that it does not consider as binding upon itself sub-paragraphs 1(c) and 1(f) of Article 16 'as they conflict with *shari'ah* law based on Holy Qur'an and *Sunna*'.[124] Iraq has declared that it is not bound by any part of Article 16, drawing attention to those provisions of the *shari'ah* which accord women rights 'equivalent to' the rights of their husbands so as to ensure a 'just balance' between them, in exactly the same terms as the Egyptian reservation.[125] Jordan has attached a reservation about Article 16(1)(c) in relation to the rights to maintenance and compensation arising upon the dissolution of marriage.[126] Tunisia and Turkey do not consider themselves bound by sub-paragraphs (1)(c), (d), and (f) of Article 16.[127] Reservations in similar vein have been attached by Kuwait, Libya, Malaysia, and Morocco.[128]

Several states outside the Muslim world have, however, reacted in a hostile manner to these types of reservations. During 1985–6 Mexico, Sweden, and the Federal Republic of Germany all objected formally to such reservations, on the basis that they were incompatible with the object and purpose of the Convention itself and therefore impermissible under Article 28(2).[129] At the Third Meeting of the state parties to the Convention in 1986 a decision was adopted by consensus to urge full respect for Article 28(2), but there was considerable tension when the matter arose shortly afterwards in a meeting of the United Nations Economic and Social Council (ECOSOC).[130] Several countries portrayed

---

[124] CEDAW/SP/1996/2, 14. '*Sunna*' refers to the deeds, statements, and sayings of the Prophet Muhammad or collectively his 'practice'.   [125] CEDAW/SP/1996/2, 20.
[126] Ibid, 22.   [127] Ibid, 32–3.   [128] Ibid, 23–5, 27–8.
[129] Ibid, 42, 44, 49–50.
[130] See generally on the controversy, Clark, B., 'The Vienna Convention Reservations Regime and the Convention on Discrimination against Women' (1991) 85 *AJIL* 281.

the issue of impermissible reservations as an attack on Islamic states by Western countries. As a result, some Third World countries such as Kenya, Nicaragua, and Mexico, which had earlier expressed their grave concerns about the reservations, found their loyalties increasingly divided and decided to remain silent. The same hostile atmosphere prevailed at subsequent General Assembly meetings, with Islamic countries accusing Western states of cultural insensitivity and interference with their sovereign right to make reservations. During 1987 the UN Committee on the Elimination of Discrimination Against Women decided to ask the United Nations to 'promote or undertake studies on the status of women under Islamic laws and customs and in particular on the status and equality of women in the family', taking into account the Islamic legal doctrine of *ijtihad*[131] (interpretation). Strong resistance from Muslim countries ensured that no such studies were authorized, but at the World Conference on Human Rights held in Vienna in 1993 there was a consensus that states should be urged to withdraw reservations which were contrary to the object and purpose of the Convention.[132] In the meantime, Denmark, Finland, the Netherlands, Norway, and Portugal had joined in the process of registering objections to the reservations made by Muslim states.[133]

AN INDIAN PERSPECTIVE

India ratified the Convention on the Elimination of All Forms of Discrimination Against Women in 1993, attaching a declaration that it would abide by the provisions of Article 16(1), albeit 'in conformity with its policy of non-interference in the personal affairs of any community without its initiative and consent'.[134] This declaration no doubt reflected India's reluctance to override or disregard the clear unwillingness of the vast majority of its Muslim population to agree to any modification or reform of their Islamic personal law,[135] while at the same time indicating that the Indian Government remained committed to its constitutional mandate to introduce at some future date a uniform civil code suitable for a secular state.[136]

---

[131] *Ijtihad* is discussed further below, p 230.
[132] Vienna Declaration and Programme of Action, II, para 39.
[133] CEDAW/SP/1996/2, 41–2, 46–9.   [134] Ibid, 19–20.
[135] See Mahmood, T., *Muslim Personal Law* (New Delhi, 1977), 134, 143, 199.
[136] Art 44 of the Constitution of India 1950 provides—'The State shall endeavour to secure for the citizens a uniform civil code throughout the territory of India'. However, there seems little realistic prospect of such a code—see Menski, W., 'The reform of Islamic family law and a uniform civil code for India' in Connors, J. and Mallat, C. (eds), *Islamic Family Law* (London, 1990), ch 13.

An Indian perspective on the problems of accommodating Muslim personal law is instructive for a number of reasons. First, many Muslims living in Britain today have their origins in that country. Secondly, during the period of Empire, Britain established the pattern of legal pluralism in family matters which prevails there to this day. In many fields individuals are governed by a system of personal law, which depends entirely upon their religious affiliations. If such a system could function satisfactorily in India under British administration why, many Muslims may ask, cannot the British Government apply the same approach at home? Of course, the basic, if rather unpalatable answer to this question is that the Imperial administration in India possessed the might and power to impose whatever legal arrangements were required to suit its needs, whereas the Muslim minority in Britain today has minimal political influence. Moreover, while the logic behind such an argument for the recognition of personal laws in England appears super-ficially compelling, it is important to bear in mind the fact that India's rulers have long had strong reservations about certain aspects of Muslim law and these have persisted since the attainment of Independence in 1947. It is this dimension in particular which is worth exploring in some detail for if India itself, a multi-cultural society in which Muslims form a very substantial minority of the population, is currently unclear about the desirability of safeguarding and retaining a system of Muslim per-sonal law, this is surely a factor which should be borne in mind in framing a suitable policy for a far smaller number and proportion of Muslims now resident in England.

An illuminating critique of the status of Muslim personal law in India has been provided by the eminent Muslim scholar Tahir Mahmood in his book *Personal Laws in Crisis*,[137] based on a series of memorial lectures delivered at the University of Bombay in 1984. In his second lecture he set out to defend the 'misunderstood' law of Islam, declaring—

No other aspect of Islam has suffered so much misconception and distortion as its personal law. And, unfortunately, in no other part of the world has the personal law of the Muslims been so much misunderstood as in India.[138]

He ascribed the emergence of a distorted image of Muslim personal law in India to the advent of the British Raj. Since direct interference with such personal law would have jeopardized Imperial interests 'the British rulers surreptitiously decided to turn the natives away from their tradi-tional laws by making them believe that they were "inhuman" and "uncivilised". So they began distorting and misinterpreting those laws'.[139] Legal education was transferred to institutions under British

---

[137] (New Delhi, 1986).   [138] At 49.   [139] Ibid, 51.

control, the religious courts of the *qadis* were abolished and their jurisdiction taken over by civil courts manned by English-trained judges, faulty treatises on Islamic law were prepared by English officials and then relied upon by the courts in reaching their decisions, and finally the precedents so established were artificially 'codified' in a textbook written by Mulla, a Parsee, and erroneously entitled *Principles of Mohammedan Law*.[140] This eventually became a classic, proceeding through no fewer than eighteen editions between 1906 and 1977, and it continues to carry great weight in the Indian courts at the present time. The petty *mullahs* at the mosques acceded to such distortions through their own ignorance of the true principles of Islamic law and eventually all these misconceptions received the widest possible publicity through the medium of popular Indian films, which presented mere caricatures of Muslim matrimonial law. By 1972 a judge of the Indian High Court, himself a Muslim, could go so far as to comment in reference to the Islamic law of divorce that his judicial conscience was 'disturbed at this monstrosity.'[141]

Tahir Mahmood went on to plead for the Indian courts to change their current attitudes and search for the true rationale of Islamic principles, so that these could be accurately applied in the future. In his third lecture he argued strongly that India should resist the fashionable tendency to regard the West as possessing better systems of family law and thus offering suitable models for reform.[142] However, for present purposes it is his analysis of certain key concepts and institutions of Islamic personal law which is of the greatest significance.

His treatment of polygamous marriages under the heading 'The Myth about Polygamy' concentrated on three points. First, he drew attention to the historical fact that the Qur'an neither introduced polygamy among the Arabian tribes nor enjoined it. Hitherto polygamy had been unrestrained; Islam subjected it to 'very strict conditions'.[143] However, in stressing the key condition laid down in the Qur'an that a husband should not become a polygamist if he fears that he may not be able to treat his co-wives justly and fairly,[144] Mahmood ignored the subjective nature of this regulation, which leaves the decision whether or not to take further wives, in legal terms, to the discretion of the husband and to his conscience, rather than to any outside body.[145]

---

[140] (Bombay, 1906).
[141] Per Justice Khalid in *Mohamed Haneefa v Pathummal* [1972] *Kerala Law Times* 512.
[142] At 95–136.   [143] Ibid, 69.
[144] *Surah* IV: 3 declares—'If ye fear that ye shall not be able to deal justly with the orphans, marry women of your choice, two or three or four; but if ye fear that ye shall not be able to deal justly with them, then only one.' Many young women and girls were orphaned by the deaths of their fathers at the battle of Uhud in 625 AD.
[145] At 71.

Secondly, Mahmood explained that very few Indian Muslims have in fact more than one wife, so that in practical terms—

. . . the so-called problem of polygamy among the Indian Muslims is quite imaginary and hence a non-issue. Authentic surveys report that in recent years the percentage of polygamy among Muslims, whose law conditionally permits it, has been far less than among those whose personal law absolutely prohibits it by the force of civil and penal sanctions.[146]

Of course, the argument that a particular social practice is not a problem because its incidence is very low tends to cut both ways. It may be harmful for the few who are directly affected and if the vast majority do not feel the need to pursue the practice, it can perhaps safely be dispensed with altogether without causing much interference in the general pattern of people's lives.

Thirdly, Mahmood made the point that the few Muslims who do marry a second wife invariably do so after forsaking, though not divorcing, their first wife.[147] This approach to polygamy is totally disapproved of by the Qur'an, which indicates that if a man finds it impossible to live in respectable harmony with his wife he should part from her in kindness through divorce.[148] Opponents of polygamy may naturally seize upon this fact to argue that if Muslims cannot be trusted to follow their own moral precepts and if they themselves distort the values of their own religion, the state is justified in intervening to prohibit polygamy altogether.

Turning to the dissolution of marriage, Mahmood declared that 'no other aspect of Islamic matrimonial law has been as much distorted in this part of the world as its law on divorce'.[149] On this score he attached blame equally to many eminent English judges, various textbook writers, and the ill-educated *mullahs* of the village mosques 'who misguided their clientele by transmitting to them their own shamefully faulty understanding of a superb divorce law'.[150] He asserted that 'true Islamic law in fact stands for what is now known as the "breakdown theory" of divorce.'[151] This theory precludes the courts from investigating the causes of marriage breakdown and Islam follows this line to the extent of largely avoiding recourse to court proceedings by providing for three methods of extrajudicial divorce, namely *talaq*, *khul'* and *mubar'at*.[152]

In his treatment of the notorious *talaq*, Mahmood portrayed this form of divorce as being simply based on irretrievable breakdown of marriage. The husband's pronouncement takes effect after the expiry of the three-month period of *'iddat* (representing the completion of three

---

[146] At 71.   [147] Ibid, 70.   [148] *Surah* II: 229.   [149] At 72.
[150] Ibid 73–4.   [151] Ibid, 74.   [152] These terms are defined above at p 207.

menstrual cycles), provided he has not revoked it.[153] The true extent of Mahmood's concern for the wife's position is apparent from the following extraordinary passage—

At the expiry of this period [of *'iddat*], if he has not revoked the divorce, the marriage is dissolved—but the couple can revive the marriage by a fresh solemnisation, *provided that the wife agrees*. And that is all. There are no complications, no complexities, no inequities in the process. However, since the husband cannot be allowed to play hide and seek with his wife by repeatedly pronouncing a divorce and then either revoking it within the permissible period of *'iddat* or offering to remarry the same woman after its expiry, the law provides that a husband can do so only twice in the whole of his life; whenever during married life he pronounces a divorce for a third time the marriage is instantly dissolved perpetually, leaving no room either for the revocation of divorce or for a novation of marriage by a fresh solemnisation.[154]

Mahmood next proceeded to compare the *talaq* procedure with the *khul'*, which he claimed is the wife's counterpart right to divorce. He categorized it as 'divorce at wife's insistence' and seemed to suggest that it is the exact equivalent of *talaq*. 'The right of divorce which Islam confers on women, if understood in its true perspective, will indeed be found dazzling.'[155] Despite energetic efforts on his part to disguise the fact, the truth is that the essence of *khul'* is that it involves the husband's agreement and is therefore a consensual form of divorce, similar to *mubar'at*. Moreover, it involves the wife in the surrender of her legal entitlement to dower. It is thus far from comparable with *talaq* and this rules out the success of any argument that Muslim divorce law does not discriminate on the ground of sex.

So far as the breakdown theory of divorce is concerned, the mere fact that one partner unilaterally repudiates the other and does not change his mind within a period of three months may indicate breakdown in some instances, but it is certainly far from furnishing the sort of proof of breakdown required in most of those legal systems where it now operates.[156] Such a repudiation may be evidence of no more than a temporary rift in the couple's relationship. A period of three months' delay may well not be sufficient to eliminate precipitate divorces and the absence of any form of judicial or administrative process may considerably restrict the exploration of the prospect of reconciliation and the use of mediation techniques in the resolution of any dispute over the future of the children. Finally, Mahmood failed to bring out clearly enough the undisputed fact

---

[153] Qur'an, *Surah* II: 228–32. [154] At 75. [155] Ibid, 77.
[156] See e.g. Law Commission Report No. 170 'Facing the Future—A discussion paper on the ground for divorce' (1988), para 4.16.

that one particular form of *talaq*, known as *talaq al bidah*,[157] albeit greatly frowned upon on moral grounds, entitles a husband to obtain an instant divorce, without even the possibility of revocation during the period of '*iddat*. There is little consolation for wives in his complaint that many Muslim husbands use this form out of sheer ignorance of the true tenets of Islam. The legal position in this regard has been accurately summarized by Esposito[158]—

Unlike the two approved forms of divorce, the following two disapproved forms (*talaq al-bidah*) do not allow for a chance to reconsider a possible capricious or hastily-made decision. These forms of divorce, similar to the husband's unfettered right to divorce in pre-Islamic Arabia, again made their way through the force of custom into common practice and were incorporated into Islamic law. They are valid but disapproved of and sinful. The first disapproved form of divorce, the *talaq al-bidah*, consists of three declarations of divorce occurring at one time. The 'triple declaration' is made during a single *tuhr*[159] by pronouncing one sentence 'I divorce thee thrice', or three separate sentences, 'I divorce thee, I divorce thee, I divorce thee' and then the marriage is irrevocably dissolved. The second version of the *talaq al-bidah* consists of one irrevocable declaration. The single pronouncement can be made in oral or written form during a *tuhr* or even at another time. At the moment of pronouncement or at the writing of the divorce, the marital tie is immediately severed. The allowance of these two forms in law directly contradicts the Qur'anic prescription: 'When ye divorce wives, divorce them at their prescribed periods, and count (accurately) their prescribed periods. . . . And fear God your Lord. . . . Those are limits set by God: and any who transgress the limits of God, does verily wrong his (own) soul.'[160] However since Islamic law permitted the *talaq al-bidah*, only the husband's conscience served as a restraint from the use of such disapproved forms of divorce.

Despite Mahmood's vigorous attempts to defend some of the most controversial aspects of Muslim family law, it is hard to find his reasoning sufficiently convincing on the major topics of polygamy and *talaq* divorce. Furthermore, his own earlier writings clearly underline the grave weaknesses of Muslim personal law as a suitable system for application in modern conditions. In 1972 Mahmood was asked, on the eve of an important gathering of Muslim leaders in India, to write down a list of those features of Muslim society which kept modern thinkers like himself awake at night. This list is to be found in his book *Muslim Personal Law*,[161] first published in 1977. Among his many concerns there are several which relate to issues raised in this chapter.

---

[157] '*Bidah*' means innovation; for the background to this form of *talaq*, see Engineer, A., *The Rights of Women in Islam* (London, 1992), 123–7.
[158] *Women in Muslim Family Law*, 32–3.
[159] '*Tuhr*' means purity and refers to the time when a woman is not experiencing menstruation.   [160] *Surah* LXV: 1.
[161] (New Delhi, 1977).

Once they have been enumerated, it may become easier to draw together some conclusions about what requires to be done if English law is to make any greater accommodation than it does at present for the needs of Muslim families in Britain. The list included the following areas of concern[162]—

(i) the diversity of legal principles within the different schools of Islamic jurisprudence, resulting in a denial of equal protection under the law to the followers of the same religion;

(ii) the absence of a systematically codified Muslim personal law, creating difficulties in discovering exactly what the law is and often leading to misapplication in the courts;

(iii) the imposition upon a girl of her guardian's choice of husband;

(iv) the 'tremendous diversity between the rights of men and women in the matter of divorce, men enjoying arbitrary power to inflict instant unilateral divorce';

(v) the unconditional effectiveness of unintentional divorces under the Hanafi school of Islamic jurisprudence, in terms of which pronouncements made in jest or anger arising from momentary provocation are fully effective;

(vi) legal recognition by Islam of the 'triple divorce' which results in an immediate, irrevocable termination of marriage, making any remarriage of the spouses conditional upon a consummated marriage of the wife to a third party;

(vii) the dependence of a wife's right to *khul'* upon the consent of the husband;

(viii) a husband's unbridled right to contract a second, polygamous marriage irrespective of whether he needs an additional wife or whether he can comply with the Qur'anic requirement of equitable justice between co-wives;

(ix) the restriction of a divorced wife's right to maintenance to the period of *'iddat* when the amount of dower actually paid is too low to support her properly;[163] and

(x) the very low share of a widow in her deceased husband's estate, which creates great hardship where her dower is nominal.

Mahmood noted that this list of 'ailments' was not the creation of Islam itself so much as the abuse and misapplication of Muslim laws.

---

[162] At 163–6.

[163] For controversy over this issue in the light of the Indian Supreme Court's decision in *Mohd Ahmed Khan v Shah Bano Begum* AIR 1985 SC 945 and the enactment of the Muslim Women (Protection of Rights on Divorce) Act 1986 by the Indian Parliament, see generally, Connors, J. and Mallat, C. (eds), *Islamic Family Law*, 283–8 (Menski) and 295–311 (Mahmood).

He accurately summed up the position in the following penetrating statement—

Troubles arise when distinction is made between strictly 'legal' and apparently 'moral' precepts in Islamic texts. To illustrate, 'man can divorce his wife' is treated as 'law' but an exhortation very relevant to this law, namely 'the most detestable thing in the eyes of God is divorce' is devoid of any legal sanction. Similarly, permission for polygamy is considered to be the 'law', but the conditions attached to this permission are treated as rules of morality or courtesy.[164]

It is this disparity between specifically legal rules enforceable through the authority of state institutions, on the one hand, and rules binding on the individual's conscience alone, on the other, which suggests that while many excellent ethical principles are to be found in Islam, it may often be gravely defective as a legal system.[165] In the light of this, as Mahmood has cogently argued, there should be no logical objection to the introduction of statutory legal reforms which seek to uphold the fundamental moral principles of Islam by imposing a check upon popular abuses of the existing rules themselves.[166]

CONCLUSIONS

What remedies might, then, be available to cure the ailments afflicting Muslim personal law outlined above? Mahmood has drawn attention to several possibilities in the Indian context,[167] some of which might conceivably be adapted to an English setting. A long-term goal might perhaps be to compile a codification of Muslim personal law, eliminating the differences between the various schools of jurisprudence by selecting the best interpretations from each of them.[168] No doubt this would be a daunting task and one that would require an enormous degree of co-operation between expert representatives of the different communities resident in England today, as well as the ultimate step of approval by Parliament. Mahmood clearly regarded such a project for India as 'utopian'.

On the assumption that the existing separate systems of Muslim personal law will be retained, if any of them were to be given formal legal recognition in England, certain of their rules would clearly have to

---

[164] *Muslim Personal Law*, 167–8.
[165] See generally, Ahmed, L., *Women and Gender in Islam*.
[166] *Muslim Personal Law*, 168.   [167] Ibid, 167–73.
[168] For an attempt to achieve such unification, see the Unified Arab Draft Law for Personal Status prepared under the auspices of the Council of Arab Ministers of Justice and reprinted in an English translation in Nasir, 260–313. No Muslim state has yet adopted the draft in its own legal system.

be modified or disregarded in the light of the criticisms of them levelled earlier. This could be accomplished either by means of English legislation specifically precluding the judicial recognition of Islamic rules concerning, for example, polygamy, forced marriages, and *talaq* divorces, or else by giving the English courts a wide discretion to decline to apply any Muslim rules which they found manifestly contrary to public policy in the sense of being against justice, equity, and good conscience.[169] No doubt, in making any such assessment the human rights dimension would be borne firmly in mind by the judges.[170]

Some Muslims in England might feel that such a 'watered-down' version of Islamic law was unacceptable and that only the undiluted classical law should be introduced here. However, it is extremely important to recognize that during the course of the twentieth century a great variety of reforms have been made in Muslim personal law by the governments of Arab and Islamic states. Since this has often been achieved against the wishes of a conservative clergy, who have maintained that Islamic law is immutable and cannot be changed, it is necessary to explain how such developments can be justified in terms of Islamic principles themselves. This last element is vital because today the vast majority of Muslims will not easily accept explanations for change which are rooted in Western models and perceptions.[171] As a leading Muslim jurist has explained—

Like members of other cultural traditions, Muslims tend to be suspicious and unreceptive towards what they perceive to be an attempt to impose alien standards. To obtain their cooperation in implementing international standards on the rights of women, we need to show the Muslims in general that these standards are not alien at all. They are, in fact, quite compatible with the fundamental values of Islam. In other words, we need to provide Islamic legitimacy for the international standards on the rights of women.[172]

While a detailed exposition of the underlying nature, sources, and development of Islamic law is beyond the scope of this chapter on account of their complexity and controversiality,[173] the following brief summary of a few key points should suffice to indicate the general drift of the argument being propounded.

The four major sources of Muslim law are the Qur'an itself, the *Sunna* (the practice of the Prophet Muhammad), *qiyas* (reasoning by analogy), and *ijma* (the general consensus of the community and of legal scholars). Three of the four Sunni schools of jurisprudence have additionally

---

[169] See above, ch 2.   [170] Ibid.   [171] See Esposito, 130–1; Ahmed, ch 8.
[172] An-Na'im, A., 'The Rights of Women and International Law in the Muslim Context' (1987) 9 *Whittier LR* 491 at 515.
[173] See generally, Anderson, J., *Law Reform in the Muslim World*.

developed and used various forms of *ijtihad* (independent interpretation or deduction) in order to ensure justice and equity. Although the broad assumption among Muslim jurists for well over a thousand years was that further change and development were neither needed nor legally possible through *ijtihad*, and that the task of Muslim lawyers was simply to follow the path of tradition (*taqlid*), this approach has had to be modified somewhat during the twentieth century in the face of modernization and social change. Such challenges to traditional perceptions of orthodoxy have naturally led to conflict between 'conservatives' and 'modernists', but the result has been that in many Muslim countries the state has intervened through legislation to bring the law more into line with current thinking and practice.

In seeking to introduce suitable reforms for the modern world, which remain in harmony with the principles and values contained in the Qur'an, it has been suggested that the processes of *ijtihad* and *ijma* may have a vital role to play.[174] If the general consensus (*ijma*) of a particular Muslim community is that legal change is needed in order to give greater effect to Qur'anic values, especially concerning the equality of women, then, it can be argued, *ijtihad* is available to provide the necessary reinterpretation of what is required. Inevitably education has a key part to play here in inculcating among the population a proper understanding of the underlying Qur'anic values. It is far from clear, however, whether such an education will be widely available in England in the immediate future.[175] As the first few generations of Muslims settle down in Britain and face a battery of problems of prejudice, discrimination, intolerance, and a clash of cultures, many of them seem likely to cling with even greater fervour to rather doctrinaire attitudes and conservative values. What is needed is an education which will give young British Muslims both a deep sense of their religious and cultural traditions and a spirit of independent thought and critical inquiry, which will enable them to find realistic solutions to family law problems in modern England.

Two illustrations of how this process of reform might work can be offered. First, in relation to polygamy, there is a widespread belief among many Muslim jurists today that the underlying message in the Qur'an is that, while polygamy is permissible, the ideal is monogamy. Since 1950 a number of states in the Middle East, North Africa, and the Indian subcontinent have, therefore, taken steps to restrict polygamy, mainly by requiring the prior authorization of a court of law or other body.[176] In Iraq and Syria a judge has to be satisfied that the husband has

---

[174] Esposito, 131–4; Engineer, 170.

[175] For criticism of the traditional education offered here by the *'ulama* (Muslim scholars), see Lewis, *Islamic Britain*, ch 5.   [176] Anderson, 61–4, 110–4; Nasir, 61–2.

a legitimate interest in taking a subsequent wife and is capable of providing the necessary financial support. In Morocco a judge can forbid polygamy if injustice among wives is feared. In Pakistan and Bangladesh prior written permission to contract a subsequent marriage must be obtained from an arbitration council. Another possible method of curbing polygamy would be to make use of the well-recognized power of the parties themselves to insert stipulations in marriage contracts. Legislation in Jordan allows a wife to incorporate a condition into her marriage contract, which gives her a right to divorce her husband if he takes a subsequent wife.

The state might, however, go much further than this and decree that all Muslim marriage contracts be in standard form and contain an outright ban on polygamy.[177] In a country such as England, where all marriages have to be registered, it might be perfectly feasible to require registration of all such Muslim marriage contracts. The consequence of breaking the ban on polygamy would not only be a risk of prosecution for the crime of bigamy but also that the subsequent marriage was devoid of legal effect and void. The essential feature of this solution would be that Muslim husbands would freely, by means of the contract, forego one of their legal privileges, and since polygamy is not positively required by Islam they would not be doing something which their religion prohibited, if they entered into such a contract. Because it is so closely tied to recognized Islamic practice this route of reform might perhaps prove more acceptable to Muslims in Britain than an outright prohibition on polygamy through legislation, which was what President Bourguiba achieved in Tunisia in 1957. He outlawed polygamy altogether on the basis of a total reinterpretation of two Qur'anic injunctions. The first was that polygamy was only permissible if the husband could treat each wife fairly and justly.[178] The second, less well-known, was 'Ye are never able to be fair and just between women even if that were your ardent desire'.[179] His argument was that, since in modern times husbands cannot in practice ever achieve fair treatment of multiple wives (and indeed that no one other than a prophet could accomplish this feat), polygamy should no longer be allowed. However, no other Muslim state has felt bold enough to follow Tunisia's unconventional lead in the ensuing period of forty years, which suggests strong reservations about the use of this revolutionary technique.

Turning next to the issue of *talaq* divorce, if the Muslim community in England and its legal experts can reach a consensus that reform is needed here, perhaps a process of reinterpretation can remove the sexual

---

[177] See Mahmood, T., *Muslim Personal Law*, 170.   [178] *Surah* IV: 3.
[179] *Surah* IV: 129.

discrimination involved and curb the worst excesses of the process on the basis of the key underlying Qur'anic principles. These are to ameliorate the legal status of women generally and to discourage divorce.[180] The Prophet is reported to have said, for example, that 'of all the permitted things, divorce is the most abominable with God'[181] and one of the verses on divorce in the Qur'an states—

And women shall have rights similar to the rights against them, according to what is equitable.[182]

Yet another verse states that if discord is feared between husband and wife two arbitrators should be appointed to attempt to reconcile them.[183] It follows that the law should endeavour to confine divorce to cases where a marriage has irretrievably broken down. In the view of several Muslim states such as Syria, Iraq, and Morocco, this requires the involvement of a court or other institution to check that the divorce is really needed and that a reconciliation is impossible.[184] Failure to seek the court's approval renders the husband liable to criminal sanctions, though admittedly the divorce itself remains valid. Tunisia, however, has gone further and declared that extrajudicial divorces are totally invalid. In Pakistan and Bangladesh a rather different line of approach has been adopted. There a husband who wishes to divorce his wife must, immediately after his pronouncement of *talaq* in any form, give written notice of the *talaq* to the chairman of an administrative council and supply a copy of the notice to his wife.[185] The effect of the notice is to 'freeze' the *talaq* for ninety days, during which period the council is given an opportunity of trying to achieve a reconciliation between the couple. It is only after the expiry of the ninety days that the divorce is effective, assuming that no reconciliation has occurred in the meantime. The requirement concerning giving notice is mandatory and if it is not complied with the divorce is ineffective and the husband is liable to a sentence of one year's imprisonment or a fine or both.

Certainly the disapproved forms of *talaq*, namely the *talaq al-bidah*, cannot be permitted in England and the rights of husbands and wives must be equalized, for example by inserting a standard term in all Muslim marriage contracts to the effect that the husband grants his wife an equal right of repudiation by means of *talaq*. It should be

---

[180] Esposito, 108–9.   [181] Ibid, 29.   [182] *Surah* II: 228.
[183] *Surah* IV: 35.   [184] Anderson, 60–1, 126–9.
[185] Muslim Family Laws Ordinance 1961. For discussion of the precise status of the Ordinance in the light of the Enforcement of Shariah Act 1991 and judicial decisions interpreting earlier trends towards 'Islamization' of the legal system, see Kennedy, C., 'Repugnancy to Islam—Who Decides? Islam and Legal Reform in Pakistan' (1992) 42 *ICLQ* 769.

stressed, however, that none of the reforms mentioned above involves requiring Muslims to violate their religious duties by performing any act that is forbidden by Islam. All that is involved is a modification of legal privileges.

Reforms have also been accomplished in many Muslim countries with a view to prohibiting the marriages of young children and preventing marriages being entered into under compulsion.[186] Recent legislation has also given increasing importance to the welfare of children in disputes after divorce.[187]

A leading British authority on Islamic law has written—

The Qur'anic precepts are in the nature of ethical norms—broad enough to support modern legal structures and capable of varying interpretations to meet the particular needs of time and place.[188]

It is now clear that in many parts of the contemporary world Muslim personal law is not regarded as immune from the power of nation states to mould new rules to meet modern conditions and promote the welfare of all their subjects. If Muslims in England cannot themselves reach a consensus on a new unified code of personal law, which might be put before the legislature for Parliamentary approval, the most that they can hope for is that, as English family law goes through the regular procedures whereby it is updated, the underlying spirit of the fundamental principles of the *shari'ah* is increasingly embodied in its provisions.[189] In this regard Muslim organizations must be encouraged to become fully involved in the general law reform process so that their views are clearly heard. It is, however, inevitable that the 'modernists' among them are likely to receive a more sympathetic hearing than those whose conservatism precludes them from envisaging any scope for the development of Islamic law beyond its classical state more than a thousand years ago.

At all events, there is no justification for acceding to the claim to a separate system of personal law for British Muslims at the present time, especially in the light of the observation of one well-informed scholar that—'soundings among ordinary Muslims seem to suggest little active support for the idea'.[190] The demand may, to a significant degree, be the product of internal institutional rivalries between different Muslim organizations and factions in this country and a desire on their part to impress the governments of Muslim states and gain their patronage and support.[191] Attention should, rather, be turned away from such a

---

[186] See Anderson, 102–5, 109.   [187] Ibid, 141–3.
[188] Coulson, N., *A History of Islamic Law* (Edinburgh, 1964), 225.
[189] See Poulter, S., 'Divorce Reform in a Multicultural Society' (1989) 19 *Fam Law* 99.
[190] Nielsen, J., *Muslims in Western Europe*, 53.
[191] Nielsen, J., 'Aux Sources des Revendications des Musulmans en Matière de Droit de la Famille en Europe' in Foblets, M.-C. (ed), *Familles-Islam-Europe* (Paris, 1996), 33 at 45.

grandiose scheme to more mundane local initiatives with a greater potential for achieving practical results.

In this sphere, the most constructive development in recent years has been the establishment of several *'shari'ah* councils' in England, devoted to the informal settlement of disputes between Muslims according to Islamic legal principles and ethical precepts. As suggested earlier, Muslim community agencies and organizations may be particularly well placed to resolve family problems through the processes of counselling, mediation, and arbitration and will often be the first 'port of call' for those in difficulty. English family law now strongly encourages the resolution of such problems by the parties themselves and will, in appropriate circumstances, give effect to negotiated agreements and compromises through 'consent orders' and similar mechanisms.[192] So long as English public policy considerations are not contravened, for instance through attempts to enforce *shari'ah* council judgments or oust the jurisdiction of the English courts, such 'private ordering' of family problems utilizing mechanisms of 'alternative dispute resolution' has gained widespread acceptance.[193] Obviously, care would need to be taken by those offering mediation to ensure that gender-based power imbalances were properly addressed and that solutions were not imposed upon women against their wishes. In any event, it would always be open to an individual Muslim to reject any proposals put forward by a *shari'ah* council or other agency and seek an adjudication from the English courts. Similarly, no agreement about the distribution of parental responsibilities for children would preclude an English court from determining their future upbringing on the basis of its own view as to what was in the best interests of the welfare of the particular children involved.[194]

A range of techniques designed to resolve family differences is employed at the *shari'ah* council which operates under the auspices of the Council of Imams and Mosques,[195] and is attached to the Muslim College in West London.[196] First, vigorous attempts are made to see if reconciliations can be promoted, on the basis that the Prophet Muhammad described divorce as 'abominable' in the eyes of God.[197] Moreover, certain forms of *talaq* are declared invalid by the council so that they are

---

[192] See e.g. Cretney, S. and Masson, J., *Principles of Family Law* 6th ed. (London, 1997), 397–408, 698–9; Eekelaar, J., *Regulating Divorce* (Oxford, 1991), 145–54.

[193] For a useful practical guide, see Haynes, J., *Alternative Dispute Resolution: Fundamentals of Family Mediation* (Horsmonden, 1993). [194] Children Act 1989, s 1.

[195] This *shari'ah* council began work in 1985 and represented the continuation of earlier arrangements organized by its secretary, Dr Zaki Badawi, when he was the director of the Islamic Cultural Centre attached to the Regents' Park Mosque.

[196] See Badawi, Z., 'Muslim Justice in a Secular State' in King, M. (ed.), *God's Law versus State Law* (London, 1995), ch 8. [197] See Esposito, 29.

ineffective in terms of Islamic law, as well as English law, for instance those pronounced in the absence of witnesses and the 'disapproved' form known as *talaq al-bidah*, described earlier. Secondly, in certain circumstances Islamic divorces are granted by the council. The most common situation is where the wife has already obtained a divorce from the English courts, but the husband has refused to pronounce a *talaq* and is thus trying to prevent any remarriage on her part from being recognized in the eyes of Muslim law. A Muslim divorce is granted by the council where the husband persists in this attitude over many months, despite several reminders from the council. A divorce may also be granted to the wife by the council where the only valid marriage to which the couple are parties is an Islamic one, for instance where a man has taken a second wife in England and her status as such is not recognized in English law because of the husband's prior subsisting marriage.[198] Thirdly, the council has drafted a form of Muslim marriage contract (with variable terms), so that Muslim couples can expressly agree upon certain matrimonial arrangements, which are in line with Islamic ethical principles, and feel that they are utilizing a distinctively Islamic technique as an integral part of the process. A standard form of will, bequeathing estates in accordance with Muslim principles of inheritance, is also available.

A characteristic feature of the work of the *shari'ah* council attached to the Muslim College is its eclectic approach to Islamic law. It is not tied to any particular school of Islamic doctrine and is prepared to offer the parties the benefits of any school which suits their particular needs, regardless of whether this conforms with the school prevailing in their country of origin, domicile, or nationality.[199] The council is thus concerned to apply the underlying spirit and general principles of Islamic law, as set out in the Qur'an and the *Sunna*, rather than let itself be constrained by narrow interpretations of classical jurisprudence (*fiqh*). Personal judgement and interpretation (*ijtihad*) are thus given free rein.

If the valuable work of the various *shari'ah* councils can be adequately publicized among the various Muslim communities and expanded to cover the major urban centres where the Muslim population is concentrated, as well as being drawn to the attention of local solicitors and court welfare officers for referral in appropriate cases, this would seem to offer a valuable method of fulfilling Muslim demands for their religious tenets to play an important role in the resolution of family problems. Of course, judges and magistrates (and indeed court staff

---

[198] Matrimonial Causes Act 1973, s 11(*b*).
[199] See Surty, M., 'The Shari'ah Family Courts in Britain and the Protection of Women's Rights in Muslim Family Law' (1991) 9 *Muslim Educational Quarterly* 59 at 63.

generally) also need to be trained to deal with Muslim litigants and their disputes in a sensitive manner, and significant initiatives in this regard have recently been taken by the Judicial Studies Board.[200] Even if, as argued above, there are sound reasons for not introducing Islamic family law into England as a separate system, Muslims must be made to feel confident that their religious and family values will be accorded due respect by the English legal system and that they will receive justice at the hands of the English courts. It is inevitable, however, that they will have to accept that in England Islam can only be followed as a religious faith and not pursued as an all-embracing way of life.[201]

---

[200] See generally, Judicial Studies Board, *Handbook on Ethnic Minority Issues* (London, 1994–5).

[201] See Lewis, B. and Schnapper, D. (eds), *Muslims in Europe* (London, 1994), 156.

7

Hindus: A Dispute about Worship at a Temple

HISTORICAL BACKGROUND

There have been Hindus living in England for at least two hundred years. During the eighteenth century British families who were returning from India developed a practice of bringing their domestic servants with them.[1] The custom seems to have been initiated by the higher officials of the British East India Company, but the trend soon extended far more widely.[2] In addition, Indian sailors known as Lascars, who were employed by the Company on its ships, naturally came ashore at several British ports and some of these remained here permanently.[3] During the course of his survey of the London poor in the 1850s Henry Mayhew encountered Hindu street traders, herbalists, tract-sellers, and beggars.[4] There were also musicians and entertainers.[5]

By this time Hindu students had begun to arrive in England to study law or medicine or obtain qualifications in other professions, and several of these subsequently settled here.[6] A notable example was Ganendra Tagore who was educated in this country and subsequently held the post of Professor of Hindu law and Bengali language at University College, London during the 1860s.[7] Nationalist politicians came to London to plead the cause of political independence for India and princes and maharajahs paid regular and often lengthy visits, both to attend formal occasions and for personal pleasure.[8] In Visram's words—

The princes mingled with the upper classes in Britain, played polo and cricket with them, and went to shooting parties. They attended state balls and dances, went to the races, and gave extravagant presents and parties. Their wealth and splendour dazzled and many of them became indispensable in Edwardian England . . . .[9]

One Hindu prince who made a special impact on the British public was the cricketer Ranjitsinji, who was later to become Maharajah the Jam

---

[1] See Fryer, P., *Staying Power: The History of Black People in Britain* (London, 1984), 69, 77–9; Visram, R., *Ayahs, Lascars and Princes: The Story of Indians in Britain 1700–1947* (London, 1986), ch 2.   [2] Visram, 12.
[3] Ibid, ch 3.
[4] See *London Labour and the London Poor* (London, 1861), I, 241–2, IV, 423–4.
[5] Visram, 59, 61.   [6] Ibid, 9–10, 63–70.   [7] Ibid, 63.
[8] Ibid, chs 5–8; Vadgama, K., *India in Britain* (London, 1984).   [9] At 172–3.

Saheb of Nawanagar.[10] Popularly known as 'Ranji', he obtained a Cambridge blue in 1893, played for Sussex between 1895 and 1920, part of the time as captain, and scored a total of nearly 25,000 runs in first-class cricket, including almost 1,000 runs for England in test matches against Australia. However, it was the grace and originality of his batting which entranced spectators as much as his prolific run-making and which led to ecstatic reviews in *Wisden*. In 1896 one news-paper described him as 'the most popular man in England'.[11] Later Gilbert Jessop wrote of him that he was 'indisputably the greatest genius who ever stepped on to a cricket field, the most brilliant figure during cricket's most brilliant period'.[12]

During the early years of the twentieth century virtually the only public manifestations of Hinduism in this country were the activities either of modern Indian religious movements, which had reinterpreted Hinduism in the light of western values, or else of Western Orientalist movements, such as the Theosophical Society, seeking a link with Indian spiritualism.[13] The Bengali monk Swami Avyaktananda, for example, established a centre for his Ramakrishna mission in London in 1935 and later he went to Bath where he founded the Vedanta Society.[14]

By the end of the Second World War there were estimated to be no more than a few thousand Hindus settled here, many of them doctors who had obtained their medical qualifications in Britain and stayed on to practise in the profession.[15] It was only during the 1950s and 1960s that immigration from India increased dramatically and this was supplemen-ted during the 1970s by those arriving from East Africa. By 1977 there were estimated to be around 307,000 Hindus living in the United King-dom, 70 per cent of whom were Gujerati and 15 per cent Punjabi.[16] The numbers of Gujeratis had increased very substantially through the influx from East Africa. Whereas their exodus had resulted from the process of 'Africanization' in civil service posts and other jobs in Kenya and Tan-zania after these countries obtained their independence (and was further accelerated by their expulsion from Uganda by Idi Amin in 1972), those who had earlier come directly from India had been reacting to pressure on the land and unemployment in Gujerat.[17] A recent estimate of the number of Hindus living in this country puts the figure at between 400,000 and 550,000.[18]

---

[10] See generally Ross, A., *Ranji: Prince of Cricketers* (London, 1983).   [11] Ibid, 77.
[12] Ibid, 240.   [13] Burghart, R. (ed), *Hinduism in Great Britain* (London, 1987), 6.
[14] Ibid.   [15] Hiro, D., *Black British, White British* (London, 1991), 11.
[16] Knott, K., *Hinduism in Leeds*, (Leeds, 1986), 9.
[17] Rose, E., *Colour and Citizenship* (London, 1969), 57.
[18] Weller, P. (ed), *Religions in the UK: A Multi-Faith Directory*, 2nd ed. (Derby, 1997), 30.

THE ATTITUDES OF THE MAJORITY COMMUNITY

It has never been easy for members of the majority community to obtain a clear idea of exactly what Hinduism entails, for to a Western mind it seems to lack many of the characteristic features which might be expected of a religion, such as a founder, a creed, a set of doctrines, and an institutional organization such as a priesthood.[19] It is not a system of theology, it does not lay down a single moral code, and the concept of God is by no means central to it. Rather it is a complex, amorphous, and evolving tradition which has developed over four or five thousand years into a major world civilization with its roots firmly in the Indian sub-continent and which is represented today by the highly diverse beliefs and practices of all those who describe themselves as Hindus.[20] Although a variety of deities are revered, it is often claimed that Hinduism is a monotheistic rather than a polytheistic faith—to the confusion of out-siders (and perhaps adherents as well). This claim is usually justified on the basis either that for each individual there is only one supreme God, all the others being subordinates[21] or by viewing the many different deities as merely the 'shapes' or 'manifestations' of God.[22]

One of the most striking elements of Hindu belief and practice—and certainly the most widely criticized—is the classification of individuals and families by caste. Social divisions are determined by birth and a person's caste affects such crucial matters as marriage partners, forms of employment, and those with whom meals may be taken. Caste taboos in the field of work are hard to maintain in an urbanized environment and hence are to a large extent being broken down, both in Indian cities and in Britain.[23] However, even where such boundaries persist in this coun-try, for example in relation to arranged marriages, attendance at social functions,[24] the formation of community associations,[25] and in the estab-lishment of separate places of worship,[26] they are largely invisible to members of the white community.[27] When confined to personal relation-ships they also provoke only limited concern in a majority society which is itself still largely influenced by class difference.[28] Other aspects of

---

[19] See generally, Chaudhuri, N., *Hinduism* (London, 1979).

[20] See e.g. Hinnells, J. (ed), *A Handbook of Living Religions* (Harmondsworth, 1985), 191–2.

[21] Ibid, 212.

[22] See e.g. Chaudhuri, 88–9 (who refers to 'polymorphous monotheism'; Bowen, D. (ed), *Hinduism in England* (Bradford, 1981), 37–8.   [23] Hiro, 131–2; Bowen, ch 5.

[24] See e.g. Henley, A., *Caring for Hindus and their Families: religious aspects of care* (Cambridge, 1983), 54–7.   [25] See Burghart, 21–6.

[26] There are several examples of temples for 'untouchables' in Britain: see e.g. Knott, 51; Bowen, 63.

[27] See 'The untouchables of London's suburbs', *Independent*, 10 Jan 1991.

[28] See e.g. Reid, I., *Social Class Differences in Britain*, 3rd ed. (London, 1989).

Hindu culture which members of the majority community find wholly repulsive and unacceptable are the traditional custom of cremating widows on their husbands' funeral pyres (*sati*) and the modern phenomenon of murdering wives because their families have provided their husbands' families with insufficient dowry upon marriage. As we have seen, although *sati* was outlawed in India in 1829 the practice has been resurrected (albeit on a very small scale) in recent years and the ban had to be reinforced in 1987.[29] Similarly, although the payment of dowries upon marriage has been a criminal offence in India since 1961,[30] there are reported to be thousands of dowry murders there every year[31] and while there is no hard evidence of any such murders having occurred in England, reports of wives dying in suspicious circumstances have recently begun to circulate.[32]

Undoubtedly the single individual Hindu who has made the most profound impact upon the consciousness of the British population as a whole was Mahatma Gandhi. He first came to this country to read for the Bar between 1887 and 1891[33] and he made a few other brief visits over the years, notably during 1931 to attend one of the three 'Round Table Conferences', which laid down a framework for India's progression to greater autonomy. In 1931 he received a very warm welcome here, especially from those living in the East End of London, where he chose to stay for the duration of the Conference. Some months earlier, however, Winston Churchill had uttered the following notorious remark—

It is alarming and also nauseating to see Mr. Gandhi, a seditious Middle Temple lawyer, now posing as a fakir of a type well known in the East, striding half-naked up the steps of the vice-regal palace, while he is organising and conducting a defiant campaign of civil disobedience, to parley on equal terms with the representative of the King-Emperor.[34]

Gandhi's sustained policies of civil disobedience and passive resistance did indeed put the British Government under very considerable pressure to grant India her independence[35] and this was eventually achieved in 1947, a year before he was assassinated. Gandhi also waged a long

[29] By the Sati (Prevention) Act 1987 discussed above, ch 2.
[30] Dowry Prohibition Act 1961.
[31] See generally, Kumari, R., *Brides are Not for Burning: Dowry Victims in India* (London, 1989).
[32] See e.g. 'Young brides beaten for dowry cash', *Observer*, 13 Dec 1987; 'Suicide or dowry murder?' *Independent on Sunday*, 11 Feb 1990.
[33] See Gandhi, M., *An Autobiography: The Story of My Experiments with Truth* (Boston, 1957), 42–80.
[34] Quoted in Ashe, G., *Gandhi: A Study in Revolution* (London, 1968), 296.
[35] See generally, Brown, J., *Gandhi: Prisoner of Hope* (London, 1989). See also Parekh, B., *Gandhi's Political Philosophy* (Basingstoke, 1989).

campaign to raise the status of the outcasts or untouchables, whom he referred to as *harijans* (children of God). The elimination of untouchability formed part of the programme of the Indian National Congress for many years prior to independence and, as was to be expected, the Indian Constitution provided for its abolition and made the enforcement of any discrimination attaching to it a criminal offence.[36]

THE ROLE OF THE TEMPLE IN HINDU WORSHIP

In the early years of South Asian settlement in Britain it appeared as if the Hindus, unlike the Muslims and the Sikhs, were wholly uninterested in establishing places of public worship in this country and were generally content to leave many of the duties and practices of the faith to their relatives in India.[37] While the impression of being 'exceptionally unobtrusive'[38] in this way may have been partly justified, it is important to bear in mind the essential nature of Hindu worship. In India most such worship occurs within the domestic setting of the family home, reflecting very diverse beliefs and practices.[39] Most homes contain a small shrine where devotional prayers are said and where flowers and little offerings of food may be placed. Visits to the temple (*mandir*) are peripheral rather than central to the practice of Hinduism and indeed in early Hindu scriptures and epic works there is no mention of temples.[40] There is no religious requirement for Hindus to go to the temple, though many do so in order to make offerings to or petition a particular deity there. Hence it is not surprising that domestic worship should have predominated among Hindus upon their arrival in England and this pattern continues to be maintained at the present time.[41]

However, during the 1960s Hindu cultural societies began to be established in Britain and in 1969 the first *mandir* was opened in Leicester.[42] Ten years later there were at least ninety-four such temples, spread around the country, and this figure represented only the larger ones and not those situated in private homes but which were nevertheless open to the public.[43] This period of expansion coincided with the arrival here of wives and children from India and of whole families from East Africa. In part it can be seen as a period of consolidation and of a growth in people's confidence that the Hindu faith (and the ethnicity of the

---

[36] See Constitution of India 1950, Art 17; see also Untouchability (Offences) Act 1955.
[37] Desai, R., *Indian Immigrants in Britain* (London, 1963), 93; Knott, 9; Burghart, 18.
[38] Hiro, 131.   [39] Chaudhuri, chs 2, 3.   [40] Ibid, 90.
[41] See e.g. Burghart, ch 2; Law, J., *The Religious Beliefs and Practices of Hindus in Derby* (Leeds, 1991), 35.   [42] Knott, 10.
[43] Ibid.

Gujeratis and Punjabis which supported it) would survive and prosper in Britain, as it had in East Africa.[44]

It has been suggested that there may well be greater temple attendance and activity by Hindus in this country today than is found in modern India.[45] If this is so, and it seems to have been the case in East Africa, one obvious explanation for this seems to lie in the invaluable opportunities furnished by temple attendance for Hindus to meet, share news, and reinforce social relationships, which would otherwise be curtailed by the patterns of urban life in this country and the organization of the British working week. However, perhaps an even more important justification is to be found in the need for members of a minority community to come together to confirm and re-assert their identity and values in the context of a climate in which different ideologies and traditions and a somewhat alien moral code prevail. This poses a particular problem for young Hindus who are exposed to these powerful competing influences at school. Knott has reached the following conclusion about the position of Hindus in Leeds, one which is almost certainly of wider application throughout the country—

Temple practice . . . has become of crucial importance in the retention of tradition and its transmission from one generation to the next. Attendance at the temple provides an opportunity for the strengthening of social relationships and cultural ties between members of like kin, caste and language groups. The ritual itself acts as a coded message which reminds participants of and reinforces them in their religious precepts, practices and beliefs. Without temple practice it is unlikely that Hinduism, in any traditional sense, could continue to exist in Leeds.[46]

Jackson has commented in similar vein about temple practice among Gujeratis in Coventry—

. . . religion in the sense of worship, fasts and festivals is a standard feature of domestic and cultural activity and its practice has a vital role to play in maintaining the community's identity. This has become increasingly true of temple worship in the 'migrant' situation. Temple worship has for centuries had an important place in Indian devotional life, alongside worship in the home, at village shrines and through pilgrimages to sacred sites. But there is no doubt that temple worship took on a new significance among Gujerati migrants in East Africa and this significance has been transferred to the British situation. The temple is no longer just a centre for devotion, but is an oasis of Indian culture in an alien environment, and a focus for social and recreational life, especially for many of the women who would otherwise be virtually housebound.[47]

---

[44] For comparable developments in the Sikh community at this time, see below, ch 8.
[45] Knott, 80, 115, 157.   [46] Ibid, 115.   [47] In Bowen (ed), 65–6.

Not only is the temple the principal vehicle chosen by Hindus to serve these purposes, it also functions as the institution most clearly identified by members of the wider society and, most significantly, its bureaucratic agencies, as accurately representing the interests of Hindus.[48] This has led temple officials to adopt policies of centralization and standardization, involving the selection of key festivals, their celebration at British weekends (even though they actually fall on a weekday), concentration on the recognition of a single God (despite the many deities of popular worship), and the identification of central texts (such as the *Vedas* and the *Bhagavad Gita*) as comparable to the holy books of other major religions.[49] Knott has described the pattern of temple worship as 'a form of retraditionalisation in which common religious beliefs and practices rather than ethnic elements are employed in the practice of group presentation'.[50]

During the late 1960s and early 1970s, at the time when Hindus from India and East Africa were consolidating their position here and expanding their cultural activities and establishing a growing number of temples, another development was occurring of major significance for the controversy highlighted later in this chapter. A variety of 'Hindu-related groups' were either being formed or were experiencing new growth, both here and in the United States, as part of a so-called 'counter culture' or 'alternative society'.[51] They attracted young, white people from educated middle class backgrounds, offering them paths of enlightenment, the possibility of self-transcendence, and techniques for personal improvement and development. These included Maharishi Mahesh Yogi's Transcendental Meditation, the Divine Light Mission, *Raja Yoga*, and the International Society for Krishna Consciousness (ISKCON), more familiarly known as the Hare Krishna movement.[52] Since the legal dispute which provides the focus of this chapter relates to a temple owned by ISKCON it is appropriate to turn next to an examination of the Society's formation and its relationship with mainstream Hinduism in England.

THE INTERNATIONAL SOCIETY FOR KRISHNA CONSCIOUSNESS[53]

ISKCON was founded in 1966 by A. C. Bhaktivedanta Swami, also known as Srila Prabhupada, a penniless monk and Sanskrit scholar. Some forty years earlier he had joined the movement associated with the name of

---

[48] Knott, 157.   [49] Ibid, 83, 231.   [50] Ibid, 237.
[51] Ibid, 10.   [52] Ibid, ch 6.
[53] See generally, Knott, K., *My Sweet Lord: The Hare Krishna Movement* (Wellingborough, 1986); Carey, S., 'The Indianization of the Hare Krishna Movement in Britain' in Burghart, R. (ed.), *Hinduism in Great Britain* (London, 1987), ch 5.

the sixteenth century Hindu saint Sri Chaitanya Mahaprabhu and had come under the influence of a guru who had established a *math* (theological college) in Calcutta in 1918. The movement is commonly referred to as Vaishnavite,[54] being committed to devotion to the deity Vishnu, and before his guru's death the Swami had been instructed to spread knowledge of Krishna to the West. In the *Bhagavad Gita* Krishna is identified with God and represents the incarnation of Vishnu, possessing the attributes of omnipotence, omniscience, and omnipresence. Devotion to him is expressed not so much in rituals as in *bhakti*, loving devotion through meditation and concentration.[55] According to some texts this devotion may be passionate and emotional to purify the heart[56] and one means of achieving this is by repetitive chanting of the holy names of God, as in the Hare Krishna '*mantra*'.

It was against this background that the Swami left for the United States in 1965 at the age of seventy and established ISKCON there a year later. The main purposes of ISKCON were set out in its charter as follows—

To systematically propagate spiritual knowledge to society at large, to educate all peoples in the techniques of spiritual life in order to check the imbalance of values in life, and to achieve real unity and peace in the world and to propagate a Consciousness of Krishna, as it is revealed in the *Bhagavad Gita*.[57]

The Swami was a vigorous proselytizer and initially he attracted many adherents among the 'hippies' and 'flower children' of that period. However, the Swami's objective was not only to save the materialistic West. He also felt that, if he could manage to acquire some Western converts, Indians would retreat from their headlong rush towards 'modernity' and return to the path of spiritual righteousness. He was, after all, operating within a long established Hindu tradition, reproducing an authentic version of a devotional movement in the hope of influencing a world dominated by Western thinking. The sight, so familiar to London shoppers since the early 1970s, of members of the Hare Krishna movement in their orange *dhotis* marching up and down Oxford Street, chanting their transcendental *mantras* to the sound of tambourines and small drums, actually had its origins in sixteenth century Bengal, for a very important part of the devotions of the followers of Chaitanya was singing and dancing to the accompaniment of an earthen drum in assemblies or processions.[58] Members of the sect wore bead-necklaces and saffron clothes and had distinctive marks on their foreheads.[59]

The first ISKCON temple in Britain was established in London during 1969 and although the initial founding group came from San Francisco

---

[54] On Chaitanya and his Vaishnavism, see Chaudhuri, 182–4, 282–90.
[55] Bowen, 70.   [56] Ibid.   [57] See Knott, *My Sweet Lord*, 31.
[58] Chaudhari, 182; Knott, *My Sweet Lord*, 14, 16, 26–7.   [59] Chaudhari, 183–4.

they were quick to reach out to the Hindu community in England. They distributed *prasad* (consecrated food) three times a week at the temple, canvassed Hindu commuters and businessmen, and were invited to dinner by the Indian High Commissioner. The Swami himself came to London to conduct the formal installation within the temple of the deities of Krishna and his consort Radhu, which had been imported from India. This early provision of good temple facilities, including a high standard of ritual worship in clean and pleasant surroundings, coupled with the opportunity for congregational worship, came at an extremely opportune time. Many Hindus arriving from East Africa were temple-goers from a Vaishnavite background and were surprised at the general absence of temples in England. They were by no means doctrinaire and were happy to make use of whatever facilities were available here. The Hare Krishna movement had acquired a high public profile, particularly through the chanting and processions of its members in Oxford Street, and this helped to increase the general awareness among Hindus of what the movement could offer, both in terms of temple worship and in the provision of religious education.

By 1987 ISKCON had acquired over 4,000 'life members', each of whom had paid a subscription fee of between £200 and £400, and the vast majority of these were Hindus from East Africa rather than Westerners. As will be seen, ISKCON has the capacity to attract very large numbers of worshippers, for example at the celebration of major festivals, but only a small number of Hindus in England confine their public worship to or undertake all their major life-cycle rituals at ISKCON shrines today. Even so, ISKCON is clearly capable of ministering very constructively to the needs of many members of the Hindu community at large and seems to be able to provide young Hindus with a knowledge of their religion and philosophy through drama productions and other forms of instruction and entertainment which capture their interest. This is achieved not only on temple visits but also in youth clubs and at cultural societies spread around the country.[60] This fact needs to be set alongside surveys which tend to indicate that many Hindu children know little about Hinduism because their parents have not taken active steps to bring them up in the faith.[61] As Knott has explained—

All Britain's Indian Hindus recognise the religion and culture of the Hare Krishna devotees. They see it as similar to their own (and thus a legitimate

---

[60] See e.g. Bowen (at 48–9) describing a visit by a theatrical group to the Hindu Cultural Society in Bradford.
[61] See e.g. Taylor, J., *The Half-Way Generation* (Slough, 1976), 78–80. For a more positive account of the transmission of Hinduism based on a survey in Coventry, see Jackson, R. and Nesbitt, E., *Hindu Children in Britain* (Stoke-on-Trent, 1993).

expression of *sanatana dharma*[62]) except in so far as it is generally practised with greater commitment, greater austerity and greater philosophical awareness. The vast majority of Indian Hindus have a profound respect for the devotees; there is no feeling amongst them that this is not 'real' Hinduism . . . . To many, the Hare Krishna devotees, unlike the members of other new Eastern-based religious groups, are the true exemplars of Hinduism in its new geographical location.[63]

THE CONTROVERSY CONCERNING BHAKTIVEDANTA MANOR TEMPLE

It is by no means unusual in Britain for religious minorities to become embroiled in disputes with planning authorities and local residents over the siting of religious buildings or the activities taking place there. Muslims have often experienced difficulties in obtaining the necessary planning permission to construct mosques or convert existing buildings into places of public worship.[64] Hindus have faced similar problems[65] and in many instances it is not uncommon for several years to elapse before a suitable site is located, planning permission granted, and local tensions defused.[66] Planning permission is required both for the construction of a new building for public worship and for the conversion of an old one, where this involves a 'material change of use'.[67] Failure to obtain the necessary permission or non-compliance with conditions imposed by the planning authority can lead to the issue of an enforcement notice ordering the cessation of unauthorized activities and ultimately to the imposition of criminal penalties if the requirements in the notice are not adhered to.[68]

No dispute over a religious building belonging to a minority faith has, at least in recent years, achieved the notoriety which has surrounded the controversy concerning ISKCON's temple at Bhaktivedanta Manor in the little village of Letchmore Heath in Hertfordshire. The village lies about four miles to the south east of Watford and is situated within both the Metropolitan Green Belt and a conservation area designated on the

---

[62] '*Sanatana dharma*' is generally understood to refer to eternal Hindu tradition, i.e. the established, correct, and authentic version of their religion—see Knott, *My Sweet Lord*, 57; Chaudhari, 28. [63] At 57.

[64] See e.g. Hodgins, H., 'Planning permission for mosques—the Birmingham experience', Research Paper No. 9, Muslims in Europe (Centre for the Study of Islam and Christian-Muslim Relations, Birmingham, 1981), 11–27.

[65] *Cherwell District Council v Vadivale* (1991) 6 Planning Appeal Decisions 433.

[66] See e.g. Bowen, 66–7, in relation to problems in Coventry between 1969 and 1978.

[67] Town and Country Planning Act 1990, s 55(1), replacing Town and Country Planning Act 1971, s 22(1); Town and Country Planning (Use Classes) Order 1987, class D1(h), replacing Town and Country Planning (Use Classes) Order 1972, class XIII.

[68] Town and Country Planning Act 1990, ss 172, 179 as amended by Planning and Compensation Act 1991, ss 5, 8, replacing Town and Country Planning Act 1971, ss 87, 89.

Hertsmere District Plan. It has a population of only about 300 inhabitants and is surrounded by undulating countryside, mainly comprising small fields with well defined hedgerows, and small woodlands. In the words of the Inspector who held a public inquiry into the dispute in 1988—

. . . the village with its houses grouped around the green, attractive old pub, duck pond and war memorial, all shaded by horse chestnut trees, has a small scale but very satisfying picturesque quality, and such unspoiled surroundings are a rarity so close to London.[69]

Legal proceedings began in earnest with the issue of an enforcement notice by the local planning authority, Hertsmere Borough Council, in January 1987. The purpose of the notice was to circumscribe future public worship at the temple. This caused an outcry on the part of a large number of Hindus, especially those living nearby in north London who feared that their freedom of worship was likely to be severely curtailed if the notice was implemented. A campaign was quickly launched against the enforcement notice, involving the formation of a committee to lobby MPs and others in defence of the temple. A delegation was despatched to India in the hope that the Indian Government could be induced to apply diplomatic pressure upon the United Kingdom. At the public inquiry in 1988 petitions to the British Prime Minister containing over 45,000 signatures were submitted in evidence, as well as numerous petitions and letters to the Queen, the Secretary of State for the Environment, and others, with signatories from many countries around the world. In 1990 the campaign committee was dissolved and re-formed as a defence movement pledged to non-violent disobedience on the Gandhi model, in pursuit of its objective of keeping the temple open for public worship.[70]

(a) Background to the dispute[71]

Bhaktivedanta Manor is a large Victorian country house standing in seventeen acres of wooded formal gardens and pastureland. It became a grade II listed building in 1985. Formerly known as Piggott's Manor it was purchased for ISKCON by George Harrison, of 'Beatles' fame, in 1973 and renamed after the founder of ISKCON. The freehold of the Manor was finally transferred to ISKCON in 1981. The principal feature of the ground

---

[69] Para 8.16 of the Inspector's Report (see note 71 below).
[70] See *New Life*, 15 June 1990.
[71] The material which follows is derived from the Inspector's Report and the decision of the Secretary of State for the Environment, dated 20 Mar 1990, under the references APP/C/87/N1920/1; APP/N1920/A/88/100747–8; E1/N1920/1/3/01.

floor of the main house is a temple room capable of accommodating 300–400 people and containing a gilden shrine together with marble figures representing the deities of Krishna, Radha, Sita, Rama, Laxman, and Hanuman. Other accommodation comprises a reception hall, a dining room seating about thirty five people, several classrooms, and a theatre with sixty seats. The upper floors comprise administrative offices, classrooms, a special suite of rooms used by Srila Prabhupada during visits to England in the period 1973–78 and kept as a memorial to him, and bedrooms for the twenty resident male devotees. In the Manor grounds are a former stable block, containing further bedrooms and classrooms as well as a kitchen, and a cottage occupied by the eight female resident devotees. The car parking facilities were substantially improved in 1979 and there are now spaces for about 120 cars.

The Manor is the only *math* or training college for Hindu priests in the United Kingdom and it welcomes as students those who wish to commit the whole or a part of their lives to an understanding of the faith and devotion to Krishna. The Manor is also generally regarded as the most sacred and important Hindu temple in Britain. Followers of the Vaishnavite branch of Hinduism in north London view the Manor as their principal place of worship and a recent survey of Hindu households in Harrow, for example, revealed that in 88 per cent of them at least one member had visited the Manor. It is also a place of pilgrimage for those living further afield. Its special attractions are the high standard of *puja* (acts of devotion) maintained there, the richness and beauty of the shrine and its deities, the tranquil wooded surroundings with their capacity to enhance meditation, and the special association of the Manor with ISKCON's founder.

There is a daily routine of devotional services at the Manor, each day starting early with the first ceremony being performed at 4.30 am, a sacred hour which cannot be altered. Other major activities carried on at the Manor include the training of Hindu priests and missionaries, the administration of ISKCON as a worldwide charity with some 5,500 life members, the running of a primary school, the organization of a programme of lectures, films, plays, and dancing (all with a religious significance), the cultivation of flowers and vegetables in connection with religious devotions, and the keeping of five cows in pursuance of the practice of cow protection. Also of particular significance is the provision of facilities for the celebration of Hindu festivals, especially those of Ramnavani (marking the birth of Rama, in April), Janmashtami (marking the birth of Krishna, in August–September), and Diwali (the festival of light, in October–November). Each of these three major festivals attracts a large number of visitors and there are other minor ones celebrated in addition. The festivals normally take place at weekends and involve a programme of services, lectures, plays, and films, as well as music and dance and congregational chanting. Apart from festival days, the most popular time for visits to the Manor is on a Sunday evening, with a peak period between 6 and 8 pm.

In 1987 a list compiled by the temple president revealed that there were fifty people who were actually resident at the Manor and another 200 who were regular visitors, including teachers, administrators, students, and schoolchildren. Some indication of the volume of traffic generated by the temple around a decade ago is available from a 24–hour survey conducted by the Hertsmere Borough Council on a non-festival Sunday at the end of 1988. This revealed that 288 cars and one coach came to the Manor, carrying a total of 723 people. ISKCON estimated that 312 of these were either residents or regular visitors, with the remaining 411 representing devotees who attended only intermittently (394) and a small number of non-devotees (seventeen).

The first Hindu festival celebrated at the Manor was held in the summer of 1973 to mark the opening of the temple. It lasted for five days, attracting between 500 and 1,000 visitors each day. Various festivals during 1974–79 attracted daily attendances estimated at between 2,500 and 6,000. The Janmashtami festival in 1980 was attended by an estimated 14,000–15,000 people and prompted several villagers to voice complaints about noise, disturbance, and traffic congestion after cars and coaches had blocked the village for several hours. This led Hertsmere Borough Council to establish a special planning sub-committee with respect to the Manor and in 1981 the first enforcement notice was served. This required ISKCON to discontinue use of the Manor for public worship and public entertainment involving visits by more than 1,000 persons in any one day, save with prior written approval from the planning authority. An appeal was immediately lodged against the notice and eventually it was withdrawn in consideration of ISKCON entering into an agreement with the authority under the provisions of section 52 of the Town and Country Planning Act 1971. This agreement, signed in 1983, after reciting that it was made without prejudice to the Council's right to serve a further enforcement notice if it was expedient to do so, provided that ISKCON should not arrange or permit to be arranged at the Manor any event involving visits to the Manor or any part thereof of more than 1,000 persons on any one day, without the consent of Hertsmere Borough Council. The agreement also contained a clause whereby the Council specifically granted its consent to attendances of more than 1,000 persons on up to six festival days each calendar year, provided it was notified of the dates prior to the end of the previous year and provided ISKCON co-operated in complying with all reasonable Council requirements for the arrangements relating to such festival events. Ever since that agreement was concluded ISKCON has duly notified the Council of festival days and co-operated with environmental health officers and the police in respect of the arrangements.

Counts carried out by the Council between 1985 and 1988 revealed that there had regularly been more than 1,000 visitors to the Manor on non-festival Sundays, the average attendance being in the region of 1,500. By 1986 the Council felt it appropriate to issue a High Court writ for an injunction to enforce the 1983 agreement on the basis that an event on Wednesday 13 November 1985, a non-festival day, had been attended by over 3,000 visitors without the Council's consent. Leggatt J, however, refused to grant an injunction, interpreting the agreement as only barring events in relation to which ISKCON actually expected the arrival of more than 1,000 visitors—which he did not consider to be the case in respect of this instance.[72] He also declared that, even if ISKCON had foreseen such numbers, he would not have granted an injunction against the Society because he did not believe the Council could sensibly restrict the number of persons attending and being admitted on a single day. Subsequently, the Council sought to persuade ISKCON to accept a form of wording which would modify and clarify the terms of the 1983 agreement, but when that approach failed to bear fruit the Council issued a further enforcement notice in 1987.

(b) Proceedings in respect of the 1987 enforcement notice

The breach of planning control alleged in the notice was that ISKCON had unlawfully made a 'material change of use' of the Manor. The Council therefore required ISKCON to discontinue, within a period of six months, use of the land for the purposes of a religious community, together with public worship and public entertainment in connection with religious festivals. ISKCON appealed against the notice on a number of grounds, all of which were rejected by the Inspector at a public inquiry which was completed in December 1988. On a further appeal to the Secretary of State for the Environment the Council's enforcement notice was upheld in March 1990, subject to two small variations in its requirements, to be described later. An appeal to the High Court was dismissed by Kennedy J in 1991[73] and leave to appeal to the Court of Appeal was refused in 1992.[74] The main issues raised were as follows.

First, ISKCON argued that the notice was invalid for a lack of clarity in its references to 'public worship', 'public entertainment', and 'religious

---

[72] *Hertsmere BC v ISKCON Ltd* (18 Apr 1986, unreported).

[73] *ISKCON v Secretary of State for the Environment and Hertsmere Borough Council* (1992) 64 P & CR 85.   [74] Decision of the Court of Appeal (16 Mar 1992, unreported).

community'. However, the Inspector found that these phrases were apt to describe in simple and clearly understood terms those activities at the Manor which the Council sought to discontinue. These included all the festivals, even though they were not specifically mentioned. The Minister subsequently accepted that the notice was 'potentially ambiguous',[75] but he agreed with the Inspector that the allegation should be construed as a whole and that the notice was not invalid. In the High Court ISKCON contended that the notice was a nullity because it neither clearly indicated what the Society had done wrong nor what steps it needed to take to remedy the situation and had thus failed to satisfy the test to this effect laid down by the Court of Appeal in *Miller-Mead v Minister of Housing and Local Government*.[76] However, Kennedy J ruled that those to whom the enforcement notice had been addressed knew precisely what was alleged and what steps they were being required to take and therefore the notice was not a nullity.

Secondly, ISKCON denied that any material change of use had in fact occurred. Prior to its acquisition for ISKCON in 1973, the Manor had been owned by the Governors of St Bartholomew's Hospital. The Hospital had used it between 1948 and 1971 as a residential college for the preliminary training of nurses. In 1973 the solicitors acting for George Harrison had applied to the planning authority for a determination, under section 53 of the Town and Country Planning Act 1971, as to whether the proposal to use the property as 'a residential educational college, being a theological college in connection with the promotion of the religion of Krishna Consciousness' would involve 'development' and, if so, whether an application for planning permission was required. The solicitors had intimated that in their view planning permission was not required since the proposed use fell within the same use class as the previous occupancy, namely 'use as a residential or boarding school, or a residential college' within Class XII of the Schedule to the Use Classes Order. The Clerk to the former Watford Rural District Council had replied to the solicitors that he had consulted Hertfordshire County Council's Divisional Planning Officer who had stated as follows—

It appears that on the information available the last use of the premises, namely a nurses' residential college, falls squarely within the same use class as a residential theological college in connection with the promotion of the religion of Krishna Consciousness. In these circumstances planning permission is not required. Although the previous use was largely residential, I gather that it was also partly educational and this appears to be the situation with the use now proposed.

[75] Para 6 of his decision.   [76] [1963] 2 QB 196.

The District Council had accepted that opinion and had determined the application under section 53 by confirming that planning permission would not be needed.

At the end of the public inquiry the Inspector concluded that the types of activities carried on at the Manor by ISKCON in recent years fell partly within Class XII (use as a residential school or college) and partly within Class XIII, which covers 'use as a building for public worship and religious instruction or for the social or recreational activities of the religious body using the building'. Since a use which has elements of two different classes, and hence is categorized in law as being *sui generis*,[77] does constitute development under the planning legislation, it did indeed require permission. As to whether there had in fact been a material change of use, the Inspector was in no doubt. While a school or college could be expected to have incidental activities such as plays, sports matches, founders' days and other events generating a large number of visitors, without there being any question of a material change of use, this was because these events would all be merely ancillary to the primary use as a residential educational establishment. However, such reliance on the concept of 'ancillary use' was quite inappropriate to describe what was happening at the Manor. In reality, the primary use of the Manor was fundamentally different in many ways from a residential theological college. There was a group of over forty residents living there communally, some of them responsible for the running of primary and Sunday schools, others for the administration of a charity controlling a worldwide religious movement, and there were services of public worship open to all as well as a wide programme of events at festivals designed to attract as many people as possible. In the words of the Inspector's Report—

The sheer numbers of people and vehicles attracted to the Manor, not only on festival days but on ordinary Sundays, take the uses for public worship and public entertainment in connection with religious festivals beyond anything that can be regarded as ancillary to a college.[78]

This ground of appeal was therefore rejected by the Inspector and his conclusion was endorsed by the Minister. The High Court similarly took the view that ISKCON's use of the Manor had gone well beyond anything that was genuinely ancillary to a Class XII use.

Thirdly, ISKCON argued that if a material change of use had actually occurred planning permission should be granted for this 'development'. In reality this aspect of the appeal amounted to a belated or deemed

---

[77] The 1972 Use Classes Order was replaced by the Town and Country Planning (Use Classes) Order 1987, but the Manor's use remained *sui generis*, with elements of both class C2 and D1(c) and (h) uses.   [78] Para 36.6.

application for the necessary permission and it went to the very heart of the dispute. In this connection the Inspector identified seven primary issues which he regarded as equally relevant in setting out the conflicting priorities, as follows—

(i) Did the present use of the Manor conflict with national and local policies for protecting the Metropolitan Green Belt? While one of the purposes of the Green Belt is to allow access to the countryside for recreational purposes by town dwellers, the Hertfordshire County Structure Plan 1986 stated that only small scale facilities for recreation were permissible, whereas at the Manor visitors were being attracted on a large scale (and on a very large scale at festivals), and their attendance regularly lasted until the late evening. The Inspector therefore concluded that the Manor's existing use was in conflict with the Plan's policies in this regard.

(ii) Did this existing use make life significantly less pleasant for residents of the village? On this issue the Inspector had some harsh words to say about ISKCON's use of the Manor. Admittedly, some of the complaints made by villagers to District Councillors were relatively trivial and unrelated to planning matters or else were simply the product of a suspicious attitude towards an unconventional way of life or arose out of a resentment of strangers. However, the Inspector was in no doubt that 'the sheer numbers of people which the Manor attracts, not only at festival times, but also every Sunday, and the vehicular and pedestrian activity in the evenings and the small hours, is not something which those living in a quiet country village should have to expect'.[79] He went on—

... to have such large numbers of strangers coming into a quiet village at weekends leaves the resident population feeling uncomfortable, and at risk of becoming a minority in the village. Not only do the appellants insist on a freedom to come and go, sometimes in comparatively large numbers at all hours of the day and night, but the long history appears to show a consistent disregard for the sensibilities of neighbours, and indeed on occasions of proper standards of hygiene. The history of complaints about such things as dumping of rubbish, overflowing drains and toilets, careless driving and parking, and floodlights left on close to bedroom windows, all add up to a lack of respect for the neighbourhood and a carelessness towards the standards of reasonable good housekeeping which an institution occupying a large country house in a village ought to show.[80]

In the Inspector's opinion, the large number of individual complaints by villagers could not be dismissed as mere prejudice and they signified a

[79] Para 37.4.   [80] Para 37.5.

considerable adverse impact on the quality of life arising out of activities at the Manor.

(iii) Did the use of the Manor accord with Structure Plan policies relating to leisure development and to development within Green Belt settlements? As to leisure development, the Inspector felt that even if ISKCON'S religious activities fell within the concept of leisure development, the Structure Plan only permitted such development to meet local needs, whereas the Manor was catering for Hindus throughout London and the Home Counties and to some extent throughout the country. Moreover, the amount of traffic generated and the disturbance caused meant that such leisure development ran counter to the policies of the Hertsmere District Plan. As to development within the settlement of Letchmore Heath itself, under the Plan this was not commonly permitted in small villages because of the requirement to maintain their character, unless there was a clear local need. The Inspector commented—

Letchmore Heath is a Green Belt settlement. Its character is predominantly residential and I would describe it as a quiet backwater, most of whose residents either work in nearby towns or are retired. It is noticeably compact, no doubt as a result of long standing Green Belt policies, and whilst individual buildings may not be of the highest architectural merit, the whole has a pleasing coherent quality and the views around the green are of a quintessential English country village. Regular influxes of car bound visitors attending large scale outdoor festivals and substantial increases of traffic outside normal working hours are wholly alien to that character.[81]

(iv) Was the use of the Manor contrary to the aims of national and local policies for preserving and enhancing the amenities of the Letchmore Heath Conservation Area?[82] The Inspector considered that the weight of these policies leant against ISKCON because of the excessive traffic and disturbance generated by its activities. ISKCON had argued that its institutional use of the Manor preserved the architectural integrity and original features of a listed building which might not be the case if the property were divided up. However, the Inspector felt that not all the buildings and grounds were very well maintained. Some of the exterior needed painting and the general condition of the grounds, at least at the time of his visit, appeared rather neglected with the cottage and former stable-block being in a somewhat ramshackle state. ISKCON'S standards of main-

---

[81] Para 37.8.

[82] The national policy is currently found in statutory form in s 72(1) of the Town and Country Planning Act 1990 which replaced s 277 of the 1971 Act, as amended by s 1(1) of the Town Amenities Act 1974. For interpretation of the statutory provisions, see *South Lakeland District Council v Secretary of State for the Environment* [1992] 1 All ER 573.

tenance were not such as to enhance the Conservation Area or justify any special consideration on that basis.

(v) Did the activities at the Manor result in a significant increase in traffic congestion and hazard potential? The Inspector was in no doubt that this was the case because the village was 'fundamentally unsuitable in traffic management terms for activities which generate very large numbers of visiting vehicles, since there is only one suitable route in and out of the village'.[83] The Manor had only one access, in the very centre of the village, where visiting traffic was likely to create maximum congestion and a degree of conflict with local residents needing to gain access to and park outside their own homes. While there had been no serious accidents, the potential hazard was clearly there.

(vi) Did the importance of the Manor as a shrine and the need to provide places of worship for the Hindu population constitute those 'very special circumstances' which justify development in the Green Belt in any event and outweigh any specific and convincing planning objections so as to justify an exception to the normal rules?[84] The Inspector accepted that the Manor had become a special place of worship and pilgrimage for the Hindu community and that there appeared to be very few Hindu places of worship in north London and nearby counties. No one could ignore the national and international concern shown about the future of the Manor, nor about the social issues posed by the possibility of restricting participation in worship there or attendance at religious festivals. Although the Manor had been allowed to be used for these activities for many years, the Inspector did not interpret this as implying toleration by the authorities of the status quo but rather concluded that the Council had been doing everything possible to avoid the confrontation inevitably provoked by the issue of an enforcement notice. While there might perhaps have been less cause for complaint on the part of villagers in recent years than formerly (and there was evidence that ISKCON had taken steps to encourage devotees to limit the number of their visits to the Manor), this was doubtless the product of the pending enforcement proceedings. There would probably be an upsurge of activity if permission were to be granted for a use which was geared to attracting people in large numbers. Despite the agreement reached in 1983 between ISKCON and the Council that there could be up to 1,000 visitors on non-festival days and six festival days with unlimited numbers of visitors, the Inspector considered that allowing 1,000 visitors per day was not an acceptable norm in planning terms. He declared—

---

[83] Para 37.11.

[84] See DoE Circular 42/55, para 5; Planning policy guidance notes, PPG 2/1988 'Green Belts', para 13.

The intimate small scale closely built character of a home counties village simply cannot accommodate the crowds attracted to a *'tirtha'* (shrine) in the Indian sub-continent, especially when most of the worshippers or pilgrims have to come in their own private transport or in coaches. When religious meetings on this scale are held in the United Kingdom, such as those by Billy Graham and other evangelists, Earls Court or Wembley Stadium are booked . . . . It also seems to me that the fact that the tenets of Krishna Consciousness prescribe that there must be devotions virtually 24 hours a day, with comings and goings very late at night, are particularly intrusive in a small village. The appellants are not pre-pared to even consider curbing their night time activities, and maintain that it would be contrary to their faith to do so. I understand what they say, but this inevitably makes the use very difficult to fit into a residential village where most people travel some distance to work, and come home expecting a measure of peace and quiet, especially at weekends when the use of the Manor is at its most active.[85]

On balance, the Inspector concluded that the interests of the village and its residents should prevail over the needs of ISKCON and Hindu wor-shippers generally, and that there was insufficient justification for setting aside the weight of Green Belt policy as well as other specific and convincing planning objections. He had this comment to make about the issues of religious freedom and discrimination—

In his submissions Counsel for the appellants expressly withdrew any allega-tions of religious or racial prejudice which had been made against the planning authority. In this, as in very many other planning decisions, it is necessary to weigh the needs of one group or interest against others, and the needs of religious or ethnic minorities, however important, cannot necessarily be allowed to override those constraints which have to apply to everyone, in planning as in other matters, in the interests of a tolerant and free society in a small and crowded country.[86]

(vii) Given the long history, the presumption in favour of development and the previous decisions by the planning authority, could any injury to amenity be met by suitable and enforceable conditions? As we have seen, ISKCON argued that, in view of the 1983 agreement reached with the Council, adequate controls could be achieved by imposing the same conditions upon use of the Manor. However, the Inspector felt that ISK-CON had chosen to disregard the spirit of the agreement and concluded that it was unwilling in principle to restrict the number of people attend-ing its premises. He had the gravest doubts as to whether such a con-dition could be enforced and the very fact that such a condition would be necessary pointed to the fundamental unsuitability of the Manor for ISKCON's activities on anything other than a purely local scale.

[85] Para 37.17.   [86] Para 37.20.

On all these questions relating to the planning merits and whether the deemed application for permission should be granted, the Secretary of State agreed with the Inspector, commenting—

After most careful consideration, it has been concluded that, even allowing for the Council's apparent acceptance, over some years, of the worshipping activities of visitors to the Manor, it would not be justified to grant a planning permission, conditionally or otherwise, which would be contrary to the Inspector's very firmly founded conclusion that the planning objections are of such force that they amply outweigh the arguments on grounds of need.[87]

In its turn, the High Court ruled that the Minister was entitled to regard the Inspector's conclusions in this regard as firmly founded. Kennedy J cited with approval the following statement by the Inspector—

It was suggested that need justified an exception to, or setting aside the Green Belt policy altogether in this particular case. However, when I weigh on one side the needs of the Appellants and their congregation and on the other not just the Green Belt policy but the actual disquiet and inconvenience to residents and add to that the positive duty which conservation area status imposes on the decision maker, not just to preserve but also to enhance the character of Letchmore Heath, I consider that the interests of the village and its residents should prevail and that there is insufficient justification for setting aside that weight of policy as well as other specific and convincing planning objections.[88]

The fourth issue revolved around whether the steps which the Council had required ISKCON to take in terms of the enforcement notice exceeded what was strictly necessary in order to remedy the breach of planning control which had occurred through ISKCON's material change of use. While some elements of the existing use went beyond what was permissible, others corresponded with the original 1973 determination of use under section 53 of the 1971 Act. The Inspector agreed that reversion could be made to the use of the Manor as a residential theological college, though no element of public entertainment in connection with religious festivals would be allowed since this could not be regarded as ordinarily ancillary to a theological college in this country. On the other hand, public worship could be so regarded and the extent to which it could be accepted as being reasonably ancillary should be specified in the enforcement notice in view of the practical problems experienced in the past. The Inspector considered that the maximum number of persons who could be expected to attend worship in the chapel or shrine of a residential theological college where there were forty to fifty resident students would be 400 persons in any one day. The vehicles generated by such numbers could be accommodated conveniently in the Manor car

---

[87] Para 12.   [88] At para 37.22.

park. The Secretary of State, however, while supporting the ban on festivals, considered that it would be very difficult, if not impracticable, to control the numbers of people attending the Manor for the purpose of ancillary public worship by means of a planning condition and he therefore deleted this from the requirements of the enforcement notice. The question whether ISKCON'S future use of the Manor for public worship went beyond what was reasonably ancillary to use as a theological college would thus be a matter for the planning authority to consider, in the first instance, as a matter of fact and degree.

Both the Inspector and the Minister agreed that there was no objection to ISKCON continuing to function at the Manor as a 'religious community' and hence the reference to this was deleted from the enforcement notice. The final version of the enforcement notice thus took the form of an order to ISKCON to discontinue use of the Manor 'for public worship, save and except for worship which is ancillary to the primary use of the premises as a residential educational college in connection with the religion of Krishna Consciousness . . . [and] for public entertainment in connection with religious festivals'.[89] In the High Court Kennedy J upheld the validity of the amendments to the notice made by the Secretary of State.

While the Inspector considered that the six-month time limit for compliance set by the Council afforded ISKCON ample opportunity to implement the necessary arrangements, the Secretary of State took the exceptional step of extending the compliance period to two years. The reason for taking this step was that, on the same day as the Minister announced his decision in the enforcement notice proceedings, he also turned down ISKCON'S appeal against the refusal of planning permission to build a new temple complex about two miles away to the south at Dagger Lane, Elstree. Hence the need for ISKCON and for Hindu worshippers generally to identify a suitable alternative site elsewhere warranted, in his view, special consideration. The needs of the Hindu population certainly appeared to be substantial. The Inspector had seemingly accepted ISKCON'S estimate that there were between 120,000 and 200,000 Hindus living in north London, with around 55,000 being resident within Brent and Harrow, the main catchment area for the temple's congregations.[90] There were very few temples in the London area ministering to the needs of mainstream Sanatan Hindus, while there were

---

[89] Para 17 of the Minister's decision.

[90] ISKCON had estimated the total Hindu population in Britain as being 750,000, but a more likely figure is in the range of 400,000–550,000—see Weller, P. (ed), *Religions in the UK: A Multi-Faith Directory*, 2nd ed. (Derby, 1997), 30.

two in north-west London serving the minority Swaminarayan community of Hindus.[91]

(c) Application for planning permission in Elstree[92]

At the end of 1987 a site at Dagger Lane, Elstree had been identified as providing a possible alternative venue for meeting many of ISKCON'S expanding needs. ISKCON had already determined that as part of its long term development it wished to bring to fruition its founder's vision of a purpose-built temple combined with a cultural centre similar to those already constructed in Bombay, Detroit, Durban, and Los Angeles. This would enable the main aspects of instruction and public worship, as well as the festivals, to be transferred away from Letchmore Heath, leaving the Manor to function purely as a residential theological college. The deities would be moved to the new site and the effect of this would be that the Manor no longer attracted more than a handful of worshippers and became chiefly of historical interest. To move Hindu deities without good reason amounts to an act of desecration, but it could be justified in the present situation provided a superior shrine was being made available to house them and better access to them would be afforded to devotees.

The Elstree site was well over twice the size of the Manor site and thus a major new building project was being contemplated. An application for planning permission in respect of the new site had been made in 1988 and, if it had been successful, it would clearly have solved many problems, not only for the villagers of Letchmore Heath but also for Hertsmere Borough Council, which was naturally anxious to respond positively both to the complaints of the villagers and to the needs of ISKCON and of thousands of Hindu devotees.

During the course of 1987 Hertsmere Borough Council had indicated publicly that it was 'prepared to lend its full weight to the quest for a further site, and would be prepared to consider applications for suitable sites even within the Green Belt'.[93] In a meeting with Council officials ISKCON representatives had indicated that they had in mind a large site of around forty to fifty acres (twenty acres of which needed to be suitable for grazing cows), which was within ten to fifteen minutes' drive of the Manor so that a close association between the two institutions could be maintained. They also wanted the new site to have direct access off the

---

[91] The construction of a major new Swaminarayan temple in Neasden was subsequently completed in 1995.

[92] The material which follows is derived from the Inspector's report and the decision of the Secretary of State for the Environment, dated 20 March 1990, under the references APP/N1920/A/88/100747 and APP/N1920/A/88/107997.   [93] Para 6.7.

principal road network and not to be adjacent to a populated area. The Dagger Lane site, comprising forty-one acres, appeared promising and its owners were identified as being London Regional Transport (LRT). Two applications for planning permission were in fact submitted—one by ISKCON and the other by LRT, the latter relating both to the construction of a temple for ISKCON and to a proposal for a separate business park on a much smaller piece of adjacent land. The idea behind the second application was that if LRT could make a substantial financial gain from the development of the business park it would be willing to sell the temple site to ISKCON for only a nominal sum. Otherwise the price of the temple site might be beyond ISKCON's means.

Pending consideration of the applications, the Council sought to reach agreement with ISKCON upon the types of conditions which would need to be incorporated in any grant of planning permission. In particular, the Council wished to restrict any residential development to an *ashram* (or hostel) accommodating no more than twenty people overnight and it sought to impose a time limit of two years on the construction of the temple, so that at the end of this period the restrictions on public worship and festivals at the Manor could be enforced without prejudicing ISKCON and its devotees. ISKCON found these terms unacceptable, being especially committed to an *ashram* for fifty residents. Although no agreement was reached on these matters, the Council's planning officers seemed not unwilling to grant the necessary permission in mid-1988, on the basis of special circumstances justifying development within the Green Belt, arguing that the temple would have only limited impact on the Dagger Lane site. Despite this, the planning committee was divided on the question and eventually turned down both applications by a majority of one, through the casting vote of the chairman.

Subsequently, however, the Council changed its mind and resolved that it was willing to grant permission in respect of either of the two applications, provided there would be no residential development on the site other than accommodation for a caretaker and an agricultural worker. Later the Council offered as an alternative solution the provision of residential accommodation for up to fifty people at the new temple but only on the condition that ISKCON would agree to sell the Manor to the Council. Clearly, neither solution was acceptable to ISKCON, which insisted upon retaining the Manor as a theological college because of its special association with its founder and upon maintaining an *ashram* of fifty at any new temple so as to ensure a very high standard of *puja*, sufficient to justify in Hindu law the transfer of the deities to the new site. Meanwhile, objections had been received from local residents as well as from the London Borough of Harrow and the county planning officer of Hertfordshire County Council, and directions had been given by the Secretary of State that no permission could be given without his express authorization. It was, therefore, against this deadlocked background that the Inspector held a public inquiry into the two appeals by ISKCON and LRT during February 1989.

ISKCON presented what appeared to be a strong case. The size of the proposed site was ideal. Twenty acres were needed as pastures for its herd of cows, which was to be expanded from the existing five cows to twenty. A further five to ten acres were required for horticulture and agriculture. Flowers had to be cultivated to adorn the shrine and vegetables had to be grown to provide the constituents of the sacred food (*prasad*) offered to the deities and to devotees. Five to ten acres would be used for formal gardens and lawns with a view to achieving a serene, sylvan setting appropriate to a Hindu temple. Finally, about five acres would be allocated to the provision of adequate car parking to accommodate visitors, especially the large influx expected at festivals.

The location of the site was also good. It had an easy, safe access, not only from the main centres of the Hindu community in the vicinity but also from further north via the M1 motorway. It was simple for newcomers to find if they were travelling by car and it was also on a bus route and not far away from three railway stations. It was not so close to a residential area as to cause disturbance to neighbours, as at the Manor. The terrain was pleasantly undulating and well suited to the extensive planting and landscaping which would be required. Although the noise from traffic on the main A1 road and the motorway was clearly a disadvantage, this could be mitigated by screening, by double glazing, and by the construction of a fountain to mask the sound of passing vehicles. The main buildings would comprise the temple itself, capable of accommodating 1,000 people, a large community hall for lectures, plays, weddings, and other functions, and residential accommodation in the form of an *ashram* so that devotees could maintain the high standard of *puja* required. The *ashram* was of vital importance because the Council had expressed considerable disquiet about the possibility of devotees commuting between the new temple and the Manor, especially late at night and early in the morning. This could only be avoided by allowing sufficient devotees to reside at the new site. Moreover, *pujaris* had to shower and change clothes frequently before conducting their devotions and hence, for very practical reasons, the temple could not be divorced from living accommodation.

Although the site formed part of the Green Belt, the temple would not detract from the sense of separation between the built-up areas of Elstree and Bushey. This area already had other major institutional developments, such as schools, and these together with their large grounds were a major stabilising factor in maintaining the integrity of the Belt and resisting unacceptable uses. With only about 2 per cent of the site being built upon people travelling past would not be conscious of any loss of rural quality or of a sense of separation between Bushey and Elstree. While the temple would be visible to those relatively few visitors to the nearby Aldenham Country Park who chose to take one of the woodland walks, it could be partly masked by additional tree planting and could also be viewed as a stimulating addition to the vistas currently available to walkers. As most of the site would not be built upon, with half of it being set aside for the pasture of cattle, and since the temple would be open to the general public, it could be seen as complementing the park in environmental and land use terms.

Financial considerations were also an important factor in the choice of site. ISKCON estimated that the likely cost of building the temple would be around £6 million. The money would have to be obtained through a massive fund-raising programme. LRT had put a value of £5 million on the temple site which meant that the whole project would be quite beyond ISKCON'S means unless the site were made available at a nominal sum as part of the wider scheme of obtaining planning permission for a business park development on the adjacent LRT land. In reality, there would be no temple without a business park as well.

On the legal side, ISKCON had to address the broad position that there is a general presumption against 'inappropriate' development in a Green Belt. This represents an exception to the normal presumption in favour of allowing applications for development.[94] Within a Green Belt approval is not given in the absence of 'very special circumstances'.[95] There was an exception for institutions, which could be regarded as 'appropriate' development, but the proposal for substantial residential accommodation at the proposed temple took it outside the normal range of institutions.[96] Hence much depended on establishing that there were very special circumstances. ISKCON'S case rested principally upon two lines of argument. First, there had been previous instances where need, special circumstances, and the institutional nature of religious buildings had combined to permit development within the Green Belt. During 1986 no fewer than three appeals against refusals of planning permission had been allowed in such circumstances. These precedents related to a mosque in Hounslow, a Roman Catholic Church in Chipperfield, and a Mormon church in Watford. Secondly, ISKCON contended that

---

[94] See e.g. Planning policy guidance notes, PPG1/1988, 'General policy and principles', para 15.

[95] See Planning policy guidance notes, PPG2/1988 'Green Belts', para 13.

[96] See paras 21.3 and 21.4 of the Inspector's Report. See also *Pehrsson v. Secretary of State for the Environment* [1990] *JPL* 764.

there was high authority for the propriety of linking together the two applications for permission in respect of the temple and the business park, in such a way as to bring in the financing of the temple as a 'material consideration' under section 29(1) of the 1971 Act. That sub-section provided that, in dealing with any application for permission, the authority should have regard not only to the provisions of the local development plan but also to 'any other material consideration'.[97] In *R v Westminster City Council, ex parte Monahan*[98] the Court of Appeal had permitted non-commercial development (in relation to the Royal Opera House at Covent Garden) to be subsidised by commercial development (in the form of offices). The decision can be regarded as authority for the proposition that financial considerations can be 'material' insofar as profits derived from permission granted in respect of one site enable desirable development to occur on another site in close proximity, even if this entails disregarding some planning objections to development in relation to the first site, on the ground that overall there would be some 'planning gain'. Hence it may be a material consideration that, even though there are policy objections to a particular planning application, to allow the development to proceed will assist in the achievement of some other planning objective. In relation to the Dagger Lane applications ISKCON argued that there would be an additional planning gain through the resolution of the problems surrounding the use of the Manor and the fulfilment of planning objectives at Letchmore Heath. The concept of overall planning gain could, ISKCON contended, justify what might otherwise be regarded as inappropriate Green Belt development.

ISKCON'S case was buttressed by LRT'S argument that the proposed business park site was situated immediately next to two similar industrial and business parks where planning permission had been granted in recent years, despite the fact that they were within the Green Belt. Nearby was a redundant bus garage which already had 'existing use' rights for general industry and was about to be redeveloped. Because of the local topography the visual impact of the area would be enhanced rather than despoiled by the creation of a new business park. The two sites had no intrinsic landscape value on their own and if they were removed from the Green Belt this would round off the existing pocket of development and leave a more logical and defensible boundary to the truly open areas. The land in question was only low grade agricultural land and very marginal to the Green Belt.

At the inquiry Hertsmere Borough Council reiterated its support in principle for the two applications, on the basis of very special

---

[97] The sub-section has since been replaced by s 70(2) of the Town and Country Planning Act 1990.   [98] [1990] 1 QB 87.

circumstances, but insisted on the need for agreement to be reached on limiting residential accommodation and on a clear timetable for completion of the new temple. In the Council's view there was no justification for duplicating residential accommodation at the new temple by permitting an *ashram* there and a timescale of eighteen months was greatly preferable to the four years proposed by ISKCON for the building of the temple.

The applications were vigorously opposed by Hertfordshire County Council and the London Borough of Harrow, as well as by many local residents, as being in direct conflict with long established Green Belt policies. In particular, the County Council contended that the three recent instances of religious institutions being granted planning permission within the Green Belt were distinguishable from the present case. The mosque in Hounslow could be justified on the ground that local plan policies there expressly provided for institutions in the Green Belt. The Roman Catholic church at Chipperfield was close to the centre of its pastoral area, whereas the Dagger Lane site did not lie in the heart of the catchment area for local Hindus, namely north-west London. The Mormon church in Watford was to replace very unsightly derelict buildings on land that was unlikely to revert to agricultural use and it was preferable to the other option of a garden centre.

The Inspector upheld the objections of the County Council (and others) and dismissed the appeals by ISKCON and LRT on the following grounds. The Hertfordshire County Structure Plan Review had declared the County Council's policy of maintaining a Green Belt in the south of the county as part of a corridor around London about twelve to fifteen miles deep in which, apart from a few exceptions, there could be no development in the absence of very special circumstances. The sites were within an area of wholly open agricultural land which represented the first clearly defined break to the north of the London conurbation before a traveller from the metropolis reached Watford or St Albans.

The Inspector seemed to doubt ISKCON's capacity to devote the time, labour, and money which would be necessary to make the temple complex blend into the surrounding area through careful landscaping and he felt that the large number of devotees attracted to festivals would generate substantial movements of vehicles and people which would tend to 'blur the distinction between town and country at this point, and detract from the remaining open character which is clearly much valued by the residents of the immediate area'.[99] The development would also detract from the look and flavour of the open countryside enjoyed by visitors to the Aldenham Country Park. It was a distinct disadvantage that the

---

[99] Para 21.9.

temple site should be so far from public transport and there would be problems in allowing overspill car parking on pasture land during festivals because of poor drainage and the land 'lying wet'. Turning to the issue of ISKCON'S requirements as representing 'very special circumstances', the Inspector felt that while there was a need for a relocation of activities away from the Manor there was no overwhelming necessity for such a large project as the one planned at Dagger Lane. This type of centre was clearly part of ISKCON'S long term aspirations, but the Society should have considered smaller sites and should have extended its search further afield than it had. It should also have explored the possibility of converting existing buildings made redundant by public bodies such as schools, rather than insisting on a green field site.

Addressing the linking of the application in respect of the temple with LRT'S proposal for a business park, the Inspector was unimpressed by the Covent Garden precedent, commenting—

. . . there is . . . a world of difference between permitting an office development in the Inner City, to generate funds to achieve an object the subject of a specific policy in the local plan, namely improvements to the Royal Opera House, and allowing commercial development in the Green Belt to facilitate another proposal which is also contrary to Green Belt policy, in order to relocate a use which is, in my view, unlawful. The link between the two developments is there, and it is a material consideration, but it does not seem to me that what was done at Covent Garden is any kind of precedent so far as the merits of this development at Elstree are concerned.[100]

The Inspector's overall conclusions were that there were specific and convincing planning objections to the proposed development on the basis of the adverse effects it would have upon the appearance, character, and function of the Green Belt. The demonstrable harm that would be caused to the Green Belt was not outweighed either by considerations of need or by 'very special circumstances'.[101]

The Secretary of State, in his turn, dismissed appeals by ISKCON and by LRT because of the considerable significance of the sites for a part of the Green Belt which was particularly vulnerable and because of the demonstrable harm which the proposed development would cause. In relation to whether there were 'very special circumstances', while the Minister accepted the pressing need to relocate some of ISKCON'S activities away from the Manor and the desirability of providing a religious and cultural centre for members of the Hindu community, these two requirements did not have to be satisfied on the same site in a single development.

---

[100] Para 22.11.

[101] Successful appeals on the grounds of 'very special circumstances' are very rare—see Elson, M. and Ford, A., 'Green Belts and Very Special Circumstances' [1994] *JPL* 594.

ISKCON had identified criteria which were too restrictive and it had limited its search to an unnecessary degree. The Minister considered that a major religious and cultural centre for Hindus on the scale proposed did not necessarily have to be located close to the Manor and it had not been demonstrated that sites away from the Green Belt, with adequate rail and road access, would not be acceptable or available. A site for the re-location of unacceptable activities at the Manor could be found separately. In the light of the Minister's simultaneous decision to extend the period for compliance with the enforcement notice on the Manor from six months to two years, ISKCON would have more time to identify a suitable alternative site. In the Minister's words—

Such sites should take into account both the need for good transport access and adequate car parking arrangements for public worship and festivals, as well as those requirements which derive from the pursuit of ISKCON'S religious activities in themselves. It will be necessary to identify a site that minimises the risk of unacceptable intrusion and disruption to any nearby residents at the times of public worship and religious festivals. While this combination of requirements is unusual, the Secretary of State has no reason to conclude that it cannot be satisfied. He does not rule out the possibility that a site located elsewhere within an area designated as Green Belt could prove acceptable.[102]

Although leave to appeal out of time against the Minister's decision was granted by the High Court, the appeal was later abandoned.[103]

THE HUMAN RIGHTS DIMENSION

After the Court of Appeal had refused leave to appeal in relation to the 1987 enforcement notice, ISKCON lodged an application with the European Commission of Human Rights, alleging the violation of several articles of the Convention.[104] The principal allegation was that the enforcement notice breached Article 9(1), which provides that—

Everyone has the right to freedom of thought, conscience and religion; this right includes . . . freedom, either alone or in community with others and in public or in private, to manifest his religion or belief, in worship, teaching, practice and observance.

The Government relied, in its defence, upon Article 9(2), which restricts Article 9(1) by providing that—

---

[102] Para 10.
[103] See *ISKCON v. Secretary of State for the Environment and Hertsmere Borough Council* (1992) 64 P & CR 85 at 87.   [104] *ISKCON v UK* (1994) 76–A Dec & Rep 90.

Freedom to manifest one's religion or beliefs shall be subject only to such limitations as are prescribed by law and are necessary in a democratic society in the interests of public safety, for the protection of public order, health or morals, or for the protection of the rights and freedoms of others.

ISKCON accepted that the enforcement notice was 'prescribed by law' and that it had the legitimate purpose of seeking to protect the rights of others, namely the villagers of Letchmore Heath, but it argued that the interference with freedom of public worship was not 'necessary in a democratic society', being unnecessarily harsh and a disproportionate response to the problem. Not only had the relevant authorities given insufficient weight to the importance of the Manor as a place of worship and inspiration for Hindus, but they had also departed (without good reason) from what had previously appeared acceptable under the 1983 agreement, namely a limit being placed upon the number of visitors to the temple, rather than public worship there being terminated altogether. ISKCON contended that it was unnecessary to impose a total prohibition on what had, over the years, become an established use of the temple, when the welfare of the local residents could be adequately safeguarded by introducing additional conditions relating to public worship there.

These arguments were rejected by the Commission. While it was prepared to assume that the issue of the enforcement notice amounted to an interference with religious freedom, justification could be found not only in the need to protect the rights of local residents but also in the protection of public order and health, which was the generally accepted purpose of modern planning legislation designed to prevent uncontrolled development. On the question whether the enforcement notice was 'necessary', the Commission followed previous rulings[105] in requiring a 'pressing social need', while stressing that states possess a certain margin of appreciation—

The task of the Convention organs is not to substitute their view for that of the competent national authorities, but rather to review under the Article at issue the decisions delivered pursuant to their power of appreciation. This does not mean that supervision is limited to ascertaining whether the respondent State exercises its discretion reasonably, carefully and in good faith; what the Convention organs have to do is to look at the interference . . . in the light of the case as a whole and determine whether it was 'proportionate to the legitimate aim pursued' and whether the reasons adduced by the national authorities to justify it are 'relevant and sufficient'.[106]

Applying these principles, the Commission found that the issue of the

---

[105] See e.g. *Sunday Times v UK* (1979) 2 EHRR 245 at 275–8.   [106] At 106.

enforcement notice was not disproportionate. Reliance could not be placed upon the 1983 agreement's provision for a limit of 1,000 visitors a day to the temple because it was implicit in the agreement that enforcement action could still be taken where it was expedient for planning reasons. Moreover, negotiations for a new agreement had broken down. As to whether sufficient weight had been accorded to ISKCON's right to religious freedom, the Commission started from the premise that Article 9 could not be used 'to circumvent existing planning legislation, provided that in the proceedings under that legislation, adequate weight is given to freedom of religion'.[107] In this regard, the Commission drew attention to the fact that the planning inspector had given detailed consideration to the 'special circumstances of the case' and concluded—

It is in any event clear from the terms of the Inspector's report and the decision letter of the Secretary of State that considerable weight was attached to the religious needs and interests of the members of ISKCON and to the importance of the Manor in relation to the religious activities of the members.[108]

ISKCON had relied strongly on statements in letters from government ministers and an official in the Department of the Environment to the effect that the decisions reached about the enforcement notice had been made solely on land-use planning grounds and that 'the religious aspects of the Society's activities at Bhaktivedanta Manor were not relevant'.[109] These statements demonstrated, in ISKCON's eyes, that freedom of worship had palpably not been afforded adequate prominence in the English proceedings. However, the Commission, perhaps rather too charitably, interpreted these statements as meaning merely that the English decisions had been reached on proper planning grounds 'and not on any objections to the religious aspects of the activities of ISKCON'.[110] The crucial point which these letters were attempting to make to ISKCON was that under English law the whole question of religious freedom was not directly relevant because there is no constitutional or statutory protection of this freedom and the planning legislation had to be interpreted and applied in its own terms rather than balanced with any right to freedom of worship.

This point formed the basis of ISKCON's further claim that the United Kingdom was in breach of another provision of the Convention, namely Article 6, which runs as follows—

In the determination of his civil rights . . . everyone is entitled to a fair and public hearing . . . by an independent and impartial tribunal established by law.

ISKCON contended that it was barred under English law from access to a

---

[107] At 107.   [108] At 107–8.   [109] At 104, 107.   [110] At 107.

proper court hearing in respect of its right to freedom of religion since any consideration of religious freedom had to be assessed by the authorities within the technicalities of planning law. The Government denied that ISKCON had a 'civil right' to freedom of religion under English law and argued that the civil right at issue was whether or not ISKCON'S religious interests and needs outweighed the planning concerns in the case. The Commission decided the point in the government's favour on the basis of a previous ruling by the European Court of Human Rights that it is not the function of Article 6 to regulate the content of civil rights.[111] Since freedom of religion has no formal status as a civil right in United Kingdom law, disputes about it are not covered by Article 6. A fair hearing of the planning aspects, including some consideration of the religious aspects, had been furnished by the appeal to the High Court, which fully met the requirements of Article 6.

Insofar as English law apparently provides no effective remedy for complaints concerning interference with religious freedom, ISKCON further alleged a violation of Article 13, which states—

Everyone whose rights and freedoms as set forth in this Convention are violated shall have an effective remedy before a national authority notwithstanding that the violation has been committed by persons acting in an official capacity.

However, the Commission rejected this contention on the ground that the jurisprudence of the European Court demonstrated that Article 13 only applied to grievances that were 'arguable',[112] which those made in the present case were not. For the reasons given above, no appearance of a violation of either Article 6 or Article 9 had been disclosed.

ISKCON'S remaining complaint alleged that the enforcement notice violated Article 1 of the First Protocol to the Convention through an interference with its property rights. Article 1 provides as follows—

Every natural or legal person is entitled to the peaceful enjoyment of his possessions. No one shall be deprived of his possessions except in the public interest and subject to the conditions provided for by law and by the general principles of international law. The preceding provisions shall not, however, in any way impair the right of the State to enforce such laws as it deems necessary to control the use of property in accordance with the general interest . . . .

The Commission doubted whether any interference had actually occurred with ISKCON'S property rights, in view of the fact that the aim of the enforcement notice was merely to limit ISKCON'S use and enjoyment of the Manor to that which was legally permissible when the property was acquired. Assuming that there had been some interference, it

---

[111] *W v UK* (1987) Series A, No. 121, para 73; see also *Lithgow et al v UK* (1986) 8 EHRR 329. [112] See *Powell and Rayner v UK* (1990) 12 EHRR 355.

amounted to 'control' rather that deprivation and thus the Commission's task was to determine, in accordance with its established jurisprudence, whether a fair balance had been struck by the United Kingdom between the protection of ISKCON's rights and the general interest of the community. As the Commission had indicated in its earlier decision in *Chater v UK*[113], a wide margin of appreciation is afforded to states in the planning field because controls are 'necessary and desirable in order to preserve and improve the amenities of residential areas'.[114] The same applies to the preservation and improvement of 'town and country landscapes'.[115] The Commission's task is therefore to 'supervise the lawfulness, purpose and proportionality'[116] of the restriction in question. On the facts, the Commission was satisfied that a proper balance had been struck between ISKCON's interests and the general interest because there was no indication in the inspector's report or the decision of the Secretary of State that the various interests were not duly taken into consideration in limiting ISKCON to using the Manor for the purposes permissible when it was acquired.

ISKCON had further alleged that there had been a violation of Article 1 of the First Protocol taken together with Article 14, which precludes discrimination on, *inter alia*, grounds of religion. ISKCON argued that Muslims, Catholics, and Protestants had been given permission to use premises for public worship within Green Belt areas, while it had been denied such permission. The Commission, however, noted that ISKCON had withdrawn allegations of racial or religious prejudice in the planning inquiry, as there was 'no evidence of bad faith on the part of the local authority in relation to the adoption of the enforcement notice. In such circumstances, alleged prejudice from individuals cannot be of relevance to the complaints under Article 1 of Protocol No. 1'.[117] No doubt, it was impossible for ISKCON to furnish hard evidence that the Green Belt policy was being administered in a discriminatory fashion.

The final outcome of ISKCON's application to the Commission was that each complaint was dismissed as manifestly ill-founded, as were similar complaints made by eight individual members of the Society. Most importantly, their right to freedom of religion was held not to have been violated, any interference being both justified and necessary in a democratic society. On the other hand, the decision to declare the application inadmissible was only reached by a majority of the Commission,[118] which to some extent detracts from its authority.

---

[113] (1987) 52 Dec & Rep 250.   [114] At 256.   [115] *ISKCON v UK* at 108.
[116] *Chater v UK* at 256; *ISKCON v UK* at 108.   [117] *ISKCON v UK* at 109.
[118] Ibid at 112.

SALVATION THROUGH THE CONSTRUCTION OF A NEW ACCESS DRIVEWAY[119]

In view of the fact that the residential part of Letchmore Heath lies to the north-east of the Manor and that the only entrances to it for vehicles and pedestrians were located on the village side, a very substantial alleviation of the disturbance caused to the villagers would be achieved if access to the Manor could be gained from the opposite direction. Indeed, considerable advantages would also accrue for visitors from such a solution, for there is much easier access to the main road network, including the A41, the A411, and the M1 motorway only a few miles to the west or south-west. Hence, in 1987–8 ISKCON had coupled an application for planning permission to legitimize the unauthorized uses at the Manor with a specific proposal to construct a new driveway running for about 700 metres across fields to the south-west to link up with a road named Hilfield Lane. This combined application had been rejected by Hertsmere Borough Council and an appeal had not been pursued at that time, apparently because one of the owners of the relevant fields was unwilling to sell part of his land to ISKCON for the purpose. However, in 1993 an agreement had ultimately been reached with the landowner in question and a fresh application for such planning permission was made and pursued in earnest once the European Commission of Human Rights had delivered its ruling in spring 1994. Hertsmere Borough Council would, nevertheless, have refused such permission had it still been seized of the issue in autumn 1994,[120] but the Secretary of State asserted jurisdiction over the application because it involved proposals giving rise to significant public controversy and he duly appointed an inspector to hold a further public inquiry.

At the inquiry, the application was opposed by about thirty local residents, as well as the Council, but ISKCON was supported by over 700 letters (including twenty-one from MPs) and some 8,900 cards (printed in standard form). In the event, the Inspector recommended that permission be granted both for the driveway and for the wider uses, and his views were broadly accepted by the Secretary of State. The final upshot was, therefore, that ISKCON achieved its longstanding goal, for the Minister's decision was that, as soon as the driveway had been constructed, the use of the Manor could be changed to 'a residential and

---

[119] The material which follows is mainly derived from the Inspector's Report and the decision of the Secretary of State for the Environment, dated 10 May 1996, under the reference APP/N1920/A/94/241083.

[120] Indeed, ISKCON was prosecuted by the Council in 1994 for breach of the enforcement notice in allowing the Janmashtami festival to proceed and a fine of £30,000 was imposed, subsequently reduced to £5,000 on appeal: *R v ISKCON Ltd*, Court of Appeal, Criminal Division, 9 July 1996 (unreported).

non-residential theological college and religious community, together with use for public worship (including the observance of religious festival days)'.[121] In order to appreciate how this dramatic *volte-face* came about, it is necessary to return to the question of development within the Green Belt since, although several other issues were raised at the inquiry, this was clearly of critical importance.

As we have seen, there is a general presumption against 'inappropriate' development within the Green Belt and approval of such development is not given unless there are 'very special circumstances'.[122] Although both the Inspector and the Secretary of State ruled that the construction of the driveway fell within the category of inappropriate development because it represented an encroachment into the countryside, which threatened its openness and permanence, they each concluded that it could be justified on the basis of 'very special circumstances'. However, they reached their separate conclusions through rather different routes. The Inspector began by expressing his view that the presence here of a Hindu community of over half a million people (many integrating into this society following persecution in Uganda), when coupled with the special significance to them of the Manor and its deities, constituted a 'material consideration' because of the wider public interest involved. He then addressed the Green Belt issue in the following way—

In dealing with the weight which I conclude should be attached to the very special circumstances in this case, I return to a matter which I believe, irrespective of its Green Belt location, is a relevant material consideration in this case— namely the extent to which it is reasonable for a significant group of the community to be able to worship according to their religious beliefs and tenets. It is a matter of undisputed fact that Bhaktivedanta Manor has a special relevance to the Hindu community and provides a level of worship and pilgrimage which is manifestly important to Hindus. In this regard Bhaktivedanta Manor is without rival or comparability elsewhere in the UK. In its present location it is well placed to serve the religious and cultural needs of Hindus living in North London, Harrow and Brent.[123]

In order to assess whether these circumstances were sufficient to outweigh the indisputable harm to the Green Belt which would arise from granting permission to ISKCON, the Inspector first took account of the fact that for about one-third of its length the driveway would be physically associated with an electricity transformer station. In view of the screening provided by existing trees and the level of additional planting planned by ISKCON, as well as the low-lying nature of part of the route,

---

[121] Para 46.   [122] See now PPG 2/1994, para 3.2, replacing PPG 2/1988, para 13.
[123] Para 396 of the Report.

the impact of the driveway on the character of the rural area would not, in his opinion, be great. As a man-made encroachment, it would not have an excessively jarring influence on the local countryside. Secondly, although ISKCON'S plans for additional car parking in the fields and the erection of tents and other temporary structures on festival days would lead to visual impairment of the openness of the area, the effects would only be felt for the limited duration of the festivals. Hence he concluded that—

... the religious, spiritual and customary needs of the Hindu community are both so fundamental and relevant to so many people that they should be considered as representing a public interest. As such they are a material consideration in this case of such weight that they represent the very special circumstances for allowing, exceptionally, a form of development which is inappropriate in Green Belt terms.[124]

He specifically made reference to the significance he had attached to the public interest factor and drew attention to the general principle that the planning system as a whole is designed to regulate development and land use in the public interest,[125] adding—

... the combination of religious importance and the scale of benefits to the Hindu community differentiate this case from one of benefits to a private interest, say to a single householder, group or organisation, [elevating it] to that of a type and scale of use which serves a public interest.[126]

The Secretary of State ruled, however, that the Inspector had not approached the 'very special circumstances' question in the correct manner, since he had apparently given overriding weight to the spiritual and religious needs of Hindu worshippers without undertaking the balancing exercise which is necessary, whether or not such circumstances exist. In this regard, it was necessary to examine all the objections to a proposal, not just those relating to the Green Belt. These included issues relating to traffic control and highway safety, parking, and residential amenity, as well as conservation area and listed building protection. The Inspector had, of course, considered each of these matters carefully and indeed the Secretary of State ultimately reached the same conclusions about them, namely that they were insufficient to outweigh the 'very special circumstances' present in this instance. However, the Secretary of State was at pains to point out that—

... the religious needs of one section of the community are not in themselves of such paramount importance that they can automatically override national or local planning policies.[127]

---

[124] Para 418. [125] See PPG 1/1994, para 2. [126] Para 460 of the Report.
[127] Para 37.

Even so, these religious needs had to be accorded 'considerable weight' and they 'clearly outweighed' the harm involved.[128]

So far as traffic control and highway safety were concerned, the Inspector and the Minister were of the view that a combination of remedial work to be done by ISKCON at the junction of the driveway with the main road (to be imposed as a planning condition), exhortation by ISKCON to worshippers to turn left at the junction, so as to gain easier access to the main road network, and implementation of a traffic management scheme for the Janmashtami festival, were adequate safeguards. As for parking congestion, a planning condition was imposed that sufficient parking space should be guaranteed in adjacent fields before festivals could be held. On the question of residential amenity, both the Inspector and the Minister were satisfied that the adverse effects on the quality of life of the villagers of Letchmore Heath arising from the influx of vehicles on festival days would substantially disappear once the new driveway was built. ISKCON had undertaken that the existing entrance on the village side could then be closed off, even for pedestrians, if the Council so required. Noise from firework displays on festival days could be restricted to certain fixed hours by means of conditions attached to the grant of planning consent. Finally, although the Minister regarded the two-year search for an alternative site, as provided for in the modified enforcement notice in 1990, as relevant to the questions of 'religious needs' and 'very special circumstances', he acknowledged that finding such a site would not have been easy, adding (perhaps rather belatedly)—

Given the special religious significance of Bhaktivedanta Manor and its location, the Secretary of State is prepared to accept that the chances of finding a viable alternative site were bound to be very low.[129]

Work on the new access driveway was completed within only a few months of the Secretary of State's decision, with the result that the wider uses of the Manor finally became officially authorized and lawful in the latter part of 1996.

CONCLUSIONS

The right to freedom of religion, including freedom to worship in community with others, is guaranteed by both Article 9 of the European Convention and Article 18(1) of the International Covenant on Civil and Political Rights. Religious minorities are given special

---

[128] Paras 37–39.   [129] Para 34.

protection in this regard, not only through provisions banning discrimination on the basis of religion[130] but also in terms of Article 27 of the International Covenant.[131]

The European Court of Human Rights has emphasized that the hallmarks of a democratic society are pluralism, the tolerance of different outlooks and philosophies, and broadmindedness.[132] In such a society a balance must be struck which ensures the 'fair and proper treatment of minorities'.[133] In *Kokkinakis v Greece*[134] the Court declared that religious freedom constituted—

. . . one of the most vital elements that go to make up the identity of believers and their conception of life, but it is also a precious asset for atheists, agnostics, sceptics and the unconcerned. The pluralism indissociable from a democratic society, which has been dearly won over the centuries, depends upon it.[135]

In elaborating the content of religious freedom, the United Nations Declaration on the Elimination of All Forms of Intolerance and of Discrimination Based on Religion or Belief[136] specifically refers to the freedom 'to worship or assemble in connection with a religion or belief, and to establish and maintain places for these purposes', as well as the freedom to 'celebrate holidays and ceremonies in accordance with the precepts of one's religion or belief'.[137] Article 7 of the Declaration then insists that these freedoms—

. . . shall be accorded in national legislation in such a manner that everyone shall be able to avail himself of such rights and freedoms in practice.

The Declaration is not legally binding and there is no express enactment in England guaranteeing freedom of religious worship in general terms. Even so, it is such a fundamental and pervasive right that it may perhaps be regarded as part of the common law, on the basis of the principle that universally recognized rules of customary international law automatically form part of English law.[138]

However, freedom of religion and in particular its manifestation in public worship cannot be regarded as unlimited, as the European Commission's decision in *ISKCON v UK* clearly demonstrated. Restrictions are permissible and state interference can be justified if it is necessary to

---

[130] ECHR, Art 14; ICCPR, Arts 2(1), 26.   [131] See above, ch 3.
[132] See e.g. *Handyside v UK* (1976) 1 EHRR 737 at 754.
[133] *Young, James and Webster v UK* (1981) 4 EHRR 38 at 57.
[134] (1994) 17 EHRR 397.   [135] At 418.
[136] UN Doc A/36/51 (1981).   [137] Art 6(a), (h).
[138] See e.g. *West Rand Central Gold Mining Co v R* [1905] 2 KB 391 at 406–7; *Trendtex Trading Corporation v Central Bank of Nigeria* [1977] QB 529 at 553–4; Higgins, R., 'The Relationship Between International and Regional Human Rights Norms and Domestic Law' [1992] *Commonwealth Law Bulletin* 1268 at 1272.

protect public order and the rights of others.[139] In relation to the enforcement notice served on ISKCON in 1987, the Commission ruled that this was not a disproportionate interference with religious freedom, in view of the need for planning laws to restrict development (especially in the Green Belt) in the wider public interest and the duty to protect the welfare and amenity of the villagers against undue disturbance, especially on festival days. With regard to the latter aspect, however, it should be borne in mind that similar 'invasions' commonly occur elsewhere and local residents are expected to tolerate them and if possible learn to appreciate the contribution these events make to the cultural, sporting, and religious life of the visitors and indeed the nation at large. The residents of Glastonbury, Henley, Notting Hill, Twickenham, Walsingham, Wembley, and Wimbledon all have to accommodate the visits of very large crowds of people for a few days each year. It is true that the very substantial crowds at Bhaktivedanta Manor could not have been anticipated by the villagers of Letchmore Heath when the property was acquired by ISKCON in 1973, but the numbers of visitors at many other venues have also increased markedly over the years and, in any event, the composition of a local population is constantly changing. Moreover, there is convincing evidence that ISKCON members, together with the police, handle the organization of the festivals, including the large volume of traffic, extremely well and relatively few complaints are levelled in this score.

Fortunately, planning permission for the construction of a new access driveway ultimately enabled a long-standing problem to be resolved in a manner in which the reasonable requirements of both worshippers and villagers could be satisfactorily accommodated. In the end, the English legal system proved capable of settling the dispute through the flexible application of its ordinary planning principles, without any need for a specific provision designed for the exclusive benefit of ISKCON or Hindus. Religious freedom was properly accorded considerable weight in determining whether, on balance, sufficient 'very special circumstances' existed to authorize 'inappropriate development' in the Green Belt and to overcome other planning objections.

---

[139] Compare *Chappell v UK* (1987) 53 Dec & Rep 241, in which the European Commission upheld a ban on Druidic ceremonies at Stonehenge at the midsummer solstice because of the risk of harm to the public through the disruption likely to be caused by 'hippies'.

8

Sikhs: Tussles over Beards and Turbans

Although the establishment of a Sikh community in England is a comparatively recent phenomenon, with the main thrust of immigration occurring from the 1950s onwards in the wake of the disruptive effects upon the Punjab of the partition of India in 1947[1], a small number of Sikhs had lived here well before this time. The 1920s and 1930s had witnessed the arrival of Sikh pedlars and hawkers, who became a familiar sight selling their wares in Oxford Street and Hyde Park, as well as in Liverpool and the Midlands.[2] Probably, many of them had been soldiers fighting in the British army in France during the First World War, who had stayed on here afterwards rather than return to India.[3] Earlier still, one notable individual made his own distinct mark on English society through his rank and personality. The life of Maharajah Duleep Singh[4] provides a pertinent historical link with one of the principal features of the relationship which developed over many years between the Sikhs and the British and which (as we shall see) is still alluded to today, namely the military connection.

Duleep was an 'acknowledged son'[5] of Ranjit Singh, the founder of the Sikh nation and 'Lion of the Punjab', who had built up a formidable modern military machine in North West India during the early part of the nineteenth century. Ranjit had driven out the Mughal emperor, but he had carefully avoided direct conflict with British forces.[6] After his death in 1839 rival factions reduced the Punjab to chaos and anarchy, hostilities broke out between his successors and British forces, and two 'Anglo-Sikh Wars' were fought in 1845–6 and 1848–9. After defeat in the first war the Sikhs were allowed to retain formal sovereignty over the

---

[1] See Rose, E., *Colour and Citizenship* (London, 1969), 70–3.

[2] See Desai, R., *Indian Immigrants in Britain* (London, 1963), 5, 64–5.

[3] See Ballard, R., 'Differentiation and Disjunction among the Sikhs' in Ballard, R. (ed), *Desh Pardesh* (London, 1994), 93.

[4] See generally, Alexander, M. and Anand, S., *Queen Victoria's Maharajah Duleep Singh, 1838–93* (London, 1980).

[5] It seems highly unlikely that Ranjit Singh himself fathered Duleep—see Alexander and Anand, 2.

[6] Mason, P., *A Matter of Honour: An Account of the Indian Army, its Officers and Men* (London, 1974), 228–9.

Punjab and Duleep was officially recognized as its Maharajah, but after the second war the Punjab was formally annexed by the Governor-General, Lord Dalhousie, and Duleep (aged eleven) was compelled to renounce all claims to his kingdom, its sovereignty, and property.[7] He was also forced to surrender the famous Koh-i-noor diamond to Queen Victoria as a token of his submission and his official title was reduced to that of Maharajah of Lahore.[8] He was quickly separated from his mother and his education and guardianship were assigned to a Scottish doctor and his wife.[9] Under such tutelage Duleep announced at the age of twelve that he was embracing Christianity (no doubt influenced by his new young English friends) and he was formally baptized into the faith three years later.[10] He then obtained permission from the Court of Directors of the East India Company in London to come to England and it was here that he was to spend most of the rest of his life.

Upon his arrival Queen Victoria immediately took him 'under her wing' and treated him as being of equal rank to a European prince.[11] He made a most favourable impression on the Queen and she entertained him at Buckingham Palace, at Windsor Castle, and at Osborne House on the Isle of Wight. During his first seven years here she took an intimate interest in his education, welfare, and development, even to the extent of seeking to influence his choice of a wife.[12] However, it was during this period, in 1857, that the Indian Mutiny or 'National Rising' occurred, involving more than twelve months of ferocious fighting and atrocities on both sides. Throughout these hostilities the Sikhs (and other Punjabis) remained loyal to the British authorities. According to Khushwant Singh—

Of the Punjabis, the role of the Sikhs in suppressing the uprising was the most significant. Sikh soldiers defended English establishments and families in Allahabad, Benares, Lucknow, Kanpur, Arrah and other centres of revolt.[13]

Bingley, a British captain in the Indian army at the end of the nineteenth century, adds further details—

. . . the Sikhs flocked in numbers to our standards and identified themselves with the British cause with a loyalty which never wavered. While the newly-raised regiments and the corps of the Frontier Force were earning fame and distinction before Delhi, their comrades of the 14th and 45th Sikhs were rendering splendid service in Oudh and the North-West Province. The former, besides saving the fort at Allahabad from falling into the hands of the rebels, took a distinguished part in Havelock's advance on Lucknow, and in the subsequent defence of the Residency. The latter, rejecting the numerous attempts made to seduce them from

---

[7] See Alexander and Anand, 12. [8] Ibid, 12–13. [9] Ibid, 12–14.
[10] Ibid, 25–38. [11] Ibid, ch 3. [12] Ibid, ch 4.
[13] *A History of the Sikhs* (Princeton, 1966), vol 2, 109.

their allegiance, took a prominent share in the suppression of the Mutiny in Behar, and gained special distinction by the gallantry of a small detachment in defending a house at Arrah against the Dinapore mutineers.[14]

This was to stand the Sikhs in very good stead in terms of recruitment to the new Indian army which was established soon afterwards.[15] Mason has written of the sympathy, mutual respect, and trust which was to exist for almost a century up to Indian independence between British officers and Sikh soldiers[16] and it is clear that after the Mutiny a new policy was adopted in army recruitment of specially favouring the 'more warlike and hardy races', amongst whom the Sikhs (and the Gurkhas) were pre-eminent.[17] Towards the end of the nineteenth century the military authorities were far more concerned with the threat from Russia than from internal disorder and needed troops capable of defeating a European enemy. Relying upon currently fashionable theories of biological determinism, Lord Roberts, who was commander-in-chief of the Indian army from 1885 to 1893, rejected as heretical the notion that one Indian was 'as good as another for purposes of war' and insisted upon the need to concentrate on the 'martial races'.[18] This attitude is graphically illustrated by the following passage in Captain R. W. Falcon's recruitment manual entitled *Handbook on Sikhs for Regimental Officers* published in 1896—

The Sikh is a fighting man and his fine qualities are best shown in the army, which is his natural profession. Hardy, brave and of intelligence; too slow to understand when he is beaten; obedient to discipline; attached to his officers; and careless of caste prohibitions, he is unsurpassed as a solider in the East and takes the first place as a thoroughly reliable, useful soldier. The Sikh is always the same, ever genial, good-tempered and uncomplaining; as steady under fire as he is eager for a charge . . . when well and sufficiently led he is the equal of any troops in the world and superior to any with whom he is likely to come into contact.[19]

Sikh soldiers fought on the Allied side in both World Wars and served with great distinction and bravery in France and Mesopotamia in the 1914–18 war and in Italy and Burma during 1939–45.[20] By the end of the First World War Sikhs accounted for about a fifth of the combat troops in the Indian army, with over 100,000 men in action.[21]

Duleep Singh returned to India for a brief visit in 1861 at the age of twenty-three and was reunited with his mother whom he brought back

---

[14] Bingley, A., *Handbook for the Indian Army: Sikhs* (Simla, 1899), 28.
[15] Khushwant Singh, 111–15; Mason, 234–6, 307–8, 313–4.   [16] Mason, 230.
[17] Ibid, 346–7.   [18] Ibid, 346.
[19] (Allahabad, 1896), 65–6; see also Bingley, 93.
[20] Mason, 414–6, 440–1, 446, 492, 502, 513.   [21] Khushwant Singh, 160.

to England. Under her influence, and sensing both his own political importance to Sikhs in India and the loss of his sovereignty in the Punjab, he began to turn his attention to the pursuit of perhaps somewhat dubious claims to various private estates of his late 'father', which he alleged had not been appropriated by the British at the conclusion of the second Sikh War.

In 1863 he acquired Elveden Hall in Suffolk and following his marriage to an Egyptian girl (of Coptic faith) he settled down to playing the role of a country squire and fashionable socialite.[22] However, while ostensibly an English gentleman in manners, dress, and lifestyle, he still thought of himself as a Sikh. In declining the Queen's offer of peerages for himself and his sons in 1876 he declared—

I thank Her Majesty most heartily and humbly convey to her my esteem, affection and admiration. Beyond that I cannot go. I claim myself to be royal. I am not English, and neither I nor my children will ever become so. Such titles—though kindly offered—we do not need and cannot assume. We love the English and especially their Monarch, but we must remain Sikhs.[23]

Eventually his extravagant lifestyle forced him into debt and he entered into a series of wrangles with the India Office over his father's estates, publicizing what he felt were the wrongs done to him and the greed of British administrators.[24] Obtaining no satisfaction, he renounced Christianity, re-embraced Sikhism and in 1886 set off for India in the hope of recovering his possessions and intent on fulfilling an eighteenth century prophecy which suggested that he might be a long-awaited Sikh religious leader or '*guru*'.[25] Anxiety on the part of the Viceroy of India that Duleep's return might lead to internal disorder and political unrest in the Punjab resulted in his detention when his ship docked at Aden.[26] From there he went to Paris, where he drafted proclamations to be published in Indian newspapers calling upon Indians to rise up and liberate themselves from British rule. He also sought Russian backing for his plans to mount an insurrection.[27] He styled himself 'Sovereign of the Sikh Nation' and claimed to have the support of 45,000 Punjabi soldiers in the Indian army.[28] He next proceeded to Moscow where he invited the Tsar to invade India,[29] but the political situation was unfavourable to Russian intervention and no action was taken. Ultimately he returned to Paris where, coming under the continued pressures of ill-health and financial stringency, he decided to send fulsome apologies to Queen Victoria for his disloyal behaviour and seek a royal pardon.[30] This was duly granted and he died soon afterwards in 1893.

[22] See Alexander and Anand, ch 5.   [23] Ibid, 120.   [24] Ibid, chs 8–12.
[25] Ibid, chs 11–12.   [26] Ibid, ch 13.   [27] Ibid, ch 14.
[28] Ibid, 239, 246–7.   [29] Ibid, 257–60.   [30] Ibid, ch 16.

A gap of more than half a century separates Duleep Singh's death from the start of the migration of Sikhs to Britain in substantial numbers. This process began in the 1950s, following the dislocation of peoples living in the Punjab around the time when India was partitioned in 1947.[31] In the face of rising communal tensions, riots, and bloodshed, Hindus and Sikhs moved east into India and Muslims moved west into the newly-created state of Pakistan. Sikh peasant farmers of the Jat 'caste',[32] who were experiencing economic hardship through high population density in the wake of an influx of refugees from West Punjab (which was to become part of Pakistan), began to send their younger adult sons abroad, both to increase their wealth and to enhance their families' prestige and honour (*izzat*). Many of them came to England and their numbers increased dramatically around 1960–62 as news emerged that immigration controls were about to be introduced by Parliament. Large numbers of wives, children, and other family members were also brought over just before the Commonwealth Immigrants Act 1962 was brought into force.

Although there were obvious economic attractions in migrating to a country which was short of labour during a period of 'boom', the Sikhs already had a well established tradition of migration since they had been settling in many parts of the Far East and North America,[33] as well as in East Africa, for some eighty years beforehand. At the end of the nineteenth century, for example, an agreement had been reached between the Government of India and the British East Africa Company to construct a railway in Uganda employing Indian labour.[34] Substantial numbers of Sikhs of the Ramgarhia (artisan) 'caste' had been recruited for this task over many years and Sikh soldiers had been despatched from the Punjab to help maintain order in East Africa.[35] Gradually, throughout the colonial period in East Africa, Sikhs had filled a variety of skilled technical, administrative, and clerical posts in both the public and the private sectors of the economies of Kenya, Uganda, and Tanganyika, as well as being commonly recruited into the local police forces.[36] Many of them were squeezed out of their positions by policies of 'Africanization' once these countries achieved their independence during the 1960s and the

---

[31] See generally, Helweg, A., *Sikhs in England*, 2nd ed. (Delhi, 1986), chs II and III; Rose, 52–4; Ballard, R., 'The context and consequences of migration: Jullundur and Mirpur compared' (1983) *New Community* 117.

[32] Formally, Sikhism rejects notions of caste, but in practical terms caste divisions still exist; see generally Kalsi, S., *The Evolution of a Sikh Community in Britain* (Leeds, 1992); Thomas, T., 'Old Allies, New Neighbours: Sikhs in Britain' in Parsons, G. (ed), *The Growth of Religious Diversity in Britain from 1945: vol 1, Traditions* (London, 1993), ch 5.

[33] Khushwant Singh, 168–81.

[34] See Mangat, J., *A History of the Asians in East Africa, c 1886 to 1945* (Oxford, 1969), 32.

[35] Ibid, 40, 42–3, 61.   [36] Ibid, 75, 142.

process was sharply accelerated by the mass deportations from Uganda ordered by President Amin in 1972. Most of those expelled came to Britain, where they form a separate and distinct group of Sikhs from those who migrated here directly from the Indian sub-continent.[37] They are predominantly middle class.[38]

There are no official statistics on the total number of Sikhs living in Britain today, but recent estimates suggest a figure between 300,000 and 500,000.[39]

THE ATTITUDES OF THE MAJORITY COMMUNITY

It is possible to identify four separate strands in the attitudes adopted over the years towards the Sikhs on the part of the majority community, or at least certain sections of it.

The first of these is represented by the strong ties of loyalty, respect, and affection which, as we have seen, developed between British officers and Sikh troops in the Indian army during the period of almost a century from the Indian Mutiny in 1857 to the end of the Second World War in 1945 and the attainment of India's independence in 1947. These bonds must have made a marked impression on the British establishment in general and would also have been communicated to a wider public through reports conveyed by former Indian army officers to their families and friends both by correspondence and, upon their return to Britain, in person.

Secondly, these feelings of respect and admiration for the Sikhs were, early in this century, to some extent matched by a sense of guilt arising from one of the most notorious acts of brutality perpetrated during the days of the Raj. In April 1919, following Mahatma Gandhi's arrest in the wake of his campaign of peaceful protests and workers' strikes, a public demonstration took place at the Jalianwallah Bagh in Amritsar, the city in which the Sikhs' holiest shrine, the Golden Temple, is situated. This meeting contravened a martial law ordinance prohibiting all public gatherings. The martial law administrator, General Dyer, ordered his troops to open fire without warning on an unarmed crowd of around 25,000, who were trapped in a confined space with no means of escape. Officially, it was estimated that 379 people died and another 2,000 were wounded,[40] but there were almost certainly a larger number of casualties.[41] Many

---

[37] See generally, Bhachu, P., *Twice Migrants: East African Sikh Settlers in Britain* (London, 1985).   [38] Hiro, D., *Black British, White British* (London, 1991), 125.
[39] See Ballard, *Desh Pardesh*, 95; Weller, P. (ed.), *Religions in the UK: A Multi-Faith Directory*, 2nd ed. (Derby, 1997), 30.   [40] Khushwant Singh, 163–4.
[41] See Furneaux, R., *Massacre at Amritsar* (London, 1963), 24.

were young children.[42] Following a public outcry and the report of an official committee of inquiry, General Dyer was forced into premature retirement by the Government of India and at Westminster Sir Winston Churchill described the massacre as 'an episode . . . without precedent or parallel in the modern history of the British Empire . . . a monstrous event, an event which stands in singular and sinister isolation'.[43] However, opinion in Britain was divided on the issue and after a motion in the House of Commons censuring General Dyer had been passed with only a small majority, the House of Lords' vote actually vindicated him.[44]

Thirdly, turning to the present day, there is perhaps an impression in Britain, formed by various media reports, that some Sikhs have carried their 'martial' traditions into extremism, violence, and terrorism in pursuit of political objectives in the Punjab and in particular the aim of establishing there, through secession, an independent Sikh state of Khalistan.[45] Certainly the events of 1984 lent credence to such perceptions. During that year the Sikh leader Sant Jarnail Singh Bhindranwale turned the Golden Temple complex at Amritsar into a military compound and was killed by government forces, who were sent to restore law and order and return the Temple to its proper function. Subsequently, the Indian Prime Minister, Mrs Indira Gandhi, who had ordered the attack, was assassinated by one of her Sikh bodyguards. However, it seems clear that only a small minority of Sikhs seriously contemplate the founding of a separate state or favour the use of violence to achieve political ends. Even so, events in India have spilled over into the Sikh community in Britain and there were some expressions of delight here at the news of Mrs Gandhi's murder. Tensions mounted between rival Sikh factions and there were running street fights between 'militants' and 'moderates' in Gravesend.[46] Moreover, during 1986–7 two moderate Sikh leaders were assassinated in Southall[47] and in 1991 three extremists involved in a terrorist plot against a leading moderate temple official in Southall were found guilty of conspiracy to murder and were sentenced to long periods of imprisonment.[48] Outrage on the part of many Sikhs at the assault upon the Golden Temple and the killing of thousands of Sikhs in communal violence in Delhi in the aftermath of Mrs Gandhi's murder heightened tensions in India and have inevitably led to an increase in the identification of Sikhs with their faith, both in India itself and in Sikh communities around the world.

The fourth aspect of the majority community's perception of Sikhs is that in the early years of their settlement here feelings of suspicion and

---

[42] Ibid, 24–9. [43] HC Debs, 131, col 1724 (7 July 1920). [44] Furneaux, 160.
[45] See generally, McLeod, W., *The Sikhs: History, Religion and Society* (New York, 1989), 1–2, 11–15. [46] Hiro, 180.
[47] Ibid. [48] *Independent*, 23 July 1991.

apprehension were engendered by their striking and unfamiliar physical appearance. One of the central tenets of the Sikh faith, to be explained more fully below, is *kesh* or uncut hair. A man's hair should be worn long, tied up and held in position by a comb (*kanga*), and covered by a turban. Similarly, men should not shave but allow their beards to grow. Early Sikh settlers here felt they were viewed by English people as 'strange' or 'barbaric' if they wore beards and turbans.[49] Many Sikhs were refused employment and accommodation purely because of their appearance and quickly realized that they needed to cut their hair and dispense with their turbans if they were to be successful in finding a job and a place to live.[50] As Beetham has reported—

Those who migrated here in the 1950s found that they could only secure a job if they were clean shaven. This was rarely openly demanded by an employer, but Sikhs soon learnt that they might present themselves one day wearing a turban and be refused, only to be accepted the next day if they applied clean shaven. The message was quickly passed on to relatives who followed.[51]

Around this time a Labour MP, John Stonehouse, indicated that Sikhs could only be integrated into British society if they abandoned their turbans, and this sentiment was endorsed from the other side of the party-political spectrum by Enoch Powell.[52]

In 1966 Khushwant Singh wrote at the end of his magisterial survey of Sikh history—

. . . whenever Sikhs are scattered among other people, the attachment to tradition declines and the rate of apostasy rises. This is most evident in the Sikh communities in foreign lands. In the United States, Canada and England the number of *keshdhari*[53] Sikhs is extremely small and ever-diminishing.[54]

In a survey of Sikh youths in Newcastle undertaken during 1968–9 Taylor found only four out of twenty-six wore turbans and virtually all the older men had dispensed with them.[55] Those boys who had worn turbans to school recounted how they had been mocked and stared at. However, in discarding their beards and turbans many Sikhs were acutely conscious of the religious implications of their actions and

[49] Aurora, G., *The New Frontiersmen: A Sociological Study of Indian Immigrants in the United Kingdom* (Bombay, 1967), 93.
[50] Ibid, 94; Desai, 10–11; John, D., *Indian Workers Associations in Britain* (London, 1969), 32; Helweg, 49; Hiro, 127–8, 149.
[51] Beetham, D., *Transport and Turbans: A Comparative Study in Local Politics* (London, 1970), 11.
[52] Bidwell, S., *Red, White and Black: Race Relations in Britain* (London, 1976), 57.
[53] Those adhering to *kesh* or uncut hair; see further below.   [54] At 304.
[55] Taylor, J., *The Half-Way Generation* (Slough, 1976), 75, 93.

were filled with shame, as one commentator has graphically pointed out—

When faced with this situation, Trilok Singh Dhami, a newcomer to Wolver-hampton, booked a passage home. But relatives and friends prevailed upon him to reconsider. He went through an agonising reappraisal of his religious identity. Reluctantly he cut his hair. 'Afterwards I felt less than a man', he later recalled. 'I didn't want to go out in the street: I didn't want to be seen by people. It was like I had got a scarred face overnight'. As with Dhami so with thousands of other Sikhs. Caught in the conflict between religious identity and economic interest, they submitted to the material need, but only at the cost of suffering a sense of spiritual degradation.[56]

Such departures from religious 'orthodoxy' were naturally viewed with alarm by the more devout members of the community and gradually the tide began to turn, as James has explained—

As the number of Sikhs in various towns increased, with wives and families, *gurdwaras*[57] were founded and self-contained communities developed, the wear-ing of *kesh* became more common—new arrivals did not shave, and some who had shaved felt shamed into growing their hair again.[58]

The leaders of this new trend were principally drawn from the Ramgar-hia caste who had come from East Africa.[59] It has been suggested that they were particularly concerned to improve their status here by encouraging a strict adherence to religious orthodoxy,[60] but others have stressed their commitment to traditionalism rather than caste riv-alry with the Jats as the crucial factor.[61] In any event the Ramgarhias were confident of the Sikhs' capacity to survive as a distinctive religious minority in Britain, in the light of their long experience of doing so successfully under British colonial rule in Africa.

From 1959 onwards a few Sikh individuals were prepared to make a personal stand on the issue, adopting a high profile and attracting a great deal of public attention in the media and generating much con-troversy. In each case a lengthy campaign had to be waged against public transport employers who were unwilling to employ Sikhs unless they were clean shaven.[62]

In 1959 Mr G. S. S. Sagar applied to Manchester City Council's trans-port department to be taken on as a bus conductor, wearing his beard and turban. He was rejected on the grounds that his turban did not conform with the current conditions of service in the department,

[56] Hiro 128; see also Aurora, 110–11; Thomas, 228–9.   [57] Sikh temples.
[58] James, A., *Sikh Children in Britain* (London, 1974), 49.   [59] See Kalsi, 88, 106–8.
[60] Ballard, R. and Ballard, C., 'The Sikhs' in Watson, J. (ed), *Between Two Cultures: Migrants and Minorities in Britain* (Oxford, 1977), 37–8.   [61] See Kalsi, 110, 186.
[62] See generally, Beetham, chs II and III.

despite the fact that the rule about busmen's caps was rarely adhered to or enforced in practice and that Mr Sagar was prepared to wear a navy blue turban with the City Council's badge on it.[63] The dispute which ensued took seven years to be resolved, including four full Council debates on the problem, and was said afterwards to have occupied more of the transport committee's time than any other single issue.[64] As part of his argument Mr Sagar drew attention to the acceptance of the turban as a suitable form of headgear in the British army throughout two world wars, in which some 80,000 Sikhs had been killed in combat and won numerous awards for gallantry.[65] If, as he so aptly put it, they could die for Britain in their turbans, why could they not also work for Britain in them?[66] However, by 1966 in view of strong trade union opposition to granting any group of workers 'special privileges', the transport committee still refused to amend the regulations about conductors' uniform and Mr Sagar appealed for support to Sant Fateh Singh, a revered Sikh religious and political leader, who happened to be on a visit to Britain.[67] He in turn took the matter up with politicians at both local and national level and reiterated the military analogy—if turbaned Sikhs could operate a tank they could surely drive a bus or ring a bell without endangering the safety of passengers or causing offence.[68] Soon afterwards the Council finally reversed its initial ruling against turbans, though by then Mr Sagar had passed the maximum age for recruitment of busmen and so could not personally benefit from the decision.

The other campaign took place in Wolverhampton. Mr Tarsem Singh Sandhu had been employed by the Council's transport department while he was clean-shaven. In 1967 he returned to work after an illness, wearing a beard and claiming to have undergone a spiritual revival. He was told by his employers that he was in breach of the regulations and must therefore go home and not return until he was clean-shaven. This dispute lasted for a period of two years and it required a mass march to the British High Commission in New Delhi, pressure from the Indian government, threats of suicide, and a visit to Wolverhampton by a minister of the British government before a decision was ultimately reached by the Council to authorize the wearing of beards and turbans by Sikh busmen.[69] Moreover, Enoch Powell, the Member of Parliament for Wolverhampton, was able to use the opportunity afforded by the controversy to issue dire warnings of the dangers of communalism arising from the presence of alien communities from 'beyond the oceans'

---

[63] Beetham, 3, 18.   [64] Ibid, 1.

[65] It has been calculated that Sikhs were awarded nearly half the medals won by members of the Indian army in the two world wars—see Collins, L. and LaPierre, D., *Freedom at Midnight* (London, 1975), 200.   [66] Beetham, 21.

[67] Ibid, 31–3.   [68] Hiro, 129.   [69] Ibid, 129–31.

insistent on preserving their own cultures here, leading to 'whole areas, towns and parts of towns' being 'occupied by different sections of the immigrant and immigrant descended populations', with the possibility of racial conflict and bloodshed.[70]

In the light of these highly publicized controversies thousands of Sikhs in Britain, who had previously resigned themselves to living with shorn hair, had to reconsider their positions. The obstinacy of various local authorities led many Sikhs to rededicate themselves to orthodox practice and several mass baptisms of adults occurred as a result.[71] Moreover, many Sikh parents prescribed long hair and turbans for their sons. By the mid-1970s, according to Helweg—

More men are growing their beards than before, and to be a Sikh is taking on greater pride. As people grow older and the community progresses through time, there is a resurgence of ethnic pride, and being a Punjabi Sikh Jat is taking on a higher meaning and greater significance for individuals and the society as a whole.[72]

In an unreported case decided in the Birmingham County Court in 1979 expert testimony was given that the proportion of Sikh men in England who adhered to the practice of wearing a turban was somewhere between two-thirds and three-quarters.[73] Although this estimate appears to have been accepted without demur by the judge, it was not based on any reliable social survey and must therefore be treated merely as conjecture. However, it can be set beside a more recent survey of 102 young Sikh women aged between sixteen and twenty, who were either born in this country or arrived here when they were under five years old.[74] Of these, 75 per cent were maintaining long hair, 54 per cent willingly and the others unwillingly, out of deference to their parents' wishes.[75] Moreover, Bhachu, writing in 1985, stated that the majority of East African Sikh men in England were wearing turbans and that their interest in doing so was on the increase.[76]

---

[70] See Holmes, C., *John Bull's Island: Immigration and British Society 1871–1971* (Basingstoke, 1988), 265.   [71] Ibid, 155; Helweg, 87–8, 91–2.

[72] Helweg, 140.

[73] *Commission for Racial Equality v Genture Restaurants Ltd.* The case is discussed further below. Only the decision of the Court of Appeal is reported in [1981] Race Relations Law Report 48.

[74] Drury, B., 'Sikh girls and the maintenance of an ethnic culture' (1991) *New Community* 387.   [75] At 390–1.

[76] At 50, 94.

BEARDS, TURBANS, AND THE NATURE OF SIKH IDENTITY

The origins of Sikhism lie in the teachings of its founder and first spiritual leader, Guru Nanak, who lived in the Punjab from 1469 to 1539.[77] He and the early gurus who succeeded him turned away from Hinduism and preached a simple monotheistic faith which stressed contemplation and hard work, while rejecting caste inequalities and the subservience of women. At the end of the seventeenth century, as Sikhism faced continuing oppression at the hands of the Mughal (Muslim) rulers of northern India, the tenth and last guru, Gobind Singh (1666–1708) institutionalized a transformation of the faith so that it took on a more militant and political stance. He had been strongly affected by the beheading of his father, Guru Tegh Bahadur, by the Mughals in 1675 and particularly distressed at the passive response of his fellow Sikhs to this event. They had shrunk from public acknowledgment of their faith, with no one being willing to come forward to claim the Guru's body for cremation.[78] From that moment Guru Gobind Singh determined that the Sikhs should be visibly distinct, so that their courage in openly declaring their faith could not fail them in the future. In dramatic fashion he established the *khalsa* ('the pure ones'), a community of baptized Sikhs who would defend the faith from all forms of attack, by force if necessary.[79] An expectant crowd had gathered at Anandpur to celebrate the new year festival in 1699 when, to everyone's astonishment, he suddenly demanded the heads of five loyal Sikhs who would be prepared to give their lives as a sacrifice for their faith. After much hesitation five volunteers came forward, each in turn being ushered into a nearby tent from which only the Guru himself emerged, carrying a blood-stained sword.

Eventually he returned to the crowd together with the five volunteers and revealed the existence of five dead goats lying in the tent. He proclaimed the five loyal followers to be the first members of a new order or brotherhood to be known as the *khalsa*, which would re-establish the foundations of Sikhism. Men who were baptized into the *khalsa* were all to adopt in common the surname of Singh (lion). This was designed to reflect their rejection of caste names and to express their fearless solidarity with one another.[80] These initiates would also be required to wear five symbols (the 'five Ks') comprising *kesh* (long hair), *kanga* (a comb), *kara* (a steel band worn on the right wrist), *kirpan* (a sword or dagger), and *kaccha* (special undershorts).[81] Guru Gobind

---

[77] See generally, Cole, W. and Sambhi, P., *The Sikhs: Their Religious Beliefs and Practices* (London, 1978), ch 2.   [78] See McLeod, 44.
[79] Khushwant Singh, vol 1, 82–3; Cole and Sambhi, 35–8; McLeod, 61–2.
[80] Women were to adopt the surname Kaur (lioness or princess).
[81] Khushwant Singh, vol 1, 84.

Singh further indicated that after his death the line of succession of human gurus would come to an end and the holy scriptures contained in the Guru Granth Sahib would henceforth provide the necessary religious teachings and guidance for adherents to the faith.[82]

Khushwant Singh has explained that observance of the five symbols defined the image of a member of the *khalsa* as representing a combination of the saint and the soldier.[83] On the one hand, long hair and a beard reflect the rejection of worldly concerns; on the other, the sword and the long undershorts would have formed part of a soldier's accoutrements in Guru Gobind Singh's time and the bangle might have given the arm some protection in military combat. The Guru himself did not give any explanation for the form of these symbols, but it seems clear that by making members of the *khalsa* easily and publicly identifiable he was seeking to make it virtually impossible for them to deny their faith when challenged. This in turn would breed a quality of defiant courage. Within a short time, according to Sikh chronicles, 20,000 men were baptized at Anandpur and many more at mass baptisms all over northern India. In the words of Khushwant Singh—

Within a few months a new people were born—bearded, be-turbaned, fully armed and with a crusader's zeal to build a new commonwealth.[84]

Since by no means all Sikhs undergo initiation into the *khalsa* or observe the 'five Ks', clear distinctions are currently recognized between at least three different groups—those who have been baptized (*amritdharis*); those who have not been baptized but nevertheless wear their hair long and do not shave (*keshdharis*); and those who fall into neither of these categories (*sahijdharis*).[85] No doubt the first two groups are widely perceived today, as in the past, as representing 'orthodox' Sikhism, but *sahijdharis* now appear equally entitled to be identified as adherents to the faith and members of the Sikh community.[86]

It is clear that during the nineteenth century there was a lengthy struggle in India over exactly who was properly qualified to be described as a Sikh, in which the British Raj played an important part.[87] Different groups in the Punjab described themselves as Sikhs, but they had separate images of what this label meant and followed a diversity of cultural practices. It was estimated that, even in Amritsar, for example, less than 10 per cent of those claiming to be Sikhs had been baptized into the *khalsa*.[88] Faced with such confusion over the nature of

---

[82] See e.g. Fox, R., *Lions of the Punjab: Culture in the Making* (Berkeley, 1985), 108–9.
[83] Vol 1, 86.　　[84] At 89–90.　　[85] McLeod, 7, 78–80.
[86] Ibid. In India the Sikh Gurdwaras Act 1925 defines a Sikh as one who believes in the Ten Gurus and the Guru Granth Sahib.　　[87] Fox, 110–11.
[88] Falcon, 120.

religious identity, those responsible for recruitment to the Indian army intervened decisively.[89] Having elected to give strong preference to the Sikhs as one of the 'martial races' and having adopted a policy of forming separate Sikh regiments and companies, they insisted upon Sikh recruits observing the full regalia of the orthodox *khalsa* identity in the belief (probably correct) that this would ensure higher morale and a stronger loyalty.[90] All those who enlisted had to undergo formal baptism in the *gurdwara* and British officers saluted or stood to attention before the book of holy scriptures, the Guru Granth Sahib.[91] All Sikh regiments and companies included *granthis*, readers of the scriptures, on their staff. In this calculating manner the British promoted their own version of what it meant to be a 'true' Sikh in pursuit of their own vested interests. Indeed, it has been suggested that recruitment into the Indian army brought about a revival in Sikhism, which had been somewhat in decline following British annexation of the Punjab in 1849. In 1899 a British officer went so far as to write—

Modern Sikhism, in fact, is to a large extent preserved from extinction by the encouragement it receives from the Indian army, which, by exacting a rigorous observance of the outward signs of the religion from all its Sikh soldiers, keeps the advantages of faith prominently before the eyes of the recruit-giving classes.[92]

Insofar, therefore, as many Sikhs living in England today attach considerable religious and cultural significance to adherence to the 'five Ks', this is at least partly due to the 'strange syncretism of British military form and Singh ritual symbolism',[93] which developed under the Raj. Their capacity to mobilize community support in recent years for the recognition of their cultural and religious distinctiveness by English institutions can thus be attributed in part to British administrative policy in India during the nineteenth century, which intensified awareness of religious differences and positively promoted the traditions of the *khalsa*.[94]

For members of the majority community in Britain the most striking characteristic of an orthodox Sikh man's appearance is undoubtedly his turban. Although not expressly included as one of the 'five Ks', pictorial representations of all the ten gurus show each of them wearing a turban and when Guru Gobind Singh instituted the *khalsa* he requested all male Sikh initiates to look like him.[95] Kalsi concludes that the fundamental

---

[89] Fox, 141–3.   [90] McLeod, 8.   [91] Fox, 141–2.
[92] Bingley, 57.   [93] Ibid, 143.
[94] See Beckerlegge, G., '"Strong cultures" and distinctive religions: the influence of imperialism upon British communities of South Asian origin' (1991) *New Community* 201 at 208.   [95] Cole and Sambhi, 110–11.

criterion of Sikh religious orthodoxy is 'the observation of the *Khalsa* discipline which means the wearing of Sikh symbols popularly known as the five K's and a turban'.[96] Wearing a turban possesses the valuable practical advantage of keeping long hair clean and tidy and in this respect complements the function of another of the five Ks, the comb (*kanga*), which holds hair fastened in a top-knot firmly in place. In this sense it may be viewed as an integral concomitant of *kesh*.[97] However, Cole and Sambhi reject the notion that its real purpose is functional and stress its symbolic importance in maintaining religious and social identity and cohesion.[98] They describe it as the 'hallmark' of a true Sikh,[99] adding—

The turban also serves as a uniform. In the Punjab, East Africa or London it makes the Sikhs stand out visibly from other men. When Gurus encouraged the wearing of the turban they did it partly to prevent non-Sikhs being picked upon and treated as Sikhs in time of local persecution and they did it also to prevent the less courageous of their followers deserting and merging with the crowd when the going became hard. A person known to hold certain beliefs is more likely to live by them; the Sikh who publicly demonstrates his allegiance by wearing a turban will be more likely to remain loyal . . . than one who dispenses with it and cuts his hair.[100]

THE LEGAL TUSSLES

As we have seen, the early years of Sikh settlement were characterized by the arrival of single men and an overriding concern for their economic welfare in terms of finding employment and housing. In this context beards and turbans were often sacrificed. However, as the community grew in size and confidence, and as families were formed or reunited here, many Sikhs increasingly turned their attention to the restoration and maintenance of their religious beliefs and cultural traditions. After the successful campaigns of the 1960s for beards and turbans to be worn by busmen in Manchester and Wolverhampton, the community and its leaders were ready to move beyond persuasion towards the demand for greater legal protection and for the acquisition of rights enshrined in law. Since the 1970s there have been several statutory changes and a number of judicial decisions in relation to these issues, each of which will be analyzed in turn.

[96] At 104.
[97] See Iqbal, M. (ed), *East Meets West: A background to some Asian faiths* (London, 1981), 103. [98] At 111.
[99] Ibid, 110. [100] Ibid, 110–11.

(a) Motor cycle helmets—the struggle for an exemption

The Road Traffic Act 1962 contained a provision authorizing the Minister of Transport to make regulations requiring persons driving or riding on motor cycles to wear protective headgear of a specified description.[101] Any person driving or riding a motor cycle in contravention of such regulations would be guilty of an offence.[102] Previous legislation had merely empowered the Minister to make regulations prescribing the types of helmet recommended as affording suitable protection to motor cyclists.[103] The provision in the 1962 Act was only brought into force in October 1971[104] and was soon afterwards incorporated in the largely consolidating Road Traffic Act 1972 as section 32. Under this section the Minister was authorized to exempt certain categories of persons from the regulations[105] and before making such regulations he was required to consult with such representative organizations as he thought fit.[106]

In April 1973 John Peyton, then Conservative Minister of Transport, received strong representations from the Sikh community requesting an exemption for those wearing turbans, but he declined to consult with any Sikh organizations and no such exemption was granted to Sikhs, or indeed any other group, in the Motor Cycles (Wearing of Helmets) Regulations[107] which came into force on 1 June 1973.[108] The Minister took the view that enforcement of the regulations would be made difficult if anyone was exempted and there was clear public support in the majority community for compulsory helmets, particularly in view of the vulnerability of young drivers and their pillion passengers and the number of serious head injuries recorded.[109] Government figures showed that around 800 motor cyclists and their passengers were killed every year, two-thirds of the deaths being attributable to head injuries.[110] It was estimated that by wearing a helmet the risk of death could be reduced by 40 per cent and the risk of serious injury by 10 per cent.[111]

Some Sikhs deliberately flouted the law and were duly convicted of the new offence, while others turned to political action. Ultimately, this 'agitation', as one critic characterized it,[112] was to prove successful. During the general election campaign in February 1974 candidates in constituencies with substantial Sikh populations were approached to see

---

[101] S 41(1).   [102] S 41(3).   [103] Road Traffic Act 1960, s 221.
[104] This was accomplished by Road Traffic Act 1962 (Commencement No. 7) Order, SI No. 1335 of 1971, following the suggestion of the Court of Appeal in *O'Connell v Jackson* [1972] 1 QB 270 at 277; the case is discussed further below.   [105] S 32(1).
[106] S 199(2).   [107] SI No. 180 of 1973, reg 3(1).
[108] Under reg 2(1) riders of scooters and mopeds were covered, as well as motor cyclists.
[109] See Bidwell, 59.   [110] HC Debs, 851, cols 342–3 (written answers).
[111] HC Debs, 853, col 234 (written answers).
[112] Lord Monson, HL Debs, 374, col 1064.

if they would support a change in the law.[113] One Sikh, Baldev Singh Chahal of High Wycombe, combined political activism with a direct challenge to the existing law. During the February 1974 election he stood as a candidate in the Ealing, Southall constituency, campaigning solely on this one issue, though he only won a few votes and lost his deposit.[114] Later, following his conviction by a magistrates' court of an offence under the 1973 regulations, he applied for an order of mandamus requiring the Aylesbury Crown Court (which had upheld his conviction) to state a case for an appeal to the High Court.[115] He contended *inter alia* that the 1973 regulations were *ultra vires* because the Minister had failed to consult with Sikh community representatives pursuant to the provisions of the 1972 Act and he argued that the Minister had failed to direct his mind to the wider policy implications of the regulations and their incompatibility with the public policy objectives underlying the Race Relations Acts 1965 and 1968 in protecting minority groups. Moreover, he alleged that the regulations were null and void as being in contravention of the guarantee of freedom of religion enshrined in the European Convention on Human Rights. None of these contentions, however, cut any ice with the Divisional Court, which dismissed his application as wholly without substance. Lord Widgery CJ declared—

No one is bound to ride a motor cycle. All that the law prescribes is that if you do ride a motor cycle you must wear a crash helmet. The effect of the Regulations no doubt bears on the Sikh community in this respect because it means that they will often be prevented from riding a motor cycle, not because of the English law but by the requirements of their religion.[116]

However, Sikhs could surely be forgiven for thinking that his Lordship was transparently wrong in stating that their faith precluded the riding of motor cycles when it clearly did not. It was the provisions of English law which had this effect.

When the Labour Government came to power as a result of victory at the general election in February 1974 the new Transport Minister, Fred Mulley, was pressed by a deputation of Labour MPs and Sikh leaders to change the law, but he declined to do so.[117] However, Sydney Bidwell, Labour MP for Ealing, Southall, a constituency with a substantial Sikh population, promptly presented a ten-minute rule bill in January 1975 proposing an exemption for turbaned Sikhs, and he gained considerable support from members of all political parties.[118] The bill failed to make progress for want of Parliamentary time, but the next Transport Minister, Dr John Gilbert, gave an undertaking that he would reconsider the

---

[113] Bidwell, 59.   [114] Ibid.
[115] *R v Aylesbury Crown Court, ex parte Chahal* [1976] RTR 489.
[116] At 492.   [117] Bidwell, 59–60.   [118] HC Debs, 885, cols 222–5.

issue.[119] Although the Government subsequently proved unwilling to take the initiative in the matter, it was prepared to adopt a neutral attitude when in December 1975 Sydney Bidwell introduced, as a private member's bill, a measure very similar to the one he had promoted in the previous session.[120] Curiously, the bill was never debated on the floor of the House of Commons itself, partly for obscure procedural reasons,[121] but there was full discussion in the relevant Standing Committee[122] and subsequently in two short debates in the House of Lords.[123] Five principal issues were raised.

First, there was some argument over whether the wearing of turbans by Sikhs was truly a religious requirement or merely a religious custom and hence whether the issue was genuinely one of religious tolerance. Lord Avebury, who had been entrusted with the task of piloting the bill through the House of Lords, asserted that there was 'absolutely no doubt whatsoever that the wearing of the turban is an essential part of the Sikh religion'.[124] He cited the practice of the ten gurus, a passage from the Guru Granth Sahib, and consultations with the *gurdwara* authorities in Bradford and Southall and he quoted from a forthcoming book by a distinguished Sikh scholar. Lord Avebury's assertion was, however, challenged by Lord Monson who declared that, according to his information, wearing a turban was merely a religious custom, not one of the basic tenets of Sikhism and not obligatory in the same way as the wearing of a *kirpan*.[125] During the course of the public campaign which had preceded the legislation Sir Herbert Thompson, the last British Resident for the Punjab States during the days of Empire, had written a letter to *The Times* to deny the claim that the wearing of a turban was a specific religious requirement[126] and Lord Monson drew attention to this refutation during the course of the debate on Third Reading.[127] Indeed Sir Herbert Thompson was clearly strongly opposed to granting any legislative exemption to the Sikhs, for in his letter he not only claimed that no one had ever suggested to him in the Punjab that Sikh soldiers should not wear helmets while on active service,[128] but he also viewed Sikh 'agitation' here as 'just another modern instance of the tendency of very small minorities to buoy up their status by establishing some privilege'. Despite this, several speakers in the Parliamentary debates seemed to accept that if many Sikhs in this country felt strongly enough

---

[119] Bidwell, 60.   [120] See HL Debs, 374, cols 1066, 1068.
[121] See HC Debs, 906, col 874; 915, cols 1142, 1295–6.
[122] *Report of HC Standing Committee 'F'*, 23 June 1976.
[123] HL Debs, 374, cols 1055–69; 376, cols 1163–75.   [124] Ibid, 374, col 1056.
[125] Ibid, col 1064.   [126] *The Times*, 11 Nov 1975.
[127] HL Debs, 376, col 1165.
[128] On the position of soldiers in the Indian army, see further below.

about the religious dimension and tradition, the central issue did become one of religious freedom and tolerance. Supporters of the Bill drew parallels with the existing specific religious dispensations for Jews in respect of Sunday trading and for Jews and Muslims in relation to the slaughter of animals.[129] Mention was also made of comparable motor cycle exemptions for Sikhs in several other common law jurisdictions, such as Western Australia, Malaysia, and Singapore.[130] The value of religious freedom was stressed by several speakers and Sydney Bidwell argued that without religious toleration and understanding 'we are lesser people'.[131]

The second question was whether the right to religious freedom should predominate over the principle of equal treatment in the enforcement of measures promoting road safety. Although such measures are primarily acts of paternalism on the part of the state, the cost of treating injuries through the National Health Service obviously has to be borne in mind. By 1976 the Ministry of Transport estimated that compulsory helmets were saving around 200 fatal and serious casualties each year.[132] Although some 80 per cent of motor cyclists had been using helmets before they were made compulsory in 1973,[133] many of those who could not be bothered to do so probably resented any special exemption being granted to the Sikhs.[134] In their view the criminal law should apply uniformly to all. The Government's position was summarized by Kenneth Marks, Under-Secretary of State for the Environment, as follows—

. . . can I dispose of the argument that a properly tied turban in itself provides adequate protection in the event of an accident involving a blow to the head? Motor cycle helmets are manufactured by very stringent British standards which lay down specifications concerning material, construction, shock absorption, resistance to penetration by a sharp object, and so on. I understand a turban has been tested and was shown to offer no measurable degree of protection. The Bill, therefore, is not based on road safety criteria. The need for road safety provisions is of tremendous importance. The Bill is based on religious tolerance and that, too, is an important and vital part of our society . . . There is no possibility of a compromise decision on this difficult choice . . . if Parliament

---

[129] *Standing Committee Report*, col 8.
[130] *Standing Committee Report*, col 9; HL Debs, 374, col 1057; see further below.
[131] *Standing Committee Report*, cols 6, 9.
[132] *Standing Committee Report*, col 10; HC Debs, 851, col 156 (written answers).
[133] Ibid. If moped and scooter riders were included the overall figure would be 75 per cent, see HC Debs, 851, cols 342–3.
[134] *Standing Committee Report*, cols 11, 16. According to a poll conducted by the magazine *Motorcycle Rider*, 69 per cent of respondents to a questionnaire had objected to any exemption being granted exclusively to Sikhs—see HL Debs, 376, col 1168.

concludes that in this case religious tolerance outweighs road safety and equality, the Government will accept that decision.[135]

Thirdly, concern was briefly expressed at possible abuse of the exemption by people masquerading as Sikhs through the simple device of donning a turban. The general feeling, however, was that the police would have little difficulty in determining the bona fides of those claiming to be Sikhs, especially in view of the co-operation likely to be forthcoming from the Sikh community itself.[136]

The fourth aspect of the debates was the stress laid by several speakers on the Anglo-Sikh military tradition. Sydney Bidwell drew attention to this as contributing substantially to the goodwill behind the bill, mentioning that he had received an account by a former general[137] of a Sikh soldier plucking bullets out of his long hair and turban 'and no one ever thought of trying to enforce a situation when he had to wear any other kind of headgear'.[138] He went on—

It is not surprising that the tradition is being carried on in the British Armed Forces. No Sikh in the Navy—I am talking of devout Sikhs—in the Army or in the Royal Air Force is obliged to wear the same kind of headgear as that worn by serving men.[139]

The Under-Secretary of State for the Environment spoke of the Sikhs' 'most prodigious record of honourable service to this country in the past'[140] and Winston Churchill referred to their contributions in two world wars, in which 'we did not then require them to wear a steel helmet in the front line of battle'.[141] Lord Mowbray and Stourton paid similar tribute and recounted an incident in which many Sikhs had given their lives at Gallipoli.[142] He went on—

. . . none of this would have been possible if we had attempted to force Sikh troops to wear tin hats . . . . This is recognised in the Indian Army today by the exemption of Sikh troops from the regulation on protective headgear. As General Sir Reginald Arthur Savory . . . who took part as a subaltern at the Gallipoli engagement which I mentioned, and who was later colonel-in-chief of the Sikh Regiment, has said, 'In our hour of need we did not press the matter of headgear on the Sikhs'. It would be downright ignoble . . . to press it now.[143]

Earl Grey, the next speaker, added a further detail—

When World War II was declared, a military order was issued stating that every soldier in the Indian Army should wear a steel helmet. The Sikhs refused to fight

---

[135] *Standing Committee Report*, col 11.   [136] See e.g. HL Debs, 374, cols 1067–8.
[137] This must have been General Sir Reginald Savory (referred to below)—see Bidwell, 57–8.   [138] *Standing Committee Report*, cols 5–6.
[139] *Standing Committee Report*, col 6.   [140] Ibid, col 10.   [141] Ibid, col 12.
[142] HL Debs, 374, col 1060.   [143] Ibid, col 1061.

if they were compelled to comply with that, and the order was later withdrawn in their favour.[144]

He was also able to cite the instance of a Sikh soldier who, having travelled from Singapore to this country to join the 10th Hussars, had unhesitatingly been granted permission by the regiment's commander-in-chief, the late Duke of Gloucester, to wear a turban displaying the regimental badge.[145]

The fifth aspect of the debates was concern that a ban on riding motor cycles without a helmet would have practical repercussions upon the employment opportunities open to Sikhs, for example as policemen or Post Office messengers or within motoring organizations such as the Automobile Association or Royal Automobile Club. Much progress had been made in gaining the acceptance by many major employers of their Sikh employees wearing turbans at work and such a ban would tend to undermine these advances.[146]

The upshot of the debates was that the Motor-Cycle Crash Helmets (Religious Exemption) Act was enacted into law in November 1976. Its main provision[147] simply inserted a new sub-section into the Road Traffic Act 1972, declaring that any requirement about helmets imposed by regulations made pursuant to section 32 'shall not apply to any follower of the Sikh religion while he is wearing a turban'.[148] This provision has since been re-enacted in the largely consolidating Road Traffic Act 1988.[149] As a result the Motor Cycle (Protective Helmets) Regulations now include a specific exemption for any Sikh wearing a turban.[150]

Neither the 1976 Act nor the section in the 1988 Act which replaced it contains any provision relating to the civil law implications of the exemption of turbaned Sikhs from criminal liability for failure to wear a helmet. If a Sikh motor cyclist is involved in an accident caused wholly by the negligence of another driver and his injuries are greater than he would have sustained had he been wearing a safety helmet, is he confined in a claim in tort against the other driver to a lower level of compensation on the basis of his decision to wear a turban rather than a helmet? Is he, to put it in technical terms, 'guilty' of 'contributory negligence'? The issue is governed by section 1(1) of the Law Reform (Contributory Negligence) Act 1945, which provides as follows—

---

[144] Ibid, cols 1061–2; Indian Army Order No. 329 of 1941 stated—'Indian Army Order No. 994 of 1940 is cancelled . . . steel helmets will not be issued to Sikhs nor will they be carried or worn by them unless the Sikhs of a particular unit unanimously ask to be allowed to do so'; see (1974) *New Community* 428.   [145] HL Debs, 374, col 1062.
[146] *Standing Committee Report*, col 7.   [147] S 1.   [148] S 32(2A).
[149] S 16(2).   [150] SI No. 1279 of 1980, as amended by SI No. 374 of 1981, reg 4(2)(c).

Where any person suffers damage[151] as a result partly of his own fault and partly of the fault of any other person or persons, a claim in respect of that damage shall not be defeated by reason of the fault of the person suffering the damage, but the damages recoverable in respect thereof shall be reduced to such extent as the court thinks just and equitable having regard to the claimant's share in the responsibility for the damage.

While the Sikh's failure to wear a helmet has clearly not contributed to the accident, it has contributed to his injuries and this is all that the section requires, provided, of course, that the Sikh's failure counts as 'fault' on his part. This involves a determination of whether he has failed to take reasonable care for his own safety. Traditionally, the standard of care expected of a plaintiff has generally been objective and impersonal in the sense of ignoring most personal idiosyncrasies, but the particular circumstances in which the plaintiff acts must also be borne in mind.[152] Hence in *Condon v Condon*[153] Bristow J took the view that a passenger in a car, who had a phobia about wearing a seat belt and was injured in an accident, should not be regarded as having failed to take reasonable care for her own safety in not wearing one.[154] In the light of this, while a judge might properly disregard a Sikh plaintiff's argument that he believed that a turban afforded as much protection as a helmet,[155] it is far less clear whether a court would be entitled to ignore his sincere religious belief that he could not conscientiously discard his turban in a public place.

There are two aspects to this dilemma. First, there seems to be a growing tendency for some judges to be willing to incorporate the notion of cultural values into an assessment of what constitutes reasonable behaviour since much behaviour is, at least in part, culturally determined. For example, in *DPP v Camplin*[156], a case on provocation, Lord Morris commented—

. . . it would now be unreal to tell a jury that the notional 'reasonable man' is someone without the characteristics of the accused . . . . If the accused is of . . . particular ethnic origin and things are said which to him are grossly insulting it would be utterly unreal if the jury had to consider whether the words would have provoked a man of different . . . ethnic origin—or to consider how such a man would have acted or reacted. The question would be whether the accused if

---

[151] 'Damage' includes loss of life and personal injury—s 4.
[152] See e.g. *Glasgow Corporation v Muir* [1943] AC 448 at 457.
[153] [1978] RTR 483.   [154] At 487–8.
[155] Cf *Froom v Butcher* [1976] QB 286 at 294 where the court stated that it was no excuse for the plaintiff to have sincerely believed that it was more dangerous to wear a seat belt in a car than not to do so.   [156] [1978] AC 705.

he was provoked only reacted as even any reasonable man in his situation would or might have reacted.[157]

Moreover, in three modern Australian cases involving personal injury claims, consideration has been given to the particular circumstances and backgrounds of immigrant plaintiffs in deciding whether they were acting reasonably or unreasonably in refusing to undergo surgical operations to mitigate injuries sustained by the negligence of the defendants.[158]

Secondly, the impact of the statutory exemption from criminal liability has to be borne in mind in assessing the reasonableness of a Sikh's behaviour in not wearing a helmet. In this regard two contrasting cases need to be examined. In *Hilder v Associated Portland Cement Manufacturers Ltd*[159] in 1961 it was held that failure on the part of a motor cyclist to wear a crash helmet did not amount to contributory negligence. At that time the wearing of helmets generally was not compulsory, nor was there any advice to take such precautions given in the current edition of the Highway Code.[160] Such advice was, however, contained in the 1968 edition of the Code and in 1971 the Court of Appeal ruled in *O'Connell v Jackson*[161] that a plaintiff who had failed to wear a helmet in such circumstances certainly was guilty of contributory negligence. The Court invoked section 74(5) of the Road Traffic Act 1960 which declared—

A failure on the part of a person to observe a provision of the Highway Code shall not itself render that person liable to criminal proceedings of any kind, but any such failure may in any proceedings (whether civil or criminal . . .) be relied upon by any party to the proceedings as tending to establish or to negative any liability which is in question in those proceedings.

Although the collision in which the plaintiff had been involved was caused wholly by the negligence of the defendant, the plaintiff had sustained additional injuries through his own fault in not wearing a helmet. The Court drew attention to the fact that under section 41 of the Road Traffic Act 1962 statutory authority already existed for the Minister of Transport to make regulations requiring the wearing of protective headgear in such cases and it indicated that it would welcome the introduction of such regulations.[162] The implication was that any

---

[157] At 721.
[158] See *Glavonjic v Foster* [1979] VR 536; *Karabotsos v Plastex Industries Pty Ltd* [1981] VR 675; *Fazlic v Milingimbi Community Inc* (1982) 38 ALR 424.
[159] [1961] 1 WLR 1434.   [160] At 1436.   [161] [1972] 1 QB 270.
[162] At 277. The court did not, however, seem to appreciate that s 41, though enacted in 1962, had still not been brought into force by the time of the hearing in the middle of 1971. This was only accomplished three months later by means of SI No. 1335 of 1971.

such statutory regulations would make the responsibility of an unhelmeted motor cyclist in a dispute over contributory negligence that much clearer.

By the time statutory compulsion was introduced in 1973 any motor cyclist would undoubtedly have been guilty of contributory negligence in failing to wear a helmet, but the creation of a specific exemption for turbaned Sikhs in 1976 has left the whole issue of the relationship between the criminal law and civil liability unclear so far as they are concerned. It would not be surprising if the courts were eventually to decide that, as a matter of law, turbaned Sikh motor cyclists riding without helmets were not to be regarded as failing to take reasonable care for their own safety. However, the question might instead be held to be one of fact,[163] namely whether a particular Sikh's failure to wear a helmet was in all the circumstances of the case a reasonable course of action for him to take. Both the inherent reduction in safety protection afforded by a turban and the extent of the plaintiff's religious commitment would then be vital matters to be considered, as well as the degree of risk involved in the particular journey undertaken.

Where the court rules that there has indeed been an element of contributory negligence, the damages recoverable by the plaintiff are to be reduced, in terms of the 1945 Act, 'to such extent as the court thinks just and equitable having regard to the claimant's share in the responsibility for the damage'.[164] The notion of such responsibility encompasses both causation and blameworthiness (or culpability)[165] and it is in relation to the latter aspect that an orthodox Sikh might expect considerable support from the court. Although blameworthiness is to be understood not in the sense of moral culpability but rather as failure to take reasonable care for one's safety,[166] it might be thought that comparatively little blameworthiness should attach to an orthodox Sikh in view of Parliament's express recognition of the compelling nature of his religious beliefs. Hence, even if in deciding the preliminary issue of fault the court adopts an entirely objective approach and ignores orthodox Sikh religious practice, it might still bear in mind the existence of the religious exemption in undertaking the exercise of apportioning damages.

This factor might well lead a court to disregard the normal tariff of reductions which, for pragmatic reasons related to cost, the courts have developed in relation, for example, to cases involving the failure to wear a seat-belt in a car. Here, regardless of whether the failure to wear the

---

[163] Cf *Hoadley v Dartford District Council* (1979) RTR 359.
[164] Law Reform (Contributory Negligence) Act 1945, s 1(1).
[165] See e.g. *Davis v Swan Motor Co (Swansea) Ltd* [1949] 2 KB 291 at 326; *Stapley v Gypsum Mines Ltd* [1953] AC 663 at 682.   [166] Cf *Pennington v Norris* (1956) 96 CLR 10 (Aus).

belt was 'entirely inexcusable or almost forgivable',[167] if the plaintiff's injuries would have been altogether avoided there is generally a reduction of 25 per cent, but if he would still have been injured, but less severely, the reduction is generally only 15 per cent.[168] While in principle there seems no difference between failure to wear a seat belt in a car and failure to wear a crash helmet on a motor cycle,[169] the courts might decide that they should be more generous to a turbaned Sikh since his failure to wear a helmet would be partly if not wholly excusable and forgivable. In *Capps v Miller*[170] a reduction of only 10 per cent was imposed upon the plaintiff motor cyclist's damages where his only fault lay in failing to fasten his helmet properly rather than neglecting to wear it at all. Whatever the precise deduction, if any, arrived at by the court in assessing the damages to be awarded to a turbaned Sikh motor cyclist, the award will undoubtedly reflect the fact that the main responsibility for his injuries lies with the person who caused the accident in the first place.[171]

(b) Indirect discrimination—reliance on a novel concept

The second sphere in which Sikhs have invoked the law has been through use of the race relations legislation. The Race Relations Act 1976 renders both direct and indirect discrimination unlawful in certain specified fields.

'Direct' racial discrimination occurs where one person treats another person less favourably than others and does so on racial grounds.[172] While it is a reasonably easy concept to understand in theory, it can be very difficult to prove in practice, for such blatant discrimination is invariably denied by the perpetrator.[173] Partly for this reason, the Act introduced into English law the novel concept of 'indirect' racial discrimination.[174] Such discrimination operates in a more subtle and insidious fashion, but it can be just as harmful to members of ethnic minority communities. It involves rules and practices which appear at first sight to be perfectly innocent and harmless because they apply the same requirements to everyone in a neutral fashion, regardless of their race or origins. However, upon closer examination these rules and practices

---

[167] *Froom v Butcher* [1976] QB 286 at 296.

[168] Ibid; these percentage reductions relate only to the category of injury causally related to the lack of a belt, e.g. head injuries. In *O'Connell v Jackson* [1972] 1 QB 270 the plaintiff motor cyclist's damages were reduced by 15 per cent because his failure to wear a helmet had partly contributed to his injuries.

[169] See *Capps v Miller* [1989] 2 All ER 333 at 339, 342.   [170] Ibid at 343.

[171] See *O'Connell v Jackson* [1972] 1 QB 270 at 278; *Froom v Butcher* [1976] QB 286 at 295.

[172] Race Relations Act 1976, s 1(l)(a).

[173] See e.g. *Khanna v Ministry of Defence* [1981] ICR 653 at 658.   [174] Section 1(1)(b).

turn out to have a disproportionately adverse impact upon members of such minority groups. The definition of indirect discrimination in the Act is extremely detailed, but in principle it should be comparatively simple to prove, if only because the perpetrator often openly admits to the rule or practice since its existence can so easily be established independently, either through the testimony of witnesses or by means of documentary evidence. The essential statutory ingredients of indirect discrimination are outlined below, prior to an examination of the particular fields in which individual Sikhs have been involved in legal proceedings with a view to asserting their rights under the Act.

The first element to be proved is the application by one person to another of 'a requirement or condition which he applies or would apply equally to persons not of the same racial group as that other'. This element relates to the apparently neutral rules and practices referred to earlier and, so far as Sikhs are concerned, these rules are usually found in the form of requirements that all males be clean-shaven and either wear no headgear at all or else only wear headgear of a particular type. The second ingredient in the definition is that the proportion of persons of the same racial group as the person to whom the requirement is being applied, who can comply with it, is considerably smaller than the proportion of persons not of that racial group who can comply with it. For example, it is obvious that the proportion of Sikh men who can comply with a 'no beards' or a 'no headgear' rule is considerably smaller than the proportion of non-Sikh men who can comply with it.[175] The phrase 'can comply' has been held to mean 'can in practice' comply or can do so 'consistently with the customs and cultural conditions' of their racial group, rather than can do so in physical terms.[176] To interpret the provision in the latter sense would be to render it devoid of any impact, since clearly even devout and orthodox Sikhs can physically shave off their beards and appear in public bare-headed. Thirdly, the application of the requirement or condition to the applicant must be to the detriment of that person owing to his inability to comply with it. This is established simply by showing that the rule has prevented the applicant from obtaining what was sought, such as access to employment, education or services. Fourthly, an allegation of unlawful indirect discrimination can only be substantiated if the discriminator cannot show the requirement or condition in question to be 'justifiable'. The defence of justifiability will be elaborated in detail below.

Of course, no complaint of unlawful indirect discrimination can

---

[175] To date there has been no clear judicial ruling as to what percentage is needed for the rate of compliance to be 'considerably smaller'.

[176] *Mandla v Dowell Lee* [1983] 2 AC 548 at 565–6.

succeed unless the claimant can demonstrate that he is a member of a distinct 'racial' group, which is disproportionately prejudiced by seemingly neutral requirements in the manner already described. At first sight Sikhs would appear not to qualify as a separate racial group, for in biological terms they are not easily distinguishable from other groups whose origins lie in the Punjab. What makes them markedly different from other Punjabis is, rather, their faith (together with its cultural manifestations), for they draw a clear line between their own religious beliefs and values and those of their Hindu and Muslim neighbours. However, while the Race Relations Act 1976 does not outlaw religious discrimination as such, the term 'racial group' is widely defined to mean 'a group of persons defined by reference to colour, race, nationality or ethnic or national origins'.[177] In the leading case of *Mandla v Dowell Lee*[178] the key question raised was whether the Sikhs could claim the protection of the Act on the basis that they did indeed constitute a racial group since they could be defined by reference to their ethnic origins. The county court judge ruled that 'ethnic' should be narrowly interpreted as meaning 'pertaining to race' and that on this basis the Sikhs did not qualify as an ethnic group, because their racial characteristics were the same as the other inhabitants of the Punjab. This decision was upheld by the Court of Appeal,[179] but it was eventually reversed by the House of Lords, who adopted a far broader construction of the word 'ethnic' and one more in keeping with modern usage. In the leading speech Lord Fraser stated—

My Lords, I recognise that 'ethnic' conveys a flavour of race but it cannot . . . have been used in the 1976 Act in a strict racial or biological sense. For one thing, it would be absurd to suppose that Parliament can have intended that membership of a particular racial group should depend on scientific proof that a person possessed the relevant distinctive biological characteristics (assuming that such characteristics exist). The practical difficulties of such proof would be prohibitive, and it is clear that Parliament must have used the word in some more popular sense. For another thing, the briefest glance at the evidence in this case is enough to show that, within the human race, there are very few, if any, distinctions which are scientifically recognised as racial.[180]

Having established that the word 'ethnic' carried wider connotations than merely 'racial' or 'biological', Lord Fraser next proceeded to identify its other ingredients as follows—

For a group to constitute an ethnic group in the sense of the 1976 Act, it must . . . regard itself, and be regarded by others, as a distinct community by virtue of

[177] S 3(1).   [178] [1983] 2 AC 548.   [179] [1983] QB 1.
[180] [1983] 2 AC 548 at 561.

certain characteristics. Some of these characteristics are essential; others are not essential but one or more of them will commonly be found and will help to distinguish the group from the surrounding community. The conditions which appear to me to be essential are these: (1) a long shared history, of which the group is conscious as distinguishing it from other groups, and the memory of which it keeps alive; (2) a cultural tradition of its own, including family and social customs and manners, often but not necessarily associated with religious observance. In addition to those two essential characteristics the following characteristics are . . . relevant; (3) either a common geographical origin, or descent from a small number of common ancestors; (4) a common language, not necessarily peculiar to the group; (5) a common literature peculiar to the group; (6) a common religion different from that of neighbouring groups or from the general community surrounding it; (7) being a minority or being an oppressed or a dominant group within a larger community, for example a conquered people . . . and their conquerors might both be ethnic groups.[181]

In reaching these conclusions about the criteria to be applied, Lord Fraser was clearly influenced both by the 1972 'Supplement to the Oxford English Dictionary'[182] and by a decision in 1979 by the New Zealand Court of Appeal,[183] both of which ascribed to 'ethnic' a broader, cultural dimension than that conveyed in earlier dictionary definitions found acceptable in the lower courts. Applying these criteria to the Sikhs, Lord Fraser drew attention to the fact that they are a distinctive and self-conscious community originally founded on religion, with a history going back to the fifteenth century, who possess a written language and who were at one time politically supreme in the Punjab.[184]

Lord Templeman, while adopting a rather narrower approach, also reached the same conclusion. For him, ethnicity required some of the characteristics of a race, namely group descent, a group of geographical origin, and a group history. He went on—

The evidence shows that the Sikhs satisfy these tests. They are more than a religious sect, they are almost a race and almost a nation . . . . As a nation the Sikhs defeated the Moghuls and established a kingdom in the Punjab which they lost as a result of the first and second Sikh wars; they fail to qualify as a separate nation . . . because their kingdom never achieved a sufficient degree of recognition or permanence. The Sikhs qualify as a group defined by ethnic origins because they constitute a separate and distinct community derived from the racial characteristics I have mentioned.[185]

The decision by the House of Lords that Sikhs and their turbans were covered by the 1976 Act corresponded with the intentions of the government of the day in framing the legislation in such a way as to outlaw

---

[181] At 562.   [182] At 561–2.   [183] *King-Ansell v Police* [1979] 2 NZLR 531.
[184] At 565.   [185] At 569.

indirect discrimination. A White Paper entitled 'Racial Discrimination' published in 1975 had specifically declared—

The provision [about indirect discrimination] will . . . apply to requirements concerning . . . clothing . . . (e.g. preventing the wearing of turbans or saris) . . . .[186]

The decision was also a triumph for commonsense, in reflecting both the popular understanding of the word 'ethnic' and the ordinary person's view about the desirability of affording a group such as the Sikhs protection from discrimination in English society. In a subsequent case Stocker LJ indicated that the Sikhs were almost self-evidently an ethnic group and that ordinary members of the public would have had little doubt about it, adding, perhaps rather too generously—

Many, if not all, of the general public would know that there had been two Sikh wars and would know that for generations regiments of Sikhs formed a part of the Indian Army and were often a symbol, through their presence on guard at British Embassies and establishments, of British Imperial power based on the Indian Army and the British Army in India . . . . They would know of their distinctive dress and probably some of their customs regarding hair and the wearing of turbans.[187]

Since 1976 Sikhs have relied upon the indirect discrimination provisions of the Act in three separate fields, namely education, entertainment facilities, and employment. The litigation in each of these fields will be examined in turn.

(i) Education

Section 17(c) of the Act provides that it is unlawful for the body responsible for an educational establishment to discriminate against a pupil 'in the way it affords him access to any benefits, facilities or services, or by refusing or deliberately omitting to afford him access to them or . . . by excluding him from the establishment or subjecting him to any other detriment'.

In *Mandla v Dowell Lee* the plaintiffs, an orthodox Sikh and his son Gurinder (both born in Kenya), claimed that the defendant, the headmaster of a private school in Birmingham, had committed an act of unlawful discrimination by refusing to admit Gurinder as a pupil. The headmaster had declined to accept Gurinder because the school's rules

---

[186] Cmnd 6234 of 1975, para 55. See also the statement of the Government spokesman, Mr Brynmor John MP, during the committee stage of the Bill—*Official Report*, Standing Committee 'A', 4 May 1976, cols 102–3.
[187] *Commission for Racial Equality v Dutton* [1989] 1 QB 783 at 809.

prescribed a particular uniform, including a cap, and required boys to have their hair cut short so as not to touch the collar, whereas Gurinder (aged thirteen) wished to observe *kesh* and wear a turban. Once the House of Lords had determined that the Sikhs constituted a racial group on the basis of their ethnic origins, the first element of indirect discrimination was close to being established. The headmaster had applied to the plaintiffs a requirement or condition, namely a rule specifying short hair and a school cap, which he applied equally to boys who were not Sikhs but which was such that the proportion of Sikhs who could comply with it was considerably smaller than the proportion of non-Sikhs who could so comply. As we have seen, the House of Lords interpreted the phrase 'can comply' as meaning 'can in practice' or 'can consistently with the customs and cultural conditions' of the racial group in question, rather than 'can physically' comply.[188] Once this point had been clarified the House of Lords took it for granted that the proportionality test was satisfied. Since a detriment had clearly been caused to Gurinder through his failure to gain a place at the school, the only remaining issue was whether the defendant could show the rule about uniform to be 'justifiable'.

The headmaster sought to argue that the school rule was justifiable on two separate grounds. The first reason given was that of practical convenience, in that the school was seeking to minimise the external differences between boys of different races and social classes, to discourage the competitive fashions which tend to exist in a teenage community, and to present a Christian image of the school to outsiders, including prospective parents. The headmaster drew attention in particular to the difficulty of explaining to a non-Sikh pupil why the rules about wearing correct school uniform were strictly enforced against him while they were relaxed in the case of a Sikh pupil. Lord Fraser held that none of these reasons either individually or collectively could provide a sufficient justification for what was *prima facie* a discriminatory school rule and hence they did not really warrant serious consideration.[189] The second attempted justification was that the headmaster was seeking to run a Christian school, while accepting pupils of a variety of faiths and races, and that he objected to the wearing of a turban because it was an outward manifestation of a non-Christian faith, indeed it represented a challenge to Christianity. While more sympathetic to this method of trying to justify the ban on turbans, Lord Fraser was compelled to reject it in the light of the wording of the Act, which requires the defendant to show that the rule is 'justifiable irrespective of the . . . ethnic . . . origins of the person to whom it is applied'.[190] Here the justification offered by

---

[188] At 565–6.   [189] At 566.   [190] Ibid.

the headmaster was not irrespective of Gurinder's ethnic origins but precisely because the display of them through his turban was so objectionable. For his part, Lord Templeman contented himself with simply adding—'The discrimination cannot be justified by a genuine belief that the school would provide a better system of education if it were allowed to discriminate'.[191]

The final upshot of the case, therefore, was that the plaintiffs obtained a declaration that the headmaster had committed an act of unlawful discrimination. This was of no practical value to Gurinder, who had completed his secondary schooling elsewhere by the time the decision of the House of Lords was announced, but a vital point of principle had been established and the public profile of the Sikhs had been enhanced both by the struggle itself and by its successful outcome.

(ii) Entertainment facilities

Section 20 of the Act makes it unlawful for any person connected with the provision to the public of facilities for entertainment, recreation or refreshment to discriminate against a person seeking to use those facilities by refusing to provide them.[192] Section 48 empowers the Commission for Racial Equality to conduct formal investigations into possible cases of discrimination and, if satisfied that a person is committing acts of discrimination, it may issue a 'non-discrimination notice' under section 58(2) requiring him to cease doing so. In *Commission for Racial Equality v Genture Restaurants Ltd*[193] the Commission had issued such a notice to the defendant company, the proprietor of Pollyanna's nightclub in Birmingham. One of the acts of discrimination complained of was a refusal by the club to grant admission to a Sikh merely because he was wearing a turban. The Commission sought to obtain an injunction under section 62 of the Act restraining any further unlawful acts of a similar nature, but first it had to establish that the club's general 'no headgear' rule amounted to indirect discrimination.

The case was decided by the Birmingham County Court in 1979 before the pronouncements of the Court of Appeal and the House of Lords in *Mandla v Dowell Lee*. The County Court found no difficulty in ruling both that the Sikhs constituted a racial group on the basis of their ethnic origins and that a considerably smaller proportion of them could comply with the club's 'no headgear' rule. On the basis of expert testimony given by Indarjit Singh, the editor of the 'Sikh Courier' and an executive member of the Sikh Cultural Society, the Court considered that only between one-quarter and one-third of Sikh men here had abandoned

---

[191] At 570.   [192] S 20(l)(*a*), (2)(*e*).   [193] [1981] Race Relations Law Report 48.

wearing the turban and hence could comply with the rule, in comparison with virtually the entire non-Sikh male population who could easily do so. The defendant company sought to show that the rule was justifiable upon a number of grounds, which were so transparently weak that the Court dismissed them all out of hand. One of these was that the rule reflected custom, good manners, and ordinary etiquette on the part of the public at large. The Court felt that the rule could only be justified in this manner if applied to the world outside the Sikh community and that the same good manners required a tolerance of rules of other ethnic groups whose religious observance demanded it.

In the event, there was no need for the Court to grant an injunction because once it had been decided that the defendant's 'no headgear' rule was unlawful, the company quickly gave an undertaking to the Court that it would not in future refuse admission to its premises or the provision of facilities for entertainment, recreation or refreshment 'to any member of the Sikh community solely by reason of his wearing a turban'.[194]

In 1984 in the case of *Gurmit Singh Kambo v Vaulkhard*[195] the Court of Appeal similarly upheld a decision by the Newcastle County Court that the licensee of a public house had unlawfully discriminated against a turbaned Sikh by refusing him admission because of a 'no-headgear' rule. However, since the discrimination was indirect and the licensee had not intended to treat the plaintiff Sikh unfavourably on racial grounds the Race Relations Act precluded the award of any damages to the plaintiff[196] and he had to be content with a declaration that the licensee's action was unlawful.

(iii) Employment

Under section 4 of the 1976 Act it is unlawful *inter alia* to discriminate against a person either in the terms upon which employment is offered or by refusing to offer employment or through dismissal from employment. There have been several cases in which Sikhs have brought proceedings under this provision alleging that discrimination had been practised against them purely on the basis that they were wearing beards or turbans.[197]

---

[194] At 52.   [195] *The Times*, 7 Dec 1984.   [196] S 57(3).

[197] For an earlier case in which a Sikh unsuccessfully brought an action for 'unfair dismissal' under the Trade Union and Labour Relations Act 1974 after being sacked for insisting upon wearing a beard in an ice-cream factory in contravention of company rules, see *Singh v Lyons Maid Ltd* [1975] IRLR 328. The main question for decision in that case was whether the employer had acted reasonably in treating the employee's conduct in refusing to shave off his beard as sufficient reason for dismissal. Since being clean-shaven was

In the first two cases, decided during 1979–80, orthodox Sikh men had applied for jobs at confectionery factories. Both men had been refused employment because the companies in question had rules prohibiting the wearing of beards by all those employees working at the particular factories to which the Sikhs had applied, who came into contact with the factories' products. In both cases it was assumed, rather than decided, that Sikhs as a group were protected by the Act, a question ultimately determined in their favour by the House of Lords in *Mandla v Dowell Lee* in 1983. In both cases it was also taken for granted that the indirect discrimination provisions were satisfied in the sense that the proportion of Sikhs who could comply with a 'no beards' rule was considerably smaller than the proportion of non-Sikhs who could do so.

In *Singh v Rowntree Mackintosh Ltd*[198] the Employment Appeal Tribunal held that the 'no beards' rule was justified on grounds of hygiene. However, the employers had to surmount the difficulty that while they enforced the rule rigidly in their factories at Edinburgh (where the complainant had applied for work) and Newcastle, they did not do so at their six other factories in the United Kingdom, and even at Edinburgh they allowed employees to have moustaches and side-whiskers. Perhaps somewhat surprisingly, the Tribunal's attitude towards the disparity between the various factories was to see it as reflecting credit upon the higher standard of hygiene maintained at the Edinburgh factory rather than undermining the logical consistency of the employers' case. Lord MacDonald concluded—

. . . in this industry at least an employer must be allowed some independence of judgement as to what he deems commercially expedient in the conduct of his business. Standards of hygiene may vary between manufacturers and indeed between sections of the consuming public. We do not consider that an employer can be said to have acted unjustifiably if he adopts a standard in one of his factories which is supported by medical advice and which has the approval of a local food and drugs officer. He cannot reasonably be said to have adopted such a standard as a matter of convenience. It could more properly be described as a commercial necessity for the purposes of his business.[199]

As to the question whether there was a reasonable alternative method of achieving the level of hygiene demanded by the employers, such as by requiring bearded employees to wear face masks, this had clearly been considered by the industrial tribunal at first instance and rejected.

a condition of his employment (and one which he had complied with for the previous six years) and since the process of manufacturing ice cream requires high standards of hygiene, the industrial tribunal ruled that his dismissal was not unfair. The case was decided before the enactment of the Race Relations Act 1976. [198] [1979] ICR 554.

[199] At 577–8.

Apparently it did not, therefore, warrant any further investigation on appeal.

In *Panesar v Nestle Co Ltd*[200] a similar overall conclusion was reached by the industrial tribunal and its ruling was upheld by the Employment Appeal Tribunal and the Court of Appeal. The industrial tribunal found, first, that all the evidence pointed to the need for improving the standards of hygiene applied within the food production industry; secondly, that while beards were not the only potential cause or even a major potential cause of bacterial infection or contamination, the company was entitled to maintain a regulation against a well recognised risk; and thirdly, that the interests of the public and of consumers were best served by taking all reasonable precautions to maintain the quality of their products.

In a third case, *Kuldip Singh v British Rail Engineering Ltd*,[201] a turbaned Sikh employed in one of British Rail's engineering workshops brought an action against his employers alleging unlawful discrimination, on the ground that he had been demoted for failure to wear a type of hard hat known as a 'bump cap'. This form of protective headgear had been introduced, on a voluntary basis, for employees working in the applicant's section of 'scotchers' long after he himself had started work there. No steps had actually been taken to enforce the wearing of these bump caps because the employers hoped that by a process of education and persuasion the workforce would gradually be willing to wear them, but the applicant had made it clear from the start of discussions that he would not do so in any circumstances because it would involve discarding his turban.

In rejecting the applicant's complaint the industrial tribunal held that the requirement to wear a bump cap was justifiable for the following reasons. First, although the risk of injury was admittedly very small and no reportable accident had occurred during the twelve-year period in which the applicant had worked in the section, the wearing of protective headgear could reduce the risk of injury still further and a reasonable and responsible management was entitled to make up for past neglect in not introducing such measures earlier. Secondly, in the absence of such a requirement, it was possible that the employers would be in breach of their duties under the Health and Safety at Work etc. Act 1974 and might leave themselves open to a claim for damages by an injured employee. Thirdly, a special exception could not be made for the applicant because this would be resented by the other (non-Sikh) members of his section, who would themselves then be likely to refuse to wear bump caps. The internal discipline of the rest of the workforce would thus probably

---

[200] [1980] ICR 144.   [201] [1986] ICR 24.

decline as a result. Exceptions made by the Army and the Police for turbaned Sikhs, as well as the statutory exemption for Sikh motor cyclists, were regarded as irrelevant by the tribunal to the specific issue in this dispute. The upshot of the case was, therefore, that while the tribunal clearly felt the employers had behaved unreasonably in demoting the applicant rather than finding him a post in an equivalent grade, no unlawful discrimination was held to have occurred. The decision was upheld by the Employment Appeal Tribunal, principally on the basis that the question whether a discriminatory requirement is justifiable is essentially one of fact for the industrial tribunal to decide and its finding in this regard could not be regarded as 'perverse'. In particular, the Employment Appeal Tribunal rejected the argument that there was no realistic possibility of the employers ever incurring any liability in permitting the applicant to work without protective headgear, declaring—

It seems to us that it would be remarkable if conscientious employers, aware of a real risk to their employee in the place of work they provide for him, and aware that they can eliminate or reduce the risk by insisting on a safety requirement, are precluded by law from such insistence. We accept that . . . the chances of an employee or his personal representative suing successfully for damages in the event of an accident are not high because of the defences open to the employers that having provided the protective headgear and urged that it be worn, it has not been in breach of its duty of care and that the damage to the employee was not caused by the breach. But we find ourselves unable to say that this is only a fanciful . . . possibility that the employer will be held liable in the particular circumstances that they had knowingly exposed an employee whom they themselves believed to be inadequately protected to a real risk known to them.[202]

So far as criminal liability was concerned, the employers had been unable to obtain an assurance from the Health and Safety Executive that they would not be prosecuted under the Health and Safety at Work etc. Act for failing to ensure the safety of their employees. Nor could any support for the applicant's case be derived from the Motor-Cycle Crash Helmets (Religious Exemption) Act, precisely because Parliament had not specifically provided a dispensation in the field of employment law for Sikhs who refused to wear protective headgear, in the same manner as it had done in road traffic law.

Eventually, in 1988 a Sikh was successful for the first time in his claim of indirect discrimination in a case in which his employers were unable to establish that their rule was justifiable. In *Kamaljeet Singh Bhakerd v Famous Names Ltd*[203] the employers, chocolate manufacturers, had a rule requiring all their employees to wear 'mob caps' which were provided

---

[202] At 27. For further discussion of a claim for damages in such circumstances, see below.
[203] Case number 19289/87, unreported, decision dated 18 Feb 1988.

by the company, kept on their premises, and laundered by them. The applicant was refused a job by the company simply because he wanted to wear a turban rather than one of these company caps. The industrial tribunal (by a majority) ruled that the company's requirement was unjustifiable because the high standards of hygiene demanded by the company in order to comply with the Food Hygiene (General) Regulations 1970 could equally well be achieved by allowing Sikhs to wear turbans as by insisting that they wore company caps. Both would prevent hair falling into the chocolates. The company could easily make a special arrangement for Sikh workers and, if necessary, insist that turbans worn in the factory be laundered on the company's premises and be inspected regularly for cleanliness. The sheer convenience of the company's rule did not mean that it was justifiable within the terms of the 1976 Act.

In the period which has elapsed since all these decisions were reached in the employment field, the higher courts[204] have established a new test of justifiability designed to bring the law on race relations into line with comparable provisions on sex discrimination.[205] As a result, employers can now only show that an act of discrimination is justifiable if they can demonstrate that there was no viable alternative method of achieving the outcome they desired.[206] They must show that the means chosen for achieving their objective 'correspond to a real need on the part of the undertaking, are appropriate with a view to achieving the objective in question and are necessary to that end'.[207] This test of 'objective necessity' had previously been rejected by the courts.[208] However, had it been adopted in *Singh v Rowntree Mackintosh, Panesar v Nestle* and *Kuldip Singh v British Rail Engineering Ltd* the outcomes might have been different, for the hygiene and safety risks were not very substantial and there might well have been satisfactory alternative methods of tackling the problems perceived by the employers, without having to bar Sikhs from wearing their beards and turbans. Beards, for instance, can be neatly covered by face masks or nets known as 'snoods'.[209] Similarly, protective headgear can sometimes be worn over a lightweight turban[210] by those engaged in hazardous activities and with this in mind special

---

[204] See *Hampson v Department of Education* [1990] 2 All ER 25 (CA); *Webb v EMO Air Cargo (UK) Ltd* [1992] 4 All ER 929 (HL).

[205] See e.g. *Rainey v Greater Glasgow Health Board* [1987] AC 224.

[206] See *Bilka-Kaufhaus v Weber von Hartz* [1986] ECR 1607.   [207] At 1629.

[208] See e.g. *Ojutiku v Manpower Services Commission* [1982] IRLR 418 at 422.

[209] Even surgeons are allowed to have beards, which they cover when performing operations.

[210] Some orthodox Sikhs, however, may not feel that they can conscientiously wear any covering over a turban; this was the view taken by the applicants in *Kamaljeet Singh Bhakerd v Famous Names Ltd* and *Kuldip Singh v British Rail Engineering Ltd* (above).

helmets have occasionally been manufactured for Sikh riders, jockeys,[211] and airmen.[212] Hence, while bans on beards and turbans for reasons of hygiene and safety are entirely plausible they may not, upon close examination, be objectively necessary to achieve the legitimate objectives of employers.

(c) Building workers—a successful campaign

In 1979 the Health and Safety Commission published a discussion document entitled 'Safety helmets on construction sites' based on work done by its Construction Industry Advisory Committee. Its principal conclusion was that safety helmets should be worn by all personnel and visitors on construction sites, save where it was absolutely clear that there was no risk of head injury.[213] The Commission recommended that the construction industry should prepare a voluntary code of practice making the wearing of such helmets a condition of employment. As a result a number of working rule agreements were signed by the National Joint Councils for the building and civil engineering sectors of the industry and these came into effect in 1981. However, a survey of their effectiveness in 1982 revealed that on nearly two-thirds of sites there had apparently been no increase in the wearing of helmets. Subsequent reports suggested that, while there had been some overall increase between 1982 and 1986, the wearing rate still did not exceed 30 per cent.[214]

This led the Construction Industry Advisory Committee to conclude that self-regulation had proved unsuccessful. Knowledge of the working rule agreements was poor, insufficient equipment was provided, and the decision whether or not to wear a helmet was largely left to the individual workers themselves. Yet analysis of head injury data for the two years 1981 and 1982 had revealed a substantial problem. Some 2000 accidents involving injury to a single location of the head and causing absence from work of more than three days had been reported to the Health and Safety Commission by the construction industry. Just over 20 per cent were classified as serious involving fractures, concussions or

---

[211] In 1984 Toby Balding, the racehorse trainer, commissioned the manufacture of a special skull cap to be fitted over the lightweight turban worn by the Sikh jockey, Daljeet Kalirai, so as to comply with the rules of the Jockey Club.

[212] See the obituary of the remarkable diplomat and sportsman Sardar Hardit Singh Malik in *The Times*, 4 Nov 1985. The first Indian to obtain a commission in the Royal Flying Corps in 1917, he had an outsize flying helmet made for him by a hatter in Picadilly, to be worn over his turban. He subsequently became Indian Ambassador to Canada (1947–49) and later to France (1949–56).

[213] See Health and Safety Commission, 'Proposals for Regulations requiring Head Protection in Construction Work' (London, 1987) 1.   [214] Ibid, 2.

internal injuries. In each year at least one death (and possibly as many as four) caused by falling objects or materials would, in the Commission's view, have been prevented by the wearing of a suitable safety helmet.[215] In the light of this the Construction Industry Advisory Committee felt that there was a need for legal regulations to be introduced making the wearing of helmets compulsory. A 'Consultative Paper' along these lines was, therefore, issued by the Health and Safety Commission in 1986, in which it was estimated that if everyone on construction sites wore helmets there could be a reduction of up to one third in non-fatal head injuries as well as the prevention of some fatalities.[216]

The Commission was aware of the difficulty such mandatory requirements would impose on Sikh building workers, of whom there were reckoned to be around 40,000, and commented—

Work in Canada[217] and by the Health and Safety Executive[218] has shown . . . that the turban provides generally poor protection and certainly does not give the same degree of protection for the head as a standard industrial safety helmet, particularly in respect of risks to the crown of the head from falling objects. Health and safety considerations therefore provide no justification for treating Sikh workers differently from other groups and they could not be excluded in Health and Safety Regulations for a purpose not connected with health and safety. The only way this could be achieved would be by primary legislation, as in the Motor-Cycle Crash Helmets (Religious Exemption) Act 1976. The Commission appreciates the strength of feeling in the Sikh community on this question and would welcome comments on it.[219]

The Commission received a large number of representations from members of the Sikh community demanding an exemption and many Members of Parliament were lobbied about the issue. The upshot was that before the Construction (Head Protection) Regulations 1989,[220] giving effect to the Commission's proposals, came into force on 30 March 1990, Parliament enacted a specific exemption for turbaned Sikhs. This was accomplished through the Government's hurried insertion, at the end of

---

[215] See Health and Safety Commission, 4.   [216] Ibid, 6.

[217] This refers to Biokinetics and Associates Ltd, 'An evaluation of the protective capabilities of Sikh turbans' (Ottawa, 1979).

[218] This refers to Rowland, F., 'Comparison of the Impact Protection Properties of Sikh Turbans and Industrial Safety Helmets' (1987) 9 *Journal of Occupational Accidents* 47. This research demonstrated that the forces transmitted to the head at comparable impact energies were almost five times greater when a turban was worn instead of an industrial safety helmet, for the major part of the head area.   [219] At 11.

[220] SI No. 2209 of 1989. In terms of these Regulations every employer must ensure, so far as it is reasonably practicable, that each of his employees wears suitable head protection unless there is no foreseeable risk of injury to his head other than by his falling (reg 4) and every employee who has been provided with suitable head protection must wear it when required to do so by rules made or directions given by his employer (reg 6). Self-employed persons are similarly obliged to wear suitable head protection pursuant to reg 6 (2) and (3).

the 1988–89 session of Parliament, of a set of amendments to the Employment Bill 1989 during the Committee stage in the House of Lords, some time after the bill had already completed its passage through all its stages in the House of Commons. Introducing the amendments, Lord Strathclyde indicated that the Government's decision to exempt Sikhs was not an easy one in view of its firm commitment to improving safety standards in the construction industry. On balance, however, it had adopted the position that 'the wider issues of religious freedom and relations with the Sikh community must take precedence'.[221] During the course of the debates in the House of Lords, and those in the House of Commons when the amended bill was brought back, a number of issues were raised by opponents of the proposed exemption. Their arguments and those used to rebut them can conveniently be summarized as follows.

First, it was alleged that the exemption constituted positive discrimination in favour of one particular religion and thus discriminated against those who were not Sikhs.[222] The Government denied that Sikhs were being afforded any special privilege, pointing out that a failure to exempt them would in itself represent an act of indirect discrimination because of the disproportionately adverse impact which the helmet requirement would have upon Sikh workers.[223]

Secondly, it was suggested by opponents that the exemption would breed resentment on the part of non-Sikh workers, who disliked wearing helmets because they were hot and gave rise to a feeling of claustrophobia.[224] Others doubted, however, whether there would be much resentment or resistance on the part of non-Sikh workers.[225] Lord Boyd-Carpenter commented—

Most of us . . . greatly respect people who take their religion sufficiently seriously to adopt this line. They must be aware of the increased risk of injury to themselves in the event of an accident. They have apparently weighed this up and have come to the conclusion that their duty to their religion, their faith in it, demands that they should not wear a helmet. The Government are right to accept that view.[226]

Thirdly, the Government's justification of the exemption on the basis of good relations with the Sikh community was severely attacked by Mr John Townend, Conservative MP for Bridlington. From the offensive tone of his speech it seems clear that, in his view, the Sikhs should never have been allowed to enter the United Kingdom in the first place, but

---

[221] HL Debs, 511, col 738.
[222] HL Debs, 511, cols 738–9; 512, cols 69, 72; HC Debs, 159, col 1109.
[223] HL Debs, 512, cols 76, 78.   [224] HL Debs, 511, col 739; HC Debs, 159, col 1109.
[225] HL Debs, 511, cols 740, 744.   [226] HL Debs, 511, col 740.

once here they should at least have been assimilated as fast as possible. He declared—

The British people have accepted millions of immigrants from the new Commonwealth since the war. As a result we have, for better or worse, ceased to be a white, homogenous society and become a multi-racial society, with all the problems that that brings. The British people were never consulted and all the polls show that if they had been consulted they would have consistently opposed mass immigration, which has fundamentally changed the country in which they live. Despite that, however, they have accepted the newcomers with a generosity and tolerance that few other countries have shown. The British people have accepted that they must integrate with the newcomers. They have accepted that everyone should be treated equally under the law and, to ensure that there is no discrimination they have rightly been told that they must accept the Race Relations Act 1976.

Since the British people have so generously accepted the newcomers, it behoves the newcomers to integrate and to become English. Whether they are brown, black, yellow or white, they should become English in England and Scots in Scotland. They should accept our laws, our history, our traditions and our tolerance. Unfortunately, the great and the good in this country are not satisfied with having created a multi-racial society—they now want a multicultural society, which will prevent assimilation and Anglicisation and will result in Britain ceasing to be one nation and becoming several nations. The new clause is fundamental to the change of policy. An ethnic minority, albeit for religious reasons, is to be treated differently under the law from the rest of the community. Separate laws for separate communities are divisive and unwise, particularly when they involve the safety of others.[227]

He went on—

When immigrants from different countries and with different beliefs come to a Christian country they should be prepared to accept our laws and our way of life. If they do not wish to do so, they have a choice. They do not need to work in the construction industry because there are plenty of other jobs available . . . .

I beg the Government to go no further down this path as it is divisive and discriminatory. We must stop encouraging the development of a multi-cultural society. We must all be equal before the law whether we are brown, black or white.[228]

This diatribe clearly left several MPs feeling distinctly uneasy[229] and several speakers in both Houses drew attention to British traditions of freedom of religion, tolerance, and respect for the cultures of others.[230] Lord Strathclyde expressed the Government's position forcefully—

---

[227] HC Debs, 159, cols 1107–8.   [228] Ibid at cols 1108–9.
[229] HC Debs, 159, cols 1112, 1115.   [230] Ibid; HL Debs 512, cols 78–9, 84.

. . . it is estimated that there are up to 40,000 Sikhs working in the construction industry who could be dismissed if they felt unable to comply with the requirements of the new regulations . . . . The effect on the Sikh communities themselves . . . would be a severe economic blow and cause unnecessary damage to their perceptions of British society and its laws . . . . Is it not more important in the longer term for our diverse society and its harmony and cohesion that we should show that we mean what we say when we speak of toleration and respect for the religions of others where—and this is an important proviso—our own core values and commitment to human rights are not at stake?[231]

After dealing with an intervention he added—

On the question of how far we should bend our laws to take account of non-Christian religions and on the question of integration, the Government have made it clear that integration is our aim, in the real sense of participation in the economy and life of this country. It is not an aim of assimilation. We have emphasised that it does not imply for those of different cultures and religions any forfeiting of their faith. Tolerance and respect for religion, as for free expression, are a part of our heritage . . . . I see no issue of core values. We are following a clear and unobjectionable precedent and are right to provide an exemption. In this case we are not yielding to religious bigotry, but giving expression to our own values of tolerance and respect for religion.[232]

Fourthly, the objections to the exemption on grounds of safety were rehearsed and opponents drew attention to the opposition of both trade unions and employers' organizations to the Government's proposals.[233] Lord McCarthy, adopting utilitarian criteria, argued that interference with the freedom of Sikhs to practise their religion could be justified if by their actions they were significantly damaging people other than themselves.[234] In his view 'the issue should turn basically on whether other workers are being damaged, on whether the employer is being put at risk and on whether there is an unnecessary and significant increase in the likelihood of accidents—even perhaps fatal accidents'.[235] Lord Houghton expressed concern that others might suffer through a Sikh worker's failure to wear a helmet and made his point in the following way -

For example, let us assume that a Sikh is not wearing a protective helmet, something hits him on the head, he falls off the scaffold, falls on somebody else, knocks him to the ground and breaks his neck.[236]

The Government's response was that the chances of this happening were pretty remote and that it was unaware of any case where injuries had

---

[231] HL Debs, 512, cols 77–8.   [232] Ibid, col 79.
[233] HL Debs, 512, cols 79–80; HC Debs, 159, col 1109.
[234] HL Debs, 511, col 744.   [235] HL Debs, 512, col 69.
[236] HL Debs, 511, col 742; see also HC Debs, 159, col 1108.

been sustained in such circumstances.[237] Moreover, as Lord Strathclyde explained—

If a third party was injured as a result of a Sikh being injured, the third party would still be able to claim against the person responsible for the act causing the Sikh's injury. Where, for example, the Sikh is injured by a falling brick which has been knocked off scaffolding by an employee, an injured third party would be able to claim against that employee or his employer if he is vicariously liable. It must be remembered that the person who causes the Sikh's injury will have been negligent in the first place, and in the case of the innocent third party it must be right that he should remain liable . . . . [It] would not be right for the Sikh to remain liable for failing to wear a helmet. One cannot exempt a person from a duty but provide that he should remain liable for failing to comply with the duty.[238]

Later, at the Committee stage of the bill, he added—

It is almost inconceivable that the accident would be solely attributable to the fact that the Sikh was not wearing a helmet. It is much more likely that it would be due to the fact that there was an unsafe system of work in the first place or that somebody acted negligently, causing injury to the Sikh.[239]

However, the fact that legal liability for such accidents would usually lie with the employers did not satisfy Lord Wedderburn, who wished to know what the position would be if the damage sustained in such an accident was more extensive than it would have been if the Sikh worker had been wearing a helmet.[240] With the helmet the Sikh might have recovered from the blow to his head and injuries to others might have been less serious. The answer given by Lord Strathclyde was that a third party's claim would not be dependent in any way on whether the Sikh's injury would have been prevented or lessened by a safety helmet,[241] but Lord McCarthy felt this would be unfair to employers who could not provide the protection they wanted to as a result of a legislative exemption, yet would still be liable to pay full compensation.[242] This helped, he stated, to explain the opposition of the Confederation of British Industry to the exemption. Equally, the hostility of the Trades Union Congress to the proposal could be explained by the fact that if an employer had not been negligent in any way a worker whose injury was partly caused by a Sikh's lack of a helmet would receive no damages in tort from the Sikh in respect of the injury.[243]

Fifthly, the existence of a large number of Sikh construction workers was utilized on both sides of the argument. For opponents, the prospect

---

[237] HL Debs, 512, col 77; HC Debs, 159, col 1114.   [238] HL Debs, 511, cols 745–6.
[239] HL Debs, 512, col 78.   [240] Ibid.   [241] Ibid.
[242] HL Debs, 512, col 80.   [243] Ibid.

of 40,000 workers being exempted from the helmet requirements seemed to pose a considerable safety risk.[244] The Government, however, after noting that there were more Sikhs employed in construction than in any other industry,[245] simply drew attention to the practical consequences of facing so many people with a stark choice between their religion and their job.[246] No official statistics were available as to how many of the accidents on construction sites each year entailing head injuries involved Sikhs.[247] Nor were any figures presented on either side as to the numbers of Sikh construction workers who actually wore turbans. Reference was, however, made by opponents of the exemption to the possibility of a helmet being worn over a turban,[248] but Lord Strathclyde indicated that the Government had been given to understand that while some Sikhs might be willing to take such a step, this solution was totally unacceptable to orthodox Sikhs and hence to the Sikh community as a whole.[249]

Finally, in moving the Government's proposals in the House of Commons, Mr Tim Eggar, Minister for State in the Department of Employment, incorporated into his arguments a characteristic reference to 'the whole British Sikh military tradition', pointing out that 'Sikhs were allowed to wear turbans instead of steel helmets when they fought for this country in the first and second world wars'.[250]

Somewhat surprisingly, no reference was made during the Parliamentary debates to the existence of two new directives from the Council of the European Communities which were in the process of being adopted during 1989. The 'parent' directive of 12 June 1989, on the introduction of measures to encourage improvements in the safety and health of workers,[251] imposes a general duty on employers to take such measures as are necessary for this purpose[252] and requires each worker to take care as far as possible for his own safety and that of others.[253] It also specifically provides that workers must 'make correct use of the personal protective equipment supplied to them'.[254] Moreover, the 'parent' directive authorizes the Council to adopt further individual directives in selected areas, including one on 'personal protective equipment'.[255] Hence, the second directive, dated 30 November 1989, establishes minimum health and safety requirements for the use by workers of such equipment.[256] In particular, mention is made of

---

[244] HL Debs, 512, col 70.

[245] The explanation for this lies largely in the fact that the traditional occupation of the Ramgarhia 'caste' was skilled work as artisans (carpenters, blacksmiths, bricklayers etc.)—see e.g. Kalsi, 5, 60, 73, 86–7.

[246] HL Debs, 511, col 744; 512, col 77; HC Debs, 159, cols 1106–7.

[247] HC Debs, 159, col 1114.   [248] HL Debs, 511, col 740; 512, col 73.

[249] HL Debs, 511, col 745.   [250] HC Debs, 159, col 1107.   [251] 89/391/EEC.

[252] Art 6(1).   [253] Art 13(1).   [254] Art 13(2)(*b*).

[255] Art 16(1); annex.   [256] 89/656/EEC.

helmets for head protection on building sites[257] and member states are enjoined to ensure that general rules are established for the use of such equipment.[258] The basic rule is that such equipment must be used when the risks cannot be avoided or sufficiently limited by technical means of collective protection or by measures, methods, or procedures of work organization.[259] No reference is made to the possibility of exemptions being permitted for religious reasons and member states were obliged to implement the directive by the end of 1992.[260] Although the Parliamentary debates on the Employment Act were completed on 8 November 1989, a draft of the second directive would obviously have been available to the British Government at that time.

In any event, the Employment Act 1989 contains two detailed sections relating to turbaned Sikhs. Section 11 begins by according them the exemption already outlined, by providing as follows—

Any requirement to wear a safety helmet which . . . would, by virtue of any statutory provision or rule of law, be imposed on a Sikh who is on a construction site shall not apply to him at any time when he is wearing a turban.[261]

The section then proceeds to exclude liability in tort in respect of any injury, loss or damage caused by a turbaned Sikh's failure to wear a safety helmet. This applies both to liability on the part of the Sikh himself and to liability on the part of 'any other person',[262] such as his employer, who would otherwise have had a duty imposed upon him in relation to the provision and maintenance of such a helmet and ensuring that it was worn.[263]

On the other hand, a turbaned Sikh who is on a construction site without a helmet and who, in consequence of any act or omission of some other person, sustains any injury, loss, or damage which is to any extent attributable to the fact that he is not wearing a safety helmet, has his legal rights very considerably restricted by section 11. The wrongdoer is only liable to the Sikh in tort to the extent that the injury, loss or damage would have been sustained by the Sikh even if he had been wearing a safety helmet complying with the statutory require-

---

[257] Annexes II, III.   [258] Art 6(1).   [259] Art 3.   [260] Art 10(1).

[261] S 11(1). By s 11(7) the expression 'construction site' means any place where any 'building operations' or 'works of engineering construction' are being undertaken and these two phrases are to have the same meanings as they have in the Factories Act 1961. In terms of s 176(1) of that Act 'building operations' means the construction, structural alteration, repair, maintenance, or demolition of a building or the laying of any foundations; 'works of engineering construction' include the construction, structural alteration, repair, and demolition of docks, harbours, tunnels, bridges, waterworks, and gasholders.

[262] S 11(2), (3), (4).

[263] Under the Construction (Head Protection) Regulations 1989, regs 3(1), 4.

ments.[264] Hence Sikh building workers who wear turbans rather than helmets are deemed by the law to take a substantial part of the risk of head injury upon themselves through the principle of 'contributory negligence'. It is highly significant, however, that the manner in which the apportionment of damages is to be undertaken has not been left to the general law of tort, but has been clearly delineated in section 11 itself and operates in a fashion which is prejudicial to the interests of Sikhs. Even if the accident causing injury to the Sikh was caused wholly through the negligent act of another worker, the Sikh will be denied any compensation at all if he would not have suffered any injury had he been wearing a helmet. By contrast, if such injuries had been sustained in a road accident, a turbaned Sikh motor cyclist would have been entitled to at least 75 per cent of the damages attributable to his injuries on the basis of precedents under the Law Reform (Contributory Negligence) Act 1945, which uses a formula related to what is 'just and equitable'.[265]

This avowed policy of ensuring that the wrongdoer is not placed in a worse position than he would have been if the victim had been wearing a helmet seems to have been formulated in rather a hurry, as the Government sought to rush through its late amendments to the Employment Bill at the end of the 1988–89 session of Parliament. Such haste was prompted by a concern to ensure that the provisions about turbaned Sikhs would be in place before the new Construction (Head Protection) Regulations 1989 came into force, as planned, on 30 March 1990. At first it seemed as if the Government was preparing to take an even tougher stance against turbaned Sikhs, disentitling them from any claims for damages at all. In announcing to the House of Lords the plans for an exemption, Lord Trefgarne stated on 14 July 1989—

The Government proposes to exempt turban-wearing Sikhs from any requirement to wear head protection in construction work. There will be a parallel exemption for employers from civil liability towards Sikhs using this exemption.[266]

However, by 16 October 1989 in moving the exemption, Lord Strathclyde modified this position when he announced—

Understandably, employers take the view that, as they will not be able to require Sikhs to wear helmets, they should not be liable for the consequences of the Sikh's failure to do so. The clause therefore provides that employers and others

[264] S 11(5). Moreover, if the Sikh is killed in such circumstances but would have survived if he had been wearing a helmet, the damages recoverable by his personal representatives are limited to those obtainable in respect of his death rather than any higher damages which might otherwise have been obtainable in respect of the hypothetical injuries he would have suffered if he had been wearing a helmet: s 11(6).
[265] See above, pp 297–301.   [266] HL Debs, 510, col 524.

will not be liable to the Sikh for an injury that he has sustained which would have been prevented had he been wearing a helmet.[267]

Even this softening of the very hard line taken initially represented a major departure from the normal principles of contributory negligence, but none of the Government spokesmen drew attention to its novelty, nor was there any discussion of its implications during the course of the Parliamentary debates on the exemption. It creates a grave anomaly in the different treatment accorded to Sikh building workers and Sikh motor cyclists, without apparent justification.

Section 12 of the 1989 Act, on the other hand, is designed to strengthen and consolidate the basic exemption described above by protecting turbaned Sikhs from discrimination at the hands of employers within the construction industry, who might otherwise refuse to employ any Sikh unwilling to wear a safety helmet or else might want to transfer their existing turbaned Sikh employees to other types of work.[268] Such employers might seek to justify what would otherwise be an instance of indirect discrimination under the Race Relations Act 1976 by reference to safety considerations, in the same way as the defendants succeeded in doing in *Kuldip Singh v British Rail Engineering Ltd*[269] in 1986. The effect of section 12 is, therefore, to preclude any defence of justification from being raised in such circumstances in the context of work on construction sites. Hence an employer who has no reasonable grounds for believing that a Sikh job applicant or existing employee would not wear a turban at all times when on such a site will be acting unlawfully if he applies to him any requirement relating to the wearing of a safety helmet there.[270] No defence of justifiability is available in any circumstances.

THE HUMAN RIGHTS DIMENSION

Broadly speaking, the Sikh community in England can claim to have emerged from the legal tussles over beards and turbans with a considerable degree of success. Parliament has been persuaded to introduce the two statutory exemptions for motor cyclists and building workers,[271]

---

[267] HL Debs, 511, col 738.

[268] HL Debs, 512, cols 81–2; HC Debs, 159, cols 1114–5.

[269] [1986] ICR 24, discussed above, pp 310–11.   [270] S 12(1).

[271] A further statutory provision was introduced in 1988 to permit Sikhs to carry their *kirpans* (swords or daggers) in public places without fear of prosecution. The Criminal Justice Act 1988, which contains provisions designed to penalize those who carry knives and other sharply pointed articles, specifically states that it is a defence for an accused to prove that he had the article with him in a public place 'for religious reasons'—see s 139(5)(*b*) and, for the legislative background, HL Debs, 489, cols 920, 924.

and a test case taken to the House of Lords has established that Sikhs are an ethnic group and hence entitled to the protection afforded by the Race Relations Act 1976 against unlawful discrimination. Sikhs have thus been prime beneficiaries of 'specific differential treatment'. However, it is worthwhile evaluating the outcomes described earlier by reference to the relevant standards set by international human rights treaties.

Article 9(1) of the European Convention provides that everyone has a right to freedom of religion, including the right to manifest this religion in practice and observance. However, Article 9(2) restricts this right as follows—

Freedom to manifest one's religion or beliefs shall be subject only to such limitations as are prescribed by law and are necessary in a democratic society in the interests of public safety, for the protection of public order, health or morals, or for the protection of the rights and freedoms of others.

Article 18 of the International Covenant on Civil and Political Rights is framed in very similar terms. The wearing of beards and turbans by 'orthodox' Sikhs is clearly a manifestation of their religion and during the course of the House of Lords debate on the Motor-Cycle Crash Helmets (Religious Exemption) Bill Lord Avebury specifically argued that the exemption was 'essential, if we are to comply with the spirit as well as with the letter of the Human Rights Convention'.[272]

As we have seen, much of the controversy over creating legislative exemptions for Sikhs has been directed at the issues of safety and health and several judicial decisions have been similarly focused, so that it is particularly significant that both public safety and public health are listed as justifications for restricting freedom of religion in Article 9(2) of the European Convention and Article 18(3) of the International Covenant. Indeed, when in *Panesar v Nestle Co Ltd*[273] counsel for the applicant specifically drew the attention of the Court of Appeal to Article 9(1), Lord Denning MR immediately recited Article 9(2) and declared that the defendant confectionery manufacturer's rule banning beards was, on all the evidence, for the protection of public health.[274] Hence, even if the Convention had formed part of English law, in his Lordship's view there would have been no breach of Article 9.

It should, however, be borne in mind that Article 9(2) requires any legal limitations upon freedom of religion to be 'necessary in a democratic society' and the concept of necessity entails both a pressing social need and a degree of proportionality between the aim being pursued by the state and the legal interference with the basic right in question.[275] It

---

[272] HL Debs, 374, col 1058.   [273] [1980] ICR 144.   [274] At 147.
[275] See e.g. *Handyside v UK* (1976) 1 EHRR 737 at 754; *Sunday Times v UK* (1979) 2 EHRR 245 at 275, 277–8; *Lingens v Austria* (1986) 8 EHRR 407 at 418.

is not enough that the general ground for the interference merely appears to belong to the class of exemptions listed in Article 9(2).[276] On the other hand, the state is allowed a 'margin of appreciation', in terms of which a considerable measure of discretion is left to the state in determining what the vital interests of the country and its people demand.[277]

In 1977 in *X v United Kingdom*[278] an application was made to the European Commission of Human Rights by a turbaned Sikh against the United Kingdom, alleging that the Motor Cycle (Wearing of Helmets) Regulations 1973 violated his freedom of religion by making the wearing of helmets compulsory in the years prior to the enactment of the exemption in 1976. Between 1973 and 1976 the applicant had been prosecuted, convicted, and fined no fewer than twenty times for failing to wear a crash helmet. The application was declared inadmissible by the Commission in the following terms—

The Commission considers that the compulsory wearing of crash helmets is a necessary safety measure for motor cyclists. The Commission is of the opinion therefore that any interference there may have been with the applicant's freedom of religion was justified for the protection of health in accordance with article 9(2). The fact that Sikhs were later granted an exemption to the traffic regulations does not in the Commission's opinion vitiate the valid health considerations on which the regulations are based.[279]

A further case has been taken to the UN Human Rights Committee under the Optional Protocol to the International Covenant on Civil and Political Rights, which allows the Committee to receive and consider communications from individuals claiming to be victims of a violation of the Covenant. In 1989 in *Bhinder v Canada*[280] the applicant claimed a violation of Article 18 guaranteeing freedom of religion, on the basis of his dismissal from employment by Canadian National Railroads solely because he had refused to wear a 'hard hat' in a newly designated hard hat area. He argued that as a devout Sikh he could only wear a turban. He had first brought a complaint of religious discrimination in the Canadian courts alleging a violation of the Canadian Human Rights Act 1976–77. However, in terms of that Act an employer's specification of a particular form of dress 'based on a bona fide occupational requirement' is perfectly acceptable and does not count as a discriminatory practice. Relying on this exemption the Supreme Court of Canada ruled

---

[276] *Sunday Times v UK* at 281.

[277] *Handyside v UK* at 754; *Sunday Times v UK* at 275–6; *Lingens v Austria* at 418. See also *X v Netherlands*, (1962) 5 YBECHR 278 at 284.

[278] (1978) 14 Dec & Rep 234.   [279] At 235.

[280] Communication 208/1986; *Report of the Human Rights Committee* (1990), II, 50.

(by a five to two majority) that no breach of the Act had occurred.[281] In the opinion of the majority a genuine job-related safety specification, such as the requirement that workers wear hard hats, negated any finding of discrimination. The dissenting judges, on the other hand, took the view that, for an occupational requirement to be truly bona fide in a case where it had a discriminatory impact on a particular person, the employer had to be able to justify its application to each individual employee (rather than as a general measure). Only if the requirement was reasonably necessary for the employer's business, in the sense that he would otherwise suffer undue hardship by exempting the particular individual concerned, could it be justified and hence bona fide. Since on the facts of this case any hardship to the defendant's business through increased liability to compensation claims through personal injury would have been minimal, the dissenting judges would have upheld the Sikh's claim.[282]

Before the Human Rights Committee the applicant argued that his right to manifest his religious beliefs had been violated contrary to Article 18(1) of the Convention and in particular that the restrictions allowed by Article 18(3) on grounds of public safety did not apply because 'any safety risk ensuing from his refusal to wear safety headgear was confined to himself'.[283] The Canadian Government submitted that no violation had occurred because the hard hat rule was a neutral legal requirement imposed for legitimate reasons and applied to all members of the relevant workforce without being aimed at any religious group. The Committee found no breach of either Article 18 or Article 26 guaranteeing freedom from discrimination, commenting—

If the requirement that a hard hat be worn is regarded as raising issues under article 18, then it is a limitation that is justified by reference to the grounds laid down in article 18(3). If the requirement that a hard hat be worn is seen as a discrimination *de facto* against persons of the Sikh religion under article 26, then, applying criteria now well established in the jurisprudence of the Committee, the legislation requiring that workers in federal employment be protected from injury . . . by the wearing of hard hats is to be regarded as reasonable and directed towards objective purposes that are compatible with the Covenant.[284]

One method of attempting to assess how far it was 'necessary', in terms of both the European Convention and the International Covenant, for the United Kingdom Parliament to introduce a general mandatory

---

[281] *Re Bhinder and Canadian National Railway Co* (1986) 23 DLR (4th series) 481.

[282] There was much criticism of the stance taken by the majority and the approach of the dissenters would seem to have been vindicated subsequently in *Alberta Human Rights Commission v Central Alberta Dairy Pool* (1990) 72 DLR (4th) 417; see Vizkelety, B., [1991] 70 *Canadian Bar Review* 335.

[283] At 53.   [284] At 54.

requirement that motor cyclists and building workers wear helmets 'in the interests of public safety' is to examine the evidence of accident rates. In both cases the British government argued strongly that compulsion was required because persuasion, propaganda, and self-regulation had failed to elicit a sufficiently positive response. In relation to motor cyclists, just prior to the introduction of the mandatory requirement in June 1973 it was estimated that, while the number of motor cyclists wearing helmets had risen from 66 per cent in 1962 to 75 per cent in 1973, this still left around 400,000 non-users.[285] In 1971 some 13,400 people were estimated to have been killed or seriously injured riding on motor cycles[286] and it was anticipated that around 300 to 400 deaths and serious injuries could be avoided each year through mandatory helmet regulations.[287] Subsequently, a comparison of the number of deaths alone occurring during the first four months of the requirement between July and October 1973 with the same period in the previous year revealed a decline from 299 to 276.[288] Moreover, in 1974 the number of deaths per 100 motor cycle involvements in injury accidents had fallen to 1.44 from 1.66 in 1972.[289] By 1975 the estimate of the number of deaths and serious injuries being prevented by the 1973 regulations had been revised down to 200 per annum,[290] but this still represented a substantial achievement. However, precise quantification of the impact of the mandatory requirement is impossible because of the number of variable factors involved and in 1984 the Secretary of State for Transport, when asked how many lives had actually been saved since mandatory crash helmets had been introduced, replied that circumstances had changed so much since 1973 that 'it was no longer possible to provide a meaningful figure of annual casualty savings'.[291]

So far as building workers are concerned, we have seen that the Health and Safety Commission hoped for a significant reduction in the number of serious head injuries occurring each year through the compulsory wearing of helmets and expected that at least one fatality (and perhaps as many as four) could be prevented in this way. Figures for reported accidents among employees during the first year of the operation of the Construction (Head Protection) Regulations were certainly encouraging, with deaths from head injuries reduced from twenty-six during the period April 1989 to March 1990 to twenty-one for the period April

[285] See HC Debs, 851, cols 342–3; 852, col 448; 854, col 770. These figures included riders of scooters and mopeds as well as of motorbikes.
[286] HC Debs, 854, cols 756, 770. Subsequent statistics put the figure at 15,582—see HC Debs, 911, cols 681–2 (written answers).   [287] HC Debs, 854, col 771.
[288] HC Debs, 871, col 426 (written answers).
[289] HC Debs, 973, col 141 (written answers).   [290] HC Debs, 884, col 109.
[291] HC Debs, 63, col 153 (written answers).

1990 to March 1991.[292] Major head injuries fell from 140 to 103 and head injuries leading to absence from work for at least three days came down from 527 to 377 over the same period. Since then such injuries have continued to decline and during 1992–93 there were fifteen fatalities and seventy major head injuries.[293]

The broad conclusion to be drawn from all these statistics is that they at least provide a prima facie justification for the general mandatory requirements for motor cyclists[294] and building workers. Of course, the absence of any specific figures for Sikh casualties in either field makes an objective appraisal of their special exemptions from a safety standpoint somewhat problematical, but it seems unlikely that their accident rates differ significantly from the rest of the population.

SOME FOREIGN COMPARISONS

During the course of his speech in the House of Lords in 1976, moving the second reading of the bill introducing the exemption for turbaned Sikh motor cyclists, Lord Avebury asserted that similar exemptions had already been granted in several Commonwealth jurisdictions and he specifically mentioned Saskatchewan, Western Australia, Singapore, and Malaysia.[295] How accurate were these assertions? In Western Australia, the Road Traffic Code 1975 authorizes the granting of exemptions there from the requirement that motor cyclists wear a protective helmet, both on medical grounds and 'for any other reason' considered 'sufficient' by the Traffic Board.[296] There is no express mention of turbaned Sikhs, but one or two of the hundred or so exemptions in force seem to have been granted on this basis.[297] Both Malaysia and Singapore have indeed created special exemptions for turbaned Sikh motor cyclists and these were already in force at the time when Parliament enacted the 1976 Act here.[298]

In relation to Saskatchewan Lord Avebury claimed that the requirement that Sikhs should wear a crash helmet had been 'ruled unconstitutional in

---

[292] See Health and Safety Commission, *Annual Report 1992/93, Statistical Supplement* (Sudbury, 1993), 13.   [293] Ibid.

[294] For the view that compulsory additional insurance is a preferable way of reducing head injuries to motor cyclists, see Feinberg, J., *The Moral Limits of the Criminal Law, Vol 3: Harm to Self* (New York, 1986), 134–42; Schonsheck, J., *On Criminalization* (Dordrecht, 1994), 120–41.   [295] HL Debs, 374, col 1057.

[296] Regulation 1607(4).

[297] Personal communication from the Australian Law Reform Commission, dated 5 Aug 1991.

[298] For Malaysia, see Motor-Cycles (Safety Helmets) Rules 1973, enacted pursuant to the Road Traffic Ordinance 1958 and exemption notification PU (B) 23/1975; for Singapore, see s 142 of Road Traffic Act (cap 276).

the Supreme Court on the grounds that it would interfere with the practice of religion'.[299] However, an extensive search has failed to reveal any Supreme Court ruling along these lines and the section in the Vehicles Act requiring motor cyclists to wear helmets, which dates back to 1967, contains no provision for exemptions of any sort.[300] On the other hand, recent developments in Canada are illuminating in a rather different context, namely the controversy over whether or not to recruit turbaned Sikhs into the ranks of the Royal Canadian Mounted Police (RCMP).[301]

In 1989 the Commissioner of the RCMP had recommended that the Federal Government should amend the statutory regulations governing the force's uniform, so as to permit orthodox Sikhs to wear turbans rather than the widebrimmed stetson which had long been designated as appropriate for ceremonial occasions. There was very significant opposition from the Western provinces to this proposal, not only in Parliament but also in the form of public petitions and even involving protesters marketing calendars, posters, car-stickers, and lapel badges. Opponents argued that Sikh tradition should not be allowed to override Canadian tradition, especially in view of the fact that the stetson had become the loved and revered distinguishing symbol of an internationally renowned police force. However, the stetson had only been introduced in around 1900 (in place of a pillbox hat), the Canadian armed forces had already authorized the wearing of turbans, and the Chief Human Rights Commissioner had lent his support to the demand for an alteration in the RCMP's dress code in order to ensure that the force complied with the religious freedom and non-discrimination provisions of the Canadian Human Rights Act[302] and the Canadian Charter of Rights and Freedoms.[303] Despite Canada's commitment to a general policy of multiculturalism,[304] it took the Federal Government over a year to agree to revision of the regulations because of the strength of opposition in the prairie provinces on such a sensitive issue. The new dress code introduced in 1990 now provides that the RCMP Commissioner may exempt any member of the force from wearing any item of uniform

---

[299] HL Debs 374, col 1057.

[300] Vehicles Act (1978 Consolidation), s 134, re-enacting s 31 of cap 82 of 1967. The Saskatchewan Multicultural Act 1974 had recently been enacted, but its provisions did not purport to grant Sikhs legal rights to exemptions of this nature.

[301] See e.g. *Canadian House of Commons Debates*, 131, 5232, 5252– 62 (27 Oct 1989); 8277, 8295 (13 Feb 1990); 9307–9 (15 Mar 1990); *Globe and Mail*, 6, 10, 16 March 1990.

[302] Canadian Human Rights Act 1976–77, ss 2, 3, 10.

[303] Canada Act 1982, sched B, ss 2, 15.

[304] Ibid, s 27; Canadian Multiculturalism Act 1988, discussed below, ch 10.

on the basis of the person's religious beliefs[305] and the first turbaned Sikh 'mountie' eventually graduated in 1991.[306]

CONCLUSIONS

In view of the two human rights decisions in *X v United Kingdom* and *Bhinder v Canada* and the pressing social need to reduce casualty rates amongst motor cyclists and building workers, it appears probable that there is no international obligation to create special exemptions for turbaned Sikhs in these fields. However, there is equally no duty placed upon states by international human rights law to use the limitation clauses in the treaties to the full and to restrict religious freedom in these spheres on grounds of public health or safety. It is the right to freedom of religion itself which is protected and guaranteed and in these two instances the United Kingdom has elected to allow the Sikhs to manifest their religious freedom in practice by wearing their turbans in place of helmets. On balance, this may be thought to have been a wise exercise of the discretion reserved to a state by the 'margin of appreciation', since there is force in the argument that the people whose safety is principally put at risk are the turbaned Sikhs themselves. 'Public safety' as such does not appear to have been significantly jeopardized by permitting them the two exemptions.[307] If they decide that the practice of their religion outweighs the greater risk of physical injury, the values of a liberal democracy are hardly imperilled in the way in which they might be if a significant degree of harm was being inflicted upon others. It is, however, somewhat anomalous that a turbaned Sikh should have a remedy against indirect discrimination if he is refused work on a building site for safety reasons, while no such remedy is available if he seeks employment elsewhere and the employer can show that a 'hard hat' rule is justifiable on the same grounds. A turbaned Sikh may thus be employed to build a steel factory without wearing a safety helmet, but would not necessarily be able to work in the same factory if engaged on equally dangerous tasks.[308]

---

[305] Royal Canadian Mounted Police Regulations 1988 (as amended), s 64(2).

[306] *Independent*, 18 Apr 1991. For an unsuccessful (and wholly unmeritorious) challenge to the constitutional validity of the new dress code brought by RCMP veterans from Alberta, see *Grant v Attorney General of Canada* (1995) 125 DLR (4th) 556.

[307] For criticism of *Bhinder v Canada* on the grounds that the Human Rights Committee confused 'public safety' with the safety of the applicant, see Tahzib, B., *Freedom of Religion or Belief: Ensuring Effective International Legal Protection* (The Hague, 1996), 294–300.

[308] See *Dhanjal v British Steel* (Birmingham Industrial Tribunal, 16 Dec 1993, unreported).

Legislation whose primary object is to protect an individual from causing injury to himself is inherently problematic[309] and, if its rationale is relentlessly pursued, logical inconsistencies soon become apparent. For example, if it is right for the state to interfere with the individual liberties of motor cyclists and building workers, it may be asked why the law does not similarly insist upon helmets being worn by pedal cyclists and workers in industries other than construction. Yet when the Secretary of State for Transport was asked to introduce compulsion in the former sphere in 1988 he replied—

There are no plans to make the wearing of pedal cycle safety helmets compulsory. It is sensible for cyclists to wear helmets. Almost half of cycle casualties suffered some form of head injury. Three-quarters of all cycle deaths involve head injuries.[310]

Equally, in relation to industrial safety, although the Government's attention was drawn in 1989 to the dangers of head injuries to workers in power stations,[311] the Construction (Head Protection) Regulations do not extend beyond construction sites. Obviously, a balance of convenience has to be struck in electing when to legislate on paternalistic principles and a democratic government needs to be sensitive to popular resentment at growing interference with personal freedom designed to protect individuals from harming themselves.[312] Moreover, while much of the cost of treating preventable injuries has to be borne by the taxpayer through contributions to the National Health Service, if this consideration were to dictate the limits on personal freedom, statutory bans would have to be imposed upon a wide range of social activities including drinking, smoking, and participation in dangerous sports. Other costs in the form of claims for damages by injured parties will generally be covered by insurance policies taken out by motorists and employers.

It therefore seems reasonable to conclude that, through the two legislative exemptions coupled with the indirect discrimination provisions of the Race Relations Act (including the current 'objective test' of justifiability), English law is able to afford orthodox Sikhs a substantial level of protection for their wearing of *kesh* and turbans without endangering the core values of society as a whole. The arguments in favour of paying specific attention to their needs through differential treatment have been

---

[309] See generally, Feinberg, Schonsheck, *op cit*; J. S. Mill took the view that people should be warned of the dangers of accidents, but not forcibly prevented from exposing themselves to them—see *On Liberty* (Himmelfarb, G., ed, Harmondsworth, 1985), 166.

[310] HC Debs, 130, col 129 (written answer). For an analysis of the rival arguments, see Hillman, M., *Cycle Helmets: the case for and against* (London, 1993).

[311] HL Debs, 511, col 739.

[312] See e.g. Wayland, D., 'Seat Belts—A Comparative Study of the Law and Practice' (1981) 30 *ICLQ* 165 at 170–4.

vindicated. There remains, however, one striking instance of injustice in the current law. Under section 11(5) of the Employment Act 1989 severe restrictions have been imposed upon the damages which turbaned Sikhs can obtain for injuries suffered as a consequence of another's act of negligence or breach of statutory duty on a construction site. As we have seen, the wrongdoer is only liable to the Sikh in tort to the extent that the injury would have been sustained even if the Sikh had been wearing a suitable safety helmet. The section thus imposes its own special brand of contributory negligence, rather than leaving the matter to be regulated by the general provisions of the Law Reform (Contributory Negligence) Act 1945. The latter scheme is far more generous to plaintiffs who fail to take sufficient precautions for their own safety, recognizing that where the accident itself is entirely attributable to the fault of the defendant, it is he who should bear the major financial responsibility for the consequences of his wrongdoing. Hence a motor cyclist who fails to wear a protective helmet in breach of the statutory requirement to do so and who is injured in a collision with a car whose driver is entirely to blame for the accident is likely to obtain at least 75 per cent of the damages attributable to his head injuries and the whole of the damages attributable to his other injuries. A turbaned Sikh motor cyclist exempted by statute from the helmet requirement may well, as suggested earlier, do even better than this.

Injuries to turbaned Sikhs working on building sites are treated in a very different manner. An accident might well occur in which a heavy object is negligently dropped from the top of a scaffold onto a turbaned Sikh who is standing halfway up the scaffold. Had he been wearing a helmet the object would have caused him merely mild concussion, entitling him perhaps to a small sum by way of compensation. However, since he was only wearing a turban he may have suffered both severe brain damage due to the force of the impact and multiple other injuries occasioned by falling to the ground from a considerable height. Instead of being able to recover very substantial damages, subject possibly to a maximum 15 per cent reduction to the award in respect of the head injuries (since a helmet would have clearly reduced but not wholly prevented his injuries[313]), he is limited by section 11(5) of the 1989 Act to a minimal sum to compensate him for mild concussion.

Even more worrying, however, is the contrast between the restricted damages recoverable by a turbaned Sikh injured on a construction site and those recoverable by any other unhelmeted building worker. Both a non-Sikh wearing a soft hat and, even more striking, a bareheaded Sikh would be entitled to have their claims for damages regulated by the

---

[313] See *Froom v Butcher* [1976] QB 286 at 296, discussed above.

provisions of the Law Reform (Contributory Negligence) Act were they to be injured, despite their clear breaches of the Construction (Head Protection) Regulations. Section 11(5) applies exclusively to Sikhs wearing turbans and thus clearly discriminates against them in favour of less observant Sikhs, as well as in favour of non-Sikhs. It may thus violate several human rights provisions designed to guarantee equality before the law to all, regardless of religion or ethnic origin.[314]

It is hard to see why a non-Sikh who refuses to wear a helmet on a hot day because of the discomfort entailed and who then suffers serious injuries as a consequence of an accident should be placed in a far better position, despite his breach of the Regulations, than a turbaned Sikh who is exempt from them. It is even harder to comprehend why an unobservant Sikh who never wears a turban should fare so much better than a turbaned Sikh in terms of a claim for compensation, when Parliament has specifically singled out observant Sikhs for special dispensation from the safety regulations. To impose such discriminatory penalties upon those whose religious faith demanded the statutory concession in the first place seems impossible to justify, especially since any claim against an employer or fellow employee would almost certainly be covered by the employer's insurance policy. In practical terms, section 11(5) of the Act may well leave observant Sikhs who are injured at work far worse off financially than other employees in the construction industry without any corresponding economic justification from the employer's point of view, since the level of his insurance premiums is unlikely to be affected by the small additional risk entailed in employing turbaned Sikh workers. The sub-section should, therefore, be repealed and the question of apportionment of damages left to regulation by the general law governing the matter.

---

[314] See e.g. International Covenant on Civil and Political Rights, Art 26; International Convention on the Elimination of All Forms of Racial Discrimination, Arts 1, 5.

9

Rastafarians: Confrontations Concerning Dreadlocks and Cannabis

HISTORICAL BACKGROUND

Although the precise origins of the Rastafarian movement in England remain obscure, they probably lie at least partly in the attempt made in 1955 by a former Rastafarian leader from Jamaica to organize a local branch in south London of the Rastafarian-orientated United Afro-West Indian Brotherhood.[1] This endeavour had only a very limited impact, but by 1958 'a group of bearded and rather conspicuously dressed young men were noted in the Brixton market area',[2] and these were identified as Rastafarians. Towards the end of the 1960s two Jamaican-born London residents, Immanuel Fox and Gabriel Adams, who were familiar with the growing importance of Rastafarian ideas in the Caribbean, established a new institution, the Universal Black Improvement Organization (UBIO), in which specifically Rastafarian themes were incorporated into a vehicle designed to raise the general level of black consciousness.[3] Fox and Adams then went to Jamaica and obtained the necessary permission from the Ethiopian World Federation (EWF) to transform the UBIO into a local branch of the EWF in London.[4] The EWF had been set up in 1937 to assist the victims of Italian aggression against Abyssinia (as the country was then known) and its African cultural focus had nourished the aspirations of early Rastafarians in Jamaica.[5] The new London branch operated initially from premises in north Kensington and soon afterwards moved to the Portobello Road.[6] A second branch was established in Birmingham in 1972.[7]

In its formative years in England (and indeed subsequently), the Rastafarian movement's main appeal was to young, black men from working class families.[8] Cashmore's research during the 1970s indicated that the vast majority of the movement's early adherents here had come to Britain from Jamaica with their parents, when they were children aged

---

[1] Patterson, S., *Dark Strangers* (London, 1963), 360.   [2] Ibid, 354.
[3] Cashmore, E., *Rastaman: The Rastafarian Movement in England*, 2nd ed. (London, 1983), 51.
[4] Ibid, 52; for the importance in black thought and tradition of the concept of 'Ethiopia' and its use to signify the whole of Africa (including Egypt), see Barrett, L., *The Rastafarians* (Kingston, 1977), ch 3.   [5] Cashmore, 52.
[6] Ibid, 53.   [7] Ibid, 53.   [8] Ibid, 70.

between six and fourteen.[9] Their arrival was part of the large migration of workers from the Caribbean, which began with the embarkation of 492 passengers on the liner *Empire Windrush* in 1948 and reached a peak of around 50–60,000 entrants per annum in 1960 and 1961.[10] Severe labour shortages in England coupled with high population density and widespread unemployment in Jamaica[11] and Barbados provided the context in which an estimated 267,900 persons of West Indian origin were resident here by 1966.[12] Indeed, almost 10 per cent of the entire Jamaican population migrated to the United Kingdom between 1955 and 1961.[13] The number of Rastafarians in England, however, has always been quite small. Although the movement expanded considerably during the 1970s in the wake of the popularity of reggae music and tours made by its leading exponent, Bob Marley,[14] so that its influence spread far beyond its actual following to 'engulf vast sections of the young West Indian community',[15] one knowledgeable commentator estimated that in 1986 it only had some 5,000 adherents.[16] No doubt, this figure is rather too low, but it is likely that the movement 'peaked' during Marley's period as a 'superstar' and declined sharply after his death in 1981.[17]

Most of the young people who joined the movement during the 1970s were rebelling against the passive responses of their parents towards the prejudice, discrimination, and disadvantage they suffered in Britain.[18] The first generation of Caribbean migrants had expected to be assimilated into mainstream society in the 'mother country', but found to their surprise that they were rejected on the basis of their colour.[19] Profoundly shocked by the experience of discovering that they were regarded both as strangers and as inferior,[20] they tended to withdraw from confrontation with white society over this issue and sought refuge instead in their religious beliefs and practices.[21] Finding to their dismay that their attendance at church was not always welcomed by English congregations,

---

[9] Cashmore, 81, 191.   [10] Rose, E., *Colour and Citizenship* (London, 1969), 66–8.

[11] See e.g. Patterson, 69–71; Foner, N., *Jamaica Farewell: Jamaican Migrants in London* (London, 1979), ch 1.

[12] See Rose, chs 6–10. This figure had increased to at least half a million by the time of the 1991 census; see ch 1 above.

[13] Peach, C., *West Indian Migration to Britain: A Social Geography* (Oxford, 1968), 21.

[14] See generally, Cashmore, ch 6.   [15] Cashmore, 58.

[16] Clarke, P., *Black Paradise: The Rastafarian Movement* (Wellingborough, 1986), 14. It is perhaps worth noting that in the 1991 census over 2,000 people born in the Caribbean classified their ethnic group as 'Black African'—see OPCS, *1991 Census: Ethnic Group and Country of Birth, Great Britain* (London, 1993), vol 1, 404.

[17] See Murphy, D., *Tales from Two Cities* (London, 1987), 231.

[18] See Pryce, K., *Endless Pressure* (Harmondsworth, 1979), ch 13.

[19] See e.g. Patterson, 80–1; Rose, 419–40.   [20] Foner, 40–3.

[21] Pryce, chs 17–18; Cashmore, 38–40.

despite their Christian upbringing and affiliation to mainstream denominations, many turned to sects such as the Pentecostalists, often feeling the need to establish their own separate congregations.[22] Involvement in the affairs of such churches served to cushion individuals and families against their experiences of racism and alienation in England.[23] Pentecostalists, for instance, attempt to transcend a hostile world by looking forward to the Day of Judgement, when spiritual salvation will compensate them for the material deprivation they have suffered during their lifetimes.[24] As Rex and Tomlinson have explained—

Pentecostalism is a phenomenon common amongst poor, exploited and black people. It involves a turning away from the world to the cultivation of an intense religious experience (possession by the Holy Spirit). Although it involves the idea of an after-life, in which the present fortunes of the rich and the poor, the wicked and the good, are reversed, this very idea serves to make life tolerable on this earth, and the consequences of belonging to the Pentecostal church might well be acquiescence of the poor and the exploited in their present condition.[25]

Such forms of evasion of reality did not appeal to many members of the second generation, who sought both an explanation for their rejection by white society and an understanding of what positive steps might be taken to improve their morale as well as ameliorate their material conditions. In very broad terms, Rastafarian beliefs and ideas were able to minister to their needs through the adoption of a perspective which accorded central importance to recognition of their African roots, the inculcation of a positive black identity, the adoption of new religious tenets, and the use of striking symbols to protest against an oppressive social order.[26] In short, they were rejecting their own 'rejection' by white society.

The various strands in this route to a new consciousness can be briefly elaborated. The small number of individuals who are generally credited as the founders of the Rastafarian movement in Jamaica during the 1930s drew much of their inspiration from the philosophy of their countryman, Marcus Garvey (1887–1940), who was for many years the moving spirit behind the Universal Negro Improvement Association (UNIA), which he had founded in 1914.[27] Among the main concerns of this extensive

---

[22] Clarke, 53; Hiro, D., *Black British, White British* (London, 1991), 30–4.

[23] See Kiev, A., 'Psychotherapeutic aspects of Pentecostal sects among West Indian immigrants to England' (1964) 15 *British Journal of Sociology* 129.

[24] See Pryce, ch 18. For an account of early black Pentecostalism in England, see Calley, M., *God's People: West Indian Pentecostal Sects in England* (London, 1955).

[25] *Colonial Immigrants in a British City* (London, 1979), 266.

[26] See generally, Pryce, chs 9, 13–15; Hiro, chs 6, 7; Cambridge, A., 'Cultural recognition and identity' in Cambridge, A. and Feuchtwang, S. (eds), *Where You Belong: Government and Black Culture* (Aldershot, 1992), 50–72.   [27] See Cashmore, 19–21.

international Association, with over five million members, was a desire to restore those black people living outside Africa to what was perceived as their proper homeland there. Although Garvey's attempts to organize a mass migration to Africa from the USA and the Caribbean through the creation of a steamship company, the Black Star Line, proved abortive (and led to his imprisonment for fraud), his major achievement was to alter the consciousness of many black people through inculcating a new image of themselves as intellectually the equal of whites, rather than as the inferior race which a long history of slavery had hitherto impressed upon them. However, for the foundation of the Rastafarian movement, of even greater significance was the attribution to Garvey of a single, undocumented utterance during the mid-1920s—'Look to Africa for the crowning of a Black King; he shall be the Redeemer'.[28] Although research has subsequently demonstrated that this statement was in fact made by one of Garvey's associates,[29] the misattribution soon elevated Garvey to the status of a prophet, for on 2 November 1930 the Prince Regent, Ras Tafari, was crowned Emperor of Ethiopia and invested with his official title Haile Selassie I, King of Kings, Lord of Lords, the all-conquering Lion of the Tribe of Judah. For many poor black Jamaicans this event signified the prospect of an imminent return to Africa, to be instigated and organized by Ras Tafari himself. Soon four preachers started to portray him as the divine redeemer and from the moment when they succeeded in obtaining a following, the Rastafarian movement can truly be said to have begun.[30] The link between Garvey's reputed prophecy and the divinity of Haile Selassie was capable of being reinforced not only by biblical references to the Lion of Judah[31] and to Ethiopia[32] but also by the following statement made by Garvey himself—

We, as Negroes, have found a new ideal. Whilst our God has no colour, yet it is human to see everything through one's own spectacles, and since the white people have seen their God through white spectacles, we have only now started out (late though it be) to see our God through our own spectacles. . . . We Negroes believe in the God of Ethiopia, the everlasting God—God the Son, God the Holy Ghost, the one God of all ages. That is the God in whom we believe, but we shall worship him through the spectacles of Ethiopia.[33]

---

[28] Barrett, 67, 81.

[29] Rev James Morris Webb, a clergyman mystic from Chicago—see White, T., *Catch a Fire: The Life of Bob Marley* (London, 1991), 8–9.

[30] The four preachers were Leonard Howell, Joseph Hibbert, Archibald Dunkley, and Robert Hinds—see Barrett, 81–6.   [31] See e.g. Book of Revelation, ch 5, v 1–5.

[32] See e.g. Psalm 68, v 31—'Princes shall come out of Egypt; Ethiopia shall soon stretch forth her hands unto God'.

[33] See Garvey, A., *The Philosophy and Opinions of Marcus Garvey* (London, 1967), 34.

However, there is no evidence that Garvey considered Haile Selassie to be divine; indeed he seems to have held him in somewhat poor esteem and even described him as 'a great coward' when he left Abyssinia in the wake of the Italian invasion in 1936.[34]

Rastafarians are generally described as followers of a religious movement or members of a religious cult and it is worth briefly exploring at this juncture the extent to which a particular focus upon religion is accurate or adequate. Acceptance of the divinity of Haile Selassie is certainly central to the movement and in Barrett's words—'It is the belief that Haile Selassie is god and the love and worship arising from that belief which makes one a Rastafarian'.[35] Since reverence for a deity is usually regarded as a key component of most religions, there seems little difficulty in acknowledging this dimension of the movement. There is also a reasonably coherent theology in the sense of a set of beliefs which provide a world view linking current practices, rituals, symbols, and convictions with African culture and history, coupled with a mechanism for deep reflection upon fundamental questions through a selective reading of the Bible and participation in group 'reasoning' sessions.[36] On the other hand, there is no agreed written statement of Rastafarian doctrine, nor is there a uniformity of ritual, worship, or practice.[37] The faith is a flexible and undogmatic one, allowing for substantial variations between individual adherents, as well as for revision and development over time.[38] There is no centralized, institutional authority endowed with the right to pronounce definitive interpretations on aspects of belief or ritual. Rastafarians have always been sceptical of the value of 'leaders', fearing that they could destroy the movement.[39]

In 1960 a report commissioned by the Jamaican Government and compiled by three scholars at the University of the West Indies summarized the position, some thirty years after the movement's foundation, in the following terms—

... Rastafari brethren are a very heterogeneous group. Rastafarians hold in common only two beliefs: that Ras Tafari is the living God, and that salvation can come to black men only through repatriation to Africa ... some wear beards, others do not; only a small minority wear the locks ... some smoke ganja; others abhor it . . . . They are very disorganized, and lacking in leadership . . . . There is

---

[34] Cashmore, 22.

[35] At 172; see also Cashmore, 6, 88, 98; Clarke, 65–6.

[36] See Owens, J., *Dread: The Rastafarians of Jamaica* (Kingston, 1976); Clarke, ch 5; Catholic Commission for Racial Justice, 'Rastafarians in Jamaica and Britain' (London, 1982), 4–7.

[37] Clarke, 63.   [38] Cashmore, 237; Clarke, 65.

[39] Barrett, 36–7, 172–3; Cashmore, 237–8.

no leader or group of leaders who can speak for the movement as a whole or define its doctrines.[40]

To outsiders many Rastafarian beliefs, for example, that Haile Selassie is divine, that the salvation of black people will be accomplished through repatriation to Ethiopia or another part of Africa, that the Israelites in the Bible were black (as was Jesus), and that Ethiopia is the true Biblical Zion,[41] appear bizarre, misguided, and demonstrably erroneous.[42] The fact that some Rastafarians perceive the notion of a return to Africa as a mental exercise (of cultural identification), as opposed to a physical project,[43] is also somewhat confusing. However, as Clarke has pointed out, these apparent defects should not render the faith any more vulnerable than others since—

. . . there is no evidence to suggest that the highly systematic, logically consistent, literal presentation of doctrine is what a majority of people want or is any less fragile than a more imprecise, ambiguous, even inconsistent presentation. The fact that Rastafarian beliefs are not highly systematized or logically interconnected, and that they are capable of a number of possible interpretations, could well be a source of strength rather than an indication of their inherent fragility.[44]

Some writers feel that the religious dimension of the Rastafarian movement has been afforded undue prominence and that the movement should primarily be viewed as a vehicle of social and political protest against oppression. Campbell, for example, has argued that the movement developed in Jamaica between 1930 and 1950 as a form of opposition by poor black people to the racial injustice of a colonial society, which graded individuals according to the lightness of the colour of their skin.[45] The movement represented a form of black nationalist resistance to the prevailing social order.[46] The importance of Ethiopia was accentuated by the invasion of that country by Mussolini, a reflection of white patterns of world domination, and the idea of salvation through repatriation to Africa arose at least partly because of the uprooting of a quarter of Jamaica's population from rural areas to allow multinational corporations to exploit the country's bauxite resources, despite an acute land shortage.[47] Today, Campbell contends, there is a wider dimension—

---

[40] Smith, M., Augier, R. and Nettlefold, R., *The Rastafari Movement in Kingston, Jamaica* (Kingston, 1960), 17–18.   [41] See Owens, 36–7, 39–41, 224–5.

[42] See e.g. Post, K., *Arise Ye Starvelings* (The Hague, 1978), 193–4 who regarded it as an ideology of 'false consciousness'.   [43] Cashmore, 236–8.

[44] At 78.   [45] *Rasta and Resistance* (London, 1985), 89–90.

[46] Ibid, 19, 121, 128. The colonial authorities certainly viewed the foundation of the movement as political, since two of the early leaders were convicted of sedition—ibid, 71–2.   [47] Ibid, 86–7, 105, 221.

The Rastafari movement, in all its contemporary manifestations, challenges not only the Caribbean but the entire Western World to come to terms with the history of slavery, the reality of white racism and the permanent thrust for dignity and self-respect by black people.[48]

The oppression and domination against which Rastafarians struggle, whether it emanates from state institutions, such as the police, or from white members of society in general, is depicted as 'Babylon'.[49] This notion is derived from Psalm 137 in which the Israelites are revealed as captives in exile—

By the rivers of Babylon, there we sat down, yea, we wept, when we remembered Zion.

Reggae music, which developed in the late 1960s and had acquired a widespread international following by the mid-1970s, focused on social inequalities, the oppression of black people, and the evils of capitalism, as well as having a religious character and providing a reminder of African roots.[50] One of the most famous reggae songs was entitled 'Get up, stand up', in which Bob Marley and Peter Tosh enjoined their audiences—'Don't give up the fight . . . stand up for your rights'.[51] This represented a call by the singers for black people to seek their salvation in this world rather than the next, employing Rastafarian concepts and ideals in preference to reliance upon Christian beliefs about heaven.[52]

While Rastafarian political ideas have suffused the understanding of social reality shared by many black people in many parts of the world and have provided a valuable stimulant towards social transformation in Jamaica,[53] they have had little practical impact upon power relations between black and white in Britain. Those who saw in the movement the potential of a revolutionary vanguard here have been disappointed, for it has evolved into a rather passive force with minimal participation in political activity. On the other hand, particularly during the 1970s, its critique of colonialism, capitalism, and racism did strike a chord with many young people (including some whites and Asians), particularly in the inner cities, and it could thus be seen as a mass, populist, urban,

---

[48] Ibid, 1.　　　　[49] Ibid, 101; Owens, 69; Cashmore, 128–32.
[50] See generally, Pryce, ch 14; Cashmore, ch 6; Campbell, ch 5; Clarke, 93–4.
[51] From the album, *Burnin'* (1973).
[52] Cashmore, 115–6. One verse of the song's lyrics ran as follows—
　　　　'Most people think great god will come from the sky,
　　　　Take away everything, make everybody feel high,
　　　　But if you know what life is worth,
　　　　You will look for yours on earth,
　　　　Now you see the light, you stand up for your rights.'
[53] Barrett, 101, 110–1, 165, 174–6.

social movement.[54] It was capable of mobilizing local community action on the basis of shared experiences of disadvantage and discrimination and articulating grievances felt to be common to a far wider group than those who were Rastafarians themselves. Following the death of Bob Marley in 1981 there was a general drift away from reggae and other Rastafarian interpretative devices towards different forms of expression and protest.

A third perspective from which to assess the movement is to see it in cultural terms. Both the religious aspects and the nature of the social and political protests outlined above can be viewed merely as elements in the creation of a wider project—the assertion of a new cultural identity,[55] or else as a 'counterculture' or 'subculture'.[56] Some of the symbols and rituals of the movement can be seen not only negatively as new marks of defiance towards 'Babylon' but also far more positively as rooted in ancient African traditions.[57] In the words of one adherent in Jamaica—

In a generic sense a Rastafarian is one who is attempting to restructure identity so that s/he can consciously live from an Africentric perspective. This covers the physical, mental and spiritual dimensions of life. Rastafari therefore provides a vehicle through which and by which the African in the Diaspora can recreate an African identity. The Rastafarian way of life thus represents a conscious departure from participation in an alien culture and a reconstruction of an African cultural orientation in terms of worldview, ethos and ideology.[58]

Cashmore argues along similar lines in an English context—

. . . the dynamic impelling the whole Rastafarian enterprise was the effort to upgrade blackness in the face of prevalent stigmatic conceptions. Central to this was the establishment of a distinct and separate culture; the focus on Africa to dig out 'roots' and 'the way of the ancients' (Ethiopians) was a desperate search for a meaningful cultural nucleus around which to build improved social lives. . . . 'Rasta', it was repeatedly stressed, was not just a religion but a 'way of life'—a total cultural experience.[59]

Cashmore also makes the valuable point that the tensions which existed between Rastafarians and British Asians during the 1970s were partly caused by the jealousy and resentment felt by the former at the latter's success in retaining their own separate and autonomous cultures and traditions in England as resources to be utilized for mutual support in

---

[54] See Gilroy, P., *There Ain't No Black in the Union Jack* (London, 1987), 187–92, 217–9.

[55] See Cambridge, 50–72.

[56] See Hebdige, D., *Subculture: The Meaning of Style* (London, 1979), ch 3.

[57] See e.g. Miles, R., *Between Two Cultures? The Case of Rastafarianism* (Bristol, 1978).

[58] Semaj, L., 'Rastafari: From Religion to Social Theory', *Caribbean Quarterly Monograph on Rastafari* (Kingston, 1985), 22.   [59] At 188.

the face of white prejudice and discrimination.[60] In general terms, Caribbean migrants found it much harder to differentiate their culture from mainstream British culture[61]—indeed most members of the first generation, at least, did not wish to do so and preferred the prospect of voluntary assimilation, if the white majority would permit it.[62]

The Rastafarians in England, therefore, embarked on a process of defining a separate cultural identity for themselves which would correspond with those held by the Muslim, Hindu, and Sikh communities. They invented a new culture based on Africa and the divinity of an Ethiopian monarch as a means of carving out an independent place for themselves in British society. A British Rastafarian has aptly portrayed the process as a cultural 'reawakening'.[63] In Clarke's words—

The Rastas feel that, as individuals and as a race, the real, true identity of black people has been destroyed. Wrenched from their homeland and 'natural', normal ways of life, treated as sub-human during the era of the slave trade, and 'indoctrinated' with western values and notions and images of 'God', they must now restore their true identity by a process of deconversion and reconstruction. They must rid themselves of any idea or feeling of inferiority and decolonize their minds. . . . Moreover, like many other second-generation members of ethnic groups, Rastas . . . are engaged on the one hand in an attempt to revitalize and preserve an old identity and on the other to forge a new one. In order to do this they have created by their rituals, language, dress, dreadlocks, and general lifestyle a sharp sense of boundary between themselves and others.[64]

One of the consequences of viewing Rastafari in essentially cultural terms is that specific cultural patterns alter, develop, and combine with others over time,[65] and we have already seen that some distinctive Rastafarian beliefs and modes of expression have been adopted by those outside the movement. While reggae music, for instance, had a profound influence on young people generally during the 1970s and early 1980s, the popular youth culture of the 1990s is increasingly tending to reflect a fusion of different musical patterns, including Punjabi *bhangra* and Caribbean *ragga* as well as 'white' music. It is hard, therefore, to define Rastafari as a distinct youth subculture today. Equally, to describe Rastafari as a religion when it is of such an amorphous nature and lacks any authoritative doctrine or controlling institutional framework may, as we shall see, give rise to practical difficulties of formal recognition by the state and its bureaucracy. However, it seems safe to conclude at this

---

[60] At 181–90.

[61] See e.g. Hutnik, N., *Ethnic Minority Identity: A Social Psychological Perspective* (Oxford, 1991), 88–91. [62] See Hebdige, 40.

[63] Bones, J., 'Rastafari: a cultural awakening' in Minority Rights Group, *Report No. 64: The Rastafarians* (London, 1984), 9–10. [64] At 13.

[65] See Cambridge, 53.

juncture that the Rastafarian movement contains religious, cultural, and political strands, all of which are deeply intertwined.

It is perhaps hardly surprising that Rastafarians should have attracted some adverse publicity, both in Jamaica[66] and in England. Whether they are viewed primarily as a new, non-Christian religion springing up in a predominantly Christian-orientated society or as a vehicle for political protest against the existing social order or as a distinctive sub-cultural group seeking to establish a visible separate identity for itself, they are undoubtedly striving to display openly their sense of 'other-ness' or 'difference'. All societies seem to find it difficult and unner-ving to have to come to terms with novel groups, who do not conform with established norms and expectations, and the initial encounter between the English majority community and the Rastafarians has certainly been no exception. As one prominent British Rastafarian perspicaciously observed, Rastas—in the eyes of members of the estab-lishment—

. . . are rebels, anarchists and intolerable deviants. Part of the strategy of attack-ing Rastas is to make the movement appear to be a great controversial affair. That is, great efforts are spent . . . to make Rastas sound and look crazy, unreal, incredible and unwanted. So ordinary folks . . . buy the negative caricature of the Rasta people and the next thing is they can only see Rasta as confusing and controversial.[67]

However, it should be borne in mind that some of the Rastafarian symbols, such as the dreadlocks, were actually intended to shock main-stream society into recognizing that Rastafarians are different and hence taking them seriously.[68] By their strange appearance, their special voca-bulary, and their limited contact and communication with outsiders, they deliberately set out to create a social distance between themselves and others, and it was inevitable that the members of the majority community should therefore initially view them with some suspicion.[69]

   Much more worrying, however, has been the stigmatization of Rasta-farians as constituting a dangerous criminal class, prone to acts of violence including riot and murder. Several media reports during the

---

[66] See, in relation to the 1960s, Barrett, x–xi; Cashmore 31–3, 204–5; Campbell, 92. A much more positive image in Jamaica emerged subsequently.

[67] Jah Bones, quoted in Minority Rights Group, *Report*, 9.

[68] Pryce, 146–7; Clarke, 95.

[69] Cashmore, 57–8; *Rastafarianism in Greater London* (London, 1984), 19.

1970s identified Rastafarians with violence and 'mugging'[70] and by 1978 'the stereotyped conception of the Rastaman as a racist thug, lurking in the ghettos of big cities and waging war on the rest of the community... had become cemented in the public consciousness'.[71] A large measure of responsibility for this dire portrayal lay in a very misleading report commissioned by the West Midlands police force, in the wake of deteriorating relations between young black people and the police in the Handsworth area of Birmingham. The Report, 'Shades of Grey',[72] published in 1977, purported to identify a 'criminalised Dreadlock sub-culture'[73] in Handsworth comprising some 200 hard-core members, mostly unemployed and living in 'squats'. The Report stated—

... the most serious police problems relate to crimes of violence against persons and personal property ... mainly committed in a particular area ... mainly at particular times—dusk and the early hours of the morning—mainly by a particular group—some 200 youths of West Indian origin or descent who have taken on the appearance of followers of the Rastafarian faith by plaiting their hair in locks and wearing green, gold and red woollen hats.[74]

The Report went on—

... apart from the specific crimes for which they are responsible, they constantly threaten the peace of individual citizens, black, brown and white, whilst making the police task both difficult and dangerous since every police contact with them involves the risk of confrontation or violence.[75]

Although the Report attempted to draw a sharp distinction between the members of this violent, criminal sub-culture and 'true Rastafarians'[76] (who were not violent), this did not appear to be borne out by the facts since, according to Cashmore's observations, the Rastafarians in Handsworth appeared to display a 'kaleidoscopic array of beliefs and actions encased in a circumambience of Rastafarian concepts and categories'.[77] No doubt some thefts and robberies were being committed, but no hard-core, structured group of Rastafarians existed to pose a general threat to the local community.[78] Although the Report was in many respects even-handed and indeed sympathetic towards the plight of young, unemployed West Indians, the reactions of the media, and the police themselves in drafting in extra officers on foot patrol, left the general public in no doubt as to the essence of being a Rastafarian—he was a violent criminal, wearing dreadlocks and sporting the Ethiopian national

---

[70] Cashmore, 58, 207–8; Campbell, 189.   [71] Cashmore, 208.
[72] Brown, J., *Shades of Grey: A Report on Police–West Indian Relations in Handsworth* (Cranfield, 1977).   [73] Ibid, 7.
[74] Ibid, 3.   [75] Ibid, 8.   [76] Ibid, 3, 7.
[77] Cashmore, 215.   [78] Ibid, 216–7, 223–4.

colours of red, gold and green.[79] This was, of course, highly misleading, for many Rastafarians in Handsworth (and elsewhere) were peaceful, law-abiding citizens and the crime rate there was unremarkable in comparison with other areas of Birmingham.[80] However, the upshot of the Report, together with the wide publicity which it generated, was that all Rastafarians tended to be ascribed a deviant role as dangerous and violent criminals.

Somewhat ironically, Cashmore, whose book on the Rastafarian movement in England did much to create a more positive image and exposed the flaws in the 'Shades of Grey' Report, may himself have contributed unwittingly to the creation of a negative stereotype. In assessing the early years of the movement in Jamaica,[81] he drew a comparison between certain actions of one of the founding preachers, Leonard Howell, and those of Charles Manson, whose 'hippy commune' in California achieved considerable notoriety through the commission of ritual murders in the 1960s. This led one commentator to accuse Cashmore of characterizing Rastafarians as potential murderers.[82]

Tensions between Rastafarians and the police seem to have continued, with each expecting to encounter hostility from the other.[83] Rastafarians have often been contemptuous of the police because they represent the oppressive system of 'Babylon', while the police have tended to view Rastafarians as 'truculent' and a threat to civil order.[84] In addition, since much police time is spent on combating the consumption of and traffic in illicit drugs, whereas Rastafarians regard the use of *ganja* (cannabis) as part of their faith and culture, some degree of conflict is inevitable.[85] The general taint of criminality often attached to Rastafarians has led to suggestions that they may have been partly responsible for some of the urban riots which occurred during the early 1980s.[86] However, in his Report on the Brixton Disorders in 1981, Lord Scarman was at pains to exonerate them from any responsibility and declared that 'their faith and their aspirations deserve more understanding and more sympathy than they get from the British public'.[87] Lord Scarman did, however, allude to the fact that 'young hooligans' had copied the outward signs of the faith and he drew attention to the risk that the wrongs they committed in the name of Rastafari might destroy the movement altogether.[88] Certainly, he was in no doubt that the use of *ganja* had done 'substantial harm to

---

[79] Cashmore, 219–33.
[80] See Rex, J. and Tomlinson, S., *Colonial Immigrants in a British City* (London, 1979), 232–5.
[81] Ibid, 26.   [82] Campbell, 8, 193.   [83] Cashmore, 173–80.
[84] See Rex and Tomlinson, 68.   [85] Ibid, 178.
[86] See e.g. Gilroy, 100 (in relation to the Bristol riots of 1980).
[87] *Report on the Brixton Disorders, 10–12 April 1981*, Cmnd 8427 of 1981, para 3.106.
[88] Ibid, para 3.107.

Rastafarian reputation in this country'.[89]

While some Rastafarians[90] have criticized Lord Scarman's distinction[91] between 'true' Rastafarians, who are 'deeply religious' and 'disciplined', on the one hand, and the 'young hooligans' masquerading as such through their adoption of outward symbols, on the other, the latter group do present the movement with some real difficulties. If these young criminals are indeed to be classed as Rastafarians, on the basis that they have adopted the political ideologies of protest and resistance to racism outlined earlier (as well as the outward symbols), their lack of religious discipline seems beside the point. If, on the other hand, they are in no sense Rastafarians but merely appear to be so, it is surely in the interests of the movement to disown them publicly, if it is not to be tarnished by their attempts at association. For this purpose, it is too simple merely to state that a Rastaman is 'self-defined' and that this autonomy is 'threatened by external definitions'.[92] Equally important, however, is that society in general should not form a negative impression of the Rastafarian movement as a whole on the basis of the criminal behaviour of a few of its members, which seems to have happened during the 1970s and early 1980s.[93] At all events, there seems to have been little recent adverse publicity concerning the movement and their relations with the police appear to have improved in the wake of a greater emphasis on 'community policing'.[94] In Handsworth, for example, far better relationships between the police and Rastafarian groups had been established by 1981[95] and by 1986 Clarke felt able to comment that—

. . . an increasing number of Rastafarians have shifted away from the goal of total separation, . . . from hostility to white society, to an emphasis on pluralism . . . a form of integration requiring mutual respect and involving considerable interaction.[96]

---

[89] Id.   [90] See e.g. *Rastafarianism in Greater London*, 15–16.
[91] See his *Report*, para 3.106.   [92] *Rastafarianism in Greater London*, 15–16.
[93] Popular perceptions of criminality among young black people in general were, of course, widespread during this period; see e.g. Hall, S. *et al*, *Policing the Crisis* (Basingstoke, 1978); Solomos, J., *Black Youth, Racism and the State* (Cambridge, 1988).
[94] Since 1984 police forces have had a statutory duty to make arrangements for obtaining the views of the local community about policing and obtaining their co-operation in crime prevention—see Police and Criminal Evidence Act 1984, s 106, subsequently replaced by Police Act 1996, ss 7(3)(*b*), 96.
[95] See Brown, J., *Policing by Multi-racial Consent* (London, 1982), 220–3.
[96] At 99.

DREADLOCKS AND ETHIOPIAN COLOURS:
THE SYMBOLS OF RASTAFARIAN IDENTITY

Rastafarians have employed the wearing of dreadlocks and the display of 'Ethiopian' colours in their clothing (notably in their woollen tams) as striking symbols of their separate identities and their social distance from mainstream society, both in Jamaica and in England. In Cashmore's words—

The somewhat exotic appearance of Rastas provided evidence of their disaffiliation with the wider society and served to solidify feelings of belongingness to a small but exclusive movement.[97]

The origins of the wearing of dreadlocks remain obscure, but they certainly go back to the early years of the movement in Jamaica. Some suggest that the founding members may have sought to emulate the appearance of Ethiopian warriors or East African tribesmen whom they had seen in photographs,[98] whilst others point to the presence of Hindu holy men in Jamaica who had long, flowing hair.[99] In any event, the practice has since been afforded a number of different justifications. First, it reflects Rastafarian beliefs about the need for man to lead a life which is in harmony with the laws of nature.[100] Left uncut, African hair grows naturally into dreadlocks, once it has been coiled, and does not require to be specially plaited or combed to achieve this effect.[101] Secondly, reference is made to Old Testament authority in support of the practice. Passages in Leviticus and Numbers proscribe shaving the head[102] and Samson is invoked as an exemplar of a successful warrior, whose long hair enabled him to defeat the Philistines.[103] Thirdly, long hair is identified with strength through comparison with a lion's mane. One of Haile Selassie's honorific titles was the 'Lion of Judah'[104] and the symbolism of 'African lionism'[105] is employed to link the raw power of 'the king of beasts' with the apocalyptic vision[106] of the Lion of Judah's success in opening the sealed book containing the secrets of life.[107] Fourthly, dreadlocks function as a form of defiance against conventional

---

[97] At 156.

[98] Smith, Augier, and Nettleford, 9, 26; Barrett, 137. Campbell (at 95–6) links the origins of Rasta dreadlocks to the long hair of members of the Mau Mau movement in Kenya, but that uprising only commenced in 1951.

[99] Mansingh, A. and Mansingh, L., 'Hindu influences on Rastafarianism', *Caribbean Quarterly Monograph on Rastafari* (1985), 96 at 109.

[100] Owens, 151–7; Barrett, 137–40; Clarke, 82–5.

[101] Cashmore, 156; Campbell, 96.   [102] Leviticus, ch 21, v 5; Numbers, ch 6 v 5.

[103] Judges, ch 16; Barrett, 137; Clarke, 90.

[104] He kept tame lions himself in his palace in Addis Ababa.

[105] Barrett, 142; Campbell, 99–100.   [106] See Book of Revelation, ch 5, v 1–5.

[107] Clarke, 90.

social norms, a rejection of the values of 'Babylon' and its imputations of black inferiority, a rebellion against the fashion of some black people to go to great lengths to straighten their hair to look more like whites.[108] The figure of 'Natty Dread', popularized by the 1974 reggae song of that title sung by Bob Marley and the Wailers, has become part of the vocabulary of resistance.[109]

The importance attached to dreadlocks can be gauged from Barrett's assertion that one of the 'chief marks' of a true Rastafarian is 'the way he wears his hair'.[110] Also of considerable, if lesser, significance are the movement's colours of red, green, black, and gold.[111] The first three of these were adopted by Marcus Garvey for his Universal Negro Improvement Association, the first two being derived from the colours of the Ethiopian flag. For Rastafarians, red signifies the blood of the martyrs of history, black their skin colour, and green the land and its natural vegetation. Gold forms part of the national colours of both Ethiopia and Jamaica.

LEGAL CONFRONTATIONS OVER DREADLOCKS

(a) Treatment in prison

Rastafarians first encountered legal problems concerning dreadlocks when, during the 1970s, the prison authorities asserted a right to apply to them the normal rule that the hair of inmates should be cut short.[112] A Home Office circular issued in 1976 stated that Rastafarians did not qualify as members of a religious denomination for the purposes of the Prison Act 1952 and therefore no special dispensations should be applied to them.[113] The practice of the authorities was apparently to encourage Rastafarians to register their religious affiliation under the Act as members of the Ethiopian Orthodox Church,[114] but the wearing of dreadlocks is, of course, no part of the ritual of that Church.[115] Hence the circular was able to instruct prison officers in the following, rather obtuse, terms—

In support of a request to be allowed to wear hair long, an inmate may claim he belongs to the Ethiopian Orthodox Church. It has been confirmed with the

[108] Barrett, 138; Cashmore, 157–9; Campbell, 95.
[109] Barrett, 138–9; Cashmore, 102, 116–17; Campbell, 96.   [110] At 137.
[111] Barrett, 143; Cashmore, 159–60.   [112] Campbell, 195–6.
[113] Circular Instruction 60/1976.
[114] Robilliard, S., 'Religion in Prison' (1980) 130 *NLJ* 800 at 801.
[115] The Church is one of the oldest in Christendom, dating back to 330 AD, and naturally repudiates any notion that Haile Selassie is divine; see Barrett, 201–9; Cashmore, 62; Clarke, 15–16, 53.

resident priests of the church that long hair is not a requirement and governors may therefore require hair to be cut.[116]

However, following the plea in Lord Scarman's Report on the Brixton Disorders in 1981 for more understanding and sympathy for the Rastafarians,[117] a reappraisal took place. The 1981 *Report on the Work of the Prison Department* stated—

The Prison Department is now reviewing its policy toward Rastafarian inmates, and giving particular consideration to the desirability of allowing further recognition of minority customs and beliefs, even when the faith cannot be accorded formal recognition as a religion. One difficulty has been that there is no central authority or point of reference for guidance on what constitutes Rastafarian custom and practice. Discussions are taking place with the Commission for Racial Equality and between the Commission and Rastafarian and other groups. In the meantime the Home Secretary decided in November 1981 that wardens in detention centres—where the general practice is to require all inmates to have their hair cut short—should give Rastafarian inmates the opportunity to retain their 'dreadlocks'.[118]

So far as the practice in prisons was concerned, Lord Belstead on behalf of the Government answered a Parliamentary question in 1981 in the following terms—

As to haircuts, a governor has the right . . . to require the hair of any inmate to be cut for the sake of hygiene or neatness. Governors generally have a tolerant approach to long hair, including Rastafarian styles.[119]

Whether such a sanguine view of the situation was justified may perhaps be doubted, since there is at least one documented report just two years earlier of a Rastafarian prisoner being held down and rendered unconscious by means of tranquilizers so that his dreadlocks could be cut off.[120] Allegations were also made around this time that Rastafarian prisoners who resisted having their dreadlocks cut off were sometimes diagnosed as schizophrenic and placed in mental institutions.[121]

In 1982 the Catholic Commission for Racial Justice published a report recommending that Rastafari be recognized as a valid religion and that Rastafarian prisoners be accorded the same privileges as those of other faiths.[122] The following year in a new Home Office circular,[123] prison governors were instructed that Rastafarians should be allowed to retain their dreadlocks and the discretion of governors to allow dreadlocks is

[116] Circular Instruction 60/1976, annex A.   [117] *Report*, para 3.106.
[118] (London, 1982), 39.   [119] HL Debs, 423, col 542 (written answer).
[120] See Gordon, P., *White Law: Racism in the Police, Courts and Prisons* (London, 1983), 129–30.   [121] See Campbell, 195–7.
[122] 'Rastafarians in Jamaica and Britain' (London, 1982), 11.
[123] Circular Instruction 2/1983.

preserved in the current circular.[124] However, no change has occurred since that time in the policy of refusing to recognize the faith officially as a religion,[125] although a curious development has recently occurred in the annual statistics compiled by the Prison Service Chaplaincy. The 1994 census of religious registrations in prison showed the number of adherents to the Ethiopian Orthodox Church over a four year period was 1991–124, 1992–163, 1993–139, and 1994–143.[126]

A note relating to the figure for 1994 explained, however, that—

For the purposes of this exercise Rastafarian inmates have been included within the Ethiopian Orthodox listing. 101 inmates out of the total of 143 recorded are in fact Rastafarian.[127]

By the following year, the transparent falsity of this approach had begun to be acknowledged. The 1995 census gave two figures for the Ethiopian Orthodox Church, namely 29 and 151, the latter including 122 Rastafarians, who were also presented separately, for the first time, under the heading 'Non-Permitted "Religions"'.[128] By 1996 the fiction had been abandoned altogether, with only 21 Ethiopian Orthodox prisoners listed.[129] A total of 131 Rastafarians appeared, together with Black Muslims and Scientologists, under the independent rubric 'Non Permitted Religions'.[130]

From this rather opaque nomenclature, it would appear that Rastafarian prisoners are currently being treated as members of a cult, rather than adherents to a religion. They are not allowed to have themselves officially recorded as Rastafarians by prison governors for the purposes of section 10(5) of the Prison Act 1952, but they are not, of course, prevented from maintaining their faith in gaol. Indeed, a recent guide states that they are 'entitled to have their needs met, such as a vegetarian diet, retaining locks and wearing suitable headwear etc.'.[131]

In principle, the Prison Chaplaincy seems keen to afford official recognition, on the grounds that all minority faiths should be treated equally, but it has imposed two pre-conditions upon giving its support to an application to the Home Office for such recognition. First, it wishes to publish detailed information about Rastafari in its *Directory and Guide on Religious Practices in HM Prison Service*,[132] so that those who work in prisons have accurate information on matters such as central beliefs,

---

[124] Circular Instruction 51/1989, annex A2.   [125] Ibid.
[126] Prison Service Chaplaincy, *Annual Census of Religious Registration in Prison 1994* (London, 1994), i.   [127] At iv.
[128] Prison Service Chaplaincy, *Annual Religious Census 1995* (London, 1995), 3, 13.
[129] Prison Service Chaplaincy, *Annual Religious Census 1996* (London, 1996), 1.
[130] Ibid, 4.
[131] Prison Reform Trust and HM Prison Service, *The Prisoners' Information Book* (London, 1996), 22.   [132] (London, 1992).

diet, dress, worship, sacred writings, and ministry. Over the last few years such information has been gathered together on a number of religions, but great difficulty has been experienced in obtaining such information concerning Rastafari. In the absence of any central authority, assistance has been sought from the Rastafarian Advisory Service in London, but so far without success. Secondly, the Chaplaincy has sought a written undertaking from the Advisory Service that, if Rastafari were formally recognized, 'ministers' of that faith would not bring cannabis into prison establishments nor seek to use it there for religious purposes. No such undertaking has yet been forthcoming, although oral assurances have been given that this would not present any problem.

While, at first glance, these requests by the Chaplaincy do not appear unreasonable, they represent substantial obstacles for a religion without an authoritative leadership or institutional framework and with only minimal doctrinal beliefs. It would be far simpler for the Home Office to afford official recognition, while making it clear to any visiting Rastafarian 'minister' that cannabis could not be brought into the prison or consumed there as an aspect of religious observance or worship. So long as cannabis remains a banned substance outside prison, its use clearly cannot be permitted inside. By no means every religious practice can be accommodated within the prison regime.[133] Information for inclusion in the *Directory and Guide on Religious Practices* can be obtained initially from published sources and then discussed with Rastafarian organizations before a final draft is agreed. Details about other religions in the *Directory* often need revision and updating and the lack of an authoritative statement about Rastafari, of all faiths, should not be an impediment to official recognition. It seems unlikely that the Jamaican Government, which apparently opposed such recognition in the 1970s, would take the same hostile stance today.

(b) Indirect discrimination in employment

In the previous chapter, the law relating to indirect discrimination in the field of employment was analyzed in the context of claims brought by Sikhs wearing beards and turbans. Conditions or requirements imposed by employers concerning facial appearance or particular headgear were identified as unlawful under the Race Relations Act 1976 if job applicants could not conscientiously comply with them, if such persons suffered a detriment as a result (by failing to obtain work), and if the

---

[133] An analogy can be drawn with the wearing of the Sikh *kirpan* (or dagger), which can lawfully be carried outside prison, but which Sikh prisoners are only permitted to keep in the form of a small symbolic replica, inlaid in a comb—see *Directory*, 76.

condition or requirement was not 'justifiable'.[134] In addition, for an action brought by an applicant to succeed he needed to demonstrate that the proportion of such persons of his own ethnic group who could in practice comply with the condition or requirement imposed by the employer was considerably smaller than the proportion of persons not of his own ethnic group.[135] In the leading case of *Mandla v Dowell Lee*[136] the House of Lords ruled that Sikhs constituted an ethnic group for the purposes of the Act and were therefore afforded legal protection against unlawful discrimination. Hence, in *Kamaljeet Singh Bhakerd v Famous Names Ltd*[137] an industrial tribunal held that the defendant company had acted unlawfully in refusing employment to the applicant, a turbaned Sikh, on the basis of a company rule that all employees had to wear 'mob caps'.

Similar problems have been encountered by Rastafarian job applicants wearing dreadlocks and multicoloured tams, who found that employers rejected their applications because of company rules about short hair and special caps. In *Cooper v British Rail*[138] in 1986 a Rastafarian had applied to British Rail for employment as a ticket collector. During his interview for the job he was told that he would have to wear a regulation BR cap. He offered instead to cover his dreadlocks with a tam in BR colours because a BR cap would not be large enough, but this was treated as a facetious remark by the BR interviewer and he was therefore refused the job. The industrial tribunal held that he had been discriminated against on religious rather than racial grounds and thus had no claim under the Race Relations Act 1976.

The same issue received much more detailed examination in *Dawkins v Department of the Environment*.[139] Here the applicant had responded to an advertisement by the Crown Suppliers for an experienced van driver for the Government's interdepartmental dispatch service, an operation later run by the Department of the Environment, and he subsequently attended an interview wearing a tam, under which his hair was arranged in the form of dreadlocks. The interviewer explained to him that the service expected its male drivers to have short hair. The interview was terminated when the applicant made it clear that he was unwilling to cut off his dreadlocks because of his religion. He was subsequently refused the job. His complaint of unlawful indirect discrimination was upheld by a majority decision of the industrial tribunal, but then rejected on appeal by a majority decision of the Employment

---

[134] Ss 1(1)(*b*), 4(1).   [135] S3(1).   [136] [1983] 2 AC 548.
[137] Case number 19289/87, unreported, decision dated 18 Feb 1988.
[138] Unreported, but described in *Independent*, 27 Nov 1986.   [139] [1993] IRLR 284.

Appeal Tribunal. This decision was subsequently affirmed by the Court of Appeal.

The central issue in the case revolved around whether or not Rastafarians constitute an ethnic group within the terms of the 1976 Act. If they fall outside the Act's protection, the common law does nothing to inhibit an employer from rejecting a job applicant simply on the basis of the length and style of his hair,[140] however arbitrary such a policy may be in the case of van drivers. At the industrial tribunal, which heard expert evidence from Dr Ernest Cashmore, the majority held that Rastafarians did qualify as an ethnic group because they possessed the two essential characteristics demanded by Lord Fraser in *Mandla v Dowell Lee*, namely a long shared history, of which the group is conscious as distinguishing it from other groups and the memory of which it keeps alive, and a cultural tradition of its own, including family and social customs, often but not necessarily associated with religious observance.[141] The tribunal found that Rastafarians also possessed some of the additional characteristics mentioned by Lord Fraser as usual, though not essential for designation as an ethnic group, namely a common geographical origin (in Jamaica), a common language (English and Jamaican patois), a distinctive literature (in the form of poetry), and having a sense of being an oppressed minority. Mention was also made of their reggae music and the need to take into account a musical tradition as well as a written or oral literary tradition. The dissenting member of the tribunal did not consider that the movement's history of nearly sixty years was long enough to meet Lord Fraser's first essential condition, but the majority felt this period was sufficient in view of the movement's continuity and persistence.

On appeal, the Employment Appeal Tribunal reversed this decision, again only by a majority. Applying Lord Fraser's test relating to the two essential elements, the majority took the view that Rastafarians did not possess a long shared history, remarking—

It cannot reasonably be said that a movement which goes back for only 60 years, ie within the living memory of many people, can claim to be long in existence. Its history, in the judgment of the majority, is insufficiently sustained.[142]

On the other hand, the second element, in the form of a distinct cultural tradition, did appear to be satisfied—

. . . our view is that Rastafarians are a group with very little structure, no apparent organisation and having customs and practices which have evolved in a somewhat haphazard way. Nevertheless, notwithstanding these reservations

---

[140] See *Allen v Flood* [1898] AC 1 at 172–3.   [141] [1983] 2 AC 548 at 562.
[142] *Dawkins v Crown Suppliers (Property Services Agency)* [1991] ICR 583 at 594.

and placing them in the context of a formerly enslaved people striving for an identity, there may be a sufficient cultural tradition to satisfy the test, and we are not prepared to disagree with the finding of the tribunal on this point.[143]

The majority also relied upon Lord Templeman's judgment in *Mandla v Dowell Lee*, in which he stressed the need for an ethnic group to have some of the characteristics of a race, namely group descent, a group of geographical origin, and a group history,[144] commenting—

. . . in our judgment, Rastafarians cannot be so described. There is in our view insufficient to distinguish them from the rest of the Afro-Caribbean community so as to render them a separate group defined by reference to ethnic origins. They are a religious sect and no more.[145]

The decision of the Employment Appeal Tribunal was endorsed by the Court of Appeal, which held that while Rastafarians possessed a strong cultural tradition including reggae music and dreadlocks, the crucial question was whether they had established a separate identity from other Jamaicans or Afro-Caribbeans by reference to their ethnic origins. Giving the word 'ethnic' a 'racial flavour', the Court ruled that they had not. In stressing that their shared history only went back for sixty years and could not be extended further to encompass the African past with which they so closely identify today, the Court also appeared to be indicating that their history was not long enough to satisfy Lord Fraser's test in *Mandla v Dowell Lee*.

During the course of the Parliamentary debates on the 1976 Act Lord Harris, the Government spokesman in the House of Lords, had stated that the phrase 'ethnic or national origins' introduced the idea of 'groups defined by reference to cultural characteristics, geographical location, social organisation and so on', rather than physical characteristics such as colour or race.[146] If the Court of Appeal had known this, their decision might possibly have been different. However, the judges declined an invitation to consult Hansard, pursuant to the rule in *Pepper (Inspector of Taxes) v Hart*,[147] on the surprising ground that the guidance given by the speeches of Lord Fraser and Lord Templeman, when read together, was 'clear and unambiguous'.[148]

The high level of disagreement among those involved in attempting to determine whether Rastafarians are an ethnic group provides a salutary reminder of the elusive nature of the concept of ethnicity.[149] It is certainly possible to argue cogently in favour of their inclusion within the concept, either on the basis that a sixty year existence is indeed sufficient to meet

---

[143] Id.   [144] [1983] 2 AC 548 at 569.   [145] [1991] ICR 583 at 594.
[146] HL Debs, 374, col 74.   [147] [1993] AC 593.
[148] At 288. For the different approaches adopted in the two speeches, see above, ch 8.
[149] See above, ch 1.

Lord Fraser's requirement of a 'long' shared history, or on the grounds that the precise length of that history should not be considered a critical factor in the definition in any event. Lord Fraser himself cited with unqualified approval[150] the following test propounded by Richardson J in the New Zealand Court of Appeal in *King-Ansell v Police*—

. . . a group is identifiable in terms of its ethnic origins if it is a segment of the population distinguished from others by a sufficient combination of shared customs, beliefs, traditions and characteristics derived from a common or presumed common past, even if not drawn from what in biological terms is a common racial stock. It is that combination which gives them an historically determined social identity in their own eyes and in the eyes of those outside the group. They have a distinct social identity based not simply on group cohesion and solidarity but also on their belief as to their historical antecedents.[151]

Adopting this perspective and in the light of the fact that Rastafarians possess almost all those characteristics which Lord Fraser depicted as 'relevant', albeit not 'essential', in commonly distinguishing ethnic groups from the surrounding community, there is surely a powerful argument for their claim to the protection of the 1976 Act to be upheld. They possess a common geographical origin, a common language, and a common religion, and they perceive themselves as an oppressed minority. To regard a sixty year history as insufficient for the construction of an ethnic group is to disregard modern anthropological perceptions of ethnicity and ethnic identity as concepts which can be fashioned, moulded, and even invented to suit particular social circumstances.[152] In this context it is certainly not unrealistic to acknowledge that a distinctive ethnic identity has been constructed over a period of two generations. On the other hand, it may be salutary if the English legal system is forced to recognize that it offers no protection against religious discrimination *per se* and that this is a defect which needs to be remedied.[153] Muslims, in particular, have identified this branch of the law as ripe for reform,[154] following tribunal rulings that they too do not constitute an ethnic group under the 1976 Act.[155]

---

[150] [1983] 2 AC 548 at 564.   [151] [1979] 2 NZLR 531 at 543.

[152] See above, ch 1.

[153] See Commission for Racial Equality, *Second Review of the Race Relations Act 1976* (London, 1992), 58–61.

[154] See e.g. UK Action Committee on Islamic Affairs, *Muslims and the Law in Multi-faith Britain: The need for reform* (London, 1993).

[155] See *Nyazi v Rymans Ltd*, EAT, 10 May 1988 (unreported); *Tariq v Young*, Birmingham IT, 19 Apr 1989 (unreported); *Commission for Racial Equality v Precision Manufacturing Services*, Sheffield IT, 26 July 1991 (unreported); *JH Walker Ltd v Hussain* [1996] IRLR 11.

THE USE OF *'GANJA'* (CANNABIS): A RELIGIOUS RITE AND CULTURAL PRACTICE

The use of *ganja* by Rastafarians in Jamaica dates back to the earliest years of the movement, following the release from prison of one of its founding preachers, Leonard Howell. He had been convicted of sedition in 1934 for, *inter alia*, advocating loyalty to Haile Selassie rather than to the British Crown,[156] but by 1940 he had established a commune of several hundred followers at a remote place named Pinnacle, high up in the hills, some twenty miles from Kingston.[157] As well as being grown as a cash crop, *ganja* was cultivated and used there for ritual purposes.[158] However, this was by no means the first instance of its consumption in Jamaica, as Barrett has explained—

Prior to the emergence of the Rastafarians, *ganja* was used by native herbalists as a folk medicine, particularly in teas and as smoking mixtures with tobacco. But as the Rastafarians emerged, *ganja* took on a new role as a religious sacrament. Its use became a reactionary device to the society and an index of an authentic form of freedom from the establishment. Although the use of *ganja* was prohibited very early in Jamaica,[159] most of the peasants were unaware of it; the Rastafarians, who were mostly urban dwellers, knew of its illegality. It would therefore be right to assume that as a protest against society, *ganja* smoking was the first instrument of protest engaged in by the movement to show its freedom from the laws of 'Babylon'.[160]

The precise origins of *ganja* consumption in Jamaica are unclear, some arguing that the practice was imported from India by indentured labourers in the 1840s,[161] while others contend that the custom may have been brought across from West Africa, either by slaves or by post-emancipation African industrial workers during the nineteenth century.[162] In any event, the Jamaican police raided the Pinnacle commune in 1941 and brought criminal charges against Howell and several of his followers for the cultivation of a dangerous drug. Twenty-eight of them were convicted and imprisoned.[163] From that time onwards Rastafarians in Jamaica have found themselves in a perpetual conflict with the state authorities over *ganja*.[164]

There are a number of separate strands in the arguments employed by Rastafarians to explain the use of *ganja* as the movement's 'principal

---

[156] Barrett, 85; Campbell, 71.   [157] Barrett, 86.   [158] Ibid, 88, 128.
[159] Legislation banning it was first introduced in 1913.   [160] At 128–9.
[161] Rubin, V. and Comitas, L., *Ganja in Jamaica* (The Hague, 1975), 36–7; Campbell, 107–8; Mansingh and Mansingh, 103, 106.
[162] Bilby, K., 'The Holy Herb: Notes on the Background of Cannabis in Jamaica', *Caribbean Quarterly Monograph on Rastafari* (Kingston, 1985), 82.   [163] Barrett, 87.
[164] Barrett, 92, 133–6; Campbell, 108–9. It should not be thought, however, that they are alone in this, since it was estimated during the 1970s that some sixty per cent of adult male Jamaicans were *ganja* smokers—see Rubin and Comitas, 37.

ritual'.[165] First, Biblical authority is cited to justify consumption of 'the holy herb', 'the weed', or 'the grass', as *ganja* is variously described. According to the Book of Genesis, for example—

. . . the earth brought forth grass, and herb yielding seed after his kind, and the tree yielding fruit, whose seed was in itself, after his kind: and God saw that it was good.[166]

Secondly, *ganja* is thought to contribute to more fruitful religious reflection and meditation, as well as to greater spiritual insights and the attainment of wisdom during 'reasoning' sessions.[167] Barrett has argued that the core of Rastafarian religiosity resides in the revelatory dimensions induced by the sacramental use of *ganja*, in which a new level of consciousness is attained.[168] Adherents to the movement are enabled more easily to perceive Haile Selassie as the true redeemer and to appreciate their own true identities.[169] *Ganja* is clearly a basic element in their belief system[170] and Owens states that the very act of smoking *ganja* is considered a form of religious worship, comparable to the sharing of communion wine by Christians in church.[171]

Thirdly, the use of *ganja* fits within Rastafarian religious views about the importance of natural living. Most are vegetarians and prefer to eat foods in their natural state, rather than processed products.[172] They also avoid alcohol.[173] *Ganja* is one of the fruits of the earth and it has long been thought to have valuable medicinal properties.[174]

So far as the use of *ganja* by Rastafarians in England is concerned, there is clear evidence of widespread consumption, as well as of dealing in relatively small quantities, both within the movement and with outsiders, especially in pubs and cafes.[175] Clearly, many Rastafarians regard the use of *ganja* as legitimate in terms of their religious and cultural norms[176] (although its consumption is certainly not obligatory on the part of adherents[177]) and this is liable to bring them into direct confrontation with English law in the form of police raids, arrests, prosecution, conviction, and punishment. Those who act in conformity with their religious beliefs and cultural traditions will automatically be in breach of English legal provisions governing the misuse of drugs. This dilemma was glossed over rather too easily in Lord Scarman's Report on the

---

[165] Clarke, 47.
[166] Ch 1, v 12; see also Genesis, ch 1, v 29, ch 3, v 18; Exodus, ch 10, v 12, Proverbs, ch 15, v 17; Psalms, ch 104, v 14; Revelation, ch 22, v 2.
[167] Owens, 162; Barrett, 128, 130; Clarke, 89.   [168] At 216.
[169] Ibid, 216–8.   [170] Rubin and Comitas, 4.   [171] At 160.
[172] Barrett, 140–1.   [173] Ibid, 131.   [174] Ibid, 129.
[175] See e.g. Pryce, 73–5; Cashmore, 178; Kerridge, R., *Real Wicked Guy: A View of Black Britain* (Oxford, 1983), 84, 92–4; Murphy, D., *Tales of Two Cities* (London, 1987) chs 11–13.
[176] Cashmore, 138.   [177] Owens, 158–9; Clarke, 89.

Brixton Disorders in 1981.[178] Jah Bones, a British Rastafarian, indicated in his evidence to the inquiry that he believed it was as legitimate to smoke cannabis as to drink alcohol.[179] However, Lord Scarman managed to extract from him an acceptance of the duty of all to obey the law of the land,[180] when in fact the conflict between the twin obligations of religion and law are not capable of resolution by examining the belief system of the 'true' Rastafarian, as Lord Scarman had supposed.[181] The consumption of *ganja* certainly appears to be a significant element in the religious practice and cultural and social life of most Rastafarians living in England today.

LEGAL CONFRONTATIONS OVER CANNABIS

(a) Development of the statutory prohibition

Early English drug control legislation was partly prompted by international pressures. In 1912 the first international Opium Convention was signed after a conference at the Hague, following US-orchestrated condemnation of Britain for exploiting its status as the world's most powerful trading nation to force China to import opium from India.[182] By the terms of the 1912 Convention the thirty-four signatory states committed themselves to using their pharmacy laws to restrict opiates and cocaine to purely medical as opposed to recreational use. At the Hague conference it was also agreed that a study of the abuse of cannabis was required. In 1919 under the Treaty of Versailles, ratification of the Hague Convention was made mandatory and Britain subsequently implemented its provisions in domestic law through the enactment of the Dangerous Drugs Act 1920. Four years earlier, however, emergency wartime measures had been taken to criminalize the possession or supply of opium and cocaine without medical prescription, following widespread use of cocaine by soldiers in the front line.[183] In 1925 a further Convention was signed at Geneva, which added cannabis to the list of drugs subject to international control, following a strong condemnation of

---

[178] Cmnd 8427 of 1981.   [179] Para 3.106.   [180] Ibid.
[181] See Kerridge, 96.
[182] Berridge, V. and Edwards, G., *Opium and the People* (London, 1987), 174; *Release White Paper on Reform of the Drug Laws* (London, 1992), 5–6. In 1829 Britain had refused to accede to a new policy of 'prohibition' introduced by the Chinese emperor, who was well aware of the evils of opium addiction, and in 1842 the matter had been settled by a British victory in the first Opium War—see Whittaker, B., *The Global Connection: The Crisis of Drug Addiction* (London, 1987), 16–20; Fortson, R., *The Law on the Misuse of Drugs and Drug Trafficking Offences*, 3rd ed. (London, 1996), 4.
[183] See Regulation 40B made under Defence of the Realm Act 1914.

'hashish' (the term by which cannabis resin is commonly known) by the Egyptian delegate.[184] This extension was incorporated into English law by the Dangerous Drugs Act 1925. International control of dangerous drugs was revised and consolidated in the Single Convention on Narcotic Drugs 1961 which, as amended by a Protocol in 1972, forms the basis of the current international regime.

The Misuse of Drugs Act 1971 represents the cornerstone of English legal controls, but before drawing attention to its main provisions it is important to examine briefly how it evolved. There seems to have been very little use of cannabis in this country until the 'youth revolution' of the 1960s when, in the context of a new mood of protest among young people, both hard and soft drugs were increasingly consumed across a wide range of social classes as part of the positive assertion of a different, often hedonistic, lifestyle.[185] Horror stories of escalation and addiction dominated media reporting[186] and in 1967 a new Dangerous Drugs Act was enacted to restrict the medical prescription of heroin and cocaine to addicts in the light of the discovery of massive overprescription by some doctors, which had led to the surplus being sold on the black market. Until the 1960s, drug addiction was regarded as a disease or a form of mental illness and as a result the role of doctors was seen as central.[187] Since that time the emphasis has shifted to a 'crime-control model', seeing drug misuse as a deviant fashion or sub-culture, warranting a penal rather than a medical response.[188] It is viewed as a social as much as a medical problem.

(b) Application of the law by the courts

The principal offences relating to cannabis in the 1971 Act cover production, cultivation, importation, possession, and supply of the drug.[189] It is also an offence for the occupier of premises knowingly to permit or suffer to take place on those premises the production, supply, or smoking of cannabis.[190] Production, for this purpose, encompasses the cultivation of cannabis plants.[191] Detailed examination of the requirements of each offence lies beyond the scope of this work,[192] which focuses instead on the practical impact of the law, especially as it affects Rastafarians. Official statistics reveal that, whereas in 1976 some 9,946 persons were

---

[184] Fortson, 5.
[185] See e.g. Young, J., *The Drugtakers* (London, 1971), 11–13; Auld, J., *Marijuana Use and Social Control* (London, 1981), 31–2; Office of Health Economics, *Drug Misuse* (London, 1992), 39.   [186] Auld, ch 1.
[187] Fortson, 6.
[188] Rutherford, A. and Green, P., 'Illegal Drugs and British Criminal Justice Policy' in Albrecht, H. and Kalmthout, A. (eds), *Drugs Policies in Western Europe* (Freiburg, 1989), 383.
[189] Ss 3–6.   [190] S 8.   [191] S 37.   [192] See generally, Fortson (1996).

found guilty, cautioned, or dealt with by compounding for drugs offences involving cannabis,[193] by 1995 this figure had risen to 76,694.[194] Cannabis-related offences comprised 82 per cent of all drug related offences, with the vast majority of offenders being dealt with for the crime of simple possession alone.[195]

Cannabis and cannabis resin are classified as Class B drugs in the 1971 Act[196] and as a result offences involving these substances attract lighter sentences than those involving Class A drugs, such as heroin and cocaine.[197] In *R v Aramah*[198] in 1983 the Court of Appeal set out detailed sentencing guidelines for drug offences, with a view to trying to achieve greater consistency, indicating what would be an appropriate range of sentences for importation, supply, and possession of both Class A and Class B drugs. While the guidelines have had to be amended to deal more harshly with those trafficking in hard drugs, in the light of the heavier maximum sentences introduced in respect of the importation and supply of Class A drugs by the Controlled Drugs (Penalties) Act 1985,[199] there has been no revision of the guidelines in relation to Class B drugs.[200] The specific guidelines for cannabis laid down by Lord Lane CJ in *R v Aramah* were as follows[201]—

(a) *Importation*

The maximum sentence is fourteen years' imprisonment.[202] Large scale or whole-sale importation of massive quantities justifies around ten years' imprisonment for those playing other than a subordinate role in the operation.[203] Medium quantities over twenty kilos should attract three to six years' imprisonment, depending upon the amount involved and all the other circumstances of the case.[204] Amounts below twenty kilos would merit between eighteen months' and three years' imprisonment, with the lowest range being reserved for those who pleaded guilty and who made only a small profit out of the transaction.[205] A courier's previous good character should not be treated as an important factor in sentencing because large scale operators tend to recruit persons of good character in the hope that they will attract the court's sympathy and escape with a light sentence.[206] An immediate custodial sentence is generally required in these

---

[193] Home Office, *Statistics of Drug Seizures and Offenders Dealt With, United Kingdom, 1986: Supplementary Tables* (London, 1988), table S2.29.
[194] Home Office, *Statistics of Drug Seizures and Offenders Dealt With, United Kingdom, 1995* (London, 1996), table 3.12. [195] Ibid, 22.
[196] Sched 2. [197] Sched 4, as amended. [198] (1982) 4 Cr App R (S) 407.
[199] See *R v Bilinski* (1987) 9 Cr App R (S) 360.
[200] *R v Hedley* (1989) 11 Cr App R (S) 298. [201] At 409–10.
[202] Customs and Excise Management Act 1979, s 170.
[203] See e.g. *R v Mitchell* (1986) 8 Cr App R (S) 472.
[204] See e.g. *R v Price* (1985) 7 Cr App R (S) 190.
[205] See e.g. *R v Daly; R v Whyte* (1987) 9 Cr App R (S) 519.
[206] See e.g. *R v Hamouda* (1982) 4 Cr App R (S) 137.

cases.[207] On the other hand, importation of very small quantities for personal use can often simply be met by a fine.

(b) *Distribution*

The maximum sentence for supplying cannabis or possessing cannabis with the intent to supply the drug is fourteen years' imprisonment.[208] The supply of massive quantities justifies a sentence in the region of ten years' imprisonment for those playing anything other than a subordinate role. Otherwise the period should be between one year and four years, depending upon the scale of the operation.[209] Wholesale distribution to the retail trade comes at the top of this bracket. On the other hand, where there is no commercial motive, for instance where cannabis is supplied at a party, the offence may not be serious enough to warrant a prison sentence.

(c) *Possession*

Simple possession carries a maximum sentence of five years' imprisonment,[210] but where only small amounts are involved for personal use the offence can often be met by the imposition of a fine.[211] However, a history of persistent flouting of the law may justify a short sentence of imprisonment.[212]

Two other offences relating to cannabis, which were not specifically dealt with in the guidelines set down in *R v Aramah*, are also worth mentioning here.

(d) *Cultivation*

Cultivation of cannabis plants carries a maximum sentence of fourteen years' imprisonment,[213] but if the plants are grown for the offender's own consumption a sentence of between three and twelve months' imprisonment is generally appropriate.[214]

(e) *Permitting use of premises*

Permitting premises to be used for the supply or smoking of cannabis is punishable by up to fourteen years' imprisonment.[215] A publican who takes no steps to prevent cannabis consumption on licensed premises after a warning by the police can expect a short prison sentence.[216]

Against this background it is possible to analyse the only three instances

---

[207] For concern relating to the imposition of long custodial sentences upon naive and impoverished couriers, see e.g. Green, P., *Drug Couriers* (London, 1991).

[208] Misuse of Drugs Act 1971, ss 4(3), 5(3), sched 4.

[209] See e.g. *R v Steventon* (1991) 13 Cr App R (S) 127; *R v Friend* (1992) 14 Cr App R (S) 77.

[210] Misuse of Drugs Act 1971, s 5(2), sched 4.

[211] See e.g. *R v Aldred* (1983) 5 Cr App R (S) 393. A community service order is also possible; see *R v Barley* (1989) 11 Cr App R (S) 158. The maximum fine was increased from £500 to £2,500 by Criminal Justice and Public Order Act 1994, s 157(2), Sched 8.

[212] See e.g. *R v Cocks* (1991) 13 Cr App R (S) 166.

[213] Misuse of Drugs Act 1971, s 6(2), sched 4.

[214] See e.g. *R v Proud* (1987) 9 Cr App R (S) 119; *R v Case* (1991) 13 Cr App R (S) 20.

[215] Misuse of Drugs Act 1971, s 8, sched 4.

[216] See e.g. *R v Pusser* (1983) 5 Cr App R (S) 225.

in which the defendants in reported cannabis cases have been specifically identified as Rastafarians. In *R v Williams*[217] the defendant and his
girlfriend had arrived in the United Kingdom from Jamaica for a
month's holiday carrying about five kilos of cannabis in the false bot-
toms of their suitcases. They both pleaded guilty to charges of importing
the drug, the defendant receiving a sentence of three years' imprisonment and his friend a suspended sentence of two years' on the ground
that she was merely acting as his assistant. The defendant successfully
appealed against his sentence and had it reduced to two years', on the
basis that he was not a professional smuggler, he had a good job in
Jamaica, his employer had given him an excellent character reference,
and he was a Rastafarian who was only intending to sell a part of the
drug to fellow members of the movement to help finance his holiday
here. However, Cantley J commented that it remained 'a serious case,
and it must not be supposed either here or in Jamaica that the courts will
regard the sale of cannabis, smuggled into this country, to Rastafarians
as a different sort of offence from smuggling drugs into this country for
any other illicit reasons'.[218]

In *R v Daudi and Daniels*[219] two Rastafarians (one of whom was a
minor) were sentenced to three months' detention and six months'
imprisonment respectively, after pleading guilty to the offence of possessing a large quantity of cannabis with the intent to supply. They were on
their way back to their homes in Bristol after purchasing the cannabis in
Manchester when their car was stopped by the police. They were planning to distribute the drugs to fifty fellow members of the movement
living in Bristol. There was no commercial motive since the fifty 'brethren' had each contributed £12 towards the total costs of the purchase
price of £600, which the defendants had paid for the drugs. The Court of
Appeal acknowledged the benefits which had accrued to the defendants
from their faith and the good work they had done for the local community in the troubled area of St Paul's. However, their sentences were held
to be at the lower end of the bracket for this offence and the law had to
be applied even-handedly. In the words of Griffiths LJ—

It would be a denial of justice to say that 'because you are a Rastafarian you are
entitled to be treated entirely differently from other members of the community if
you choose to break the law relating to the supply and distribution of cannabis'.
Therefore this Court has come to the conclusion that . . . there are no grounds
upon which it would be right or indeed fair to the community as a whole, to
discriminate in their favour. Sadly they must pay the price of consciously and
knowingly breaking the law.[220]

---

[217] (1979) 1 Cr App R (S) 5. [218] At 6. [219] (1982) 4 Cr App R (S) 306.
[220] At 307.

In *R v Dallaway*[221] the defendant's principal defence to a charge of possession with intent to supply was that the small parcels of cannabis found in his flat were not for sale but for fellow Rastafarians to smoke when they came to visit him. However, it is clear that the word 'supply' in section 5(3) of the Act is not confined to sales of drugs but covers all forms of distribution.[222] A sentence of one year's imprisonment was upheld on appeal.

(c) Police practice

As we have seen, the number of people dealt with for cannabis related offences in 1995 was 76,694, yet estimates of the total numbers of those using cannabis each year tend to be expressed in terms of millions.[223] Clearly, the police lack the capacity to enforce the law rigorously to anywhere near its full extent. In many instances they are aware of well-established patterns of consumption and small-scale distribution of cannabis at particular locations and elect to ignore the situation. Not unnaturally, they prefer to devote scarce resources to more important tasks. Even where they do apprehend someone who has been breaking the law, they commonly choose to administer a formal 'caution' rather than institute criminal proceedings. Well-publicized raids on 'cannabis pubs' and mass arrests of black people may often prove counterproductive in terms of community relations, though obviously certain inner-city districts cannot be allowed to become 'no-go areas', in which no attempt is ever made to enforce the law relating to the misuse of hard drugs for fear of sparking off civil disorder. However, it is common knowledge that Rastafarians disapprove of hard drugs[224] and will often be prepared to co-operate with the police in their suppression.[225]

The police discretion to issue cautions is currently governed by guidelines issued by the Home Office in 1994, which refer to the need for 'greater consistency between police force areas'.[226] However, in recent years uniformity of approach has been notably absent in relation to cannabis. According to one report—

In some police authorities, up to three quarters of those found in possession of small amounts are cautioned. In others, all those caught are arrested and charged. Courts vary widely in their imposition of fines, conditional discharges or probation.[227]

---

[221] (1983) 148 JPN 31.   [222] See s 37(1).
[223] See e.g. Office of Health Economics, *Drug Misuse* (London, 1992); *Release White Paper*, 8; Coffield, F. and Gofton, L., *Drugs and Young People* (London, 1994), 3.
[224] Owens, 200; Murphy, 268–9.   [225] Murphy, 263.
[226] Home Office Circular 18/1994, para 1.   [227] *Independent* editorial, 20 Jan 1992.

Such variations on the part of different police forces were officially confirmed by the Home Office in 1995.[228] Although the 1994 guidelines indicate that offenders cannot normally expect to receive more than one caution,[229] it is clear that the huge rise in the number of cautions issued in recent years was maintained in 1995. During that year, just over half of all drug offenders were dealt with by means of a caution, compared with only 1 per cent in 1981.[230] Possession of cannabis attracted a caution in 56 per cent of cases in 1995, compared with 16 per cent ten years earlier.[231]

A major danger inherent in discretionary justice, whether administered by the police through their power to 'turn a blind eye' or issue a caution, or applied by the courts through their selection of appropriate sentences, is that it may be exercised in a racially discriminatory manner. Perceptions of such discrimination within the legal system on the part of many members of the black community,[232] whatever the true position may be,[233] are mirrored by Rastafarian ideas of 'Babylon' as an oppressive force operating against their interests. It has been alleged, for example, that some police officers use the cannabis prohibition law as a tool to exert control over local black populations[234] and one study has shown that a higher proportion of blacks than whites were convicted of drugs offences (mainly involving cannabis) in the West Midlands during 1989.[235] This is not surprising in view of the fact that black people are more frequently arrested for cannabis dealing than whites by police officers who stop and search black people more often than whites.[236] The practice of cautioning amounts in effect to a judicial decision which is not subject to public scrutiny since, although it obviously lacks the status of a conviction, it is recorded on the Police National Computer and can be cited in subsequent criminal proceedings.[237]

THE HUMAN RIGHTS DIMENSION

Article 9(1) of the European Convention provides that everyone has a right to freedom of religion, including the right to manifest this religion

---

[228] Home Office, *Statistics of Drug Seizures, 1995*, 15–16.
[229] Home Office Circular 18/1994, para 8. [230] *Statistics of Drug Seizures*, 18.
[231] Ibid, 20.
[232] See e.g. Runnymede Trust, *Racial Justice and Criminal Justice: A Submission to the Royal Commission on Criminal Justice* (London, 1992), 20–3.
[233] See generally, Reiner, R., 'Race and Criminal Justice' (1989) *New Community* 5; Hudson, B., 'Discrimination and Disparity: the influence of race on sentencing' (1989) *New Community* 23; Green, R., 'Probation and the Black Offender' (1989) *New Community* 81; Hood, R., *Race and Sentencing* (Oxford, 1992). [234] *Release White Paper*, 14.
[235] Hood, 53–4, 180.
[236] Ibid, 5; Amin, K., 'Police Stop and Searches: Who, Where and Why' (1995) 283 *Runnymede Bulletin* 6. [237] See Enright, S., 'Charge or Caution' (1993) 143 *NLJ* 446.

in practice and observance. However, Article 9(2) limits this right by
providing—

Freedom to manifest one's religion or beliefs shall be subject only to such
limitations as are prescribed by law and are necessary in a democratic society
in the interests of public safety, for the protection of public order, health or
morals, or for the protection of the rights and freedoms of others.

Article 18 of the International Covenant on Civil and Political Rights is in
similar vein and Article 27 of the same Covenant buttresses the position
of members of religious and ethnic minorities by giving them the right to
practise their own religion and enjoy their own culture. Religious discrimination is outlawed in certain circumstances by Article 14 of the
Convention and Articles 2(1) and 26 of the Covenant.

The official denial of the right of Rastafarian prisoners to record their
faith as such would appear to contravene the basic right of freedom of
religion. There is sufficient evidence of the usual attributes of a religion,
including reverence for a deity,[238] to warrant such recognition, and even
Pagan prisoners are now permitted to record their religion officially.[239]
The pre-conditions imposed by the Prison Chaplaincy for supporting an
application for recognition of the faith by the Home Office cannot be
justified by reference to Article 9(2) of the European Convention because
they are not 'necessary' in a democratic society. As we have seen, the
practical problems which the pre-conditions seek to address can be
easily solved in other ways. In addition, the discrimination against
Rastafarian prisoners is disproportionate and hence violates Article 14
because of the drastic nature of the means employed to deal with these
minor administrative problems.[240]

So far as the issue of wearing dreadlocks at work is concerned, it is
important to bear in mind that Article 14 of the European Convention
does not provide an independent, free-standing guarantee of non-discrimination on grounds of religion. As noted in Chapter 3, it only bars
discrimination in relation to other rights contained within the Convention. Since employment rights are not included in the Convention, Article 14 cannot offer any guarantee against employment being refused to a
Rastafarian on account of his dreadlocks. However, Article 26 of the
Covenant on Civil and Political Rights offers a more comprehensive
safeguard and its guarantee of equal protection of the law is not

---

[238] See e.g. *Re South Place Ethical Society: Barralet v Attorney-General* [1980] 1 WLR 1565.
[239] See e.g. *Annual Religious Census 1996*, 3. A clear distinction can be drawn with the
earlier unsuccessful application by a Pagan prisoner for registration of his membership of
the 'Wicca religion' (modern witchcraft) in *X v UK* (1978) 11 Dec & Rep 55, since in that case
the Commission ruled that no facts had been adduced from which it was possible to
establish the existence of such a religion.
[240] See e.g. *Belgian Linguistic Case (No 2)* (1968) 1 EHRR 252 at 284.

restricted to a prohibition of discrimination in relation to other Covenant rights, but applies to any field regulated and protected by public authorities.[241] Hence, it has been held by the Human Rights Committee to be applicable in relation to the enjoyment of economic, social, and cultural rights,[242] including employment rights.[243] Doubts do exist as to whether the ban on discrimination in Article 26 extends to the activities of private individuals, firms, and companies rather than merely to state organizations and public bodies,[244] but it is significant that in 1989, in its General Comment on Article 26, the Human Rights Committee indicated that it wished to know, from periodic reports supplied by states—

... if there remain any problems of discrimination in fact, which may be practised either by public authorities, by the community, or by private persons or bodies. The Committee wishes to know the legal provisions and administrative measures directed at diminishing or eliminating such discrimination.[245]

In the light of this, it seems probable that an evolution of international human rights law is occurring in this sphere since the earlier UN Declaration on the Elimination of All Forms of Intolerance and of Discrimination Based on Religion or Belief (1981) provides in Article 2 -

No one shall be subject to discrimination by any State, institution, group of persons or person on the grounds of religion or belief.

Article 4(1) provides, equally strongly—

All States shall take effective measures to prevent and eliminate discrimination on the grounds of religion or belief in the recognition, exercise and enjoyment of human rights and fundamental freedoms in all fields of civil, economic, political, social and cultural life.

Although the Declaration is not binding on states, it furnishes cogent evidence of the direction in which the law is developing. Reference can also be made to the provisions of the International Covenant on Economic, Social and Cultural Rights, in which states recognize the right to work and guarantee that this right will be exercised without religious discrimination.[246] However, state parties only commit themselves to

---

[241] See General Comment 18 (1990), para 12.

[242] *Zwann-de Vries, Broeks v Netherlands*, communication 182/1984.

[243] *Bwalya v Zambia*, communication 314/1988.

[244] See Lester, Lord and Joseph, S., 'Obligations of Non-Discrimination' in Harris, D and Joseph, S. (eds), *The International Covenant on Civil and Political Rights and United Kingdom Law* (Oxford, 1995), 582–4.

[245] General Comment No. 18, UN Doc CCPR/C/Rev1/Add1 (1989), para 9.

[246] Arts 2(2), 6.

achieve the progressive realization of such rights, rather than their immediate implementation.[247]

Alternatively, reliance can be placed on the guarantees of religious freedom contained in Article 9 of the European Convention and Article 18 of the International Covenant on Civil and Political Rights, but the restrictions in the limitation clauses need to be kept in mind. As we have seen, employers may justifiably impose general rules and conditions upon their existing employees, which impair their religious freedom, for instance where this is necessary to protect public health and safety[248] or to preserve the rights and freedoms of others.[249] However, with respect to most forms of employment, it is thought that it would be impossible to justify, on such grounds, a ban on dreadlocks being worn for religious reasons.

Turning next to the use of *ganja*, Article 8(2) of the European Convention authorizes state interference with the right to respect for a person's private life only if the interference is—

... such as is in accordance with the law and is necessary in a democratic society in the interests of national security, public safety or the economic well-being of the country, for the prevention of disorder or crime, for the protection of health or morals, or for the protection of the rights and freedoms of others.

Hence the central question would appear to revolve around whether the restrictions imposed by the Misuse of Drugs Act 1971 are 'necessary in a democratic society' for the protection of public health.[250] A century has now elapsed since the first thorough investigation of the possible health risks of cannabis consumption was undertaken by the Indian Hemp Drugs Commission in 1894. Its report concluded that 'moderate use has no physical, mental or moral ill-effects whatsoever'.[251] Fifty years later the New York Academy of Medicine found that cannabis was non-addictive, did not lead on to the use of hard drugs, and had no effect on the user's underlying personality.[252] In 1968, after reviewing all the available evidence, the Wootton Sub-Committee of the British Government's Advisory Committee on Drug Dependence expressed its agreement with the conclusions of these two earlier reports, commenting that 'long-term consumption of cannabis in *moderate* doses has no harmful effects'.[253] Six years later the US Shafer Report found that cannabis

---

[247] Art 2(1).   [248] See e.g. *Bhinder v Canada*, discussed in ch 8 above.
[249] See e.g. *Ahmad v UK*, discussed in ch 3 above.
[250] See generally, Whittaker, 220–3.
[251] *Report of the Indian Hemp Drugs Commission, 1893–94* (Simla, 1894), 264.
[252] Mayor's Committee on Marijuana, *The Marijuana Problem in the City of New York* (Lancaster, 1944).
[253] Home Office, *Cannabis: Report by the Advisory Committee on Drug Dependence* (London, 1968), 6–7.

causes no psychological deterioration, either in motivation or intellect, does not result in physical dependence, and that the overwhelming majority of users do not escalate to other drugs.[254] In 1982 the British Government's Advisory Council on the Misuse of Drugs reported that, although there was insufficient evidence to enable it to reach any incontestable conclusions as to the effects of cannabis use, 'much of the research undertaken so far has failed to demonstrate positive and significant harmful effects . . . attributable solely to the use of cannabis.'[255]

From these and other reports on the available research evidence it seems clear that, while the use of cannabis (like any other drug) does involve some health hazards,[256] especially if consumption is taken to excess over a substantial period, for most casual users in Britain the risks of real harm are minimal. Cannabis can obviously be dangerous if it is abused or if it is used in inappropriate circumstances, for instance by those operating machinery, flying aircraft or driving motor vehicles, or by pregnant women or by those with a predisposition to mental illness.[257] However, the dangers to health are far smaller than in the case of the consumption of tobacco or alcohol.[258]

Recent surveys suggest that cannabis smoking is a well-established leisure activity of up to 10 per cent of young adults, rather than a sign of an affiliation to an alternative lifestyle.[259] According to one newspaper report—

Anecdotal evidence suggests that the habit is more popular now than at any time since the sixties, having become the recreational drug of choice for many middle-class teenagers.[260]

Since the vast majority of these are using the drug for social or recreational purposes, rather than as part of a religious ritual, it seems helpful to examine the human rights dimension in the context of the right to privacy guaranteed by both the International Covenant on Civil and

[254] National Commission on Marijuana and Drug Abuse, *Marijuana: A Signal of Misunderstanding* (Washington, 1972).

[255] Advisory Council on the Misuse of Drugs, *Report of the Expert Group on the Effects of Cannabis Use* (London, 1982), 4.

[256] Inciardi, J. (ed), *The Drug Legalization Debate* (London, 1991), 49–51.

[257] Negrete, J., 'What's Happened to the Cannabis Debate?' (1988) 83 *Brit J of Addiction* 359 at 365–9. For reservations about some diagnoses of mental illness among Afro-Caribbeans, see Ranger, C., 'Race, culture and "cannabis psychosis": the role of social factors in the construction of a disease category' (1989) *New Community* 357.

[258] Inciardi, 37–8; this fact is not even mentioned in the recent White Paper, *Tackling Drugs Together: A Strategy for England 1995–1998*, Cm 2846 of 1995.

[259] See Office of Health Economics, 20.

[260] *Independent*, 20 Jan 1992; for detailed figures, see *Tackling Drugs Together: A Consultation Document on a Strategy for England 1995–1998*, Cm 2678 of 1994, 83; Miller, P. and Plant, M., 'Drinking, smoking and illicit drug use among 15 and 16 year olds in the United Kingdom' (1996) 313 *BMJ* 394.

Political Rights and the European Convention.[261] Arbitrary state interference with privacy is prohibited by the former treaty, while the latter only permits interference by a public authority where this is necessary in a democratic society in the interest of, *inter alia*, the protection of health or the prevention of disorder or crime.[262] Can it be argued that the cannabis provisions in the Misuse of Drugs Act are necessary for the prevention of disorder or crime, assuming that the argument on the basis of health is at best a borderline one? This position is difficult to sustain in view of the fact that penalizing simple possession of cannabis turns large numbers of otherwise entirely law-abiding citizens into criminals, with possibly profound repercussions for their family life, reputations, career prospects, and freedom to travel abroad. A policy of prohibition tends to inflate the street value of cannabis and leads many unemployed young people to commit robbery, burglary, or theft in order to finance their consumption. The black market fosters the creation of criminal gangs for the purpose of acquisition, importation, and distribution. Particular harm is done to relations between Rastafarians (and other black people) and the police because of the stereotypical ascription of criminality to black people in the public mind, based on well-publicized drugs raids in inner-city areas.[263] Moreover, a massive and wholly disproportionate amount of police and court time is expended on cannabis offences compared with offences relating to hard drugs such as heroin and cocaine and indeed with other measures of law enforcement.[264] Finally, laws which fail to command public respect and are widely perceived as wrong (as well as unenforceable) tend to bring the legal system as a whole into disrepute and can themselves lead to further law breaking.[265] For many people, the interference with individual liberty and freedom of choice entailed by the law's distinction between cannabis, on the one hand, and alcohol and tobacco, on the other, is demonstrably arbitrary. As one commentator pertinently asks—'Where is the morality of a society that imprisons cannabis dealers while according peerages and fortunes to nicotine and alcohol pushers?'[266] J. S. Mill's famous 'harm principle' would, of course, preclude any such forms of legal paternalism, on the ground that the individual should be sovereign over decisions which solely concern his or her own mind and body.[267] As a principle of public policy, legal paternalism in this field has, in the words

[261] Arts 17 and 8 respectively.   [262] Art 8(2).
[263] See e.g. Murphy, 229–30, 264.   [264] JUSTICE, *Drugs and the Law* (London, 1991), 4.
[265] *Release White Paper*, 14.   [266] Whittaker, 371.
[267] *On Liberty* (Himmelfarb, G., ed., Harmondsworth, 1985), 68–9; see ch 1 above.

of one commentator, 'an acrid moral flavour, and creates serious risks of governmental tyranny'.[268] Schur has also rightly pointed out that—

It is widely recognized by disinterested students of crime that whatever drastic methods are employed, law enforcement efforts in the victimless crime area are bound to meet with very limited success.[269]

Removal of the ban would also reduce the mystique of cannabis and should limit the chances of users having to come into contact with suppliers who would lead them on to hard drugs. In human rights terms, a policy of legal prohibition on the use of cannabis by Rastafarians (and indeed others) does not appear to be 'necessary' in a democratic society.

SOME FOREIGN COMPARISONS

Holland is perhaps the most striking example of a country which has altered its policy on cannabis in recent years, in the light of clear evidence that the imposition of criminal penalties often does more harm to the user than is done by the drug itself.[270] Drug problems there are generally viewed as being primarily for health workers rather than for the police and the courts, and it is felt that they should be tackled pragmatically and without excessive drama or moralizing. Cannabis is seen as normally causing little, if any, harm to consumers and the law was therefore amended in 1976 to draw a clear distinction between 'drugs presenting unacceptable risks' (such as heroin and cocaine) and 'traditional hemp products' (such as cannabis). Whereas penalties for illicit trafficking in drugs in the former category were greatly increased, the maximum penalty for possession of up to 30g of cannabis for personal use was lowered to one month's detention or a fine of 5,000 florins. Moreover, fresh government guidelines issued to the prosecuting authorities indicated that individuals should not be charged with an offence if this would not reduce health risks but rather cause the person concerned further problems. In practice this means that the prosecution of offences involving possession or cultivation of cannabis has very low priority and possession of less than 30g is never prosecuted. The Dutch authorities have broadly rejected the hypothesis that the use of cannabis is likely of

---

[268] Feinberg, J., 'Legal Paternalism' (1971) *Can Jnl of Philosophy* 105 at 116; see also his general critique of legal paternalism, *The Moral Limits of the Criminal Law, Vol 3: Harm to Self* (New York, 1986).　　　　[269] *Our Criminal Society* (New Jersey, 1969), 199.
[270] See generally, Van de Wijngaart, G., 'A Social History of Drug Use in the Netherlands' (1988) 18 *Jnl of Drug Issues* 481; Engelsman, E., 'Dutch Policy on the Management of Drug-related Problems' (1989) 84 *Brit Jnl of Addiction* 211; Whittaker, 53–4.

itself to lead consumers to hard drugs, but in an attempt to keep separate the markets for hard and soft drugs they have licensed a small number of youth centres and coffee shops (mainly in Amsterdam) where up to 5g of cannabis[271] can be purchased by individuals over the age of eighteen for their personal use. As a result of these reforms the use of cannabis has, contrary to some predictions, declined rather than increased. Holland remains a full party to the 1961 Single Convention. Possession of small quantities of cannabis for personal use has also been decriminalized in Spain and Germany.

By way of contrast, the long-standing strategy in the United States has essentially been to wage a war on all drugs in an uncompromising fashion, accentuated during the late 1980s by a belief in the White House that public tolerance for drug abuse should be reduced to zero.[272] Even so, during the 1970s eleven states reduced the penalties for possession of cannabis to the status of civil fines of around 100 dollars and Alaska went a stage further by permitting its cultivation for private and personal use.[273]

However, perhaps of even greater salience in the context of this chapter is the fact that in over twenty American states a special exemption from the narcotics laws has been created for adherents to the Native American Church, in their use for religious purposes of the drug *peyote* (a mescaline-based hallucinogen).[274] In some states such as New Mexico[275] and Montana,[276] this exemption was introduced by means of legislation, while in others such as California,[277] Arizona,[278] and Oklahoma,[279] it was achieved through judicial decision.[280] The most celebrated instance of judicial intervention occurred in *People v Woody*[281] in 1964 when the Supreme Court of California ruled that the state could not constitutionally apply its narcotics law to prohibit bona fide use of *peyote* by a group of Navajos in pursuit of their faith. Justice Tobriner declared—

[271] The figure was reduced from 30g to 5g in 1996.   [272] See Inciardi, 11.

[273] Ibid, 151; Gettman, J., 'Decriminalizing Marijuana' (1989) 32 *American Behaviourial Scientist* 243; DiChiara, A. and Galliher, J., 'Dissonance and Contradictions in the Origins of Marijuana Decriminalization' (1994) 28 *Law & Soc Rev* 41.

[274] See *Employment Division, Department of Human Resources of Oregon v Smith* 110 SC 1595 (1990) at 1618.   [275] New Mexico Statutes (1959) 54–5–16.

[276] Montana Statutes (1959) 94–35–123.   [277] *People v Woody* (1964) 40 Cal Rptr 69.

[278] *State v Whittingham* 19 Ariz App 27, 504 P 2d 950 (1973).

[279] *Whitehorn v State* 561 P 2d 539 (1977).

[280] A similar exemption was refused by an Oregon court in *State v Soto* 21 Or App 794, 537 P 2d 142 (1975); for discussion of the cases, see Doyle, J., 'Constitutional Law: Dubious Intrusions—Peyote, Drug Laws, and Religious Freedom' (1980) 8 *American Indian LR* 79.

[281] (1964) 40 Cal Rptr 69.

. . . the right to free religious expression embodies a precious heritage of our history. In a mass society, which presses at every point toward conformity, the protection of a self-expression, however unique, of the individual and the group becomes ever more important. The varying currents of the subcultures that flow into the mainstream of our national life give it depth and beauty. We preserve a greater value than an ancient tradition when we protect the rights of the Indians who honestly practised an old religion in using peyote one night at a meeting. . . .[282]

There are several points of similarity and difference between the decision in *People v Woody* and the question of exempting the Rastafarian use of cannabis in England. First, on the health side, *peyote* was found by the Court (on the basis of expert evidence) to 'work no permanent deleterious injury to the Indian', nor was there any evidence 'to suggest that Indians who use peyote are more liable to become addicted to other narcotics than non-peyote-using Indians'.[283] Cannabis is also properly classified as a hallucinogen[284] and, as we have seen, the health risks associated with its moderate use appear to be small and there is no evidence to support the theory that its use leads on to hard drugs. After ten years of studying Rastafarians in Jamaica, Barrett observed 'no physical, mental, or psychic effects' on them, adding that 'most older brethren have been smoking for twenty years and are still as witty, hard working, and creative as other citizens'.[285] It is generally accepted that the social and cultural context within which a particular drug is used, its 'set' and 'setting', determine whether or not it is viewed as harmful[286] and Rastafarian consumption is regulated both in Jamaica and England primarily by informal social controls (rather than legal constraints), which keep it within reasonable bounds.

Secondly, the Californian Court found that the Native American Church claimed no official pre-requisites to membership, had no written membership rolls, and possessed no recorded theology.[287] It would thus appear to be as difficult for outsiders to define exactly who is included as an adherent of the Church as it is to define a Rastafarian with any precision. Self-ascription and acceptance by the group itself are crucial in both instances. Estimates of membership of the Native American Church range from 30,000 to 250,000, which of themselves furnish some idea of the diffuse understandings among the members themselves as to who was included and what was entailed.[288]

Thirdly, sacramental use of *peyote* at special 'meetings', which were solemn occasions, was found by the Court to lie at the heart of the

---

[282] At 77–8.   [283] At 74.   [284] Whittaker, 84, 215.
[285] At 132; see also Rubin and Comitas, 165–6.
[286] See e.g. Auld, chs 3, 4; Office of Health Economics, 3.   [287] At 73.
[288] Ibid.

Church's theology.[289] *Peyote* enabled members to enter into direct contact with God. On the other hand, not all those present at a 'meeting' had to partake of *peyote*.[290] 'Meetings' involved prayers and other rituals and lasted from sunset to sunrise. Some similarity clearly exists between Church meetings and Rastafarian 'reasoning' sessions, though the latter seem far less formal and are by no means the only occasions on which *ganja* is smoked. The difficulty of separating social or recreational use of *ganja* from its specific consumption at reasoning sessions for purposes of religious inspiration certainly poses a major problem for regulation by means of a legal exemption.

The question of fraudulent claims to religious immunity was, however, dealt with by the Californian Court in a very robust fashion. Justice Tobriner indicated that the problem was no greater than in other areas in which courts have to detect fraud and he commented that spurious claims should present only comparatively minor enforcement problems.[291] On the other hand, the decision of the California Supreme Court in *In re Grady*,[292] handed down on the same day as *People v Woody*, provides some idea of the difficulties which might arise from an attempt to furnish an exemption in English law for bona fide religious use of *ganja* by Rastafarians. Grady alleged that his use of *peyote* had been for religious purposes, but he was unable to demonstrate any connection with the Native American Church or any other organized religion. The Court wished to be satisfied that he had 'actually engaged in good faith in the practice of a religion', as opposed to seeking to 'wear the mantle of religious immunity merely as a cloak for illegal activities',[293] and this question was sent for trial as an issue of fact. Furthermore, the US Supreme Court has ruled that individual states are under no constitutional obligation to create exemptions from their drugs laws for the religious use of *peyote*[294] and US courts have also held that neither Rastafarians nor members of the Ethiopian Zion Coptic Church can rely on the constitutional protection of the free exercise of religion to exempt them from criminal liability for the consumption of marijuana.[295]

It would clearly be extremely difficult for the police and the courts in England to operate a system which provided exemptions from the ordinary law on cannabis either for those who were 'Rastafarians' or for those who were 'acting bona fide in the practice of a religion'. Problems in defining Rastafari, of distinguishing religious from social practice, and of verifying a person's bona fides, all militate against the

---

[289] At 73–4.   [290] At 73.   [291] At 75, 77.
[292] (1964) 39 Cal Rptr 912.   [293] At 913.
[294] *Employment Division, Department of Human Resources v Smith* 110 SC 1595 (1990).
[295] See e.g. *US v Middleton* 690 F 2d 820 (1982); 103 SC 1497 (1983); *Whyte v US* 471 A 2d 1018 (1984); *Olsen v Iowa* 808 F 2d 652 (1986).

introduction of such a scheme. Whereas in the United States there are currently sound policy reasons for safeguarding an 'ancient tradition'[296] of the Indians, we have already seen that one of the features of Rastafari is its very modernity. A history of sixty years, only about two-thirds of which has involved a presence in England, is surely too short to warrant the creation of a special statutory exemption in an area where the state of the law is so controversial and the proportion of cannabis users who are Rastafarians is so minute. Widespread popular opposition to the present law on possession would be converted into a stream of resentment against Rastafarians, who would be widely regarded as the beneficiaries of a privilege through the process of 'reverse discrimination'. Such allegations could only be rebutted if lawful Rastafarian use of cannabis was confined to consumption for purely religious or cultural reasons, a practical impossibility.

CONCLUSIONS

So far as the use of cannabis is concerned, there would seem to be a strong case for a reform of the law to reflect first, respect for the religious beliefs and cultural practices of the Rastafarians and the need for better relations between them and the police generally, and secondly, the fact that a policy of prohibition cannot be justified on health grounds and has proved in practice to be unenforceable to such a degree that justice is not being dispensed on an equal basis to all sections of the population throughout the country.

In 1991 a Report by a Committee of JUSTICE[297] argued that it was inappropriate for such a high proportion of public resources to be devoted to control of the use of cannabis, in view of the fact that it is 'significantly less harmful'[298] than Class A and other Class B drugs. The Report proposed that cannabis be reclassified as a Class C drug (with a consequential reduction in maximum penalties), in line with the recommendations of the Advisory Council on the Misuse of Drugs in 1979 and 1981, but argued that its possession should remain an arrestable offence (unlike other Class C drugs) so as not to unduly hamper police powers. Lesser maximum penalties were also suggested for those who supplied drugs in the course of social intercourse rather than as part of a business concern.[299]

However, these proposals are far too timid and fall well short of what is required. For cannabis possession to remain an arrestable offence

---

[296] See *People v Woody* at 78. [297] *Drugs and the Law* (London, 1991).
[298] Ibid, 9. [299] Ibid, 14.

would perpetuate a situation in which the police can unduly harass black users. Furthermore, the Committee appeared to place too great an emphasis upon the strictest possible literal adherence to the 1961 Single Convention,[300] without sufficiently appreciating the flexible interpretation given to it by Holland. Article 36 of the Convention, after declaring that both possession and distribution of cannabis should be punishable offences, states—

Notwithstanding the preceding sub-paragraph, when abusers of drugs have committed such offences the Parties may provide either as an alternative to conviction or punishment or in addition to conviction or punishment, that such abusers shall undergo measures of treatment, education, after-care, rehabilitation and social re-integration.

It is perfectly possible, therefore, for a state party to the Convention to provide education in lieu of a conviction, or where necessary in particular instances, treatment and rehabilitation, while retaining the offence on the statute book for very serious cases. The Dutch policy possesses considerable merits and could be implemented immediately.[301] A more far-reaching reform, involving formal decriminalization of possession, legalization of licensed supply (with proper quality controls), a programme of health education and treatment funded by taxation of sales, and restrictions on glamorous advertising would no doubt require amendment of the Convention. However, widespread disillusion with current policies has led to powerful advocacy of such developments[302] and they may ultimately prove more acceptable to public opinion than they are today.[303]

In the meantime, is there any case for affording Rastafarian users of cannabis specific differential treatment? The current policy of applying a uniform standard in determining guilt or innocence, regardless of the religious beliefs or cultural traditions of the defendant, is in line with long established general principle.[304] The creation of a special statutory exemption would be fraught with difficulty, as we have seen. Similar problems would also arise if, instead of a statutory exemption from criminal liability, the courts were to apply differential rules in the sen-

---

[300] Ibid, 9.   [301] See Coffield and Gofton, 29.

[302] See e.g. Whittaker, 356; Inciardi, chs 1, 7; *Release White Paper on Reform of the Drug Laws* 16–27; Schonsheck, J., *On Criminalization* (Dordrecht, 1994), ch 6. For earlier advocacy of such policies see *Cannabis: A Report of the Commission of Inquiry into Non-Medical Use of Drugs* (Ottawa, 1972) 303–10.

[303] For evidence that around 30 per cent of the general population favours some form of legalization, see Leitner, M., Shapland, J. and Wiles, P., *Drug Usage and Drugs Prevention* (London, 1993), ch 9; Jowell., R. *et al*, *British Social Attitudes: The 13th Report* (Aldershot, 1996), 96–7.

[304] See *R v Esop* (1836) 7 C & P 456; *R v Barronet and Allain* (1852) Dears CC 51; *R v Senior* [1899] 1 QB 283, discussed in ch 2 above.

tencing process, giving Rastafarians more lenient treatment. We saw in Chapter 2, however, that English judges have been prepared in certain circumstances to take account of religious and cultural values in deciding upon an appropriate sentence. A notable example is the case of *R v Bibi*,[305] where a Muslim widow, who had been involved in the importation of cannabis, had her sentence of imprisonment reduced from three years to six months because of her social isolation and dependence upon her brother-in-law, resulting from the doctrine of *purdah*. On the other hand, this decision was clearly reached in the light of the particular circumstances of the case, whereas a policy of differential sentencing of Rastafarians would have to operate in every case. In *R v Bibi* the religious and cultural background of the defendant was merely incidental to the offence, whereas in cases involving Rastafarians this aspect would lie at the heart of the offence.

Another factor militating against specific differential treatment in either the determination of guilt or the selection of sentence is that cannabis use among Rastafarians does not appear to be an essential ingredient of religious practice. Not all Rastafarians use cannabis[306] and those who do may not always be doing so for religious reasons. Finally, it is arguable that many Rastafarians themselves would prefer to help bring pressure on the Government to introduce legal reforms applicable to the British population as a whole, rather than to carve out an exclusive exemption for themselves. While the movement has in the past contained strands of an ideology of separation from 'Babylon', in recent years there has been a greater tendency to seek to influence the content and development of British culture at large, a striking example being the impact of reggae music and concepts of 'style' in popular youth culture.

While it is felt that identical rather than differential treatment is required in relation to cannabis law reform, it is worth noting that at present some ethnic minority communities fare much better than others under the drug laws. The stimulant *qat*, which is used for social recreation by groups of Somalis and Yemenis in particular in Britain,[307] is not regulated by the Misuse of Drugs Act and thus may be freely imported, sold, and consumed here. Yet in terms of health risks there appears very little to differentiate *qat* from cannabis.[308] *Qat* contains an alkaloid analogous to amphetamine and has been chewed for centuries by various peoples in north-east Africa and the Middle East[309] and this cultural tradition has naturally been maintained by some small communities

---

[305] [1980] 1 WLR 1193.   [306] Owens, 158–9; Clarke, 58, 89.
[307] See Halliday, F., *Arabs in Exile: Yemeni Migrants in Urban Britain* (London, 1992), 124–8.
[308] Ibid, 125–6.   [309] Whittaker, 63–4, 89–90.

upon their settlement here. While this anomaly benefits Muslims from these communities and perhaps compensates them for the fact that their religion precludes the use of Britain's most popular and lawful dangerous drug, alcohol, it does not assist Rastafarians who, as we have seen, equally reject alcohol.

Turning to the wearing of dreadlocks and the decision of the Court of Appeal in *Dawkins v Department of the Environment*, it would appear that the time is ripe for religious discrimination in employment to be outlawed by statute so as to bring domestic English law into line with developments in international human rights law. For similar reasons, Rastafarian prisoners should be permitted to have their religious affiliation officially recorded in England by prison governors.

PART III
The Way Ahead

10

Conclusions

In 1978 UNESCO expressed its confidence both in the intrinsic worth of the different cultures found throughout the world and in their potential for fruitful interaction, when it declared its conviction that—

. . . all peoples and all human groups, whatever their composition or ethnic origin, contribute according to their own genius to the progress of the civilizations and cultures which, in their plurality and as a result of their interpenetration, constitute the common heritage of mankind.[1]

The Sri Lankan jurist H. L. De Silva has also extolled the capacity of distinctive ethnic cultures to unify disparate groups of people and give them a special sense of community and identity through a common language and religion—

Ethnic divisions are an integral part of human existence and have by their very diversity and uniqueness contributed richly to the sum total of man's happiness. They symbolise the glories of human civilization and are therefore worthy of preservation for the future.[2]

However, coming from a country which has in recent years witnessed terrible ethnic strife, he freely acknowledged the ambivalence of ethnic divisions within a single state and their disturbing ability to impede the growth of that unity of outlook and vision which is so vital to cope with modern problems, adding—

The tensions which are produced by such differences and the prejudices which are engendered by ethnic differences are a great obstacle to progress and a colossal waste in terms of human effort and available resources.[3]

It is clear that England has become a much more ethnically diverse society since 1945 and officially a general policy of cultural pluralism (within limits) has been adopted since 1966, in order to pursue the twin objectives of equal opportunity and cultural diversity within a tolerant social atmosphere. However, the creation of a democratic pluralist society which is 'both socially cohesive and culturally diverse',[4] based on shared core values, is by no means easy to accomplish. Rex has

---

[1] UNESCO Declaration on Race and Racial Prejudice, 27 Nov 1978, preamble.
[2] 'Pluralism and the Judiciary in Sri Lanka' in Tiruchelvam, N. and Coomaraswamy, R., (eds) *The Role of the Judiciary in Plural Societies* (London, 1987), 3.   [3] Ibid, 2.
[4] See 'Education for All' (Swann Committee Report), Cmnd 9453 of 1985, 6.

painted a pessimistic picture of the likely short-term prospects of such a policy—

Conflict will go on about the place of multi-culturalism in education; British nationalism and racism are likely to continue in ways which deny ethnic minority cultures recognition and individual members of these minorities equality of opportunity; efforts to ensure equality of opportunity and equality of outcomes for ethnic minority members will continue to provoke a backlash in the indigenous community; many members of the indigenous working class will continue to pursue strategies of usurpationary closure against the minorities, particularly if economic circumstances are such that their own livelihood seems threatened; ethnic minority cultures may continue to be attacked by human rights activists; and finally, minority cultures may be slow to adapt to living in a secular multicultural society, the more so if their adherents feel that they are not fully members of that society.[5]

By contrast, Gross is much more sanguine about the prospects of a pluralist society—

Pluralism is not a plan for a society free of conflicts. To the contrary, tensions and non-violent conflicts or opposition of goals and conduct are a normal social experience. However, the problem of resolution and reduction of such tension is paramount . . . . Without a spontaneous acceptance of rules of procedure and without core . . . values a pluralistic society is unable to function.[6]

The best way of searching for solutions to such conflicts is through the processes of dialogue, negotiation, and compromise, as well as by utilizing the mechanisms of education and law. The law has a vital role to play in establishing the broad framework within which settlements of such controversies and disputes can be achieved, as well as the outcomes in particular instances. It furnishes proper procedural rules and reflects the formal, institutional, core values of society as a whole. In the case studies presented in Part II of this work detailed examination has been made of the practical application of the wide range of legal responses which are available to handle ethnic diversity and which were outlined in Chapter 2. Specific differential treatment has been recognized as both desirable and justifiable in the context of Sikh turbans and the production of *kosher* food for Jews (and *halal* meat for Muslims), as well as in relation to the publicly-funded provision of sites for gypsy encampments. Such treatment is not, however, required to satisfy the demand of Hindus for freedom of public worship; rather the existing law needs to guarantee that liberty for members of all faiths, subject only to those

---

[5] 'The Political Sociology of a Multi-Cultural Society' (1991) 2 *European Journal of Intercultural Studies* 7 at 17–18. For a view that conflict is endemic in a multicultural society, see Raz, J., *Ethics in the Public Domain* (Oxford, 1994), 164.
[6] *Ideologies, Goals and Values* (Westport, 1985), 311.

planning restrictions which are necessary in a democratic society in order to safeguard the rights and freedoms of others. Identical treatment with the rest of the population is similarly appropriate for Rastafarians in respect of the consumption of cannabis. Nor can specific treatment be justified in relation to the claim by some Muslims for a separate Islamic system of personal law to govern the family relations of all British Muslims. Indeed, certain aspects of Islamic law are so unacceptable that their observance in practice here can justifiably be restrained or prevented. Techniques of suppression, invalidity, and exclusion are the appropriate response when minimum standards are in serious danger of being breached. In each of the above situations English law has had to find a method of delivering fair and equitable treatment to members of the ethnic minority communities, whilst upholding and guaranteeing the basic human rights set down in international instruments to which every individual in this country is properly entitled.

In just the same way as ignorance of ethnic minority cultures can lead members of the majority community to hold false and prejudiced opinions about the values and practices of members of other faiths and groups, so can a lack of understanding of key principles of international human rights law result in blind adherence to simplistic beliefs concerning the concept of 'equality before the law'. This principle, especially hallowed since Dicey extolled it as part of the doctrine of 'the rule of law' in 1888,[7] was never intended to preclude differential treatment if the situation warranted it. Hence, while it generally requires English law to be colour-blind and precludes racial discrimination, it does not bar legal recognition of important religious and cultural differences. Lord Mackay, then Lord Chancellor, placed special emphasis upon this point in an address to legal practitioners in 1990—

. . . any lawyer, to be worthy of that name ought to be a part of a wider search for a rational basis for the relationships between groups and individuals in the community. It can never be acceptable for a lawyer to seek to succeed by appeals to prejudice or even to tradition. This does not mean, however, that every client has to be treated alike: on the contrary, this framework is intended to deal with diversity. A client who does not speak the language of the majority inevitably needs more help than one who does. A client who is an immigrant is inevitably at a disadvantage in understanding the ways of those who were born and grew up in the community—and this also means that the lawyer has to understand and be objective about what is distinctive about the majority community, if he is a member of that community. Nor does it mean that the law has to be exactly the same for everyone: there may be good reason why groups are treated differently,

[7] See now Dicey, A., *An Introduction to the Study of the Law of the Constitution*, 10th ed. (London, 1959), ch IV.

for instance, out of respect for religious convictions. But the process, in terms of access to the machinery of justice, ought to be the same for everyone.[8]

Are there, then, any further steps which need to be taken to ensure that English law is sufficiently responsive to ethnic and cultural diversity? This question will be addressed here from two rather broad policy perspectives rather than with a view to making a list of suggestions for specific reforms.

GENERAL POLICY STATEMENTS

In Chapter 1 it was explained that the current official guiding philosophy of cultural pluralism dates back to the mid-1960s and in particular, to a speech made by Roy (now Lord) Jenkins on 'integration' when he was Labour Home Secretary. Subsequent statements along similar lines have been made by several Conservative ministers. However, it is still not possible to point to any prominent formal policy document where this approach is identified as constituting the general standpoint of the state. More specific official clarification and greater public awareness would seem highly desirable and in this regard it is worth considering steps taken within the last few years in two liberal democracies in the Commonwealth with which Britain has much in common, namely Canada and Australia. Both are former 'dominions' with predominantly white, Anglo-Saxon, nominally Christian populations, which have comparatively recently taken in significant numbers of immigrants from very different backgrounds to add to their respective indigenous populations of Inuits (Eskimos), Indians, and Aborigines.

In 1988 the Canadian Parliament enacted legislation for the promotion of multiculturalism, with a view to buttressing the statement in its constitutional Charter of Rights and Freedoms that the Charter itself had to be interpreted 'in a manner consistent with the preservation and enhancement of the multicultural heritage of Canadians'.[9] Section 3(1) of the Multiculturalism Act[10] takes the unusual course of declaring it to be 'the policy of the Government of Canada' to—

(a) recognize and promote the understanding that multiculturalism reflects the cultural and racial diversity of Canadian society and acknowledges the freedom

---

[8] 'The Role of the Profession in Securing Access to Justice' in *Conference Papers of the Ninth Commonwealth Law Conference* (Auckland, 1991), 59.

[9] Canada Act 1982, sched B, s 27; for an account of the impact of s 27, see Bottos, D., 'Multiculturalism: section 27's application in charter cases thus far' (1988) 26 *Alberta Law Review* 621. For discussion of the development of the policy of multiculturalism, see Kallen, E., *Ethnicity and Human Rights in Canada*, 2nd ed. (Toronto, 1995), 170–6.

[10] Ch 93 of the Laws of Canada.

of all members of Canadian society to preserve, enhance and share their cultural heritage; . . .

(c) promote the full and equitable participation of individuals and communities of all origins in the continuing evolution and shaping of all aspects of Canadian society and assist them in the elimination of any barrier to such participation; . . .

(e) ensure that all individuals receive equal treatment and equal protection under the law, while respecting and valuing their diversity;

(f) encourage and assist the social, cultural, economic and political institutions of Canada to be both respectful and inclusive of Canada's multicultural character . . . .

All federal institutions are to ensure equality of opportunity for every-one, enhance the contributions of all to the country's evolution, promote respect for diversity, and generally carry on their activities in a manner that is responsive to the multicultural reality of Canada.[11] A designated minister is given special responsibility for encouraging and promoting a co-ordinated approach to the implementation of the policy and is authorized to provide advice and assistance in the development and implementation of programmes and practices.[12] Annual reports on the operation of the Act have to be laid before Parliament.[13] Legislation of this sort clearly provides such a policy with a very high public profile and affords an easy reference point for developing widespread apprecia-tion of the basic requirements of living in a multicultural society. Diver-sity is valued, everyone is encouraged to contribute, and equal opportunities are promoted.

A slightly different strategy, albeit with the same end in view, has been adopted in Australia. In 1989 the then Prime Minister, Bob Hawke, launched amidst a fanfare of publicity a 'National Agenda for a Multi-cultural Australia',[14] following over two years of consultation, research, and development of ideas on the issue.[15] The National Agenda, which has bipartisan support, is a statement of the federal government's public policy response to the changing ethnic composition of Australian society. Recent growth in immigration from many different parts of the world has resulted in about a quarter of all Australians now having no Anglo-Celt background and less than half the population is today of pure Anglo-Celt descent,[16] compared with 90 per cent in 1947. Over 140 ethnic groups and a hundred different first languages are now reflected in the composition of Australian society. 'Multiculturalism' is defined in the Agenda as a policy for 'managing the consequences of diversity in

---

[11] S 3(2).   [12] Ss 2, 4.   [13] S 9.
[14] Department of the Prime Minister and Cabinet, Office of Multicultural Affairs, *National Agenda for a Multicultural Australia* (Canberra, 1989).
[15] For the background to the development of the Agenda, see ibid, 57–60.
[16] Ibid, 5.

the interests of the individual and society as a whole'[17] and it possesses three different dimensions.[18] The first of these is cultural identity, the right of all Australians, within carefully defined limits, to express and share their individual cultural heritage, including their language and religion. People should not be coerced, by antiquated structures or inflexible attitudes, into surrendering their cultural identity as the price of being considered 'Australian'. The second strand relates to social justice, the right of all Australians to equality of treatment and opportunity and the removal of barriers of race, ethnicity, culture, religion, language, gender, or place of birth. The third aspect is economic efficiency, the need to maintain, develop, and utilize effectively the skills and talents of all Australians, regardless of background, so that everyone is allowed and encouraged to contribute their skills and talents to the public good.

Although the precise limits of the first of these dimensions, namely cultural identity, have not yet been finally determined, the Agenda specifies the broad boundaries within which multicultural policies are to operate with a view to preserving social cohesion.[19] The key premise is that all Australians should have an overriding and unifying commitment to Australia's interests. Everyone also has to accept the basic structures and principles of Australian society, namely the constitution and the rule of law, tolerance and equality, Parliamentary democracy, the freedoms of speech and religion, sexual equality, and the status of English as the official language of the country. In return for the right to express their own culture and beliefs, everyone is under a reciprocal responsibility to respect the rights of others to do likewise and express their own views and values.

Within this broad framework of limitations there is scope for legal reform to redefine the extent to which Australian laws should reflect and recognize cultural diversity and in 1989 the Australian Law Reform Commission (ALRC) was asked to report on whether various provisions in the fields of criminal law, family law, and contract law were appropriate for a society made up of people from different cultural backgrounds and from ethnically diverse communities.[20] Several recommendations for alterations to the law were contained in the Commission's report in 1992.[21] It bore in mind that one of the objectives of the National Agenda is the promotion of equality before the law through the

---

[17] National Agenda, vii.   [18] Ibid, vii, 51–2.
[19] Ibid, vii.
[20] See ALRC, Issues Paper No. 9: 'Multiculturalism and the Law' (1990).
[21] ALRC, Report No. 57: 'Multiculturalism and the Law' (1992); for subsequent reforms, see e.g. Crimes and Other Legislation Amendment Act 1994, s 10; Family Law Reform Act 1995, s 68F.

systematic examination of the implicitly cultural assumptions which the legal system makes. These may unintentionally act to the disadvantage of certain groups. Another objective is to promote an environment which is tolerant and accepting of social and cultural diversity, and which respects and protects the associated rights of individuals.[22] Of course, as the Commission pointed out, the success of a multicultural society depends—

> . . . not just on legal measures, but also on acceptance by the general community and by legal institutions and the legal profession of the right of people to be different, to have different opinions, religions and traditions . . . . The law can help to encourage tolerant attitudes; but to be effective it should be supplemented by knowledge, understanding and communication of ideas.[23]

The Agenda also required the Office of Multicultural Affairs to examine whether it would be desirable to enact a Multiculturalism Act for Australia to define the principles and limits of the policy.[24] This could also provide a legislative basis for the Government's closely related 'Access and Equity Strategy', which requires government agencies to review, monitor, and evaluate all services, programmes, and policies to ensure that they take account of the diverse linguistic, cultural, and racial characteristics of Australian society.[25]

In the light of these developments some considered thought should be given to the adoption of a clear public agenda for promoting the future of a plural society in Britain, perhaps culminating in the enactment of a Multiculturalism Act. In such a sensitive area careful and detailed planning would be required, with wide-ranging consultation at both local and national levels before any official documents were produced. Considerable opposition can be expected, as the Canadian experience demonstrates. According to a public opinion poll conducted there in 1993, a 'white backlash' had occurred with nearly three-quarters of respondents rejecting the idea that Canada is a multicultural nation and 62 per cent expressing the opinion that people should 'adapt to the value system and the way of life of the majority in Canadian society'.[26] Even so, the challenge of multiculturalism has to be faced openly and honestly.

---

[22] *National Agenda*, 17.   [23] Report No. 57, 15.   [24] *National Agenda*, 18.
[25] See ALRC, Report No. 57, 71.
[26] Kallen, 33, 225; see also Abu-Laban, Y. and Stasiulus, D., 'Ethnic Pluralism under Siege: Popular and Partisan Opposition to Multiculturalism' (1992) 18 *Canadian Public Policy* 365.

THE HUMAN RIGHTS DIMENSION

The importance of a human rights dimension has been stressed throughout the preceding chapters and it is significant that both Canada and Australia take their international obligations in this field very seriously. The Canadian Constitution 1982 contains a Charter of Rights and Freedoms,[27] which supplements the statutory protection afforded by the Human Rights Act 1976. While no comparable legislation exists in Australia, the Government's reference to the Australian Law Reform Commission of the issue of multiculturalism in 1989 made specific reference to the country's obligations under the International Covenant on Civil and Political Rights and the International Convention on the Elimination of All Forms of Racial Discrimination.[28] These and other human rights treaties were used by the Commission as a source of principles transcending cultural, political, and economic differences, which enabled different rights to be balanced and accorded their proper weight.[29]

Further support for the value of reliance upon such treaties, in the context of a Western democracy coming to terms with an increasingly multicultural population, is available much closer to home. In 1989 three girls of North African extraction were excluded from their school in Creil in northern France because they insisted upon wearing their 'Muslim' headscarves in class.[30] In the view of their headmaster, their action constituted a violation of the long-standing republican tradition of *laïcité* (secularism) in the public sector of education in France. Media reports of the contretemps in Creil caused a national furore, as extreme right-wing politicians and others expressed concern that Islamic *intégrisme* ('fundamentalism') had spread to the heart of the country. Even those on the left were deeply divided over the issue, with many socialists arguing that only in a totally secular school environment could children be saved from 'the obscurantist particularism of religion'.[31] The state system of education was described by one group of socialist intellectuals in terms

[27] Schedule B.
[28] See ALRC, Issues Paper No. 9: Multiculturalism and the Law (1990).
[29] See ALRC, Report No. 57, 12–13.
[30] For accounts of the background to and repercussions of the dispute, see Silverman, M., *Deconstructing the Nation: Immigration, Racism and Citizenship in Modern France* (London, 1992), 111–18; Nielsen, J., *Muslims in Western Europe* (Edinburgh, 1992), 162–4; Beriss, D., 'Scarves, Schools and Segregation: The *Foulard* Affair' (1990) 8 *French Politics and Society* 1; Bell, J., 'Religious observance in secular schools: A French solution' (1990) 2 *Education and the Law* 121; Poulter, S., 'Muslim Headscarves in School: Contrasting Legal Approaches in England and France' (1997) 17 *OJLS* 43; for the most penetrating examination of the issues involved, based on interviews with 100 veiled Muslim girls and young women, see Gaspard, F. and Khosrokhavar, F., *Le Foulard et la République* (Paris, 1995).
[31] Silverman, 112.

of 'a rhetoric of emancipation, neutrality, universality and liberty in opposition to the constitution of a mosaic of ghettos'.[32]

To calm the situation, the Minister of Education sought a legal opinion (*avis*) from the Conseil d'Etat on three issues.[33] First, in view of the relevant constitutional and statutory principles and the rules governing state schools, was the wearing of religious insignia compatible with the principle of *laïcité*? Secondly, if so, what conditions could be applied to such display by means of ministerial instructions, school rules, and decisions of headteachers? Thirdly, if the wearing of such insignia was banned, or conditions applied to such display were not fulfilled, what steps were available to the school in terms of non-admission or exclusion and subject to what procedural safeguards? The Conseil's opinion was that although France was a secular state, with a principle of neutrality towards religion in all its public services, any discrimination on the basis of religious belief was unconstitutional. Hence pupils had a right to express and manifest their religious beliefs within state schools, so long as they respected pluralism and the freedom of others. This was not incompatible with the principle of *laïcité*. However, the right to freedom of religion was not absolute and, the Conseil advised, pupils could not wear insignia which—

. . . by their character, by the circumstances in which they were worn individually or collectively, or by their ostentatious or campaigning nature, constituted an act of pressure, provocation, proselytism, or propaganda, or which were aimed at the dignity or freedom of other pupils or members of the school community, or compromised their health or safety or disturbed good order and the peaceful running of the school.

Rules implementing these basic principles could be expressed in ministerial instructions.[34] Disciplinary matters should be governed by school rules and headteachers should take appropriate steps when the occasion demanded. Procedural safeguards should be complied with before serious decisions, such as expulsion, were reached.

To the English eye, perhaps the most striking feature of the *avis* given by the Conseil was its copious citation of international human rights law, in addition to its reference to the relevant constitutional and statutory provisions of French law. The Conseil drew attention to France's obligations under the European Convention on Human Rights, the two International Covenants, and the Convention against Discrimination in

---

[32] Ibid.

[33] See *Avis du 27 Novembre 1989*, (1990) *L'Actualité juridique—Droit administratif* 39; [1990] *Public Law* 434.

[34] For the subsequent ministerial circular, issued on 12 Dec 1989, see (1990) 6 *Revue Française de Droit Administratif* 20.

Education. Collectively, these obliged France to afford education to pupils free from any religious discrimination,[35] to guarantee freedom of conscience for all together with the right to manifest religious beliefs,[36] to respect the rights of parents to ensure education in conformity with their religious convictions,[37] and to take the necessary measures to provide education which promotes understanding and tolerance among racial and religious groups.[38] However, since the state's duty under international human rights law to guarantee religious freedom is not absolute, legal limitations could be imposed where they were necessary for the protection of public health or safety, public order, or the rights and freedoms of others.[39] It was these restrictions which enabled the Conseil d'Etat to declare that the display of religious insignia should not involve pressure, proselytism, propaganda, or provocation, nor disrupt good order, nor pose a threat to health or safety. A balanced and sensible compromise was thus achieved in a tense and complex situation through the application of legal principles relating to human rights rather than through a settlement negotiated between the interested parties on the basis of purely pragmatic political considerations.[40] It was also a brave ruling on the part of the Conseil d'Etat in view of France's traditional propensity to refuse recognition of the separate cultural identities of minority groups.[41] In subsequent litigation arising out of further expulsions of Muslim pupils, the Conseil has resolutely re-affirmed these principles.[42]

As we have seen, the English courts have increasingly been taking account of the human rights dimension through reference to the provisions of the European Convention,[43] and the incorporation of the Convention and its Protocols into English law by statute is imminent.[44] One important consequence of taking such a step is that the right to religious freedom will for the first time be set down clearly in writing as a legal principle in English law. This will convey a valuable message to the population at large that respect for freedom of religion is embodied in the core of the English legal system, albeit subject to restrictions on religious practice and observance deemed necessary to protect certain public interests. Furthermore, the very act of formally prescribing a list

---

[35] ECHR, Art 14 and 1st Protocol, Art 2; ICESR, Arts 2(2), 13, CADE, Art 2.
[36] ECHR, Art 9(1); ICCPR, Art 18(1).
[37] ECHR, 1st Protocol, Art 2; ICCPR, Art 18(4); ICESR, Art 13(3).
[38] ICESR, Art 13(1); CADE, Art 5.   [39] ECHR, Art 9(2); ICCPR, Art 18(3).
[40] See Corbett, A., 'Keeping Faith with the Rights of Man', *Guardian*, 1 Dec 1989.
[41] See above, ch 3 and Lloyd, C., 'Concepts, models and anti-racist strategies in Britain and France' (1991) *New Community* 63 at 65–7.
[42] See *Kherouaa* [1992] *Revue du Droit Public* 220; *Yilmaz* [1995] *Revue du Droit Public* 249; *Aoukili* (1995) *Dalloz* 365.   [43] See above, ch 2.
[44] Legislation is expected in 1998.

of the basic legal rights of citizens should encourage people to claim them and help to create a healthier climate for the development of equal respect and justice for all. A charter of rights affords both a basis of legitimacy for the framing of claims and a form of leverage for minorities.

It is sometimes suggested that, unlike the French, whose welcome to foreigners is often felt to be confined to those prepared to immerse themselves in French culture and become thoroughly 'gallicized',[45] the English have a greater propensity to respect those who are firmly rooted in and proud of their own cultural traditions and religious values, and consequently are less flattered by attempts at imitation.[46] Whether or not this is a fair and accurate reflection of popular attitudes[47] in the two countries,[48] a liberal spirit of tolerance coupled with an appreciation of diversity must continue to be developed among members of the majority community in Britain. Many of them are, however, often prone to ask why they should extend tolerance to those from countries overseas whose governments are undemocratic, oppressive, and themselves intolerant of diversity and dissent. In their view, an element of reciprocity of treatment is required. To insist upon such reciprocity, however, would entail lowering the standards of treatment to the levels of the most discreditable regimes around the world, whereas the task of a liberal democracy such as the United Kingdom must be to maintain and foster the high standards set by widely ratified international human rights conventions. That such norms are broadly accepted and implemented here is one of the principal reasons why so many members of the ethnic minority communities appreciate living in this country, identify themselves as British, and choose to stay here, despite the persistence of widespread prejudice and discrimination.[49] They are entitled to insist that they are accorded in practice the legal rights which should accrue to all within a liberal democracy and to play a full part in developing a fair and just society for all. They must be regarded as members of the British nation in the fullest sense irrespective of cultural and ethnic differences

[45] See e.g. Silverman, ch 1.
[46] See e.g. Freedman, M., *A Minority in Britain* (London, 1955), 242.
[47] For doubts about this hypothesis, see Modood, T., 'The Indian Economic Success' (1991) 19 *Policy and Politics* 177 at 185; Holmes, C., *John Bull's Island: Immigration and British Society 1871–1971* (Basingstoke, 1988), 300 ('There was . . . a persistent opposition between 1871 and 1971 towards groups which tended to preserve their own cultural identity . . . . Jewish and Chinese minorities were particular targets for such antipathy before 1914 and the emphasis of Powellism, and other less sophisticated sources in the 1960s, on the perils and damage wreaked by strange, alien cultures, was a forceful reminder of the continuity of such concern'). [48] For French public policy, see above, ch 3.
[49] See generally, Stopes-Roe, M. and Cochrane, R., *Citizens of This Country: The Asian British* (Clevedon, 1990), especially chs 6–10.

since, as is commonly remarked, a civilized country is judged according to the treatment it affords to its minorities.

Equality in law and recognition of diversity must, of course, be carefully balanced, for too great an emphasis upon cultural differences can destroy the cohesion of a society, as many deeply-divided and war-torn countries in the world today bear awesome testimony.[50] Members of ethnic communities must not be made to feel that they are 'caught between two cultures', but rather that they can benefit substantially from each through the possession of a repertoire of multiple cultural identities.[51] Their lives must blossom and flower, but in the manner of hybrid plants and shrubs, reflecting in their vigour and distinction their dual heritage and cross-fertilization. To employ another metaphor to convey the same idea, the culture of English society as a whole must become a richer tapestry in which the strands of non-European civilizations are interwoven with older textures already knitted together in previous centuries through the joint efforts of diverse European communities such as the Saxons, Vikings, Normans, Flemings, Lombards, and Huguenots, as well as of European Jews and gypsies.

In a moving modern account of a migrant's long and difficult search for a balanced sense of identity in a new country, Eva Hoffman has written of her acquisition of 'a second unconscious'[52] and stressed the need to 'translate' herself and acquire certain common assumptions of her adopted country in order to avoid a 'mild cultural schizophrenia'.[53] However, as she points out—

. . . if I'm to achieve this without becoming assimilated—that is absorbed—by my new world, the translation has to be careful, the turns of the psyche unforced. To mouth foreign terms without incorporating their meaning is to risk becoming bowdlerised. A true translation proceeds by the motions of understanding and sympathy; it happens by slow increments . . . .[54]

Easing the process of integration is a task which involves the law as well as other social institutions. Law contributes to a common sense of citizenship and should reflect shared values which transcend ethnic differences. The state's commitment to the values of tolerance, liberty, pluralism, justice, equality, and respect may to a large degree be judged by reference to its legal system.

---

[50] As one experienced commentator has pointed out—'Ethnic conflict does not require great differences; small will do'; see Moynihan, D., *Pandaemonium: Ethnicity in International Politics* (Oxford, 1993), 15.

[51] See generally, Hutnik, N., *Ethnic Minority Identity: A Social Psychological Perspective* (Oxford, 1991); see also Hall, S. 'Politics of Identity' in Ranger, T., Samad, Y., and Stuart, O., (eds) *Culture, Identity and Politics* (Aldershot, 1996), ch 12.

[52] *Lost in Translation: Life in a New Language* (London, 1991), 221.

[53] Ibid, 211.   [54] Id.

The ability of the English courts to mould the law to take account of an increasingly diverse population was reiterated at the highest level in 1991 when Lord Keith emphasized that the common law was 'capable of evolving in the light of changing social, economic and cultural developments'[55] and it is to be hoped that judges in future cases will follow this approach.

Perhaps the last word, by way of guidance for the future, should be left to an early and very distinguished migrant worker, who was to exert a profound influence upon a civilization other than that in which he was born and grew up. In the fourth century, Saint Augustine left his native region of Numidia in North Africa to spend several years teaching in Rome and Milan, before returning to serve as Bishop of Hippo in what is now Algeria. He is reputed to have issued the following injunction—

In necessities, unity; in doubtful things, liberty; in all things, charity.

While English law should broadly approach other cultures in a charitable spirit of tolerance and, when in doubt, lean in favour of affording members of ethnic minority communities freedom to observe their diverse traditions here, there will inevitably be certain key areas where minimum standards, derived from shared core values, must of necessity be maintained, if the cohesiveness and unity of English society as a whole is to be preserved intact. The elucidation of these cardinal principles has been the primary aim of this book.

[55] *R v R* [1992] AC 599 at 616; see also *Gillick v West Norfolk and Wisbech Area Health Authority* [1986] AC 112 at 171, where Lord Fraser had earlier drawn attention to the need for the law to have regard to major changes in social customs.

Bibliography

Abu-Laban, Y., and Stasiulus, D., 'Ethnic Pluralism under Siege: Popular and Partisan Opposition to Multiculturalism' (1992) 18 *Canadian Public Policy* 365.

Adams, B., Okely, J., Morgan, D., and Smith, D., *Gypsies and Government Policy in England* (Heinemann, London, 1975).

Advisory Council on the Misuse of Drugs, *Report of the Expert Group on the Effects of Cannabis Use* (HMSO, London, 1982).

Ahmed, L., *Women and Gender in Islam* (Yale University Press, New Haven, 1992).

Akhtar, S., *Be Careful with Muhammad* (Bellew, London, 1989).

Alderman, G., *The Jewish Community in British Politics* (Clarendon Press, Oxford, 1983).

—— 'Power, Authority and Status in British Jewry: The Chief Rabbinate and Shechita' in G. Alderman and C. Holmes (eds.), *Outsiders and Outcasts* (Duckworth, London, 1993).

—— 'The defence of *shechita*: Anglo-Jewry and the "humane conditions" regulations of 1990' (1995) *New Community* 79.

Alexander, C., *The Art of Being Black: The Creation of Black British Identities* (Clarendon Press, Oxford, 1996).

Alexander, M., and Anand, S., *Queen Victoria's Maharajah Duleep Singh, 1838–93* (Weidenfeld and Nicholson, London, 1980).

Allen, C., *Law in the Making*, 7th ed. (Clarendon Press, Oxford, 1964).

Allott, A., *New Essays in African Law* (Butterworths, London, 1970).

—— 'What is to be done with African Customary Law?' [1984] *Journal of African Law* 56.

Al-Rasheed, M., 'The Other-Others: Hidden Arabs?' in C. Peach (ed.), *Ethnicity in the 1991 Census, vol 2, The Ethnic Minority Populations of Great Britain* (HMSO, London, 1996).

Alston, P. (ed.), *The United Nations and Human Rights: A Critical Appraisal* (Clarendon Press, Oxford, 1992).

Amin, K., 'Police Stop and Searches: Who, Where and Why' (1995) 283 *Runnymede Bulletin* 6.

—— and Richardson, R., *Politics for All: Equality, Culture and the General Election 1992* (Runnymede Trust, London, 1992).

Anderson, J., *Law Reform in the Muslim World* (Athlone Press, London, 1976).

An-Na'im, A., 'The Islamic Law of Apostasy and its Modern Applicability: A case from the Sudan' [1986] 16 *Religion* 197.

—— 'Religious Minorities under Islamic Law and the Limits of Cultural Relativism' (1987) 9 *Human Rights Quarterly* 1.

—— 'The Rights of Women and International Law in the Muslim Context' (1987) 9 *Whittier Law Review* 491.

Anwar, M., *The Myth of Return: Pakistanis in Britain* (Heinemann, London, 1979).

—— 'Muslims in Britain: 1991 Census and other statistical sources', Centre for the Study of Islam and Muslim-Christian Relations, Birmingham, 1993.

Appiah, K., 'Identity, Authenticity, Survival' in A. Guttman (ed.), *Multiculturalism*, 2nd ed. (Princeton University Press, Princeton, 1994).

Appignanesi, L., and Maitland, S., *The Rushdie File* (Fourth Estate, London, 1989).

Applebaum, S., 'Were there Jews in Roman Britain?' (1951–2) XVII *Transactions of the Jewish Historical Society of England* 189.

Armstrong, K., *Holy War: The Crusades and their Impact on Today's World* (Macmillan, London, 1988).

Ashe, G., *Gandhi: A Study in Revolution* (Heinemann, London, 1968).

Auld, J., *Marijuana Use and Social Control* (Academic Press, London, 1981).

Aurora, G., *The New Frontiersmen: A Sociological Study of Indian Immigrants in the United Kingdom* (Popular Prakashan, Bombay, 1967).

Australian Law Reform Commission, *Report No. 31: The Recognition of Aboriginal Customary Laws* (Government Publishing Service, Canberra, 1986).

—— *Issues Paper No.9: Multiculturalism and the Law* (Government Publishing Service, Canberra, 1990).

—— *Report No. 57: Multiculturalism and the Law* (Government Publishing Service, Canberra, 1992).

Badawi, Z., 'Muslim Justice in a Secular State' in M. King (ed.), *God's Law versus State Law: The Construction of an Islamic Identity in Western Europe* (Grey Seal, London, 1995).

Bagley, C., *Back to the Future: Section 11 of the Local Government Act 1966: Local Authorities and Multicultural/Antiracist Education* (National Foundation for Educational Research, Slough, 1992).

Bagley, I., *General Principles and Problems in the Protection of Minorities* (Imprimeries Populaires, Geneva, 1950).

Ballantine, J., *The Life of David Roberts, R.A.* (A. and C. Black, Edinburgh, 1886).

Ballard, R., 'The Context and consequences of migration: Jullundur and Mirpur compared' (1983) *New Community* 117.

—— 'New Clothes for the Emperor?: The conceptual nakedness of the race relations industry in Britain' (1992) *New Community* 481.

—— 'Differentiation and Disjunction among the Sikhs' in R. Ballard (ed.), *Desh Pardesh: The South Asian Presence in Britain* (Hurst, London, 1994).

—— (ed.), *Desh Pardesh: The South Asian Presence in Britain* (Hurst, London, 1994).

—— and Ballard, C., 'The Sikhs' in J. Watson (ed), *Between Two Cultures: Migrants and Minorities in Britain* (Blackwell, Oxford, 1977).

—— and Kalra, V., *The Ethnic Dimensions of the 1991 Census: A Preliminary Report* (University of Manchester, Manchester, 1994).

Banks, M., *Ethnicity: Anthropological Constructions* (Routledge, London, 1996).

Banton, M., *Racial and Ethnic Competition* (Cambridge University Press, Cambridge, 1983).

Baring, E., 1st Earl of Cromer, *Modern Egypt*, 2 vols, (Macmillan, London, 1908).

Barnett, H., 'A Privileged Position? Gypsies, Land and Planning Law' [1994] *Conveyancer* 454.

Baron, S., *Ethnic Minority Rights* (Oxford University Press, Oxford, 1985).

Barrett, L., *The Rastafarians* (Sangster, Kingston with Heinemann, London, 1977).

Barth, F. (ed.), *Ethnic Groups and Boundaries* (Allen and Unwin, London, 1969).

Baumann, G., *Contesting Culture: Discourses of Identity in Multi-ethnic London* (Cambridge University Press, Cambridge, 1996).

Beale, A., and Geary, R., 'Abolition of an Unenforced Duty' (1995) 145 *New Law Journal* 47.

Beckerlegge, G., '"Strong cultures" and distinctive religions: the influence of imperialism upon British communities of South Asian Origin' (1991) *New Community* 210.

Beetham, D., *Transport and Turbans: A Comparative Study in Local Politics* (Oxford University Press, London, 1970).

—— (ed.), *Politics and Human Rights* (Blackwell, Oxford, 1995).

Bell, J., 'Religious observance in secular schools: A French solution' (1990) 2 *Education and the Law* 121.

Benn, S., and Gaus, G. (eds.), *Public and Private in Social Life* (Croom Helm, London, 1983).

Beriss, D., 'Scarves, Schools and Segregation: The *Foulard* Affair' (1990) 8 *French Politics and Society* 1.

Berridge, V., and Edwards, G., *Opium and the People* (Yale University Press, London, 1987).

Berting, J. (ed.), *Human Rights in a Pluralist World: Individuals and Collectivities* (Meckler, London, 1990).

Bhachu, P., *Twice Migrants: East African Sikh Settlers in Britain* (Tavistock, London, 1985).

Bidwell, S., *Red, White and Black: Race Relations in Britain* (Gordon and Cremonesi, London, 1976).

Bilby, K., 'The Holy Herb: Notes on the Background of Cannabis in Jamaica', *Caribbean Quarterly Monograph on Rastafari* (Kingston, 1985).

Bilder, R., 'Can Minorities Treaties Work?' in Y. Dinstein and M. Tabory (eds.), *The Protection of Minorities and Human Rights* (Martinus Nijhoff, Dordrecht, 1992).

Bingham, T., 'The European Convention on Human Rights: Time to Incorporate' (1993) 109 *Law Quarterly Review* 390.

Bingley, A., *Handbook for the Indian Army: Sikhs* (Central Printing Office, Simla, 1899).

Blackman, D., Humphreys, P., and Todd, P. (eds.), *Animal Welfare and the Law* (Cambridge University Press, Cambridge, 1989).

Board of Deputies of British Jews, *Report on the Jewish Method of Killing Animals* (Board of Deputies, London, 1905).

Boggan, S., 'A Law unto Themselves', *Independent on Sunday*, 11 Aug. 1991.

Bones, J., 'Rastafari: a cultural awakening' in *Report No. 64: The Rastafarians* (Minority Rights Group, London, 1984).

Bottos, D., 'Multiculturalism: section 27's application in charter cases thus far (1988) 26 *Alberta Law Review* 621.

Bowen, D. (ed.), *Hinduism in England* (Bradford College, Bradford, 1981).

—— *The Satanic Verses: Bradford Responds* (Bradford and Ilkley Community College, Bradford, 1992).

Brand, C., *Mobile Homes and the Law* (Sweet and Maxwell, London, 1986).

Brennan, K., 'The Influence of Cultural Relativism on Human Rights Law: Female Circumcision as a Case Study' (1989) 7 *Law and Inequality* 367.

Brook, S., *The Club: The Jews of Modern Britain* (Constable, London, 1989).

Brown, C., *Black and White Britain: The Third PSI Survey* (Heinemann, London, 1984).

—— and Gay, P., *Racial Discrimination: 17 Years After the Act* (Policy Studies Institute, London, 1985).

Brown, J., *Shades of Grey: A Report on Police–West Indian Relations in Handsworth* (Cranfield Institute of Technology, Cranfield, 1977).

—— *Policing by Multi-racial Consent* (Bedford Square Press, London, 1982).

Brown, J., *Gandhi: Prisoner of Hope* (Yale University Press, London, 1989).

Brown, L., *Cruelty to Animals* (Macmillan, Basingstoke, 1988).

Burghart, R. (ed.), *Hinduism in Great Britain* (Tavistock, London, 1987).

Burton, R., *A Plain and Literal Translation of the Arabian Nights' Entertainments* (Burton Club, London, 1884–6).

—— *The Jew, The Gypsy and El Islam*, W.H. Williams ed. (Hutchinson, London, 1898).

Calley, M., *God's People: West Indian Pentecostal Sects in England* (Oxford University Press, London, 1955).

Cambridge, A., 'Cultural Recognition and Identity' in A. Cambridge and S. Feuchtwang (eds.), *Where You Belong: Government and Black Culture* (Avebury, Aldershot, 1992).

Campbell, H., *Rasta and Resistance* (Hansib, London, 1985).

Cannabis: A Report of the Commission of Inquiry into Non-Medical Use of Drugs (Information Canada, Ottawa, 1972).

Capotorti, F., *Study on the Rights of Persons belonging to Ethnic, Religious and Linguistic Minorities* (United Nations, New York, 1991).

Carey, S., 'The Indianization of the Hare Krishna Movement in Britain' in R. Burghart (ed.), *Hinduism in Great Britain* (Tavistock, London, 1987).

Carter, P., 'The Role of Public Policy in English Private International Law' (1993) 42 *International and Comparative Law Quarterly* 1.

Casese, A., *International Law in a Divided World* (Clarendon Press, Oxford, 1986).

Cashmore, E., *Rastaman: The Rastafarian Movement in England*, 2nd ed. (Counterpoint, London, 1983).

Catholic Commission for Racial Justice, 'Rastafarians in Jamaica and Britain', London, 1982.

Chambers, G., and McCrudden, C. (eds.), *Individual Rights and the Law in Britain* (Clarendon Press, Oxford, 1994).

Charlton, R., and Kaye, R., 'The Politics of religious slaughter: an ethno-religious case study' (1985–86) *New Community* 490.

Chaudhuri, N., *Hinduism* (Chatto and Windus, London, 1979).

Cheshire and North's Private International Law, 12th ed. (Butterworths, London, 1992).

Clark, B., 'The Vienna Convention Reservations Regime and the Convention on Discrimination against Women' (1991) 85 *American Journal of International Law* 281.

Clarke, P., *Black Paradise: The Rastafarian Movement* (Aquarian Press, Wellingborough, 1986).

Clarke, P., and Linzey, A. (eds.), *Political Theory and Animal Rights* (Pluto Press, London, 1990).

Claude, I., *National Minorities: An International Problem* (Harvard University Press, Massachusetts, 1955).

Cochran, C., *Religion in Public and Private Life* (Routledge, New York, 1990).

Coffield, F., and Gofton, L., *Drugs and Young People* (Institute for Public Policy Research, London, 1994).

Cole, W., and Sambhi, P., *The Sikhs: Their Religious Beliefs and Practices* (Routledge, London, 1978).

Collins, L., and La Pierre, D., *Freedom at Midnight* (Collins, London, 1975).

Comments by the Jewish Community on the Farm Animal Welfare Council 'Report on the Welfare of Livestock When Slaughtered by Religious Methods' (Board of Deputies of British Jews, London, 1985).

Commission for Racial Equality, *Chartered Accountancy Contracts* (Commission for Racial Equality, London, 1987).

—— *Law, Blasphemy and the Multi-Faith Society* (Commission for Racial Equality, London, 1990).

—— *Free Speech* (Commission for Racial Equality, London, 1990).

—— *Britain: A Plural Society* (Commission for Racial Equality, London, 1990).

—— *Second Review of the Race Relations Act 1976* (Commission for Racial Equality, London, 1991).

Commonwealth Immigrants Advisory Council, *Second Report*, Cmnd 2266 (HMSO, London, 1964).

Commonwealth Secretariat, *Developing Human Rights Jurisprudence* (Commonwealth Secretariat, London, 1988).

Connors, J., and Mallat, C. (eds.) *Islamic Family Law* (Graham and Trotman, London, 1990).

Conservative Party, *The Best Future for Britain: The Conservative Manifesto 1992* (Conservative Central Office, London, 1992).

Corbett, A., 'Keeping Faith with the Rights of Man', *Guardian*, 1 Dec. 1989.

Coulson, N., *A History of Islamic Law* (Edinburgh University Press, Edinburgh, 1964).

Cranston, M., 'John Locke and the Case for Toleration' in S. Mendus and D. Edwards (eds.), *On Toleration* (Clarendon Press, Oxford, 1987).

Cretney, S., and Masson, J., *Principles of Family Law*, 6th ed. (Sweet and Maxwell, London, 1997).

Cripps, J., *Accommodation for Gypsies: A Report on the Working of the Caravan Sites Act 1968* (HMSO, London, 1977).

Daly, C., Kallweit, E., and Ellendorf, F., 'Cortical function in cattle during slaughter; conventional captive bolt stunning followed by exsanguination compared with shechita slaughter' (1988) 122 *Veterinary Record* 325.

Daly, M., *Anywhere But Here: Travellers in Camden* (London Race and Housing Research Unit, London, 1990).

Daniel, N., *Islam and the West: The Making of an Image* (Edinburgh University Press, Edinburgh, 1960).

Daniels, W., *The Common Law in West Africa* (Butterworths, London, 1964).

Darsh, S., *Muslims in Europe* (Ta-Ha Publishers, London, 1980).

Dearing, R., *The National Curriculum and its Assessment: Final Report* (School Curriculum and Assessment Agency, London, 1994).

Department of the Environment, *The Accommodation Needs of Long Distance and Regional Travellers* (Department of the Environment, London, 1982).

—— *Urban Programme: User Guide* (Department of the Environment, London, 1991).

—— 'Gypsy Sites Policy and Illegal Camping: Reform of the Caravan Sites Act 1968' (Department of the Environment, London, 1992).

Derrett, D., 'Justice, Equity and Good Conscience' in N. Anderson (ed.), *Changing Law in Developing Countries* (Allen and Unwin, London, 1963).

Desai, R., *Indian Immigrants in Britain* (Oxford University Press, London, 1963).

De Silva, H., 'Pluralism and the Judiciary in Sri Lanka' in N. Tiruchelvam and R. Coomaraswamy (eds.), *The Role of the Judiciary in Plural Societies* (Pinter, London, 1987).

Dicey, A., *An Introduction to the Study of the Law of the Constitution*, 10th ed. (Macmillan, London, 1959).

Dicey and Morris on the Conflict of Laws, 12th ed. (Sweet and Maxwell, London, 1993).

Di Chiara, A., and Galliher, J., 'Dissonance and Contradictions in the Origins of Marijuana Decriminalisation' (1994) 28 *Law and Society Review* 41.

Dickson, B., 'The United Nations and Freedom of Religion' (1995) 44 *International and Comparative Law Quarterly* 327.

Donelly, J., 'Cultural Relativism and Universal Human Rights' (1984) 6 *Human Rights Quarterly* 400.

Dorkenoo, E., and Elworthy, S., *Female Genital Mutilation: Proposals for Change* (Minority Rights Group, London, 1992).

Doyle, J., 'Constitutional Law: Dubious Intrusions – Peyote, Drug Laws and Religious Freedom' (1980) 8 *American Indian Law Review* 79.

Dresner, S., and Siegel, S., *The Jewish Dietary Laws* (Burning Bush Press, New York, 1966).

Drury, B., 'Sikh girls and the maintenance of an ethnic culture' (1991) *New Community* 387.

Duffy, M., *Men and Beasts: An Animal Rights Handbook* (Granada, London, 1984).

Dugard, J., *Human Rights and the South African Legal Order* (Princeton University Press, Princeton, 1978).

Dummett, A., and Nicol, A., *Subjects, Citizens, Aliens and Others* (Weidenfeld and Nicholson, London, 1990).

Dworkin, R., *Taking Rights Seriously* (Duckworth, London, 1977).

Edmonds, R., 'Gypsies and the Law' (1968) 31 *Modern Law Review* 567.

Edwards, J., *Positive Discrimination, Social Justice, and Social Policy* (Tavistock, London, 1987).

Eekelaar, J., *Regulating Divorce* (Clarendon Press, Oxford, 1991).

Elias, T., *British Colonial Law* (Stevens, London, 1962).

Elson, M., and Ford, A., 'Green Belts and Very Special Circumstances' [1994] *Journal of Planning and Environmental Law* 594.

Engelsman, E., 'Dutch Policy on the Management of Drug-related Problems' (1989) 84 *British Journal of Addiction* 211.

Engineer, A., *The Rights of Women in Islam* (Hurst, London, 1992).

Eriksen, T., *Ethnicity and Nationalism* (Pluto Press, London, 1993).

Ermacora, F., 'The Protection of Minorities before the United Nations' (1983) IV *Recueil des Cours* 247.

Esposito, J., *Women in Muslim Family Law* (Syracuse University Press, Syracuse, 1982).

Falcon, R., *Handbook on Sikhs for Regimental Officers* (Government Printing Press, Allahabad, 1896).

Farm Animal Welfare Council, *Report on the Welfare of Livestock (Red Meat Animals) at the Time of Slaughter* (HMSO, London, 1984).

—— *Report on the Welfare of Livestock When Slaughtered by Religious Methods* (HMSO, London, 1985).

Faruqi, I., 'The Rights of Non-Muslims under Islam' in *Muslim Communities in Non-Muslim States* (Islamic Council of Europe, London, 1980).

Feinberg, J., 'Legal Paternalism' (1971) *Canadian Journal of Philosophy* 105.

—— *The Moral Limits of the Criminal Law, Vol 3: Harm to Self* (Oxford University Press, New York, 1986).

Feldman, D., *Civil Liberties and Human Rights in England and Wales* (Clarendon Press, Oxford, 1993).

Finnis, J., *Natural Law and Natural Rights* (Clarendon Press, Oxford, 1986).

Foner, N., *Jamaica Farewell: Jamaican Migrants in London* (Routledge and Kegan Paul, London, 1979).

Fonseca, I., *Bury Me Standing: The Gypsies and Their Journey* (Chatto & Windus, London, 1995).

Forrester, B., *The Travellers' Handbook* (Interchange Books, London, 1985).

Fortson, R., *The Law on the Misuse of Drugs, 3rd ed.* (Sweet and Maxwell, London, 1996).

Fox, R., *Lions of the Punjab: Culture in the Making* (University of Calfornia Press, Berkeley, 1985).

Freedman, M. (ed.), *A Minority in Britain: Social Studies of the Anglo-Jewish Community* (Vallentine, Mitchell and Co., London, 1955).

Fryer, P., *Staying Power: The History of Black People in Britain* (Pluto Press, London, 1984).

Furneaux, R., *Massacre at Amritsar* (Allen and Unwin, London, 1963).

Galligan, D., 'Preserving Public Protest: The Legal Approach' in L. Gostin (ed.), *Civil Liberties in Conflict* (Routledge, London, 1988).

Gandhi, M., *An Autobiography: The Story of My Experiments with Truth* (Beacon Books, Boston, 1957).

Gann, L., and Duignan, P., *The Rulers of British Africa 1870–1914* (Croom Helm, London, 1978).

Gardner, J., 'Private Activities and Personal Autonomy: At the Margins of Anti-Discrimination Law' in B. Hepple and E. Szyszczak (eds.), *Discrimination: The Limits of Law* (Mansell, London, 1990).

Gartner, L., *The Jewish Immigrant in England 1870–1914*, 2nd ed. (Allen and Unwin, London, 1976).

Garvey, A., *The Philosophy and Opinions of Marcus Garvey* (Cass, London, 1967).

Gaspard, F., and Khosrokhavar, F., *Le Foulard et la République* (La Découverte, Paris, 1995).

Geaves, R., *Sectarian Influences within Islam in Britain* (Department of Theology and Religious Studies, University of Leeds, Leeds, 1996).

Gettman, J., 'Decriminalizing Marijuana' (1989) 32 *American Behavioural Scientist* 243.

Gilbert, G., 'The Council of Europe and Minority Rights' (1996) 18 *Human Rights Quarterly* 160.

Gilroy, P., *There Ain't No Black in the Union Jack: The Cultural Politics of Race and Nation* (Routledge, London, 1987).

Glazer, N., and Moynihan, D., *Beyond the Melting Pot* (Harvard University Press, Massachusetts, 1963).

—— (eds.), *Ethnicity: Theory and Experience* (Harvard University Press, Massachusetts, 1975).

Godfrey, J., 'Flourishing Sites Help Gypsies Settle', *Local Government Chronicle*, 30 Sept 1988, 14.

Golub, J., *British Attitudes toward Jews and other Minorities* (American Jewish Committee, New York, 1993).

Gomien, D., 'The Rights of Minorities under the European Convention on Human Rights and the European Charter on Regional and Minority Languages' in J. Cator and J. Niessen (eds.), *The Use of International Conventions to Protect the Rights of Migrants and Ethnic Minorities* (Churches' Commission for Migrants in Europe, Strasbourg, 1994).

Goodkin, S., 'The Evolution of Animal Rights' (1987) 18 *Columbia Human Rights Law Review* 259.

Gordon, P., *White Law: Racism in the Police, Courts and Prisons* (Pluto Press, London, 1983).

Gostin, L. (ed.), *Civil Liberties in Conflict* (Routledge, London, 1988).

Goulbourne, H., 'Varieties of Pluralism: The Notion of a Pluralist, Post-Imperial Britain' (1991) *New Community* 211.

—— *Ethnicity and Nationalism in Post-Imperial Britain* (Cambridge University Press, Cambridge, 1992).

Green, P., *Drug Couriers* (Howard League for Penal Reform, London, 1991).

Green, R., 'Probation and the Black Offender' (1988) *New Community* 81.

Greenawalt, K., *Discrimination and Reverse Discrimination* (Knopf, New York, 1983).

Gross, F., *Ideologies, Goals, and Values* (Greenwood Press, Westport, 1985).

Gwynn, R., *Huguenot Heritage* (Routledge and Kegan Paul, London, 1985).

Hall, S., 'Politics of Identity' in T. Ranger, Y. Samad and O. Stuart (eds.), *Culture, Identity and Politics* (Avebury, Aldershot, 1996).

—— et al, *Policing the Crisis: Mugging, the State, and Law and Order* (Macmillan, Basingstoke, 1978).

Halliday, F., *Arabs in Exile: Yemeni Migrants in Urban Britain* (I.B. Tauris, London, 1992).

Hamilton, C., *Family, Law and Religion* (Sweet & Maxwell, London, 1995).

Harris, D., O'Boyle, M., and Warbrick, C., *Law of the European Convention on Human Rights* (Butterworths, London, 1995).

Harte, J., 'Worship and Religious Education under the Education Reform Act 1988 – a Lawyer's View' (1991) *British Journal of Religious Education* 152.

Hartmann, E., *The Movement to Americanize the Immigrant* (AMS Press, New York, 1967).

Hassan, R., 'Rights of Women Within Islamic Communities' in J. Witte and J. van der Vyver (eds.), *Religious Human Rights in Global Perspective: Religious Perspectives* (Nijhoff, The Hague, 1996).

Hatch, E., *Culture and Morality: The Relativity of Values in Anthropology* (Columbia University Press, New York, 1983).

Hawes, D., and Perez, B., *The Gypsy and the State* (SAUS, Bristol, 1995).

Haynes, J., *Alternative Dispute Resolution: Fundamentals of Family Mediation* (Old Bailey Press, Horsmonden, 1993).

Health and Safety Commission, 'Proposals for Regulations requiring Head Protection in Construction Work' (HSC, London, 1987).

—— *Annual Report 1993/94, Statistical Supplement* (HSC, Sudbury, 1994).

Hebdige, D., *Subculture: The Meaning of Style* (Methuen, London, 1979).

Hecht, J., *Continental and Colonial Servants in Eighteenth Century England* (Smith College, Massachusetts, 1954).

Helweg, A., *Sikhs in England*, 2nd ed. (Oxford University Press, Delhi, 1986).

Henkin, L., 'The Universality of the Concept of Human Rights' (1989) 506 *Annals of the American Academy of Political and Social Science* 10.

Henley, A., *Caring for Hindus and their Families: Religious Aspects of Care* (DHSS and King's Fund, Cambridge, 1983).

Henriques, H., *The Jews and the English Law* (Oxford University Press, Oxford, 1908).

Herskovits, M., *Cultural Relativism: Perspectives in Cultural Pluralism* (Random House, New York, 1972).

Higgins, R., 'The Relationship Between International and Regional Human Rights Norms and Domestic Law' (1992) 18 *Commonwealth Law Bulletin* 1268.

Hillman, M., *Cycle Helmets: The Case For and Against* (Policy Studies Institute, London, 1993).

Hinnells, J. (ed.), *A Handbook of Living Religions* (Penguin, Harmondsworth, 1985).

Hiro, D., *Black British, White British*, 2nd ed. (Grafton Books, London, 1991).

Hodgins, H., 'Planning Permission for Mosques – The Birmingham Experience'

(Centre for the Study of Islam and Christian-Muslim Relations, Birmingham, 1981).

Hoffman, E., *Lost in Translation: Life in a New Language* (Minerva, London, 1991).

Holder, W., 'Public Policy and National Preferences: The Exclusion of Foreign Law in English Private International Law' (1968) 17 *International and Comparative Law Quarterly* 926.

Holgate, G., 'The Government's Consultation Paper "Reform of the Caravan Sites Act 1968" – A Solution to Gypsy Site Provision?' [1993] *Conveyancer and Property Lawyer* 39, 111.

Holmes, C., 'The German Gypsy Question in Britain 1904–06' (1978) *Journal of the Gypsy Lore Society* 248.

—— *Anti-Semitism in British Society, 1876–1939* (Edward Arnold, London, 1979).

—— *John Bull's Island: Immigration and British Society, 1871–1971* (Macmillan, Basingstoke, 1988).

Homa, B., *Shechita* (Soncino Press, London, 1967).

Home, R., 'Planning Problems of Self-Help Gypsy Sites' [1982] *Journal of Planning and Environmental Law* 217.

—— 'Planning Aspects of the Government Consultation Paper on Gypsies' [1993] *Journal of Planning and Environmental Law* 13.

Home Office, *Cannabis: Report by the Advisory Committee on Drug Dependence* (HMSO, London, 1968).

—— *Statistics of Drug Seizures and Offenders Dealt With, United Kingdom, 1986: Supplementary Tables* (Government Statistical Service, London, 1988).

—— 'Policy Criteria for the Administration of Section 11 Grant' (Home Office, London, 1990).

—— *13th UK Periodic Report to the UN Committee on the Elimination of All Forms of Racial Discrimination Relating to the Period up to 31 July 1994* (Home Office, London, 1995).

—— *Statistics of Drug Seizures and Offenders Dealt With, United Kingdom, 1995* (Government Statistical Service, London, 1996).

Honeyford, R., *Integration or Disintegration* (Claridge Press, London, 1988).

Hood, R., *Race and Sentencing* (Clarendon Press, Oxford, 1992).

Hooker, M., *Legal Pluralism* (Clarendon Press, Oxford, 1976).

Horowitz, G., *The Spirit of Jewish Law* (Central Book Co, New York, 1953).

Horrell, M., *Laws Affecting Race Relations in South Africa* (South African Institute of Race Relations, Johannesburg, 1978).

Horton, J. (ed.), *Liberalism, Multiculturalism and Toleration* (Macmillan, Basingstoke, 1993).

Horton, J., and Mendus, S. (eds.), *Aspects of Toleration* (Methuen, London, 1985).

Hourani, A., *A History of the Arab Peoples* (Harvard University Press, Massachusetts, 1991).

House of Commons, Home Affairs Committee *Racial Attacks and Harrassment* (HC 71, 1994) (HMSO, London, 1994).

Howard, R., 'Dignity, Community and Human Rights' in A. An-Na'im (ed.), *Human Rights in Cross-Cultural Perspectives* (University of Pennsylvania Press, Philadelphia, 1992).

—— 'Cultural Absolutism and the Nostalgia for Community' (1993) 15 *Human Rights Quarterly* 315.

Hudson, B., 'Discrimination and Disparity: The Influence of Race on Sentencing' (1989) *New Community* 23.

Hull, J., 'The Religious Education Clauses of the 1993 Education Bill' (1993) 15 *British Journal of Religious Education* 1.

Humane Slaughter Association, *Slaughter By Religious Methods* (HSA, South Mimms, 1995).

Humphrey, J., 'The Universal Declaration of Human Rights: Its History, Impact and Judicial Character' in B. Ramcharan (ed.), *Human Rights: Thirty Years after the Universal Declaration* (Martinus Nijhoff, The Hague, 1979).

Hunt, M., *Using Human Rights Law in English Courts* (Hart, Oxford, 1997).

Hutchinson, J., and Smith, A. (eds.), *Ethnicity* (Oxford University Press, Oxford, 1996).

Hutnik, N., *Ethnic Minority Identity: A Social Psychological Perspective* (Oxford University Press, Oxford, 1991).

Hyamson, A., *A History of the Jews in England* (Chatto and Windus, London, 1908).

—— *The London Board for Shechita* (London Board for Shechita, London, 1954).

Hyman, M., *Sites for Travellers* (Runnymede Trust, London, 1989).

Ignatieff, M., 'Why "Community" is a Dishonest Word', *Observer*, 3 May 1992.

Inciardi, J. (ed.), *The Drug Legalization Debate* (Sage, London, 1991).

Institute for Public Policy Research, *Survey on Prejudice* (IPPR, London, 1997).

Iqbal, M. (ed.), *East Meets West: A Background to Some Asian Faiths* (Commission for Racial Equality, London, 1981).

Iqra Trust, 'Research on Public Attitudes to Islam', Iqra Trust, London, 1991.

Jackson, D., *Immigration Law and Practice* (Sweet & Maxwell, London, 1996).

Jackson, R., and Nesbitt, E., *Hindu Children in Britain* (Trentham Books, Stoke-on-Trent, 1993).

James, A., *Sikh Children in Britain* (Oxford University Press, London, 1974).

Jeffery, P., *Migrants and Refugees: Muslim and Christian Families in Bristol* (Cambridge University Press, Cambridge, 1976).

Jenkins, R., *Essays and Speeches* (Collins, London, 1967).

John, D., *Indian Workers Associations in Britain* (Oxford University Press, London, 1969).

Jowell, R., *et al* (eds.), *British Social Attitudes: The 9th Report* (Gower, Aldershot, 1992).

—— *British Social Attitudes: The 13th Report* (Dartmouth, Aldershot, 1996).

Judicial Studies Board, *Handbook on Ethnic Minority Issues* (JSB, London 1994–5).

JUSTICE, *Drugs and the Law* (JUSTICE, London 1991).

—— 'Response to Consultation Paper on the Reform of the Caravan Sites Act 1968' (JUSTICE, London, 1992).

Kabbani, R., *Europe's Myths of Orient* (Pandora, London, 1986).

Kahn-Freund, O., 'Reflections on Public Policy in the English Conflicts of Laws' (1953) 39 *Transactions of the Grotius Society* 39.

Kallen, E., *Ethnicity and Human Rights in Canada*, 2nd ed. (Oxford University Press, Toronto, 1995).

Kallen, H., *Cultural Pluralism and the American Idea* (University of Pennsylvania Press, Philadelphia, 1956).

Kalsi, S., *The Evolution of the Sikh Community in Leeds* (Department of Theology and Religious Studies, University of Leeds, Leeds, 1992).

Kaye, R., 'The politics of religious slaughter of animals' (1993) *New Community* 235.

Kennedy, C., 'Repugnancy to Islam – Who Decides? Islam and Legal Reform in Pakistan' (1992) 42 *International and Comparative Law Quarterly* 769.

Kenrick, D., and Bakewell, S., *On the Verge: The Gypsies of England*, 2nd ed. (University of Hertfordshire Press, Hatfield, 1995).

Kerridge, R., *Real Wicked Guy: A View of Black Britain* (Blackwell, Oxford 1983).

Khadduri, M., *War and Peace in the Law of Islam* (John Hopkins Press, Baltimore, 1955).

Kiernan, V., 'Britons Old and New' in C. Homes (ed.), *Immigrants and Minorities in British Society* (Allen and Unwin, London, 1978).

Kiev, A., 'Psychotherapeutic Aspects of Pentecostal Sects among West Indian Immigrants to England' (1964) 15 *British Journal of Sociology* 129.

King, A., and Reiss, M., (eds.), *The Multicultural Dimension of the National Curriculum* (Falmer Press, London, 1993).

King, P., *Toleration* (George Allen and Unwin, London, 1976).

Klug, B., 'Overkill – the polemic against ritual slaughter' (1989) 134 *Jewish Quarterly* 38.

Knight, W., 'Public Policy in English Law' (1922) 38 *Law Quarterly Review* 207.

Knott, K., *Hinduism in Leeds* (University of Leeds, Leeds, 1986).

—— *My Sweet Lord: The Hare Krishna Movement* (Aquarian Press, Wellingborough, 1986).

Knott, K., and Khokher, S., 'Religion and Ethnic Identity Among Young Asian Women in Bradford' (1993) *New Community* 593.

Kumari, R., *Brides are Not for Burning: Dowry Victims in India* (Sangam Books, London, 1989).

Kushner, T., 'Stunning Intolerance: A Century of Opposition to Religious Slaughter' (1989) 133 *Jewish Quarterly* 16.

—— *The Persistence of Prejudice: Antisemitism in British Society During the Second World War* (Manchester University Press, Manchester, 1989).

—— 'The impact of British Anti-semitism 1918–1945' in D. Cesarani (ed.), *The Making of Modern Anglo-Jewry* (Oxford University Press, Oxford, 1990).

Kymlicka, W., *Liberalism, Community and Culture* (Clarendon Press, Oxford, 1991).

—— *Multicultural Citizenship* (Oxford University Press, Oxford, 1995).

Latham, R., and Matthews, W. (eds.), *The Diary of Samuel Pepys* (G. Bell and Sons, 1971).

Law, J., *The Religious Beliefs and Practices of Hindus in Derby* (University of Leeds, Leeds, 1991).

Law Commission, *Report No. 170, Facing the Future: A Discussion Paper on the Ground for Divorce* (HMSO, London, 1988).

—— *Report No. 192, The Ground for Divorce* (HMSO, London, 1990).

Lawrence, J., *Some Aspects of Shechita* (Council of Christians and Jews, London, 1971).

Lee, S., *The Cost of Free Speech* (Faber, London, 1990).

Leitner, M., Shapland, J., and Wiles, P., *Drug Usage and Drugs Prevention* (HMSO, London, 1993).

Lerner, N., *Group Rights and Discrimination in International Law* (Martinus Nijhoff, Dordrecht, 1991).

Lester, A., and Bindman, G., *Race and Law* (Penguin, Harmondsworth, 1972).

Lester, Lord and Joseph, S., 'Obligations of Non-Discrimination' in D. Harris and S. Joseph (eds.), *The International Covenant on Civil and Political Rights and United Kingdom Law* (Clarendon Press, Oxford, 1995).

Lewis, B., 'Legal and Historical Reflections on the Position of Muslim Populations under Non-Muslim Rule' in B. Lewis and D. Schnapper (eds.), *Muslims in Europe* (Pinter, London, 1994).

Lewis, P., *Islamic Britain: Religion, Politics and Identity among British Muslims* (I.B. Tauris, London, 1994).

Liberty, 'Rights and Freedoms of Gypsies and Travellers' (Liberty, London, 1993).

Lipman, V., *A History of the Jews in Britain since 1858* (Leicester University Press, Leicester, 1990).

Lloyd, C., 'Concepts, models and anti-racist strategies in Britain and France' (1991) *New Community* 63.

Lloyd, D., *Public Policy* (Athlone Press, London, 1953).

Long, A., 'Taking the Horror Out of the Ritual Slaughter of Animals', *Independent*, 28 Aug. 1987.

Lustgarten, L., 'Liberty in a Culturally Plural Society' in P. Griffith (ed.), *Of Liberty* (Cambridge University Press, Cambridge, 1983).

—— 'Racial Inequality, Public Policy and the Law: Where Are We Going?' in B. Hepple and E. Szyszcak (eds.), *Discrimination: The Limits of Law* (Mansell, London, 1992).

McGoldrick, D., *The Human Rights Committee* (Clarendon Press, Oxford, 1991).

Machiavelli, N., *The Prince and the Discourses*, M. Lerner ed. (Modern Library, New York, 1940).

Mackay, Lord, 'The Role of the Profession in Securing Access to Justice' in *Conference Papers of the Ninth Commonwealth Law Conference* (Auckland, 1990).

McLeod, W., *The Sikhs: History, Religion and Society* (Columbia University Press, New York, 1989).

Mahmood, T., *Muslim Personal Law* (Vikas, New Delhi, 1977).

—— *Personal Laws in Crisis* (Metropolitan, New Delhi, 1986).

Mangat, J., *A History of the Asians in East Africa c 1886 to 1945* (Oxford University Press, Oxford, 1969).

Mansingh, A., and Mansingh, L., 'Hindu influences on Rastafarianism', *Caribbean Quarterly Monograph on Rastafari* (Kingston, 1985).

Marie, J.-B., 'International Instruments Relating to Human Rights: Classification and Status of Ratifications as of 1 January 1996' (1996) 17 *Human Rights Law Journal* 61.

Marquand, D., 'Human rights protection and minorities' [1994] *Public Law* 359.

Mason, P., *A Matter of Honour: An Account of the Indian Army, its Officers and Men* (Cape, London, 1974).

Massil, S. (ed.), *The Jewish Year Book 1996* (Vallentine Mitchell, London, 1996).

Mayall, D., *Gypsy-Travellers in Nineteenth Century Society* (Cambridge University Press, Cambridge, 1988).

—— 'The making of British gypsy identities c 1500–1800' (1992) 11 *Immigrants and Minorities* 21.

Mayer, A., *Islam and Human Rights: Tradition and Politics* (Pinter, London, 1991).

Mayhew, H., *London Labour and the London Poor* (Frank Cass, London, 1861).

Mayor's Committee on Marijuana, *The Marijuana Problem in the City of New York* (Jacques Cattell Press, Lancaster, 1944).

Mendus, S. (ed.), *Justifying Toleration: Conceptual and Historical Perspectives* (Cambridge University Press, Cambridge, 1988).

—— *Toleration and the Limits of Liberalism* (Macmillan, Basingstoke, 1989).

Mendus, S., and Edwards, D. (eds.), *On Toleration* (Clarendon Press, Oxford, 1987).

Menski, W., 'The Reform of Islamic Family Law and a Uniform Civil Code for India' in J. Connors and C. Mallat (eds.), *Islamic Family Law* (Graham and Trotman, London, 1990).

Mernissi, F., *Women and Islam: An Historical and Theological Enquiry* (Blackwell, Oxford, 1991).

Meron, T., 'On a Hierarchy of International Human Rights' (1986) 80 *American Journal of International Law* 1.

—— *Human Rights and Humanitarian Norms as Customary Law* (Clarendon Press, Oxford, 1989).

Miles, R., *Between Two Cultures? The Case of Rastafarianism* (Social Science Research Council, Bristol, 1978).

Mill, J., *On Liberty*, G. Himmelfard (ed.) (Penguin, Harmondsworth, 1985).

—— *Utilitarianism, On Liberty, Considerations on Representative Government*, G. Williams (ed.), (J.M. Dent, London, 1993).

Miller, D., 'Socialism and Toleration' in S. Mendus (ed.), *Justifying Toleration: Conceptual and Historical Perspectives* (Cambridge University Press, Cambridge, 1988).

Miller, P., and Plant, M., 'Drinking, smoking and illicit drug use among 15 and 16 year olds in the United Kingdom' (1996) 313 *British Medical Journal* 394.

Milne, A., *Human Rights and Human Diversity* (Macmillan, Basingstoke, 1986).

Ministry of Housing and Local Government, *Gypsies and Other Travellers* (HMSO, London, 1967).

Mir-Hosseini, Z., *Marriage on Trial: A Study of Islamic Family Law* (I.B. Tauris, London, 1993).

Modood, T., '"Black", Racial Equality and Asian Identity' (1988) *New Community* 397.

—— 'Alabama Britain', *Guardian*, 22 May 1989.

—— 'Catching up with Jesse Jackson: Being Oppressed and Being Somebody' (1990) *New Community* 85.

—— 'British Asian Muslims and the Rushdie Affair' (1990) 61 *Political Quarterly* 143.

—— 'The Indian Economic Success: A Challenge to Some Race Relations Assumptions' (1991) 19 *Policy and Politics* 177.

—— 'Cultural Diversity and Racial Discrimination in Employment Selection' in B. Hepple and E. Szyszcak (eds.), *Discrimination: The Limits of Law* (Mansell, London, 1992).

—— *Racial Equality, Colour, Culture and Justice* (Institute for Public Policy Research, London, 1994).

Modood, T., Beishon, S., and Virdee, S., *Changing Ethnic Identities* (Policy Studies Institute, London, 1994).

Modood, T., Berthoud, R., *et al.*, *Ethnic Minorities in Britain: Diversity and Disadvantage* (Policy Studies Institute, London, 1997).

Montgomery, J., 'Legislating for a Multi-faith Society: Some Problems of Special Treatment' in B. Hepple and E. Szyszcak (eds.), *Discrimination: The Limits of Law* (Mansell, London, 1992).

Morris, P., 'Judaism and Pluralism' in I. Hamnett (ed.), *Religious Pluralism and Unbelief* (Routledge, London, 1990).

Moynihan, D., *Pandaemonium: Ethnicity in International Politics* (Oxford University Press, Oxford, 1993).

Mulla, D., *Principles of Mohammedan Law* (N.M. Tripathi, Bombay, 1906).

Murphy, D., *Tales from Two Cities* (John Murray, London, 1987).

Murphy, T., 'Toleration and the Law' in J. Horton and H. Crabtree (eds.), *Toleration and Integrity in a Multi-Faith Society* (Department of Politics, University of York, York, 1992).

Nasir, J., *The Islamic Law of Personal Status* (Graham and Trotman, London, 1986).

National Agenda for a Multicultural Australia (Department of the Prime Minister and Cabinet, Office of Multicultural Affairs, Canberra, 1989).

National Commission on Marijuana and Drug Abuse, *Marijuana: A Signal of Misunderstanding* (Government Printing Office, Washington, 1972).

National Curriculum Council, *Guidance Document No. 3: 'The Whole Curriculum'* (Department of Education and Science, London, 1990).

Negrete, J., 'What's Happened to the Cannabis Debate?' (1988) 83 *British Journal of Addiction* 359.

Newark, F., 'The Case of Tanistry' (1952) 9 *Northern Ireland Law Quarterly* 215.

Nielsen, J., *Muslims in Western Europe* (Edinburgh University Press, Edinburgh, 1992).

—— 'Aux Sources des Revendications des Musulmans en Matière de Droit de la Famille en Europe' in M.-C. Foblets (ed.), *Familles – Islam – Europe* (Harmattan, Paris, 1996).

Nygh, P., 'Foreign Status, Public Policy and Discretion' (1964) 13 *International and Comparative Law Quarterly* 39.

O'Brien, C., 'What Rights Should Minorities Have?' in G. Ashworth (ed.), *World Minorities* (Quartermaine House, Sunbury, 1977).

O'Donovan, K., *Sexual Divisions in Law* (Weidenfeld and Nicholson, London, 1985).

Office of Health Economics, *Drug Misuse* (OHE, London, 1992).

Office of Population, Censuses and Surveys, *1991 Census: Ethnic Group and Country of Birth, Great Britain* (HMSO, London, 1993).

Okely, J., *The Traveller-Gypsies* (Cambridge University Press, Cambridge, 1983).

Owens, J., *Dread: The Rastafarians of Jamaica* (Sangster, Kingston, 1976).

Palley, C., *The United Kingdom and Human Rights* (Stevens, London, 1991).

Parekh B., *Gandhi's Political Philosophy* (Macmillan, Basingstoke, 1989).

—— 'Britain and the Social Logic of Pluralism' in *Britain: A Plural Society* (Commission for Racial Equality, London 1990).

—— 'Equality, Fairness and the Limits of Diversity' (1994) 7 *Innovation* 289.

—— (ed.), *Colour, Class and Consciousness* (George Allen and Unwin, London, 1984).

Patterson, S., *Dark Strangers* (Tavistock, London, 1963).

—— *Immigration and Race Relations in Britain 1960–1967* (Oxford University Press, London, 1969).

—— 'Immigrants and Minority Groups in British Society' in S. Abbott (ed.), *The Prevention of Racial Discrimination in Britain* (Oxford University Press, London, 1971).

Peach, C., *West Indian Migration to Britain: A Social Geography* (Oxford University Press, Oxford, 1968).

—— 'Introduction' in C. Peach (ed.), *Ethnicity in the 1991 Census, vol 2, The Ethnic Minority Populations of Great Britain* (HMSO, London, 1996).

—— 'Black Caribbeans: class, gender and demography' in C. Peach (ed.), *Ethnicity in the 1991 Census, vol 2, The Ethnic Minority Populations of Great Britain* (HMSO, London, 1996).

Peach, C., and Glebe, G., 'Muslim Minorities in Western Europe' (1995) 18 *Ethnic and Racial Studies* 26.

Pearl, D., *A Textbook on Muslim Personal Law*, 2nd ed. (Croom Helm, London, 1987).

—— 'Three Decades of Executive, Legislative and Judicial Amendments to Islamic Family Law in Pakistan' in J. Connors and C. Mallat (eds.), *Islamic Family Law* (Graham and Trotman, London, 1990).

Pedley, D., 'Animal rights: some are more equal than others' (1990) 140 *New Law Journal* 1415.

Phillips, A., and Morris, H., *Marriage Laws in Africa* (Oxford University Press, London, 1971).

Pollis, A., and Schwab, P. (eds.), *Human Rights: Cultural and Ideological Perspectives* (Praeger, New York, 1980).

Post, K., *Arise Ye Starvelings* (Martinus Nijhoff, The Hague, 1978).

Poulter, S., '*Hyde v Hyde*: A Reappraisal' (1976) 25 *International and Comparative Law Quarterly* 475.

—— 'Polygamy—New Law Commission Proposals' (1983) 13 *Family Law* 72.

—— *English Law and Ethnic Minority Customs* (Butterworths, London, 1986).

—— 'Recognition of Foreign Divorces: The New Law' (1987) 84 *Law Society Gazette* 253.

—— 'Divorce Reform in a Multicultural Society' (1989) 19 *Family Law* 99.

—— 'The Claim to a Separate Islamic System of Personal Law for British Muslims in J. Connors and C. Mallat (eds.), *Islamic Family Law* (Graham and Trotman, London, 1990).

—— 'The Religious Education Provisions of the Education Reform Act 1988' (1990) 2 *Education and the Law* 1.

—— 'Towards Legislative Reform of the Blasphemy and Racial Hatred Laws' [1991] *Public Law* 371.

—— 'Gypsy Sites: An Unacceptable Volte-Face' (1992) 260 *Runnymede Bulletin* 10.

—— 'Muslim Headscarves in School: Contrasting Legal Approaches in England and France' (1997) 17 *Oxford Journal of Legal Studies* 43.

Prison Reform Trust and H.M. Prison Service, *The Prisoners' Information Book 1996* (Prison Reform Trust and H.M. Prison Service, London, 1996).

Prison Service Chaplaincy, *Annual Census of Religious Registration in Prison 1994* (Prison Service Chaplaincy, London, 1994).

—— *Annual Religious Census 1995* (Prison Service Chaplaincy, London, 1995).

—— *Annual Religious Census 1996* (Prison Service Chaplaincy, London, 1996).

Pritchard, A., *Squatting* (Sweet and Maxwell, London, 1981).

Prothro, J., and Grigg, C., 'Fundamental Principles of Democracy: Bases of Agreement and Disagreement' (1960) 11 *Journal of Politics* 276.

Pryce, K., *Endless Pressure* (Penguin, Harmondsworth, 1979).

Pumfrey, P., and Verma, G. (eds.), *Cultural Diversity and the Curriculum: The Foundation Subjects and Religious Education in Secondary Schools* (Falmer Press, London, 1993).

Raison, T., 'Cultural diversity, adaptation and participation' (1980) *New Community* 96.

Ranger, C., 'Race, culture and "cannabis psychosis": the role of social factors in the construction of a disease category.' (1989) *New Community* 357.

Rankin, G., *Background to Indian Law* (Cambridge University Press, Cambridge, 1946).

Rastafarianism in Greater London (Greater London Council, London, 1984).

Rawls, J., 'Kantian Constructivism in Moral Theory' (1980) 77 *Journal of Philosophy* 543.

Raz, J., *The Morality of Freedom* (Clarendon Press, Oxford, 1986).

—— 'Autonomy, Toleration and the Harm Principle' in S. Mendus (ed.), *Justifying Toleration: Conceptual and Historical Perspectives* (Cambridge University Press, Cambridge, 1988).

—— *Ethics in the Public Domain* (Clarendon Press, Oxford, 1994).

Regan, T., *The Case for Animal Rights* (Routledge and Kegan Paul, London, 1983).

Reid, I., *Social Class Differences in Britain*, 3rd ed. (Fontana, London, 1989).

Reiner, R., 'Race and Criminal Justice' (1989) *New Community* 5.

Release White Paper on Reform of the Drug Laws (Release, London, 1992).

Renteln, A., 'Relativism and the Search for Human Rights' (1988) 90 *American Anthropologist* 56.

—— 'A Cross-Cultural Approach to Validating International Human Rights: The

Case of Retribution Tied to Proportionality' in D. Cingranelli (ed.), *Human Rights: Theory and Measurement* (Macmillan, Basingstoke, 1988).

—— *International Human Rights: Universalism versus Relativism* (Sage, London, 1990).

Report of the Admiralty Committee on the Humane Slaughtering of Animals, Cd 2150 (HMSO, London, 1904).

Report of the Committee of Inquiry into the Education of Children from Ethnic Minority Groups, Cmnd 9453 (HMSO, London, 1985).

Report of the Indian Hemp Drugs Commission, 1893–94 (Government Printing Office, Simla, 1894).

Report of the Royal Commission on Population, Cmnd 7695 (HMSO, London, 1949).

Rex, J., *Race and Ethnicity* (Open University Press, Milton Keynes, 1986).

—— 'The concept of a multi-cultural society' (1987) *New Community* 218.

—— 'The Political Sociology of a Multi-Cultural Society' (1991) 2 *European Journal of Intercultural Studies* 7.

Rex, J., and Mason, D. (eds.), *Theories of Race and Ethnic Relations* (Cambridge University Press, Cambridge, 1986).

Rex, J., and Tomlinson, S., *Colonial Immigrants in a British City* (Routledge and Kegan Paul, London, 1979).

Roberts-Wray, K., *Commonwealth and Colonial Law* (Stevens, London, 1966).

Robilliard, S., 'Religion in Prison' (1980) 130 *New Law Journal* 800.

Robinson, V., *Transients, Settlers and Refugees: Asians in Britain* (Cambridge University Press, Cambridge, 1986).

Rocker, S., 'Shechita defence lobby moves up a gear', *Jewish Chronicle*, 19 Aug. 1994, 15.

Rollin, C., *Animal Rights and Human Morality* (Prometheus Books, New York, 1981).

Rose, E., *Colour and Citizenship* (Oxford University Press, London, 1969).

Ross, A., *Ranji: Prince of Cricketers* (Collins, London, 1983).

Roth, C., *A History of the Jews in England* (Clarendon Press, Oxford, 1941).

Rowland, F., 'Comparison of the Impact Protection Properties of Sikh Turbans and Industrial Safety Helmets' (1987) 9 *Journal of Occupational Accidents* 47.

Royal Society for the Prevention of Cruelty to Animals, *Legalised Cruelty* (RSPCA, London, 1948).

—— *Humane Slaughter* (RSPCA, Horsham, 1981).

—— *Ritual Slaughter* (RSPCA, Horsham, 1984).

—— *Farm Animals: Religious Slaughter* (RSPCA, Horsham, 1995).

Rubin, V., and Comitas, L., *Ganja in Jamaica* (Mouton, The Hague, 1975).

Runnymede Commission on Antisemitism, *A Very Light Sleeper: The persistence and dangers of antisemitism* (Runnymede Trust, London, 1994).

Runnymede Commission on British Muslims and Islamophobia, *Islamphobia: its features and dangers* (Runnymede Trust, London, 1997).

Runnymede Trust, *Racial Justice and Criminal Justice: A Submission to the Royal Commission on Criminal Justice* (Runnymede Trust, London, 1992).

Rutherford, A., and Green, P., 'Illegal Drugs and British Criminal Justice Policy' in H. Albrecht and A. Kalmthout, (eds.), *Drugs Policies in Western Europe*, (Max Planck Institute, Freiburg, 1989).

Ruthven, M., *A Satanic Affair* (Chatto & Windus, London, 1990).

Sachdeva, S., *The Primary Purpose Rule in British Immigration Law* (Trentham Books, Stoke-on-Trent, 1993).

Sachs, J., *The Persistence of Faith* (Weidenfeld and Nicolson, London, 1991).

Saghal, G., and Yuval-Davis, N. (eds.), *Refusing Holy Orders: Women and Fundamentalism in Britain* (Virago, London, 1992).

Said, E., *Orientalism* (Penguin, Harmondsworth, 1985).

Sandford, J., *Gypsies* (Secker and Warburg, London, 1973).

Sandland, R., 'Travelling: Back to the Future' (1994) 144 *New Law Journal* 750.

Sawyer, A., 'Judicial Manipulation of Customary Family Law in Tanzania' in S. Roberts (ed.), *Law and the Family in Africa* (Mouton, The Hague, 1977).

Scarman, Lord, *Report on the Brixton Disorders, 10–12 April 1981*, Cmnd 8427 (HMSO, London, 1981).

—— 'Toleration and the Law' in S. Mendus and D. Edwards (eds.), *On Toleration* (Clarendon Press, Oxford, 1987).

Schmool, M., and Miller, S., *Women in the Jewish Community: Survey Report* (Office of the Chief Rabbi, London, 1994).

Schonsheck, J., *On Criminalization: An Essay in the Philosophy of the Criminal Law* (Kluwer, Dordrecht, 1994).

Schur, E., *Our Criminal Society* (Prentice-Hall, New Jersey, 1969).

Semaj, L., 'Rastafari: From Religion to Social Theory', *Caribbean Quarterly Monograph on Rastafari* (Kingston, 1985).

Shaw, A., *A Pakistani Community in Britain* (Blackwell, Oxford, 1988).

Shibutani, T., and Kwan, K., *Ethnic Stratification: A Comparative Approach* (Macmillan, New York, 1965).

Shyllon, F., *Black People in Britain 1555–1833* (Oxford University Press, London, 1977).

Sieghart, P., *The Lawful Rights of Mankind* (Clarendon Press, Oxford, 1985).

Sillitoe, A., *Britain in Figures* (Penguin, Harmondsworth, 1973).

Silverman, M., *Deconstructing The Nation: Immigration, Racism and Citizenship in Modern France* (Routledge, London, 1992).

Singh, K., *A History of the Sikhs*, 2 vols, (Oxford University Press, Princeton, 1963–66).

Smith, A., *The Ethnic Origin of Nations* (Blackwell, Oxford, 1986).

Smith, M., Augier, R., and Nettlefold, R., *The Rastafari Movement in Kingston, Jamaica* (University of the West Indies, Kingston, 1960).

Sohn, L., 'The Rights of Minorities' in L. Henkin (ed.), *The International Bill of Rights* (Columbia University Press, New York, 1981).

Sollors, W. (ed.), *The Invention of Ethnicity* (Oxford University Press, New York, 1989).

Solomos, J., *Black Youth, Racism and the State* (Cambridge University Press, Cambridge, 1988).

Stein, P., and Shand, J., *Legal Values in Western Society* (Edinburgh University Press, Edinburgh, 1974).

Steiner, H., 'Ideals and Counter-Ideals in the Struggle Over Autonomy Regimes for Minorities' (1991) 66 *Notre Dame Law Review* 1539.

Stopes-Roe, M., and Cochrane, R., *Citizens of This Country: The Asian British* (Multilingual Matters, Clevedon, 1990).

Surty, M., 'The Shariah Family Courts of Britain and the Protection of Women's Rights in Muslim Family Law' (1991) 9 *Muslim Educational Quarterly* 59.

Tahzib, B., *Freedom of Religion or Belief: Ensuring Effective International Legal Protection* (Nijhoff, The Hague, 1996).

Taylor, J., *The Half-Way Generation* (National Foundation for Educational Research, Slough, 1976).

Teson, F., 'International Human Rights and Cultural Relativism' (1985) 25 *Virginia Journal of International Law* 869.

Thomas, P., 'Housing Gypsies' (1992) 142 *New Law Journal* 1714.

—— and Campbell, S., *Housing Gypsies* (Cardiff Law School, Cardiff, 1992).

Thomas, T., 'Old Allies, New Neighbours: Sikhs in Britain' in G. Parsons (ed.), *The Growth of Religious Diversity in Britain from 1945: vol 1, Traditions* (Routledge, London, 1993).

Thornberry, P., *International Law and the Rights of Minorities* (Clarendon Press, Oxford, 1991).

—— and Estebanez, M., *The Council of Europe and Minorities* (Council of Europe, Strasbourg, 1994).

Todd, D., and Clark, G., *Gypsy Site Provision and Policy* (HMSO, London, 1991).

—— *Good Practice Guidelines for Gypsy Site Provision by Local Authorities* (HMSO, London, 1991).

Tomlinson, S., 'The Multicultural Task Group: The Group That Never Was' in A. King and M. Reiss (eds.), *The Multicultural Dimension of the National Curriculum* (Falmer Press, London, 1993).

Tyler, A., 'Slaughterhouse Tales', *Independent*, 13 Mar. 1989.

UK Action Committee on Islamic Affairs, *Muslims and the Law in Multi-faith Britain: The need for reform* (UKACIA, London, 1993).

Union of Muslim Organisations of UK and Eire, *Why Muslim Family Law for British Muslims* (UMO, London, 1983).

Vadgama, K., *India in Britain* (Robert Royce, London, 1984).

Van den Bergh, P., *The Ethnic Phenomenon* (Elsevier Press, New York, 1981).

Van de Wijngaart, G., 'A Social History of Drug Use in the Netherlands' (1988) 18 *Journal of Drug Issues* 481.

Van Dyke, V., *Human Rights, Ethnicity and Discrimination* (Greenwood Press, London, 1985).

Vincent, R., *Human Rights and International Relations* (Cambridge University Press, Cambridge, 1986).

Viney, T., and Dermody, T., 'Beyond the Pale' (1986–87) 65 *Poverty* 9.

Visram, R., *Ayahs, Lascars and Princes: Indians in Britain 1700–1947* (Pluto Press, London, 1986).

Walvin, J., *Black and White: The Negro and English Society, 1555–1945* (Allen Lane, London, 1973).

Ward, M., *Jewish Kosher—should it be permitted to survive in a new Britain?* (A.H. Stockwell, Ilfracombe, 1945).

Waterman, S., and Kosmin, B., *British Jewry in the Eighties* (Board of Deputies of British Jews, London, 1986).

Wayland, D., 'Seat Belts—A Comparative Study of the Law and Practice' (1981) 30 *International and Comparative Law Quarterly* 165.

Webster, R., *A Brief History of Blasphemy* (Orwell Press, Southwold, 1990).

Weeramantry, C., *Islamic Jurisprudence: An International Perspective* (Macmillan, Basingstoke, 1988).

Weller, P. (ed.), *Religions in the UK: A Multi-Faith Directory*, 2nd ed. (University of Derby, Derby, 1997).

White, T., *Catch a Fire: The Life of Bob Marley* (Omnibus Press, London, 1991).

Whittaker, B., *The Global Connection: The Crisis of Drug Addiction* (Jonathan Cape, London, 1987).

Wibberley, G., *A Report on the Analysis of Responses to Consultation on the Operation of the Caravan Sites Act 1968* (Department of the Environment, London, 1986).

Winfield, P., 'Public Policy in the English Common Law' (1928–9) 42 *Harvard Law Review* 76.

Young, J., *The Drugtakers* (MacGibbon and Kee, London, 1971).

Young JUSTICE, *The primary purpose rule: a rule with no purpose* (JUSTICE, London, 1993).

Zellick, G., *The Law, Religion and the Jewish Community* (Jews' College, London, 1987).

Index